Litigation Practice
E-Discovery and Technology

Thomas F. Goldman, JD
Attorney at Law
Thomas Edison State College
Professor Emeritus
Bucks County Community College

Prentice Hall
Boston Columbus Indianapolis New York San Francisco Upper Saddle River
Amsterdam Cape Town Dubai London Madrid Milan Munich Paris Montréal Toronto
Delhi Mexico City São Paulo Sydney Hong Kong Seoul Singapore Taipei Tokyo

Editorial Director: Vernon Anthony
Executive Acquisitions Editor: Gary Bauer
Editorial Assistant: Tanika Henderson
Director of Marketing: David Gessel
Marketing Manager: Stacey Martinez
Marketing Assistant: Les Roberts
Senior Managing Editor: JoEllen Gohr
Project Manager: Christina Taylor
Senior Operations Specialist: Pat Tonneman
Senior Art Director: Diane Ernsberger
Cover Art: David Graham
Full-Service Project Management and Composition: Integra-Chicago
Printer/Binder: Edwards Brothers
Cover Printer: Lehigh-Phoenix Color Corp./Hagerstown
Text Font: 11/13 Goudy

Credits and acknowledgments borrowed from other sources and reproduced, with permission, in this textbook appear on appropriate page within text.

Library of Congress Cataloging-in-Publication Data

Goldman, Thomas F.
Litigation practice : e-discovery and technology / Thomas F. Goldman.
p. cm.
Includes bibliographical references and index.
ISBN 978-0-13-237315-9
1. Electronic discovery (Law)—United States. 2. Electronic evidence—United States. 3. Electronic records—Law and legislation—United States. I. Title.
KF8902.E42G65 2012
347.73′50285—dc22

2011002657

10 9 8 7 6 5 4 3 2 1

Prentice Hall
is an imprint of

www.pearsonhighered.com

ISBN 10: 0-13-237315-7
ISBN 13: 978-0-13-237315-9

DEDICATION

It is not easy keeping life and what is important in perspective.

This book is for Sara and Rob, who have given me strength in difficult times and continue to amaze and delight me with their maturity and accomplishments as they have grown to adulthood.

TFG

BRIEF CONTENTS

CONTENTS

UNIT 3 EVIDENCE AND E-DISCOVERY PRACTICE

UNIT 4 TECHNOLOGY APPLICATIONS IN THE COURTHOUSE AND LITIGATION

ABOUT THE AUTHOR

THOMAS F. GOLDMAN, JD, is an experienced trial attorney who has represented nationally known insurance companies and corporations. He developed the Advanced Litigation Support and Technology Certificate Program at Thomas Edison State College, where he is both a member of the Paralegal Studies Program Advisory Board and a mentor. He is Professor Emeritus at Bucks County Community College, where he was a professor of Law and Management; Director of the Center for Legal Studies; and Director of the ABA-approved Paralegal Studies Program.

Professor Goldman is an author of textbooks in paralegal studies and technology, including *The Paralegal Professional*, in its third edition; *Civil Litigation: Process and Procedures*, in its second edition; *Accounting and Taxation for Paralegals; Technology in the Law Office*, in its second edition; *AbacusLaw: A Hands-On Tutorial and Guide;* and *SmartDraw: A Hands-On Tutorial and Guide*. In addition, he is the executive producer of the Paralegal Professional video series, in which he occasionally appears.

An accounting and economics graduate of Boston University and Temple University School of Law, Professor Goldman has an active international law, technology law, and litigation practice. He has worked extensively with paralegals and has received the Boss of the Year award of the Legal Support Staff Guild.

He was elected the Legal Secretaries Association Boss of the Year for his contribution to cooperative education by encouraging the use of paralegals and legal assistants in law offices. He also received the Bucks County Community College Alumni Association Professional Achievement Award.

He has been an educational consultant on technology to educational institutions and major corporations and a frequent speaker and lecturer on educational, legal, and technology issues. In October 2005, he was appointed to the American Association for Paralegal Education Board of Directors, where he served as the founding chair of the Technology Task Force and initiated the Train the Trainer program.

TO THE STUDENT

Being part of a litigation team taking a client's case to court is one of the most exciting experiences and greatest honors in the field of law. Truly, the ultimate show of trust a person can give another is to allow him or her to represent and present a critical moment in the person's life. In the civil litigation world, the outcome of litigation can result in financial reward or ruin. The hope for a decent future for an injured client may depend on a successful verdict, one that provides enough financial resources to pay doctors and put the client's life back together, at least financially. For a person wrongly accused of negligent conduct, a potential verdict against him or her may result in bankruptcy and shattered dreams of putting children through school and retiring. The outcome of each verdict can thus affect the rest of a client's life for better or worse.

Going to court, even in a supporting role, should never be taken lightly. Clients depend on all members of the legal team to do their best. In the modern age, this requires knowledge of the technology used in litigation. With so much at stake for the client, a member of the team may be deemed incompetent if he or she does not have at least some knowledge about electronic discovery and technology. In addition, everyone involved in a client's case must at least be aware of what he or she does not know and when it is necessary to call in technology experts.

In the pages of this text, I have tried to provide you with the fundamentals of e-discovery and the tools of technology that are frequently used in the processing of a civil case from inception to trial.

Reading this text will not make you an expert in the technology used in litigation. However, it will provide you with the opportunity to practice using the legal technology tools of office management, case management, discovery, graphic creation, and trial presentation used in the real world. There are many different computer programs used in each area of practice. The ones made available to you in your course will provide a basic understanding of the fundamentals and the terminology associated with each.

Each law firm in which you work in the future may use a different program or version than the one you are familiar with. However, a basic understanding of how these programs work will provide you with the ability to quickly learn a newer version or a competitive program. A human resources director told me that she was less concerned with new hires knowing the specific programs used in her firm than with them understanding the basic functions of the programs. In her experience, someone with prior knowledge and experience using a legal program can learn a new program and features customized to her office quickly and usually without the need for outside training.

TO THE INSTRUCTOR

This text is a direct result of the requests of many of my fellow educators for a book that develops practical contemporary litigation skills that incorporate the use of technology. Just knowing the fundamental concepts of litigation is no longer enough for graduates to be able to obtain and keep jobs in the very competitive litigation field. The courts, both federal and state, are increasingly requiring the use of technology in the courtroom; and attorneys, already burdened with keeping current with rapidly changing litigation concepts, are increasingly requiring support staff to play a larger role in their preparation for trial.

This textbook is designed to give students the experience of assisting in every aspect of preparing for litigation using the tools found in a contemporary law office. Throughout this text, a real case, as reported by the National Transportation Safety Board (NTSB), presents a **sample fact pattern that is used to illustrate the concepts presented in each chapter.** This sample fact pattern is also used in the illustrations of legal software program applications discussed in the text, from initial office setup in an office management program through trial preparation and courtroom presentation. The text also provides students with a template to use to complete assignments involving the **additional case studies provided in the textbook appendix.**

Accompanying the case studies in the text is a set of **documents, reports, images, videos, and simulations** that students can download from the new student resource site, **MyLegalStudiesKit.** These resources may be used to prepare a multimedia trial presentation using trial presentation software or in the form of an oral classroom report.

You may assign your own case studies or use one of those provided in the appendix to give students an opportunity to use and learn the fundamentals of each type of legal software program, including office management: AbacusLaw; case management: Lexis-Nexis CaseMap; e-discovery: Concordance; trial graphics: PowerPoint and SmartDraw; and trial presentation: Sanction. **Short tutorials,** along with directions for accessing and using online tutorials to learn more about the programs, are provided in the appendix to get students started.

Free demonstration versions of these software programs may be downloaded by students from my technology website at www.pearsonhighered.com/goldman. **Extended-term access codes** allowing use of the software for up to two or three years, packaged with a tutorial guide, are also available for select programs. Contact your Pearson representative for the most up-to-date list of packages.

A newly revised **Civil Litigation Video Series** also accompanies the book and allows students to see key aspects of handling a civil litigation case from initial interview through trial summation, jury charge, and appeal. For many students, this will be their first look into what happens in a courtroom or behind the closed doors of the judge's chambers. These videos may be used as the basis for written assignments or to stimulate classroom discussion of ethical concepts and practice issues. These video scenarios also work well as the basis for role-playing exercises. For example, after the class observes how a deposition is conducted, you may want to ask students to play the roles of witnesses or opposing counsel as part of a classroom exercise. The NTSB cases in the appendix provide enough information to support this type of role playing, up to and including trial. Links are provided for downloading the full NTSB reports.

Finally, throughout the text, you will find assignments encouraging students to **create a portfolio** of their work that will demonstrate to potential employers their knowledge of the field and practice and their ability to work in a contemporary law office.

ORGANIZATION OF THE BOOK

The book is divided into four units:

UNIT 1, LITIGATION—FOUNDATIONS FOR E-DISCOVERY AND TECHNOLOGY, provides a review of basic litigation concepts, including the specific application of legal ethics to litigation practice and the rules of evidence. The changes brought about by, and the impact of, technology in litigation and discovery in particular are reviewed and discussed to provide students with an understanding of the traditional roles, practices, and procedures in litigation and the changes technology has brought to the field.

UNIT 2, E-DISCOVERY—THE FUNDAMENTALS, provides a framework of the fundamental changes that have impacted discovery with the introduction of computers and electronic storage of documents. The federal rules are used as a frame of reference since these rules and the related court decisions are what most state courts have followed in establishing their own guidelines and rules.

UNIT 3, EVIDENCE AND E-DISCOVERY PRACTICE, provides the practical procedural and practice rules that have developed from case law, and includes the leading cases in the field and the words of the court from the most respected jurists in the field of e-discovery. Because this is a constantly evolving area in law, it is important for students to have an appreciation of the seminal cases in the field upon which other case law will be based in the future.

UNIT 4, TECHNOLOGY APPLICATIONS IN THE COURTHOUSE AND LITIGATION, provides an opportunity to put together all of the elements of a case using the tools of the profession to organize and present a case in trial. While not everyone on a trial team will make a presentation to a judge or jury, each member must appreciate the underlying elements that must be presented and how the contemporary multimedia tools may be used in the courtroom.

CHAPTER PEDAGOGY AND FEATURES

Litigation Practice: E-Discovery and Technology follows the same design used in the author's *Civil Litigation: Practice and Procedure*, 2e, text to provide a consistent look and feel for those using both books. Chapter features include:

■ OPENING SCENARIOS: THE CIVIL LITIGATION TEAM AT WORK

Each chapter contains a scenario designed to focus the reader's attention on the relationship between the chapter's content and civil litigation practice. The scenarios offer insight into the operation of a civil litigation law firm that a professional might encounter on the job. The scenarios revolve around activities in a fictional multi-location law office that is handling a major tort action through to the trial presentation.

■ VIDEO ADVICE FROM THE FIELD INTERVIEWS

These features present professional advice straight from the experts on litigation support, in the areas of acquiring videotaped depositions, working with court reporters, and using specialty legal software.

■ ETHICAL PERSPECTIVES

These features raise students' awareness of ethical issues encountered by a litigation team and direct the students to resources to resolve those issues.

■ PRACTICE TIPS

The goal of this feature is to provide practical tips, based on experience, for the litigation team. Typical advice can incorporate the simple (*Always check the local rules*), the practical (*Call the courthouse to determine the electronic features available in the courtroom*), and the obtuse (*Make sure the file formats are supported by the program you select*).

■ SKILL-BUILDING EXERCISES USING CASE RESOURCE MATERIALS

End-of-chapter practice materials, continuing case studies, and a comprehensive case study reflect the actual activities of professionals working in the civil litigation area. Samples are placed throughout the chapters for reference and guidance in preparing the assignments.

■ VIDEO CASE STUDIES

Litigation Practice: E-Discovery and Technology is supported by forty-six scenario-based video segments dealing with practice, procedures, and ethical issues in civil litigation practice that allow you to bring the world of the practicing paralegal into the classroom. Twenty-four of the case studies feature situations dealing with the school bus–truck accident case included in Appendix II.

■ BUILDING YOUR PROFESSIONAL PORTFOLIO

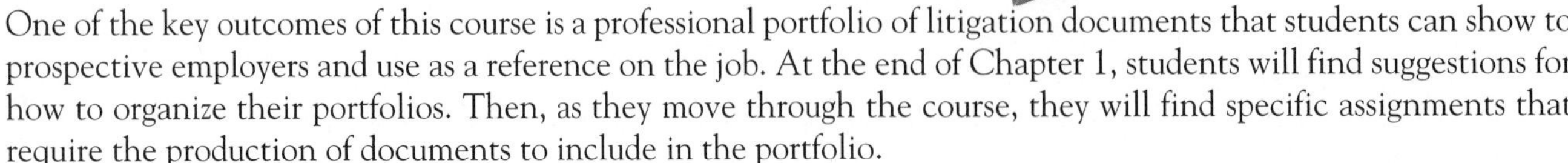

One of the key outcomes of this course is a professional portfolio of litigation documents that students can show to prospective employers and use as a reference on the job. At the end of Chapter 1, students will find suggestions for how to organize their portfolios. Then, as they move through the course, they will find specific assignments that require the production of documents to include in the portfolio.

THE CIVIL LITIGATION VIDEO SERIES

The forty-six video cases in this series illustrate each step of the litigation process and demonstrate a wide variety of practice and procedural scenarios. Students can view the cases within MyLegalStudiesKit, and instructors can receive the videos on DVD upon adoption of this book for classroom use.

A complete twenty-five-minute videotaped deposition of an expert witness and accompanying written transcript (in .txt and .doc format) are provided for use in creating a deposition summary; these could also be used in conjunction with trial or deposition programs such as Sanction.

CASE RESOURCES AVAILABLE IN TEXT AND ONLINE

A variety of video scenarios, case materials, and documents are available for use in completing assignments throughout the course. In addition to the material available to support the continuing case study, three additional case studies in the appendix are supported with videos and related documents to provide a simulation of real cases; see the details below. These case studies may be completed as individual or group assignments. Detailed information shown for the continuing case study of the school bus–truck accident may be used as a template for completion. All of the material shown below may be downloaded from MyLegalStudiesKit.

CONTINUING CASE STUDY: SCHOOL BUS–TRUCK ACCIDENT CASE

A. Documents

- Pleadings

B. Videos

- Video Conferencing: Strategy Discussions
- Administrative Agency Hearing
- Settlement Conference with Judge
- Truck Driver's Deposition
- Attorney Meet and Confer: Electronic Discovery
- Remote Video Conference: Taking Fact Witness Video Deposition
- Real-Time Reporting Witness Testimony: Deposing a Minor
- Mechanic's Deposition
- Preparing for Trial: Preparing for Deposition and Trial
- Jury Selection: Potential Juror Challenged for Cause
- A Salesman's Courtroom Testimony
- Trial: Direct and Cross-Examination of a Witness
- Preliminary Jury Instructions Before Trial
- Closing Argument: A Lawyer's Last Chance
- Judge Charges the Jury
- A Corporate Officer Seeks Legal Advice
- Deposition in Aid of Execution: Transferring Corporate Assets to Avoid Paying a Judgment

SIMPLE MOTOR VEHICLE PROPERTY DAMAGE CLAIM CASE

A. Documents

- Police Incident Report
- Estimate of Repairs from Acme Garage
- Notes of Client Interview (from Video)
- Notes of Witness Interview (from Video)

B. Videos

- UPL Issue: Interviewing a Client
- UPL Issue: Working with a Witness

INJURED STUDENT MEDICAL TREATMENT DELAYED CASE

A. Documents

- School Incident Report
- Emergency Room Report
- Treating Physician, Dr. Lee, Report
- Dr. Lee's Medical Bills
- Medical Records
- HIPAA Release Form Signed by Parent

B. Videos

- Solicitation in the ER: Ethical Duties of the Profession
- Court Hearing to Decide Who Represents a Minor: The Court's Duty to Protect the Child
- Video Deposition of a Treating Doctor, Dr. Lee
- Fact or Expert: Resolving Objection in Videotaped Deposition
- Three-Judge Appellate Panel

CIVIL ASSAULT ON BUS CASE

A. Documents

- School Incident Report
- Psychologist for Attacker Report (Antisocial with Psychotic Tendency)
- Report of School Nurse on Search
- HIPAA Release Form
- Notice to Opposing Counsel Requesting Medical Records
- Medical Records of Victim Davis Hilary

B. Videos

- Altercation on the School Bus
- School Principal Reacts
- Arbitration Before Three-Member Panel
- Preparing for Arbitration

LEGAL SOFTWARE RESOURCES

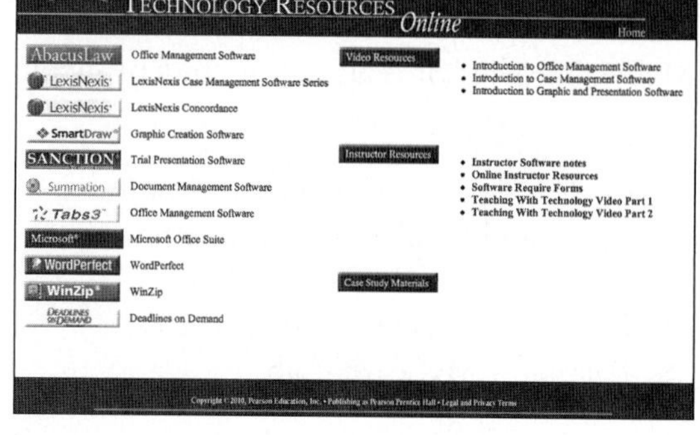

Students can download the latest (time-limited) versions of the most popular legal software from the Technology Resources Website at www.pearsonhighered.com/goldman. There they will find links to software tutorials, video overviews, teaching notes, and a variety of other useful resources, including forms for requesting lab copies of software from vendors.

OFFICE MANAGEMENT AND ACCOUNTING SOFTWARE

Office management and accounting software is used extensively in most law firms, from the sole practitioner to large, multi-office practices. It is used to keep accurate calendars of appointments, schedules, and deadlines; to track time and billing information, client funds, and costs; and to prepare accurate billing records. **AbacusLaw** is one of the most popular and best-supported office management software programs.

CASE ORGANIZATION AND MANAGEMENT SOFTWARE

Case management software can be used to organize the cast of characters in a case, the documents, the relevant timetables, the issues involved, legal authority, and other desired information. Top programs are **LexisNexis CaseMap** and **LexisNexis TimeMap.**

LITIGATION SUPPORT SOFTWARE

Litigation support software such as **Clustify** and **Concordance** provides specialty application software programs for managing electronic documents.

PRESENTATION AND TRIAL GRAPHICS SOFTWARE

Graphic creation programs such as **SmartDraw** are used to create graphics for either standalone presentations or as part of a graphics presentation, such as a PowerPoint presentation. The obvious advantage to this class of software is the ability of the legal team to create its own graphics without the need of graphic artists and outside consultants.

THE ELECTRONIC COURTHOUSE

Litigation support software such as **Sanction** is used in trial to display documentary evidence, graphic presentations, and simulations of accident cases in court. Relevant portions of illustrations and documents can be displayed as a witness testifies without having to pass around paper copies to everyone.

EXTENDED-USAGE SOFTWARE PACKAGES

AbacusLaw Tutorial and Guide with three-year Access Code (ISBN: 0-13-249071-4)
SmartDraw Tutorial and Guide with two-year Access Code (ISBN: 0-13-262523-7)

Check with your Pearson representative to find out about other new tutorial guides with extended-usage software.

STUDENT RESOURCES

MYLEGALSTUDIESKIT FOR LITIGATION PRACTICE

MyLegalStudiesKit is an online student supplement that contains access to the following study aids:

- **Chapter Objectives**
- **Civil Litigation Video Case Studies**
- **Cases and Resource Documents**
- **Advice From the Field Videos**
- **Key Term Electronic Flashcards**
- **Pearson's MySearchLab.**

To order *Litigation Practice: E-Discovery and Technology* value packages with a MyLegalStudiesKit Access Code, order ISBN: 0-13-275532-7.

A Standalone MyLegalStudiesKit Access Code can also be purchased separately at www.pearsonhighered.com.

INSTRUCTOR RESOURCES

INSTRUCTOR'S MANUAL

The *Instructor's Manual*, written by Thomas Goldman, Kathleen Smith, and David Freeman, contains sample syllabi, chapter outlines and summaries, Web Resources results, answers to questions and exercises, and teaching notes.

The *Instructor's Manual* can be downloaded from the Instructor's Resource Center. To access supplementary materials online, instructors need to request an instructor access code. Go to **www.pearsonhighered.com/irc,** where you can register for an instructor access code. Within forty-eight hours of registering, you will receive a confirming email that includes an instructor access code. Once you have received your code, locate your text in the online catalog and click on the Instructor Resources button on the left side of the catalog product page. Select a supplement and a log-in page will appear. Once you have logged in, you can access instructor material for all Pearson textbooks.

ACKNOWLEDGMENTS

A special thanks to the people who have given so generously of their time in reviewing the manuscript and offering suggestions for this text, particularly my friends David Freeman and Kathy Smith, who offered guidance and important suggestions for content and presentation of material and spent part of their vacation to help me develop this text. My continuing gratitude to Bob Elliott of AbacusLaw for helping develop the tutorials and rallying the great people of AbacusLaw, including Judd Kessler and Bryan Hays, to get the latest version online for student use. Thanks also to Mike Hahn at Sanction for endless support and advanced copies of preliminary versions of the newest software and for generously giving his time and enlisting the resources of Esquire in producing the Video Advice from the Field segments. My thanks to Steve d'Alencon of Case Central and Tom Fishborne, the fabulous cartoonist, not only for the use of his works in the pages of the text but also for delivering a new cartoon every Monday to my mailbox that I eagerly awaited to help put e-discovery and the law into perspective.

To the software companies who have generously provided software and support, a special thank you:

AbacusLaw
LexisNexis Concordance
SmartDraw
ALCoder
Clustify by Hot Neuron
LexisNexis CaseMap
Sanction by Sanction Solutions
Tab 3
CaseCentral
Deadlines on Demand

"To me the law seems like a sort of maze through which a client must be led to safety, a collection of reefs, rocks and underwater hazards through which he or she must be piloted."

–John Mortimer,
Clinging to the Wreckage, 1982, Ch. 7

Litigation Practice

CHAPTER 1

OPENING SCENARIO

The law firm of Mason, Marshall and Benjamin evolved from the sole proprietorship of Owen Mason and paralegal Edith Hannah, to a partnership with Ariel Marshall and Ethan Benjamin and two offices, with Mrs. Hannah acting as practice manager and Caitlin Gordon in one office and her twin sister, Emily Gordon, in the other office as lead paralegals. The firm was gaining a reputation as a leading-edge litigation practice that was experienced in the use of technology in litigation and in managing a multi-office, growing practice. The partners realized that they had to use technology to keep the two offices in touch with each other and to provide everyone with access to needed up-to-date information on files and cases. In addition, they found themselves working with outside co-counsel on a number of cases. With the use of outside trial co-counsel, it was also important to have systems in place that allowed everyone to have secure access to case information from outside the two main offices.

LEARNING OBJECTIVES

After studying this chapter, you should be able to:

1. Understand how technology has changed civil litigation practice.
2. Describe the rules of court and evidence related to electronic discovery.
3. Describe the ethical duties and obligations of the legal team.

VIDEO INTRODUCTION

A. An introduction to the use of technology in the law.

After watching the video in MyLegalStudiesKit, answer the following question.

- How has technology changed the practice of law?

B. An introduction to ethics in a technology world.

After watching the video in MyLegalStudiesKit, answer the following question.

- How has technology changed the traditional ethics rules of the legal profession?

INTRODUCTION TO LITIGATION PRACTICE FUNDAMENTALS

civil litigation
Resolution of legal disputes between parties seeking a remedy for a civil wrong or to enforce a contract.

evidence
Testimony, documents, and tangible things that tend to prove or disprove a fact.

Civil litigation involves legal disputes between parties seeking a remedy for a civil wrong or to enforce a contract. It includes a number of steps including discovery, analysis, and presentation of relevant evidence. It is a process that requires locating information and **evidence,** analysis of facts and law, preparation of material for trial presentation and posttrial appeals, and execution of judgments. The basic functions performed by the litigation team have not changed with the introduction of technology; only the methods and the tools have changed. How information and evidence are located, analyzed, and presented has changed as increasing amounts of information and evidence are saved in electronic format instead of on paper. Discovery now requires technological expertise to locate and obtain production of potential evidence. The analysis of large volumes of data obtained through electronic discovery requires the use of computers and specialized software to locate the relevant information and potential evidence. Courtroom exhibits that in the past might have been exclusively large foam board posters are now presented using computers and presentation software in electronically equipped courtrooms.

documentary evidence
Writings, recordings, and photographs, which include X-ray films, electronic recordings, or any other data compilation.

For the litigation team, what previously only required knowledge of the law now requires knowledge of technology. Most **documentary evidence** today is in electronic format, with a lesser amount in hard-copy (paper) form. In preparing for litigation, conducting discovery, and presenting cases in court the legal team must understand the ways in which the potential evidence was created and stored or filed. It may be e-mails, word processor documents, electronic spreadsheets, or financial data stored in databases. Frequently, locating and retrieving this information requires the help of a computer or information technologist. All professions, including the computer or data management fields, have their own language, with a lexicon of terms that have specific meanings to them. The litigation team must have a working knowledge of the terminology of technology and the ability to communicate with non-traditional members of the legal team, especially those supporting the technology needs of the litigation team in discovering, analyzing, and presenting information and evidence. In addition to the traditionally required familiarity with the rules of court and evidence, success in electronic discovery and computerized trial presentation requires a working knowledge of the tools and related terminology used in creating, storing, retrieving, and presenting electronically stored information.

As technology has become an increasingly important element in civil litigation, the added burden on the courts and judges has been met with increasing demand on opposing counsel to work together in a collaborative manner to resolve discovery issues without court intervention.

THE CHANGING ROLE OF THE LITIGATION TEAM

LEARNING OBJECTIVE 1
Understand how technology has changed civil litigation practice.

In some law firms, lawyers specialize, with some specializing in litigation and others counseling clients, like the English system with Solicitors, who only counsel clients, and Barristers, who only try cases. In most smaller and midsized firms, the distinction is not as clear, with lawyers serving the roles of counselors and trial attorneys. The advantage of having a specialized trial bar is the ability to learn and understand the rules of court and rules of evidence by continued practice and use in trial. With litigation specialization and division of responsibilities come the increasing need to have systems in place to facilitate communication among all members of the legal team, the litigation team, and the client.

The introduction of technology in business and personal life has impacted the practice of law and civil litigation and the functions and role of the trial bar. The introduction of computers and word processors changed the way documents could be created and stored. No longer did everything have to be kept on paper or as hard copy; it could be stored electronically. With the development of electronic databases, financial records and other business records could also be kept electronically. With the introduction of the Internet to the law office, e-mail has become the most commonly used method of communication. And don't forget the use of text messaging and social networks, with people communicating via Facebook and Twitter. With the increased use of technology has come the need for members of the litigation team to have technology expertise. It may be the civil litigation paralegal with some technology skills or a litigation support specialist who has learned the tools of specialty areas like electronic discovery or computerized trial presentation support. The courts have imposed new duties on the litigation team members that require them to work more closely with clients, their employees, and information technologists, not only in preserving potential trial evidence but also in counseling them on appropriate retention methods of records in advance of any litigation.

Discovery and Technology

The challenge for the legal profession and the litigation team in particular during discovery is locating and obtaining the electronic documentation previously kept in paper form. In the traditional paper discovery process, a typical document request might be, "Produce all the engineering records related to the design and manufacture of…." The result might be anything from a few file boxes of paper copies and microfilm or microfiche images, to a tractor trailer full of boxes, to a warehouse full of paper documents that had to be reviewed manually by a team of litigation support personnel that might have included paralegals, law students, or contract attorneys.

With the advent of technology, the discovery process has changed as the forms in which documents are stored has changed. For many years records were copied

VIDEO ADVICE FROM THE FIELD

Jennifer McCoy—National Litigation Service Coordinator

A discussion on how technology has impacted litigation.

After watching the video in MyLegalStudiesKit, answer the following question.

- Why is knowledge of technology important in litigation?

onto film in the form of microfilm or microfiche; these are photographic copies of documents such as the bank records or cancelled checks. Today, storage of documents may be in the same electronic format as the original document, such as a word processing program format or a copy of a paper document—not photographically copied but instead electronically scanned and saved in electronic format. Modern discovery requires knowledge of how documents are stored electronically, how they are indexed, and how to obtain them in a useful, reviewable format. Litigation support personnel and trial counsel must have a basic understanding of the technology used in creating, storing, and retrieving **electronically stored information (ESI)** and the terminology used by the information technology specialist to be able to effectively communicate the needs and requirements for litigation.

electronically stored information (ESI)
Any type of information that can be stored electronically.

The courts have addressed the use of technology by implementing rules of court and of evidence specifically related to electronic discovery. The federal courts first introduced rules on electronic discovery by amending the Federal Rules of Civil Procedure (FRCP) in 2006. These rules were restated in 2007. Congress reacted to initial concerns of the courts and trial counsel about privilege and confidentiality issues by enactment of Federal Rules of Evidence (FRE) rule 502 in 2008, shown in Appendix VII. State courts have also introduced new rules on electronic discovery, with many based on the federal rules.

As with anything new in the law, there is a period during which different legal theories of practice and procedures are tested through court challenges. As a result of these court challenges in the area of electronically stored information, there have been a number of well-regarded court decisions. The courts have addressed these challenges with court opinion that defines the duties and responsibilities of counsel and of their clients involved in litigation. Among these rules are those on **spoliation of evidence,** mandating protection of the potential evidentiary data against loss, and new obligations on lawyers to cooperate in the process and ensure protection of the electronically stored information. Among the new rules and obligations imposed on counsel are those defining the **legal hold** on potential evidence and the responsibility of trial counsel to supervise actively the preservation and collection of evidence.

spoliation of evidence
Destruction of records that may be relevant to ongoing or anticipated litigation, government investigation, or audit. Courts differ in their interpretation of the level of intent required before sanctions may be warranted.

legal hold
An affirmative duty to preserve potential evidence.

Locating Electronically Stored Information

A key component of the process of civil litigation is investigation and finding of evidence supporting the facts as alleged. Success in electronic discovery requires knowledge of the tools of document creation and storage. Historically, file memos and correspondence were a fruitful source of information. Correspondence and, to some extent, memos have been replaced with e-mails, text messages using cell phones, and comments on social networking sites. Evidence of actionable wrongdoing based on age, sex, or other discrimination in the work place may only exist in electronic form in an e-mail chain among executives of a company. Proof of actionable financial wrongdoing in the corporate world may become evident only by careful analysis of the pattern and code words used in e-mails. As shown in Exhibit 1.1, these patterns of connection between senders and receivers of e-mail are expansive, as they were in Enron Corporation.

Obtaining Records

In many litigation cases, copies of documents that have been stored electronically will have to be obtained. Knowing that documents have been stored in particular locations or on specific devises is only part of the process. Knowing how and where information is stored will help in being satisfied that all records have been delivered.

Exhibit 1.1 E-mail patterns in Enron Corporation

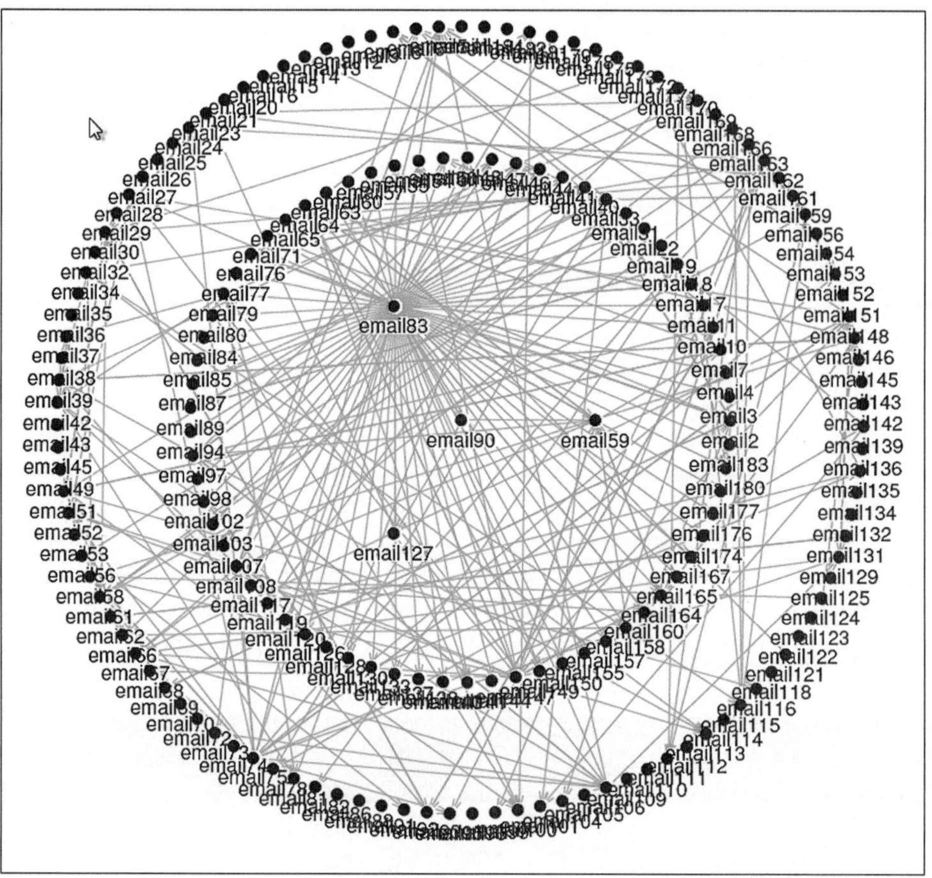

Source: "Scan Statistics on Enron Graphs" by Carey E. Priebe, et al. from *Computational & Mathematical Organization Theory,* October 1, 2005. Copyright © 2005 Springer Netherlands. Used with permission.

What is obtained from the opposing party must be an authentic copy in a usable form for analysis and review. In an international contract dispute, the documents may be in a language other than English, such as Spanish, Chinese, Japanese, Russian, or another written or spoken language. In these cases, translators or translation services may be brought in if there is no one on the legal team with that language skill.

Electronically stored information may also be delivered in different formats; think of them as computer languages. It may be simple word processing format differences like the difference between documents saved using Microsoft Word or WordPerfect. Each is a different format that may or may not be readable using the other program. Other forms of data, from financial records to database items, may be provided in the original format of creation, called **native form,** or in reproduced formats like **PDF** or **TIFF** image files. In most cases, the format of delivery will not be an issue, but in others it may prevent the ability to authenticate the document because the information about the creation of the document, called **metadata,** has been removed. It may also make electronic searching and review of the documents difficult or impossible without additional, costly steps.

Reviewing Records

Traditional review of records looks for consistencies and inconsistencies with the client's story and that of other witnesses. With limited numbers of documents, it is possible to economically conduct a manual review. But, as the numbers of

native form (native file format)
Electronic documents have an associated file structure defined by the original creating application. This file structure is referred to as the "native format" of the document. Because viewing or searching documents in the native format may require the original application (e.g., viewing a Microsoft Word document may require the Microsoft Word application), documents are often converted to a standard file format (e.g., TIFF) as part of electronic document processing.

PDF
Portable Document Format.

TIFF
Tagged Image File Format, one of the most widely used formats for storing images. TIFF graphics can be black and white, gray-scaled, or color.

metadata
Information about a particular data set that may describe, for example, how, when, and by whom it was received, created, accessed, and/or modified and how it is formatted.

PRACTICE TIP

Virtually every word processing format may be opened and read using Corel WordPerfect. The same cannot be said for some other, competitive programs, which can only be used to read their own proprietary formats.

documents increases to the thousands, tens of thousands, and even more, economical review initially requires the use of computers and software searches for names, phrases, and other key terms. The first steps are to eliminate duplicates, called **de-duping.** Think about the e-mails that you have received that were also sent to twenty or thirty others on an e-mail chain. There is no need to read each of them; the content is the same. What might be of importance is who the recipients are, their relation to the sender, or their role in the underlying potential cause of action or actual involvement in wrongdoing.

de-duping
The process of comparing electronic records based on their characteristics and removing duplicate records from the data set.

Organizing and Managing Case Files

As cases become more complex, software programs are being used to organize and manage case files. These programs allow a central repository for information on contacts (people), dates (calendars), locations of documents, and in some cases time and expenses on a case. It may be lists of names or clients, witnesses, opposing parties for a document, the name and phone number of the opposing counsel, or a copy of the complaint. Crucial to case management is recording deadlines, such as the **statute of limitations** for filing a complaint, the due date of a pleading or motion, and the conference date with the assigned judge. Some law firms do this manually using a file card system; others use case management software that automatically calculates deadlines based on the local rules of court.

statute of limitations
The time frame within which an action must be commenced or the party will lose their right to use the courts to seek redress.

ADVICE FROM THE FIELD

DISCONNECT BETWEEN LEGAL AND IT GETTING WORSE, RECOMMIND SURVEY REVEALS

Second Annual Survey Shows Collaboration Between Departments has Decreased Dramatically in Last Year, Threatening Effective eDiscovery Response

SAN FRANCISCO, CA, JUNE 16, 2010–Recommind, the leader in search-powered information risk management (IRM) software, today released results from its second annual survey that examines the working relationship between corporate IT and legal departments. While the inaugural survey revealed that a lack of collaboration between both teams was greatly hindering eDiscovery efforts, the 2010 installation demonstrates that this disconnect has dramatically worsened. The survey of senior IT managers at enterprises averaging 13,000 employees reveals that IT and legal teams aren't collaborating on buying decisions and question each other's commitment to and understanding of eDiscovery and regulatory compliance. This further endangers effective eDiscovery and regulatory responses at the exact time such activities are skyrocketing.

While legal and IT have been historically disparate, the exponential increase in content creation and the rising complexities and risks of eDiscovery and regulatory scrutiny have inexorably linked the needs and responsibilities of each department. With the average U.S. company facing 305 lawsuits at any given time–a number that jumps to 556 for companies with more than $1 billion in revenue–enterprises urgently need to ensure close collaboration between these critical departments or face massive financial, competitive and reputational risks as [a] result. Recommind's survey reveals that communication between legal and IT has become decidedly worse in 2010. For example:

- In 2009, 67% of respondents described the relationship between the two departments as "good" or "very good"; in 2010, that number has dropped to 54%.
- In 2009, 37% of respondents reported that IT and legal were working more closely together than the year before; that number has dropped to 27% in 2010.
- In 2009, 40% of respondents stated that their IT department considered eDiscovery to be a high to very high priority; in 2010, that number has dropped to 26%.
- In 2009, 82% of respondents said that IT was "very involved" in eDiscovery technology purchasing decisions, with legal being "very involved" 48% of the

(continued)

(continued)

time. In 2010, IT's involvement has remained largely the same, dropping from 82% to 78%. The involvement of the legal department, however, has dropped dramatically, decreasing from 48% to 33%.

In addition to measuring collaboration, the survey also examined the formalized processes between IT and legal and inter-departmental perceptions, focusing specifically on how the teams communicate with and evaluate each other. For example:

- 72% of respondents report that their IT and legal teams meet once a quarter or less; 52% meet once a year or less and 23% never meet at all.
- When it comes to actually implementing eDiscovery processes, the focus of each department is also quite different: the primary goal of the IT department is "executing as quickly as possible" (35%), while the primary goal of the legal department is "complying with federal regulations and court orders" (61%).

Finally, earlier this year, Gartner Group recommended that global organizations start adding legal support managers—a hybrid position that helps mediate between IT and legal—to create policies and schedule and execute eDiscovery processes. It would appear that Gartner's advice is not yet being heeded; nearly 75% of the enterprises surveyed do not currently have this position filled.

"How can enterprises expect to avoid trouble in this hyper-regulatory and increasingly litigious environment when their legal and IT teams hardly talk? Effective responses to regulatory scrutiny and eDiscovery events are too complex, expensive and dangerous to have this level of miscommunication and mistrust between key departments," said Craig Carpenter, vice president of marketing, Recommind. "Having the right technology and processes in place are crucial, but everything starts with communication. Hopefully the fact that these problems are being exposed will serve as a clarion call for enterprises and the industry in general, because enterprises need a real sense of urgency if they want to avoid becoming front-page news for all the wrong reasons."

About Recommind Inc.

Recommind's search-powered Information Risk Management (IRM) platform automatically accesses, organizes, collects, and analyzes large volumes of information from myriad sources to address an enterprise's critical eDiscovery, compliance, e-mail categorization, and knowledge management needs. With faster, more accurate access to and greater control over information, organizations can lower risk, improve productivity, increase the value of information assets, and improve competitiveness and profits. Recommind customers include Bertelsmann, BMW, DLA Piper, Eversheds, Novartis, Shearman & Sterling, and Verizon. Recommind is headquartered in San Francisco and has offices in New York, Atlanta, Boston, Chicago, Houston, Washington, D.C., London, and Bonn, Germany. For more information, e-mail info@recommind.com, or go to www.recommind.com.

RULES OF EVIDENCE AND COURT

LEARNING OBJECTIVE 2
Describe the rules of court and evidence related to electronic discovery.

The courts, federal and state, have created rules of court to ensure fairness and the orderly administration of justice through trials and other court proceedings. Each jurisdiction is free to establish its own rules, and some judges even have their own localized rules for their courtroom. See those of Judge Padova in Exhibit 1.2. Rules of evidence provide the framework for the presentation and use of evidence in trials. In the federal system, these are the Rules of Civil Procedure, Rules of Criminal Procedure, and the Federal Rules of Evidence. Many states pattern their rules of court and of evidence on the federal rules, but generally have no obligations to do so. Over the many years of litigation, a body of opinions has been created interpreting the pre-electronic discovery rules and offering guidance to counsel and the courts.

Electronic discovery did not suddenly appear, nor did the rules enacted by the federal courts in 2006. They were a response to a growing uncertainty of how existing rules of discovery should be applied and which rules would apply to the new form of documentary evidence in electronic form.

Exhibit 1.2 Policies and procedures of United States District Judge Padova

The Honorable John R. Padova
United States District Judge
Room 17613, U.S. Courthouse
601 Market Street
Philadelphia, PA 19106
215-597-1178
Fax: 215-580-2272

Deputies: Gerrie Keane (Civil Case Management and Scheduling)
Jenniffer Cabrera (Criminal Case Management and Scheduling)

Policies and Procedures

(Revised August, 2005)

. . . .

Discovery Conferences and Dispute Resolution

Judge Padova normally does not hold discovery conferences, but encourages the use of telephone conferences in lieu of motion practice to resolve discovery disputes. When a **discovery *default*** occurs, Judge Padova encourages counsel to file a motion to compel, which he will usually grant upon presentation pursuant to Local Civil Rule 26.1(g). When a **discovery *dispute*** occurs, and counsel have been unable to resolve it themselves or with Judge Padova's assistance by telephone, he requires a motion to compel. Judge Padova expects discovery to be voluntary and cooperative in accordance with the Federal Rules of Civil Procedure and the Plan.

Confidentiality Agreements

Parties may agree privately to keep documents and information confidential. The Court may enter an Order of Confidentiality only after making a specific finding of good cause based on a particularized showing that the parties' privacy interests outweight the public's right to obtain information concerning judicial proceedings. See Pansy v. Borough of East Stroudsburg, 23 F.3d 772, 786 (3d Cir. 1994).

Expert Witnesses

Counsel are required to identify expert witnesses and provide curriculum vitae and, as to all experts, voluntarily exchange the information referred to in Federal Rule of Civil Procedure 26(a)(2)(B) by expert report, deposition or answer to expert interrogatory in accordance with the dates outlined in the Court's scheduling orders. Except for good cause, expert testimony will be limited at trial to the information provided.

The federal courts adopted, effective December 2006 and restated effective December 2007, a set of rules of civil procedure that recognize the impact of technology on discovery and trial practice:

- Rule 16 Pretrial Conferences: Scheduling Management
- Rule 26 General Provisions Governing Discovery; Duty of Disclosure
- Rule 33 Interrogatories to Parties
- Rule 34 Productions of Documents, Electronically stored information, and things and entry upon land for inspection and other purposes
- Rule 37 Failure to make Disclosures or Cooperate in Discovery; Sanctions
- Rule 45 Subpoeña

The courts also added a new form:

- Form 35 Report of Parties Planning Meeting

After a brief experience with the December 2006 version of the rules, the federal courts tried to bring greater clarity to the field by restating the rules in 2007. These new Federal Rules of Civil Procedure provide a framework for requesting

IN THE WORDS OF THE COURT...

Zubulake v. UBS Warburg LLC, (S.D.N.Y. 2004) 229 F.R.D. 422

Judge Shira Scheidlin

...When this case began more than two years ago, there was little guidance from the judiciary, bar associations or the academy as to the governing standards. Much has changed in that time. There have been a flood of recent opinions–including a number from appellate courts–and there are now several treatises on the subject.... In addition, professional groups such as the American Bar Association and the Sedona Conference have provided very useful guidance on thorny issues relating to the discovery of electronically stored information.... Many courts have adopted, or are considering adopting, local rules addressing the subject.... Most recently, the Standing Committee on Rules and Procedures has approved for publication and public comment a proposal for revisions to the Federal Rules of Civil Procedure designed to address many of the issues raised by the discovery of electronically stored information....

Now that the key issues have been addressed and national standards are developing, parties and their counsel are fully on notice of their responsibility to preserve and produce electronically stored information. The tedious and difficult fact finding encompassed in this opinion and others like it is a great burden on a court's limited resources. The time and effort spent by counsel to litigate these issues has also been time-consuming and distracting. This Court, for one, is optimistic that with the guidance now provided it will not be necessary to spend this amount of time again. It is hoped that counsel will heed the guidance provided by these resources and will work to ensure that preservation, production and spoliation issues are limited, if not eliminated.

and satisfying requests for documents in electronic format, like e-mails, electronically stored word processor documents, and information in electronic databases. Unlike other well-tested rules, court opinions continue to define the duties and responsibilities of the legal team as it relates to the issues of electronic discovery. Among the leading opinions on the subject are the series of opinions written by Judge Shira Scheidlin in *Zubulake v. UBS Warburg LLC*, a case of alleged work place discrimination.

ETHICAL DUTIES AND OBLIGATIONS OF THE LITIGATION TEAM

LEARNING OBJECTIVE 3
Describe the ethical duties and obligations of the legal team.

Every profession has a set of rules that members of that profession are expected to follow. These rules typically set forth the minimum in ethical behavior—the very least that each professional should do. In the field of law, these rules are referred to as "the rules of **ethics**" or "the rules of professional responsibility." With only a few exceptions, most states have adopted some form of the current or former version of the American Bar Association's **Model Rules of Professional Conduct.**

ethics
Minimally acceptable standards of conduct in a profession.

Model Rules of Professional Conduct
The American Bar Association set of proposed ethical standards for the legal profession.

Among the ethical obligations of the attorney and the legal team acting as agent of the attorney are:

Rule 1.1, Competency,
Rule 1.6(A), Confidentiality,
Rule 1.7, Conflicts Of Interest,
Rule 3.3, Candor,

Rule 3.4, Fairness To Opposing Party And Counsel, and
Rules 5.1 and 5.3, Duty to Supervise.

As with the opinions interpreting the rules of court and rules of evidence in federal and state courts, there is a body of ethics opinions in each jurisdiction. These opinions clarify and apply the ethics rules to specific situations. With the increased use of computers and technology in the law office, in court, and in marketing law practices, many new opinions have been written interpreting the rules and applying them to contemporary issues of legal practice.

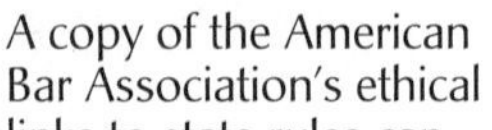

WEB RESOURCES

A copy of the American Bar Association's ethical rules and links to state rules can be viewed at www.abanet.org/cpr

Competency

competent
Having the requisite knowledge and skill, thoroughness, and preparation necessary for representation.

Competent representation requires the legal knowledge, skill, thoroughness, and preparation reasonably necessary for the representation. The minimum standards clearly require an understanding of the rules of court and the rules of evidence. These rules continue to grow in number and complexity, including the adoption of rules regarding electronic discovery. New rules require a new level of knowledge to competently represent clients. Further, lawyers must be able to communicate with clients in the language of technology about methods of creation, storage and sources of electronic documents and the methods for retrieving them and processing them for submission to opposing counsel and the court. Increasingly, the courts have been critical of lawyers who do not possess the requisite technology skills. As stated by U.S. Magistrate Judge Facciola:

> "I have indicated how dangerous it is for lawyers to opine on technical matters when they lack the necessary understanding and training." See, e.g., *United States v. O'Keefe*, 537 F. Supp. 2d at 24.

WEB RESOURCES

Ethical Perspectives

Review the most current version and comments to Rule 1.6 on Confidentiality of Information of the American Bar Association Model Rules of Professional Conduct at the American Bar Association's website: http://www.abanet.org/cpr/mrpc/rule_1_6.html

Confidentiality

confidentiality
Ethical obligation to keep client information confidential (not disclose) founded on the belief that clients should be able to tell their attorneys everything about their case so the attorney can give proper legal advice to the client.

attorney–client privilege
Rule of evidence that protects the client from the attorney being required to reveal the confidential information.

The ethical obligation to keep client information confidential is founded on the belief that clients should be able to tell their attorneys everything about their case so that the attorneys can give proper legal advice to the client. **Confidentiality** is an ethical obligation. For the attorney, the American Bar Association (ABA) Model Rules require, in Rule 1.6, that lawyers "not reveal information relating to representation of a client" until the client gives informed consent to the disclosure after being advised of the consequences of disclosure, except for disclosures that are "impliedly authorized." Everything the lawyer or the members of the legal team learn about the case from every possible source is to be kept confidential. For example, the client's case is written up in the local daily newspaper, which sets out details of the case. Even though these details are made public, the members of the legal team are not free to discuss them. They are still to be kept confidential. They may not be discussed with someone else who has read the newspaper but who is not on the team.

All communication between the client and the lawyer for the purpose of obtaining legal advice is protected by the attorney–client privilege. The **attorney–client privilege** is a rule of evidence that protects the client from the attorney's being required to reveal the information. (Note that the information is also confidential, but the privilege is different from the duty of confidentiality.) The privilege only applies when the lawyer is questioned under oath.

It is now accepted that the efficient administration of justice requires lawyers to engage others, such as legal assistants, accountants, and other experts. This would not be possible if the privilege did not extend to these agents of the attorney, including, most recently, public relations firms.

work product doctrine
A limited protection for material prepared by the attorney, or those working for the attorney, in anticipation of litigation or for trial.

The **work product doctrine** provides a limited amount of protection for material prepared by the attorney, or those working for the attorney, in anticipation of litigation or for trial. The work product doctrine is different from both the attorney–client privilege and the duty of confidentiality. The attorney–client privilege and the duty of confidentiality relate to the information provided by the clients regardless of whether the information involves potential litigation.

The basic concepts of privilege and confidentiality have not changed with the introduction of technology. The problem arises of preserving the privilege and confidentiality when the information may be buried in potentially millions of documents that are produced as part of the discovery process. As communication methods have changed, communication between attorneys and clients has also changed. What was once in written paper form may now be in an e-mail, text message, or other electronically stored document. While every safeguard is undertaken by counsel before turning over ESI to the opposing party, occasionally something that is privileged or confidential may be inadvertently turned over. The question of the ongoing confidential or privileged nature of the information is not always clear. The implementation of Federal Rules of Evidence 502 was an attempt to bring uniformity to the issue. But, courts still have different views on the potential waiver of privilege, depending on the actions made to avoid inadvertent disclosure and the steps taken to retrieve the document.

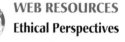

WEB RESOURCES

Ethical Perspectives

Review the most current version and comments to Rule 1.7 on Conflict of Interest of the American Bar Association Model Rules of Professional Conduct at the American Bar Association website at http://www.abanet.org/cpr/mrpc/rule_1_7.html

ETHICAL Perspectives

ARIZONA ETHICS RULES

ER 1.6. Confidentiality of Information.

(a) A lawyer shall not reveal information relating to the representation of a client unless the client gives informed consent, the disclosure is impliedly authorized in order to carry out the representation or the disclosure is permitted or required by paragraphs (b), (c) or (d), or ER 3.3(a)(3).
(b) A lawyer shall reveal such information to the extent the lawyer reasonably believes necessary to prevent the client from committing a criminal act that the lawyer believes is likely to result in death or substantial bodily harm.
(c) A lawyer may reveal the intention of the lawyer's client to commit a crime and the information necessary to prevent the crime.
(d) A lawyer may reveal such information relating to the representation of a client to the extent the lawyer reasonably believes necessary:
    (1) to prevent the client from committing a crime or fraud that is reasonably certain to result in substantial injury to the financial interests or property of another and in furtherance of which the client has used or is using the lawyer's services;
    (2) to mitigate or rectify substantial injury to the financial interests or property of another that is reasonably certain to result or has resulted from the client's commission of a crime or fraud in furtherance of which the client has used the lawyer's services;
    (3) to secure legal advice about the lawyer's compliance with these Rules;
    (4) to establish a claim or defense on behalf of the lawyer in a controversy between the lawyer and the client, to establish a defense to a criminal charge or civil claim against the lawyer based upon conduct in which the client was involved, or to respond to allegations in any proceeding concerning the lawyer's representation of the client; or
    (5) to comply with other law or a final order of a court or tribunal of competent jurisdiction directing the lawyer to disclose such information.

WEB RESOURCES

Contrast and compare the **Arizona Rules of Professional Conduct** at http://www.myazbar.org/Ethics/rules.cfm with the American Bar Association Model Rules of Professional Responsibility at http://www.abanet.org/cpr/mrpc/mrpc_toc.html, and the ethical rules in your jurisdiction.

Conflicts of Interest

conflict of interest
Situations where the interests or loyalties of the lawyer and client may be or may appear to be adverse or divided.

The basis of the **conflict of interest** rule is the belief that a person cannot be loyal to two clients. Lawyers cannot represent two clients with potentially conflicting interests, such as a husband and wife in a domestic relations case, nor represent a client when the attorney has a financial interest in the subject matter of the case, such as being a partner in a real estate transaction. Loyalty to the client is the essence of ethics Rule 1.7 on Conflict of Interest. A lawyer should not represent another client if "representation of one client will be directly adverse to another client" (ABA Model Rules of Professional Conduct Rule 1.7), unless both clients give their informed consent to the dual representation, and the consent is confirmed in writing. The lawyer's personal interests or those of third parties who are not clients, such as family members, may also create a risk of a conflict that must be avoided.

The increased use of computerized case management software makes checking for conflicts easier and more reliable than some earlier, paper-based card systems, where a missing card could result in a faulty search for conflicts. With a highly mobile legal workforce, the names of past clients of the firm and of other firms at which the legal team members—including paralegals, litigation support, and attorneys—have worked can be easily searched. Where conflicts may exist, they may not necessarily disqualify the firm but may be used to create a conflict wall around legal team members who must be shielded from any access to a client or file because of a potential or actual conflict.

Candor

It is the duty of the advocate to avoid any conduct that undermines the integrity of the process. The duty to the client to persuasively present the case is a qualified duty, qualified by the ethical obligation (**candor**) to not mislead the court or opposing counsel with false statements of law or of facts that the lawyer knows to be false. It may be a simple ethical duty to competently research and present the current case and statutory law, even when the most current version is not favorable to the position taken. In the technology age, this duty requires making a complete search for ALL the law, statutory enactments and case law, and not just the part that is favorable to the client's position.

candor
Ethical obligation to not mislead the court or opposing counsel with false statements of law or of facts that the lawyer knows to be false.

ETHICAL Perspectives

RHODE ISLAND RULES OF PROFESSIONAL CONDUCT

Rule 3.3 Candor Toward the Tribunal

(a) A lawyer shall not knowingly:
  (1) make a false statement of fact or law to a tribunal or fail to correct a false statement of material fact or law previously made to the tribunal by the lawyer;
  (2) fail to disclose to the tribunal legal authority in the controlling jurisdiction known to the lawyer to be directly adverse to the position of the client and not disclosed by opposing counsel; or
  (3) offer evidence that the lawyer knows to be false. If a lawyer, the lawyer's client, or a witness called by the lawyer, has offered material evidence and the lawyer comes to know of its falsity, the lawyer shall take reasonable remedial measures, including, if necessary, disclosure to the tribunal. A lawyer may refuse to offer evidence, other than the testimony of a defendant in a criminal matter, that the lawyer reasonably believes is false.

WEB RESOURCES

Contrast and compare the **Rhode Island Rules of Professional Conduct** at http://www.courts.ri.gov/supreme/pdf-files/Rules_Of_Professional_Conduct.pdf with the American Bar Association Model Rules of Professional Responsibility at http://www.abanet.org/cpr/mrpc/mrpc_toc.html, and the ethical rules in your jurisdiction.

(b) A lawyer who represents a client in an adjudicative proceeding and who knows that a person intends to engage, is engaging or has engaged in criminal or fraudulent conduct related to the proceeding shall take reasonable remedial measures, including, if necessary, disclosure to the tribunal.
(c) The duties stated in paragraphs (a) and (b) continue to the conclusion of the proceeding, and apply even if compliance requires disclosure of information otherwise protected by Rule 1.6.
(d) In an ex parte proceeding, a lawyer shall inform the tribunal of all material facts known to the lawyer that will enable the tribunal to make an informed decision, whether or not the facts are adverse.

Fairness to Opposing Party and Counsel

The ethical rule of fairness to opposing counsel and parties is an attempt to set the guidelines to ensure justice is done even if one's client loses the case. Each side is expected to use its best skills and knowledge and present fairly its position in the form of evidence for the trier of fact to determine where the truth lies. Destroying, falsifying, or tampering with evidence destroys the fabric of the system. If people lose confidence in the system because of these unfair tactics, society loses confidence in the system and it breaks down. Just consider the criminal cases where the prosecutor does not turn over, as required, exculpatory evidence that might show the defendant innocent.

Courts have encouraged a spirit of civility if not cooperation between counsels. The increased complexity and importance of electronic discovery have seen both an increased cooperation in some litigation circles and an increase in what can be described as gamesmanship at best or unfair delaying tactics at worst. Federal rules of court require counsel to confer early in a case to discuss issues

IN THE WORDS OF THE COURT . . .

United States District Court, District of Columbia.
COVAD COMMUNICATIONS COMPANY, Plaintiff,
V.
REVONET, INC., Defendant.
Civil No. 06-1892 (CKK/JMF).
August 17, 2009.

MEMORANDUM OPINION

JOHN M. FACCIOLA, **Magistrate Judge.**

In this particular case, the spirit and letter of rules requiring attorneys to meet and confer are often treated in a perfunctory manner or completely disregarded. I will not discourage the few examples of cooperation in this case. Indeed, if the efforts of the federal courts to reduce the costs of discovery and, in particular electronic discovery, are to be taken seriously, then counsel will have to know that judicial orders and local rules requiring meaningful discussions between counsel before discovery motions are filed mean what they say. If attorneys insist on "drive by" meetings and conferrals, or they think that exchanging nasty e-mails about how they will not talk and will not cooperate satisfies the requirements will suffice, then they have to know that they are going to get hit where it hurts—in their pocketbooks.

information technologist
A member of the legal team who has legal and technological skills and primarily support electronic discovery activities.

about discovery. When attended by cooperating counsel with the requisite technological knowledge or a knowledgeable **information technologist (IT),** it can result in a saving of time and money in the discovery process. When counsel does not have sufficient knowledge about electronically stored information in general or the client's system in particular, it can be the start of a process involving needless discovery motions, delays, and increased costs of discovery.

ETHICAL Perspectives

OREGON RULES OF PROFESSIONAL CONDUCT (12/01/06)

Rule 3.4 Fairness to Opposing Party and Counsel

A lawyer shall not:

(a) knowingly and unlawfully obstruct another party's access to evidence or unlawfully alter, destroy or conceal a document or other material having potential evidentiary value. A lawyer shall not counsel or assist another person to do any such act;

(b) falsify evidence; counsel or assist a witness to testify falsely; offer an inducement to a witness that is prohibited by law; or pay, offer to pay, or acquiesce in payment of compensation to a witness contingent upon the content of the witness's testimony or the outcome of the case; except that a lawyer may advance, guarantee or acquiesce in the payment of:

   (1) expenses reasonably incurred by a witness in attending or testifying;
   (2) reasonable compensation to a witness for the witness's loss of time in attending or testifying; or
   (3) a reasonable fee for the professional services of an expert witness.

(c) knowingly disobey an obligation under the rules of a tribunal, except for an open refusal based on an assertion that no valid obligation exists;

(d) in pretrial procedure, knowingly make a frivolous discovery request or fail to make reasonably diligent effort to comply with a legally proper discovery request by an opposing party;

(e) in trial, allude to any matter that the lawyer does not reasonably believe is relevant or that will not be supported by admissible evidence, assert personal knowledge of facts in issue except when testifying as a witness, or state a personal opinion as to the justness of a cause, the credibility of a witness, the culpability of a civil litigant or the guilt or innocence of an accused;

(f) advise or cause a person to secrete himself or herself or to leave the jurisdiction of a tribunal for purposes of making the person unavailable as a witness therein; or

(g) threaten to present criminal charges to obtain an advantage in a civil matter unless the lawyer reasonably believes the charge to be true and if the purpose of the lawyer is to compel or induce the person threatened to take reasonable action to make good the wrong which is the subject of the charge.

Adopted 01/01/05 http://www.osbar.org/_docs/rulesregs/orpc.pdf

WEB RESOURCES

Contrast and compare the **Oregon Rules of Professional Conduct** at http://www.osbar.org/_docs/rulesregs/orpc.pdf with the American Bar Association Model Rules of Professional Responsibility at http://www.abanet.org/cpr/mrpc/mrpc_toc.html, and the ethical rules in your jurisdiction.

DUTY TO SUPERVISE

Ethical behavior is expected and required of every member of the legal team: attorney, paralegal, litigation support, information technologist, and outside consultant. The supervising attorney of every legal team must follow the ethics rules and ensure that the members of the legal team follow the same rules as the supervising attorney. These rules are as much a part of the administration of justice as the rules of civil or criminal procedure and the rules of evidence. The obligation to ensure ethical conduct is that of the **supervising attorney** under the ethical obligation to supervise all who work on the case for the attorney, under Rules 5.1 and 5.3. The duty of supervision is required of partners, and lawyers with managerial authority in the firm, to ensure that other lawyers' conduct conforms to the ethical code.

supervising attorney
Member of the legal team to whom all others on the team report and who has the ultimate responsibility for the actions of the legal team.

CONCEPT REVIEW AND REINFORCMENT

KEY TERMS

civil litigation 4
evidence 4
documentary evidence 4
electronically stored information (ESI) 6
spoliation of evidence 6
legal hold 6
native form 7
PDF 7
TIFF 7
metadata 7
de-duping 8
statute of limitations 8
ethics 11
Model Rules of Professional Conduct 11
competent 12
confidentiality 12
attorney–client privilege 12
work product doctrine 12
conflict of interest 14
candor 14
information technologist (IT) 16
supervising attorney 17

CHAPTER SUMMARY

Introduction to Litigation Practice Fundamentals	Civil litigation involves remedies for legal disputes and includes a number of steps including discovery, analysis, and presentation of relevant evidence. For the litigation team, knowledge of technology must be added to the required knowledge of the law.
The Changing Role of the Litigation Team	Introduction of technology, including computers and word processors, has changed the way discovery is conducted from the days of paper documentation. The litigation team must have a basic understanding of the technology used in creating, storing, and retrieving electronically stored information and the terminology used by the information technology specialist.
Locating Electronically Stored Information	A key component of the process of civil litigation is investigation and finding evidence supporting the facts alleged.
Obtaining Records	In many litigation cases it is necessary to obtain copies of documents that are stored electronically. These electronically stored items may be delivered in different formats, including in original form, called native form, or in reproduced formats like PDF or TIFF image files.
Reviewing Records	With increases in the number of documents to be reviewed, the first step is to eliminate duplicates, called de-duping.
Organizing and Managing Case Files	As cases become more complex, software programs are used to organize and manage case files.

Rules of Evidence and Court	To ensure fairness and the orderly administration of justice, the state and federal courts have created rules of court and rules of evidence. Each court may create its own rules. To address the issue of electronic discovery, the federal courts adopted in December 2006 new rules and forms to meet the needs of electronically stored information.
Ethical Duties and Obligations of the Litigation Team	Ethics is the minimally acceptable standards of conduct in a profession. Ethical guidelines are enforced by the court in the jurisdiction where the attorney is practicing or where the case is being tried. The supervising attorney of every legal team must follow the ethics rules and ensure the members of the legal team follow the same rules as the supervising lawyer.
Competency	Ethical guidelines require lawyers to provide competent representation.
Confidentiality	Confidentiality is an ethical obligation. Attorneys have a duty to treat client information obtained in the course of representation of a client in confidence under ABA Rule 1.6.
Conflicts of Interest	A lawyer should not accept an engagement (representation) if the lawyer's personal interests or desires will, or if there is a reasonable probability that they will, adversely affect the advice to be given or services to be rendered to the prospective client.
Candor	It is the duty of the advocate to avoid any conduct that undermines the integrity of the process.
Fairness to Opposing Party and Counsel	Lawyers are expected to use their best skills in presenting a case and to avoid destruction or tampering with evidence or ignoring rules of court.
Duty to Supervise	All lawyers and partners in law firms are required to supervise everyone over whom they have supervisory authority. All ethical breaches by members of the legal team are ultimately those of the supervising attorney.

3

REVIEW QUESTIONS AND EXERCISES

1. What is ethics?
2. What is the purpose of the confidentiality rule in the legal setting?
3. What is the difference between the duty of confidentiality and the attorney–client privilege?
4. What are the judicial approaches to the inadvertent disclosure of confidential information?
5. What ethical guidelines, if any, does your state follow?
6. What is the ethical obligation of a paralegal to the firm's client?
7. What is the ethical obligation of the paralegal to the court?
8. What is the ethical obligation of a litigation support staff member to the client? To the court? Of a litigation support person from an outside firm or consultant? Explain.
9. In addition to the attorney–client relationship, are there others where there is a privilege? Why would the privilege apply to others not in an attorney–client relationship?
10. How is a claim of privilege made?
11. Why is conflict of interest an issue for the legal team?
12. What are the ethical issues for a law firm using outside computer or technology consultants?
13. What is protected by the work product doctrine?
14. Should a technology consultant be considered an "other representative" under the Federal Rules of Civil Procedure, Rule 26? Why or why not?

15. Describe some of the applications of legal ethics in the use of technology.
16. How has technology changed the concept of competence for lawyers?
17. Do the ethical rules of "fairness" prevent lawyers from aggressively advocating their client's position?
18. Why would a partner in a law firm be required to supervise the other lawyers in the firm?
19. How can members of the legal team demonstrate that they have been adequately supervised?

BUILDING YOUR PARALEGAL SKILLS

INTERNET AND TECHNOLOGY EXERCISES

1. Find the web link to a copy of the most current version of the Model Rules of Professional Conduct as published by the American Bar Association. Save the web address in your bookmarks or favorites for future reference.
2. Use the Internet to locate the most current version of the ethical rules as used in your jurisdiction. Save the web address in your bookmarks or favorites for future reference.
3. Find any websites that have ethics opinions or sources of information on ethics in your jurisdiction.

CIVIL LITIGATION VIDEO CASE STUDIES

Parent and Child Consult the Legal Team: Confidentiality Issues

A student accused of assaulting another student on a school bus and his parents are meeting with the lawyer provided by their homeowner's insurance company. While the parents are talking with the lawyer, the student is interviewed by a paralegal; all confide what they consider to be confidential information.

After viewing the video at MyLegalStudiesKit, answer the following questions.

1. To whom does the attorney owe a duty of confidentiality?
2. Are the conversations covered by the attorney–client privilege?
3. What is the difference between confidentiality and privilege?

Solicitation in the ER

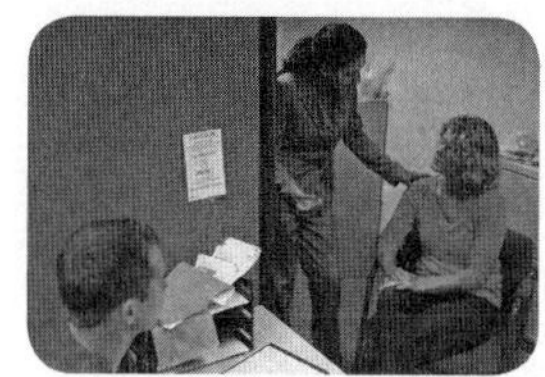

The mother of an injured child is approached in the emergency room and offered representation by a paralegal introduced by the emergency room clerk.

After viewing the video at MyLegalStudiesKit, answer the following questions.

1. What are the ethical guidelines in soliciting cases in your jurisdiction?
2. Are the rules of confidentiality the same for the medical profession as for the legal profession?
3. Has the paralegal engaged in the unlawful practiced of law?

CHAPTER OPENING SCENARIO CASE STUDY

1. Prepare a policy for the two offices to keep current with the activities of the other.
2. Prepare a memo to the partners of the firm on a method for the firms to follow in working on the same case.
3. Prepare an office policy on how members of the firm should keep current in the law and local procedures.
4. Maintain a time log of your activity in the course.

COMPREHENSIVE CASE STUDY

SCHOOL BUS–TRUCK ACCIDENT CASE

Review the assigned case study in Appendix II.

1. What are the ethical issues in representing a number of parties involved in the same accident case?
2. What is the minimum knowledge necessary to meet the ethical obligation of competency in a case involving potential brake failure, serious injuries, and death?
3. How can technology be used to manage a case involving a large number of plaintiffs and defendants?
4. Use the Internet to locate and prepare the required fee agreement for use in this case as required by your jurisdiction.

BUILDING YOUR PROFESSIONAL PORTFOLIO

PORTFOLIO EXERCISES: CIVIL LITIGATION TEAM AT WORK

Over time, experienced members of the litigation team accumulate reference information; policy issues, like password policies; forms, like checklists for filing pleadings; procedural issues, like statute of limitation information; and contacts, like the phone numbers of the technology support person in the local courthouse. Many also add samples of pleadings and sample letters that can be used as references in the future.

The Building Your Professional Portfolio Exercises at the end of each chapter are designed to help you create your own personal law office and litigation practice reference manual. The main heading: POLICY, FORMS, PROCEDURES, and CONTACTS AND RESOURCES are starting points. You may wish to further subdivide these by area of law or alphabetically to make finding a desired item easier. There are many different formats for the contents themselves. Policy statements may be in the form of formal or informal memos, and they may follow a specified format used by an organization. Forms may follow court requirements, or they may be a checklist of your own design. Contacts and resources may use the format of address books, computerized contact formats, or preprinted forms. Samples of possible formats are shown below. Additional formats for templates of memos and contacts may be downloaded from the samples provided in computerized office suites such as Microsoft Office or Corel WordPerfect.

Initially, set up a binder with a tab for each general category:

POLICY,
FORMS,
PROCEDURES, and
CONTACTS AND RESOURCES.

You may also want to set up an electronic file folder entitled PORTFOLIO, with subfolders for the tab categories, on your computer or a removable storage device. For example:

Portfolio

- Policy
- Forms
- Procedures
- Contacts and Resources

Most chapters suggest items to add to your portfolio. Add additional items that you may want to have for future reference.

Creating the Portfolio

Information included in the portfolio will come from a variety of sources, such as the Internet, library reference materials, and textbooks. One of the most widely used sources of information today is the Internet. In some cases, the same website may be a source of information on a number of topics; for example, the American Bar Association website, www.abanet.org, contains a copy of the model rules of professional responsibility and links to individual state legal resources. The website of the Cornell University Law School, www.law.cornell.edu, has online copies of cases, rules, and legal reference material.

An invaluable part of any portfolio is a current list of websites that provide necessary information. Be sure to add these Internet addresses (URL) to your list of favorites or bookmarks on your computer and to keep a current list with you when your personal computer is not available. When you copy material from the Internet, always include the source in the same document and in your portfolio. This way, you can refer back to it when you want to update or confirm the information, such as when your colleague or a judge asks, "Where did you get that information?"

Your learning objective in doing the portfolio exercises in each chapter is to give you real world experience finding information frequently needed in litigation. With practice, the ability to locate desired information and complete assigned tasks becomes easier, helping you become the "go to person" that everyone relies on for answering legal questions.

When completing the assignments, use the text as your guide and starting point, but do not limit yourself to a single source. Think outside the box.

Policy

A policy is a set of guidelines; they may be voluntary or mandatory, formal or informal, such as everyone is asked to cover their coffee cup when walking in the halls; or, no one may bring any food or drinks into the courtroom.

Forms

Forms may include helpful checklists for completing tasks or for obtaining information, such as a new client interview form or a checklist to obtain documents needed to open the new case. They also may be a mandated form required to file documents, such as a new case coversheet required to file a complaint in federal or state court.

Procedures

Procedures are the required methods of completing tasks. Procedures include the required time frames for taking action, such as the procedural time limits within which to file an appeal, as well as the required documentation required to file an appeal.

Contacts and Resources

Contacts and resources include everyone you will or may need to contact during any phase of the processing of a case, such as obtaining a client, setting up the case, investigating the facts, and trying the case in court.

EXAMPLES OF A POLICY, FORM, PROCEDURE, AND CONTACT RECORD

Policy

Exhibit 1.3

Password Policy

Created by or for the SANS Institute. Feel free to modify or use for your organization. If you have a policy to contribute, please send e-mail to stephen@sans.edu.

1.0 Overview

Passwords are an important aspect of computer security. They are the front line of protection for user accounts. A poorly chosen password may result in the compromise of <Company Name>'s entire corporate network. As such, all <Company Name> employees (including contractors and vendors with access to <Company Name> systems) are responsible for taking the appropriate steps, as outlined below, to select and secure their passwords.

2.0 Purpose

The purpose of this policy is to establish a standard for creation of strong passwords, the protection of those passwords, and the frequency of change.

3.0 Scope

The scope of this policy includes all personnel who have or are responsible for an account (or any form of access that supports or requires a password) on any system that resides at any <Company Name> facility, has access to the <Company Name> network, or stores any non-public <Company Name> information.

4.0 Policy

4.1 General

- All system-level passwords (e.g., root, enable, NT admin, application administration accounts, etc.) must be changed on at least a quarterly basis.
- All production system-level passwords must be part of the InfoSec administered global password management database.
- All user-level passwords (e.g., email, web, desktop computer, etc.) must be changed at least every six months. The recommended change interval is every four months.
- User accounts that have system-level privileges granted through group memberships or programs such as "sudo" must have a unique password from all other accounts held by that user.
- Passwords must not be inserted into email messages or other forms of electronic communication.
- Where SNMP is used, the community strings must be defined as something other than the standard defaults of "public," "private" and "system" and must be different from the passwords used to log in interactively. A keyed hash must be used where available (e.g., SNMPv2).
- All user-level and system-level passwords must conform to the guidelines described below.

4.2 Guidelines

A. General Password Construction Guidelines

Passwords are used for various purposes at <Company Name>. Some of the more common uses include: user level accounts, web accounts, email accounts, screen saver protection, voicemail password, and local router logins. Since very few systems have support for one-time tokens (i.e., dynamic passwords which are only used once), everyone should be aware of how to select strong passwords.

(*continued*)

Exhibit 1.3 *(continued)*

Poor, weak passwords have the following characteristics:

- The password contains less than fifteen characters
- The password is a word found in a dictionary (English or foreign)
- The password is a common usage word such as:
    - Names of family, pets, friends, co-workers, fantasy characters, etc.
    - Computer terms and names, commands, sites, companies, hardware, software.
    - The words "<Company Name>", "sanjose", "sanfran" or any derivation.
    - Birthdays and other personal information such as addresses and phone numbers.
    - Word or number patterns like aaabbb, qwerty, zyxwvuts, 123321, etc.
    - Any of the above spelled backwards.
    - Any of the above preceded or followed by a digit (e.g., secret1, 1secret)

Strong passwords have the following characteristics:

- Contain both upper and lower case characters (e.g., a-z, A-Z).
- Have digits and punctuation characters as well as letters e.g., 0-9, !@#$%^&*()_+|~-=\`{}[]:";'<>?,./).
- Are at least fifteen alphanumeric characters long and is a passphrase (Ohmy1stubbedmyt0e).
- Are not a word in any language, slang, dialect, jargon, etc.
- Are not based on personal information, names of family, etc.
- Passwords should never be written down or stored on-line. Try to create passwords that can be easily remembered. One way to do this is create a password based on a song title, affirmation, or other phrase. For example, the phrase might be: "This May Be One Way To Remember" and the password could be: "TmB1w2R!" or "Tmb1W>r~" or some other variation.

NOTE: Do not use either of these examples as passwords!

B. Password Protection Standards

Do not use the same password for <Company Name> accounts as for other non-<Company Name> access (e.g., personal ISP account, option trading, benefits, etc.). Where possible, don't use the same password for various <Company Name> access needs. For example, select one password for the Engineering systems and a separate password for IT systems. Also, select a separate password to be used for an NT account and a UNIX account.

Do not share <Company Name> passwords with anyone, including administrative assistants or secretaries. All passwords are to be treated as sensitive, Confidential <Company Name> information.

Here is a list of "dont's":

- Don't reveal a password over the phone to ANYONE
- Don't reveal a password in an email message
- Don't reveal a password to the boss
- Don't talk about a password in front of others
- Don't hint at the format of a password (e.g., "my family name")
- Don't reveal a password on questionnaires or security forms
- Don't share a password with family members
- Don't reveal a password to co-workers while on vacation

If someone demands a password, refer them to this document or have them call someone in the Information Security Department.

Do not use the "Remember Password" feature of applications (e.g., Eudora, OutLook, Netscape Messenger).

(continued)

Exhibit 1.3 *(continued)*

Again, do not write passwords down and store them anywhere in your office. Do not store passwords in a file on ANY computer system (including Palm Pilots or similar devices) without encryption.

Change passwords at least once every six months (except system-level passwords which must be changed quarterly). The recommended change interval is every four months.

If an account or password is suspected to have been compromised, report the incident to InfoSec and change all passwords.

Password cracking or guessing may be performed on a periodic or random basis by InfoSec or its delegates. If a password is guessed or cracked during one of these scans, the user will be required to change it.

C. Application Development Standards
Application developers must ensure their programs contain the following security precautions. Applications:

- should support authentication of individual users, not groups.
- should not store passwords in clear text or in any easily reversible form.
- should provide for some sort of role management, such that one user can take over the functions of another without having to know the other's password.
- should support TACACS+ , RADIUS and/or X.509 with LDAP security retrieval, wherever possible.

D. Use of Passwords and Passphrases for Remote Access Users
Access to the <Company Name> Networks via remote access is to be controlled using either a one-time password authentication or a public/private key system with a strong passphrase.

E. Passphrases
Passphrases are generally used for public/private key authentication. A public/private key system defines a mathematical relationship between the public key that is known by all, and the private key, that is known only to the user. Without the passphrase to "unlock" the private key, the user cannot gain access.

Passphrases are not the same as passwords. A passphrase is a longer version of a password and is, therefore, more secure. A passphrase is typically composed of multiple words. Because of this, a passphrase is more secure against "dictionary attacks."

A good passphrase is relatively long and contains a combination of upper and lowercase letters and numeric and punctuation characters. An example of a good passphrase:

"The*?#>*@TrafficOnThe101Was*&#!#ThisMorning"

All of the rules above that apply to passwords apply to passphrases.

5.0 Enforcement
Any employee found to have violated this policy may be subject to disciplinary action, up to and including termination of employment.

6.0 Definitions

Terms	**Definitions**
Application Administration Account	Any account that is for the administration of an application (e.g., Oracle database administrator, ISSU administrator).

7.0 Revision History

Source: http://www.sans.org/security-resources/policies/Password_Policy.pdf

Forms

Exhibit 1.4a

JS 44C/SDNY
REV. 5/2010

CIVIL COVER SHEET

The JS-44 civil cover sheet and the information contained herein neither replace nor supplement the filing and service of pleadings or other papers as required by law, except as provided by local rules of court. This form, approved by the Judicial Conference of the United States in September 1974, is required for use of the Clerk of Court for the purpose of initiating the civil docket sheet.

PLAINTIFFS | DEFENDANTS

ATTORNEYS (FIRM NAME, ADDRESS, AND TELEPHONE NUMBER | ATTORNEYS (IF KNOWN)

CAUSE OF ACTION (CITE THE U.S. CIVIL STATUTE UNDER WHICH YOU ARE FILING AND WRITE A BRIEF STATEMENT OF CAUSE)
(DO NOT CITE JURISDICTIONAL STATUTES UNLESS DIVERSITY)

Has this or a similar case been previously filed in SDNY at any time? No? ☐ Yes? ☐ Judge Previously Assigned

If yes, was this case Vol. ☐ Invol. ☐ Dismissed. No ☐ Yes ☐ If yes, give date ______________ & Case No. ______________

(PLACE AN [x] IN ONE BOX ONLY) NATURE OF SUIT

TORTS

CONTRACT

[ ] 110 INSURANCE
[ ] 120 MARINE
[ ] 130 MILLER ACT
[ ] 140 NEGOTIABLE INSTRUMENT
[ ] 150 RECOVERY OF OVERPAYMENT & ENFORCEMENT OF JUDGMENT
[ ] 151 MEDICARE ACT
[ ] 152 RECOVERY OF DEFAULTED STUDENT LOANS (EXCL VETERANS)
[ ] 153 RECOVERY OF OVERPAYMENT OF VETERAN'S BENEFITS
[ ] 160 STOCKHOLDERS SUITS
[ ] 190 OTHER CONTRACT
[ ] 195 CONTRACT PRODUCT LIABILITY
[ ] 196 FRANCHISE

PERSONAL INJURY

[ ] 310 AIRPLANE
[ ] 315 AIRPLANE PRODUCT LIABILITY
[ ] 320 ASSAULT, LIBEL & SLANDER
[ ] 330 FEDERAL EMPLOYERS' LIABILITY
[ ] 340 MARINE
[ ] 345 MARINE PRODUCT LIABILITY
[ ] 350 MOTOR VEHICLE
[ ] 355 MOTOR VEHICLE PRODUCT LIABILITY
[ ] 360 OTHER PERSONAL INJURY

PERSONAL INJURY

[ ] 362 PERSONAL INJURY - MED MALPRACTICE
[ ] 365 PERSONAL INJURY PRODUCT LIABILITY
[ ] 368 ASBESTOS PERSONAL INJURY PRODUCT LIABILITY

PERSONAL PROPERTY

[ ] 370 OTHER FRAUD
[ ] 371 TRUTH IN LENDING
[ ] 380 OTHER PERSONAL PROPERTY DAMAGE
[ ] 385 PROPERTY DAMAGE PRODUCT LIABILITY

ACTIONS UNDER STATUTES

FORFEITURE/PENALTY

[ ] 610 AGRICULTURE
[ ] 620 OTHER FOOD & DRUG
[ ] 625 DRUG RELATED SEIZURE OF PROPERTY 21 USC 881
[ ] 630 LIQUOR LAWS
[ ] 640 RR & TRUCK
[ ] 650 AIRLINE REGS
[ ] 660 OCCUPATIONAL SAFETY/HEALTH
[ ] 690 OTHER

LABOR

[ ] 710 FAIR LABOR STANDARDS ACT
[ ] 720 LABOR/MGMT RELATIONS
[ ] 730 LABOR/MGMT REPORTING & DISCLOSURE ACT
[ ] 740 RAILWAY LABOR ACT
[ ] 790 OTHER LABOR LITIGATION
[ ] 791 EMPL RET INC SECURITY ACT

IMMIGRATION

[ ] 462 NATURALIZATION APPLICATION
[ ] 463 HABEAS CORPUS- ALIEN DETAINEE
[ ] 465 OTHER IMMIGRATION ACTIONS

BANKRUPTCY

[ ] 422 APPEAL 28 USC 158
[ ] 423 WITHDRAWAL 28 USC 157

PROPERTY RIGHTS

[ ] 820 COPYRIGHTS
[ ] 830 PATENT
[ ] 840 TRADEMARK

SOCIAL SECURITY

[ ] 861 HIA (1395ff)
[ ] 862 BLACK LUNG (923)
[ ] 863 DIWC/DIWW (405(g))
[ ] 864 SSID TITLE XVI
[ ] 865 RSI (405(g))

FEDERAL TAX SUITS

[ ] 870 TAXES (U.S. Plaintiff or Defendant)
[ ] 871 IRS-THIRD PARTY 26 USC 7609

OTHER STATUTES

[ ] 400 STATE REAPPORTIONMENT
[ ] 410 ANTITRUST
[ ] 430 BANKS & BANKING
[ ] 450 COMMERCE
[ ] 460 DEPORTATION
[ ] 470 RACKETEER INFLUENCED & CORRUPT ORGANIZATION ACT (RICO)
[ ] 480 CONSUMER CREDIT
[ ] 490 CABLE/SATELLITE TV
[ ] 810 SELECTIVE SERVICE
[ ] 850 SECURITIES/ COMMODITIES/ EXCHANGE
[ ] 875 CUSTOMER CHALLENGE 12 USC 3410
[ ] 890 OTHER STATUTORY ACTIONS
[ ] 891 AGRICULTURAL ACTS
[ ] 892 ECONOMIC STABILIZATION ACT
[ ] 893 ENVIRONMENTAL MATTERS
[ ] 894 ENERGY ALLOCATION ACT
[ ] 895 FREEDOM OF INFORMATION ACT
[ ] 900 APPEAL OF FEE DETERMINATION UNDER EQUAL ACCESS TO JUSTICE
[ ] 950 CONSTITUTIONALITY OF STATE STATUTES

REAL PROPERTY

[ ] 210 LAND CONDEMNATION
[ ] 220 FORECLOSURE
[ ] 230 RENT LEASE & EJECTMENT
[ ] 240 TORTS TO LAND
[ ] 245 TORT PRODUCT LIABILITY
[ ] 290 ALL OTHER REAL PROPERTY

ACTIONS UNDER STATUTES

CIVIL RIGHTS

[ ] 441 VOTING
[ ] 442 EMPLOYMENT
[ ] 443 HOUSING/ ACCOMMODATIONS
[ ] 444 WELFARE
[ ] 445 AMERICANS WITH DISABILITIES - EMPLOYMENT
[ ] 446 AMERICANS WITH DISABILITIES -OTHER
[ ] 440 OTHER CIVIL RIGHTS

PRISONER PETITIONS

[ ] 510 MOTIONS TO VACATE SENTENCE 20 USC 2255
[ ] 530 HABEAS CORPUS
[ ] 535 DEATH PENALTY
[ ] 540 MANDAMUS & OTHER
[ ] 550 CIVIL RIGHTS
[ ] 555 PRISON CONDITION

Check if demanded in complaint:

☐ CHECK IF THIS IS A CLASS ACTION UNDER F.R.C.P. 23

DO YOU CLAIM THIS CASE IS RELATED TO A CIVIL CASE NOW PENDING IN S.D.N.Y.?
IF SO, STATE:

DEMAND $__________ OTHER __________ JUDGE ____________________ DOCKET NUMBER__________

Check YES only if demanded in complaint
JURY DEMAND: ☐ YES ☐ NO

NOTE: Please submit at the time of filing an explanation of why cases are deemed related.

Exhibit 1.4b

(PLACE AN x IN ONE BOX ONLY) **ORIGIN**

☐ 1 Original Proceeding
☐ 2a. Removed from State Court
☐ 2b. Removed from State Court **AND** at least one party is pro se.
☐ 3 Remanded from Appellate Court
☐ 4 Reinstated or Reopened
☐ 5 Transferred from (Specify District)
☐ 6 Multidistrict Litigation
☐ 7 Appeal to District Judge from Magistrate Judge Judgment

(PLACE AN x IN ONE BOX ONLY) **BASIS OF JURISDICTION** ***IF DIVERSITY, INDICATE CITIZENSHIP BELOW. (28 USC 1322, 1441)***

☐ 1 U.S. PLAINTIFF ☐ 2 U.S. DEFENDANT ☐ 3 FEDERAL QUESTION (U.S. NOT A PARTY) ☐ 4 DIVERSITY

CITIZENSHIP OF PRINCIPAL PARTIES (FOR DIVERSITY CASES ONLY)

(Place an [X] in one box for Plaintiff and one box for Defendant)

	PTF	DEF		PTF	DEF		PTF	DEF
CITIZEN OF THIS STATE	[ ] 1	[ ] 1	CITIZEN OR SUBJECT OF A FOREIGN COUNTRY	[ ] 3	[ ] 3	INCORPORATED and PRINCIPAL PLACE OF BUSINESS IN ANOTHER STATE	[ ] 5	[ ] 5
CITIZEN OF ANOTHER STATE	[ ] 2	[ ] 2	INCORPORATED or PRINCIPAL PLACE OF BUSINESS IN THIS STATE	[ ] 4	[ ] 4	FOREIGN NATION	[ ] 6	[ ] 6

PLAINTIFF(S) ADDRESS(ES) AND COUNTY(IES)

DEFENDANT(S) ADDRESS(ES) AND COUNTY(IES)

DEFENDANT(S) ADDRESS UNKNOWN
REPRESENTATION IS HEREBY MADE THAT, AT THIS TIME, I HAVE BEEN UNABLE, WITH REASONABLE DILIGENCE, TO ASCERTAIN THE RESIDENCE ADDRESSES OF THE FOLLOWING DEFENDANTS:

Check one: THIS ACTION SHOULD BE ASSIGNED TO: ☐ WHITE PLAINS ☐ MANHATTAN
(DO NOT check either box if this a PRISONER PETITION.)

DATE SIGNATURE OF ATTORNEY OF RECORD

ADMITTED TO PRACTICE IN THIS DISTRICT
[ ] NO
[ ] YES (DATE ADMITTED Mo. ______ Yr. ______)
Attorney Bar Code #

RECEIPT #

Magistrate Judge is to be designated by the Clerk of the Court.

Magistrate Judge ______________________________ is so Designated.

Ruby J. Krajick, Clerk of Court by ____________ Deputy Clerk, DATED ______________.

UNITED STATES DISTRICT COURT (NEW YORK SOUTHERN)

Procedures

Exhibit 1.5

UNITED STATES DISTRICT COURT
SOUTHERN DISTRICT OF NEW YORK

CHIEF JUDGE LORETTA A. PRESKA
RUBY J. KRAJICK, CLERK OF COURT

About the Court | Attorney | Cases | ECF | Fees | Forms | Judges | Jury Duty | Local Rules | Naturalization | Part 1 | Trial Support

Welcome to the Southern District of New York

Forms Index
Forms Required to Start an Action
Misc. Pleadings and Motions
Transcripts
Judgments
Appeals
Criminal Justice Act (CJA)
Pro Se
Attorney Services
ECF Registration Only
Interpreters' Forms
Law Student Intern Appearance

All official Court forms must be used without modification.

Forms Required to Start an Action

Civil Cover Sheet
Contains Fields to Complete on-line (print out for filing)
JS 44C/SDNY (Rev. 05/10)

Summons in a Civil Case
Contains fields to complete on-line (print out for filing).
AO 440 (Rev. 12/09)

Fee Schedule

Waiver of Service of Summons
Contains Fields to Complete on-line (print out for filing)
AO 399 (Rev. 01/09)

Notice of Lawsuit and Request for Waiver of Service of Summons
Contains Fields to Complete on-line (print out for filing)
AO 398 (Rev. 01/09)

Consent to Proceed Before US Magistrate Judge
Contains Fields to Complete on-line (print out for filing)
AO 85 (Rev. 01/09)

Consent to Proceed Before US Magistrate Judge Over a Specific Motion
Contains Fields to Complete on-line (print out for filing)
AO 85A (Rev. 01/09)

Appearance
Sample PDF Form

Rule 7.1 Statement
Contains Fields to Complete on-line (print out for filing)

Getting Started

Starting an Action
24 Hour Filing | PACER
Attorney Admission | Representing Yourself (Pro Se)

Electronic Case Filing

Training Courses Schedules
Sign up to become a Point of Contact (POC)

CJA

Revised Plan for Furnishing Representation Pursuant to the Criminal Justice Act (18 U.S.C. § 3006A)

Individual Practices of Judges

U.S. District Judges
U.S. Magistrate Judges

Privacy and Security Notice | RSS Feeds

500 Pearl Street, New York, New York 10007-1312 • 300 Quarropas Street, White Plains, New York 10601-4150

Source: http://www.nysd.uscourts.gov/forms.php

Contacts and Resources

Exhibit 1.6a

Please enter your contact information below

Last name [ ] Check for duplicates
First name
Dear
Addressee
treet Address 1
treet Address 2
treet Address 3
Zip
City State
Email address
Work Phone ( ) -
Home Phone ( ) -
Cell Phone ( ) -
Fax Number ( ) -
Referred By

Please enter a brief description of the case (no more than 100 words).

Note

Exhibit 1.6b

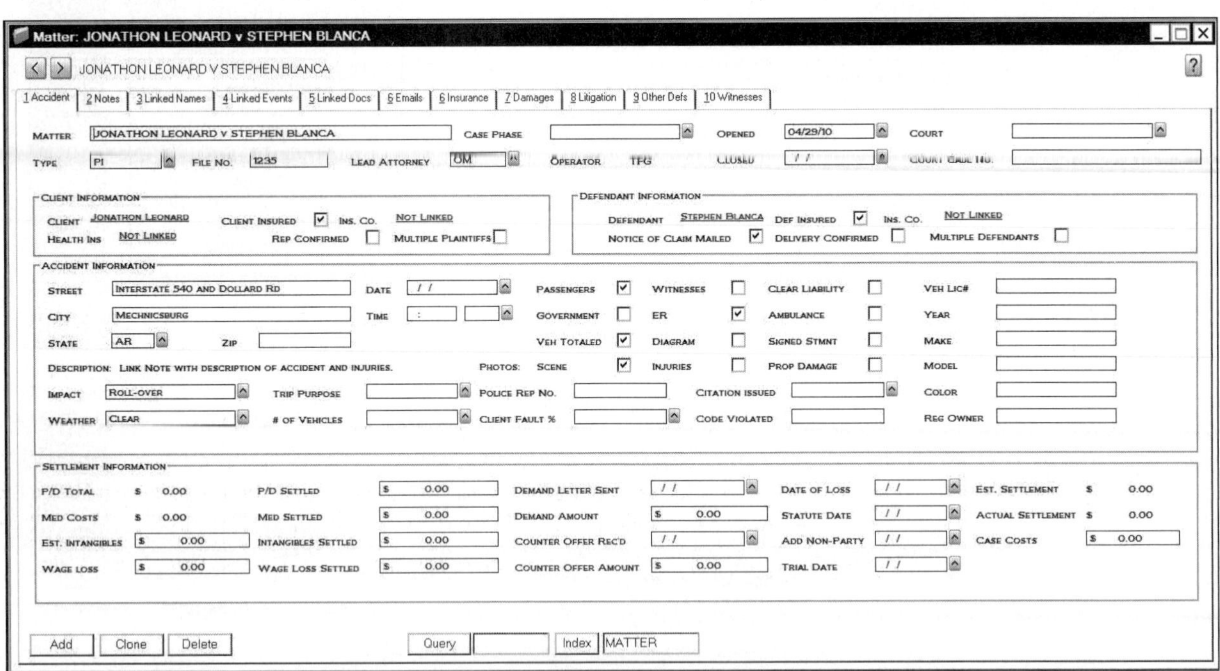

Matter: JONATHON LEONARD v STEPHEN BLANCA

JONATHON LEONARD V STEPHEN BLANCA

1 Accident | 2 Notes | 3 Linked Names | 4 Linked Events | 5 Linked Docs | 6 Emails | 6 Insurance | 7 Damages | 8 Litigation | 9 Other Defs | 10 Witnesses

MATTER: JONATHON LEONARD v STEPHEN BLANCA — CASE PHASE — OPENED: 04/29/10 — COURT
TYPE: PI — FILE NO.: 1235 — LEAD ATTORNEY: OM — OPERATOR: TFG — CLOSED: / / — COURT CASE NO.

CLIENT INFORMATION
CLIENT: JONATHON LEONARD — CLIENT INSURED ☑ — INS. CO.: NOT LINKED
HEALTH INS: NOT LINKED — REP CONFIRMED ☐ — MULTIPLE PLAINTIFFS ☐

DEFENDANT INFORMATION
DEFENDANT: STEPHEN BLANCA — DEF INSURED ☑ — INS. CO.: NOT LINKED
NOTICE OF CLAIM MAILED ☑ — DELIVERY CONFIRMED ☐ — MULTIPLE DEFENDANTS ☐

ACCIDENT INFORMATION
STREET: INTERSTATE 540 AND DOLLARD RD — DATE: / / — PASSENGERS ☑ — WITNESSES ☐ — CLEAR LIABILITY ☐ — VEH LIC#
CITY: MECHNICSBURG — TIME: : — GOVERNMENT ☐ — ER ☑ — AMBULANCE ☐ — YEAR
STATE: AR — ZIP — VEH TOTALED ☑ — DIAGRAM ☐ — SIGNED STMNT ☐ — MAKE
DESCRIPTION: LINK NOTE WITH DESCRIPTION OF ACCIDENT AND INJURIES. — PHOTOS: SCENE ☑ — INJURIES ☐ — PROP DAMAGE ☐ — MODEL
IMPACT: ROLL-OVER — TRIP PURPOSE — POLICE REP NO. — CITATION ISSUED — COLOR
WEATHER: CLEAR — # OF VEHICLES — CLIENT FAULT % — CODE VIOLATED — REG OWNER

SETTLEMENT INFORMATION
P/D TOTAL $ 0.00 — P/D SETTLED $ 0.00 — DEMAND LETTER SENT / / — DATE OF LOSS / / — EST. SETTLEMENT $ 0.00
MED COSTS $ 0.00 — MED SETTLED $ 0.00 — DEMAND AMOUNT $ 0.00 — STATUTE DATE / / — ACTUAL SETTLEMENT $ 0.00
EST. INTANGIBLES $ 0.00 — INTANGIBLES SETTLED $ 0.00 — COUNTER OFFER REC'D / / — ADD NON-PARTY / / — CASE COSTS $ 0.00
WAGE LOSS $ 0.00 — WAGE LOSS SETTLED $ 0.00 — COUNTER OFFER AMOUNT $ 0.00 — TRIAL DATE / /

Add | Clone | Delete | Query | Index | MATTER

BUILDING YOUR PROFESSIONAL PORTFOLIO

CIVIL LITIGATION TEAM AT WORK

Procedures

1. Prepare a list of citations for your jurisdiction's various statutes of limitation for civil action.
2. Prepare a list of the statute or court rules that specify the time frames for responding to pleadings in your jurisdiction.

Contacts and Resources

1. Prepare a list of the publisher of the rules of court and of evidence for your jurisdiction, with contact information and titles. Include any websites where the rules of court and of evidence are also available.
2. Prepare a list of the judges in your jurisdiction with their mailing addresses and their website addresses and web links to their personal procedural rules or rules for their court.

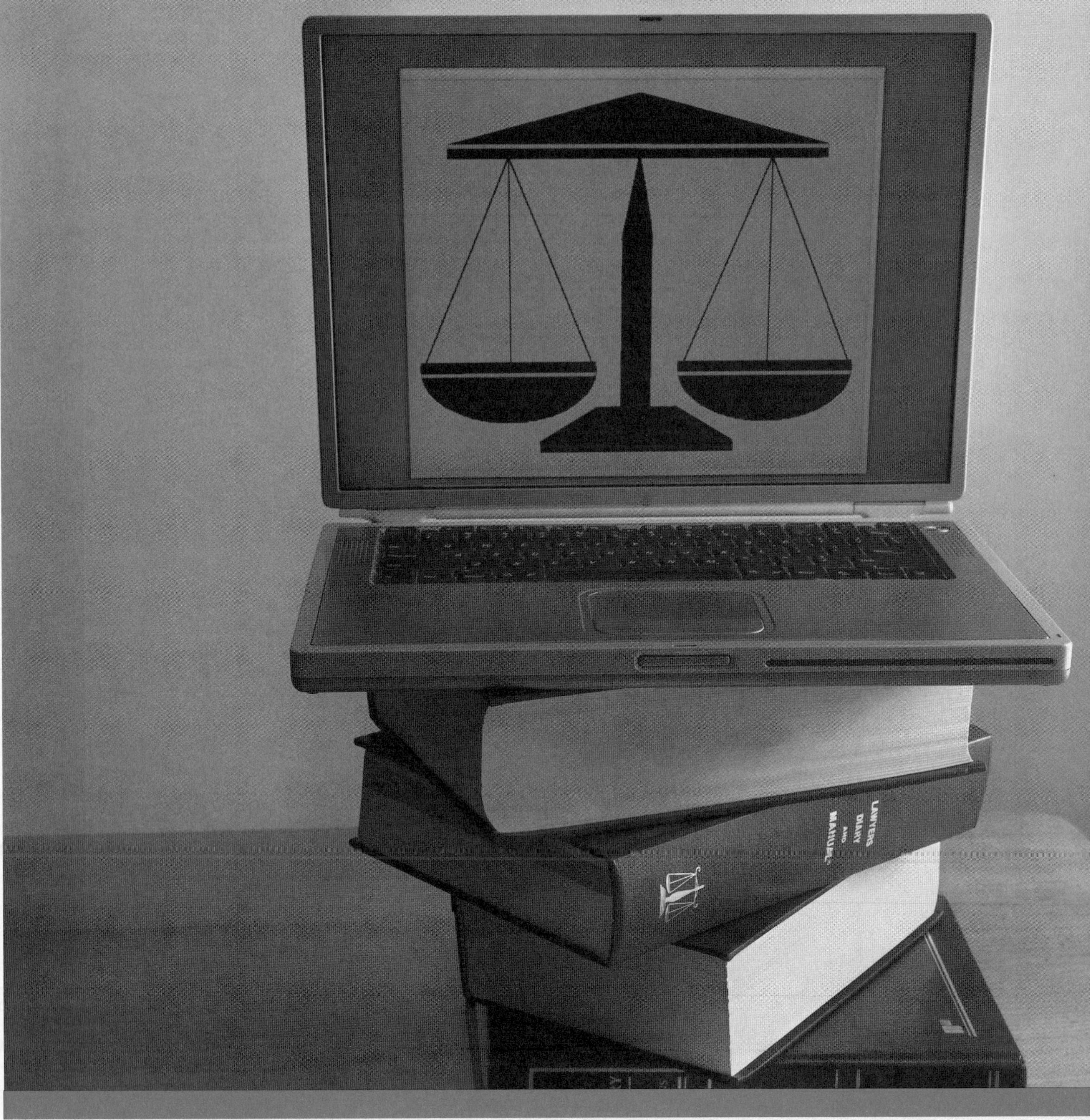

"Losing metadata is like losing all the colors, folders, staples, dates and page numbers that help paper records make sense...."

—Craig Ball,

EDD for Everybody, January 2010
Legal Technology News, Vol. 17, No.1

Technology in Civil Litigation—Concepts

CHAPTER 2

OPENING SCENARIO

The members of the firm had achieved recognition as being knowledgeable in the use of technology in the office and in court. As a result, the paralegals had been asked to make informal presentations at local paralegal association meetings, and the lawyers in the firm had been asked to do the same at a continuing education seminar for the local bar association. The firm received a number of calls from other law offices seeking information and advice. Many of the calls were from the support staff seeking advice or help with technology issues in litigation office management areas. Increasingly, as members of the bar realized the importance of technology in handling litigation cases and their own lack of expertise, they asked the firm of Mason, Marshall and Benjamin to act on a co-counsel basis, and some cases were being referred outright. The partners were glad they had made the decision to support technology with the purchase of the necessary equipment and software, even though the cost had seemed hard to justify when they were struggling as a start-up law office. The discussion at the most recent firm meeting turned to the need to maintain the skills necessary to use the computer tools. It was clear that everyone in the firm, including the lawyers, paralegals, and other support staff, had to be committed to keeping current and that they had to develop a plan and a budget for continuing education.

LEARNING OBJECTIVES

After studying this chapter, you should be able to:

1. Understand the differences in the use of paper and electronic documents in civil litigation.
2. Define and describe the different types of metadata.
3. Describe the different electronic document formats and the reasons for using them in litigation.
4. Explain the uses of optical character recognition and scanning software.
5. Describe the function and elements of electronic database software.

VIDEO INTRODUCTION

An introduction to electronic database programs.

After watching the video in MyLegalStudiesKit, answer the following question.

- How are databases used in the law office and in litigation?

INTRODUCTION TO TECHNOLOGY IN CIVIL LITIGATION

Technology is being introduced and used in every aspect of civil litigation as clients, law firms, and courts transition from a paper-based system to a computer-based system. Computerization of business and society is increasing the amounts of data created by clients that become a part of the litigation process. With this increased amount of data has also come the demand by clients for efficient, cost-effective solutions to litigation discovery and analysis.

The ethical obligation of competency requires the litigation team to have a basic knowledge of the uses and operation of the tools used in the management of cases, and the methods of creating, storing, and retrieving electronically stored information.

Software programs for managing cases, discovery, and trial presentation are based on four main components: word processing, electronic spreadsheets, databases, and presentation programs. Of these core elements, the most fundamental is that of the database. It is the heart of typical office management programs, case management programs, and electronic discovery document management programs. While helpful, it is not necessary for the litigation team to know how to create databases. It is, however, essential for the team's members to understand the concepts and, more importantly, the terminology used by the litigation support consultants and internal staff to effectively communicate the needs of the litigation team.

FROM PAPER TO ELECTRONICALLY STORED INFORMATION

LEARNING OBJECTIVE 1
Understand the differences in the use of paper and electronic documents in civil litigation.

electronically stored information (ESI)
Any type of information that can be stored electronically.

Electronically stored information, ESI, is a main or featured topic in litigation conferences, continuing education seminars, and court cases. To many, the issues of electronically stored information seem to have suddenly appeared. However, electronically stored information did not suddenly replace paper documents nor did computers suddenly replace typewriters. The conversion from paper-based to electronic environments has evolved over time. The change started in the 1960s with the introduction of the memory typewriter into law and business offices. The ability to create documents electronically demonstrated a new, cost-effective method of producing what had been a labor-intensive process. The memory typewriter demonstrated the concept; the introduction of the relatively low-cost computer and dedicated word processing software proved the value. Advances in computer technology have resulted in lower-cost, higher-performance tools that have in turn led to computer-created and electronically stored information in every aspect of business and personal life.

Some people, businesses, and government agencies still prefer paper documentation. This is gradually changing as more and more businesses—such as the health care industry, and government agencies like the federal Internal Revenue Service—require a switch to paperless systems. However, paper-based documents continue to be an important part of litigation. Many cases are still dependent on documentation created before the implementation of computers or used in many situations where access to computers was not practical at the time. For example, it has only been recently that police accident reports have been created electronically through the use of inexpensive portable computers in police and emergency vehicles. Previously, reports were handwritten or typed and then filed in hard (paper) copy.

Older medical records and business records are still in paper form or are in photographic forms like microfilm and microfiche and have not been converted to alternative storage. These older storage methods are gradually being phased out in most cases in favor of electronic duplication and storage.

Until recently, uncertain that the "new" technology worked, many businesses and law offices kept both paper and electronic versions. The paper copy was the final version and the electronic file was a copy for use as a template or for making changes to the "final" paper document. As computers gained acceptance, financial records and other types of records were created and stored electronically, ultimately in many cases only in electronic form.

Also until recently, paper copies were the dominant items requested in discovery. Responses to interrogatories frequently came with paper records attached and only rarely with any electronic response. Many cases today still require access to paper records. For example, a medical malpractice filed today may have its origins ten to eighteen years ago, when the plaintiff was a child and the statute of limitation extended until the minor reached the age of majority. At that time, hospitals and doctors kept records in paper form or converted them to a paper substitute, such as microfilm or microfiche. Other examples are the product-defect or liability cases such as the tobacco industry litigation, which started before records were routinely kept electronically.

Documents in Litigation

In the past there was little choice in how to handle document requests or document processing when received in response to interrogatories. The responding party would have to search manually through each document to find the requested documentation, a process that in large, complex cases could take large teams of

VIDEO ADVICE FROM THE FIELD

Charlotte Harris—Manager, Litigation Support, Hess Corporation

Discussion of the role of the paralegal in litigation support.

After watching the video in MyLegalStudiesKit, answer the following questions.

1. What are the challenges for litigation support?
2. How can someone enter the litigation support field?

paralegals, law students, and lawyers days, weeks, and months. Upon receipt by the requesting party, the documents would have to be reviewed for relevancy and materiality and potential clues to other documentation to be requested.

Advances in copier technology made it easier to make multiple copies, using high-speed copy machines, for multiple people to review. Additional advances in software technology permitted electronic copies to be printed out directly from computers in a variety of image formats, and ultimately to be produced not in a paper form but in a computer-readable image format, like a photograph of the document that allowed reviewers to review the documents on a computer screen instead of in a paper form.

At some point in this technological development process, technology-savvy litigation counsel realized that data about the creation and changes to the underlying documents—like dates of creation, changes, and persons who worked on the document—called metadata, could be viewed using the same programs that had been originally used to create the documentation when documents were supplied in electronic forms. Depending on whether they were providing documentation or requesting documentation, counsel would either ask for delivery in electronic format, with the underlying metadata included, or, if asked to produce documentation, would do so in a format that did not allow review of the underlying metadata: either the metadata had been removed or the document had been provided in a printed or hard-copy, paper form. This underlying metadata about documents has become an area of interest when the authenticity and genuineness of the document are questioned. For example, did someone after the institution of suit make changes to the original document after receiving discovery interrogatories?

Native Format

With an appreciation that there might be "hidden data" about the document, technology-knowledgeable counsel wanted the original files, or at least copies of the files in their original format, called **native format.** The difficulty with native file delivery is that being able to open and read the document usually requires a copy of the original program used to create the document. Historically, there has not been a universal set of operating systems or standard software. As the technology has developed, many companies have competed for the business using proprietary computer systems, operating systems, and programs to capture and create electronic documents. There have been many failed efforts to develop and gain acceptance of a universal computer operating system and its programs—for example, Apple, Microsoft, and Linux operating systems and related software suites of programs using those operating systems. Even within the same operating systems, there continue to be competing programs, such as Microsoft Word and Corel WordPerfect for the Windows operating system. In the area of accounting and database software, there are also competing systems, each of which has its own format for the creation, storage, and retrieval of electronic files. For the litigator without access to the original computer or copies of the software originally used in creating the ESI, paper copies or image copies readable on other available computers are the only solution.

native format (native file format) An associated file structure defined by the original creating application of electronic documents.

Computer Format

In cases with large amounts of data, finding the relevant information is critical. Records, documents, and data files that are in a computer-usable format are easier to search and analyze using computer programs that have word search capabilities. When documents are not delivered in a computer-usable format, they can usually

DEFINITION

"Native format" is defined as follows by The Sedona Conference Glossary:

> Electronic documents have an associated file structure defined by the original creating application. This file structure is referred to as the "native format" of the document. Because viewing or searching documents in the native format may require the original application (for example, viewing a Microsoft Word document may require the Microsoft Word application), documents may be converted to a neutral format as part of the record acquisition or archive process. "Static" formats (often called "imaged formats"), such as TIFF or PDF, are designed to retain an image of the document as it would look viewed in the original creating application but do not allow metadata to be viewed or the document information to be manipulated. In the conversion to static format, the metadata can be processed, preserved and electronically associated with the static format file. However, with technology advancements, tools and applications are becoming increasingly available to allow viewing and searching of documents in their native format, while still preserving all metadata.

Source: From *The Sedona Conference® Glossary*, 3rd edition, 2010. (available at www.thesedonaconference.org). Reprinted with permission of The Sedona Conference®.

be processed and saved in one of the other usable computer formats, but without the metadata about the original files. In computer-friendly formats, documents may be searched for key words, terms, or names as part of a records review. Where documents are not provided in usable electronic formats, service bureaus may be used to convert the paper to a searchable electronic format, with some service bureaus coding the document by the key words contained and providing indexes by key word, creator, recipient, and similar characteristics.

Subject to time and cost-effectiveness, advances in computer technology now allow some of this conversion from paper to electronic form to take place within the law office. In many law offices, some of the most used software programs are imaging and **optical character recognition (OCR)** programs. OCR programs allow the litigation team to convert paper documents into searchable electronic documents and, after conversion, to store them within litigation support programs for easy recovery.

optical character recognition (OCR)
A technology that takes data from a paper document and turns it into editable text data. The document is first scanned, then OCR software searches the document for letters, numbers, and other characters.

metadata
Information about a particular data set that may describe, for example, how, when, and by whom it was received, created, accessed, and/or modified and how it is formatted.

METADATA

LEARNING OBJECTIVE 2
Define and describe the different types of metadata.

When documents are converted from paper copies to computer-usable formats, the original, hidden electronic file information about the document, called **metadata,** is lost. Metadata is frequently referred to as data about data, and every electronic document has that information about the document—such as who created it; the date it was created, modified, or accessed; and other information related to its creation and location—contained within the document's electronic file.

Metadata is divided into two areas. The resource or **system metadata** is data about the content or application information. The resource metadata is used to track or locate the file containing the data such as file names, size, and location. **Content (application) metadata** is the data in the file itself, such as the author of the document, any tracked changes, and the version. An example of the metadata for the word processing file for this chapter in Microsoft Word 2010 is shown in Exhibit 2.1.

system metadata
Data such as file name, size, and location.

content (application) metadata
Information about the contents of a document.

Each time a file is sent as an e-mail or an attachment to an e-mail, metadata is part of the transmission. The recipient can frequently see the content or application metadata like the author and version by using a function in the program used to view the documents, such as Word or WordPerfect for word processing documents.

Access to the metadata provides some ability to verify some of the issues related to authentication, such as the last date a change was made or who actually

Exhibit 2.1 Metadata for document in Word 2010

Source: Microsoft product screen shot(s) reprinted with permission from Microsoft Corporation; Metadata® is a registered trademark of Metadata, LLC.

Exhibit 2.2 Word 2010 Document Inspector

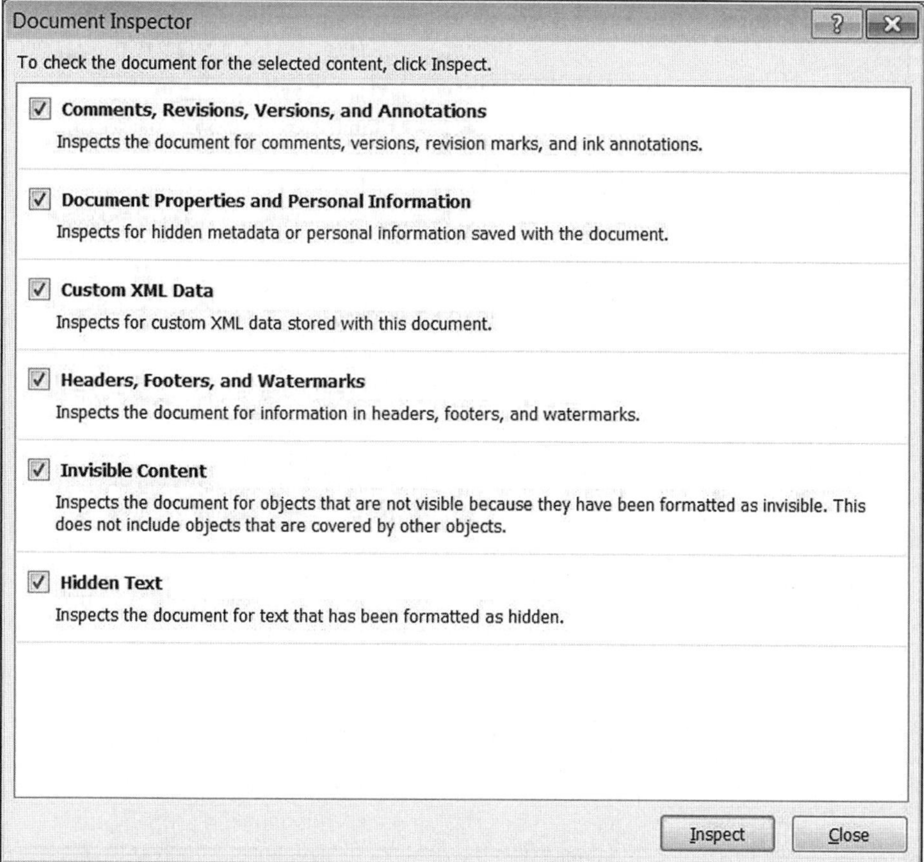
Document Inspector

To check the document for the selected content, click Inspect.

Comments, Revisions, Versions, and Annotations
Inspects the document for comments, versions, revision marks, and ink annotations.

Document Properties and Personal Information
Inspects for hidden metadata or personal information saved with the document.

Custom XML Data
Inspects for custom XML data stored with this document.

Headers, Footers, and Watermarks
Inspects the document for information in headers, footers, and watermarks.

Invisible Content
Inspects the document for objects that are not visible because they have been formatted as invisible. This does not include objects that are covered by other objects.

Hidden Text
Inspects the document for text that has been formatted as hidden.

Inspect Close

Source: Microsoft product screen shot(s) reprinted with permission from Microsoft Corporation.

created the document. Some formats of delivery may have the metadata included, such as delivery of documents in native format. However, it is also possible to remove the metadata before delivery even in native format using features of the original programs like the Microsoft Word 2010 Document Inspector (Exhibit 2.2), which reviews the document for metadata and allows its removal before saving the document.

ADVICE FROM THE FIELD

PRODUCING METADATA IN E-DISCOVERY—WHAT YOU NEED TO KNOW

By Leonard Deutchman and Brian Wolfinger

As e-discovery requests and productions increase exponentially, many of those requests will, implicitly or explicitly, seek the production of metadata. This article will help you understand metadata production by discussing what "metadata" is, how to preserve and gather metadata, what form of production e-discovery with metadata should take, and issues regarding its production. By understanding the technical and legal issues regarding metadata, you can diminish the occasions upon which you will have to produce metadata and insure that when it is produced it is done so properly.

What Is Metadata?

The Committee Note to the amended F.R.Civ.P. 26(f) defines "metadata" as "information describing the history, tracking, or management of an electronic document." In the

(continued)

(continued)

influential opinion, *Williams v. Sprint*, 230 F.R.D. 640, 646-647 (D. Kan. 2005), the court cited with favor the description of metadata in The Sedona Guidelines (The Sedona Conference Working Group Series, Sept. 2005 Version) as "information about a particular data set which describes how, when and by whom it was collected, created, accessed, or modified and how it is formatted (including data demographics such as size, location, storage requirements and media information.)" The Sedona Guidelines noted that metadata included "all of the contextual, processing, and use information needed to identify and certify the scope, authenticity, and integrity of active or archival electronic information or records."

File- and Application-Level Metadata

It is important to distinguish between two types of metadata a file could have associated to it, "File-Level" metadata ("FLM") and "Application-Level" metadata ("ALM"). All files have FLM, while certain files, such as Microsoft Word documents, Excel spreadsheets, etc. will have both. While there are some exceptions, FLM is generally stored separately from where the actual file content is stored on a hard drive, while ALM is commingled with the file content.

"File-Level" Metadata

"File-level" (or "file system") metadata about a computer file may include its size, the date/time of its creation or modification, if it is able to be written to further (as opposed to being read-only) and other information. File-level metadata is created by the computer's file system and changed due to end-user interactions with the file on that computer. Some FLM file attributes include Last Modified, Last Accessed and Creation dates and times ("MAC times"), File Physical and Logical Size, File Name and File Path.

Different user or system actions will "trip" the MAC times, causing them to be updated. Opening a new MS Office document, typing something and then saving the file to a disk or server will stamp the Created attribute with the date/time of this first save, and the Accessed and Modified attributes will show the same, since the user did all of these things to the file. On the other hand, when files are transferred between drive volumes and/or between pieces of computer media (i.e., saved from one location to another without modification) the Created date of the file is normally changed to reflect the time of the creation of the copy, but the Modified date will remain the same. This will often result in the counterintuitive situation of having file-level metadata that shows a file was modified before it was created.

"Application-Level" Metadata

In addition to FLM, certain files contain "Application-Level" metadata, that is, additional metadata within themselves. Microsoft Office documents such as PowerPoint, Excel, and Word have ALM, as do other files such as PDF files. The following is a list of some ALM file attributes that are tracked by Microsoft Office: Track changes, comments and deleted text; Author–assigned during installation of the application software (e.g., Microsoft Office) on the computer; Company–same type of value as Author, assigned during installation of the software; Revision Number–a count of every instance where the file was opened, edited and saved; Creation date and time–the Date/Time a document was first saved by a user with the stored value in the "Author" field; and, Last Save date and time–the Date/Time a document was last saved by a user with the stored value in the "Last Author" field.

Data Gathering to Preserve Metadata

As the discussion above about copying files to other media makes clear, if data is not gathered properly, metadata such as the dates of file creation, last access and last modification can be changed. If that happens, you simply cannot produce accurate metadata.

Forensic data gathering avoids this problem by gathering all data initially, and exactly as it was on the media imaged. Even if only a handful of files are sought from a hard drive, for example, an exact, "bit stream" image of the hard drive should be made and, later, forensically searched. The image would be verified by submitting both it and the original to a complex algorithm to generate identical "hash values." Bit stream imaging with hash value verification is the standard practice of law enforcement and widely accepted by peer groups and courts as scientifically reliable.

Forensic data gathering through a vendor is more expensive than in-house copying of files by the client. However, if metadata must be produced, the data has to be gathered properly, period.

So, what do you do if you are handed some DVDs produced by the client, you have no idea how the data was copied to the DVDs and you have to produce file creation and last accessed and modified dates? You must make clear that you cannot do that–that is, your firm cannot discharge its discovery duties–unless the data is properly collected.

This will not make you the most popular person at the firm, but you will be doing your job properly.

(continued)

(continued)

The Form of Production

Form of production will dictate access to metadata. If you produce the data in TIFF or PDF form, the only access to any metadata will be what is found in the fields for each record in the database. If, however, the data is produced with a link to the file in its native form, then the user, i.e. your opponent, can view the metadata as found in the file....

About the Authors: Leonard Deutchman, Esquire, is General Counsel and Managing Partner, and Brian Wolfinger, CIFI, is Vice President of Electronic Discovery and Forensic Services LegisDiscovery, LLC, a firm based in Fort Washington, PA, and McLean, VA, that specializes in electronic digital discovery and digital forensics. You may contact them at ldeutchman@legisdiscovery.com and bwolfinger@ legisdiscovery.com.

Source: "Producing metadata in e-discovery—what you need to know," *Litigation Support Today,* May 2007. Copyright © 2007 Conexion. Used with permission.

IN THE WORDS OF THE COURT...

COVAD COMMUNICATIONS COMPANY, Plaintiff, v. REVONET, INC., Defendant.
Civil Action No. 06-1892 (CKK/JMF).
United States District Court, D. Columbia.
March 31, 2010

As I explained in my earlier order, Rule 34 of the Federal Rules of Civil Procedure explicitly indicates that, when no form for producing electronically stored information has been specified, it must be produced in a reasonably usable form. Fed.R.Civ.P. 34(b)(2)(E)(ii). Earlier in this case, I found the production of 35,000 e-mails in hard copy to be unacceptable, because no reasonable person could believe that Revonet, in its day to day operations, prints out all of its electronic communications on paper and then preserves them. Covad II, 254 F.R.D. at 150-51. The conversion to paper was therefore a bit of gamesmanship that I was not obliged to tolerate. Covad, however, would like me to take the current case law a step further and determine that electronically stored data produced in hard copy is inherently unusable and unacceptable under the Rules, because it lacks the metadata available in the native format. Mot. Hr'g Tr. 121:18-23. Thus, Covad asks the Court to hold that only native production, with metadata, of electronically stored information, is reasonably usable under Rule 34(b)(2)(E)(ii). But, the rule itself permits production *either* in the format in which e-mail is ordinarily maintained, *i.e.* "native format," *or* another usable format. Thus, by its exact terms, the Rule provides an alternative to the native format, contradicting Covad's claim that native, electronic format is absolutely obligatory.

graphic image format
A computer image that is stored and displayed as a set of colored points in a rectangular grid.

portable document format (PDF)
Portable Document Format.

ELECTRONIC DOCUMENT FORMATS—COMPARISON OF PDF AND TIFF

LEARNING OBJECTIVE 3
Describe the different electronic document formats and the reasons for using them in litigation.

In addition to the native format, documents may now be saved in a **graphic image format** or a **portable document format (PDF).** These graphic images may not be easily or readily changed by the recipient. The two formats competing for use as a common format for large-scale case use are the TIFF and the PDF formats. The up-front costs to convert from the native file format to TIFF or PDF formats are about the same. Many programs used to create the original documents, like WordPerfect and Word, have a built-in feature allowing files to be saved automatically as

PDF files. In addition, most litigation support software programs, such as AD Summation and Lexis Nexis Concordance, support both TIFF and PDF formats. The advantage of conversion to either format is that the new files can be searched across the different computer platforms.

TIFF was developed in the 1980s as a format for scanning paper documents. Adobe Systems now holds the copyright for the TIFF specification. Many lawyers latched onto this format and continue to prefer it. Some attorneys prefer the TIFF format because TIFF files cannot be altered. Adobe invented PDF in 1992 as a replacement for the TIFF format and has not supported any new activity for TIFF since then. PDF files have the advantage of being usable across many different platforms (computer systems) and software programs regardless of how the files were originally created.

One of the differences between TIFF and PDF is the amount of memory required to store one document. Because of the built-in file compression in the PDF format, PDF files are normally about one-tenth the size of TIFF files. The actual file size will vary depending on which of the many compression methods is used in saving the TIFF file. If you have ever sent an e-mail with an attachment, consider the additional time it took to send a TIFF file rather than a PDF file of the same document.

The disadvantage from the receiving party's point of view is that hidden data (or metadata) of the original (or native) format document cannot be seen in TIFF files.

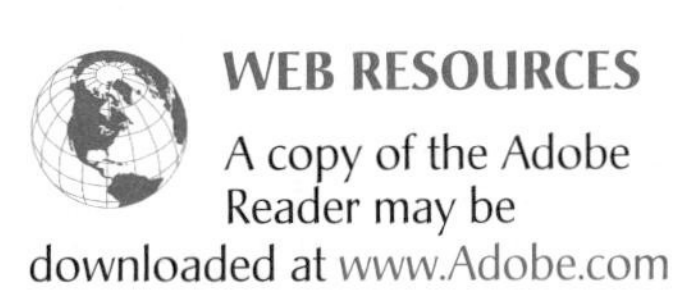

WEB RESOURCES

A copy of the Adobe Reader may be downloaded at www.Adobe.com

The ability to save documents in a format that cannot be easily changed through the use of a computer is one of the basic requirements of a system that allows for electronic documentation. Anyone who has received a word processing document file knows that he or she may change it, save it, and present it as an original unless access has been restricted, such as by use of password restriction.

The creation of documents in PDF format requires specialty software such as Adobe Acrobat. To encourage use of the PDF format as a standard, Adobe Systems, the developer of the PDF format, allows everyone to download a free Adobe Reader to view these documents, adding to the acceptance of the PDF format. With the acceptance of this format has come a willingness to scan and store documents electronically and eliminate or return to the client the original paper copies. Companies like Adobe Systems frequently provide free, limited versions of their programs, downloadable from their website, that allow the opening and reading of files created using their proprietary software formats, such as Adobe's PDF file format. Many websites that provide programs using these proprietary formats, such as the forms website of the Internal Revenue Service, contain links to these programs. These programs are limited in that they allow the user to open and read files but do not allow the creation of new document files, which requires the full version of the program.

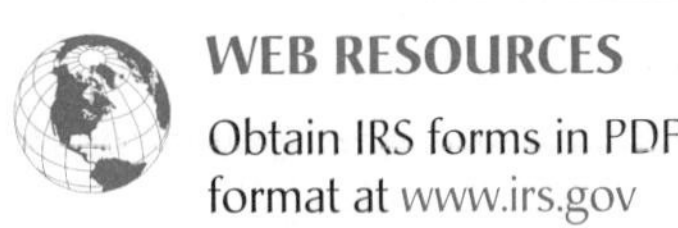

WEB RESOURCES

Obtain IRS forms in PDF format at www.irs.gov

Adobe Acrobat

Adobe Acrobat has become a standard software tool in many paperless offices for creating PDF files. With each new version or update to the original program, additional features have been added to allow greater sharing of documents, a higher level of security, and better collaboration on document preparation.

Creators of PDF documents using the newer versions of Adobe Acrobat (versions 5 and above) can limit the ability of the receiver to print the document by requiring a password to allow printing. This password feature allows the legal team to send documents that others on the legal team can view, and about which they can make and submit comments to the documents' originator, but cannot make changes to.

In typical use, the attorney or paralegal creates the document in a word processor such as Word or WordPerfect and uses Adobe Acrobat to convert the document to a PDF. The PDF format reduces the risk of sending the document metadata found in the native or original word processor document.

PDF Converter

Nuance's PDF Converter is a lower-cost alternative to the widely used Adobe Acrobat. In addition to creating PDF documents, the PDF converter also provides a number of other options. For instance, the converter feature can be used to convert PDF files into fully formatted Word, WordPerfect, and Excel documents.

An interesting additional feature of PDF Converter is its ability to convert documents into audio files that can be played back through a computer or an MP3 player, like an Apple iPod. Anyone who has tried to proofread, by herself, technical language in a document or the legal description in a real estate agreement or deed will appreciate the ability to have the language "read to her" while following the language in the document to verify accuracy.

As with Acrobat, PDF Converter allows the same type of security settings for documents created with the program, including password limitations for changes and printing.

WEB RESOURCES

Obtain a free Nuance PDF reader at www.nuance.com

Examining a PDF for Hidden Content

Adobe Acrobat is used to create PDF format documents, sometimes in the mistaken belief that the file does not have metadata. Every document has metadata—data about the document—as part of the document file.

In the Preference selections window, one of the options in Acrobat is to set the preference to Examine Documents. Two options exist: (1) examining *before* sending the e-document electronically and (2) examining *before* saving. Both practices might prevent information being sent that is not intended for the recipient.

SCANNING

LEARNING OBJECTIVE 4
Explain the uses of optical character recognition and scanning software.

scanning
Copying a document by converting the image into an electronic format.

Documents may be copied by **scanning** the original and then saving the scanned image in a desired electronic format such as a PDF, image, or with OCR software, a word processing document format. Originally, scanning hardware was costly and frequently unreliable. Modern scanners provide double-sided (front and back) scanning of documents with a high degree of accuracy at a relatively low cost. Scanning today has become a common feature of office printers and copy machines. Double-sided scanning is also found today in multifunction devices containing printing, scanning, copying, and faxing features, at prices sometimes under $100. These devices, when coupled with document management software such as Nuance's PaperPort, allow virtually anyone to create electronic documents. An automatic document feed scanner allows for single or multiple sheet-fed scanning, which is a time-saver when scanning multiple-page documents. A flatbed scanner allows for scanning sheets as well as documents that can't be fed through a page feeder, such as books or labels on packages.

Scanning Software

The process of scanning large numbers of documents requires the ability to organize the scanned documents. Scanning, organizing, and storing paper documents have become easier with the development of document management software such as PaperPort by Nuance. This software provides easy-to-use, high-speed scanning and document capture. As a document management

Exhibit 2.3 PaperPort document management desktop screen

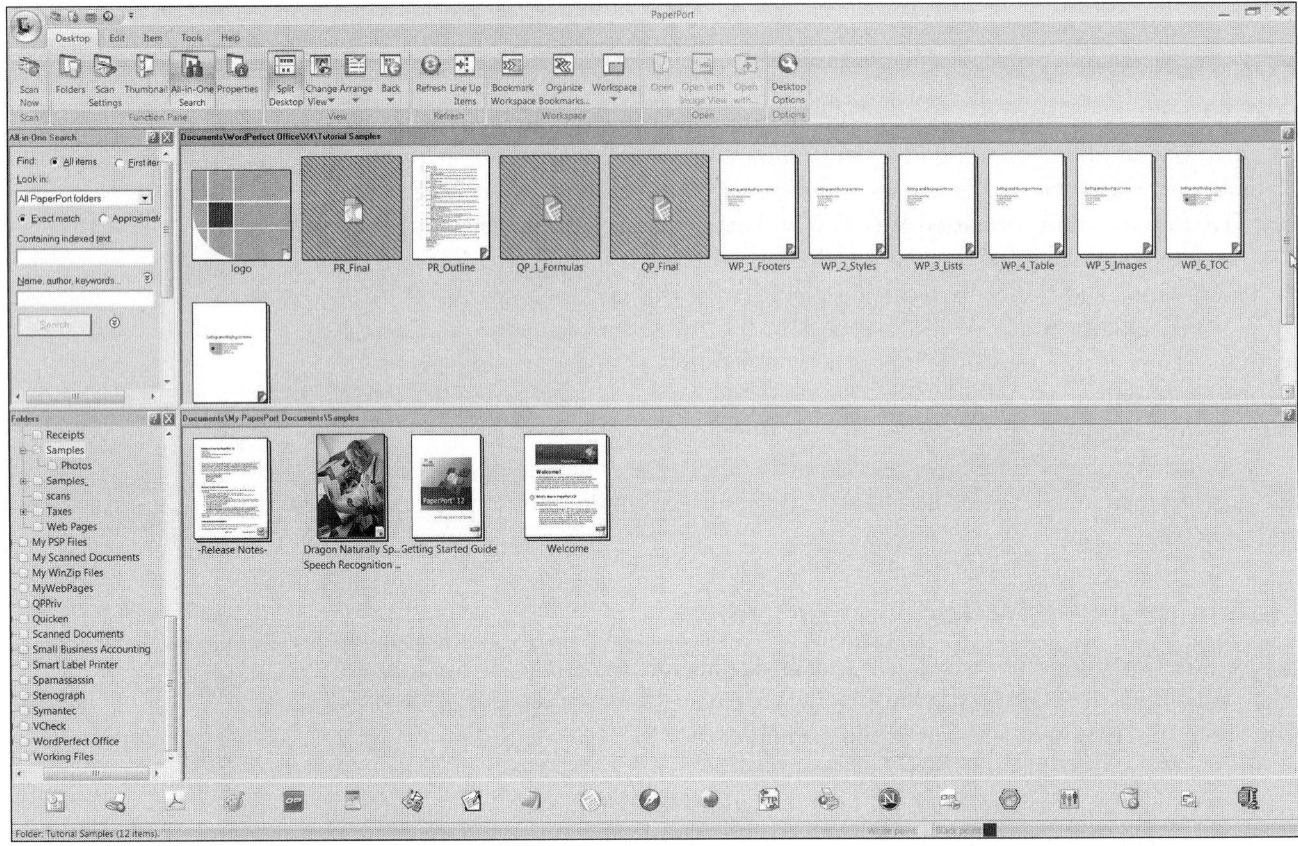

software application, it allows for the organization, finding, and sharing of paper and digital documents, permitting the elimination of paper documents, as shown in Exhibit 2.3.

Optical Character Recognition

There are obviously times when documents need to be converted from graphic images to a format that allows for editing or other use in an office suite of applications. These software applications have come to be referred to as OCR, or optical character recognition applications. Products such as OmniPage, by Nuance, provide document conversion solutions by permitting any scanned page, PDF file, or other image or document file to be converted quickly and accurately into one of a number of different editable formats, including Microsoft Word or Corel WordPerfect.

DATABASES IN LITIGATION

LEARNING OBJECTIVE 5
Describe the function and elements of electronic database software.

Litigation involves obtaining, sorting, and analyzing information about the parties, fact witnesses, expert witnesses, and others involved with a case. It also involves the accumulation of potentially massive amounts of information in the form of documents and data. Data that is obtained as part of the investigation of the case or as part of the discovery process must be organized and analyzed. Without computers, paper indexes have to be created to organize the material stored in paper form in file folders, file cabinets, and file boxes. The use of computers makes the storage of and access to the information easier and more efficient through the computer's search capabilities. The underlying programs that are used in this storage and retrieval process are databases.

ELECTRONIC DATABASE BASICS

database
A collection of similar records.

Databases are programs used to store information. After word processing programs, database programs are the most frequently used type of computer program. The advantage of a database program is its ability to search for individual or groups of words or numbers, to sort the results in some meaningful way such as by date, and then to show the results on a computer screen or in a hard-copy printout. For example, demographic data collected may be sorted by zip code, which by itself is not a very meaningful result. But adding to this result a search by zip code and income, sex, and number of children provides a good picture of the demographics of an area, such as the surveys conducted by the Census Bureau every ten years.

Electronic discovery software permits documents to be entered into a database and stored by key terms, phrases, or other criteria that then can be sorted to find patterns and connections. With a few keystrokes, lists of documents can be prepared for manual review, like an Internet search that produces a list of locations to check for desired content or products.

In addition to the obvious use of avoiding accepting a client with a potential conflict of interest, the information in a database of contacts and clients may be used in firm public relations and marketing activities. Many firms use the information to send holiday, birthday, and anniversary greetings and to collect information on updates of specific changes in the law for which a client has previously consulted the firm.

Data Repositories

A database program is a repository of information of all types that can be sorted and presented in a desired, meaningful manner. The word "database" is just computer talk for a collection of information. For example, a Contact Database in a case management program is nothing more than a collection of information about people: their names, phone numbers, addresses, and maybe birthdays or other related information.

Besides names, other information like occupations, children's names, or any other combination of information. In pre-computer days, databases frequently were a box or boxes of cards with the information about clients or important dates. These were the heart of the conflict of interest or deadline databases. The date database was checked daily and a list made up for the legal team of such things as deadlines, statutes of limitations, and appointments. Conflicts of interest were also checked in the same way, via a search of the cards maintained alphabetically in the boxes. In some offices, a card was prepared for all opposing parties. Each of these "decks of cards" was a database.

The electronic database is nothing more than a version of the cards in the boxes—except that more information can be automatically checked more quickly and more accurately—no more misfiled cards out of alphabetical order. A database is essentially an electronic card with information that can be searched using a set of things to look for and presented in a predefined manner, or report. When information about a person is needed, the report showing the information is compiled by asking the database program to look up the person's

Exhibit 2.4 AbacusLaw contact management intake template and input form

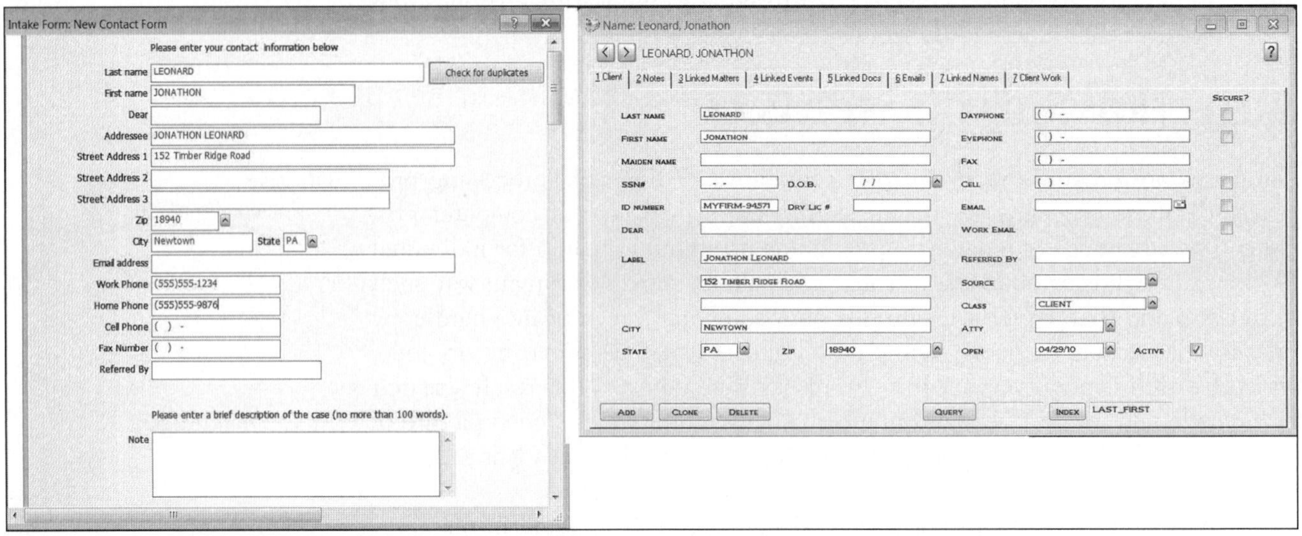

Source: © 2010 Abacus Data Systems, Inc. All rights reserved.

information and show it on the computer screen, or in a printed format called a report. Any combination of information, or queries, can be requested for a report about a single person or a list of all people or contacts with the same information such as zip code; or a more detailed report can be prepared combining specifics items, such as zip code and male or female, with a birthday before or after a certain date.

Exhibit 2.4 shows an intake template and a contact form for the input of information into a contacts management database for one record. One of the advantages of the modern database is its ability to search across a number of different sets of information and sort the data according to a predefined set of criteria. Some have likened the World Wide Web to a big database that can be searched using a search engine. The database is the place where information is stored until a request is made for a report showing some or all of the information in a certain format or appearance.

NAVIGATING ELECTRONIC DATABASES

Electronic databases use standard terminology to describe parts of the database: **table, field, cell,** and **record,** as shown in Exhibit 2.5.

Databases are collections of tables. Tables contain fields of information (data); a field is one type of information, like last names. A record is all the information about one item or person; for example, Exhibit 2.6 shows a record of information for one person. Think of the database as being a file cabinet; a table being a file drawer for a specific set of information like business contacts; the record being individual files for each contact; and the field being individual pieces of information about the person.

table
Data that is organized in a format of horizontal rows and vertical columns.

fields
Information located in vertical columns.

cell
In a spreadsheet, the box at the intersection of a row and column for text or numerical data.

record
In a database, the information in a horizontal row.

Microsoft Access is a database widely used because of its inclusion with the Microsoft Office Suite. The Microsoft Access layout shown in Exhibit 2.6 is one way of presenting the basic elements of a database—the fields, records, and cells. The same elements may appear in a different layout, such as the Contact Details in Exhibit 2.7.

Exhibit 2.5 Parts of the database: table, field, cell, and record

This entire group of records represents the SalesDeptContactInfo table

Microsoft Access - [SalesDeptContactInfo : Table]

File Edit View Insert Format Records Tools Window Help

Type a question for help

ContactID	First Name	Last Name	CompanyName	Street Address	City	State	Business Phone
1	Susan	Scantosi	eWidgetPlus	363 Rogue Street	St. Louis	MO	(612) 444-1236
2	Thomas	Mazeman	BooksRUs	2165 Piscotti Ave	Springfield	IL	(888) 234-6983
3	Douglas	Seaver	Printing Solutions	7700 First Ave	Topeka	KS	(888) 988-2678
4	Amir	Ramiv	TechStands	1436 Riverfront Place	St. Louis	MO	(877) 867-7656
5	Franklin	Scott	WorksSuite	8789 Ploughman Drive	Tulsa	OK	(800) 864-2390
6	Ronald	Komeika	Creekside Financia	1264 Pond Hill Road	Toledo	OH	(343) 333-3333
7	Barbara	Mitchell	Market Tenders	9823 Bridge Street	LaPorte	IN	(888) 238-2123
(AutoNumber)							

The category First Name is a field

All the information for Douglas Seaver represents one record

Source: Microsoft product screen shot(s) reprinted with permission from Microsoft Corporation.

Tables Databases can and frequently do contain two or more tables. For example, a database used in a legal office may have one table for employees of the firm, another for clients of the firm, a third for opposing attorneys, and a fourth for the opposing parties in cases the firm has handled.

Reports **Reports** present the data from the database in an organized presentation. A report may present just the information from one table, such as employee birthdays. Frequently, a report shows the outcome of searching multiple tables and displays the relationships between the information and data from the different tables, such as a report of the employees that have ever worked for an opposing counsel in a case against a client.

reports
Information from a search of a database or databases.

Exhibit 2.6 Record for business contact

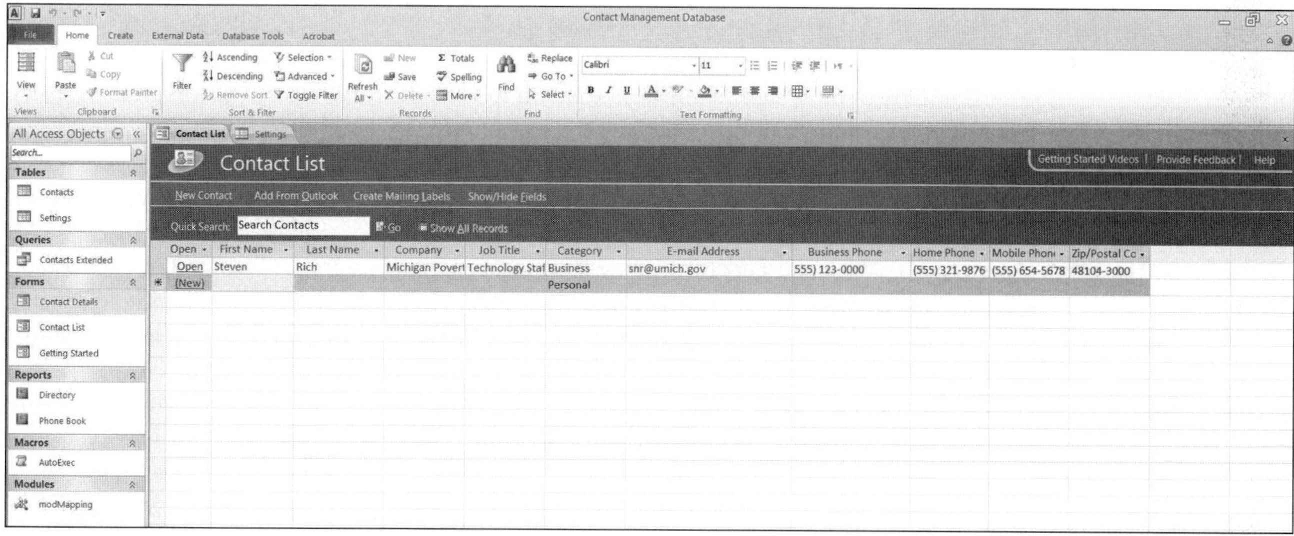

Source: Microsoft product screen shot(s) reprinted with permission from Microsoft Corporation.

Exhibit 2.7 Contact details

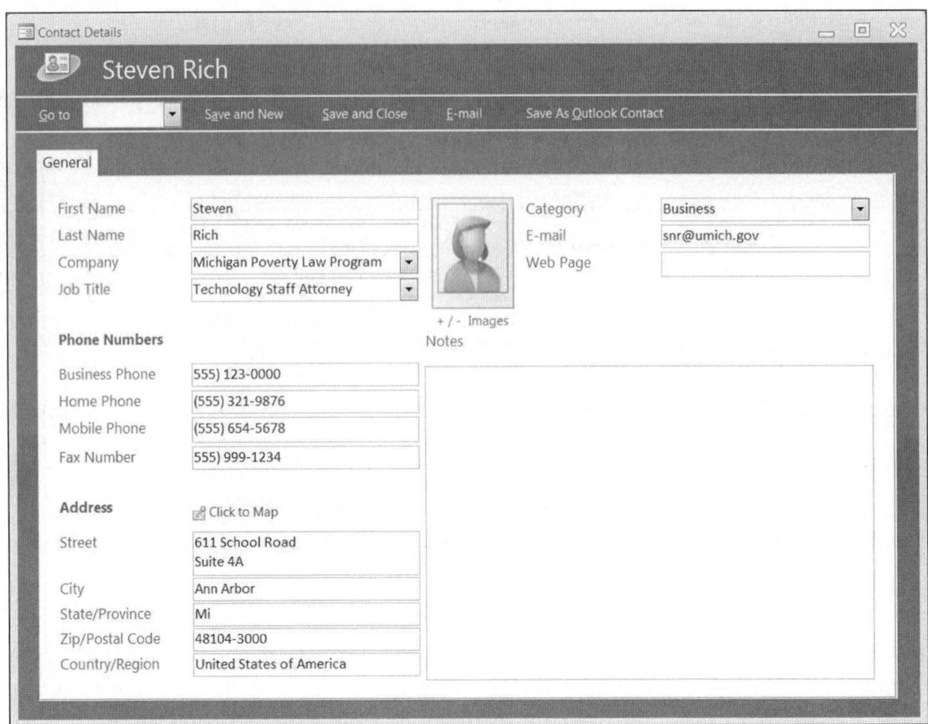

Source: Microsoft product screen shot(s) reprinted with permission from Microsoft Corporation.

Database Terminology Summary

Databases are collections of **tables.**
Tables contain **records.**
A **record** is all the information about one item or person; for example, **records** contain **fields** of information (data).
Fields contain **cells.**
A **field** is one type of information.
A **cell** is the box containing the individual field information, like a last name.

DATABASE EXAMPLE

One of most significant legal cases in modern history was the Enron case, in which many individuals and institutions lost millions of dollars. The underlying case was built from an analysis of the e-mails and other documents created and stored electronically at Enron. Databases were an important tool in accessing the information contained within the thousands of e-mails and documents in the investigation by the Federal Energy Regulatory Commission, or FERC, an independent agency that regulates the interstate transmission of natural gas, oil, and electricity. FERC makes available the ESI by use of the Internet and a third party electronic document review software called iCONECT nXT, as shown in the exhibit below. This is a good example of the use of the Internet or **cloud computing,** where information is made available for all those needing access over the Internet via a remote, hosted, secure electronic case review tool, as illustrated in Exhibit 2.8.

cloud computing
The access over the Internet of a secure depository by authorized users.

Exhibits 2.9 and 2.10 of iCONECT nXT show an example of access to a database, in this example, the case material in the investigation of Enron, with the results of searches of the e-mail database using selected terms.

Exhibit 2.8 Secure remote access

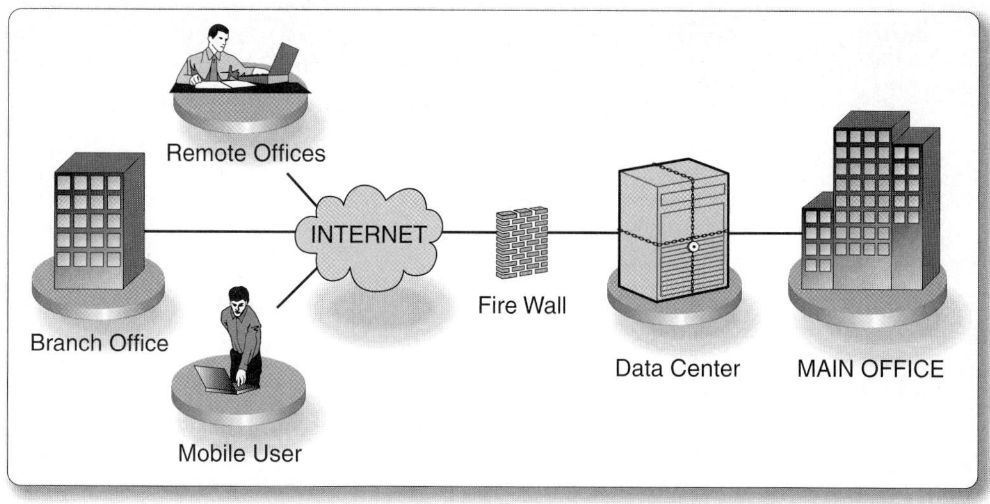

One of 1,368,775 e-mails is shown sorted by the following database fields:

SDOC_NO
FROM
TO
DATE
TIME
ORIGIN
FOLDER
ATTACHMENT

The results of a subsequent query using the name WILLIAMS from the initial search above is shown in Exhibit 2.11.

A summary report can be customized by the user to generate a comprehensive overview of relevant material as shown in Exhibit 2.12 on page 49.

Exhibit 2.9 FERC investigation material on a cloud-based system

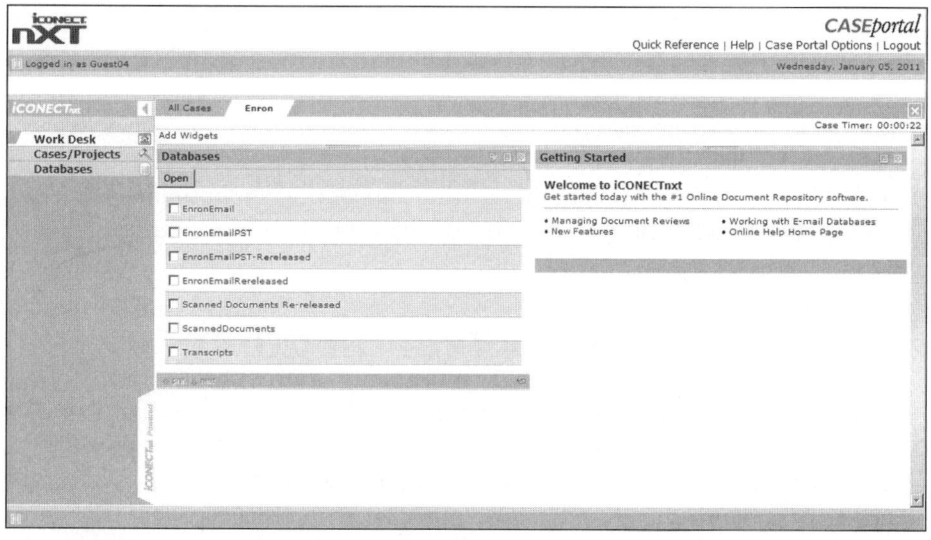

Exhibit 2.10 E-mails sorted by selected database fields

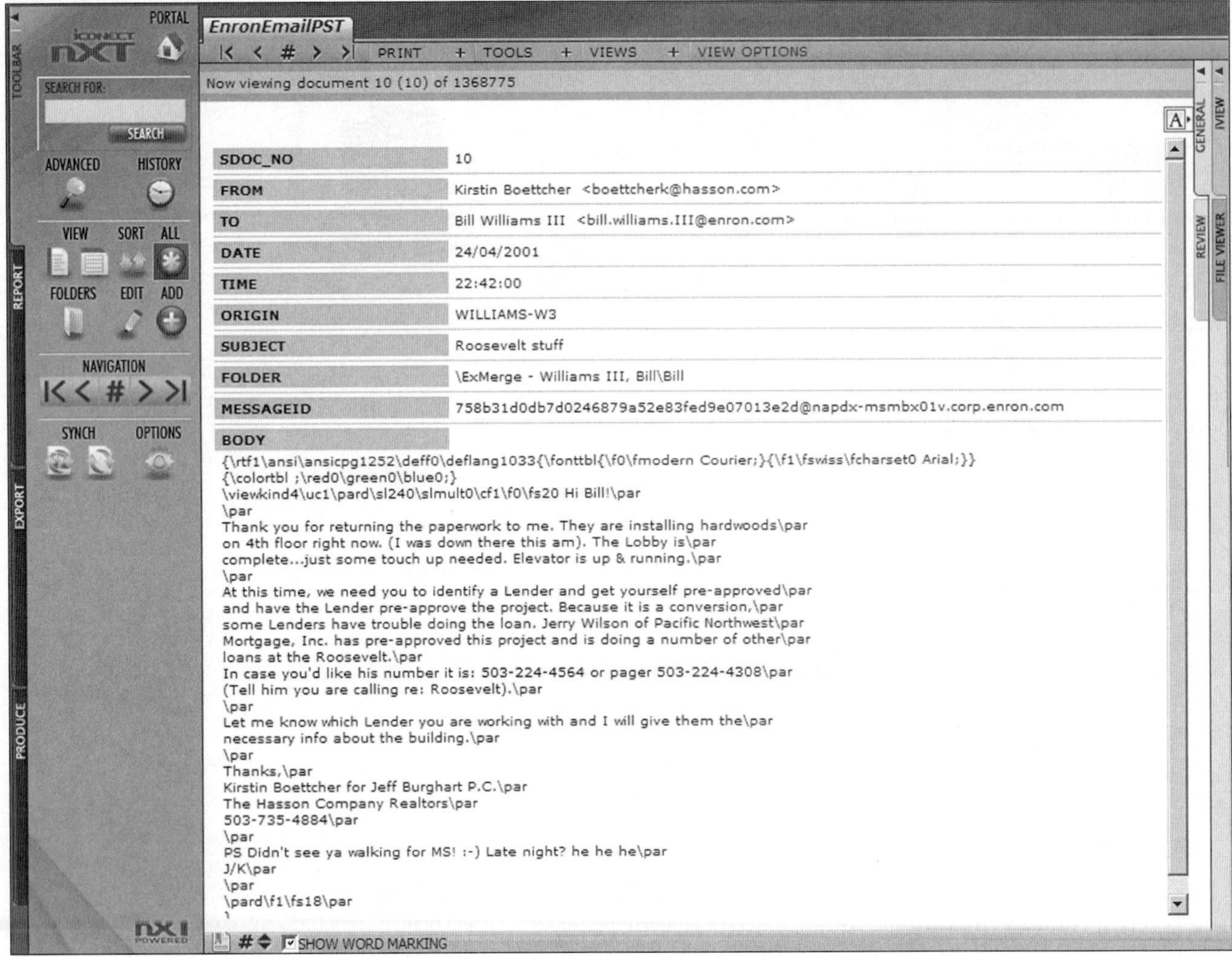

PORTAL
TOOLBAR
SEARCH FOR:
SEARCH
ADVANCED
HISTORY
VIEW
SORT
ALL
FOLDERS
EDIT
ADD
NAVIGATION
SYNCH
OPTIONS
REPORT
EXPORT
PRODUCE
EnronEmailPST
PRINT + TOOLS + VIEWS + VIEW OPTIONS
Now viewing document 10 (10) of 1368775
SDOC_NO 10
FROM Kirstin Boettcher <boettcherk@hasson.com>
TO Bill Williams III <bill.williams.III@enron.com>
DATE 24/04/2001
TIME 22:42:00
ORIGIN WILLIAMS-W3
SUBJECT Roosevelt stuff
FOLDER \ExMerge - Williams III, Bill\Bill
MESSAGEID 758b31d0db7d0246879a52e83fed9e07013e2d@napdx-msmbx01v.corp.enron.com
BODY
{\rtf1\ansi\ansicpg1252\deff0\deflang1033{\fonttbl{\f0\fmodern Courier;}{\f1\fswiss\fcharset0 Arial;}}
{\colortbl ;\red0\green0\blue0;}
\viewkind4\uc1\pard\sl240\slmult0\cf1\f0\fs20 Hi Bill!\par
\par
Thank you for returning the paperwork to me. They are installing hardwoods\par
on 4th floor right now. (I was down there this am). The Lobby is\par
complete...just some touch up needed. Elevator is up & running.\par
\par
At this time, we need you to identify a Lender and get yourself pre-approved\par
and have the Lender pre-approve the project. Because it is a conversion,\par
some Lenders have trouble doing the loan. Jerry Wilson of Pacific Northwest\par
Mortgage, Inc. has pre-approved this project and is doing a number of other\par
loans at the Roosevelt.\par
In case you'd like his number it is: 503-224-4564 or pager 503-224-4308\par
(Tell him you are calling re: Roosevelt).\par
\par
Let me know which Lender you are working with and I will give them the\par
necessary info about the building.\par
\par
Thanks,\par
Kirstin Boettcher for Jeff Burghart P.C.\par
The Hasson Company Realtors\par
503-735-4884\par
\par
PS Didn't see ya walking for MS! :-) Late night? he he he\par
J/K\par
\par
\pard\f1\fs18\par
}
GENERAL
IVIEW
REVIEW
FILE VIEWER
SHOW WORD MARKING

Source: iCONECT Development, LLC. All rights reserved.

DATABASE ISSUES IN LITIGATION

The litigation team is the interface between the client, and the opposing side and the court. Discovery requests are filtered through counsel. It is the trial counsel's duty to obtain accurate responses to the legitimate discovery requests for electronic discovery. Trial counsel and the litigation team must know enough about the client's system for creating and storing and ultimately deleting electronically stored information to avoid claims of dilatory conduct and a lack of candor to the court.

SEARCHES—CONSTRUCTING THE QUERY

Anyone who has ever conducted a search on the Internet using a single word or even a combination of a few words knows that such a search may not produce the desired results. Searching legal databases is also frequently frustrating if the exact, proper term is not entered as used in those databases. Searching electronically stored information when there are no universal, common terms or phrases such as the

Exhibit 2.11 Results of query using the name WILLIAMS

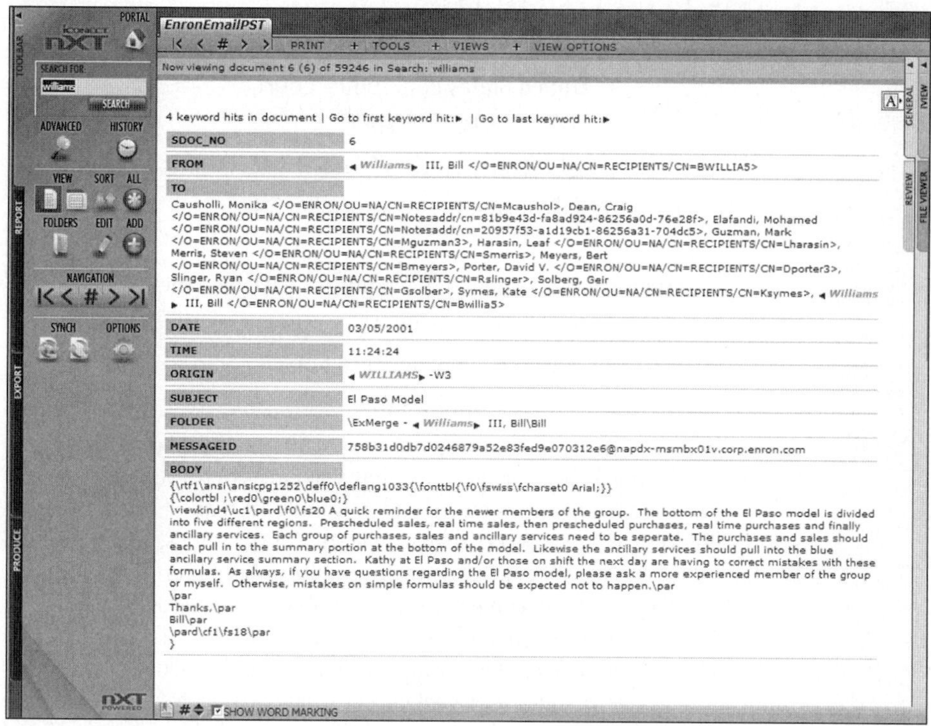

Exhibit 2.12 Custom summary reports

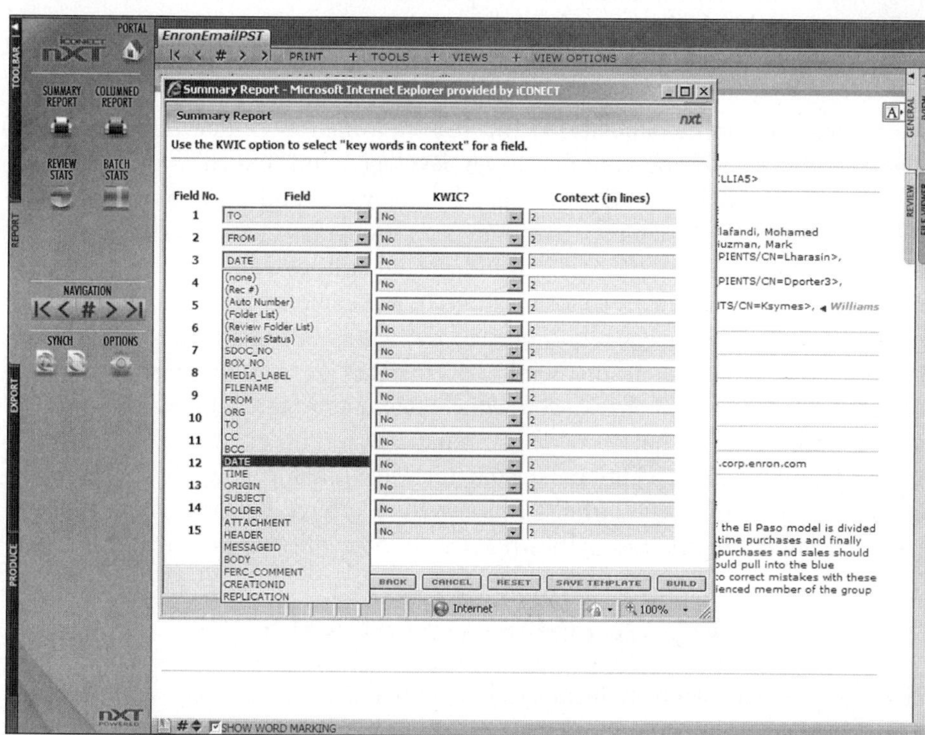

IN THE WORDS OF THE COURT...

United States Bankruptcy Court,
S.D. New York.
In re A & M FLORIDA PROPERTIES II, LLC, Debtor.
GFI Acquisition, LLC, et al., Plaintiffs,
v.
American Federated Title Corporation, Defendant.
Bankruptcy No. 09-15173 (AJG).
Adversary No. 09-01162 (AJG).
April 7, 2010.

...While the delays in discovery were not caused by any intentional behavior, GFI's counsel did not fulfill its obligation to find all sources of relevant documents in a timely manner. Counsel has an obligation to not just request documents of his client, but to search for sources of information....Counsel must communicate with the client, identify all sources of relevant information, and "become fully familiar with [the] client's document retention policies, as well as [the] client's data retention architecture." *Zubulake v. UBS Warburg LLC,* 229 F.R.D. 422, 432 (S.D.N.Y.2004)....Nash failed in his obligation to locate and produce all relevant documents in a timely manner. A diligent effort would have involved some sort of dialogue with Garfinkle and any key figures at GFI to gain a better understanding of GFI's computer system. *See Phoenix Four, Inc.,* 2006 WL 1409413, at *5 (stating that counsel's effort to discover all sources of relevant information "would involve communicating with information technology personnel and the key players in the litigation to understand how electronic information is stored."). Had he posed the proper questions in these dialogues, Nash would have gained a more nuanced understanding of how GFI employees stored e-mails much earlier in the discovery process....Assuming GFI was operating in good faith, it is almost certain that the archive folders would have been mentioned.

Boolean search
A search model that uses keywords and connectors.

West Keywords can be difficult. For this reason, a number of new search methods have been developed and continue to be developed and refined to overcome the limitation of the traditional **Boolean search** using words and connectors like AND, OR, and NOT. Some database software search engines can isolate and identify previously unknown patterns or trends in large amounts of data. Conceptual searching, a type of search that looks for meaning, not specific letters in words, looks for information that is conceptually similar to the words in the search query, For example, a conceptual search for the phrase "breakfast foods" returns items of foods eaten for breakfast. One- or two-word conceptual queries rarely return good results, whereas more detailed queries, such as "what is eaten at a Sunday Mother's Day brunch," would result in additional related items like "champagne," the mixed drinks served, and, potentially, all other items served at a large buffet. A sample search query in a discrimination case is shown in the following *Bellinger v. Astrue* case.

THE REALITY OF USING DATABASES

The reality is that legal team members, lawyers, paralegals, and legal assistants rarely create their own databases. In some cases, a simple database of a single table might be used to sort or organize some information, such as the client list or conflict list.

Exhibit 2.13

IN THE WORDS OF THE COURT . . .

CELIA BELLINGER, Plaintiff.

v.

MICHAEL J. ASTRUE, Commissioner of Social Security, Defendant.

No. CV-06-321 (CBA).

United States District Court, E.D. New York.

April 1, 2010.

...Plaintiff next demands that defendant search the email boxes of employees McGinley, Infiesta, Freeburn and Corva, listing numerous terms for which she seeks to have searches conducted. The breadth of plaintiff's demands, and her use of common terms with the potential to yield a substantial number of irrelevant documents, are plain from a review of Document Request 85, which reads as follows:

> Produce for inspection all email strings with their attachments for the following email requests, certifying that a reasonable search was conducted in all accessible places where computer generated information is archived, stored, and retained, including defendant's: a) centralized email server at the ROCC in Jamaica ROCC, b) McGinley's hard drive(s) of his desktop computer and notebook computer and c) all other places where computer generated documents are archived, kept or stored including all other servers.
>
> > Search 1. All Email strings, and attachments sent directly from John McGinely (*sic*) to anyone containing Celia Bellinger's name in whole or in part by her Employee Identification Number for the period of January 1, 2002 to January 31, 2006.
> >
> > Search 2. All Email strings and attachments sent directly from John McGinley or directly to John McGinley containing the search terms "energy lady" or "maven" or "temporary position" or "princess" or "discrimination" or "EEO" or "CREO" or "shamu" or "ass" or "tits" or "disciplinary" or "discipline" or "warning" or "complainant" or

(*continued*)

"061-05NY" or "disparate" or "counseling" or "6B201" or "Molly" or "1D251" or "95U530" or "Investigator" or affidavit" or "plaintiff" or "defendant" for the time period of January 1, 2005 to January 31, 2006.

Search 3. All email strings and attachments sent directly from John McGinley to Eric Schlesinger containing the search terms "energy lady" or "maven" or "temporary position" or "princess" or "incumbent" or "discrimination" or "complaint" or "complained" or "EEO" or "investigate" or "investigation" or "investigator" [or] "CREO" or "shamu" or "Steve Hunchik" or "Hunchik" or "ass" or "FTE" or "disciplinary" or "discipline" or "reprimand" or "warning" or "Chung" or "Schmidt" or "complainant" or "plaintiff" or "defendant" or "vacancy announcement" or "061-05NY" or "disparate" or "counseling" or "selectees" or "Chung" or "Schmidt" or "6B201" or "Molly" or "1D251" or "95U530" for the time period of January 1, 2002 to January 31, 2005.

Search 4. All email strings and attachments from directly John McGinley to Irene Corva containing the search terms "temporary position" or "princess" or "support service specialist" or "incumbent" or "discrimination" or "complaint" or "complained" or "complained of" or "EEO" or "CREO" or "investigate" or "investigation" or "investigator" or "ass" or "discipline" or "disciplinary" or "warning" or "Chung" or "Schmidt" or "complainant" or "061-05NY" or "disparate" or "counseling" or "selection process" or "selectees" or "selected" or "6B201" or "Molly" or "1D251" or "95U530" for the time period of January 1,2005 to January 31, 2006.

Search 5. All email strings and attachments sent from John McGinley directly to Julio Infiesta containing the search terms "temporary position" or "princess" or "discrimination" or "complaint" or "complained" or "investigate" or "investigation" or "CREO" or "EEO" or "ass" or "tits" or "legs" or "disciplinary" or "warning" or "discipline" or "reprimand" or "061-05NY" or "disparate" or "counseling" or "selection process" or "selectees" or "6B201" or "Molly" or "Mavis" or "1D251" or "95U530" for the time period of January 1, 2003 to January 31, 2005.

Search 6. All email strings and attachments sent from John McGinley directly to anyone in Civil Rights & Equal Opportunity (CREO) containing the search terms "energy lady" or "maven" or "temporary position" or "princess" or "discrimination" or "complaint" or "plaintiff" or "defendant" or "complained" or "EEO" or "Mavis" or "investigate" or "investigation" or "position description" or "shamu" or "ass" or "disciplinary" or "discipline" or "warning" or "reprimand" or "Chung" or "Schmidt" or "Bellinger" or "complainant" or "vacancy announcement" or "6B201" or "Molly" or "Schlesinger" or "1D251" or "95U530" for the time period of January 1, 2002 to December 31, 2006.

Search 7. All email strings and attachments sent from John McGinley to anyone in the Human Resources Center containing the search terms "temporary position" or "princess" or "discrimination" or "complaint" or "complained" or "investigate" or "investigation" or "ass" or "disciplinary" or "discipline" or "warning" or "reprimand" or "complainant" or "1D251" or "95U530" or "plaintiff" or "complainant" for the time period of January 1, 2005 to January 31, 2006.

So why do we need to learn about databases? While members of the legal team may not actually create their own databases, they do use them all the time. Virtually every law office's specialty application program for managing the office, cases, or documents in litigation is a database. Software vendors have created applications for the legal community. They have custom-designed the Form Views for input of information, and the query forms for generating the desired reports, and set up the search and presentation algorithms (formulas for searching). When special applications are required, many of the software vendors will create custom tables and report generators, such as those for a particular area of practice like estates.

Knowing what a database is and the associated terminology makes working with the software developer, in-house IT professional, or outside consultant easier and more productive in obtaining what is needed, wanted, and possible. Knowing how a database works and is organized makes the software applications that are based on database designs easier to use and work with. As electronic discovery becomes a more significant part of litigation, database programs will play an increasing role in the discovery process. In-house and electronic discovery vendor programs use databases to perform the functions of search, analysis, and reporting. Members of the litigation team must have a good basis in database operations and terminology to be able to communicate with the technical and litigation support members of the litigation team as well as to avoid claims by the court of lack of competency in the e-discovery process.

CONCEPT REVIEW AND REINFORCEMENT

KEY TERMS

electronically stored information (ESI) 32
native format 34
optical character recognition (OCR) 35
metadata 35
system metadata 35
content (application) metadata 39
graphic image format 39
portable document format (PDF) 39
scanning 41
database 43
table 44
fields 44
cell 44
record 44
reports 45
cloud computing 46
Boolean search 50

CHAPTER SUMMARY

Introduction to Technology in Civil Litigation	Technology is being introduced and used in every aspect of civil litigation as business and society have increasing amounts of data created by computerization.
From Paper to Electronically Stored Information	Electronically stored information is a dominant factor in litigation today. While some still prefer to do business using paper, electronically stored information is becoming the norm.
Documents in Litigation	In the past, requests for documents in response to interrogatories were met with the delivery of paper documents. During the transition period from paper to electronic documentation, issues have arisen with regard to the proper format for the delivery of requested documentation.
Native Format	Native format, the format in which the original files were created and saved, contains the hidden data about the document known as metadata.
Computer Format	Documents that are delivered in computer-usable formats are easier to search and analyze using computer programs designed for those purposes. When documents are not delivered in computer-usable format, they can usually be processed and saved in such a format but will not have any of the hidden data associated with the original files.
Metadata	Metadata is frequently referred to as data about data. Metadata is divided into two types. Resource or system metadata is information about the content or application. This is used to track or locate the files and contains the information such as file names, sizes, and location. Content metadata is in the file itself, such as who the author of the document is and any change wthat has been made.
Data Gathering to Preserve Metadata	If data is not gathered properly, metadata such as the dates of file creation, last access, and last modification can be changed. If that happens, you simply cannot produce accurate metadata.
Electronic Document Formats—Comparison of PDF and TIFF	The two most common formats for large-scale document delivery are the TIFF and PDF formats. Neither of these formats contains the original metadata of the native format document. It is for this reason that some counsel prefer to deliver documents in these formats to avoid revealing associated metadata.
Scanning	Scanning software today permits the scanning of tape or documents and conversion into a computer-readable format by the use of optical character recognition software. This conversion enables the document to be searched by other computer programs.

Databases in Litigation	Databases are used in the litigation process to store, sort, and analyze information.
Electronic Database Basics	Databases are programs used to store information. Stored information may then be sorted by key terms, phrases, or other criteria. Among the frequent uses of databases is to sort through lists of names in performing a conflict of interest check.
Data Repositories	A database program is a repository of information of all types that can be sorted and presented in a desired, meaningful manner. Although a database is nothing more than an electronic version of cards in a card file, it can be searched more effectively and efficiently than a paper-based system.
Navigating Electronic Databases	Electronic databases use standard terminology to describe parts of a database: **table,** which contains fields of information **field,** which is one type of information **record,** all the information about one item **cell,** which is the location of the field with one type of information **reports,** which present the data from the database in an organized way
Database Issues in Litigation	The litigation team, the interface between the client and the opposing party and the court, has the obligation to locate and produce the required or requested information from the client's databases.
Searches—Constructing the Query	The traditional method of searching databases is using the Boolean search method, which uses connectors such as AND, OR, and NOT.
The Reality of Using Databases	It is rare that the legal team creates its own database. Virtually every law office's specialty application program for managing the office, managing cases, or managing presentations in litigation is a database, and the litigation team must understand the terminology to be able to communicate with those creating, maintaining, or working on the databases.

4

REVIEW QUESTIONS AND EXERCISES

1. Why is electronically stored information a featured topic in litigation conferences?
2. What are some records to provide in paper format?
3. What are the issues in reviewing documents in paper format?
4. What is meant by native format?
5. Why is there no universal standard for delivery of electronic documents?
6. How can paper documents be converted to electronic format?
7. What is metadata?
8. What is the significance of knowing what the metadata is in a document for litigation purposes?
9. What is the difference between system metadata and content metadata?
10. What is the disadvantage of receiving documents in TIFF or PDF format?
11. What are the advantages of delivering documents in TIFF or PDF format?
12. Of what use is optical character recognition software to the litigation team?
13. What is the function of a database?
14. Identify the parts of a database record.
15. Give examples of the search terms that might be used to search e-mails.
16. Do members of the litigation team have to know how to create a database? Explain.
17. Prepare examples of searches using Boolean terms.
18. Why is it important for the litigation team to understand the terminology used in databases?

BUILDING YOUR PARALEGAL SKILLS

INTERNET AND TECHNOLOGY EXERCISES

1. Locate tutorial information on creating and using a database on the Internet or in your office suite of programs.
2. Use the database included in Microsoft Office Access or WordPerfect Office Quattro Pro to create a database of names, addresses, and phone numbers. Create separate fields for first, last, and middle names; number, street, city, state, and zip code; area code and phone number for your family, your class, or your study group. Sort the individual records by fields.
3. Prepare a new resume or update your current resume. Use the features of your word processor to review the document and locate its metadata. What kind of metadata is it?
4. If you have a scanner available to you, scan your resume or other document and save it in at least three different formats.

CIVIL LITIGATION VIDEO CASE STUDIES

Privilege Issue: Misdirected E-mail

A paralegal advises his supervising attorney that he has inadvertently sent an e-mail with confidential and privileged content to the opposing attorney.

After viewing the video in MyLegalStudiesKit, answer the following questions.

1. What steps should be taken when confidential material is sent inadvertently to the other side?
2. What is the rule on inadvertent disclosure in your jurisdiction?
3. How can the inadvertent sending of e-mails be prevented?
4. What precautions can be introduced to avoid anyone reading e-mails not intended for him or her?

CHAPTER OPENING SCENARIO CASE STUDY

1. What information should the law firm capture and maintain in a database?
2. How can the database be used by the firm?

COMPREHENSIVE CASE STUDY

SCHOOL BUS–TRUCK ACCIDENT CASE

Review the assigned case study in Appendix II.

1. Prepare a list of potential search queries that might be used if the case does involve a brake failure as a potential cause of the accident.
2. Prepare a list of documents that may be requested for review as part of discovery.

BUILDING YOUR PROFESSIONAL PORTFOLIO

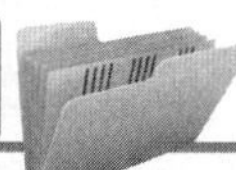

CIVIL LITIGATION TEAM AT WORK

Forms

Prepare a template for use in recording contact information for:

a. Clients
b. Business contacts
c. Personal contacts

Procedures

Prepare a step-by-step procedure to check for a conflict of interest using a database such as a MS Access database, or a software program that may be used for that purpose such as AbacusLaw.

"The leading rule for the lawyer, as for the man of every other calling, is diligence. Leave nothing for tomorrow which can be done today. Never let your correspondence fall behind. Whatever piece of business you have in hand, before stopping, do all the labor pertaining to it which can then be done."

–Abraham Lincoln in 1850

Technology in Civil Litigation

CHAPTER 3

OPENING SCENARIO

The firm's weekly staff meeting was upbeat with the discussion of the influx of new cases. Mr. Mason listened to the discussion about the new cases that had come in and the reports of those cases in progress. He wondered out loud how they were going to manage the volume of cases. He commented to his partners that when they had had fewer cases and only one office, everyone seemed to work on all the cases together with divided responsibilities, one partner concentrating on liability issues and another on damages, as they had been doing in the school bus case. With more and larger, complex cases, on some of which they were working with outside co-counsel, the required access to case file information was becoming an issue. The paralegals commented that they needed a protocol for how information was to be added to the files and updated. Another issue was the cases with divided responsibility between the two remote offices because of the need for each office to be able to add information and the other to retrieve or access that information. Mrs. Hannah, the office manager, suggested that with the proper procedures in place and the use of office management, case management, and litigation management software, this would not be a problem.

LEARNING OBJECTIVES

After studying this chapter, you should be able to:

1. Understand the functions and value to the law firm of case management software.
2. Understand the functions and value to the law firm of case analysis software.
3. Explain the use of timelines in civil litigation.
4. Explain the use of calendaring programs in civil litigation.
5. Use the Internet as part of the investigation of a case.
6. Explain the reason for using encryption in litigation.

VIDEO INTRODUCTION

A. An introduction to office management software in the law office.

After watching the video in MyLegalStudiesKit, answer the following question.

- What role does office management software play in litigation?

B. An introduction to integrated law office software AbacusLaw and Tabs3.

After watching the video in MyLegalStudiesKit, answer the following question.

- How can programs like AbacusLaw and Tabs3 support the litigation function?

C. An introduction to LexisNexis CaseMap case management software.

After watching the video in MyLegalStudiesKit, answer the following question.

- How can CaseMap be used to organize a case?

INTRODUCTION TO TECHNOLOGY IN CIVIL LITIGATION

Law firms are generally under pressure to reduce the costs associated with performing legal services. The practice of law today requires efficiency in a reduced-cost environment. Computers and appropriate software are being adopted and used to reduce errors and improve productivity with fewer personnel. Office and case management software is increasingly used to manage all aspects of client and case file information, contact information, calendaring of important and critical dates, and document generation. Conflicts of interest checks previously performed manually with a paper-based system of card files or lists of names are now performed using case and office management database software programs.

Some courts, including the federal courts, have implemented electronic filing. In increasing numbers of courts, it is not an option whether to file electronically but a requirement, using a prescribed electronic file format. Even the sole practitioner handling a relatively small, routine matter may need to file documents electronically with the court. As a result of this new requirement to use computerized filing, law offices are implementing the tools for electronic preparation of pleadings and electronic filing.

The increased dependence on the use of electronically stored information has forced law firms to learn and use the software for electronic discovery to obtain data, documents, and emails that may be evidence for use in trial or may contain statements that can be used to impeach the other party or its witnesses. Litigators are recognizing the importance of electronic presentation tools in trial for presenting exhibits of electronically stored information, static presentations, simulations, and videotaped deposition in court.

Computers and the Internet are being used in every aspect of civil litigation, from initial case organization to trial presentation. Economic pressures from clients require greater law office efficiency and productivity. Computers with legal specialty software programs are used for managing case information and electronic discovery. By eliminating manual searching of documents and records and by providing a central repository for all aspects of case materials, litigation teams can work more efficiently and be more productive. Except in smaller cases, the reality is that without computers and specialty software, some functions, like electronic discovery, cannot be performed in a timely and accurate manner. Manual processing of large quantities of data typically requires extensive labor pools of paralegals, attorneys, law students, and other specialists. Even with each person performing at optimum speed, there is a physical time limit that cannot be reduced.

As cases become more complex, the legal team members' access to case file data becomes a major issue, with more people on the legal team working on the same case, some at remote locations or even in different locations in the same building. Manually locating and accessing case material filed in large binders and file boxes is not productive or, in some cases, physically possible. Use of legal-specific case management software and the Internet can allow large numbers of people on a legal team located anywhere in the world to access all the information about a case using no more than a portable computer.

CASE AND PRACTICE MANAGEMENT SOFTWARE

LEARNING OBJECTIVE 1
Understand the functions and value to the law firm of case management software.

It is rare that a litigation team works from beginning to end on one case at a time. Indeed, the legal team may work on a number of cases simultaneously, with each case in a different stage of preparation for trial. Frequently, different members of the legal team work on different aspects of the same case. With the team approach to handling cases, each member of the team must be able to access case information and know what the other members of the team have done and what still needs to be done. In the traditional paper file case management approach, the physical file is the repository of everything from interview notes to pleadings and exhibits. With many people accessing and removing case material, it is not unusual for items to be "missing" because someone forgot to insert into the file cabinet or file box a note or card indicating that he or she has the file.

In cases with voluminous records including days' or weeks' worth of deposition transcripts, only by use of computer software can relevant documents or appropriate deposition portions be accessed quickly and efficiently. The creation of documents in electronic format and the scanning of existing paper documents into electronic format allow the storage and shared access of documents from data storage devices. Using the Internet, case files may be stored on remote file servers of outside consultants and vendors in other states or even in other countries; these remote storage systems are sometimes called **e-repositories** or *online document repositories*. Remote access to the e-repository is permitted only to those having authorization. Business and government use of computers for email and document storage has

e-repository (online document repository)
An electronic data storage facility accessed using the Internet.

Checklist ✓ CASE FILE

A typical case file contains documentation of the:

- interview of the client;
- interviews of fact and expert witnesses;
- investigation reports;
- expert reports;
- documents;
- evidence;
- research memoranda;
- pleadings; and
- trial preparation material.

resulted in a massive increase in the number of potential documents that may have to be reviewed, tracked, and made available to opposing counsel in a case. Managing cases and litigation with massive amounts of data has thus become increasingly difficult. As the number of documents has increased and cases have become more complex, the number of members of the legal team working on a given case also has increased. These factors have led to greater use of the computer to manage the case files and the litigation process. Exhibit 3.1 shows the steps in a typical personal injury case and how an automated case management system can be used to avoid mistakes.

Using Case Management Systems

case management system Software for organizing the parts of a case in a central repository that can be shared by all members of the legal team.

Efficient use of a **case management system** allows all authorized members of the legal team to access the case information day or night. Effective case management, therefore, requires some central repository of the information created or gathered by each of the team members, as well as the ability of each to access the case information added by others. Depending on available Internet access and

Exhibit 3.1 The steps in a typical personal injury case

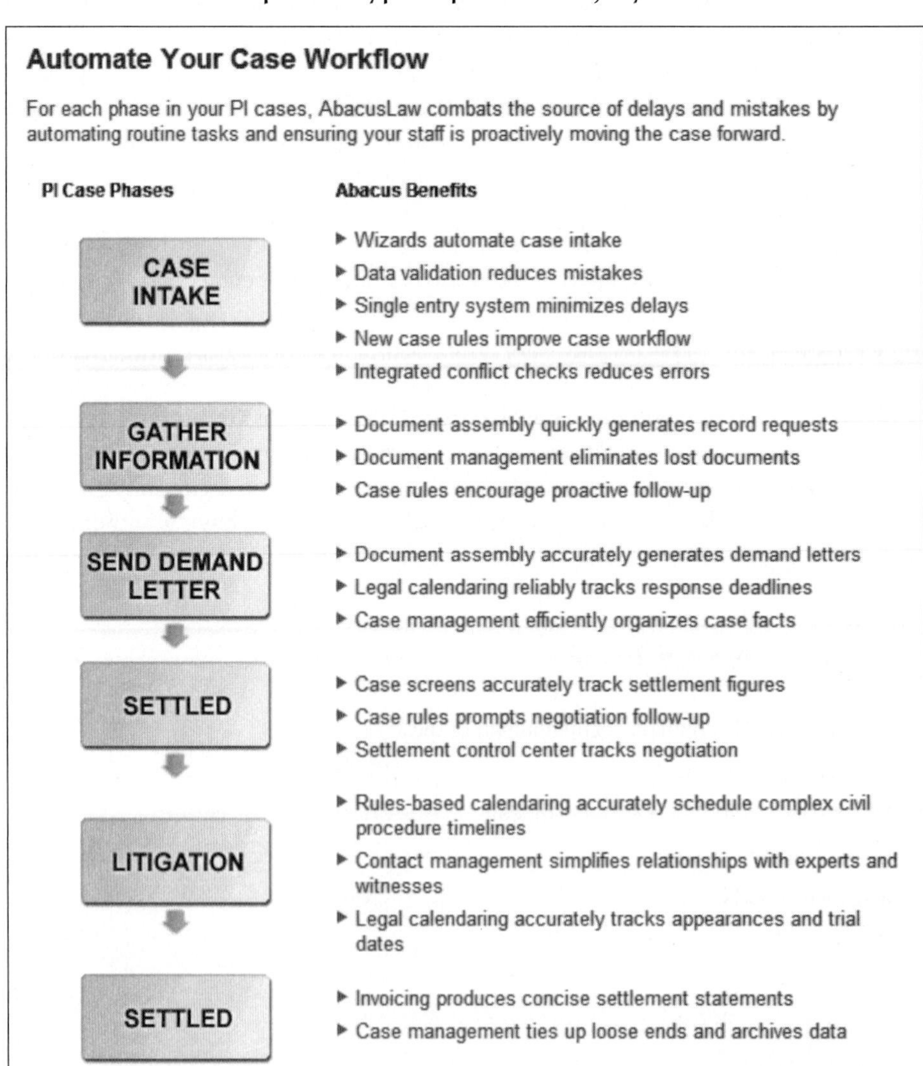

Source:

Internet connection speed, members of the legal team may all be able to access the same information from remote locations across town, across the country, and sometimes around the world.

Collaboration among members of the legal team is becoming common practice, even in smaller law offices. In part, this collaboration is a result of the increased complexity of cases, the shortened time in which to prepare for trial under court rules, and the procedures put in place by the courts to get the backload of cases reduced and to increase the speed of justice. In many smaller, specialized practices, the resources or the expertise may not be available to handle the occasional large or complex case. For example, a small firm of tax attorneys who have expertise in tax evasion issues but not trial experience may collaborate with a small trial or litigation boutique, with each firm supplying the expertise in one area and sharing all the case files and information to better serve the client. An example of the tools that may be used in collaborative situations is the form in CaseMap for individual assessment of the issues in a case, as shown in Exhibit 3.2.

Exhibit 3.2 CaseMap form for individual assessment of the issues

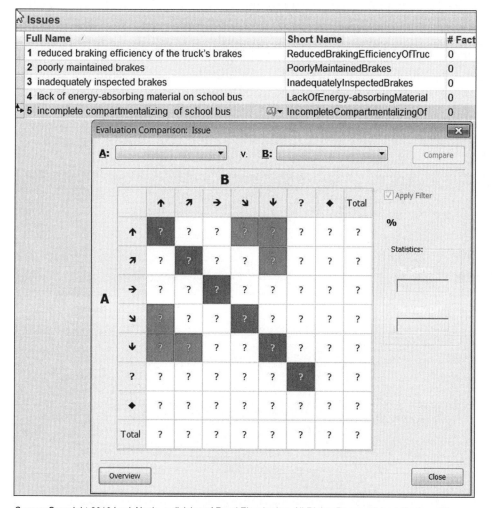

Issues

Full Name	Short Name	# Fact
1 reduced braking efficiency of the truck's brakes	ReducedBrakingEfficiencyOfTruc	0
2 poorly maintained brakes	PoorlyMaintainedBrakes	0
3 inadequately inspected brakes	InadequatelyInspectedBrakes	0
4 lack of energy-absorbing material on school bus	LackOfEnergy-absorbingMaterial	0
5 incomplete compartmentalizing of school bus	IncompleteCompartmentalizingOf	0

Evaluation Comparison: Issue

A: v. B: Compare

B

A	↑	↗	→	↘	↓	?	◆	Total
↑	?	?	?	?	?	?	?	?
↗	?	?	?	?	?	?	?	?
→	?	?	?	?	?	?	?	?
↘	?	?	?	?	?	?	?	?
↓	?	?	?	?	?	?	?	?
?	?	?	?	?	?	?	?	?
◆	?	?	?	?	?	?	?	?
Total	?	?	?	?	?	?	?	?

Apply Filter

%

Statistics:

Overview

Close

Source: Copyright 2010 LexisNexis, a division of Reed Elsevier Inc. All Rights Reserved. LexisNexis and the Knowledge Burst logo are registered trademarks of Reed Elsevier Properties Inc. TimeMap and CaseMap are registered trademarks of LexisNexis CourtLink, Inc. Used with the permission of LexisNexis.

File Access and Confidentiality

Many clients seeking legal advice do not want their names or the subject matter for which they have sought legal counsel known, making even their names a subject of confidentiality. Case management systems contain confidential information that requires the same protection against access as any other source of confidential or privileged client information. Access in all cases should be limited to those with a need to know: only legal team members working on that particular case. Exhibit 3.3 shows the range of security and access settings for AbacusLaw, a typical case and office management system.

Conflict of Interest Checks

With a case management system in the law office, information may be entered about current clients and cases. These systems may also be used to store information about former clients and cases. Cases on which and clients for whom members of the legal team worked before coming to work for the current firm may also be entered for the limited purpose of conflict checking. It is not unusual for a prospective firm employee to provide a list of names of clients on whose cases he or she has worked in prior firms so that the new law firm can check its records to ensure there will be no conflicts of interest. These lists are generally considered confidential, with access limited to senior firm management for the limited purpose of conducting a conflict check to allow the firm to create an ethics wall shielding the new employee from any access to information for which there might be a conflict—for example, by not allowing a lawyer or paralegal who had worked on a defense team to now work on the plaintiff's side at a new firm, because the lawyer or paralegal will know the defense trial strategy if he or she had helped prepare the case's work product.

Exhibit 3.3 Security setting options

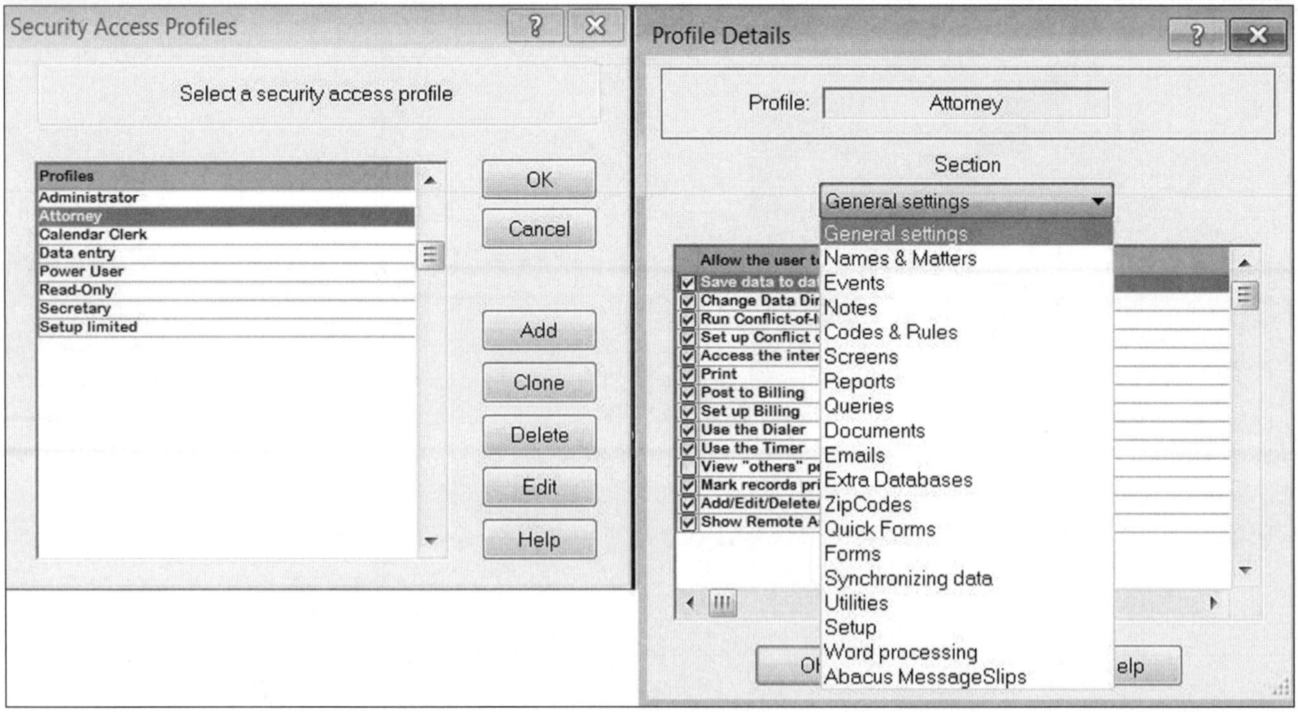

Exhibit 3.4 Conflict of interest generator window

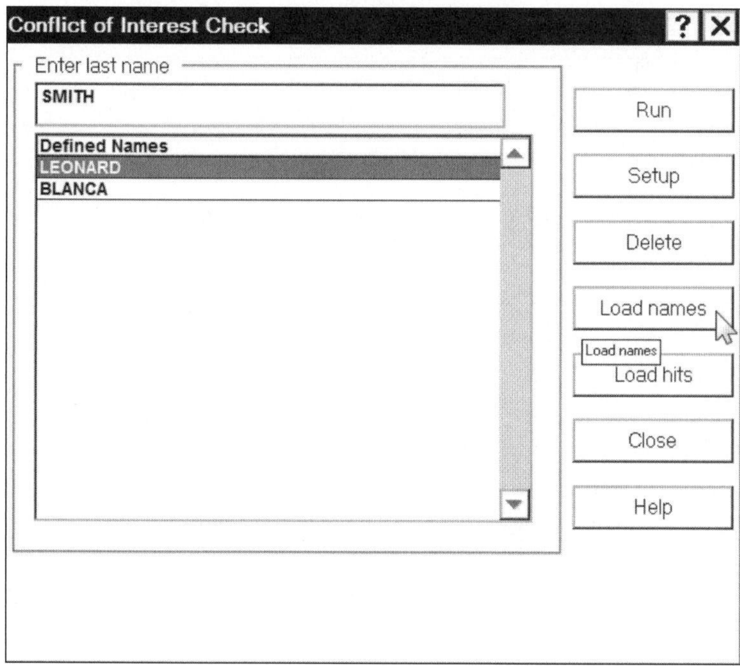

Source: © 2010 Abacus Data Systems, Inc. All rights reserved.

Some offices still use a manual card system to keep track of the names of clients and opposing parties. These cards are physically searched to find possible conflicts of interest before accepting new clients or matters. This system may work for the small office with few cases or clients; but for the larger office with multiple attorneys and possibly multiple offices, timely entry and searching of large amounts of information manually is not realistic. With a computerized database and the report generators in case management systems, timely, accurate access to information may be obtained by every authorized member of the legal team. Some reports of information, such as comparing the name of a potential client against all current clients' names, can be presented in specialized case and office management programs as a standard report, like the **conflict report generator** in AbacusLaw shown in Exhibit 3.4 above.

conflict report generator
A preconfigured report in a contacts database.

With a few keystrokes, a list can be prepared to check for potential conflicts of interest, or a computer search can be performed with a printout of any matter or litigation where a name appears, as shown in Exhibit 3.5 below.

Input—Entering Information

Case management programs provide, at the least, a basic set of screens for entering different types of information, as shown in Exhibit 3.6. Some programs provide or allow the user to create customized forms for practice specialties, such as the personal injury matter form shown in Exhibit 3.7. Information that may be entered directly into the form field and stored includes the names, addresses, contact information, and personal data (such as birth dates) of every client, every opposing party, every fact witness and expert witness, and every opposing counsel with whom any member of the firm has ever had contact in litigation, contract negotiations, or counseling sessions, or met in any business or legal setting.

PRACTICE TIP

In addition to the obvious use of avoiding accepting a client with a potential conflict of interest, the information frequently is used in maintaining client relations. Many firms use the information to send birthday and anniversary greetings and updates on specific changes in the law for which the client has consulted the firm previously.

Exhibit 3.5 Conflict report

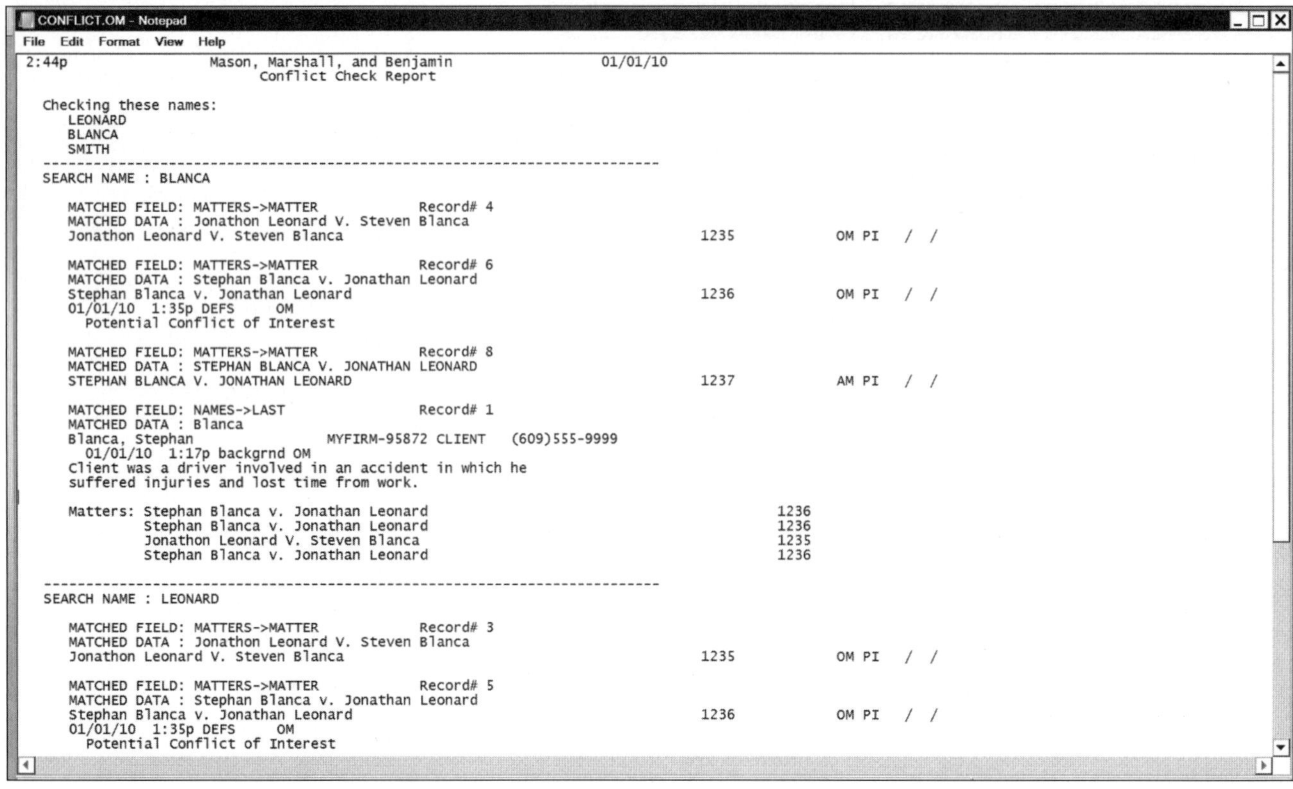

```
CONFLICT.OM - Notepad
File  Edit  Format  View  Help
2:44p                 Mason, Marshall, and Benjamin                   01/01/10
                          Conflict Check Report

  Checking these names:
     LEONARD
     BLANCA
     SMITH
  ------------------------------------------------------------------------
  SEARCH NAME : BLANCA

     MATCHED FIELD: MATTERS->MATTER           Record# 4
     MATCHED DATA : Jonathon Leonard V. Steven Blanca
     Jonathon Leonard V. Steven Blanca                                         1235         OM PI   / /

     MATCHED FIELD: MATTERS->MATTER           Record# 6
     MATCHED DATA : Stephan Blanca v. Jonathan Leonard
     Stephan Blanca v. Jonathan Leonard                                        1236         OM PI   / /
     01/01/10  1:35p DEFS      OM
       Potential Conflict of Interest

     MATCHED FIELD: MATTERS->MATTER           Record# 8
     MATCHED DATA : STEPHAN BLANCA V. JONATHAN LEONARD
     STEPHAN BLANCA V. JONATHAN LEONARD                                        1237         AM PI   / /

     MATCHED FIELD: NAMES->LAST               Record# 1
     MATCHED DATA : Blanca
     Blanca, Stephan                MYFIRM-95872 CLIENT   (609)555-9999
       01/01/10  1:17p backgrnd OM
     Client was a driver involved in an accident in which he
     suffered injuries and lost time from work.

     Matters: Stephan Blanca v. Jonathan Leonard                                        1236
              Stephan Blanca v. Jonathan Leonard                                        1236
              Jonathon Leonard V. Steven Blanca                                         1235
              Stephan Blanca v. Jonathan Leonard                                        1236

  ------------------------------------------------------------------------
  SEARCH NAME : LEONARD

     MATCHED FIELD: MATTERS->MATTER           Record# 3
     MATCHED DATA : Jonathon Leonard V. Steven Blanca
     Jonathon Leonard V. Steven Blanca                                         1235         OM PI   / /

     MATCHED FIELD: MATTERS->MATTER           Record# 5
     MATCHED DATA : Stephan Blanca v. Jonathan Leonard
     Stephan Blanca v. Jonathan Leonard                                        1236         OM PI   / /
     01/01/10  1:35p DEFS      OM
       Potential Conflict of Interest
```


Exhibit 3.6 Blank matter window

Adding a new Matter

Save Cancel ?

1 Standard | 2 Notes | 3 Linked Names | 4 Linked Events | 5 Linked Docs | 6 Emails

Matter

File/case# 1237

Court

Attorney

Court Case #

Case Code

Opened / /

Closed / /

User-defined fields:

User1

User3

User2

User4 / /

Add Clone Delete Query Index MATTER

Exhibit 3.7 Personal injury matter form

Matter: LEONARD v BLANCA
LEONARD V BLANCA
1 Accident | 2 Notes | 3 Linked Names | 4 Linked Events | 5 Linked Docs | 6 Emails | 6 Insurance | 7 Damages | 8 Litigation | 9 Other Defs | 10 Witnesses
MATTER LEONARD v BLANCA CASE PHASE 0. PROSPECTIVE CLIENT OPENED 04/19/10 COURT
TYPE PI-VEH FILE NO. 1236 LEAD ATTORNEY OM OPERATOR TFG CLOSED / / COURT CASE NO.
CLIENT INFORMATION
CLIENT Not Linked CLIENT INSURED INS. CO. Not Linked
HEALTH INS Not Linked REP CONFIRMED MULTIPLE PLAINTIFFS
DEFENDANT INFORMATION
DEFENDANT Not Linked DEF INSURED INS. CO. Not Linked
NOTICE OF CLAIM MAILED DELIVERY CONFIRMED MULTIPLE DEFENDANTS
ACCIDENT INFORMATION
STREET INTERSTATE 540 AT DOLLARD RD DATE / / PASSENGERS WITNESSES CLEAR LIABILITY VEH LIC#
CITY MECHANICSBURG TIME GOVERNMENT ER AMBULANCE YEAR
STATE ARKANS ZIP VEH TOTALED DIAGRAM SIGNED STMNT MAKE
DESCRIPTION: LINK NOTE WITH DESCRIPTION OF ACCIDENT AND INJURIES. PHOTOS: SCENE INJURIES PROP DAMAGE MODEL
IMPACT TRIP PURPOSE POLICE REP NO. CITATION ISSUED COLOR
WEATHER # OF VEHICLES CLIENT FAULT % CODE VIOLATED REG OWNER
SETTLEMENT INFORMATION
P/D TOTAL $ 0.00 P/D SETTLED $ 0.00 DEMAND LETTER SENT / / DATE OF LOSS / / EST. SETTLEMENT $ 0.00
MED COSTS $ 0.00 MED SETTLED $ 0.00 DEMAND AMOUNT $ 0.00 STATUTE DATE / / ACTUAL SETTLEMENT $ 0.00
EST. INTANGIBLES $ 0.00 INTANGIBLES SETTLED $ 0.00 COUNTER OFFER REC'D / / ADD NON-PARTY / / CASE COSTS $ 0.00
WAGE LOSS $ 0.00 WAGE LOSS SETTLED $ 0.00 COUNTER OFFER AMOUNT $ 0.00 TRIAL DATE / /
Add Clone Delete Query Index MATTER

Source:

Exhibit 3.8 shows another method of entering basic information using an **intake form.** The intake form may be filled out with the information used to automatically fill in (populate) the appropriate spaces (fields) in the appropriate screens by the legal staff or prepared by the client using a word processor or in some cases an Internet browser.

intake form
A template used to enter information into a computer program such as a case management program.

OUTPUT–REPORTS

In programs that do not have preset or predesigned reports, a search or query screen may be used to identify the information or combinations of information desired in the report. A sample set of report formats for presenting information requested is shown in Exhibits 3.9 and 3.10. While most programs permit it, some programs do not allow the user to modify or customize reports and instead require the software vendor or other expert assistance to modify report formats. Among the specialty reports and documents in CaseMap are **trial notebook** information and privilege logs.

trial notebook
A summary of the case, usually contained in a tabbed, three-ring binder with sections such as pleadings, motions, law, pretrial memos, and witnesses.

CASE ANALYSIS SOFTWARE

LEARNING OBJECTIVE 2
Understand the functions and value to the law firm of case analysis software.

Unlike television court dramas, in real life, cases are rarely presented to litigation teams organized and in perfect time-order sequence. From the client's perspective, an injury or loss has been sustained, or a notice of a lawsuit has been served on him or her. Through a process of interviews and investigations, facts and timelines become clearer, and from the process of discovery, additional facts and potential evidence are found. To this mix are added legal theories or defenses based on current case and statutory law and regulation. Ideally, a small case is handled by one person who has only that one case to deal with to the exclusion of all else, thus allowing him or her to retain all the facts and law in his or her head. Fortunately or

Exhibit 3.8 Intake form for setting up a new matter

Intake Form: PI Case Intake Form

Please enter information about the case.

Plaintiff v. Defendant: Stein v Curtis [Check for duplicates]
Court:
Court Case Number:
Opened: 03/04/10
Attorney: AM
User1:
User2:
User3:
User4: / /

Please enter the client's contact information below

Last name: Stein [Check for duplicates]
First name: Elisabeth
Dear: Elisabeth
Addressee: Elisabeth Stein
Street Address 1: 1000 School Drive
Street Address 2:
Street Address 3:
Zip: 18940
City: George School State: PA
Email address:
Work Phone: ( ) -
Home Phone: ( ) -
Cell Phone: ( ) -
Fax Number: ( ) -

Select the WHO code for calendared Events.

Responsible Attorney: AM

Please enter the other driver's contact information below.

Last name: [Check for duplicates]
First name:
Dear:
Addressee:
Address 1:
Address 2:
Address 3:
Zip:
City: State:
Work Phone: ( ) -

unfortunately, this is rarely the situation. Even supposedly simple cases may require efforts by paralegals, investigators, experts, and legal researchers, all of whom are working on a number of other cases at the same time. In larger cases there may be a team of lawyers located in different cities, each with a support staff of other lawyers, paralegals, investigators, and information specialists.

Case information can generally be divided into categories—for example, parties, witnesses, documents, case law, statutory law, and reports—which in a paper-based system might be kept in a folder or set of folders. CaseMap™ from LexisNexis® is a case management and analysis software tool that acts as a central repository for critical case knowledge. As facts are gathered, parties identified, and documents and research assembled, they may be entered into the program, allowing for easy organization and exploration of the facts, the cast of characters, and the issues by any member of the legal team, as shown in the sample case in Exhibit 3.11.

Exhibit 3.12 shows the flow of information in a typical case using CaseMap as a case management tool.

Exhibit 3.9 AbacusLaw preset report list

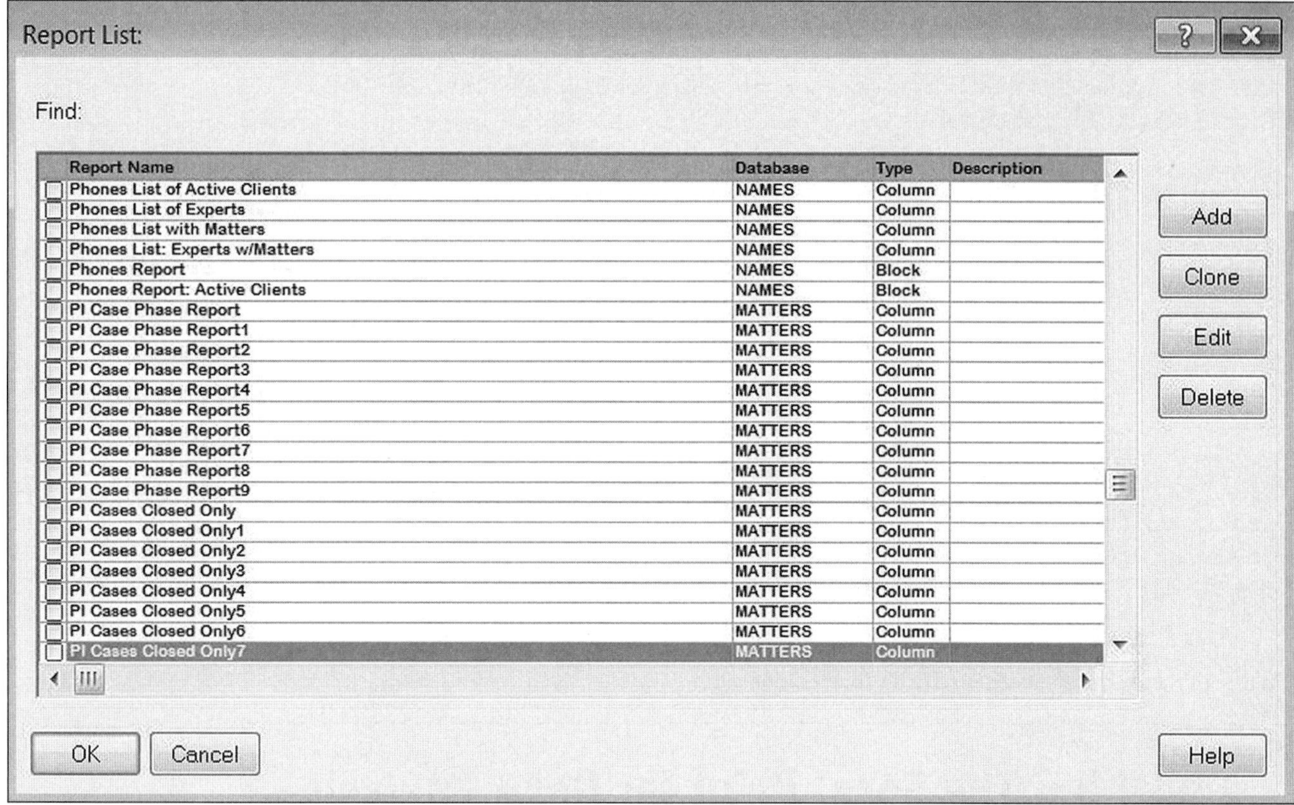

Source: © 2010 Abacus Data Systems, Inc. All rights reserved.

Exhibit 3.10 CaseMap reports–ReportBooks option

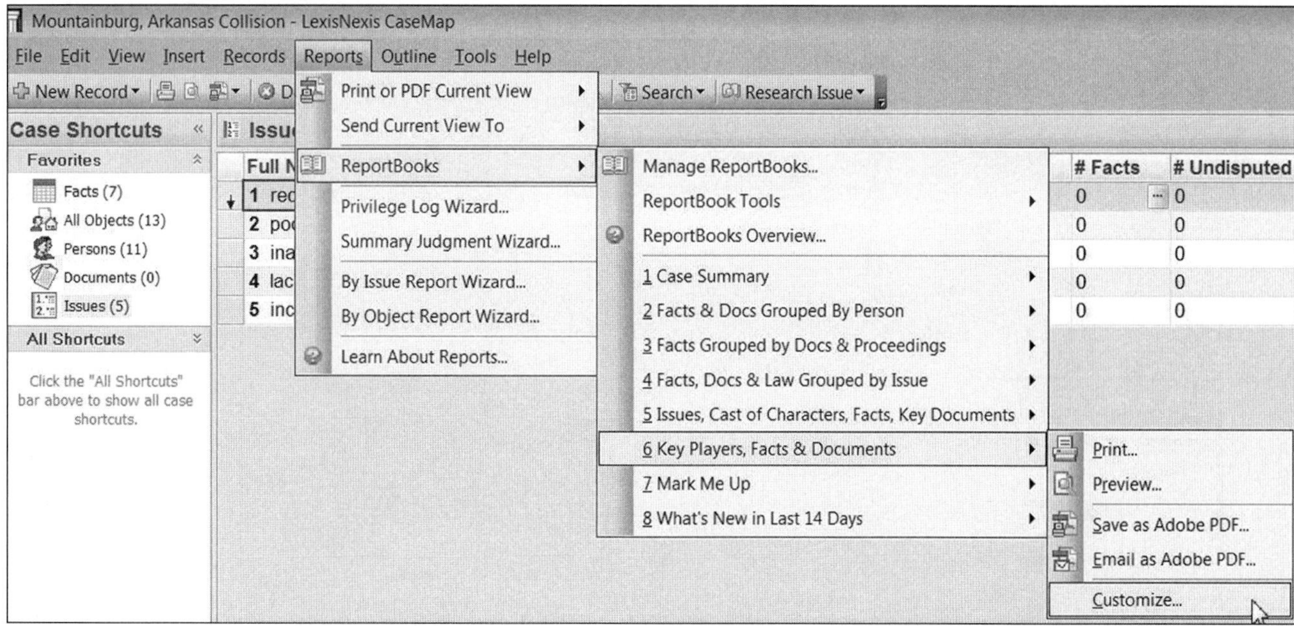

Source: Copyright 2010 LexisNexis, a division of Reed Elsevier Inc. All Rights Reserved. LexisNexis and the Knowledge Burst logo are registered trademarks of Reed Elsevier Properties Inc. TimeMap and CaseMap are registered trademarks of LexisNexis CourtLink, Inc. Used with the permission of LexisNexis.

Exhibit 3.11 CaseMap All Objects view

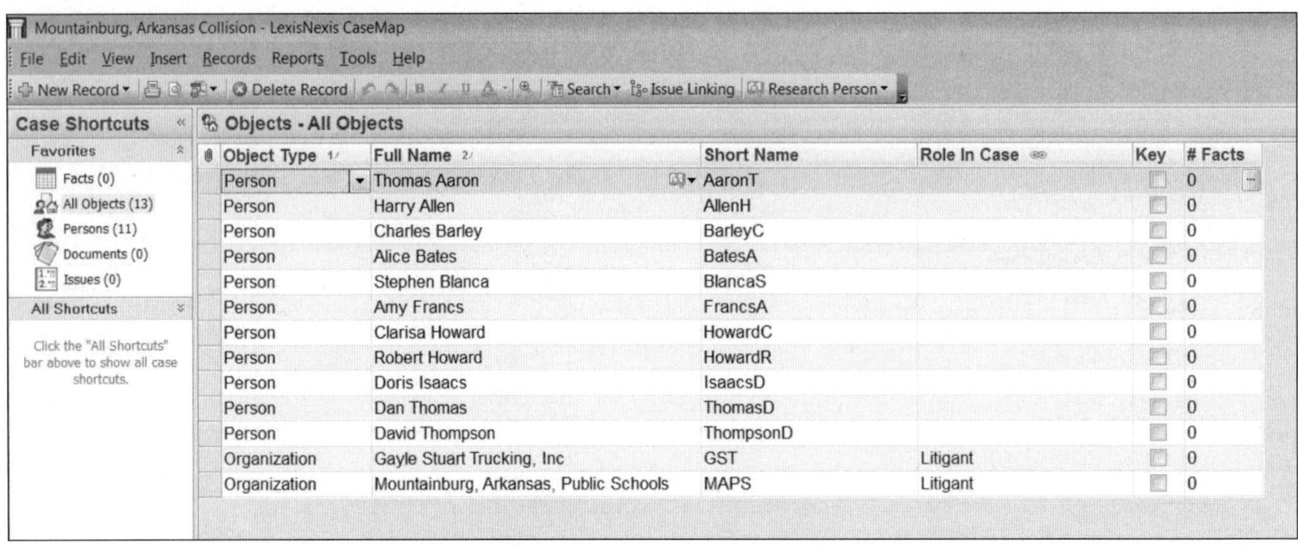

Exhibit 3.12 Case organization flowchart

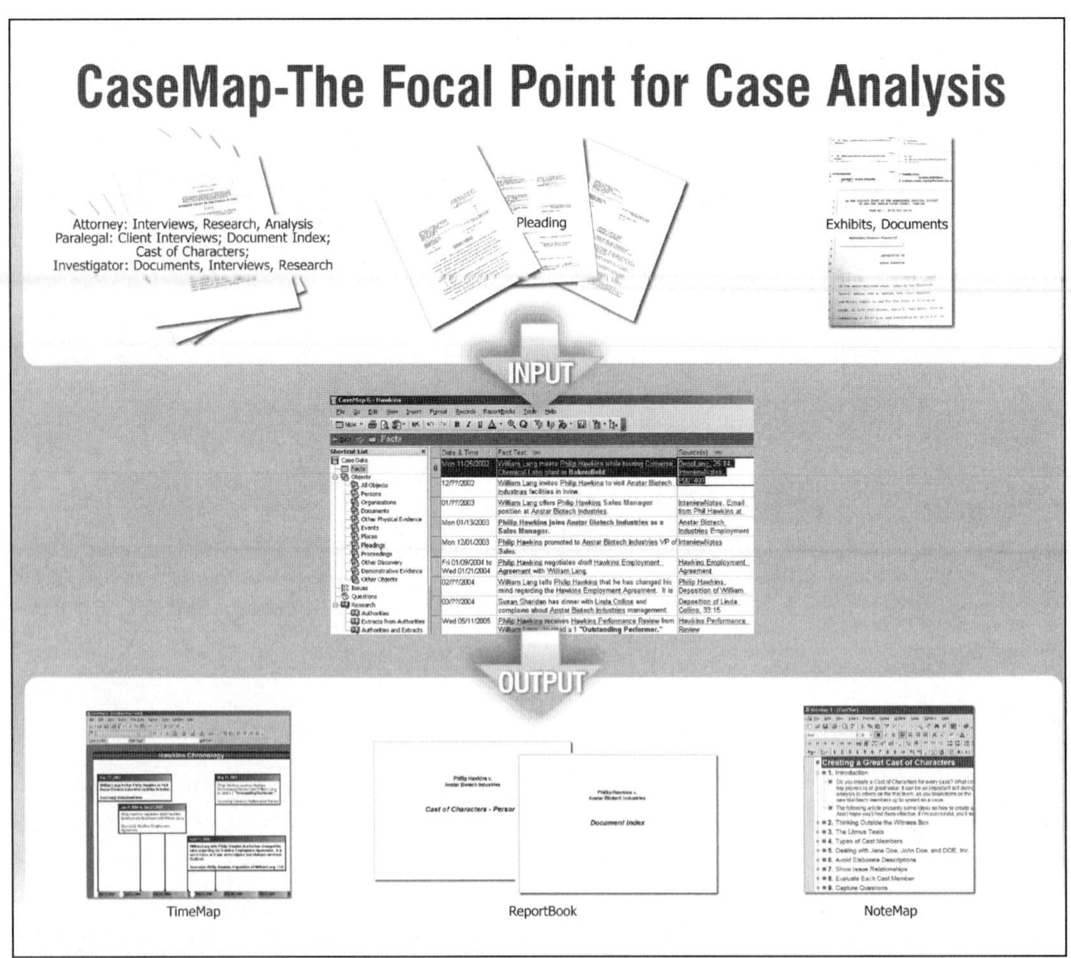

VIDEO ADVICE FROM THE FIELD

Don Swanson–President, Five Star Legal Services

A discussion of the electronic discovery process and the roles of the litigation team.

After watching the video in MyLegalStudiesKit, answer the following questions.

1. What are the skills necessary for the paralegal in the electronic discovery process?
2. What is the emerging role of the paralegal in the litigation process?

Setting Up a New Case in CaseMap

Exhibits 3.13 to 3.16 present an abbreviated sequence of screens showing the automated process for setting up a new case in CaseMap. For the purposes of these screens, the case study in Appendix II has been used.

Exhibit 3.13 Getting started with CaseMap–New case wizard

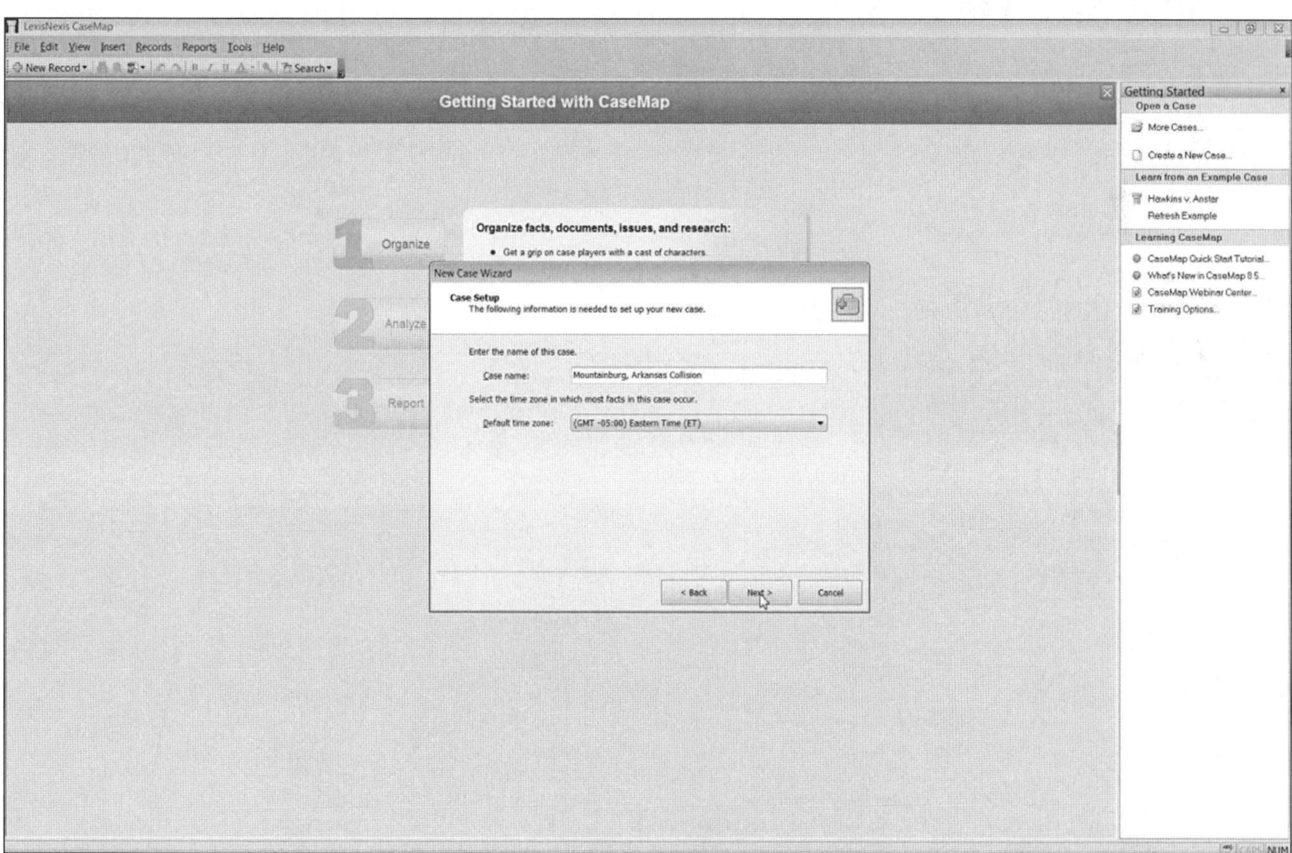

Source: Copyright 2010 LexisNexis, a division of Reed Elsevier Inc. All Rights Reserved. LexisNexis and the Knowledge Burst logo are registered trademarks of Reed Elsevier Properties Inc. TimeMap and CaseMap are registered trademarks of LexisNexis CourtLink, Inc. Used with the permission of LexisNexis.

Exhibit 3.14 Entering the parties

Mountainburg, Arkansas Collision - LexisNexis CaseMap

File Edit View Insert Records Reports Tools Help

New Record Delete Record Search Issue Linking Research Other Object

Objects - All Objects

Object Type	Full Name	Short Name	Role In Case	Key	# Facts
Other Object					0

Navigation Pane

Case Jumpstart Wizard

Overview
✔ Litigants
Judge
Opposing Counsel
Witnesses
Other People
Other Organizations
Finish

Who are the parties in this case?

Type:	Party:
Organization	Gayle Stuart Trucking, Inc
Organization	Mountainburg, Arkansas, Public Schools
Person	Robert Howard
Person	Stephen Blanca
Person	Alice Bates
Person	Amy Francs
Person	Clarisa Howard
Person	Doris Isaacs
Person	Harry Allen
Person	Charles Barley

Show when opening a new case   Back   Next   Finish   Cancel

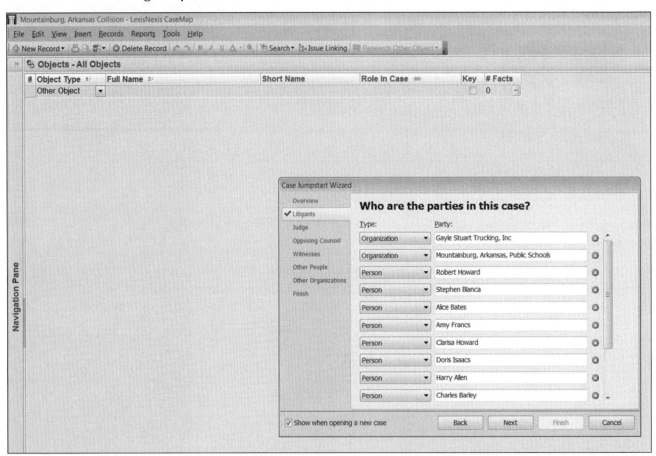

Exhibit 3.15 CaseMap object–All Objects view

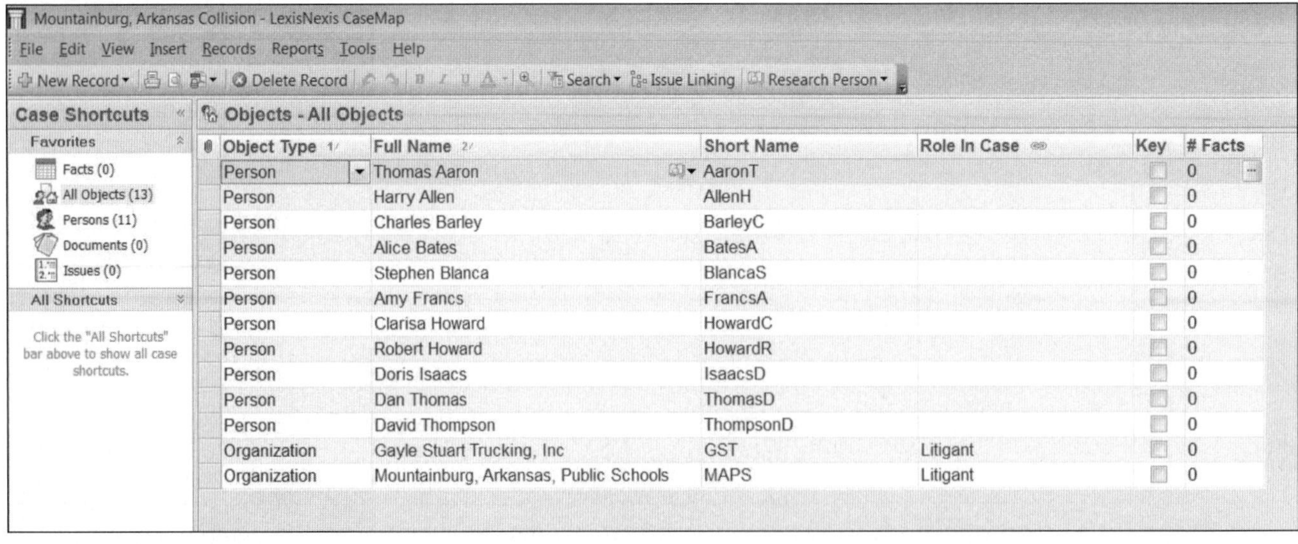

Object Type	Full Name	Short Name	Role In Case	Key	# Facts
Person	Thomas Aaron	AaronT			0
Person	Harry Allen	AllenH			0
Person	Charles Barley	BarleyC			0
Person	Alice Bates	BatesA			0
Person	Stephen Blanca	BlancaS			0
Person	Amy Francs	FrancsA			0
Person	Clarisa Howard	HowardC			0
Person	Robert Howard	HowardR			0
Person	Doris Isaacs	IsaacsD			0
Person	Dan Thomas	ThomasD			0
Person	David Thompson	ThompsonD			0
Organization	Gayle Stuart Trucking, Inc	GST	Litigant		0
Organization	Mountainburg, Arkansas, Public Schools	MAPS	Litigant		0

Exhibit 3.16 CaseMap Issues view

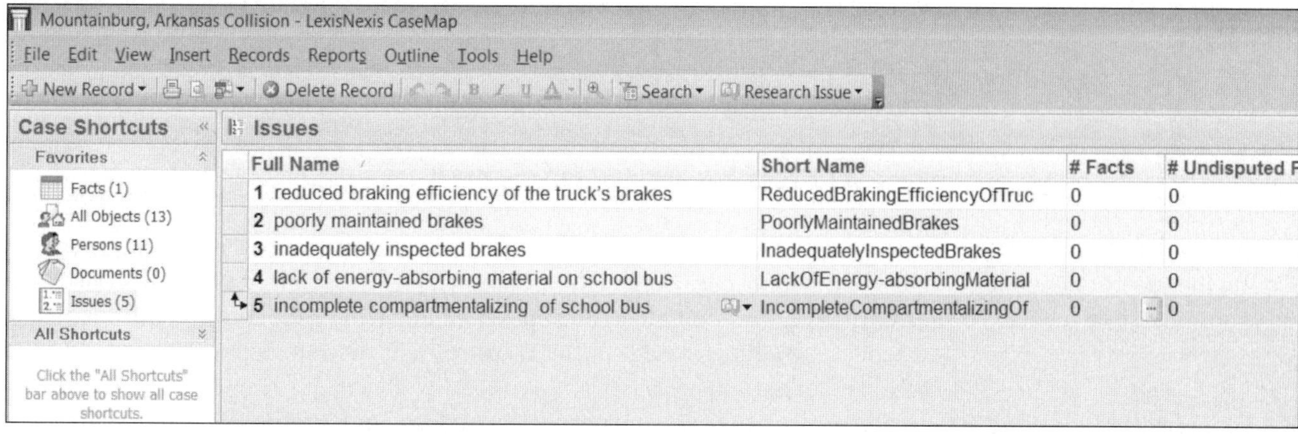

TIMELINES IN LITIGATION

LEARNING OBJECTIVE 3
Explain the use of timelines in civil litigation.

A **timeline** of the facts of a case and a procedural timeline are useful in analyzing the case and avoiding missing deadlines in the process. Factual analysis of most cases is time based, a sequence of events that happens over a period of time for which the trial team must obtain documentation to use at trial. The timeline may ultimately be a useful tool in showing the jury the sequence of events leading to the injury or damage. Exhibit 3.17 is a timeline created directly from the CaseMap file for the case study in Appendix II. Having a fact timeline during depositions helps ensure that questions will be asked about every significant time-based event.

timeline
A graphic representation of the facts or procedural steps in a case.

In cases with accelerated trial schedules, the times for completing discovery and pretrial activity may be short and every date an important factor to have in front of

Exhibit 3.17 TimeMap timeline of case

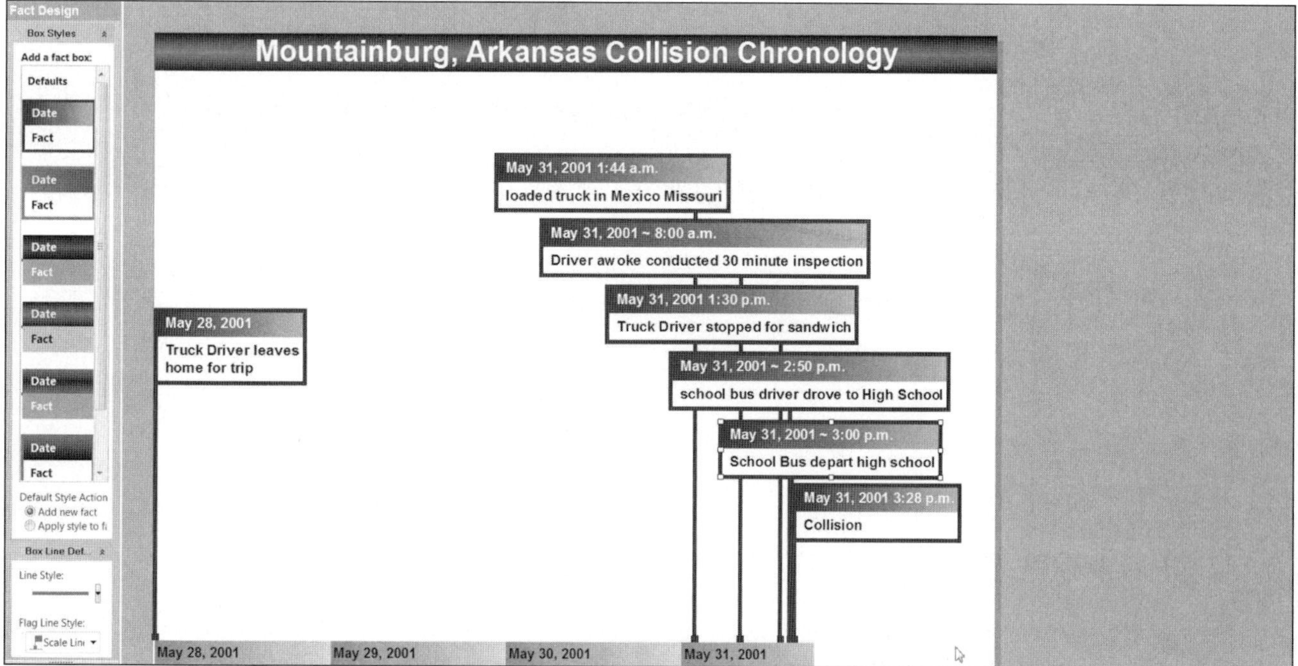

every member of the team as a reminder. With time-based statute of limitations and procedural time deadlines for filing pleading, motions, and appeals, it is important that an accurate timeline be constructed based on the individual type of case, such as automobile personal injury or death claim from an airplane crash, and the specific jurisdiction, such as the Federal District Court for the Western District of New York.

CALENDAR PROGRAM OVERVIEW

LEARNING OBJECTIVE 4
Explain the use of calendaring programs in civil litigation.

rules-based calendaring
A calendar or date calculator based on rules of court that set time limits and deadlines for cases and procedures in court.

As with all technology, calendar programs are constantly being improved. A calendar system may consist of a paper calendar, an electronic calendar (such as Outlook), or a complex **rules-based calendaring** program that automatically calculates deadlines based on the court rules of the selected jurisdiction, type of case, and event selected.

According to the American Bar Association's Profile of Legal Malpractice Claims 2004–2007, calendar-related errors are the leading cause of malpractice claims. Both CompuLaw and AbacusLaw provide rules-based calendaring software with built-in court rules databases. Exhibit 3.18 shows the AbacusLaw rules calculator. Calendaring software must have current information, with the rules updated with changes that take into account holidays for the particular jurisdiction. AbacusLaw is a standalone system that works on a local network or personal computer. CompuLaw offers a web-based, pay-per-use version of their software that is designed for small firms, Deadlines On Demand (www.deadlines.com). Exhibits 3.19 to 3.21 are screen shots from Deadlines On Demand showing how to use such a system.

Most calendaring programs will automatically sync the deadlines in the calendar in Outlook with built-in reminders, which provide a copy of your calendar without duplicate entries. This is highly recommended because it gets the calendar in as many places as possible without the error-prone task of re-entering the information. It is also recommended to have a firm-wide, centralized system and advance notification of upcoming deadlines. Informing the office staff of the importance of accurate entry of deadline dates is also a key factor, as a calendaring program is only as good as the information entered. Malpractice insurance carriers

Exhibit 3.18 AbacusLaw statute of limitations rules calculator

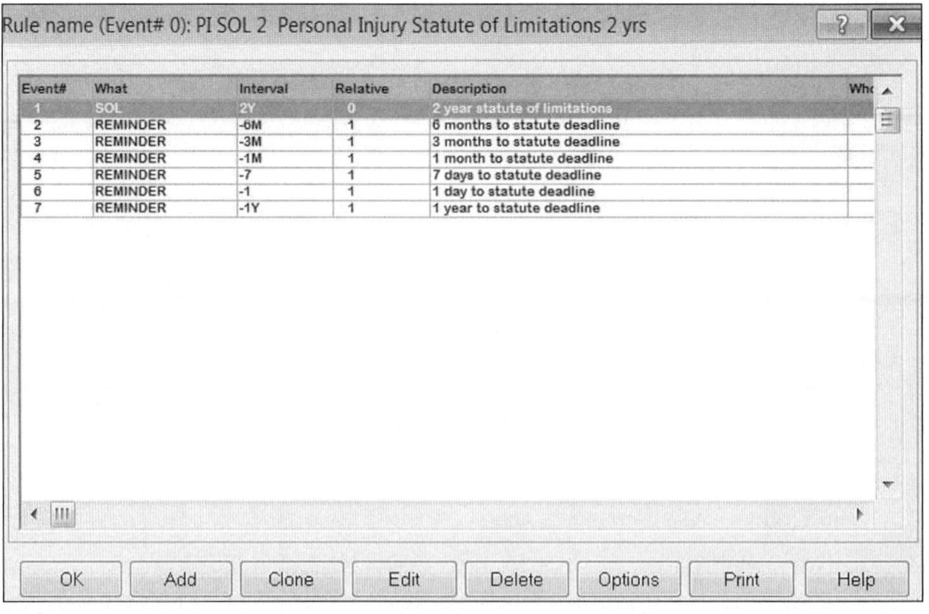

Rule name (Event# 0): PI SOL 2 Personal Injury Statute of Limitations 2 yrs
Event# | What | Interval | Relative | Description | Whe
1 | SOL | 2Y | 0 | 2 year statute of limitations
2 | REMINDER | -6M | 1 | 6 months to statute deadline
3 | REMINDER | -3M | 1 | 3 months to statute deadline
4 | REMINDER | -1M | 1 | 1 month to statute deadline
5 | REMINDER | -7 | 1 | 7 days to statute deadline
6 | REMINDER | -1 | 1 | 1 day to statute deadline
7 | REMINDER | -1Y | 1 | 1 year to statute deadline
OK
Add
Clone
Edit
Delete
Options
Print
Help

Source: © 2010 Abacus Data Systems, Inc. All rights reserved.

Exhibit 3.19 CompuLaw **Step 1: Select jurisdiction**

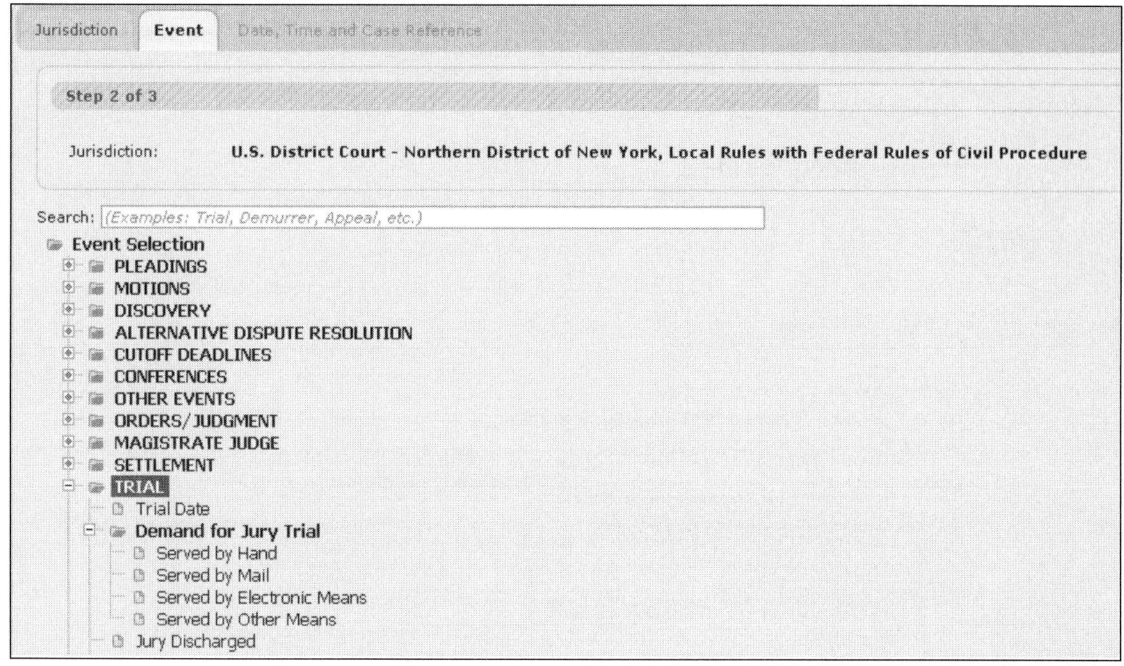

Source: Copyright 2010 CompuLaw LLC. All Rights Reserved.

recognize the risk, and many offer discounts on insurance premiums for those who use an automated, rules-based system.

THE INTERNET IN LITIGATION

LEARNING OBJECTIVE 5
Use the Internet as part of the investigation of a case.

The Internet has become an important tool in the litigation process. Many clients first learn of a firm's litigation capabilities by searching the Internet for an attorney to handle a specific type of case. In some firms, the initial information about

Exhibit 3.20 CompuLaw **Step 2: Select event**

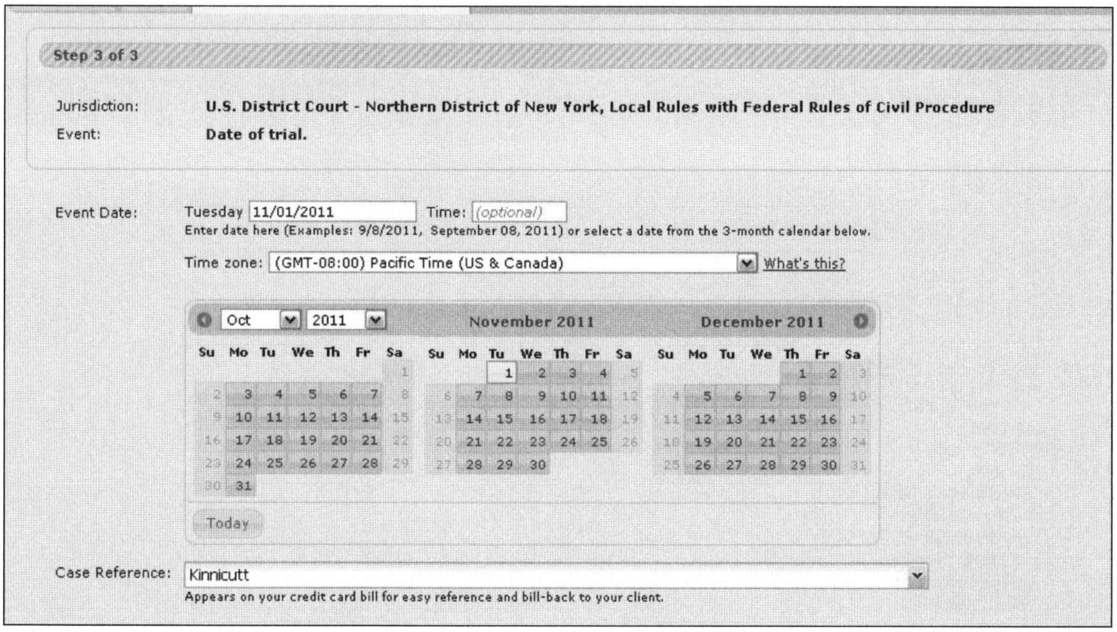

Source: Copyright 2010 CompuLaw LLC. All Rights Reserved.

Exhibit 3.21 CompuLaw Step 3: Enter event date and case reference

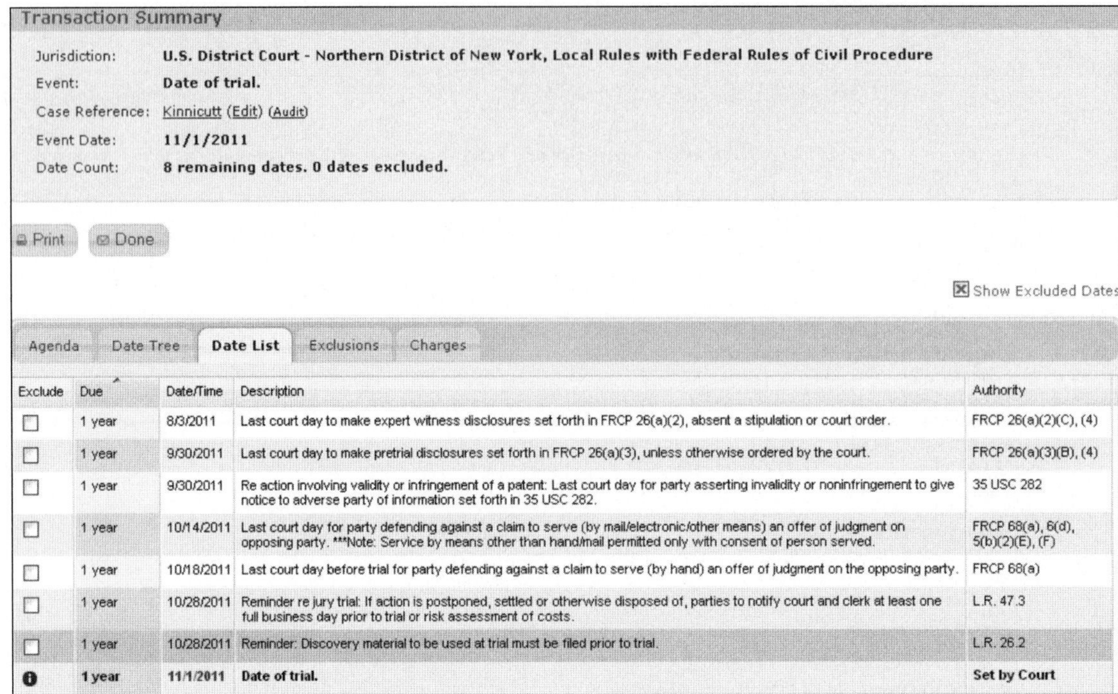

Transaction Summary
Jurisdiction: U.S. District Court - Northern District of New York, Local Rules with Federal Rules of Civil Procedure
Event: Date of trial.
Case Reference: Kinnicutt (Edit) (Audit)
Event Date: 11/1/2011
Date Count: 8 remaining dates. 0 dates excluded.
Print
Done
Show Excluded Dates
Agenda
Date Tree
Date List
Exclusions
Charges
Exclude | Due | Date/Time | Description | Authority
1 year | 8/3/2011 | Last court day to make expert witness disclosures set forth in FRCP 26(a)(2), absent a stipulation or court order. | FRCP 26(a)(2)(C), (4)
1 year | 9/30/2011 | Last court day to make pretrial disclosures set forth in FRCP 26(a)(3), unless otherwise ordered by the court. | FRCP 26(a)(3)(B), (4)
1 year | 9/30/2011 | Re action involving validity or infringement of a patent: Last court day for party asserting invalidity or noninfringement to give notice to adverse party of information set forth in 35 USC 282. | 35 USC 282
1 year | 10/14/2011 | Last court day for party defending against a claim to serve (by mail/electronic/other means) an offer of judgment on opposing party. ***Note: Service by means other than hand/mail permitted only with consent of person served. | FRCP 68(a), 6(d), 5(b)(2)(E), (F)
1 year | 10/18/2011 | Last court day before trial for party defending against a claim to serve (by hand) an offer of judgment on the opposing party. | FRCP 68(a)
1 year | 10/28/2011 | Reminder re jury trial: If action is postponed, settled or otherwise disposed of, parties to notify court and clerk at least one full business day prior to trial or risk assessment of costs. | L.R. 47.3
1 year | 10/28/2011 | Reminder: Discovery material to be used at trial must be filed prior to trial. | L.R. 26.2
1 year | 11/1/2011 | Date of trial. | Set by Court

Source: Copyright 2010 CompuLaw LLC. All Rights Reserved.

a client and the case is obtained over the Internet before the decision is made to accept or reject the client and the matter. Some legal-specific software applications like AbacusLaw and CaseMap have provisions that allow the client to complete client and case information input forms and submit them using the Internet, with the information automatically entered into the case or office management program. Exhibit 3.22 shows an example of jurisdiction-specific forms in AbacusLaw.

Exhibit 3.22 Sample jurisdiction-specific forms in AbacusLaw

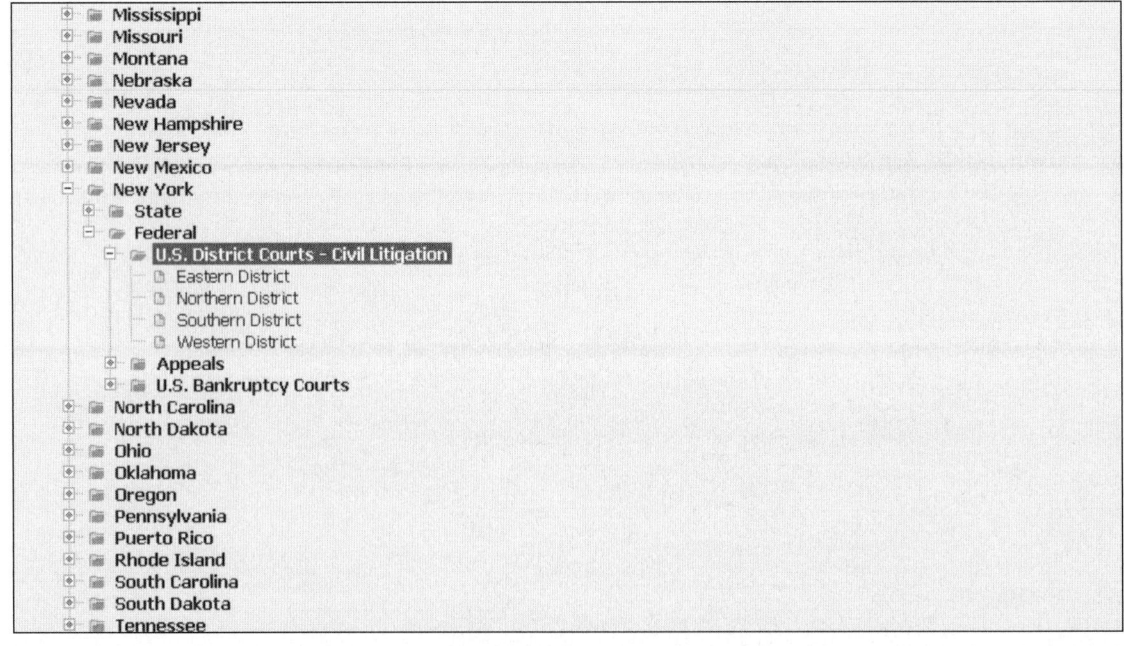

Source: © 2010 Abacus Data Systems, Inc. All rights reserved.

Exhibit 3.23 Aerial view of accident scene

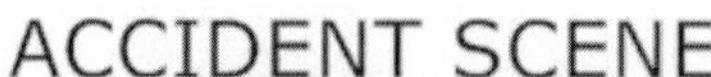

The initial investigation of a case frequently involves having an investigator or other member of the litigation team physically visit a location, such as an accident scene, to obtain photographs or to create diagrams of the location. Internet tools like Google Earth facilitate the retrieval of aerial images of locations and in many cases street-level views of buildings and surrounding views. Exhibit 3.23 is an aerial view of the overall view of the scene of the accident in the case study from Appendix II. Exhibit 3.24 is a street-level view of the ramp used by the truck to exit the highway. Exhibit 3.25 is the bus driver's view of the accident scene approaching the scene.

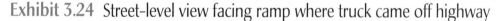

Exhibit 3.24 Street-level view facing ramp where truck came off highway

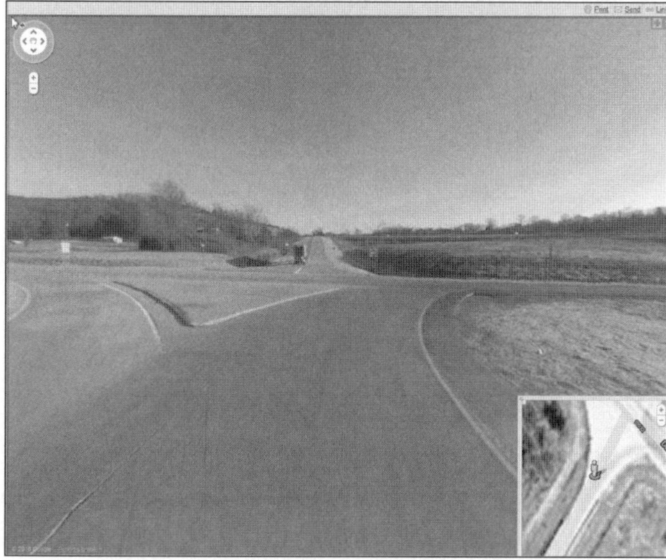

Exhibit 3.25 Bus driver's view of accident scene approaching the scene

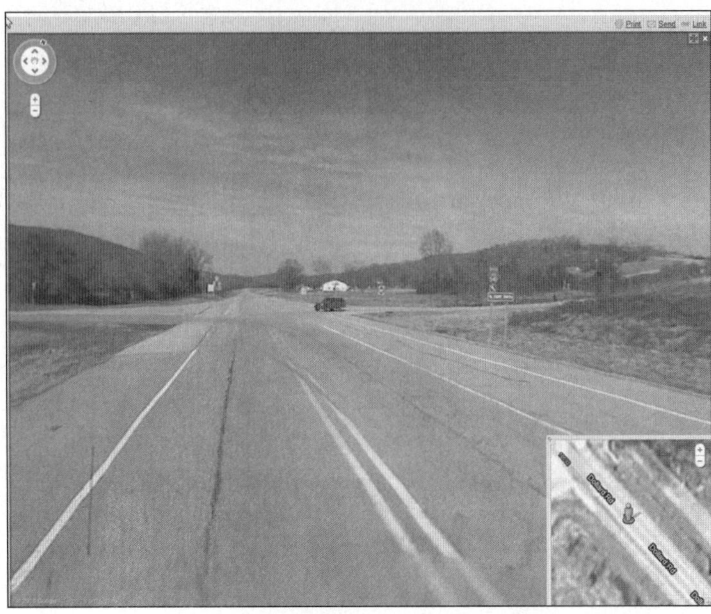

Additional information about cases may frequently be obtained from news accounts, particularly in cases of accidents, fires, or issues in complex litigation such as claims against pharmaceutical companies. Exhibit 3.26 is an example of a news program providing additional information about one of the case studies from Appendix III.

Exhibit 3.26 News report on web

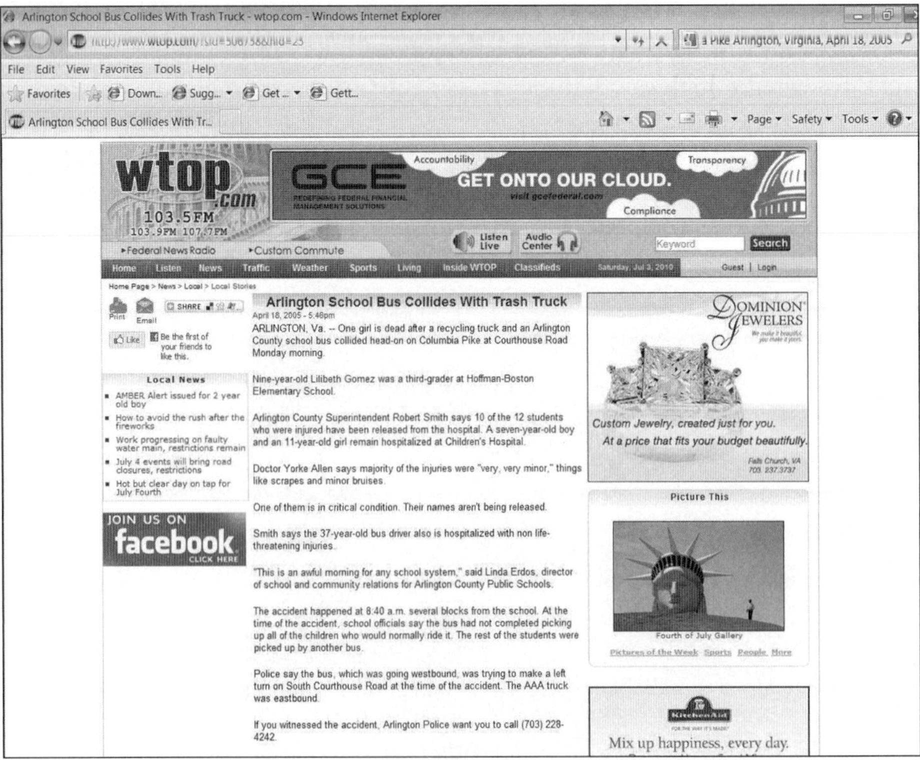

Home Page > News > Local > Local Stories

Arlington School Bus Collides With Trash Truck

April 18, 2005 - 5:46pm

ARLINGTON, Va. -- One girl is dead after a recycling truck and an Arlington County school bus collided head-on on Columbia Pike at Courthouse Road Monday morning.

Nine-year-old Lilibeth Gomez was a third-grader at Hoffman-Boston Elementary School.

Arlington County Superintendent Robert Smith says 10 of the 12 students who were injured have been released from the hospital. A seven-year-old boy and an 11-year-old girl remain hospitalized at Children's Hospital.

Doctor Yorke Allen says majority of the injuries were "very, very minor," things like scrapes and minor bruises.

One of them is in critical condition. Their names aren't being released.

Smith says the 37-year-old bus driver also is hospitalized with non life-threatening injuries.

"This is an awful morning for any school system," said Linda Erdos, director of school and community relations for Arlington County Public Schools.

The accident happened at 8:40 a.m. several blocks from the school. At the time of the accident, school officials say the bus had not completed picking up all of the children who would normally ride it. The rest of the students were picked up by another bus.

Police say the bus, which was going westbound, was trying to make a left turn on South Courthouse Road at the time of the accident. The AAA truck was eastbound.

If you witnessed the accident, Arlington Police want you to call (703) 228-4242.

Source: Courtesy of wtop.com.

Exhibit 3.27 Web search results

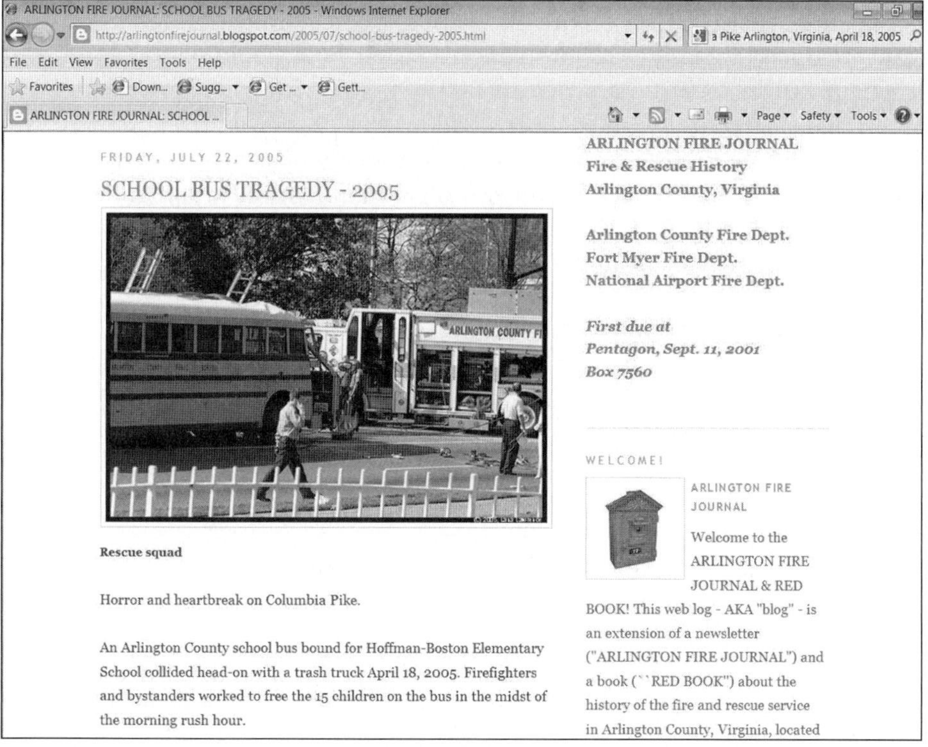

Source: Photo: Copyright © Lana Lawrence. Used with permission.

Information about individuals, including clients, fact witnesses, or expert witnesses, is also frequently available through the use of Internet search engines such as Google.com, Yahoo.com, Ask.com, or Bing.com. While a search using one of the search engines may not produce results directly, secondary sources that perform searches for free, such as the Arlington Fire Journal website shown in Exhibit 3.27, are usually shown on the search results page, and they may provide the needed information.

ENCRYPTION TECHNOLOGY

Encryption technology permits a computer user to basically put a lock around his or her computer information in order to protect that information from being read by others. Encryption technology is like a lock on a house. Without the lock in place, unwanted persons can easily enter the house and steal its contents; with the lock in place, it is more difficult for unwanted persons to enter and take the house's contents. Encryption software serves a similar function in that it lets computer users scramble information so that only those who have the encryption code can enter the database and find the information.

LEARNING OBJECTIVE 6
Explain the reason for using encryption in litigation.

encryption
Technology that allows computer users to put a "lock" around information to prevent discovery by others.

Encryption

Confidential or privileged information sent over the Internet is frequently encrypted by the sender and unencrypted by the receiver because of the concerns that the information will be intercepted while it is being transmitted over the Internet. Encryption programs use algorithms (mathematical formulas) to scramble documents. Without the proper password or encryption key, unauthorized persons are not able to read the files and determine their content.

To understand the levels of protection offered by the different encryption programs, think of the protection offered by a combination lock. The least amount of security is provided by the type of two-number combination lock frequently found with inexpensive luggage. As the numbers required for opening the lock increase to three, four, or more numbers, the security also increases. It is not hard to see how a two-digit combination lock can be quickly opened while a four-digit lock requires much time and effort. For an amateur computer hacker with a simple encryption-breaking program, a basic encryption program might be thought of as equivalent to a two- or three-number combination lock. A higher-level program, with tougher algorithms designed to thwart a professional code-breaker, would require combinations of four or more numbers. As computers become faster, more sophisticated methods will be required.

Email Encryption

The use of email for communication in the legal environment presents one of the biggest potentials for breach of confidentiality. Emails between attorney and client frequently contain confidential information. Clients provide the details necessary for the attorney to give legal advice and answer legal questions; attorneys reply with legal advice intended solely for the client. A misdirected or intercepted email with confidential content may be a breach of attorney–client confidentiality and be a waiver of the attorney–client privilege.

WinZip Courier is a program that both compresses, or zips a file, and encrypts documents that are attached to emails. While this does not eliminate all risks, it does offer a level of protection for an attachment that contains confidential or privileged information. The email itself is still readable and potentially open to others having access without the password. The recipient, who is provided with the agreed-on password in another communication (either in person, by telephone, or by another method), can open the attachment.

Password security as part of the encryption process depends on the quality or strength of the password. As stated in the WinZip manual:

> You should keep the following considerations in mind when choosing passwords for your files:
>
> In general, longer passwords are more secure than shorter passwords. In fact, taking maximum advantage of the full strength of AES encryption requires a password of approximately 32 characters for 128-bit encryption and 64 characters for 256-bit encryption.
>
> Passwords that contain a mixture of letters (upper and lower case), digits, and punctuation are more secure than passwords containing only letters.
>
> Because you can use spaces and punctuation, you can create "pass phrases" that are long enough but still easy to remember and type.
>
> Avoid using easily guessed passwords such as names, birthdays, Social Security numbers, addresses, telephone numbers, etc.
>
> Be sure to keep a record of the passwords you use and to keep this record in a secure place. WinZip has no way to access the contents of an encrypted file unless you supply the correct password. Before storing your only copies of critical information in encrypted form, you should carefully consider the risks associated with losing or forgetting the passwords involved.
>
> *Source:* Copyright © 2011 WinZip Computing, S.L., A Corel Company. WinZip is a registered trademark of WinZip International LLC.

CONCEPT REVIEW AND REINFORCEMENT

KEY TERMS

e-repository 59
case management system 60
conflict report generator 63
intake form 65
trial notebook 65
timeline 71
rules-based calendaring 72
encryption 77

CHAPTER SUMMARY

TECHNOLOGY IN CIVIL LITIGATION

Introduction to Technology in Civil Litigation	Law firms are under pressure to reduce costs. Computers and appropriate software are being adopted and used to reduce errors and improve productivity with fewer personnel. Office and case matter software is increasingly being used to manage all aspects of client and case file information.
Case and Practice Management Software	Efficient use of a case management system provides all authorized members of the legal team with access to all the case information day or night. Computer systems today even permit members of the legal team to access the same information from remote locations. One of the tools in collaborative situations is the individual assessment of the importance of items in the case. All members of the team must have the ability to input and use information for the tasks assigned to them.
Using Case Management Systems	Complex litigation may involve millions of documents and hundreds of witnesses. The use of computers for email and document storage by businesses and government has caused a massive increase in the number of potential documents that may have to be reviewed, tracked, and made available. Case management systems permit collaboration among the members of the legal team.
Case Analysis Software	Case information can generally be divided into the categories of parties, witnesses, documents, case law, statutory law, reports, and issues. A case management and analysis software program acts as a central repository for this critical case information. As facts are gathered, parties identified, and documents and research assembled. They may be entered into the program for easy organization. The program also allows for creating specialty reports including trial notebook information and privilege logs.
Timelines in Litigation	Timelines, chronological listings of the facts of a case, are frequently presented graphically.
The Internet in Litigation	The Internet has become an important tool in the litigation process. Many clients first learn of firms through the Internet. Some legal-specific software applications allow clients to complete client and case information using the Internet and input forms. The Internet also provides investigative tools such as photographs of accident scenes through programs like Google Earth.

Encryption Technology	With the increased use of the Internet and online document repositories, it is necessary to protect the information and preserve client confidences and attorney–client privileged items. Encryption allows computer users to put "locks" around computer information and protect it from those who are not authorized to access the information.

REVIEW QUESTIONS AND EXERCISES

1. What are the tasks involved in managing a litigation case?
2. How is the trial notebook used in managing a case?
3. What are some of the issues in using a trial notebook for the litigation team?
4. How does the paperless office make it easier for members of the legal team to handle litigation?
5. What is the relationship between office management and case management software?
6. How were documents in complex litigation processed before the use of computers in litigation?
7. What are some of the parts of a case file?
8. Why is the maintenance of calendaring dates critical to the litigation function?
9. What are the organizational functions of a good case management program?
10. How does any case management system aid in the collaboration among the members of the legal team?
11. What are timelines?
12. How can timelines be used to assist the litigation team?
13. Explain the use of software for managing cases.
14. What are the steps that may be taken in organizing a new case file?
15. What are some of the advantages in using a case management software program?
16. What are the advantages of timelines in litigation? Give examples of how they can be used by the legal team and in the law office.

BUILDING YOUR PARALEGAL SKILLS

INTERNET AND TECHNOLOGY EXERCISES

1. Use a search engine to locate information on "case management software."
2. Prepare a list of the case management software programs that provide online tutorials for learning how to use the programs.
3. Visit the websites for the case management programs listed in this chapter. Determine the minimum operating requirements for a computer to run the software properly.
4. Locate information on companies that provide online document repository services.

CIVIL LITIGATION VIDEO CASE STUDIES

Need to Know Circle

Two paralegals from the same firm meet in the coffee room and discuss a case that only one of them is working on.

After viewing the video at MyLegalStudiesKit, answer the following questions.

1. Can a member of the legal team discuss any of the information about a client or a case with anyone who works in the same law office?

2. Do conversations between members of the same firm breach the ethical obligation of confidentiality or attorney–client privilege?
3. Do the rules of confidentiality and privilege apply to anyone other than the attorneys working on a case?

CHAPTER OPENING SCENARIO CASE STUDY

Use the Opening Scenario for this chapter to answer the following questions.

1. Prepare an outline of the issues in handling a case with so many plaintiffs and potential witnesses.
2. Prepare a memo explaining how a case management program might be used to organize the case.
3. What are the items that will need to be tracked using the case management program?
4. Answer the following question raised by one of the attorneys: "Can't we make our own database or spreadsheet to track the information and save money?"
5. How can using a program like CaseMap help in preparing for trial and during trial? Explain in a memo for the above attorney's review.

COMPREHENSIVE CASE STUDY

For the assigned case study from Appendix III:

1. From the Technology Resources Website, www.pearsonhighered.com/goldman, download and install on your computer the demo versions of AbacusLaw, CaseMap, and TimeMap.
2. Use AbacusLaw to enter all the information for the case.
3. Use LexisNexis CaseMap to set up a new file for the case.
4. Create a timeline using LexisNexis TimeMap from the facts in the case study in Appendix III.

BUILDING YOUR PROFESSIONAL PORTFOLIO

CIVIL LITIGATION TEAM AT WORK

Policy

1. Prepare a written policy on the creation and use of passwords.
2. Prepare a policy on who should be allowed access to the information in case management and office management programs.

Forms

1. Prepare a new case client interview form for capturing contact information and details of the new case that will be needed to set up a new file in a case management system and office management system.
2. Prepare a case interview form for capturing required information from fact witnesses for entry into a case management system and office management system.
3. Prepare a case interview form for capturing required information from expert witnesses for entry into a case management system and office management system.

Contact and Resources

Prepare a list of case management and office management software programs with website addresses and local contact information for companies or people who are certified to install the program or who offer training in the use of the software.

"It's called fishing, man, not catching!"

—Denny Crane,
Boston Legal

The Changing Face of Discovery—Basics of E-Discovery

CHAPTER 4

OPENING SCENARIO

The partners and support staff of Mason, Marshall and Benjamin were having their weekly meeting. As was the customary agenda, new cases were discussed, and follow-up assignments made. Most of the work to date had concentrated on a few large federal court cases. After a discussion of the facts of a new case, it appeared that jurisdiction existed in their state, in the adjacent state, as well as in federal court under diversity jurisdiction. It was suggested that the adjacent state court might be a better place to try the case. Each of the partners, in addition to being admitted to the local and federal courts, had been admitted to the other state court. Caitlin, the paralegal who was assigned to work on the case, indicated that she had never done any cases in either state court and asked if the rules were the same as what she was used to in the federal court.

Owen Mason questioned aloud whether Caitlin should work on a case in a jurisdiction in which she had never handled a case. After a discussion, it was clear that everyone in the firm needed to understand the similarities and the differences in the state courts in which they practiced as well as in the federal court. Emily, the paralegal in the other office, suggested that it might be a good idea to put together a comparison of the differences in the rules and the court opinions to be sure the legal firm was making the correct decision in starting suit in the other jurisdiction. It seemed like a good solution, but the partners wondered whether that was truly the correct decision and agreed it was something they needed to discuss at the partners' meeting.

LEARNING OBJECTIVES

After studying this chapter, you should be able to:

1. Describe the changes to the federal rules to meet the needs of discovery of electronically stored information.
2. Describe the procedures and times for discovery under the federal rules.
3. Explain the purpose and the expected outcomes of the attorney meet and confer.
4. Explain what is discoverable.
5. Describe the function and use of depositions.
6. Explain how the litigation team can protect privileged or confidential information under the federal rules.
7. Describe the scope of the potential solutions for inadvertent disclosure of confidential or privileged material or work product under the federal rules.

VIDEO INTRODUCTION

A. An introduction to electronic discovery-the fundamentals in the law office.

After watching the video in MyLegalStudiesKit, answer the following questions.

1. What is discovery?
2. What does successful discovery require?

B. An introduction to e-discovery rules and procedures in the law office.

After watching the video in MyLegalStudiesKit, answer the following question.

- What is the difference between the discovery of paper and electronic document?

INTRODUCTION TO THE LAW OF E-DISCOVERY

The fundamental purpose of discovery remains the same whether the legal team is dealing with paper or electronic documentation: to obtain any evidence that may be used in trial or may lead to any evidence that may be used in trial. Excluding demonstrative or physical evidence, documentary evidence in the past was in the form of paper documents, while today it is increasingly in electronic format. Initial changes in discovery practice were the result of the switch from paper to electronically stored information. As government, businesses, and individuals started to save records in electronic form, the litigation discovery procedures had to be updated.

As with most new technologies, initially there were no standards for how electronic information should be created or stored. For example, some offices used WordPerfect and others Microsoft Word for creating and storing word documents, and each program has its own electronic file format. In addition to these word processing programs are many lesser-known programs used in many major corporations. Added to these word processor–format variations are the many specialized formats used for financial and other data creation and storage. Even after the passage of many years since the introduction of operating systems and programs, there is still no universally accepted standard or common set of programs. Among the issues this creates is that some programs cannot read other programs' formats or even different versions of the same program. In the area of operating systems, there is no standard among Apple, Microsoft, and Linux, three of the mostly widely used systems competing for the office and personal computer market.

With the advances in technology have come new sources of potential trial evidence in the forms of video and sound recordings, emails, text messages, and social network Internet site data, each presenting its own technical issues in locating, retrieving, and reviewing sources for their potential use in trial. As technology's playing field changes, the courts are faced with enabling, through court rules, the discovery of electronically stored information in known and currently unknown sources in a manner that preserves affordable justice for all.

PRACTICE TIP

Corel WordPerfect, unlike most of the other popular word processors, will open and save documents in virtually all formats, as shown in the following list from WordPerfect 4X. In addition, documents may be opened in one format and saved in another.

Ami Pro 1.2
Ami Pro 1.2a
Ami Pro 1.2b
Ami Pro 2.0
Ami Pro 3.0
ANSI (Windows) Delimited Text
ANSI (Windows) Generic Word Processor
ANSI Windows Text
ASCII (DOS) Delimited Text
ASCII (DOS) Generic Word Processor
ASCII DOS Text
DisplayWrite 4.0
DisplayWrite 4.2
DisplayWrite 5.0
EDGAR
IBM DCA FFT
IBM DCA RFT
Lotus 123 1.0 for Windows
Lotus 123 3.0
Lotus 123 3.1
Lotus 123 4.0 for Windows
MS Excel 3.0
MS Excel 4.0
MS Word 4.0
MS Word 5.5
MS Word 5.0
MS Word 6.0/7.0 for Windows
MS Word 97/2000/2002/2003
MS Word for Windows 1.0
MS Word for Windows 1.1
MS Word for Windows 1.1a
MS Word for Windows 1.2/1.2a
MS Word for Windows 2.0
MS Word for Windows 2.0a
MS Word for Windows 2.0b
MS Word for Windows 2.0c
MultiMate 3.3
MultiMate 3.6
MultiMate 4.0
MultiMate Advantage II 1.0
Navy DIF Standard
OfficeWriter 6.0
OfficeWriter 6.1
OfficeWriter 6.11
OfficeWriter 6.2
Professional Write 1.0
Professional Write 2.2
Quattro Pro 1.0 for Windows
Quattro Pro 5.0 for Windows
Quattro Pro 6.0 for Windows
Rich Text Format (RTF)
RTF Help File
RTF Japanese
Spreadsheet DIF
UNICODE Text
Wolkswriter 4
Windows Write
WordPerfect 4.2
WordPerfect 5.0
WordPerfect 5.1/5.2
WordPerfect 6-X4
WordPerfect Compound File
WordStar 2000 1.0
WordStar 2000 2.0
WordStar 2000 3.0
WordStar 3.3
WordStar 3.31
WordStar 3.4
WordStar 4.0
WordStar 5.0
WordStar 5.5
WordStar 6.0
WordStar 7.0
XyWrite III Plus 3.55
XyWrite III Plus 3.56
XyWrite III Plus 4.0

AMENDMENTS TO THE FEDERAL RULES OF CIVIL PROCEDURE

The adoption of the electronic discovery rules to the Federal Rules of Civil Procedure in 2006 offered guidance on the issues surrounding discovery of **electronically stored information (ESI)** and a framework for requesting and satisfying requests for documents in electronic format, like emails, electronically stored word processor documents, and information in electronic databases. Initially, it seemed to some in the legal community that the electronic storage of documents had suddenly burst onto the scene. The reality was that it had been coming for some time before the issuance of the new rules. A few well-reasoned opinions written before the rules were adopted, including those in the *Zubulake* case, addressed the issues of ESI and the problems with its discovery (and proposed solutions that the rules encompassed), offering a broad-based set of national standards.

LEARNING OBJECTIVE 1
Describe the changes to the federal rules to meet the needs of discovery of electronically stored information.

electronically stored information (ESI)
Data or information saved in a computerized (electronic) format.

The initial rules change, effective December 2006 and restated a year later (Exhibit 4.1), amended six rules and provided one new form:

Rule 16 Pretrial Conferences; Scheduling; Management

... amendment to Rule 16(b) is designed to alert the court to the possible need to address the handling of discovery of electronically stored information early in the litigation if such discovery is expected to occur...

Rule 26 General Provisions Governing Discovery; Duty of Disclosure

...amended to direct the parties to discuss discovery of electronically stored information if such discovery is contemplated in the action....a party must disclose electronically stored information as well as documents that it may use to support its claims or defenses...

Exhibit 4.1 Federal Rules of Civil Procedure numbering scheme reference guide

Federal Rules of Civil Procedure – Numbering Scheme Reference Guide

On December 1, 2007, the amendments to the numbering scheme of the Federal Rules of Civil Procedure (FRCP) became effective in an effort to improve the style of the rules, replacing long convoluted paragraphs with smaller subparts and headings.

The following chart summarizes the changes to the FRCP numbering scheme related to the electronically stored information (ESI) provisions.

Provision	Previous Rule	Current Rule
Contents of Pretrial Scheduling Order	16(b)(5)	16(b)(3)(B)
Initial Disclosures of ESI	26(a)(1)(B)	26(a)(1)(A)(ii)
Accessibility of ESI	26(b)(2)(B)	26(b)(2)(B)
Discovery Limitations - Nature and Extent	26(b)(2)(C)	26(b)(2)(C)
Claiming Work Product Privilege	26(b)(5)(A)	26(b)(5)(A)(i)-(ii)
Conference of the Parties - ESI Discovery Plan	26(f)(3)	26(f)(3)(C)
Production of ESI	34(a)(1)	34(a)(1)(A)
Party Requesting to Specify Form of ESI Production	34(b)	34(b)(1)(C)
Responding to Request for ESI	34(b)	34(b)(2)(D)
Producing ESI	34(b)	34(b)(2)(E)(i)-(iii)
Sanctions - Motion to Compel Disclosure	37(a)(2)(A)	37(a)(3)(A)
Sanctions - Motion to Compel Discovery Response	37(a)(2)(B)	37(a)(3)(B)
Sanctions - Payment of Expenses	37(a)(4)	37(a)(5)
Sanctions - Safe Harbor	37(f)	37(e)
Subpoena - Contents	45(a)(1)(C)	45(a)(1)(A)(iii)
Subpoena - Form of Production of ESI	45(a)	45(a)(1)(C)
Subpoena - Objections	45(c)(2)(B)	45(c)(2)(B)(i)-(ii)
Subpoena - Production of ESI	45(d)(1)	45(d)(1)(A)-(D)

TRIALGRAPHIX. DISCOVERY • TRIAL CONSULTING • PRESENTATIONS | KROLL ONTRACK®

Rule 33 Interrogatories to Parties

...recognizing the importance of electronically stored information....the Rule 33(d) option should be available with respect to such records as well.

...Special difficulties may arise in using electronically stored information, either due to its form or because it is dependent on a particular computer system. Rule 33(d) allows a responding party to substitute access to documents or electronically stored information for an answer only if the burden of deriving the answer will be substantially the same for either party...

Rule 34 Production of Documents, Electronically Stored Information, and Things and Entry Upon Land for Inspection and Other Purposes

...amended to include discovery of data compilations, anticipating that the use of computerized information would increase...

Rule 37 Failure to Make Disclosures or Cooperate in Discovery; Sanctions

...absent exceptional circumstances, sanctions cannot be imposed for loss of electronically stored information resulting from the routine, good-faith operation of an electronic information system.

Rule 45 Subpoena

...amended to recognize that electronically stored information, as defined in Rule 34(a), can also be sought by subpoena....

Form 35 Report of Parties' Planning Meeting

...a report to the court about the results of this discussion. (under Rule 26)

PROCEDURES AND TIMELINES IN DISCOVERY

The federal rules provide a time line and a set of obligations that attorneys must follow. The discovery process starts with an attorney conference and culminates with a meeting with the judge, as provided for in Rule 16.

LEARNING OBJECTIVE 2
Describe the procedures and times for discovery under the federal rules.

Rule 16 Pretrial Conferences; Scheduling; Management

(a) Purposes of a Pretrial Conference.

In any action, the court may order the attorneys and any unrepresented parties to appear for one or more pretrial conferences for such purposes as:

(1) expediting disposition of the action;
(2) establishing early and continuing control so that the case will not be protracted because of lack of management;
(3) discouraging wasteful pretrial activities;
(4) improving the quality of the trial through more thorough preparation; and
(5) facilitating settlement.

(b) Scheduling.

(1) Scheduling Order.

Except in categories of actions exempted by local rule, the district judge—or a magistrate judge when authorized by local rule—must issue a scheduling order:

(A) after receiving the parties' report under Rule 26(f); or
(B) after consulting with the parties' attorneys and any unrepresented parties at a scheduling conference or by telephone, mail, or other means.

(2) Time to Issue.

The judge must issue the scheduling order as soon as practicable, but in any event within the earlier of 120 days after any defendant has been served with the complaint or 90 days after any defendant has appeared.

Exhibit 4.2 Comments of the advisory committee on civil rules of the judicial conference committee on rules of practice and procedure

The Advisory Committee on Civil Rules of the Judicial Conference Committee on Rules of Practice and Procedure comments explain the reason for the change:

"The amendment to Rule 16(b) is designed to alert the court to the possible need to address the handling of discovery of electronically stored information early in the litigation if such discovery is expected to occur. Rule 26(f) is amended to direct the parties to discuss discovery of electronically stored information if such discovery is contemplated in the action. Form 35 is amended to call for a report to the court about the results of this discussion. In many instances, the court's involvement early in the litigation will help avoid difficulties that might otherwise arise."

Insight to the rule change may be found in the comments to the rules, as shown in Exhibit 4.2.

Attorney Conference–Meet and Confer

The federal rules provide an initial timeline for pretrial procedures, as shown in Exhibit 4.3.

Discovery may not begin until the lawyers for the parties have conferred and developed a proposed discovery plan, as required in Fed. R. Civ. P. 26(f) and Fed. R. Civ. P. 26(d). This meet and confer step is required before the required scheduling conference with the assigned judge.

F.R.C.P. Rule 26. Duty to Disclose; General Provisions Governing Discovery

(d) Timing and Sequence of Discovery.

(1) Timing.

A party may not seek discovery from any source before the parties have conferred as required by Rule 26(f), except in a proceeding exempted from initial disclosure under Rule 26(a)(1)(B), or when authorized by these rules, by stipulation, or by court order.

(f) Conference of the Parties; Planning for Discovery

(1) Conference Timing.

Except in a proceeding exempted from initial disclosure under Rule 26(a)(1)(B) or when the court orders otherwise, the parties must confer as soon as practicable—and in any event at least 21 days before a scheduling conference is to be held or a scheduling order is due under Rule 16(b).

(2) Conference Content; Parties' Responsibilities.

In conferring, the parties must consider the nature and basis of their claims and defenses and the possibilities for promptly settling or resolving the case; make or arrange for the disclosures required by Rule 26(a)(1); discuss any issues about preserving discoverable information; and develop a proposed discovery plan. The attorneys of record and all unrepresented parties that have appeared in the case are jointly responsible for arranging the conference, for attempting in good faith to agree on the proposed discovery plan, and for submitting to the court within 14 days after the conference a written report outlining the plan. The court may order the parties or attorneys to attend the conference in person.

Exhibit 4.3 Timeline in federal court from filing of the complaint to the scheduling conference

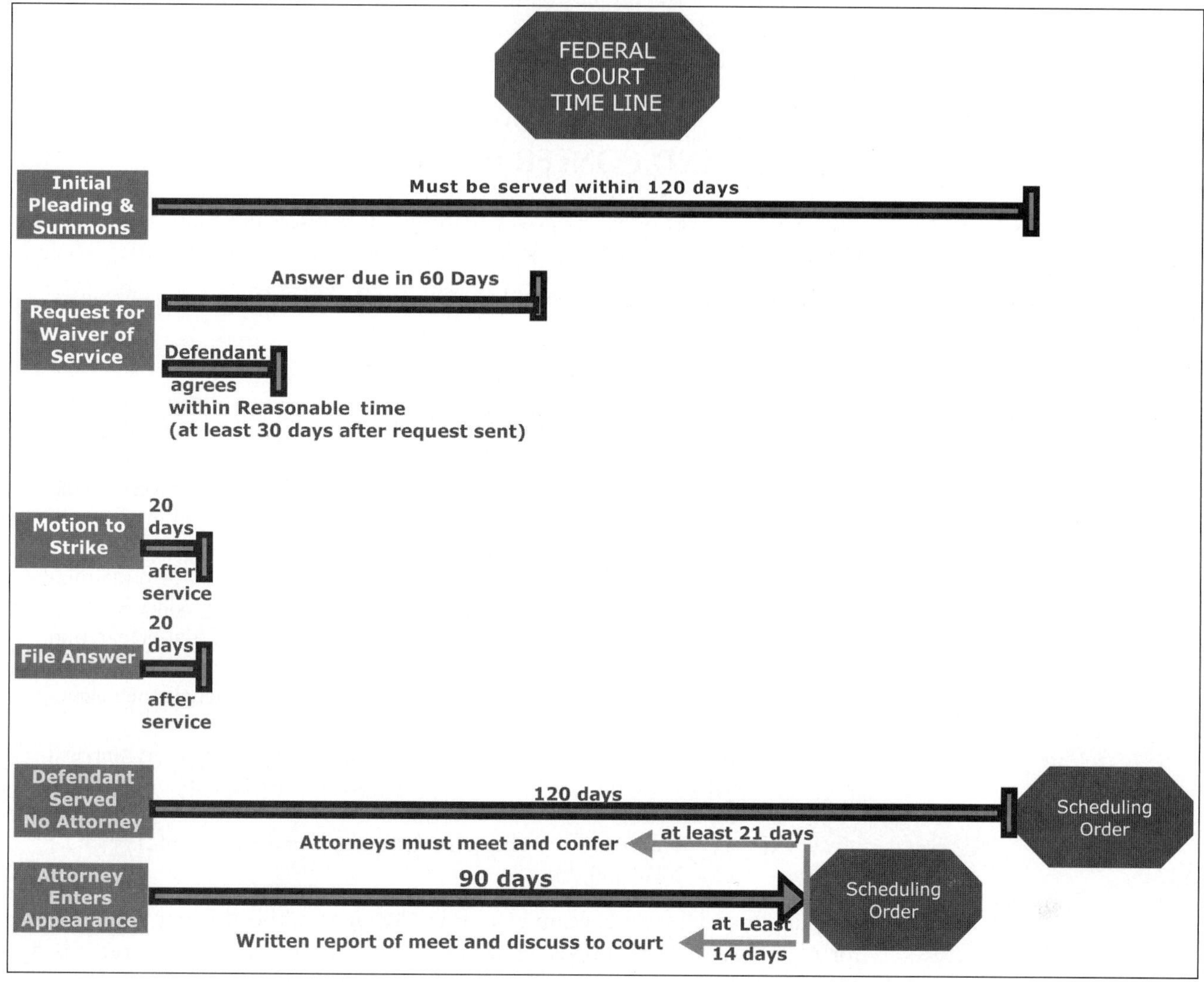

Discovery Timing

The scheduling conference occurs within 90 days after the **entry of appearance** by the attorney who will represent the defendant (or 120 days after the defendant is served with the complaint). The meet and confer must occur at least 21 days before the scheduling conference with the judge, thereby allowing 99 days for the meet and confer session. Following the meet and confer conference between counsel, a written statement memorializing the items discussed is required to be submitted to the court within 14 days.

entry of appearance
An attorney for one of the litigants files papers officially identifying himself or herself as representing the client before the court.

The required meet and confer conference is between the attorneys and without a judge present. It affords them the opportunity to amicably agree on a discovery schedule that can be submitted to the court. This process of discussing and planning discovery is particularly important in complex litigation and in those cases involving large volumes of electronically stored documentation.

The conference of the attorneys is linked in time and responsibility to the Rule 16(b) scheduling conference with the judge. Under the federal rules, a judge is assigned to the case from the time the complaint is filed. The judge will usually take an active role in setting a time line for discovery and trial. The attorneys have an opportunity to participate in that process by issuing the report of their conference and participating in the scheduling conference with the judge. The judge will usually give great deference to the recommendation of the attorneys in scheduling deadlines for discovery.

The goal of the conference between counsel is to discuss the nature of the claims and the likelihood of settlement, to arrange for mandatory disclosure under Rule 26(a), and to develop a discovery plan in the event one is necessary.

MEET AND CONFER ISSUES

LEARNING OBJECTIVE 3
Explain the purpose and the expected outcomes of the attorney meet and confer.

The meet and confer is supposed to result in a discovery plan as outlined in FRCP 26, shown below.

F.R.C.P. Rule 26. Duty to Disclose; General Provisions Governing Discovery

(3) Discovery Plan.
A discovery plan must state the parties' views and proposals on:
(A) what changes should be made in the timing, form, or requirement for disclosures under Rule 26(a), including a statement of when initial disclosures were made or will be made;
(B) the subjects on which discovery may be needed, when discovery should be completed, and whether discovery should be conducted in phases or be limited to or focused on particular issues;
(C) any issues about disclosure or discovery of electronically stored information, including the form or forms in which it should be produced;
(D) any issues about claims of privilege or of protection as trial-preparation materials, including—if the parties agree on a procedure to assert these claims after production—whether to ask the court to include their agreement in an order;
(E) what changes should be made in the limitations on discovery imposed under these rules or by local rule, and what other limitations should be imposed; and
(F) any other orders that the court should issue under Rule 26(c) or under Rule 16(b) and (c).

In a case that does not contain electronic documents, the attorney could prepare for a conference with opposing counsel by reviewing the client's records and the investigative file and come prepared with a list of parties to be deposed and records sought from the other side that could be produced in paper form, or occasionally in the form of X-rays or other similar forms.

In the electronic document cases, preparation is not as simple. Critical commitments and demands for access and delivery of electronic data require a technological skill set that many lawyers do not possess. Lawyers for the most part are trained in the procedural and substantive areas of law, not in the science of computer data storage. Without the knowledge of the technology, methods of storage used by the client, location and format of the files, and other technical issues, lawyers may find themselves agreeing to a document production plan that is not physically possible, or is extremely costly. A growing number of skilled litigators will take with them, to the meet and confer, a member of the IT or litigation support staff who is knowledgeable in the procedures and methods of e-discovery to ensure that proper requests are made and realistic agreements given. When clients have unique or complex computer systems, a person familiar with the technical aspects of the clients' system may also be brought in to offer insight and guidance to electronic discovery issues.

WEB RESOURCES
The form may be downloaded from the U.S. Courts website in WordPerfect or MS Word format at http://www.uscourts.gov/RulesAndPolicies/FederalRulemaking/RulesAndForms/IllustrativeCivilRulesForms.aspx

Form 52 from the FRCP, shown in Exhibit 4.4, may be used to complete the report to the court of the meet and confer meeting.

Exhibit 4.4 Form 52, report of the parties' planning meeting

UNITED STATES DISTRICT COURT
for the
<________________> DISTRICT OF <________________>

<Name(s) of plaintiff(s)>,	)	
Plaintiff(s)	)	
	)	Civil Action No. <number>
v.	)	
<Name(s) of defendant(s)>,	)	
Defendant(s)	)	

REPORT OF THE PARTIES' PLANNING MEETING

1. The following persons participated in a Rule 26(f) conference on <Date> by <State the method of conferring>:
   <Name>, representing the <plaintiff>
   <Name>, representing the <defendant>
2. Initial Disclosures. The parties [have completed] [will complete by <Date>] the initial disclosures required by Rule 26(a)(1).
3. Discovery Plan. The parties propose this discovery plan:
   <Use separate paragraphs or subparagraphs if the parties disagree.>
   (a) Discovery will be needed on these subjects: <Describe>.
   (b) <Dates for commencing and completing discovery, including discovery to be commenced or completed before other discovery.>
   (c) <Maximum number of interrogatories by each party to another party, along with the dates the answers are due.>
   (d) <Maximum number of requests for admission, along with the dates responses are due.>
   (e) <Maximum number of depositions by each party.>
   (f) <Limits on the length of depositions, in hours.>
   (g) <Dates for exchanging reports of expert witnesses.>
   (h) <Dates for supplementations under Rule 26(e).>
4. Other Items:
   (a) <A date if the parties ask to meet with the court before a scheduling order.>
   (b) <Requested dates for pretrial conferences.>
   (c) <Final dates for the plaintiff to amend pleadings or to join parties.>
   (d) <Final dates for the defendant to amend pleadings or to join parties.>
   (e) <Final dates to file dispositive motions.>
   (f) <State the prospects for settlement.>
   (g) <Identify any alternative dispute resolution procedure that may enhance settlement prospects.>
   (h) <Final dates for submitting Rule 26(a)(3) witness lists, designations of witnesses whose testimony will be presented by deposition, and exhibit lists.>
   (i) <Final dates to file objections under Rule 26(a)(3).>
   (j) <Suggested trial date and estimate of trial length.>
   (k) <Other matters.>

Date: <Date>

<Signature of the attorney or unrepresented party>

____

<Printed name>
<Address>
<E-mail address>
<Telephone number>

Date: <Date>

<Signature of the attorney or unrepresented party>

____

<Printed name>
<Address>
<E-mail address>
<Telephone number>

Source: http://www.uscourts.gov/uscourts/RulesAndPolicies/Rules/Usable_Rules_Forms_Civil/CIV52-Report_of_the_Parties-_Planning_Meeting.wpd

IN THE WORDS OF THE COURT...

Louis H. Hopson, et al. Plaintiffs,

v.

The Mayor and City Council of Baltimore, A Municipal Corporation of the State of Maryland, and the Baltimore City Police Department, Defendants.

UNITED STATES DISTRICT COURT FOR THE DISTRICT OF MARYLAND

232 F.R.D. 228; 244-245

November 22, 2005, Decided

...as this case graphically demonstrates, it is no longer acceptable for the parties to defer good faith discussion of how to approach discovery of electronic records until they have complied with the briefing schedule in Local Rule 104.8. Rather, as the proposed changes to Rule 16(f) make clear, counsel have a duty to take the initiative in meeting and conferring to plan for appropriate discovery of electronically stored information at the commencement of any case in which electronic records will be sought. In the absence of any guidance in the court's scheduling order, or in the local rules of court, the parties are not without resources that will assist them in determining what to discuss at their meeting. Indeed, the newly revised Civil Discovery Standards for the American Bar Association Section on Litigation 40 contain detailed information about the issues that the parties should discus in their effort to agree upon an electronic records discovery plan. At a minimum, they should discuss: the type of information technology systems in use and the persons most knowledgeable in their operation; preservation of electronically stored information that may be relevant to the litigation; the scope of the electronic records sought (i.e. e-mail, voice mail, archived data, back-up or disaster recovery data, laptops, personal computers, PDA's, deleted data); the format in which production will occur (will records be produced in "native" or searchable format, or image only; is metadata sought); whether the requesting party seeks to conduct any testing or sampling of the producing party's IT system; the burdens and expenses that the producing party will face based on the Rule 26(b)(2) factors, and how they may be reduced (i.e. limiting the time period for which discovery is sought, limiting the amount of hours the producing party must spend searching, compiling and reviewing electronic records, using sampling to search, rather than searching all records, shifting to the producing party some of the production costs); the amount of pre-production privilege review that is reasonable for the producing party to undertake, and measures to preserve post-production assertion of privilege within a reasonable time; and any protective orders or confidentiality orders that should be in place regarding who may have access to information that is produced.

It cannot be emphasized enough that the goal of the meeting to discuss discovery is to reach an agreement that then can be proposed to the court. The days when the requesting party can expect to "get it all" and the producing party to produce whatever they feel like producing are long gone. In many cases, such as employment discrimination cases or civil rights cases, electronic discovery is not played on a level field. The plaintiff typically has relatively few electronically stored records, while the defendant often has an immense volume of it. In such cases, it is incumbent upon the plaintiff to have reasonable expectations as to what should be produced by the defendant....

SCOPE OF DISCOVERY

LEARNING OBJECTIVE 4
Explain what is discoverable.

The discovery process is not limited to obtaining only the items that will be used in trial. In many cases, the actual items that will be used as evidence in trial may not be obvious. The proverbial "smoking gun" evidence may be found indirectly in a serendipitous series of events where one innocuous document leads to another that leads to a final relevant, admissible document. The general rule is that anything that may lead to relevant evidence is discoverable.

Under Rule 26 of the Federal Rules of Civil Procedure, everything is discoverable that is not privileged and is relevant or may lead to relevant evidence.

FRCP 26

(b) Discovery Scope and Limits.

(1) Scope in General.

Unless otherwise limited by court order, the scope of discovery is as follows: Parties may obtain discovery regarding any nonprivileged matter that is relevant to any party's claim or defense—including the existence, description, nature, custody, condition, and location of any documents or other tangible things and the identity and location of persons who know of any discoverable matter. For good cause, the court may order discovery of any matter relevant to the subject matter involved in the action. Relevant information need not be admissible at the trial if the discovery appears reasonably calculated to lead to the discovery of admissible evidence. All discovery is subject to the limitations imposed by Rule 26(b)(2)(C).

Documents and information that may be obtained through the discovery process are considerably broader than those that may be used or admissible at trial under the Federal Rules of Evidence (FRE). Any item of information is **relevant** for purposes of discovery where it has a relationship to evidence about the litigation and is likely to lead to admissible evidence. For discovery purposes, it is not required that an item of information meet the requirements of the Rules of Evidence for admission at trial. Admissibility of evidence requires additional scrutiny such as that of authentication under FRE Rule 901, Requirement of Authentication or Identification.

relevant
That which tends to prove the existence of facts important to the resolution of a case or may lead to such evidence which is admissible.

Federal Rules of Evidence Rule 901. Requirement of Authentication or Identification

(a) General provision.

The requirement of authentication or identification as a condition precedent to admissibility is satisfied by evidence sufficient to support a finding that the matter in question is what its proponent claims.

Mandatory Disclosure Requirements

Rule 26(a) makes mandatory the disclosure of certain information that for years was available only after a formal written discovery request was issued. For many cases, no action was taken on a file until one side moved the case forward with a formal discovery request. Under current rules, everything the legal team intends to rely upon to prove its claims must be disclosed early in the litigation. Insufficient time to investigate the claim is not a valid excuse for failure to comply. The benefits of mandatory disclosure are twofold:

1. The early evaluation and settlement of claims
2. The reduction in the amount, nature, and time necessary to conduct formal discovery

While the new rules contemplate a specific time frame for disclosure, they do permit the attorneys to agree to some other time frame for the disclosure. Although the attorneys may agree to extend that time, the judge at the scheduling conference may encourage them to conclude discovery at a faster pace.

From a practical standpoint, the plaintiff's legal team must be prepared for disclosure at or shortly after the filing of the complaint. The investigation that might have occurred after filing suit under prior rules must now be completed before filing suit. For the defense team, the time to investigate and comply is very short. Thus there is no time for procrastination in investigating and establishing the grounds to defend the claims.

PRACTICE TIP

In criminal cases, the prosecution must turn over to the defense all exculpatory information in its possession. See *Brady v. Maryland,* 373 U.S. 83, 87 (1963).

Information Subject to Mandatory Disclosure

Almost anything relied upon in developing the claim, regardless of whether it is admissible at trial, must be disclosed. This disclosure includes the identity of witnesses, copies of documents, a computation of damages, and a copy of any insurance policy that may be used to satisfy a judgment obtained in the litigation.

The computation of damages traditionally represents the plaintiff attorney's thought process and was typically not released as part of discovery under the work product privilege. Under the current rule, the attorney's value on the case is made known within months of the complaint being filed.

From the defense standpoint, the disclosure of insurance coverage, which is not admissible at trial, is a significant change from traditional discovery. A key element in settling most cases is the existence of and limitations on insurance coverage. The chances for fruitful settlement discussions are enhanced with both the plaintiff's calculation of damages and the defendant's ability to pay based upon insurance being known within months of filing the lawsuit.

Experts and Witnesses

An **expert witness** expected to be called at trial must also be identified and a copy of the expert's qualifications as an expert provided to the other side, including a list of the expert's publications from the preceding ten years, a statement of compensation, and a list of other cases in which the expert has testified. The most critical element to be shared is the written report of the expert's opinion. The report represents what the expert is expected to say at trial. The written report must include the opinion of the expert, the basis of that opinion including the information relied upon, and any assumptions made. The disclosure of the expert and his or her report must be made at least ninety days prior to trial. Some courts require the disclosure of the expert at the time of the initial disclosure or within thirty days of receipt of the expert's report. Many lawsuits become a battle of the experts. The early disclosure of the expert and his or her opinion will often lead to early resolution of the case.

expert witness
A person qualified by education, training, or experience to render an opinion based on a set of facts that are outside the scope of knowledge of the fact finder.

F.R.C.P. Rule 26. Duty to Disclose; General Provisions Governing Discovery

(2) Expert Witness.
For an expert whose report must be disclosed under Rule 26(a)(2)(B), the party's duty to supplement extends both to information included in the report and to information given during the expert's deposition. Any additions or changes to this information must be disclosed by the time the party's pretrial disclosures under Rule 26(a)(3) are due.

General Provisions

There are some general limitations on discovery that are imposed by the federal rules. The rules seek to eliminate duplicative, burdensome, and oppressive discovery requests. Requests are duplicative or burdensome when the information sought has already been provided or is more easily obtained from another source.

Another obligation that continues throughout the litigation is the duty to supplement or revise responses should additional or different information become known. A typical example is an answer to an interrogatory that indicates the identity and address of a witness. When it is learned at some later point in time that the witness has relocated, that information must be shared with opposing counsel.

PRACTICE TIP

To advise on trial preparation issues, some law firms hire independent experts (whom they do not intend to call as witnesses), in order to protect the information as work product.

F.R.C.P. Rule 26. Duty to Disclose; General Provisions Governing Discovery

(e) Supplementation of Disclosures and Responses.

(1) In General.

A party who has made a disclosure under Rule 26(a)—or who has responded to an interrogatory, request for production, or request for admission—must supplement or correct its disclosure or response:

(A) in a timely manner if the party learns that in some material respect the disclosure or response is incomplete or incorrect, and if the additional or corrective information has not otherwise been made known to the other parties during the discovery process or in writing; or

(B) as ordered by the court.

ETHICAL Perspectives

ILLINOIS RULES OF PROFESSIONAL CONDUCT OF 2010

RULE 3.4: FAIRNESS TO OPPOSING PARTY AND COUNSEL

A lawyer shall not:

(a) unlawfully obstruct another party's access to evidence or unlawfully alter, destroy or conceal a document or other material having potential evidentiary value. A lawyer shall not counsel or assist another person to do any such act;

(b) falsify evidence, counsel or assist a witness to testify falsely, or offer an inducement to a witness that is prohibited by law;

(c) knowingly disobey an obligation under the rules of a tribunal, except for an open refusal based on an assertion that no valid obligation exists;

(d) in pretrial procedure, make a frivolous discovery request or fail to make reasonably diligent effort to comply with a legally proper discovery request by an opposing party;

(e) in trial, allude to any matter that the lawyer does not reasonably believe is relevant or that will not be supported by admissible evidence, assert personal knowledge of facts in issue except when testifying as a witness, or state a personal opinion as to the justness of a cause, the credibility of a witness, the culpability of a civil litigant or the guilt or innocence of an accused; or

(f) request a person other than a client to refrain from voluntarily giving relevant information to another party unless:

(1) the person is a relative or an employee or other agent of a client; and

(2) the lawyer reasonably believes that the person's interests will not be adversely affected by refraining from giving such information.

Adopted July 1, 2009, effective January 1, 2010.

Source: http://www.state.il.us/court/supremecourt/rules/art_viii/ArtVIII_NEW.htm#3.4

WEB RESOURCES

Illinois Ethics Rules

Contrast and compare the Illinois Rules of Professional Conduct at http://www.state.il.us/court/supremecourt/rules/art_viii/default_new.asp with the American Bar Association Model Rules of Professional Responsibility at http://www.abanet.org/cpr/mrpc/mrpc_toc.html, and the ethical rules in your jurisdiction.

Production of Documents or Things

Production of documents or things under Rule 34 makes available for discovery documents and other physical objects, like defective products, relevant to the lawsuit. A sample request under Rule 34 is shown in Exhibit 4.5. The process of production of documents is a written request addressed to a party to the litigation. The party must respond in writing to each request. The response may also include a paper (hard copy) or electronic copy of the documents or the items requested. Examples include medical records of an injured plaintiff, a copy of a liability insurance policy, a police accident report, or an employee personnel file.

Exhibit 4.5 Civil Form 50, Request to Product Documents and Tangible Things, or to Enter onto Land Under Rule 34

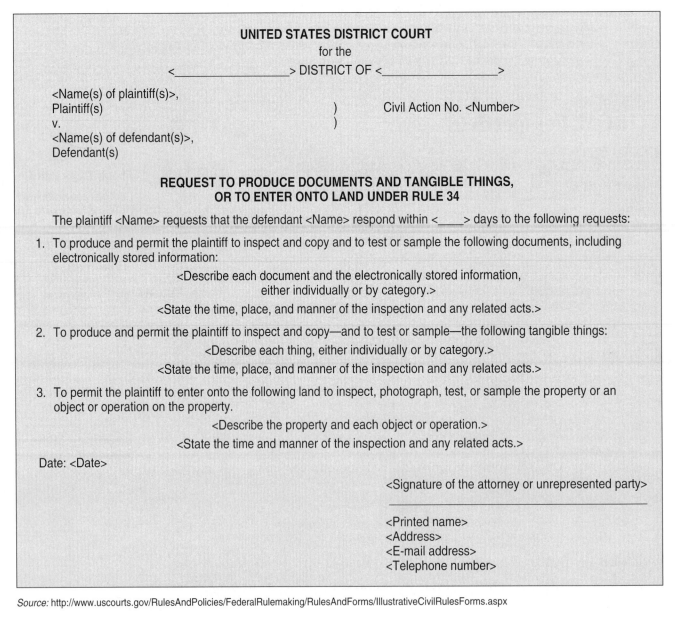

UNITED STATES DISTRICT COURT
for the
<________________> DISTRICT OF <________________>

<Name(s) of plaintiff(s)>,
Plaintiff(s)) Civil Action No. <Number>
v.)
<Name(s) of defendant(s)>,
Defendant(s)

REQUEST TO PRODUCE DOCUMENTS AND TANGIBLE THINGS, OR TO ENTER ONTO LAND UNDER RULE 34

The plaintiff <Name> requests that the defendant <Name> respond within <____> days to the following requests:

1. To produce and permit the plaintiff to inspect and copy and to test or sample the following documents, including electronically stored information:

   <Describe each document and the electronically stored information, either individually or by category.>

   <State the time, place, and manner of the inspection and any related acts.>

2. To produce and permit the plaintiff to inspect and copy—and to test or sample—the following tangible things:

   <Describe each thing, either individually or by category.>

   <State the time, place, and manner of the inspection and any related acts.>

3. To permit the plaintiff to enter onto the following land to inspect, photograph, test, or sample the property or an object or operation on the property.

   <Describe the property and each object or operation.>

   <State the time and manner of the inspection and any related acts.>

Date: <Date>

<Signature of the attorney or unrepresented party>

____

<Printed name>
<Address>
<E-mail address>
<Telephone number>

Source: http://www.uscourts.gov/RulesAndPolicies/FederalRulemaking/RulesAndForms/IllustrativeCivilRulesForms.aspx

Rule 34. Producing Documents, Electronically Stored Information, and Tangible Things, or Entering onto Land, for Inspection and Other Purposes

(a) In General.

A party may serve on any other party a request within the scope of Rule 26(b):

(1) to produce and permit the requesting party or its representative to inspect, copy, test, or sample the following items in the responding party's possession, custody, or control:

(A) any designated documents or electronically stored information—including writings, drawings, graphs, charts, photographs, sound recordings, images, and other data or data compilations—stored in any medium from which information can be obtained either directly or, if necessary, after translation by the responding party into a reasonably usable form; or

(B) any designated tangible things; or

(2) to permit entry onto designated land or other property possessed or controlled by the responding party, so that the requesting party may inspect, measure, survey, photograph, test, or sample the property or any designated object or operation on it.

Where the "thing" is not capable of delivery, such as a building or other large object, this discovery tool includes the right to enter onto the land of another for purposes of inspection. This discovery tool may also be used in cases where the volume of documentary evidence or electronic records is too large for practical delivery, such as a warehouse with thousands of cartons of paper files.

Example: The parties dispute the contents of the hard drive of the defendant. The plaintiff may believe that relevant information may have been erased or not delivered. Inspection of the computer hard drive by a forensic expert would be permissible under the rules.

DEPOSITIONS

LEARNING OBJECTIVE 5
Describe the function and use of depositions.

Depositions have historically allowed parties the out-of-court opportunity to spontaneously question parties and witnesses, under oath, without the limitation of carefully prepared, written answers to interrogatories. Depositions are, within the confines of court rules and procedures, opportunities to ask open-ended questions, obtain spontaneous responses, and follow up with additional questions. The costs of taking depositions can be significant. In addition to the cost for counsel and their assistants, there is a cost for the court reporter to transcribe the testimony. In videotaped depositions, this may include a court reporter and one or more videographers or technicians, and in some cases the cost of videoconferencing connections.

Rule 30. Deposition by Oral Examination

... (b) Notice of the Deposition; Other Formal Requirements.

(1) Notice in General.

A party who wants to depose a person by oral questions must give reasonable written notice to every other party. The notice must state the time and place of the deposition and, if known, the deponent's name and address. If the name is unknown, the notice must provide a general description sufficient to identify the person or the particular class or group to which the person belongs.

Videotaped depositions are used in many cases to preserve the testimony of a witness who might otherwise be unable to attend the trial—for example, an aged or infirmed witness who may not be physically able to attend the trial or who may not live until the trial, or an expert witness who because of personal or professional schedules is unable to sit around waiting to be called, such as a medical expert.

Because of their potential use in trial, these depositions are conducted with the same formality of a trial proceeding, with the witness sworn in and the lawyers asking questions and making objections. Unlike trial, however, the objections are addressed by the court after the fact, after the deposition is concluded but before presentation in court.

Rule 30. Deposition by Oral Examination

(c) Examination and Cross-Examination; Record of the Examination; Objections; Written Questions.

(1) Examination and Cross-Examination.

The examination and cross-examination of a deponent proceed as they would at trial uzznder the Federal Rules of Evidence, except Rules 103 and 615. After putting the deponent under oath or affirmation, the officer must record the testimony by the method designated under Rule 30(b)(3)(A). The testimony must be recorded by the officer personally or by a person acting in the presence and under the direction of the officer.

(2) Objections.

An objection at the time of the examination—whether to evidence, to a party's conduct, to the officer's qualifications, to the manner of taking the deposition, or to any other aspect of the deposition—must be noted on the record, but the examination still proceeds; the testimony is taken subject to any objection. An objection must be stated concisely in a nonargumentative and nonsuggestive manner. A person may instruct a deponent not to answer only when necessary to preserve a privilege, to enforce a limitation ordered by the court, or to present a motion under Rule 30(d)(3).

Rule 30(b). Deposition

In cases involving corporate or institutional defendants[,] it is critical to have a representative at the deposition who is actually knowledgeable about the issues of the case. Not every corporate officer or employee has the knowledge that may be needed. The problem for the opposing party is identifying the proper person with the required information. In case[s] involving ESI, the person must be able to identify the sources of discoverable information and the methods used to create, store and retrieve what may be needed.

Deposing the correct person with the needed information is important. As stated in the Heartland Surgical case:

> For a Rule 30(b)(6) deposition to operate effectively, the deposing party must designate the areas of inquiry with reasonable particularity, and the corporation must designate and adequately prepare witnesses to address these matters. If the rule is to promote effective discovery regarding corporations the spokesperson must be informed. 2007 WL 1054279 (D. Kan. 2007)

Failure to properly present a responsive witness who can answer questions about the company's electronic filing systems can result in sanctions for the costs incurred by the requesting party. In cases where electronically stored documents are involved, the proper person may be a technical person and not necessarily the traditional custodian of documents, which in paper-based document cases might be an office manager.

IN THE WORDS OF THE COURT...

Covad Communications Company v. Revonet, Inc. (D.C. 3-31-2010)
Covad Communications Company, Plaintiff, v. Revonet, Inc., Defendant.
Civil Action No. 06-1892 (CKK/JMF).
United States District Court, D. Columbia.
March 31, 2010

...As I have stated before, one of the "primary purposes of the Rule 30(b)(6) deposition is to 'curb the 'bandying' by which officers or managing agents of a corporation are deposed in turn but each disclaims knowledge of the facts that are clearly known to the organization and thereby to it.'" Banks, 241 F.R.D. at 372-73 (citing Fed.R.Civ.P. 30(b)(6) advisory committee notes). Accordingly, upon receiving notice of the deposition that contains a description, with reasonable particularity, the matters on which examination is requested, a corporation must: (1) designate a deponent knowledgeable on the topic; (2) designate multiple deponents if more than one is necessary to respond to all designated topics; and (3) prepare the deponent so that he or she can testify on matters both within his or her personal knowledge as well as those "reasonably known by the responding entity." Banks, 241 F.R.D. at 373 (citing *Alexander v. Fed. Bureau of Investigation,* 186 F.R.D. 137, 139-41 (D.D.C.1998)). A court "must guard against the gamesmanship of a company avoiding deposition topics by, for example, naming as a 30(b)(6) witness a person who knows nothing about the topics and does nothing to inform himself about them so that his deposition threatens to be a series of cynical 'I do not know' statements." Banks, 241 F.R.D. at 375 (citing In re *Vitamins,* 216 F.R.D. at 168)....

COMPLIANCE AND COURT INTERVENTION

Theoretically, the process of discovery should be accomplished in a cooperative fashion without court intervention. Often that is not the case. Whatever the reason, the legal team's response to discovery requests is often delayed—or, worse, forgotten. The litigation team members must be sure they have a system in place to comply with discovery deadlines. That means establishing an internal calendaring system and obtaining client cooperation. Because there will be times when it is not possible to comply, the litigation team needs to know the steps to take to obtain an extension of the time to comply. Alternatively, they must also know the manner in which to use court intervention to make the opposing party come into compliance.

Most judges disfavor involvement in the discovery process. The mindset of the bench is that counsel should be able to resolve these issues without court intervention. Many practitioners find that court intervention is like a trip to the principal's office after a disagreement on the school bus: unpleasant and leaving a bad impression with the authority figure. Thus the litigation teams should anticipate problems that might arise in the discovery process, resolve them during the Rule 26(f) conference, and document their agreement as to discovery issues via the scheduling order.

Seeking Compliance

As the Recipient of Discovery Requests. The litigation paralegal or support staff will typically have primary responsibility for preparation of responses within the specified time frame. Developing a procedure that ensures client participation

Exhibit 4.6 Sample Motion to Compel and Order

UNITED STATES DISTRICT COURT - NORTHERN DISTRICT OF NEW YORK

B.K., a minor by her Parents and Guardians, Janice Knowles and Steven Knowles, Plaintiff	:	No.: ______________
	:	PLAINTIFF'S MOTION TO COMPEL DEFENDANT LOWER COUNCIL SCHOOL DISTRICT'S ANSWERS TO INTERROGATORIES
v.	:	
	:	CIVIL ACTION - NEGLIGENCE
Ronald Clemmons, Lower Council School District, Bud Smith, and Ace Trucking Company, Defendants	:	Jury Trial Demanded
	:	Attorney ID No. 124987

Plaintiff in the action files this Motion for relief and alleges as follows:

1. On July 15, 2011, Plaintiff served by first class mail Interrogatories addressed to the Defendant Lower Council School District.
2. Answers to the Interrogatories were due on August 15, 2011.
3. On August 18, 2011, counsel for plaintiff contacted defense counsel by telephone and confirming letter to ascertain the reason for the delay in response and to obtain a time frame within which answers would be provided. Defense counsel indicated an additional 30 days was required. A true and correct copy of the confirming letter dated August 18, 2011 is attached as Exhibit A.
4. On September 20, 2011 more than 30 days had passed and still the answers to Interrogatories were outstanding. Plaintiff's counsel attempted to telephone and left numerous messages for defense counsel, none of which were returned.
5. On September 25, 2011 Plaintiff's counsel issued a letter advising defense counsel of the intention to file the within Motion to Compel.A true and correct copy of the letter dated September 25, 2011 is attached as Exhibit B.
6. To date, Defendant has neither answered nor objected to the Interrogatories.
7. To date, Defendant has filed neither a Motion for Enlargement of Time to Respond nor a Motion for Protective Order.
8. Plaintiff has incurred costs in conjunction with seeking the compliance of Defendant Lower Council School District. Attached as Exhibit C is an affidavit of the time expended in informal means if contacting Defendant as well as for the preparation, filing and service of the within Motion.

WHEREFORE, it is respectfully requested this Honorable court enter and order compelling Defendant Lower Council School District to issue answers to Interrogatories within 10 days, prohibiting Defendant for raising any objection to answer and awarding attorneys fees and costs in a reasonable sum.

Respectfully submitted,

(continued)

and cooperation in the preparation of responses is crucial. The meeting with the client in a case involving e-discovery should be used to determine the sources, locations, types, and formats of electronic documents. Sufficient information must be obtained about the methods of storage of electronic files and the retention policies to allow the attorney to go to the meet and confer conference with enough information to properly work out a meaningful discovery plan and timetable.

Exhibit 4.6 *(continued)*

UNITED STATES DISTRICT COURT - NORTHERN DISTRICT OF NEW YORK

B.K., a minor by her Parents and Guardians, Janice Knowles and Steven Knowles, Plaintiff	:	No.: ____________
	:	PLAINTIFF'S MOTION TO COMPEL DEFENDANT LOWER COUNCIL SCHOOL DISTRICT'S ANSWERS TO INTERROGATORIES
v.	:	
	:	CIVIL ACTION - NEGLIGENCE
Ronald Clemmons, Lower Council School District, Bud Smith, and Ace Trucking Company, Defendants	:	Jury Trial Demanded
	:	Attorney ID No.124987

ORDER

AND NOW this __________ day of __________________, 2011 the matter having been brought before the court on Plaintiff's Motion to Compel and after consideration of the Reply and hearing on this matter it is hereby ORDERED that Defendant Lower Council School District shall within ten (10) days of the date hereof answer completely, fully and without objection the Interrogatories served upon it by the Plaintiff on July 15, 2011. Failure to comply with the terms of this Order will result in the imposition of sanctions in accordance with Fed.R.Civ.P. 37; FURTHER ORDERED, Defendant Lower Council School District shall within ten (10) days of the date hereof pay to Plaintiff the sum of $1,500.00, the reasonable attorney's fees and costs associated with obtaining compliance with the discovery requested.

BY THE COURT:

______________________________ J.

As the Issuer of Discovery Requests. It may be necessary to seek relief from the court when the responding party is not cooperative. It may be a matter of recalcitrance or that the party is not able to comply with the agreement made at the meet and confer conference because of a lack of knowledge of the client's system by the attorney in making the agreement. The court will almost always ask whether a good faith attempt was made to secure the information before granting any orders compelling compliance. A sample Motion to Compel and Order is shown in Exhibit 4.6.

VIDEO ADVICE FROM THE FIELD

Debra Weaver–Certified real time court reporter

Discussion of the role of the court reporter in depositions and how to prepare witnesses for depositions before a court reporter.

After watching the video in MyLegalStudiesKit, answer the following questions.

1. What is the role of the court reporter?
2. What types of instruction should be given to witnesses before the taking of their deposition?

PROTECTING CONFIDENTIAL OR PRIVILEGED MATERIALS

LEARNING OBJECTIVE 6
Explain how the litigation team can protect privileged or confidential information under the federal rules.

The attorney has an ethical obligation to preserve the confidences of clients (see Rule 1.6 of the ABA Model Rules of Professional Conduct). This ethical duty is recognized in the Federal Rules of Civil Procedure and the Federal Rules of Evidence. Rule 26 of the Federal Rules of Civil Procedure provides a framework for the process at FRCP 26(5), and FRCP 16 provides for the court to make any agreement on inadvertent disclosure agreed upon by the parties part of the court's Scheduling Order (FRPC 16(3)(iv)).

FRCP 26 specifically recognizes that parties may withhold information otherwise discoverable, and it provides within the rule a framework for the process, as shown in Exhibit 4.7.

When vast numbers of electronic files are delivered as part of the discovery process, it may not always be possible, within the limited time frames required for compliance, to check each of the documents before handing them over to opposing counsel. Many times the documents will be part of an answer to a request for electronically stored documents that will be delivered on computer tape, CD, DVD, or other computer storage media. The electronic documents delivered may contain confidential material, like emails between attorney and client, work product materials, or a client's proprietary information or trade secret.

claw-back provision
A provision contained in the report of counsel's meet and confer and included in the court's scheduling order that describes what to do with privileged materials that are disclosed inadvertently through e-discovery. The provision should address return of the materials and waiver of the privilege.

The rules provide for a **"claw back" provision** as part of the discovery plan.

Rule 26. Duty to disclose; General provisions governing discovery

... (5) Claiming Privilege or Protecting Trial-Preparation Materials.

(A) *Information Withheld.* When a party withholds information otherwise discoverable by claiming that the information is privileged or subject to protection as trial-preparation material, the party must:
(i) expressly make the claim; and
(ii) describe the nature of the documents, communications, or tangible things not produced or disclosed—and do so in a manner that, without

Exhibit 4.7 Fed. R. Civ. P. 26(5)(A) and (B) procedures for claiming protection for privileged on work product materials

Rule 26. General Provisions Governing Discovery; Duty of Disclosure

(5) Claims of Privilege or Protection of Trial Preparation Materials.

(A) Information Withheld.
When a party withholds information otherwise discoverable under these rules by claiming that it is privileged or subject to protection as trial-preparation material, the party shall make the claim expressly and shall describe the nature of the documents, communications, or things not produced or disclosed in a manner that, without revealing information itself privileged or protected, will enable other parties to assess the applicability of the privilege or protection.

(B) Information Produced.
If information is produced in discovery that is subject to a claim of privilege or of protection as trial-preparation material, the party making the claim may notify any party that received the information of the claim and the basis for it. After being notified, a party must promptly return, sequester, or destroy the specified information and any copies it has and may not use or disclose the information until the claim is resolved. A receiving party may promptly present the information to the court under seal for a determination of the claim. If the receiving party disclosed the information before being notified, it must take reasonable steps to retrieve it. The producing party must preserve the information until the claim is resolved.

revealing information itself privileged or protected, will enable other parties to assess the claim.

(B) *Information Produced.* If information produced in discovery is subject to a claim of privilege or of protection as trial preparation material, the party making the claim may notify any party that received the information of the claim and the basis for it. After being notified, a party must promptly return, sequester, or destroy the specified information and any copies it has; must not use or disclose the information until the claim is resolved; must take reasonable steps to retrieve the information if the party disclosed it before being notified; and may promptly present the information to the court under seal for a determination of the claim. The producing party must preserve the information until the claim is resolved.

Here is the "claw-back" provision under FRCP 16:

Rule 16. Pretrial Conferences; Scheduling; Management

(3) Contents of the Order.

(A) *Required Contents*. The scheduling order must limit the time to join other parties, amend the pleadings, complete discovery, and file motions.

(B) *Permitted Contents*. The scheduling order may:

(iv) include any agreements the parties reach for asserting claims of privilege or of protection as trial-preparation material after information is produced…

In theory, with a claw-back, or **non-waiver agreement** between counsel as it is also called, if privileged or confidential material is inadvertently disclosed, the material may be recovered without waiver of privilege or confidentiality. The use of the claw-back agreement alone does not relieve the attorney of his or her obligations regarding confidential client information. The legal team must still take necessary steps to protect the confidences of clients. The claw- back is only a safety device for inadvertent disclosure after reasonable methods, under the circumstance, have been used to otherwise protect and preserve confidential material.

non-waiver agreement
An agreement between counsel that any privileged or confidential information inadvertently submitted does not lose its status as privileged or confidential. Also called a claw back clause. Agreement may be included in courts discover order.

To address the issue at the federal level, Congress passed an amendment to the Federal Rules of Evidence that was signed into law by the president on September 19, 2008. The new rule, Federal Rules of Evidence Rule 502, Attorney-Client Privilege and Work Product; Limitations on Waiver, has provided a framework but not a total solution, as lawyers challenge provisions and courts interpret this new rule.

INADVERTENT DISCLOSURE OF CONFIDENTIAL OR PRIVILEGED MATERIALS

LEARNING OBJECTIVE 7
Describe the scope of the potential solutions for inadvertent disclosure of confidential, privileged, or work product material under the federal rules.

When vast numbers of electronic files are part of the discovery process, it is not always possible, within the time limits and cost constraints imposed by clients, to check every document manually to be sure it does not contain privileged, confidential, or work product material before handing it over to opposing counsel. The lack of uniformity in application of rules by the courts with regard to the inadvertent disclosure resulted in the passage by Congress of the amendment to the Federal Rules of Evidence addressing the issue of the inadvertent disclosure. Congress passed, and the president signed, the law in 2008, adding Rule 502 to the Federal Rules of Evidence.

The adoption of Rule 502 was thought to bring uniformity to the issue of inadvertent disclosure. However, as with most laws and rules of court, it is now being challenged and tested by lawyers unsatisfied with the court's application of this rule to their particular case. The litigation bar has increasingly been incorporating

IN THE WORDS OF THE COURT...

Victor Stanley, Inc., Plaintiff v. Creative Pipe, Inc., et al., Defendant
CIVIL ACTION NO. MJG-06-2662
UNITED STATES DISTRICT COURT FOR THE DISTRICT OF MARYLAND
2008 U.S. Dist. LEXIS 42025
May 29, 2008, Decided

...the Defendants initially sought to enter a non-waiver agreement such as discussed in *Hopson,* but then abandoned this effort. Should the issue of privilege waiver by inadvertent production of voluminous ESI be considered by the Fourth Circuit at some time in the future, it may be hoped that the court will be cognizant of the unique problems presented with regard to avoiding privilege waiver presented by ESI discovery, as well as the fact that the approval of Proposed Evidence Rule 502 by the Committee on the Rules of Evidence, as well as the Judicial Conference, recognizes a need to provide relief in this difficult area. The substantive law of privilege is not rigid and inflexible, *Hopson,* 232 F.R.D. at 240 (citing *Jaffee v. Redmond,* 518 U.S. 1, 8, 116 S. Ct. 1923, 135 L. Ed. 2d 337 (1996)), [*23] but is governed by principles of the common law as interpreted "by the courts of the United States in the light of reason and experience." *Fed. R. Evid. 501.* Experience has now shown that ESI discovery presents unique, heretofore unrecognized, risks of waiver of privilege or work-product protection even when the party asserting the privilege or protection has exercised care not to waive it. The approval of Proposed Evidence Rule 502 by the Judicial Conference, is a reasoned response to this new experience, but still pending in Congress. For those courts that have yet to decide which approach to follow regarding the inadvertent disclosure of privileged material during ESI discovery, the commentary to the proposed rule is worthy of consideration.

...As noted in *Continental Casualty Co. v. Under Armour, Inc.,* 537 F. Supp. 2d 761 (D. Md. 2008), if documents qualify as both attorney-client privileged and work-product protected, separate analysis is required to determine whether inadvertent production constitutes waiver. However, the majority view is that disclosure of work-product material in a manner that creates a substantial risk that an adversary will receive it waives the protection. *Id. at 772-73* [*24] (citing *Restatement (Third) of the Law Governing Lawyers § 91* (2000)). In this case, Defendants' voluntary, though inadvertent, production of the 165 documents directly to counsel for the Plaintiff waived any work-product protection they may have had. *Id....*

the provisions and the philosophy of the new rule within its suggested language so that it will be included in the court's scheduling order.

FRE Rule 502. Attorney-Client Privilege and Work Product; Limitations on Waiver

(a) Scope of waiver.

In federal proceedings, the waiver by disclosure of an attorney-client privilege or work product protection extends to an undisclosed communication or information concerning the same subject matter only if that undisclosed communication or information ought in fairness to be considered with the disclosed communication or information.

(b) Inadvertent disclosure.

A disclosure of a communication or information covered by the attorney-client privilege or work product protection does not operate as a waiver in a state or federal proceeding if the disclosure is inadvertent and is made in connection with federal litigation or federal administrative proceedings—and if the holder of the privilege or work product protection took reasonable precautions to prevent disclosure and took reasonably prompt measures, once the holder knew or should have known of the disclosure, to rectify the error, including (if applicable) following the procedures in Fed. R. Civ. P. 26(b)(5)(B).

(c) Selective waiver.
In a federal or state proceeding, a disclosure of a communication or information covered by the attorney-client privilege or work product protection—when made to a federal public office or agency in the exercise of its regulatory, investigative, or enforcement authority—does not operate as a waiver of the privilege or protection in favor of non-governmental persons or entities. The effect of disclosure to a state or local government agency, with respect to non-governmental persons or entities, is governed by applicable state law. Nothing in this rule limits or expands the authority of a government agency to disclose communications or information to other government agencies or as otherwise authorized or required by law.

(d) Controlling effect of court orders.
A federal court order that the attorney-client privilege or work product protection is not waived as a result of disclosure in connection with the litigation pending before the court governs all persons or entities in all state or federal proceedings, whether or not they were parties to the matter before the court, if the order incorporates the agreement of the parties before the court.

(e) Controlling effect of party agreements.
An agreement on the effect of disclosure of a communication or information covered by the attorney-client privilege or work product protection is binding on the parties to the agreement, but not on other parties unless the agreement is incorporated into a court order.

(f) Included privilege and protection.
As used in this rule:
(1) "attorney-client privilege" means the protection provided for confidential attorney-client communications, under applicable law; and
(2) "work product protection" means the protection for materials prepared in anticipation of litigation or for trial, under applicable law.

Privilege in Electronic Discovery

Withholding the document claimed to be a privileged document sounds like a simple matter of not giving it to anyone. With paper documents, this may be true. However, in the age of electronics it is easy to accidentally send a privileged document by email or fax just by pushing the wrong speed dial or address book entry. With vast quantities of data transferred electronically, the matter becomes even more complicated. Which of the thousands of potential documents is privileged?

Claim of Privilege

Privilege is not automatically invoked. The person claiming the privilege—usually the client—has the burden to establish its existence, called **claim of privilege.**

claim of privilege
The person claiming the privilege–usually the client–has the burden to establish its existence.

> "To sustain a claim of privilege, the party invoking it must demonstrate that the information at issue was a communication between client and counsel or his employee, that it was intended to be and was in fact kept confidential, and that it was made in order to assist in obtaining or providing legal advice or services to the client."
>
> *SR International Bus. Ins. Co v. World Trade Center* Prop No 01 Civ 9291 (S.D.N.Y. 2002), quoting *Bowne of New York City, Inc v. Ambase Corp.*

To claim documents as privileged requires the submission of a **privilege log** identifying the item and the reason for the privilege as shown in Exhibit 4.8.

privilege log
A list of documents claimed by the submitting party to contain material subject to privilege or work product exclusion.

Exhibit 4.8 CaseMap privilege log

Case: Phillip Hawkins v. Anstar Biotech Industries **Created: 12/23/10 1:55:40 PM**

BATES - BEGIN	DATE	TYPE	AUTHOR(S)	RECIPIENT(S)	DESCRIPTION	PRIVILEGE
P001267	09/27/05	Letter	William Lang	Carol Sanders	Redacted. Letter from William Lang to his employment counsel re RIF preparations.	Atty-Client
P002019	04/19/05 6:01:01 p.m.	E-mail	Philip Hawkins	Gregory Poole	Philip Hawkins contacts attorney Gregory Poole regarding his situation re Anstar Biotech Industries and his feelings that he was fired due to his age, not his job performance.	Atty-Client
P002020	04/19/05 6:30:01 p.m.	E-mail	Philip Hawkins	Gregory Poole	More details in follow-up email from Philip Hawkins to Gregory Poole regarding William Lang and the loss of Philip Hawkins employment.	Atty-Client
P002021	04/20/05	Letter	Gregory Poole	Philip Hawkins	Letter from Gregory Poole to Philip Hawkins with general advice re discrimination and specific advice re contact with William Lang and other staff at Anstar Biotech Industries.	Atty Work Product
P002022	04/20/05	E-mail	Gregory Poole	Philip Hawkins	Email advising Philip Hawkins that letter from Gregory Poole has been mailed via regular mail.	Atty-Client and Atty Work Product

IN THE WORDS OF THE COURT...

Ruling on Plaintiff's Motion to Compel and Motion for Protective Order

Breon v. Coca-Cola Bottling Company of New England, (Conn. 2005)

Civil No. 3:04-CV-00374 (CFD) (TPS).

United States District Court, D. Connecticut.

November 4, 2005

Thomas Smith, Magistrate Judge

...B. Attorney-Client & Work-Product Claims

To protect from abuse, discovery must have limiting principles aside from the low threshold of relevance. One of these principles is that matters are not discoverable, under certain circumstances, if they are privileged. Fed.R.Civ.P. *26*(b)(1). Here, the defendant claims that a number of requests for production are inappropriate because they ask for information protected by either the attorney-client privilege or work-product doctrine.

The attorney-client privilege prevents disclosure of a communication from a client to a lawyer, where that communication relates to a fact of which the attorney was informed (a) by his client (b) without the presence of strangers (c) for the purpose of securing primarily either (i) an opinion on the law or (ii) legal services or (iii) assistance in some legal proceeding, and not (d) for the purpose of committing a crime or tort; and (4) the privilege has been (a) claimed and (b) not waived by the client. *United States v. United Shoe Machinery Corp.,* 89 F.Supp. 357, 358 (D. Mass. 1950); *Colton v. United States,* 306 F.2d 633, 637 (2d Cir. 1962). The rationale behind the privilege is to foster open and honest communication between a client and his lawyer. *United States v. Schwimmer,* 892 F.2d 237, 443 (2d Cir. 1989). Because of this underlying rationale, communication running from the lawyer to the client is not protected unless it reveals what the client has said. *SCM Corp. v. Xerox Corp.,* 70 F.R.D. 508, 522 (D. Conn. 1976); *Clute v. Davenport Co.,* 118 F.R.D 312, 314 (D. Conn. 1988).

Completely distinct from the attorney-client privilege is the work-product doctrine. The work-product doctrine, as codified in the Federal Rules[,] states: a party may obtain discovery of documents and tangible things otherwise discoverable...and prepared in anticipation of litigation or for trial by or for another party or by or for that other party's representative (including the other party's attorney, consultant, surety, indemnitor, insurer, or agent) only upon a showing that the party seeking discovery has substantial need of the materials in the preparation of the party's case and that the party is unable without undue hardship to obtain the substantial equivalent of the materials by other means.

Fed.R.Civ.P. *26*(b)(3). "The work-product doctrine...is intended to preserve a zone of privacy in which a lawyer can prepare and develop legal theories and strategy with an eye toward litigation, free from unnecessary intrusion by his adversaries." *United States v. Adlman,* 134 F.3d 1194, 1196 (2d. Cir. 1998) (internal quotations omitted). As the rule itself makes clear, work-product enjoys only limited immunity from discovery. For "fact" work-product, that is[,] work-product that does not contain legal opinions or conclusions, the party seeking discovery must meet the "substantial burden" and "undue hardship" tests outlined in Rule 26. *Maloney v. Sisters of Charity Hosp.,* 165 F.R.D. 26, 30 (W.D.N.Y. 1995). Opinion work product, on the other hand, constitutes thoughts, strategies, legal opinions and conclusions by an attorney. *See Loftis v. Amica Mut. Ins. Co.,* 175 F.R.D. 5, 11 (D. Conn. 1997). Opinion work-product is given stronger protection and only discoverable in rare circumstances where the party seeking discovery can show extraordinary justification. *Id.; S.N. Phelps & Co. v. Circle K. Corp.,* 1997 U.S. Dist. LEXIS 713, No. 96 CV 5801 (JFK), 1997 WL 31197, at *7 (S.D.N.Y. 1997).

Under both the attorney-client privilege and work-product doctrine the party asserting the claim has the initial burden of showing it applies. *See Cornelius v. Consolidated Rail Corp.,* 169 F.R.D. 250, 253 (N.D.N.Y. 1996) (party claiming work-product protection must show three elements, "[f]irst, the material must be a document or tangible thing. Second, it must have been prepared in anticipation of litigation. Third, it must have been prepared by or for a party or its representative."); *In re Horowitz,* 482 F.2d 72, 82 (2d Cir.), *cert denied,* 414 U.S. 867 (1973) ("the person claiming the attorney-client privilege has the burden of establishing all essential elements").

To assist the court and counsel, both Federal and Local Rules require that the party asserting a privilege provide the court with a privilege log. Fed.R.Civ.P. *26*(B)(5); D. Conn. L.Civ. R. 37(a)(1) When a party withholds information otherwise discoverable under these rules by claiming that it is privileged or subject to protection as trial preparation material, the party shall make the claim expressly and shall describe the nature of the documents, communications, or things not produced or disclosed in a manner that, without revealing information itself privileged or protected, will enable other parties to assess the applicability of the privilege or protection.

Fed.R.Civ.Pro. *26*(B)(5). A party seeking to avoid discovery cannot hide behind bald statements of "privilege" and "work-product" and expect the court to supply the rational to support the claims. *See Obiajulu v. City of Rochester Dep't of Law,* 166 F.R.D. 293, 295 (W.D.N.Y. 1996). At the very least, the log should identify each document's author and recipient, as well as reasons why the information is claimed to be privileged. *See United States v. Construction Prod. Research,* 73 F.3d 464, 473 (2d Cir. 1996). The privilege log is not simply a technicality, it is an essential tool which allows the parties and the court to make an intelligent decision as to whether a privilege or immunity exists. *See Bowne v. Ambase,* 150 F.R.D. 465, 474 (S.D.N.Y. 1993). Preparation of a privilege log is a critical step in discharging one's burden of establishing the existence of a privilege.

ADVICE FROM THE FIELD

SAILING ON CONFUSED SEAS

Privilege Waiver and the New Federal Rules of Civil Procedure

John M. Facciola*

VII. THE FUTURE

Lawyers and judges face a difficult future in dealing with privileged information stored in a computer's memory. As server space increases and the cost of memory decreases, the tendency of computer users to save everything and organize none of it will increase. As noted earlier, the new Federal Rules justify extremely limited relief in one situation, the "claw back," and leave other solutions, including "sneaking a peek" or agreements as to waiver, where it found them. Furthermore, waiver agreements cannot bind the rights of strangers to the litigation and, therefore, are full of peril where third-person litigation against one of the parties to the agreement is even a remote possibility. Indeed, the Tenth Circuit recently rejected a claim that disclosure to a government agency of computer information, pursuant to a confidentiality agreement, was not a waiver of the privilege as to third parties. That result is sobering not only for its rejection of any notion of the legitimacy of any kind of "selective waiver," but also for its insistence that the attorney-client privilege not be extended an inch further than necessary to accomplish its purposes and its niggardly reading of the circumstances under which waiving it can be avoided. Thus, it can be said that, without the dramatic intervention of a new rule adopted by Congress providing that disclosure pursuant to court-ordered agreements is not a waiver, lawyers will have to confront the reality that their clients either (1) authorize what may be a king's ransom to do a full-scale privilege review or (2) permit them to enter into an agreement that eliminates the need for such a detailed review and take the risk that the agreement will not prevent a third party from seeing privileged information.

Perhaps an answer may lie in the technology. Word processing is now dominated by two companies and one wonders why they have not sought to market a program that would prevent a user from saving a document unless the user indicated that it was privileged. Electronic marking of such documents and their segregation into a privileged file would, at least, narrow what must be reviewed.

Absent the technology, one wonders when American corporations will adopt records retention policies that are reasonable, applicable without exception in all departments, and enforced by a corporate manager with real power to discipline those employees who refuse to follow them. It is hard to imagine a greater waste of money than paying a lawyer $250 an hour to look at recipes, notices of the holiday party, and NCAA Final Four pool entries while doing a privilege review. A company that permits that situation to occur is wasting its shareholders' money as surely as if it were burning it in the parking lot.

In the meantime, the staggering costs of a privilege review will grow, driving the costs of litigation ever upward and probably increasing the tendency of parties to avoid the federal courts for other fora to resolve their disputes. One thing is certain: without relief from somewhere, that associate will never sail on the Chesapeake Bay.

About the Author: *John M. Facciola, is a United States Magistrate Judge in the United States District Court for the District of Columbia in re *Qwest Comm. Int'l, Inc.*, 450 F.3d 1179 (10th Cir. 2006).

Source: Federal Courts Law Review September 2006. Copyright © *The Federal Courts Law Review*.

CONCEPT REVIEW AND REINFORCEMENT

KEY TERMS

electronically stored information (ESI) 85
entry of appearance 89
relevant 93
expert witnesses 94
claw-back provision 102
non-waiver agreement 103
claim of privilege 105
privilege log 105

CHAPTER SUMMARY

Introduction to the Law of E-Discovery	The law of discovery has not changed with the adoption of electronically stored information; only the methods used to attain the information have changed.

Amendments to the Federal Rules of Civil Procedure	Effective December 2006 and since amended in 2007 are six new rules and one new form or attitude toward the Federal Rules of Civil Procedure used to address the issues of electronic discovery, including: Rule 16 Pretrial Conferences; Scheduling; Management Rule 26 General Provisions Governing Discovery; Duty of Disclosure Rule 33 Interrogatories to Parties Rule 34 Productions of Documents, Electronically Stored Information, and Things and Entry Upon Land for Inspection and Other Purposes Rule 37 Failure to Make Disclosures or Cooperate in Discovery; Sanctions Rule 45 Subpoena Form 35 Report of Parties' Planning Meeting
Procedures and Time Lines in Discovery	The federal rules provide a timeline and a set of obligations including an initial conference between counsel and a report to the court in a meeting with the trial judge.
Discovery Timing	The scheduling conference occurs within 90 days after the entry of appearance or 120 days after the defendant has been served with the complaint. Counsel must meet at least 21 days before the scheduling conference with the judge and submit a report to the court within 14 days.
Meet and Confer Issues	A primary purpose of the meet and confer is to develop a discovery plan.
Scope of Discovery	Under the federal rules, everything is discoverable that is not privileged and that is or may lead to relevant evidence.
Mandatory Disclosure Requirements	Federal Rule 26(a) makes disclosure of certain information mandatory.
Information Subject to Mandatory Disclosure	Disclosures include identity of witnesses, copies of documents, computation of damages, and copies of insurance policies.
Experts and Witnesses	The names of expert witnesses expected to be called, together with their qualifications, lists of publications, statements of compensation, and cases on which they have testified, must be provided to the opposing counsel.
Production of Documents or Things	Production of documents is by written request addressed to a party to litigation. When things are not capable of delivery, such as a building or other large object, discovery rules provide a right to enter onto the land of another for purposes of inspection.
Compliance and Court Intervention	Under ethical guidelines and court rules, the discovery process is supposed to be conducted in a cooperative fashion without court intervention. Courts are reluctant to intervene in the discovery process and look to the litigation teams to resolve the issues among themselves.
Seeking Compliance	Each side may seek court intervention when necessary to attain information or to protect information.
Protecting Confidential or Privileged Materials	According to Rule 1.6 of the model rules of professional conduct, an attorney has an ethical obligation to preserve the confidences of clients. Under Rule 26 of the Federal Rules of Civil Procedure, parties may withhold such information by expressly making the claim and describing the nature of the documents, or things not produced or disclosed in such a way as to enable the opposing party to understand the claim made.

Counsel may seek to protect inadvertently disclosed information by agreement in a "claw-back provision" under Rule 16, which permits agreements by the parties for asserting claims of privilege or protection as trial preparation material is produced. These agreements may be included in the requested court scheduling order.

REVIEW QUESTIONS AND EXERCISES

1. What is the purpose of discovery?
2. How has the production of electronically stored information changed the discovery process?
3. List some of the sources of potential evidence maintained in electronic format.
4. What is the duty of disclosure of electronically stored information?
5. Is there a penalty for the innocent destruction of information during a routine operation of an electronic information system?
6. For purposes of discovery, what is considered to be relevant?
7. Is all relevant information admissible in trial?
8. What provisions exist for discovery of information that cannot be delivered in paper or electronic form?
9. Within what time frame must the initial meeting of counsel of be, under the federal rules?
10. When should the initial scheduling conference with the judge occur, under the federal rules?
11. What is included in a discovery plan?
12. How is a meet and confer in a case involving electronically stored information different from one involving only paper documents?
13. How have the mandatory disclosure rules changed the rules for discovery?
14. What information must be disclosed regarding potential expert witnesses?
15. What are the general limitations on discovery imposed by the federal rules?
16. Which of the model rules of professional conduct impact discovery?
17. What is the procedure for obtaining information that the other side refuses to produce?
18. What is the obligation of the litigation team to protect the confidences of clients?
19. What is the procedure for claiming the privilege of protecting trial preparation materials under the federal rules?
20. What is meant by a claw-back clause? What provisions can be made to obtain court sanctions for the language of a claw-back clause?

BUILDING YOUR PARALEGAL SKILLS

INTERNET AND TECHNOLOGY EXERCISES

1. Locate and save as a favorite or bookmark an electronic version of the Federal Rules of Civil Procedure and the Federal Rules of Evidence.
2. Locate and save as a favorite or bookmark an electronic version of your local rules of procedure and evidence.

CIVIL LITIGATION VIDEO CASE STUDIES

Conference with Judge: Discovery Issue Resolution

Opposing counsel meet with the judge in his chambers prior to the start of trial. The judge reviews the strengths and weaknesses of each side in an attempt to facilitate settlement of the case prior to trial.

After viewing the video in MyLegalStudiesKit, answer the following questions.

1. What is the purpose of the scheduling conference?
2. In federal court, what must be done before the scheduling conference?

Videotape of Expert Witness

An expert witness's deposition is videotaped for use at trial.

After viewing the video in MyLegalStudiesKit, answer the following questions.

1. Was the witness properly qualified?
2. What are the pros and cons of using the videotape of the expert in the trial?
3. What is required by the federal rules before an expert may be deposed?

Fact or Expert: Resolving Objection in Videotaped Deposition

The attorneys appear before the trial judge in chambers to resolve the objections that were made during the videotaped deposition of a treating physician who is also offered as an expert witness.

After viewing the video in MyLegalStudiesKit, answer the following questions.

1. What is required to qualify a person as an expert witness?
2. What is the difference between the witness acting as a treating physician and as a medical expert?

CHAPTER OPENING SCENARIO CASE STUDY

Use the Opening Scenario for this chapter to answer the following questions.

1. What policies or procedures should a litigation firm with practices in multiple jurisdictions have in place?
2. Is it necessary for the litigation support staff to be kept current on the local practices and procedures in the various courts?

COMPREHENSIVE CASE STUDY

SCHOOL BUS–TRUCK ACCIDENT CASE

– After viewing the video Attorney Meet and Confer in MyLegalStudiesKit, prepare the Report of the Parties' Planning Meeting using Form 35 for submission to the court.

BUILDING YOUR PROFESSIONAL PORTFOLIO

CIVIL LITIGATION TEAM AT WORK

Policy

Prepare a policy for when an information or technology expert should attend the attorneys' meet and confer conference.

Forms

1. Prepare a checklist for use in a meet and confer conference that involves electronic word information.
2. Prepare a Motion to Compel discovery.
3. Prepare a Motion for a Protective Order in discovery.
4. Download copies of the Federal Rules Forms on a storage device in both WordPerfect and Word formats for future use.

Procedures

1. List the procedural steps and requirements to obtain a Motion to Compel in your state and federal jurisdictions.
2. List the procedural steps and requirements to obtain a Protective Order in discovery in your state and federal jurisdictions.

"The litigants and their lawyers are supposed to want justice, but in reality there is no such thing as justice, either in or out of court. In fact, the word cannot be defined. So, for lack of proof, let us assume that the word "justice" has a meaning, and that the common idea of the definition is correct, without even seeking to find out what is the common meaning. Then how do we reach justice through the courts? The lawyer's idea of justice is a verdict for his client, and really this is the sole end for which he aims."

—Clarence Darrow

Evolving Issues in E-Discovery

CHAPTER 5

OPENING SCENARIO

Owen Mason, Ariel Marshall and Ethan Benjamin were having their monthly face-to-face, partners-only lunch meeting. These sessions allowed the partners to discuss things with each other that they might not want to discuss in the weekly firm meetings. The first item on everyone's mind was the issue of practice in multiple jurisdictions. Ariel asked her partners whether they saw any ethical issues in their staff working on cases in a jurisdiction for the first time. Ethan pointed out that it is not much different than each of them keeping current in the courts to which they had been admitted to practice as lawyers. They each took continuing legal education courses and discussed whether the support staff should be required to attend with them.

Ethan then mentioned that he felt the same uncertainty that members of the support staff had expressed about the appropriate policies and procedures to follow regarding electronically stored information. He expressed his feeling that the rules and procedures on electronic discovery in federal courts were only slowly becoming clarified, with the state courts in many situations looking to the federal rules as the basis for their own rules and decisions. Ariel reminded Ethan that ultimately, it was their own responsibility, and that as lawyers, they all needed to supervise the staff more closely to avoid any problems.

Owen summed up their general concern by saying that in many areas of practice, there is no certainty, only guiding principles like those advising clients on document management, where it is a question of what comes first: the obligation to save information or the institution of suit. Ethan echoed the feeling with the comment, "What came first, the chicken or the egg?" Everyone agreed that

LEARNING OBJECTIVES

After studying this chapter, you should be able to:

1. Explain the purpose of a litigation hold and the duty to preserve evidence.
2. Define spoliation.
3. Describe the potential sanctions for spoliation of evidence.

VIDEO INTRODUCTION

An introduction to litigation support in the law office.

After watching the video in MyLegalStudiesKit, answer the following question.

- Why is technology important in the contemporary litigation case?

the new rules had not solved all the issues; that everyone on the team needed to keep current on trends and decisions; and that it was the partners' responsibility to be more vigilant in checking the rules and case law in each jurisdiction since there did not seem to be any consistent view. They also agreed that they would need to include this topic at the regular staff meetings to be sure the staff was kept current on rules and court decisions.

INTRODUCTION TO THE EVOLVING ISSUES IN E-DISCOVERY

There are no absolute answers in the area of electronic discovery. The law is still evolving, with each jurisdiction applying the rules at it sees necessary to promote justice. Decisions on similar fact patterns vary widely from jurisdiction to jurisdiction. It is thus essential that the litigation team carefully monitor the changes in the law, the rules of civil procedure, the rules of evidence, and the case law interpreting them in each jurisdiction in which the team practices. It is also important to monitor the leading cases from other jurisdictions that may be persuasive to a local court, even if the local case law may not currently support that position.

There are some cases that are looked at for guidance more than others; that is, some judges are read more often than others. Among the most widely read cases are those of Judge Shira Scheindlin, who wrote the opinions in the widely reported *Zubulake* case.

OPINIONS IN *ZUBULAKE*

Zubulake I	May 13, 2003 217 F.R.D. 309
Zubulake II	May 13, 2003 230 F.R.D. 290
Zubulake III	July 24, 2003 216 F.R.D. 280
Zubulake IV	October 22, 2003 220 F.R.D. 212
Zubulake V	July 20, 2004 229 F.R.D. 422
Zubulake VI	February 2, 2005
Zubulake VII	March 6, 2005

These opinions were written before the 2006 adoption of the amended Federal Rules of Civil Procedure on electronic discovery. This group of opinions is widely quoted as a well-reasoned approach to the issue of electronic discovery.

What is now informally referred to as the *Pension Committee* case—also widely reported and read—was also written by Judge Scheindlin, who titled the opinion "Zubulake Revisited: Six years later." This case is an update on the issues and potential solutions to many of the problems in electronic discovery practice not solved by the initial rules' adoption. While not everyone agrees with the holding or the proposals, they are carefully looked at for guidance and are considered by many other courts to be persuasive arguments.

The cost of electronic discovery is a concern because it is a potential reason for the decline in actual litigation and the reason for the restriction on access to the courts by those without deep pockets to pay the cost of litigation. It can be expected that the courts will look for methods and procedures to reduce this cost burden by encouraging cooperation amount counsel and imposing standards of proportionality.

The courts and Congress have adopted rules to address some of the issues that the earlier procedural changes did not properly address in the protection of attorney–client privileged materials and work product. With the increased cost of document review to identify and protect privileged material from inadvertent disclosure, each federal and state jurisdiction has had to develop rules on how inadvertently disclosed material should be treated. Congress passed a law adding a new rule to the Federal Rules of Evidence to try to establish a national standard and reduce the costs for document review by avoiding the negative potential for waiver of privilege and confidentiality caused by inadvertent disclosure. As with other areas of the law, there are still challenges to aspects of this law in federal courts in which the law applies and in state courts in which it does not apply, requiring a careful review on a jurisdiction-by-jurisdiction basis.

DISCOVERY OF ELECTRONICALLY STORED INFORMATION

LEARNING OBJECTIVE 1
Explain the purpose of a litigation hold and the duty to preserve evidence.

E-discovery is a term used to describe the process of discovery of documents created, disseminated, and stored via electronic means. Until the adoption of the 2006 Federal Rules of Civil Procedure, lawyers and the courts relied on the traditional Request for Production of Documents to obtain paper copies and electronically stored information. However, electronic data creation and storage has increased the numbers of items created and stored. It has also made the deletion of items easier. The new rules address three specific concerns, namely: (1) preserving electronic materials, (2) producing electronic materials, and (3) destruction of electronic materials.

e-discovery
Discovery of documents created, disseminated, and stored via electronic means.

Lawyers and paralegals are concerned about their responsibilities in dealing with electronically stored information in litigation, in advising clients of their responsibilities in this area, and in the impact of the rules on business practices,

VIDEO ADVICE FROM THE FIELD

Jennifer McCoy–National Litigation Service Coordinator

A discussion of the roles of litigation support l, paralegals and information technologist.

After watching the video in MyLegalStudiesKit, answer the following questions.

1. What is the role of litigation support?
2. How does the role of the paralegal differ from that of litigation support?
3. What is the difference between litigation support and information technology?

retention policy
A formal process for retaining and destroying files and electronically stored information.

like **retention policies** for electronic data. These concerns extend from small-scale litigation involving individual clients who create and maintain documents electronically, which represents the majority of litigation, to complex litigation involving major corporations. For example, in a typical construction case, blueprints and construction documents are being replaced by electronic files created with computer graphics programs and sent electronically to architects, builders, subcontractors, suppliers, and clients. When written documentation in the form of emails and other word processor documents is added, the number and location of individual documents needed in the litigation process may number in the thousands or more. How do the client and the legal team know how long to keep these documents, how do they review documents in response to a request for production, and who bears the cost of retrieval?

Document Management

Lawyers are often asked, "How long do I have to keep records or documents?" and "What happens if I destroy them?" With paper or other physical evidence, the issues frequently are ones of space, with file cabinets or boxes of paper taking up valuable and costly storage space, and the constant concern for the flammability of paper records if not stored in fireproof or sprinklered areas. The electronic era has changed some of these issues. Paper is still important, but electronic documents and emails are becoming more prevalent as the source of business records. With tape and CD storage of electronic documents, thousands of documents can be saved and stored in the space formerly taken up by a few sheets of paper. So the question then becomes, "How long should these be saved?" *Forever* is one answer, but what about an email hidden in the old files that would conclusively impeach or destroy the credibility of a witness or be evidence that conclusively determines an issue—the "smoking gun"? And what are the consequences if the old files are stored on a tape or other storage media for which the original device used to write and read the information is no longer available? For example, in the past some companies used floppy disks to store documents, or other forms of magnetic tape using proprietary tape formats and tape drives to write and read the information. As the technology has improved, some computers no longer have floppy drives. Additionally, older tapes are subject to deterioration, and some of the companies that made the tape drives have gone out of business, rendering the tapes costly to recover and convert to a readable format on more technologically advanced computers.

The answer is somewhere between forever and the practical realities of business economics and the need to preserve documents for potential litigation.

Litigation Hold

At what point should an individual or business save materials about a particular matter? A client that is concerned about a potential lawsuit could easily destroy evidence contained in electronic files, sometimes as easily as pushing the delete key. It is true that paper documents can also be deleted, but usually with more effort and a good paper shredder. The amendments to the rules of civil procedure seem to suggest that once a client has a reasonable belief that litigation may arise from a dispute, a duty arises to preserve all documents related to that dispute, both paper and electronic. The requirement is not that a lawsuit has been filed or a complaint served, only that a reasonable belief exists that litigation may arise. An emerging line of cases suggests that the duty to preserve information arises if the party knows or should have known of the possibility of litigation. Preservation may require placing a matter and all documents related to it on **litigation hold.** This term, or some equivalent, serves as

litigation hold
A process whereby a company or individual determines that an unresolved dispute may result in litigation and as a result, documents should not be destroyed or altered.

a red flag to the company and its employees not to destroy or alter, but instead to save in their present condition, all documents related to the dispute. The individual or a company must cease any activity that will result in the destruction or loss of records when litigation is filed, or when there is a reasonable expectation of litigation.

When litigation is actually commenced, counsel should issue a litigation hold letter to the client. Lawyers have, as expressed in court opinions, an affirmative duty to follow up with the client to ensure that the litigation hold procedures are implemented and followed. This burden applies to both inside counsel and outside counsel.

Duty to Preserve

There is a common law duty to preserve evidence that is well recognized.

> "Case law has developed the rule that when it is reasonably foreseeable that a claim may be asserted, a party must preserve relevant information." *Shamis v. Ambassador Factors Corp.*, 34 F. Supp. 2d 879, 888-889 (S.D.N.Y. 1999); *Wm. T. Thompson Co. v. General Nutrition Corp.*, 593 F. Supp. 1443, 1455 (C.D. Cal. 1984); *Carlucci v. Piper Aircraft Corp.*, 102 F.R.D. 472, 485-86 (S.D. Fla. 1984); *Bowmar Instrument Corp. v. Texas Instruments, Inc.*, 25 Fed. R. Serv. 2d (Callaghan) 423, 427, 1977 U.S. Dist LEXIS 16078, at *11 (N.D. Ind. May 2, 1977);... *Advisory Committee on the Civil Rules of the Committee on Rules of Practice and Procedure of the Judicial Conference of the United States*, 2-1-2001

It is clear that when actual notice of litigation is received, the duty to preserve potential evidence exists. The question for lawyers advising clients is: "When does the duty arise before litigation?" The case law is not consistent, with some cases taking the position that any preliminary activity that may lead to litigation creates the duty. For example, in the *Pension Committee* case, the court found that when two of the numerous (potential at that point) plaintiffs hired counsel for themselves to look into the situation before the entire group of plaintiffs hired common council, the duty arose.

In what appears a contrary view, one district court came to a decision holding that the duty did not arise even though there was a litigation strategy that was part of a licensing strategy. The court further ruled that the routine destruction according to the company document management and destruction policy was not a violation of the duty to preserve. *Rambus, Inc. v. Infineon Technologies*, 222 F.R.D. 280 (ED Va. 2004). In a subsequent suit in front of a different court, *Micron Technology v. Rambus*, 255 F.R.D. 135 (D. Del 2009), the court ruled that Rambus's failure to preserve relevant data from which the court could determine whether its patents were proper was grounds for a sanction declaring Rambus's patent unenforceable against Micron.

With no universal rule, the only clear lesson is that until there is a national standard, the litigation team must be aware of the local court rules and findings. In addition, taking a more conservative approach may be better than taking a liberal one, and what is reasonable under the circumstances may be the best test. If a party has knowledge of a potential for suit or one is reasonably foreseeable, and that potential for suit is known or discovered by the other side, there will be a potential claim for a remedy for the destruction of potential evidence. While the client may win, it is not a certainty, depending as it does on the particular court and that court's review of the facts.

The opinions of Judge Scheindlin in the *Zubulake* and *Pension Committee* cases are among the most read and discussed. These cases are used as the basis for suggested litigation hold letters to clients such as that of the State Bar of Alaska shown in Exhibit 5.1, which includes the language that "it may not be the law in any jurisdiction but is or may be persuasive."

Exhibit 5.1 Alaska Bar sample litigation hold letter

________________________, Esq.

ATTORNEY-CLIENT PRIVILEGED
CONTAINS ATTORNEY WORK PRODUCT

[Title]
[Client Name]
[Client Address]

Re: *Case Caption*
[Court No.]
Our File No.
Litigation Hold re Documents and Electronic Data

Dear ____:

This letter is to provide guidance with respect to the preservation and retention of all documents and electronic information relating in any way to this lawsuit and the allegations init. The recent Federal District Court decision in *Zubulake v. UBS Warburg, LLC,*[1] addressed the issues of evidence preservation with an emphasis on electronically stored information and the duties of the parties and counsel. Although it is a Federal decision from New York, the guidance and standards set out by United States District Judge Scheindlin may be deemed persuasive by our judge and therefore applied to documents, electronically stored information, and other materials that fall within the scope of discovery in this case.[2]

The *Zubulake* standards, in one form or another, are now being followed by other Federal and state courts. *See e.g., Housing Rights Center v. Sterling,* 2005 WL 3320739 at *4-5 (C.D. Cal. 2005) adopting the *Zubulake* standards.[3] This letter is, therefore, written to conform to the guidelines set out by Judge Scheindlin in the *Zubulake* case. Many of the guidelines may not seem to apply in this case, but as counsel retained to represent [Client] it is my duty to make sure that I have done everything possible to ensure the preservation of all evidence. Both Judge Scheindlin in *Zubulake,* and other courts,[4] not only place counsel's discovery duties in the context of the Rules of Civil Procedure, but also in terms of counsel's ethical duties.

Judge Scheindlin summarized what she described as a "litigant's preservation obligations"[5] as follows:

> Once a party reasonably anticipates litigation, it must suspend its routine document retention/destruction policy and put in place a "litigation hold" to ensure the preservation of relevant documents. As a general rule, that litigation hold does not apply to inaccessible back up tapes (e.g. those typically maintained solely for the purpose of disaster recovery), which may continue to be recycled in the schedule set forth in the company's policy. On the other hand, if back up tapes are accessible (i.e. actively used for information retrieval), then such tapes *would* likely be subject to the litigation hold.[6]

Judge Scheindlin's admonition also includes the following guidelines:

> A party's discovery obligations do not end with the implementation of a "litigation hold" – to the contrary, that's only the beginning. Counsel must oversee compliance with the litigation hold, monitoring the party's efforts to retain and produce the relevant documents. Proper communication between a party and her lawyer will ensure (1) that all relevant information (or at least all sources of relevant information) is discovered, (2) that relevant information is retained on a continuing basis, and (3) that relevant nonprivileged material is produced to the opposing party.[7]

In identifying the duties, Judge Scheindlin said that counsel not only has a duty to locate relevant information, but that there is also a continuing duty to "oversee compliance"[8] and ensure preservation. In accordance with these duties, counsel must make certain that all sources of potential, relevant information are identified and placed on hold. According to Judge Scheindlin:

> To do this, counsel must become fully familiar with the client's data retention architecture. This will invariably involve speaking with information technology personnel, who can explain the system-wide back up procedures and the actual implementation of the firm's recycling policy. It will also involve communicating with the "key players" in the litigation in order to understand how they stored information.[9]

Judge Scheindlin observed that if it is not possible for there to be actual verbal contact with the key players, other methods should be implemented to accomplish the same goal and that once all potential relevant information has been identified, there is a duty to retain that information and to produce it in response to an opposing party's discovery request. In addition, there is always a continuing duty to supplement discovery responses.

Accordingly, at a minimum, the following steps should be taken:[10]

1. All destruction of documents of any type, including electronic information, pertaining in any way to this matter must immediately stop, even if your document retention policy would otherwise call for routine destruction. All such documents and electronic information must be retained.

2. I need to have you identify for me the "key players" relating to your document retention and destruction policies, the creation, storage, and retention of electronic information, and your primary IT people.

3. Ideally, in keeping with the Zubulake guidelines, I should meet or confer with each such person to be fully briefed by them regarding document retention and destruction policies so that I am fully familiar with them and can effectuate my duty to insure proper retention and proper disclosure, as well as my continuing duty to monitor the litigation hold that has been placed on all such information. We can, however, discuss other ways that will provide the same level of assurance.

I presume that the manner in which [Client] normally operates diminishes the risk of improper document destruction and, therefore, the matters set out in this letter may appear unnecessary or "overkill." However, the rapidly developing doctrine of spoliation, which includes the negligent or intentional destruction of evidence, is being used by opposing counsel with greater frequency and with increasing success. Furthermore, opposing counsel are increasingly making discovery requests that attempt to "set up" companies for spoliation claims. It is this type of situation that can result in devastating consequences, including sanctions imposed upon the offending company, personnel within the company, and counsel. In addition, the courts have other mechanisms to punish for spoliation, including the striking of certain defenses and/or a jury instruction that the documents and evidence that were destroyed should be presumed to have been harmful to the party that destroyed them. These risks can be avoided or minimized if we work together to ensure the retention and preservation of documents and electronic information.

If you have any questions, please advise.

Very truly yours,

[1] 2004 WL 1620866 (S.D.N.Y. 2004).
[2] Alaska has recognized a remedy for spoliation of evidence. "In tort law when a party has destroyed records, it is sometimes appropriate to employ a rebuttable presumption that the records would have established facts unfavorable to the party who destroyed the documents." *Starek v. Kenai Peninsula Borough,* 81 P.3d 268, 272 (Alaska 2003), citing *Sweet v. Sisters of Providence in Washington,* 895 P.2d 484, 492 (Alaska 1995).
[3] *Zubulake,* 2004 WL 1620866 at *2 (S.D.N.Y. 2004) (recognizing counsel's "common law duty to preserve relevant evidence…"). See also A.B.A. Civil Discovery Standards, Standard 10 Preservation of Documents (August 1999). *See also* Devin K. Isom, *Electronic Discovery Primer for Judges,* 2005 Fed.Cts.L.Rev.1 (2005).
[4] *Metropolitan Opera Association, Inc. v. Local 100, Hotel Employees and Rest. Employee Int'l Union,* 212 F.R.D. 178 (S.D.N.Y. 2003), prior opinion adhered to on reconsideration as clarified, 2004 WL 1943099 (S.D.N.Y. 2004).
[5] *Zubulake,* 2004 WL 1620866 at *7.
[6] *Id.* citing *Zubulake v. UBS Warburg, LLC,* 220 F.R.D. 212, 218 (S.D.N.Y. 2003).
[7] *Zubulake,* 2004 WL 1620866 at *7.
[8] *Id.*
[9] *Id.* at *8.
[10] Id. at *7.

IN THE WORDS OF THE COURT . . .

Rimkus Consulting Group, Inc., Plaintiff,
v. Nickie G. Cammarata, et al., Defendants.

CIVIL ACTION NO. H-07-0405

UNITED STATES DISTRICT COURT FOR THE SOUTHERN DISTRICT OF TEXAS, HOUSTON DIVISION

2010 U.S. Dist. LEXIS 14573

February 19, 2010, Decided

February 19, 2010, Filed

OPINION BY: Lee H. Rosenthal
OPINION
MEMORANDUM AND OPINION

…

B. When Deletion Can Become Spoliation

Spoliation is the destruction or the significant and meaningful alteration of evidence. *See generally* The Sedona Conference, The Sedona Conference

(continued)

WEB RESOURCES

Alaska Ethics Rules

Contrast and compare the **Alaska Rules of Professional Conduct at** http://www.courts.alaska.gov/prof.htm with the American Bar Association Model Rules of Professional Responsibility at http://www.abanet.org/cpr/mrpc/mrpc_toc.html, and the ethical rules in your jurisdiction.

Glossary: E-DISCOVERY & DIGITAL INFORMATION MANAGEMENT (SECOND EDITION) 48 (2007) ("Spoliation is the destruction of records or properties, such as metadata, that may be relevant to ongoing or anticipated litigation, government investigation or audit."). Electronically stored information is routinely deleted or altered and affirmative steps are often required to preserve it. Such deletions, alterations, and losses cannot be spoliation unless there is a duty to preserve the information, a culpable breach of that duty, and resulting prejudice.

Generally, the duty to preserve arises when a party "has notice that the evidence is relevant to litigation or … should have known that the evidence may be relevant to future litigation." Generally, the duty to preserve extends to documents or tangible things (defined by Federal Rule of Civil Procedure 34) by or to individuals "likely to have discoverable information that the disclosing party may use to support its claims or defenses." *See, e.g., Zubulake IV*, 220 F.R.D. at 217–18.

These general rules are not controversial. But applying them to determine when a duty to preserve arises in a particular case and the extent of that duty requires careful analysis of the specific facts and circumstances. It can be difficult to draw bright-line distinctions between acceptable and unacceptable conduct in preserving information and in conducting discovery, either prospectively or with the benefit (and distortion) of hindsight. Whether preservation or discovery conduct is acceptable in a case depends on what is *reasonable*, and that in turn depends on whether what was done–or not done–was *proportional* to that case and consistent with clearly established applicable standards.[8] As Judge Scheindlin pointed out in *Pension Committee*, that analysis depends heavily on the facts and circumstances of each case and cannot be reduced to a generalized checklist of what is acceptable or unacceptable.[9]…

[8] *See* THE SEDONA PRINCIPLES: SECOND EDITION, BEST PRACTICES RECOMMENDATIONS & PRINCIPLES FOR ADDRESSING ELECTRONIC DOCUMENT PRODUCTION 17 cmt. 2.b. (2007) ("Electronic discovery burdens should be proportional to the amount in controversy and the nature of the case. Otherwise, transaction costs due to electronic discovery will overwhelm the ability to resolve disputes fairly in litigation.").

[9] *Pension Comm. of the Univ. of Montreal Pension Plan v. Banc of Am. Sec., LLC*, No. 05 Civ. 9016, 2010 WL 184312, at *3 (S.D.N.Y. Jan. 15, 2010). For example, the reasonableness of discovery burdens in a $550 million case arising out of the liquidation of hedge funds, as in *Pension Committee*, will be different than the reasonableness of discovery burdens in a suit to enforce noncompetition agreements and related issues, as in the present case.

SPOLIATION

Destruction of Electronic Records

LEARNING OBJECTIVE 2
Define spoliation.

spoliation
Destruction of records that may be relevant to ongoing or anticipated litigation, government investigation, or audit. Courts differ in their interpretation of the level of intent required before sanctions may be warranted.

Many court opinions have addressed the issue of spoliation of evidence. **Spoliation** is

> "the destruction or significant alteration of evidence or the failure to preserve property for another's use as evidence in pending or reasonably foreseeable litigation"
>
> *West v. Goodyear Tire & Rubber Co.*, 167 F.3d 776, 779 (2d Cir. 1999).

It may be the destruction of physical evidence such as the disposal, crushing, or other destruction of a motor vehicle showing evidence of the cause of an accident. It may be the shredding or burning of a letter or handwritten note confirming the existence of a promise or other obligation. In the electronic world, it may be the deleting of electronically stored documents on a computer or the erasing of the backup tapes containing critical emails and documents.

As stated by Judge Rothenthal in the *Rimkus* case:

> Spoliation of evidence—particularly of electronically stored information—has assumed a level of importance in litigation that raises grave concerns. Spoliation allegations and sanctions motions distract from the merits of a case, add costs to discovery, and delay resolution. The frequency of spoliation allegations may lead to decisions about preservation based more on fear of potential future sanctions than on reasonable need for information. Much of the recent case law on sanctions for spoliation has focused on failures by litigants and their lawyers to take adequate steps to preserve and collect information in discovery.

IN THE WORDS OF THE COURT . . .

Pension Committee of the University of Montreal Pension Plan, et al
Against
Banc of America Securities, LLC, et al
05 Civ 9016 (SAS) January 11, 2010
***Zubulake* Revisited: Six Years Later**

Shira A. Scheindlin, U.S.D.J.:

. . . II. AN ANALYTICAL FRAMEWORK AND APPLICABLE LAW

From the outset, it is important to recognize what this case involves and what it does not. This case does not present any egregious examples of litigants purposefully destroying evidence. This is a case where plaintiffs failed to timely institute written litigation holds and engaged in careless and indifferent collection efforts after the duty to preserve arose. As a result, there can be little doubt that some documents were lost or destroyed.

The question, then, is whether plaintiffs' conduct requires this Court to impose a sanction for the spoliation of evidence. To answer this question, there are several concepts that must be carefully reviewed and analyzed. The first is plaintiffs' level of culpability–that is, was their conduct of discovery acceptable or was it negligent, grossly negligent, or willful. The second is the interplay between the duty to preserve evidence and the spoliation of evidence. The third is which party should bear the burden of proving that evidence has been lost or destroyed and the consequences resulting from that loss. And the fourth is the appropriate remedy for the harm caused by the spoliation. . . .

. . . A failure to preserve evidence resulting in the loss or destruction of relevant information is surely negligent, and, depending on the circumstances, may be grossly negligent or willful. For example, the intentional destruction of relevant records, either paper or electronic, after the duty to preserve has attached, is willful. Possibly after October, 2003, when *Zubulake IV* was issued, and definitely after July, 2004, when the final relevant *Zubulake* opinion was issued, the failure to issue a *written* litigation hold constitutes gross negligence because that failure is likely to result in the destruction of relevant information. . . .

. . . The next step in the discovery process is collection and review. Once again, depending on the extent of the failure to collect evidence, or the sloppiness of the review, the resulting loss or destruction of evidence is surely negligent, and, depending on the circumstances may be grossly negligent or willful. For example, the failure to collect records–either paper or electronic–from key players constitutes gross negligence or willfulness as does the destruction of email or backup tapes

(continued)

after the duty to preserve has attached. By contrast, the failure to obtain records from *all* employees (some of whom may have had only a passing encounter with the issues in the litigation), as opposed to key players, likely constitutes negligence as opposed to a higher degree of culpability. Similarly, the failure to take all appropriate measures to preserve ESI likely falls in the negligence category....

...The common law duty to preserve evidence relevant to litigation is well recognized. The case law makes crystal clear that the breach of the duty to preserve, and the resulting spoliation of evidence, may result in the imposition of sanctions by a court because the court has the obligation to ensure that the judicial process is not abused.

It is well established that the duty to preserve evidence arises when a party reasonably anticipates litigation. "[O]nce a party reasonably anticipates litigation, it must suspend its routine document retention/destruction policy and put in place a 'litigation hold' to ensure the preservation of relevant documents." "A plaintiff's duty is more often triggered before litigation commences, in large part because plaintiffs control the timing of litigation...."

c. Burdens of Proof

The third preliminary matter that must be analyzed is what can be done when documents are no longer available. This is not an easy question. It is often impossible to know what lost documents would have contained. At best, their content can be inferred from existing documents or recalled during depositions. But this is not always possible. Who then should bear the burden of establishing the relevance of evidence that can no longer be found? And, an even more difficult question is who should be required to prove that the absence of the missing material has caused prejudice to the innocent party.

The burden of proof question differs depending on the severity of the sanction. For less severe sanctions–such as fines and cost-shifting–the inquiry focuses more on the conduct of the spoliating party than on whether documents were lost, and, if so, whether those documents were relevant and resulted in prejudice to the innocent party..., for more severe sanctions–such as dismissal, preclusion, or the imposition of an adverse inference–the court must consider, in addition to the conduct of the spoliating party, whether any missing evidence was relevant and whether the innocent party has suffered prejudice as a result of the loss of evidence....

In short, the innocent party must prove the following three elements: that the spoliating party (1) had control over the evidence and an obligation to preserve it at the time of destruction or loss; (2) acted with a culpable state of mind upon destroying or losing the evidence; and that (3) the missing evidence is relevant to the innocent party's claim or defense....

SANCTIONS FOR SPOLIATION

LEARNING OBJECTIVE 3
Describe the potential sanctions for spoliation of evidence.

Spoliation of evidence is punishable by court-imposed sanctions against the party who destroyed the evidence. Sanctions may include a negative inference instruction to the jury, advising them of the destruction of documents that they may interpret as being documents that would have been favorable to the other side and negative to the case of the party that destroyed or lost the document. Another sanction may deny the party an opportunity to defend the claims that arise out of the destroyed document. With such serious consequences for destruction of information, the question becomes "Must we save everything?" The legal team working with electronic materials must advise a client to put in place a procedure that will allow the destruction of records without penalty.

Record Retention

A client should have a standard operating procedure for the retention and destruction of records. **Record retention** is the practice of retaining documents for a period of time. Various terms are used to refer to the organized policies of document retention: *information management*, *document management*, or *record management*. What needs to be retained and for how long depends on a number of factors including governmental regulations, the need to defend against potential action, and the reasonable belief in the pendency of litigation. In some professions and businesses, the retention and destruction policies may be dictated by the laws regulating that industry, such as the obligations imposed by securities laws and the federal regulation of the pharmaceutical industry and the health care community. For example, federal regulation under HIPAA (Health Information Portability and Accountability Act) dictates that in a medical practice, all files with no activity for a period of three years be destroyed. Against these issues are balanced the costs of preservation, storage, and potential retrieval.

record retention
Keeping documents and electronically stored information for a period of time.

In a perfect world, clients would have some system in place long before a dispute arises or a lawsuit is filed. Instituting and observing this retention policy demonstrates the good faith and ordinary course of business destruction the court views favorably. Where there is good faith, it is unlikely sanctions will be imposed.

In conjunction with a record retention policy should be a litigation hold policy. The client needs to establish a set of rules for determining which matters may result in litigation and being sure not to destroy those records under the standard retention policy. In a medical practice this might include the records of patients who have complained about their medical treatment or failed to pay their bills. Files that meet either of these criteria would be placed on a litigation hold and not destroyed until some later date, usually after the statute of limitations expires.

Checklist ☑ LITIGATION HOLD

Sedona Guideline 8 explains an organization's need to ensure that legal hold recipients receive "actual, comprehensible and effective notice of the requirement to preserve information." A legal hold is most effective and shows a good faith effort when it:

1. Is issued in writing by a person of authority who commands attention
2. Is worded with appropriate urgency and sensitivity
3. Clearly describes the scope of the hold (e.g., type of content, data repositories, and time frame)
4. Clearly articulates what actions are to be taken (instructions to recipient)
5. Clearly delineates how long the hold remains in effect (and if it is an ongoing duty)
6. Clearly defines any terminology (e.g., "ESI" or "record")
7. Requests acknowledgment (i.e., that the hold has been received is applicable to the recipient, that the recipient understands and agrees to comply with the notice)
8. Requests notification about other employees, departments or systems that may be responsive
9. Includes contact information regarding questions or concerns (now or in the future)
10. Clearly articulates expectations of compliance and the implications of failing to do so

Source: "Ensuring Effective Preservation for e-Discovery–Managing the Legal Hold Process," Fios, Inc. Copyright © 2010 FIOS, Inc. www.fiosinc.com.

Spoliation Remedies

The court has the power to create and impose remedies for spoliation of evidence. The extent of the remedy can vary from monetary penalty to dismissal or adverse instruction to the jury. There is no national standard on the sanctions or on the extent of the conduct that will elicit a sanction. Different jurisdictions and courts may apply different sanctions under what appear to be the same circumstances, thus requiring the litigation team to carefully monitor the individual courts in which they practice.

IN THE WORDS OF THE COURT ...

United States District Court, D. Minnesota.

3M Innovative Properties Company and
3M Company, Plaintiff,
v.
Tomar Electronics, Defendant.

Civil No. 05-756 (MJD/AJB).

Sept. 18, 2006.

MICHAEL J. DAVIS, District Court

...

B. This Court's Authority to Impose Sanctions for Discovery Abuse

The authority of the court to impose sanctions for misconduct committed in the course of discovery arises from two distinct authorities. The Federal Rules of Civil Procedure expressly provides authority for this court to impose sanctions for abuse of the discovery process. *See* Fed.R.Civ.P. 37. The court may impose sanctions when, *inter alia,* a party fails to comply with an order from the court or when a party fails to amend or correct a response to a discovery request. *Id.* The court may also impose sanctions based on its inherent authority to control its own judicial proceedings. *Stevenson v. Union Pac. R.R. Co.,* 354 F.3d 739, 745 (8th Cir.2004) (citing *Chambers v. NASCO, Inc.,* 501 U.S. 32 (1991)); *see also Arctic Cat, Inc. v. Injection Research Specialists, Inc.,* 210 F.R.D. 680, 683 (D.Minn.2002) ("In assessing the need for sanctions, a Federal District Court has the inherent authority, and responsibility, to regulate and supervise the bar practicing before it.").

IN THE WORDS OF THE COURT . . .

Goodman v. Praxair Services, Inc. (**D. Md. 2009**)

632 F. Supp.2d 494

Marc B. Goodman, Plaintiff, v. Praxair Services, Inc., Defendant.

Case No. MJG-04-391.

United States District Court, D. Maryland.

July 7, 2009.

MEMORANDUM OPINION

PAUL W. GRIMM, United States Magistrate Judge.

... The lesson to be learned from the cases that have sought to define when a spoliation motion should be filed in order to be timely is that there is a particular need for these motions to be filed as soon as reasonably possible after discovery of the facts that underlie the motion. This is because resolution of spoliation motions are fact intensive, requiring the court to assess when the duty to preserve commenced, whether the party accused of spoliation properly complied with its preservation duty, the degree of culpability involved, the relevance of the lost evidence to the case, and the concomitant prejudice to the party that was deprived of access to the evidence because it was not preserved. *See, e.g., Silvestri,* 273 F.3d at 594–95. Before ruling on a spoliation motion, a court may have to hold a hearing, and if spoliation is found, consideration of an appropriate remedy can involve determinations that may end the litigation or severely alter its course by striking leadings, precluding proof of facts, foreclosing claims or defenses, or even granting a default judgment. And, in deciding a spoliation motion, the court may order that additional discovery take place either to develop facts needed to rule on the motion or to afford the party deprived of relevant evidence an additional opportunity to develop it from other sources. The least disruptive time to undertake this is *during* the discovery phase, not after it has closed. Reopening discovery, even if for a limited purpose, months after it has closed or after dispositive motions have been filed, or worse still, on the eve of trial, can completely disrupt the pretrial schedule, involve significant cost, and burden the court and parties. Courts are justifiably unsympathetic to litigants who, because of inattention, neglect, or purposeful delay aimed at achieving an unwarranted tactical advantage, attempt to reargue a substantive issue already ruled on by the court through the guise of a spoliation motion, or use such a motion to try to reopen or prolong discovery beyond the time allotted in the pretrial order....

The first issue mentioned by the court in the *Pension Committee* case is that of culpability; the following chart is a summary from that opinion and order:

Conduct of Discovery	Level of Culpability
Failure to adhere to contemporary standards after a duty to preserve arises	Gross Negligence
Failure to issue written litigation hold	Gross Negligence
Failure to identify key players	Gross Negligence
Failure to ensure preservation of ESI of key players	Gross Negligence
Failure to cease deletion of email	Gross Negligence
Failure to preserve records of former employees in party's possession, custody or control	Gross Negligence
Failure to preserve backup tapes when sole source of relevant information or relate to key players	Gross Negligence
Intentional destruction after duty attaches	Willful Negligence
Failure to obtain from ALL employees	Negligence
Failure to take all appropriate measures to preserve ESI	Negligence
Failure to assess accuracy and validity of selected search terms	Negligence

Cooperation in Discovery

The leading source of guidance on e-discovery is the Sedona Conference®, a nonprofit organization that regularly conducts conferences for litigators, academics, and judges. It produced a *Cooperation Proclamation* that by the end of 2009 had the endorsement of almost one hundred judges, including that of Supreme Court Justice Breyer, who called on litigants to "act cooperatively in the fact finding process." With cooperation, counsel are able to limit the discovery demands by negotiating discovery agreements, which is a trend supported by the judiciary.

As stated by Magistrate Judge Paul Grimm in *Hopson v. the Mayor of Baltimore*,

> ...The cost-benefit balancing factors listed in Rule 26(b)(2) provide useful analytical tools to enable a producing party to marshal the specific facts that would justify less than full pre-production privilege review. The amount of discovery of electronically stored information that should be permitted in a particular case will be a function of the issues in the litigation, the resources of the parties, whether the discovery sought is available from alternative sources that are less burdensome, and the importance of the evidence sought to be discovered by the requesting party to its ability to prove its claims. As this court noted in *Thompson v. HUD*, 219 F.R.D. 93 (D. Md. 2003), courts have nearly limitless ability under Rule 26(b)(2) to fashion reasonable limits to potentially burdensome discovery requests, but the parties must get beyond the posturing that all too often takes place and provide the court with particularized information and reasonable suggestions how to do so. 232 F.R.D. 228 at 244.

A number of courts have discussed the need for cooperation among counsel in discovery:

> "In my view, the *Cooperation Proclamation* correctly recognizes that while counsel are retained to be zealous advocates for their clients, they bear a professional obligation to conduct discovery in a diligent and candid manner.... Cooperation does not conflict with the advancement of their clients' interests—it enhances them. Only when lawyers confuse *advocacy* with *adversarial conduct* are these twin duties in conflict....Counsel are on notice that, henceforth, this court will expect them to confer in good faith and make reasonable efforts to work together[,] consistent with well-established case law and the principles underlying *The Cooperation Proclamation*." *Cartel Asset management v Ocwen Financial Corp.*, 2010 WL 502721(D. Colo. Feb 8 2010)

IN THE WORDS OF THE COURT...

IN THE UNITED STATES DISTRICT COURT
FOR THE NORTHERN DISTRICT OF CALIFORNIA
2009 WL 3009059 (N.D. Cal. Sept. 17, 2009)
Oracle USA, Inc., et al.,
Plaintiffs,
v.
SAP AG, et al.,
Defendants.
No. C-07-01658 PJH (EDL)

ORDER GRANTING DEFENDANTS' MOTION FOR PRECLUSION OF CERTAIN DAMAGES EVIDENCE PURSUANT TO FEDERAL RULES OF CIVIL PROCEDURE 0 37(C)(1) AND 16(f)

ELIZABETH D. LAPORTE
United States Magistrate Judge

...This Court has closely monitored discovery in this complex litigation, holding thirteen discovery conferences addressing the progress of discovery and providing guidance on the numerous complex issues that have arisen, and six contested hearings on discovery motions. The production of electronic data in this case has been huge. For example, Plaintiffs' production of a collection of databases relating to the Customer Connection database totaled two terabytes, and Defendants' production of their Data Warehouse contained over ten terabytes of data....Discovery has already cost each party millions of dollars. For example, Defendants spent approximately $100,000 per custodian on document review and production alone, and the parties have agreed to a limit of 140 custodians....

From the first discovery conference that this Court held on May 6, 2008, the Court has repeatedly emphasized that the scope of this case required cooperation in prioritizing discovery and in being mindful of the proportionality requirement of Federal Rule of Civil Procedure 26. Rule 26 requires the Court to limit discovery if "the burden or expense of the proposed discovery outweighs its likely benefit," after consideration of a number of factors. Fed. R. Civ. P. 26(b)(2)(C). Further, production of electronically stored information may be limited if the sources of the information are "not reasonably accessible because of undue burden or cost." Fed. R. Civ. P. 26(b)(2)(B). Thus, proportionality has required that both parties focus on the amount of damages at issue from the outset of the case....

Proportionality

proportionality
Weighing the cost against the benefits of preserving and obtaining evidence against the amount in controversy.

An emerging concept in the areas of preservation and e-discovery is that of **proportionality.** As the potential cost of preservation and e-discovery increases, the courts are increasingly becoming concerned that litigation will be available only to the wealthy. As stated by Magistrate Judge Facciola in a conference on e-discovery, "We have to use common sense." ABA e-discovery Conference, May 2010. Not everything that can be preserved or discovered is needed to resolve a case. What must be weighed is the cost in proportion to the benefit. If the potential evidence is only marginally relevant, is it worth the cost to obtain it? The wealthier client or the company with the deeper pockets may demand "everything" from "everyone," but is it relevant to the resolution of the case or merely a tactic to drive the opponent out of the case and force a settlement? The courts are increasingly looking at the issue and limiting the number of document custodians whose electronically stored information may be obtained without permission of the court upon good cause.

IN THE WORDS OF THE COURT...

As stated by Judge Scheindlin in the *Pension Committee* case:

"... The determination of an appropriate sanction for spoliation, if any, is confined to the sound discretion of the trial judge and is assessed on a case-by-case basis."[38]

Where the breach of a discovery obligation is the non-production of evidence, a court has broad discretion to determine the appropriate sanction.[39] Appropriate sanctions should "(1) deter the parties from engaging in spoliation; (2) place the risk of an erroneous judgment on the party who wrongfully created the risk; and (3) restore 'the prejudiced party to the same position [it] would have been in absent the wrongful destruction of evidence by the opposing party.'"[40] It is well accepted that a court should always impose the least harsh sanction that can provide an adequate remedy. The choices include–from least harsh to most harsh–further discovery,[41] cost-shifting,[42] fines,[43] special jury instructions,[44] prec1usion,[45] and the entry of default judgment or dismissal (terminating sanctions).[46] The selection of the appropriate remedy is a delicate matter requiring a great deal of time and attention by a court. *Pension Committee of the University of Montreal Pension Plan, et al v Banc of America Securities, LLC, et al* 05 Civ. 9016 U.S. Dist. Crt. S.N.Y. 2010 at 18-20.

[38] *Fujitsu,* 247 F.3d at 436.

[39] *See Residential Funding,* 306 F.3d at 107. *See also Fujitsu,* 247 F.3d at 436 (reiterating the Second Circuit's "case-by-case approach to the failure to produce relevant evidence" in determining sanctions); *Reilly,* 181 F.3d at 267 ("Trial judges should have the leeway to tailor sanctions to insure that spoliators do not benefit from their wrongdoing–a remedial purpose that is best adjusted according to the facts and evidentiary posture of each case.").

[40] *West v. Goodyear Tire & Rubber Co.,* 167 F.3d 776, 779 (2d Cir. 1999) (quoting *Kronisch,* 150 F.3d at 126).

[41] *See, e.g., Treppel,* 249 F.R.D. at 123-24 (ordering additional discovery, including forensic search of adversary's computer).

[42] *See, e.g., Green (Fine Paintings) v. McClendon,* No. 08 Civ. 8496, 2009 WL 2496275, at *7 (S.D.N.Y. Aug. 13, 2009) (awarding monetary sanctions to the movant).

[43] *See, e.g., United States v. Philip Morris USA, Inc.,* 327 F. Supp. 2d 21,25 (D.D.C. 2004) (ordering defendant to pay $2.75 million in fines).

[44] *See, e.g., Arista Records LLC v. Usenet.com, Inc.,* 608 F. Supp. 2d 409, 443-44 (S.D.N.Y. 2009) (ordering an adverse inference instruction as a sanction for defendants' spoliation of evidence).

[45] *See, e.g., Brown v. Coleman,* No. 07 Civ. 1345,2009 WL 2877602, at *4 (S.D.N.Y. Sept. 8, 2009) (precluding certain evidence from being introduced at trial).

[46] *See, e.g., Gutman,* 2008 WL 5084182, at *2 (granting a default judgment for defendants' intentional destruction of evidence).

While sanctions can range from ordering additional discovery to monetary penalties, they may, in appropriate cases, include an adverse jury instruction as a sanction for spoliation, such as that in the *Pension Committee* case.

IN THE WORDS OF THE COURT...

University of Montreal Pension Plan, et al v Banc of America Securities, LLC, et al 05 Civ. 9016 U.S. Dist. Crt. S.N.Y. 2010 at 81-83

With respect to the grossly negligent plaintiffs–2M, Hunnicutt, Coronation, the Chagnon Plaintiffs, Bombardier Trusts, and the Bombardier Foundation–I will give the following jury charge:

The Citco Defendants have argued that 2M, Hunnicutt, Coronation, the Chagnon Plaintiffs, Bombardier Trusts, and the Bombardier Foundation destroyed relevant evidence, or failed to prevent the destruction of relevant evidence. This is known as the "spoliation of evidence."

Spoliation is the destruction of evidence or the failure to preserve property for another's use as evidence in pending or reasonably foreseeable litigation. To demonstrate that spoliation occurred, the Citco Defendants bear the burden of proving the following two elements by a preponderance of the evidence:

First, that *relevant* evidence was destroyed after the duty to preserve arose. Evidence is relevant if it would have clarified a fact at issue in the trial and otherwise would naturally have been introduced into evidence; and

Second, that 2M, Hunnicutt, Coronation, the Chagnon Plaintiffs, Bombardier Trusts, and the Bombardier Foundation were grossly negligent in their failure to preserve the evidence.

I instruct you, as a matter of law, that each of these plaintiffs failed to preserve evidence after its duty to preserve arose. As a result, you may presume, if you so choose, that such lost evidence was relevant, and that it would have been favorable to the Citco Defendants. In deciding whether to adopt this presumption, you may take into account the egregiousness of the plaintiffs' conduct in failing to preserve the evidence.

However, each of these plaintiffs has offered evidence that (1) no evidence was lost; (2) if evidence was lost, it was not relevant; and (3) if evidence was lost and it was relevant, it would not have been favorable to the Citco Defendants.

If you decline to presume that the lost evidence was relevant or would have been favorable to the Citco Defendants, then your consideration of the lost evidence is at an end, and you will *not* draw any inference arising from the lost evidence.

However, if you decide to presume that the lost evidence was relevant and would have been unfavorable to the Citco Defendants, you must next decide whether any of the following plaintiffs have rebutted that presumption: 2M, Hunnicutt, Coronation, the Chagnon Plaintiffs, Bombardier Trusts, or the Bombardier Foundation. If you determine that a plaintiff has *rebutted* the presumption that the lost evidence was either relevant or favorable to the Citco Defendants, you will *not* draw any inference arising from the lost evidence against that plaintiff. If, on the other hand, you determine that a plaintiff has *not rebutted* the presumption that the lost evidence was both relevant and favorable to the Citco Defendants, you may draw an inference against that plaintiff and in favor of the Citco Defendants–namely that the lost evidence would have been favorable to the Citco Defendants.

(continued)

Each plaintiff is entitled to your separate consideration. The question as to whether the Citco Defendants have proven spoliation is personal to each plaintiff and must be decided by you as to each plaintiff individually.

University of Montreal Pension Plan, et al v Banc of America Securities, LLC, et al 05 Civ. 9016 U.S. Dist. Crt. S.N.Y. 2010 at 81-83

CONCEPT REVIEW AND REINFORCEMENT

KEY TERMS

e-discovery 115
retention policy 116
litigation hold 116
spoliation 120
record retention 123
proportionality 128

CHAPTER SUMMARY

Introduction to the Evolving Issues in E-Discovery	There are no absolute answers in the area of electronic discovery. The law is still evolving, with each jurisdiction applying the rules at it sees necessary to promote justice. Decisions on similar fact patterns vary widely from jurisdiction to jurisdiction.
Discovery of Electronically Stored Information	E-discovery is used to describe the process of discovery of documents created, disseminated, and stored via electronic means. Until the adoption of the 2006 Federal Rules of Civil Procedure, lawyers and the courts relied on the traditional Request for Production of Documents to obtain paper copies and electronically stored information.
Document Management	Legal counsels are often asked: "How long do I have to keep records or documents?" The answer is somewhere between forever and the practical realities of business economics and the need to preserve documents for potential litigation.
Litigation Hold	The amendments to the Rules seem to suggest that once a client has a reasonable belief that litigation may arise from a dispute, a duty arises to preserve all documents, paper and electronic, related to that dispute. The requirement is not that a lawsuit has been filed or a complaint served, only that a reasonable belief exists that litigation may arise.
Duty to Preserve	There is a common law duty to preserve evidence that is well recognized. It is clear that when actual notice of litigation is received, the duty to preserve potential evidence exists.
Spoliation	Spoliation is "the destruction or significant alteration of evidence or the failure to preserve property for another's use as evidence in pending or reasonably foreseeable litigation." It may be the destruction of physical evidence such as the disposal, crushing, or other destruction of a motor vehicle showing evidence of the cause of an accident. It may be the shredding or burning of a letter or handwritten note confirming the

	existence of a promise or other obligation. In the electronic world it may be the deleting of electronically stored documents on a computer or the erasing of the backup tapes containing critical emails and documents.
Sanctions for Spoliation	Spoliation of evidence is punishable by sanctions against the party who destroyed the evidence. Sanctions may include giving a negative inference instruction to the jury by advising the jury of the destruction of documents that they may interpret as being documents that would have been favorable to the other side and negative to the case of the party that destroyed or lost the document. Sanctions may also include denying the party an opportunity to defend the claims that arise out of the destroyed document.
Record Retention	Record retention is the practice of retaining documents for a period of time. Various terms are used to refer to the organized policies of document retention: *information management, document management or record management.* What needs to be retained and for how long depends on a number of factors including governmental regulations, the need to defend against potential action, and the reasonable belief in the pendency of litigation.
Spoliation Remedies	The court has the power to create and impose remedies for spoliation of evidence. The extent of the remedy can vary from monetary penalty to dismissal or adverse instruction to the jury. There is no national standard on the sanctions or on the extent of the conduct that will elicit a sanction. Different jurisdictions and courts may apply a different sanction under what appear to be the same circumstances.
Cooperation in Discovery	Judges are calling on litigants to act cooperatively in the discovery process.
Proportionality	Not everything that can be preserved or discovered is needed to resolve a case. What must be weighed is the cost in proportion to the benefit. If the potential evidence is only marginally relevant, is it worth the cost to obtain it? The wealthier client or the company with the deeper pockets can demand "everything" from "everyone," but is it relevant to the resolution of the case or a tactic to drive the opponent out of the case and force a settlement? The courts are increasingly looking at this issue and limiting the number of document custodians whose electronically stored information may be obtained without permission of the court upon good cause.

REVIEW QUESTIONS AND EXERCISES

1. What is the impact of the new Federal Rules of Civil Procedure on the procedural practice of law?
2. Where can the litigation team look for guidance on the procedure for trying cases involving electronic documentation?
3. Define spoliation and give examples.
4. What is the duty to preserve documents?
5. Has the introduction of electronically stored documents changed the duty to preserve documents?
6. Explain some of the emerging issues in electronic discovery.
7. What is the legal team's duty to preserve client confidences?
8. What are the possible costs associated with electronic discovery?
9. What are the ethical issues in protecting confidential or privileged information in an age of electronic documents?
10. May a firm or client regularly destroy files and records? Explain fully.
11. Does an attorney have a duty to learn about the issues in e-discovery?

BUILDING YOUR PARALEGAL SKILLS

INTERNET AND TECHNOLOGY EXERCISE

1. Use the Internet to locate a current version of the Federal Rules of Civil Procedure 16, 26, 33, 34, 37, and 45.

CIVIL LITIGATION VIDEO CASE STUDIES

Handling Evidence: Zealous Representation Issue

A paralegal has discovered a document that is detrimental to the law firm's client. No one else is aware of its existence.

After viewing the video in MyLegalStudiesKit, answer the following questions.

1. Is there any ethical or legal reason not to hide or destroy a document if no one else knows of its existence?
2. Does the law firm have any duty to make available to the opposing side evidence that is detrimental to its case?

CHAPTER OPENING SCENARIO CASE STUDY

Use the Opening Scenario for this chapter to answer the following questions.

1. Prepare a motion that might be used if it is found that the opposing side has not preserved vital evidence after notice of the lawsuit.
2. Prepare a discovery plan proposal for use at the meet and confer.
3. Prepare a memo outlining the potential sanctions that can be requested from the judge in the initial meeting with the court if it is decided that the opposing party has not honored all the mandatory and other discovery requests.
4. Prepare a memo from the IT staff to the trial team explaining what issues they should be aware of and suggestions for obtaining and protecting the needed data in the meet and confer.

COMPREHENSIVE CASE STUDY

SCHOOL BUS–TRUCK ACCIDENT CASE

For the case study from Appendix II:

1. Prepare a protocol for the litigation team to use in reviewing documents for a claim of privilege for the accident case in Appendix II.
2. As defense counsel, prepare a list for expert and factual witnesses that you would call at trial.
3. List the other mandatory disclosures that must be made under the federal rules.

BUILDING YOUR PROFESSIONAL PORTFOLIO

CIVIL LITIGATION TEAM AT WORK

Procedures

Prepare a protocol for the litigation team to follow to insure a litigation hold is instituted and complied with by a client.

Forms

Prepare a litigation hold letter to a client.

"Ignorantia juris quod quisque scire tenetur non excusat."

—(Ignorance of the law, which everybody is supposed to know, does not constitute an excuse.)
Legal maxim

E-Discovery—The Process

CHAPTER 6

OPENING SCENARIO

The litigation team working on the school bus case had what at first seemed to be a simple vehicle collision case between a school bus and a truck. However, the information and evidence obtained as part of discovery of the possibility of a defect in the truck, either through maintenance or defective parts, raised new issues and options. It was becoming clear that the areas for discovery would have to be expanded and additional areas explored. At the very least, the truck had to be inspected by their own experts, and the trucking company records had to be reviewed for anything related to the truck, including its use, maintenance, and repairs.

The team working on the new airplane crash case was also concerned that the mass of information and data from federal investigators and individual corporate defendants could potentially overwhelm them. In addition, they were representing only one of the potential plaintiffs in the case, with a number of other attorneys representing the other victims' families. All of the attorneys needed access to the same data and had to be able to sift through it to find the usable evidence to support their legal theory for their client. This was the first case Mason, Marshall and Benjamin had handled where the defendants were large national firms with massive amounts of electronically stored data, not to mention the federal agencies and their similarly large amounts of electronically stored information.

LEARNING OBJECTIVES

After studying this chapter, you should be able to:

1. Describe the electronic discovery process and the role of information management.
2. Describe the methods used to identify relevant information.
3. Explain the issues in locating evidence.
4. Describe the issues in creating search queries in electronic discovery.
5. Describe the role of the forensic examiner in digital discovery.

INTRODUCTION TO EVIDENCE AND DISCOVERY

Each case has at least two sides, the plaintiff's and the defendant's. There may be other interested parties who are potential litigants or have an interest in the litigation, such as governmental agencies. Each side comes into the litigation process from a different perspective. The attorneys representing the parties have their own perspectives as well. For the plaintiff, it frequently is a simple matter of a wrong against him or her for which he or she wants compensation or vindication. It may also be a question of the timing of the action and where to institute suit. For the plaintiff's attorney, it is a matter of finding the evidence to process and present the case. The defendant frequently is in the position of not knowing if or when a suit will be brought for which he or she will need a defense, and therefore defendants do not necessarily know what records need to be preserved or for how long. For the defense counsel, it is a question of counseling the client while protecting the client's rights against unwarranted claims and intrusion into the business process. Corporate or in-house counsel are concerned with the costs not only of potential litigation but also of preservation of documentation and related costs of potential review.

What to save and how long to save it is a recurring issue faced by everyone, from individuals wondering about the need to save financial records and tax returns to the business who has the same question but substantially greater numbers of documents, including those for products purchased, manufactured, and sold. With documents in all formats ranging from paper to electronic, saving the items is only one part of the problem; finding the needed, relevant documents is the other. For both plaintiff and defense counsel, it also is a matter of protecting confidential or privileged material from disclosure and a search for the relevant documents, which might include an unwanted discovery of a "gotcha" document. It is important for the legal team to understand both positions regardless of the side they are on in any particular case.

ELECTRONIC DISCOVERY—THE PROCESS

LEARNING OBJECTIVE 1
Describe the electronic discovery process and the role of information management.

Electronic Discovery Reference Model
A suggested model of the procedures in electronic discovery.

Electronic discovery, or e-discovery, should be thought of as a process and not a single event. As shown in the **Electronic Discovery Reference Model** in Exhibit 6.1, it involves a number of steps or individual processes: information management; identification; preservation and collection; processing, review, and analysis; production; and presentation. The ultimate goal is to reduce the total number of potential items to those that are relevant, and of those that are relevant, to ultimately be sure that they can meet the test of authenticity for presentation and admission in trial.

Information Management

As shown in the EDRM model in Exhibit 6.1, the e-discovery process starts with information management or, as it is also called, document management. Information or document management policies are concerned with how documents are created and stored as well as the policy on document destruction. While not always the case, the plan should be in effect before litigation creates the need. As part of attorneys' counseling function, the importance of having a policy should be a topic of discussion with clients.

Where there is a document or information management policy in place, the first step for the litigation team is to learn the details and procedures of

Exhibit 6.1 EDRM—Electronic Discovery Reference Model

The Electronic Discovery Reference Model was created to address the lack of standards and guidelines in the electronic discovery (e-discovery) market. The completed model was placed in the public domain in May 2006.

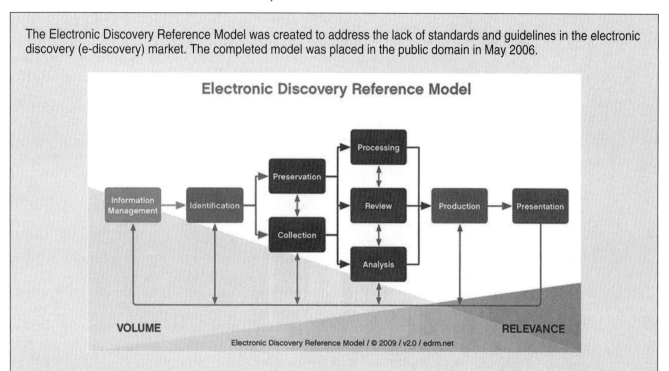

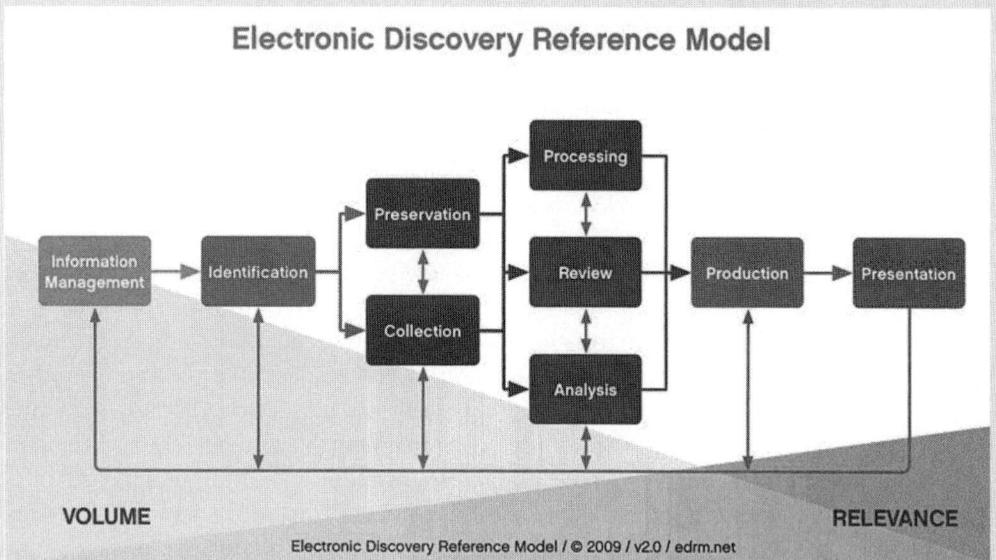

Information Management
Getting your electronic house in order to mitigate risk & expenses should e-discovery become an issue, from initial creation of electronically stored information through its final disposition.

Identification
Locating potential sources of ESI & determining its scope, breadth & depth.

Preservation
Ensuring that ESI is protected against inappropriate alteration or destruction.

Collection
Gathering ESI for further use in the e-discovery process (processing, review, etc.).

Processing
Reducing the volume of ESI and converting it, if necessary, to forms more suitable for review & analysis.

Review
Evaluating ESI for relevance & privilege.

Analysis
Evaluating ESI for content & context, including key patterns, topics, people & discussion.

Production
Delivering ESI to others in appropriate forms & using appropriate delivery mechanisms.

Presentation
Displaying ESI before audiences (at depositions, hearings, trials, etc.), especially in native & near-native forms, to elicit further information, validate existing facts or positions, or persuade an audience.

each of the litigant parties' retention policies and those of any potential third parties, such as a supplier of the parties that may have relevant supporting information.

Document retention policies that provide for the periodic destruction of stored information are permissible. In the often quoted U.S. Supreme Court case of *Arthur Andersen v. U.S.*, the court said:

> Document retention policies, which are created in part to keep certain information from getting into the hands of others, including the Government, are common in business.... It is, of course, not wrongful for a manager to instruct his employees to comply with a valid document retention policy under ordinary circumstances. 544 U.S. 696 (2005)

With paper records there is a very real need to periodically destroy the files because of the physical space their storage requires. In some cases, storage requires the rental of off-site warehouse space in secure, temperature- and humidity-controlled facilities. While it might be desirable to save everything forever, the economics of this cost of retention frequently dictates a planned destruction program. Many document or information management systems provide a timetable for removal to an off-site warehouse location and a date for destruction. To facilitate removal and destruction, the dates for each are marked on the physical boxes used for the storage. Economic considerations notwithstanding, the time frames for destruction of documentation are frequently dictated by government regulations such as health records maintenance regulations, securities laws, or tax regulations. In some cases the time frame is dictated by the potential for suit within a set statute of limitation, such as the two-year statute of limitation for tort claims in some areas.

Initially it was thought that the shift from paper to electronic storage would eliminate the need for any physical storage space or off-site storage and therefore limit the cost of data retention. Experience has shown this not to be true. While the total space necessary to store items electronically is less than that for physical document storage, the cost is still potentially substantial. In addition to the cost of maintaining the computer systems and the storage of currently used items is also the cost of generating backup and archival storage for disaster recovery as a part of information management or because of the requirements of government regulation. In many cases, companies use multiple remote, off-site data storage services for disaster recovery and archival purposes, which adds to the cost of information retention.

The use of technology has seen an explosion in the numbers of documents, far more than previously anticipated. Consider the growth in the numbers of electronically generated email and text messages. In the past, written communication took the form of letters and occasionally memos; today it consists of email, text messages, and new forms of social website communications like Twitter and Facebook. Where a letter or memo might have gone to one person with a copy to another, an email may be sent to multiple parties, all of whom send it on to multiple others—thus replicating and increasing the amount of message storage required to save potential data.

Email has become a major source of evidence and has spawned the need to archive emails, which itself requires additional computing power and cost. Because the use of computers makes saving documents easier than when they were strictly in paper format, people save more information of every type than ever before, including every draft of every document and every item they see and can download from the Internet, including still and video photographs and sound files, all of which use up large amounts of storage space. As a result, companies as well as individuals are saving and backing up more and more data.

The question clients want answered is: "Is it safe to routinely delete electronically stored information?" The federal rules, specifically Rule 37, provide a **Safe Haven** for routine, good faith operation and destruction of ESI.

Safe Haven
Procedures and circumstances under which a party will not be penalized.

Rule 37. Failure to Make Disclosures or to Cooperate in Discovery; Sanctions

(e) Failure to Provide Electronically Stored Information.
Absent exceptional circumstances, a court may not impose sanctions under these rules on a party for failing to provide electronically stored information lost as a result of the routine, good-faith operation of an electronic information system.

What is deemed routine, good faith operation will in part be determined by a company's compliance with a written policy that is monitored by those in charge to ensure its rigorous compliance by all employees on all computer systems under the control of the company. Remember, though, that this does not change the obligation, when a party reasonably anticipates litigation, to suspend its destruction policy and preserve relevant documentation under a litigation hold. Clients must be properly notified of their obligation. For the litigation team, an added ethical obligation to preserve evidence exists under Model Ethics Rule 3.4.

A lawyer shall not:

(a) unlawfully obstruct another party's access to evidence or unlawfully alter, destroy or conceal a document or other material having potential evidentiary value. A lawyer shall not counsel or assist another person to do any such act....

WEB RESOURCES
Contrast and compare the ABA's Model Rule 3.4 at www.abanet.org/CPR with that of your local jurisdiction.

Cost of Saving ESI

Technology has both advantages and disadvantages. One of its biggest advantages is the efficient, economical creation and sharing of information in electronic form. Initially, the word processor and some financial data creation and saving programs provided the bulk of ESI, in formats that were relatively easy to store and save on backup tapes and later on hard drives and other forms of memory media. Advances in technology have resulted in new methods for creating ESI, including emails, text messages, and Internet social networking sites, as well as for creating and saving every conceivable form of graphic and other type of documentation used in business and government.

One of technology's disadvantages is the cost of preserving ESI that results from the uncertainty businesses have about how much information to save and for how long. Saving and archiving ESI in secure, multi-location storage facilities as required by court action, company policy, and government regulation incurs a cost that increases as the volume increases.

Document retention policies are receiving close scrutiny as to what is needed in the context of what is economically reasonable. Somewhere there is a balance between the business need for information and the cost of creating and saving it, and the litigation need and the cost of saving everything. It is a balance between the duty to preserve and the cost to do so. The **Information Management Reference Model (IMRM)** shown in Exhibit 6.2 is a topic of discussion and study in trying to come to terms with the changes dictated by the needs of business and litigation.

Information Management Reference Model (IMRM)
A proposed model for e-discovery that balances business and litigation needs.

Exhibit 6.2 Information Management Reference Model (IMRM)

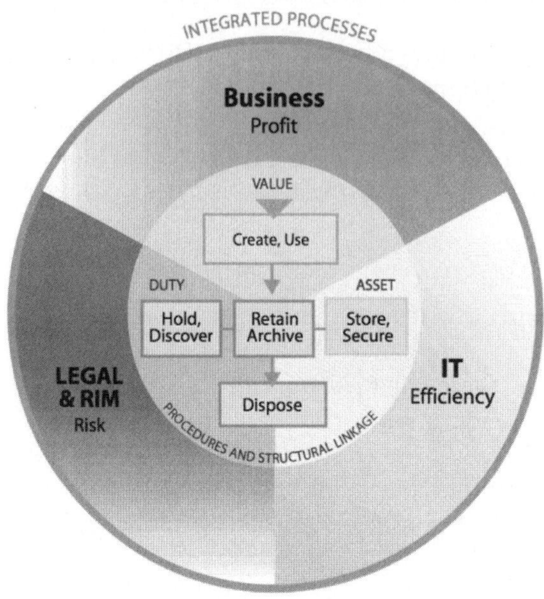

Duty: Legal Obligation for specific information

Value: Utility or business purpose of specific information

Asset: Specific container of information

Source: Courtesy of EDRM (edrm.net).

■ IDENTIFICATION

LEARNING OBJECTIVE 2
Describe the methods used to identify relevant information.

The initial step in the discovery process, traditional and electronic, is to determine what documents are needed, who has those documents, the format of the documents, the value of those documents in the case, and the potential costs of retrieving those documents. A properly prepared electronic document request, based on the federal or local rules, can then be prepared. Many different types of documents are considered a "record" by the court and may be part of the discovery request. "Record" has been defined as:

> a. As used in this Order, "record" means any book, bill, calendar, chart, check, compilation, computation, computer or network activity log, correspondence, data, database, diagram, diary, document, draft, drawing, e-mail, file, folder, film, graph, graphic presentation, image, index, inventory, invoice, jotting, journal, ledger, machine readable material, map, memo, metadata, minutes, note, order, paper, photograph, printout, recording, report, spreadsheet, statement, summary, telephone message record or log, transcript, video, voicemail, voucher, webpage, work paper, writing, or worksheet, or any other item or group of documentary material or information, regardless of physical or electronic format or characteristic, and any information therein, and copies, notes, and recordings thereof. *Jicarilla Apache Nation v U.S.* No. 02-25L U.S. Court of Fed. Claims (2004)

LOCATING EVIDENCE

LEARNING OBJECTIVE 3
Explain the issues in locating evidence.

Locating information and documentation begins with a good understanding of the types of records that are maintained, by whom and where, and the document retention policies of the client as well as those of opposing parties and potential third parties with relevant information to the case. One of the third party documents in an automobile property damage case might be the police report, tow truck dispatch log, auto body repair shop bill, rental replacement vehicle bill, and possibly a bill for the firefighters' response to clean up the gasoline or oil spill from the collision.

Before computerization, all of these would have been paper records. After a complete interview of the client, together with some intuition based on the litigation experience of the legal team, a request of appropriate agencies or businesses would be made or copies of the above documents requested in writing from the opposing party as part of the discovery interrogatories.

If a personal injury is involved, the team might add a request for medical records from doctors or hospitals and related bills for services and treatments. In each case, a written request would list the names of the parties, the dates of the incident, and known treatment dates. Any issues of misspelled names or incorrect dates would require some human intervention to find out whether there was a person with a similar name and which person was being referred to.

Discovery of electronically stored information has for the most part eliminated the human interface. In some cases, the requests are made by the litigation support staff using the Internet and searching records using computer search queries. Only the specific databases requested may be searched instead of all the databases that exist. Thus, requests for searches of ESI must be specific. The advantage to the electronic search is that there are no longer any missed documents caused by misfilings or overlooked physical paper files. The disadvantage is the loss of the human interface that could find a related document, like a second accident by one of the parties, as she or he scanned manually through the paper copies.

There is a tendency to speak of electronic documents as generic, homogeneous items when discussing discovery, particularly electronic discovery issues. The danger of doing so is that one tends to forget the specialty nature of the contents of the documents when conducting computer search queries. Finding the desired document requires an appreciation of the types of records kept, by whom they are kept, where they are kept, and the language used by the creators of the records and those indexing them. Every occupation has its own lexicon of terms and type of document used to record its activity. Without the knowledge of the terms and phrases used, a search may not produce the desired documents.

Interrogatories and Depositions

Depending on which side of the case the litigation team finds itself, it may be as important to know what is routinely deleted as what has been preserved in the opposing party's electronically stored information records. For the litigation team, the issues may also include what their own client has deleted or destroyed as part of its document retention or information management system. Counsel must therefore know the issues that it will have to face as it meets its obligations, not only to the client but also to opposing counsel and the court, including its ethical obligations.

The traditional use of the courts was to right a wrong. Today, litigation or the threat of litigation is used as part of marketing or licensing strategies, or to silence, intimidate, and censor critics, in what is referred to as a SLAPP suit (strategic lawsuit against public participation). These are suits in which the plaintiff selects the timing and controls evidence that may in the future be part of the lawsuit. For example, in *Rambus v. Micron*, the court found:

> ...because the document retention policy was discussed and adopted within the context of Rambus litigation strategy[,] the court finds that Rambus knew or should have known, that a general implementation of the policy was inappropriate because the documents destroyed would become material at some point in the future.... *Micron v Rambus* Civ. No. 00-792-SLLR US Dist. Crt. Dist. of Del. (2009)

In the *Micron* case, the penalty was that Rambus could not assert its patents against Micron. To obtain this result, the burden was on Micron, as the injured party, to prove "...that the document[s] destroyed were discoverable and the type of documents would be relevant to the instant litigation." *Micron* at page 32.

As stated by Judge Scheindlin:

> ...The innocent party must also show that the evidence would have been helpful in proving its claims or defenses—i.e. that the innocent party is prejudiced without the evidence....In short, the innocent party must prove the following three elements: that the spoliating party (1) had control over the evidence and an obligation to preserve it at the time of destruction or loss; (2) acted with a culpable state of mind upon destroying or losing the evidence; and that (3) the missing evidence is relevant to the innocent party's claim or defense.... *Pension Committee, et al v Banc of America, et al* 05- Civ.9016 at page 14.

For the litigation team seeking electronically stored information, the task is not just to find existing documentation but also to find evidence of any documents destroyed as part of a plan intended to lead to litigation, such as the marketing plans of Rambus to "...establish a royalty rate and validate its patents...." In this case, the "smoking gun" was a PowerPoint slide, prepared for a Rambus board meeting, that showed:

> ...further that the [b]est route to IP credibility is through victory over a major DRAM manufacturer.... *Micron* at pages 21, 30

Rule 33. Interrogatories to Parties

(a) In General.

(1) Number.

Unless otherwise stipulated or ordered by the court, a party may serve on any other party no more than 25 written interrogatories, including all discrete subparts. Leave to serve additional interrogatories may be granted to the extent consistent with Rule 26(b)(2).

(2) Scope.

An interrogatory may relate to any matter that may be inquired into under Rule 26(b). An interrogatory is not objectionable merely because it asks for an opinion or contention that relates to fact or the application of law to fact, but the court may order that the interrogatory need not be answered until designated discovery is complete, or until a pretrial conference or some other time.

(b) Answers and Objections.

(1) Responding Party.

The interrogatories must be answered:

(A) by the party to whom they are directed; or

(B) if that party is a public or private corporation, a partnership, an association, or a governmental agency, by any officer or agent, who must furnish the information available to the party.

(2) Time to Respond.
The responding party must serve its answers and any objections within 30 days after being served with the interrogatories. A shorter or longer time may be stipulated to under Rule 29 or be ordered by the court.

(3) Answering Each Interrogatory.
Each interrogatory must, to the extent it is not objected to, be answered separately and fully in writing under oath.

(4) Objections.
The grounds for objecting to an interrogatory must be stated with specificity. Any ground not stated in a timely objection is waived unless the court, for good cause, excuses the failure.

(5) Signature.
The person who makes the answers must sign them, and the attorney who objects must sign any objections.

(c) Use.
An answer to an interrogatory may be used to the extent allowed by the Federal Rules of Evidence.

(d) Option to Produce Business Records.
If the answer to an interrogatory may be determined by examining, auditing, compiling, abstracting, or summarizing a party's business records (including electronically stored information), and if the burden of deriving or ascertaining the answer will be substantially the same for either party, the responding party may answer by:

(1) specifying the records that must be reviewed, in sufficient detail to enable the interrogating party to locate and identify them as readily as the responding party could; and

(2) giving the interrogating party a reasonable opportunity to examine and audit the records and to make copies, compilations, abstracts, or summaries.

Interrogatories

Interrogatories are written questions that are required to be answered by the opposing party. These questions rarely result in any surprises, such as might be obtained in a face-to-face question session. The written requests are submitted to opposing counsel, who reviews both the questions and the client's answers carefully to ensure that only required information is supplied. The answers do, however, provide a basic framework from which additional discovery will follow, including depositions and request for production of documents and other things.

interrogatories
A form of discovery in which written questions are addressed to a party to a lawsuit requiring written answers made under oath.

Document discovery starts with interrogatories seeking the necessary information not just about current documents but about retention policies and identification of the items or types of items that may have been destroyed, whether as part of the routine policy or otherwise, obviously not an easy task. It is suggested that a starting point is identifying all the key players at the company or opposing party who might have created or received any relevant ESI. Exhibit 6.3 is a portion of sample interrogatories related to the discovery of electronic data.

Rule 30 Deposition

With the information from the interrogatories, the next step in obtaining the needed information that may lead to existing or destroyed ESI is the Rule 30 deposition of a knowledgeable person in the opposing party's system.

Exhibit 6.3 Sample interrogatories and requests for production

INTERROGATORIES AND REQUESTS FOR PRODUCTION

Interrogatory No. X:

Describe the computer system(s) including, but not limited to, network servers, workstations, laptops, backups/archives and hand-held computers (including, but not limited to, personal organizers) used by [PARTY] currently and at any time within [TIME PERIOD], including, but not limited to, for each such system, the brand and model; the amount of memory and capacity of the hard disk(s); the make, model and capacity of any removable media or near-line storage systems; the name and version of the operating system; the name and version of network software, if any; the brand and model of all peripheral devices including tape drives, external disk drives, other storage devices and modems; the brand and version of major software in use on the system(s) during such period (including, but not limited to, electronic mail programs, workgroup collaboration programs or groupware, and scheduling software); and the name of all online (electronic) services accessed with the system(s) during such period.

Response:

Interrogatory No. X:

Provide the name, employer, title, business and home addresses and telephone numbers for each person with operational or maintenance responsibility for the computer system(s) described above during [TIME PERIOD], including, but not limited to, the person(s) who maintain the hardware described above; the person(s) responsible for installing software on the system(s); the person(s) responsible for the day-to-day operation of the system(s); the person(s) responsible for making backups or archiving files and data on the system(s); and the person(s) who can provide any passwords that may be necessary to access the appropriate computer system(s) or files.

Response:

Interrogatory No. X:

If not the same person(s) as identified in your answer to the immediately preceding interrogatory, identify by job title, job description, and business address and telephone number, the person(s) employed by [PARTY] who is/are the most knowledgeable about the policies, procedures and actual practices for retention and destruction of documents at [PARTY].

Response:

Interrogatory No. X:

Describe all efforts and procedures taken by [PARTY] since the notice of this action to gather and secure documents, including, but not limited to, electronically generated or stored word processing files, spreadsheets or other electronic documents, electronic mail, and backup copies of information that may be relevant to the facts of this case. Describe the manner in which the notice of such efforts or procedures was communicated to [PARTY'S] employees.

Response:

Interrogatory No. X:

Has [PARTY] created any images of any computer since notice of this litigation? If so, identify each computer, the date the image was created, and the current location of the media containing the image.

Source:

deposition
A form of discovery available to ask questions and obtain oral answers under oath from a witness or party to a lawsuit. Questions and answers are recorded stenographically.

A **deposition** is a form of discovery that allows the out-of-court questioning of a witness under oath

Rule 30. Deposition by Oral Examination

(6) Notice or Subpoena Directed to an Organization.
In its notice or subpoena, a party may name as the deponent a public or private corporation, a partnership, an association, a governmental agency, or other entity and must describe with reasonable particularity the matters for examination. The named organization must then designate one or more officers, directors, or managing agents, or designate other persons who consent to testify on its behalf; and it may set out the matters on which each person designated will testify. A subpoena must advise a nonparty organization of its duty to make this designation. The persons designated must testify

> about information known or reasonably available to the organization. This paragraph (6) does not preclude a deposition by any other procedure allowed by these rules.

A sample notice of deposition that provides the details of the questions that the deponent will be asked to answer is shown in Exhibit 6.4.

> **Rule 26. Duty to Disclose; General Provisions Governing Discovery.**
>
> **(2) Limitations on Frequency and Extent.**
>
> (A) *When Permitted.* By order, the court may alter the limits in these rules on the number of depositions and interrogatories or on the length of depositions under Rule 30. By order or local rule, the court may also limit the number of requests under Rule 36.
>
> (B) *Specific Limitations on Electronically Stored Information.* A party need not provide discovery of electronically stored information from sources that the party identifies as not reasonably accessible because of undue burden or cost. On motion to compel discovery or for a protective order, the party from whom discovery is sought must show that the information is not reasonably accessible because of undue burden or cost. If that showing is made, the court may nonetheless order discovery from such sources if the requesting party shows good cause, considering the limitations of Rule 26(b)(2)(C). The court may specify conditions for the discovery.
>
> (C) *When Required.* On motion or on its own, the court must limit the frequency or extent of discovery otherwise allowed by these rules or by local rule if it determines that:
>
> (i) the discovery sought is unreasonably cumulative or duplicative, or can be obtained from some other source that is more convenient, less burdensome, or less expensive;
>
> (ii) the party seeking discovery has had ample opportunity to obtain the information by discovery in the action; or
>
> (iii) the burden or expense of the proposed discovery outweighs its likely benefit, considering the needs of the case, the amount in controversy, the parties' resources, the importance of the issues at stake in the action, and the importance of the discovery in resolving the issues.

COLLECTION

The collection phase is part of the e-discovery process that includes finding and obtaining electronically stored information for review and analysis. The collection process may require the retaining of outside professionals experienced in the techniques of searching databases. Depending on the computer systems used or programs for creating, storing, or archiving the ESI, specialists may be required to retrieve the data in a usable form. For example, some older stored information may have been created and stored on types of storage media for which there are no modern computers capable of accessing the information. In the early days of computer development, the technology had not yet developed to allow the type of memory media used today such as the removable thumb drive, DVD, or hard disk drive system. In the 1970s 15-inch floppy disks were being used, which in the 1980s were replaced with the 5-inch floppy. These were then replaced in the 1990s with the 3½-inch floppy. In the 2000s, floppies were replaced altogether by DVDs and "thumb drives," each of which is capable of holding the equivalent amount of data of thousands of the original 15-inch floppies. But if the critical information needed is still on a 15-inch floppy, a specialist may need to be found who has a floppy disk drive, a copy of the original programs that can read the original, and a system capable of printing the information.

Exhibit 6.4 Notice of Rule 30 deposition

UNITED STATES DISTRICT COURT
[XX] DISTRICT OF [STATE]

[NAME NAME], Plaintiff, v. [NAME NAME], Defendant.	No. XXX-XXXX NOTICE OF DEPOSITION PURSUANT TO FED. R. CIV. P. 30(b)(6)

TO: **[DEPONENT'S NAME]**
AND TO: [ATTORNEY'S NAME], attorney of record

PLEASE TAKE NOTICE that the testimony of [DEPONENT] will be taken upon Oral Examination pursuant to Fed. R. Civ. P. 30(b)(6) at the request of the [PARTY] in the above-entitled and numbered action, before a Notary Public on [DATE] at [TIME] at the offices of [LOCATION, ADDRESS].

This deposition shall be subject to continuance or adjournment from time-to-time and place-to-place until completed, and will be taken on the ground and for the reason that this witness will give evidence material to the establishment of [PARTY'S] case.

Pursuant to Federal Rule of Civil Procedure 30(b)(6), [PARTY'S] corporate designee(s) shall be prepared to testify regarding the following subjects, all with respect to [PARTY'S] information technology systems:

I. SYSTEM PROFILE

1. Types of data processing and data storage devices used by company in the course of business.
2. Network architecture and usage policies.
3. Number, types, and locations of computers (including desktops, laptops, PDAs, cell phones, etc.) currently in use or in use at any time during the past [XX] years.
4. Brands and versions of software used on computer system(s).
5. File naming and saving conventions.
6. Identity of the person(s) responsible for the ongoing operation, maintenance, expansion, backup, and upkeep of computer systems and how frequently these activities occur (according to policy and actual practice).
7. Policies and practices for usage of home computers for business purposes.
8. Any modification of use of computers since notice of litigation.
9. Utility programs used to permanently "wipe files" from computer(s) in the company and date(s) used since notice of litigation.
10. Upgrades to computer hardware in the past [XX] months.
11. Upgrades or replacements to computer software in the past [XX] months.

II. BACKUP AND RETENTION

1. Electronic records management policies and procedures.
2. Steps taken to ensure preservation of electronic data.
3. Deletion of any documents since lawsuit commenced or since deponent received notification about litigation or pending litigation.
4. Instructions about preservation of electronic documents due to the lawsuit: Who provided notification? How was it disseminated? What procedures were in place for verification of receipt?
5. Backup software program(s) used (e.g., ARCserve, Backup Exec, StorageExpress, etc.).
6. Any modification of backup procedures since notice of litigation.
7. Information about disaster recovery plans in place currently and during past [XX] years.
8. Backup tape or archival disk naming/labeling conventions.
9. Location of backup tapes and other backup media.
10. Method and schedule used if files are ever deleted from the computer system(s).
11. Location(s), if any, where files are "archived" off the system.
12. Dates, if any, when data was restored from backup tapes within the past [XX] months. If so: What data was restored? Why was the data restored?

III. POLICIES AND PROCEDURES

1. Policy regarding purging of individual directories when an employee leaves the company (on desktop, laptop, and server systems).

2. Policy regarding reassigning workstations to incoming employees.
3. Policy regarding disposal/recycling/sale of hardware.
4. Procedures for handling used disks or drives before destruction or sale.
5. Policy and procedure for use of outside contractors to upgrade either hardware or software for system maintenance.

IV. DATABASES
1. Types of databases used (CRM, accounting, etc.).
2. Type(s) and names of database software used (e.g., Oracle, dBASE, Advanced Revelation, Access, proprietary, etc.).
3. The fields of information used in the database(s).
4. Identity of person(s) responsible for database design, database maintenance, report design, database backup.
5. Identity of person(s) who enter information into the database.
6. Ways and by whom the database is accessed.
7. Identification of any standard reports prepared on a routine basis.
8. Incidents and dates on which database files have been re-indexed, purged, repaired, or archived.
9. Protocol for using passwords or encrypted files are used on any of the computer systems, including name(s) of person(s) who manage this process.
10. Policy for changing/revoking passwords and access codes when an employee leaves the company.
11. Method used for those outside the company to access the computers (VPN or other).

V. EMAIL SYSTEMS
1. Identity of person(s) responsible for administering the email system(s).
2. Identification of all type(s) of email programs currently in use, including name(s) and version number(s), installation date(s), and number of users.
3. Location of users' email files (e.g., mail messages stored in a central location—a server—or locally on users' desktops, or both?).
4. Ways, if any, users can access their email remotely (e.g., from outside the office via BlackBerry or other wireless device, or via a web mail application).
5. Protocol for routinely changing email passwords.
6. Policy for running "janitorial" programs to purge email.
7. Identification of any other email systems used in the past [XX] years.
8. Details about email retention policies and practices (e.g., retention period, auto-delete features, deletion procedures, etc.)
9. Restoration of any mailboxes from backup tapes within the past [XX] months/years. If applicable, identify: What mailbox(es) was/were restored? Was the restoration operation successful? What resources were required to perform the restoration (labor hours, equipment, drive space, etc.).
10. Special active email retention settings.
11. Incidents and dates on which email databases have been re-indexed, purged, repaired, or archived.
12. Protocol for using passwords or encrypted files are used on any of the computer systems, including name(s) of person(s) who manage this process.
13. Policy for changing/revoking passwords and access codes when an employee leaves the company.
14. Method used for those outside the company to access the computers (VPN or other).

VI. MISCELLANEOUS
1. Information about production of electronic documents in other litigation or legal proceedings: Which cases were produced? What was produced, in what format?
2. Information about any persons who examined any of the company's computers since learning of this lawsuit, including details about reasons for examination and protocol utilized.

DATED this XX day of [MONTH, YEAR].

[LAW FIRM NAME]

By ______________________________

[ATTORNEYS]

Attorneys for [PARTY]

Source: LexisNexis Applied Discovery

SEARCH QUERIES

LEARNING OBJECTIVE 4
Describe the issues in creating search queries in electronic discovery.

search queries
Specific words used in a computerized search.

Boolean
A search model that uses keywords and connectors.

A **search query** is a set of parameters that are used to search through electronic data to find relevant material. Lawyers and paralegals are trained to use keywords in conducting searches of legal literature. The most familiar search query is the keyword search method using the **Boolean** model. The Boolean model uses keywords with connectors such as AND and OR. Selecting the right keyword and the right connectors is critical to obtaining good results from the search. What is clear to anyone who has conducted a Boolean search is that it is not always reliable. If the wrong words are used or combinations are not properly structured in the query, the computer, without human input reviewing the documents, may not find the specific combination requested. This unsuccessful search may be the result of not knowing the specific terms used in a particular industry or profession. It may also result if the creator of the document has used unrelated terms as identifiers to throw off anyone

IN THE WORDS OF THE COURT . . .

WILLIAM A. GROSS CONSTRUCTION ASSOCIATES, INC., :
Plaintiff, : 07 Civ. 10639 (LAK) (AJP)
-against- : OPINION AND ORDER
AMERICAN MANUFACTURERS MUTUAL INSURANCE COMPANY, :

ANDREW J. PECK, United States Magistrate Judge:

This Opinion should serve as a wake-up call to the Bar in this District about the need for careful thought, quality control, testing, and cooperation with opposing counsel in designing search terms or "keywords" to be used to produce emails or other electronically stored information ("ESI"). While this message has appeared in several cases from outside this Circuit, it appears that the message has not reached many members of our Bar.

DISCUSSION

This case is just the latest example of lawyers designing keyword searches in the dark, by the seat of the pants, without adequate (indeed, here, apparently without any) discussion with those who wrote the emails. Prior decisions from Magistrate Judges in the Baltimore-Washington Beltway have warned counsel of this problem, but the message has not gotten through to the Bar in this District. As Magistrate Judge Paul Grimm has stated:

> While keyword searches have long been recognized as appropriate and helpful for ESI search and retrieval, there are well-known limitations and risks associated with them, and proper selection and implementation obviously involves technical, if not scientific knowledge.
>
> * * *
>
> Selection of the appropriate search and information retrieval technique requires careful advance planning by persons qualified to design effective search methodology. The implementation of the methodology selected should be tested for quality assurance; and the party selecting the methodology must be prepared to explain the rationale for the method chosen to the court, demonstrate that it is appropriate for the task, and show that it was properly implemented.

Victor Stanley, Inc. v. Creative Pipe, Inc., 250 F.R.D. 251, 260, 262 (D. Md. May 29, 2008) (Grimm, M.J.).

searching the records, such as the code words used by companies like Apple and Microsoft to hide the existence of a project that is developing a new product.

Words are not static; they change over time as their meaning changes or as they are applied to new areas. Consider the contemporary use of the word "bad" to mean "good," or the specialty use of the word "head" as a part of an engine to an automotive engineer, the top of a beer to a bartender, or a bathroom to a sailor.

Other search types include:

- Adaptive pattern recognition
- Associative retrieval
- Combined word search
- Full-text search
- Fuzzy search
- Indexing
- Keyword search
- Natural language search
- Numeric range search
- Phonic search
- Phrase search
- Proximity search
- Range search
- Similar document search
- Sound-alike search
- Synonym search
- Term search
- Topical search
- Variable weighted search
- Weighted relevance search
- Wildcard search
- Stemming

Boolean search queries are acknowledged to not have the degree of accuracy desired. A number of other search methods have thus been developed and are used by different search engines and electronic discovery software in an attempt to improve search accuracy. Among these are the algebraic search, where a mathematical model is created that retrieves documents based on the proximity of certain words to others, and the concept search, which relies on the use of alternative words to replace other words.

IN THE WORDS OF THE COURT . . .

UNITED STATES DISTRICT COURT
FOR THE DISTRICT OF COLUMBIA

United States of America,

Vs

Michael John O'Keefe, Sr.,

Sunil Agrawal,

Defendants. v. Cr. No. 06-249 (PLF/JMF)

MEMORANDUM OPINION

. . .

3. Search Terms and Other Deficiencies

As noted above, defendants protest the search terms the government used. Whether search terms or "keywords" will yield the information sought is a complicated question involving the interplay, at least, of the sciences of computer technology, statistics and linguistics.... Indeed, a special project team of the Working Group on Electronic Discovery of the Sedona Conference is studying that subject and their work indicates how difficult this question is....

Given this complexity, for lawyers and judges to dare opine that a certain search term or terms would be more likely to produce information than

(continued)

WEB RESOURCES

Sedona Conference® working group 1 documents on Electronic Document Retention and Production may be viewed at: http://www.thesedonaconference.org/content/miscFiles/publications_html?grp=wgs110

the terms that were used is truly to go where angels fear to tread. This topic is clearly beyond the ken of a layman and requires that any such conclusion be based on evidence that, for example, meets the criteria of Rule 702 of the Federal Rules of Evidence. Accordingly, if defendants are going to contend that the search terms used by the government were insufficient, they will have to specifically so contend in a motion to compel and their contention must be based on evidence that meets the requirements of Rule 702 of the Federal Rules of Evidence.

Text Retrieval Conference

Accurate searches are essential to reducing the cost of electronic discovery. The more searches that must be run because of poor search techniques, the greater the cost. The need for high degrees of search accuracy is not limited to the legal profession or for e-discovery. It is a broad based concern in every area of business and scientific endeavor. It is accepted that no search will be one hundred percent effective every time. But, a high rate of success is required. The issue of search accuracy has become the subject of an annual conference to encourage research in information retrieval from large text collections: the Text Retrieval Conference (TREC) co-sponsored by the National Institute of Standards and Technology, an agency of the U.S. Commerce Department.

WEB RESOURCES

Review the efforts of the Legal Track at the websites for Information Technology Laboratory (ITL) and Intelligence Advanced Research Projects Activity (IARPA) at http://trec.nist.gov/overview.html.

One of the conference tracks is the Legal Track, whose purpose is to develop search technology that meets the needs of lawyers to engage in effective discovery in digital document collections. As part of the annual meeting a set of simulated complaints are prepared and used as the basis for the creation of an appropriate search query that will locate the ESI desired in the case. The process includes a collaborative effort of plaintiff and defense counsel in creating the query as shown below based on the fictitious case of *Jensen v Smokin' Cigarettes*. A number of topics are run to test the systems. In this example the portion related to topic 145–All documents concerning actual or projected sales–is used as the example, where the final agreed search using a Boolean search query resulted in an accuracy of 55%.

PLAINTIFF'S REQUESTS FOR PRODUCTION OF DOCUMENTS

Pursuant to Rule 34 of the Federal Rules of Civil Procedure, Plaintiff Jenny Je[n]sen requests that Smokin' Cigarettes, Inc. and Jesse Winston (collectively, "Defendants") produce all responsive documents requested herein at the office of undersigned counsel as soon as practicable.

INSTRUCTIONS

1. These requests require the production of all responsive documents within the sole or joint possession, custody or control of the Defendants, including their agents, departments, attorneys, directors, officers, employees, consultants, investigators, insurance companies, or other persons subject to Defendants' custody or control.
2. All documents that respond, in whole or in part, to any portion of these Requests must be produced in their entirety, including all attachments and enclosures.
3. For purposes of these requests, the words used are considered to have, and should be understood to have, their ordinary, everyday meanings. Plaintiffs refer Defendants to any dictionary in the event Defendants assert that the wording of a request is vague, ambiguous, unintelligible, or confusing.

(continued)

DEFINITIONS

4. The words "and," "or," "each," "any," "all," "refer," and "discuss," shall be construed in their broadest form and the singular shall include the plural and the plural shall include the singular whenever necessary so as to bring within the scope of these Requests all documents (defined below) that might otherwise be construed to be outside their scope.
5. The phrase "advertising, marketing or promotion" of cigarettes includes public relations activities involving smoking and health.
6. For present purposes, the term "defendants" includes Smokin' Cigarettes Inc. as well as those companies whose records are found in the Tobacco Master Settlement Agreement database.
7. Solely for the purpose of the TREC 2008 legal track, "document" means all text-searchable data, information or writings stored in the Tobacco Master Settlement Agreement database, including without limitation: any written, electronic or computerized files, data or software; memoranda; emails; correspondence; OCR scanned images; communications; reports; summaries; studies; analyses; evaluations; notes or notebooks; indices; spreadsheets; logs; books; pamphlets; binders; calendar or diary entries; ledger entries; press clippings; graphs; tables; charts; printouts; drawings; maps; meeting minutes; transcripts. The term "document" encompasses all metadata associated with the document. The term also includes all drafts associated with any particular document.
8. "Person" or "individual" means natural persons, corporations, firms, partnerships, unincorporated associations, trusts, and any other legal entity.
9. The term "plans" means tentative and preliminary proposals, recommendations, or considerations, whether or not finalized or authorized, as well as those that have been adopted.
10. The term "relating to" means in whole or in part constituting, containing, concerning, discussing, describing, analyzing, identifying or stating.

FIRST SET OF REQUESTS FOR PRODUCTION:

Plaintiffs request that Defendants produce all responsive documents on the following topics:

[TOPIC 145] All documents concerning actual or projected sales.

Topic 145 (2008-H-4)

Request Text: All documents concerning actual or projected sales.

Initial Proposal by Defendant: "actual sales" OR "projected sales"

Rejoinder by Plaintiff: (estimate! OR anticipate! OR forecast! OR actual OR project!) w/5 sales

Final Negotiated Boolean Query: (estimate! OR anticipate! OR forecast! OR actual OR project!) w/2 sales

Sampling: 6910192 pooled, 2500 assessed, 419 judged highly relevant, 258 other judged relevant, 1816 judged non-relevant, 7 gray, \C"=5.60

Est. Rel.: 461322.3 (including 143094.7 estimated highly relevant)

Final Boolean Result Size (B): 40315, F1: 8.4%, (Precision: 55.0%, Recall: 4.6%)

Sampling

sampling
The testing of a search query by running it against a limited set of documents to measure the accuracy of the response to a search query.

Sampling is the testing of a search query by running it against a limited set of documents to measure the accuracy of the response to a search query. Consider a simplistic query looking for information about product defects in automobiles

IN THE WORDS OF THE COURT . . .

United States Court of Appeals,
District of Columbia Circuit.

In re FANNIE MAE SECURITIES LITIGATION.

No. 08-5014.

Decided Jan. 6, 2009.

Pursuant to the stipulated order, the individual defendants submitted over 400 search terms, which covered approximately 660,000 documents. OFHEO objected on the grounds that the stipulated order limited the individual defendants to "appropriate search terms," but the district court disagreed, ruling on November 2, 2007 that the stipulated order gave the individual defendants sole discretion to specify search terms and imposed no limits on permissible terms. Although the district court made this ruling in an off-the-record chambers conference, the parties agree on its meaning.

OFHEO undertook extensive efforts to comply with the stipulated order, hiring 50 contract attorneys solely for that purpose. The total amount OFHEO spent on the individual defendants' discovery requests eventually reached over $6 million, more than 9 percent of the agency's entire annual budget.

manufactured by major automobile producers. Using words such as "car" or "automobile" would result in substantial numbers of records, most of which would probably not reflect the specific documents sought. One example of an expanded set of terms is the search for the Fannie Mae securities litigation, in which over four hundred search terms were used covering 660,000 documents, as described below. As this case demonstrates, at the very least it can be a waste of time and money to search on a large database of ESI using a query with terms and phrases that are not properly selected.

COMPUTER FORENSICS

LEARNING OBJECTIVE 5
Describe the role of the forensic examiner in digital discovery.

Computer forensics is the application of computer investigation and analysis techniques to gather evidence suitable for presentation in a court of law. The goal of computer forensics is to perform a structured investigation while maintaining a documented chain of evidence to find out exactly what happened on a computer and who was responsible for it. (SearchSecurity.com)

There are times when one has the belief that documents have been modified or deleted. In this case, the dates of the original creation and those of any modifications or changes may be very relevant and material. The metadata for documents will typically show the relevant dates of creation and any changes. Qualified forensic experts can examine the original computer hard drive to determine if there were any changes or deletions of material. Where forensic data collection is required, it is important to have an expert who can obtain the information without changing anything on the original storage media. Remember, each time a document is opened, the metadata changes. The data must therefore be obtained without making any changes to the original data.

WEB RESOURCES
To learn more about computer forensics, go to http://searchsecurity.techtarget.com/sDefinition/0,,sid14_gci1007675,00.html

ADVICE FROM THE FIELD

LEXISNEXIS APPLIED DISCOVERY TECH TIPS: UNDERSTANDING THE DIFFERENCE BETWEEN COMPUTER FORENSICS AND DATA GATHERING

As the field of electronic discovery has evolved over the past several years, there has been increasing confusion about the difference between computer forensics—a specialized application of scientific principles and practices—and data gathering, the process for collecting documents and other electronic evidence from computers. Without understanding the differences between these services, many attorneys have paid to retain "forensics experts" in cases involving electronic discovery, when all they really needed was some good advice or hands-on assistance with collecting electronic files from their clients' computers.

Think of computer forensics as taking an "autopsy" of a computer hard drive. The science of computer forensics can be of great value in certain circumstances. For example, allegations of attempts to delete incriminating documents from a computer may be confirmed or refuted with the assistance of a forensic expert. Similarly, information from computer equipment damaged in a fire or flood may be recoverable with the assistance of a forensic data recovery expert. A forensic investigation can take heroic efforts and many hours of an expensive consultant's time to find the electronic needle in the haystack. Fortunately, most cases involving electronic discovery do not warrant such a burdensome expenditure.

	Computer Forensics	**Data Gathering**
Goal	To locate hidden or deleted files.	To capture potentially responsive documents.
Tools Required	Highly specialized, expensive hardware and software.	Relatively inexpensive tools utilized by most client IT departments.
Expertise Required	Computer forensics experts.	IT staff trained by or assisted by electronic discovery service provider.
Relative Expense	Can cost thousands of dollars to analyze a single hard drive.	Cost efficient methods employed to leverage the client's own resources.

Many attorneys facing an electronic discovery request need only basic assistance with data gathering. While it is critical to employ forensically sound data collection practices, in many cases, this may be as simple as providing procedures for how to intelligently and safely copy data from a computer hard drive to a CD-ROM, tape, or other transportable media. These forensically sound practices will ensure that metadata is not altered when data is copied from its original location. They will also help attorneys understand how best to save and store the copied information for use with electronic discovery review tools.

In other cases, attorneys may need on-site assistance to collect data from multiple physical locations or to assist with chain of custody tracking. In these circumstances, chain of custody tracking would include detailed documentation of the data collection procedures, who had custody of the electronic data, who collected it from its original location, and where the data was located when collected. Further tracking measures should include application of bar codes to individual pieces of media and storage in a secured evidence room.

Electronic discovery often presents unique circumstances that depend on how well the client's documents are sorted and organized in the ordinary course of business. Your electronic discovery service provider should be able to advise you on how best to approach the particular circumstances of a given case.

CHAIN OF CUSTODY

chain of custody
A written record showing the identity of everyone accessing evidence and showing that the evidence was not altered while in possession of the law firm.

Many people who watch the current crime and forensic television shows know the term **chain of custody** and have some idea of what it means. In the criminal case, it starts with the use of paper or plastic bags for the collection and storage of evidence. Steps are taken to ensure that evidence is properly collected and preserved, and that the possession of the evidence is properly documented and accounted for at all steps in the processing, pretrial, and trial phases. The point is generally made that any failure to follow a prescribed protocol can result in the evidence lacking credibility at the time of trial. The same may be said for electronic evidence. Computer sources such as hard disk drives and other storage media and the electronic documents they contain must be properly handled, accessed, and preserved to ensure the reliability of the electronic files. Every time an electronic file is opened or accessed, the metadata (file information or history) changes electronically to reflect the change, unless proper steps are taken to ensure it is not changed. For example, each time you open a Word document on your computer and then save it, even if you made no changes to the content of the document, the metadata such as the date of last access changes to reflect the latest date of access. If the original words and the original date of creation are important to a case, the original version must be preserved to avoid changes of any type to the underlying metadata. Where the physical storage devices are critical, the same procedures used when saving other evidence, including the use of sealed evidence bags such as that shown in Exhibit 6.5, may be used. In this way, a chain of custody is maintained, in case the original must be accessed, to prove no changes have occurred. If a claim is made of spoliation, the legal team may offer proof that the forensic examination was properly conducted.

RESOURCES THAT SUPPORT E-DISCOVERY

Service Companies

Law firms often retain a service bureau or consulting company to help in the electronic discovery process. There are many reasons for using an outside consultant, such as a lack of in-house expertise or a workload that will not permit another case to be handled in-house. Some full-service companies offer a range of services from the basic, like scanning paper documents into electronic form, to the complex, like forensic recovery and investigation of lost, destroyed, or missing files. In some cases, allowing a specialist to prepare and deliver the documents in a form for attorney review and use at trial may be a better allocation of resources and costs.

The trend for companies that support the electronic discovery process is to offer a complete range of products and services, from standalone software that may be used on the law firm's own computers to cloud computing systems that store and process ESI and allow any authorized member of the litigation team to access the ESI from anywhere in the world using the Internet.

AD Summation Software

The AD Summation family of products provides solutions from the standalone Iblaze to CaseVault's comprehensive, end-to-end electronic discovery services and CaseVantage's advanced, web-based review platform. As the number of documents increases in a case, the ability to locate relevant documents in a timely fashion becomes more and more critical, and managing the documents is crucial to successful litigation outcomes. In cases involving potentially millions of documents, it is essential to be able to find the relevant information quickly, sometimes in the middle of the direct or cross-examination of a witness.

AD Summation–type programs allow for easy search and retrieval of all of the evidence—whether documents, testimony, photographs, or electronic files—with

Exhibit 6.5 Evidence Bag

CONTROL NO: M 1365614

INVESTIGATOR'S RECEIPT: Tear along perforated line and retain for your records.

Case Number: ______

Evidence Bag Sealed by: ______ Date Sealed: ______

Description of Enclosed Evidence: ______

WARNING: ATTEMPTS TO OPEN THIS SEAL WILL DISTORT THESE LINES

Glue Line Glue Line

CONTROL NO: M 1365614

EVIDENCE

(TO BE OPENED BY AUTHORIZED PERSONNEL ONLY)

NOTE

A) Do not use this bag for any evidence that has wet/damp body fluids on it.
B) To seal bag, peel off blue release liner, then seal bag by pressing down on red glue line.

Case Number: ______

Description of Enclosed Evidence: ______

Submitting Agency: ______

Telephone Number: ______

Evidence Recovered By: ______ (PRINT NAME)

Victim's Full Name: ______

Suspect's Full Name: ______

Evidence Bag Sealed By: ______ (PRINT NAME)

______ (SIGNATURE)

Date Sealed: ______ Time Sealed: ______ AM PM

CHAIN OF CUSTODY

FROM	TO	DATE

FOR CRIME LAB PERSONNEL ONLY

CONDITION OF EVIDENCE BAG UPON RECEIPT AT LAB:

☐ SEALED ☐ OTHER ______ (DESCRIBE)

CRIME LAB CASE NO: ______

NOTES: ______

www.tritechusa.com

CUT HERE TO OPEN

ADVICE FROM THE FIELD

BLUEPRINT FOR CLOUD-BASED EDISCOVERY—ON DEMAND TECHNOLOGY

A Framework for eDiscovery Cloud Computing Security, Privacy, Control, Risk and Cost Concerns

Bringing eDiscovery in-house: eDiscovery cloud versus on-premise software

When considering a cloud-based eDiscovery application versus an on-premise application, one must consider not only the audience and focus for the application being delivered, but also the hardware, systems, data centers and human capital necessary to deliver the application. For corporations and law firms looking to bring eDiscovery in-house, cloud-based eDiscovery can be very attractive. Cloud-based eDiscovery is often less risky, less costly and more efficient than purchasing, installing and maintaining on-premise software. eDiscovery practitioners control the process, data and access without incurring the costs, risks and time delays[3,4] inherent in on-premise software deployments or the headaches involved [in] lobbying your IT department to modify your corporate firewall and security standards to allow outside parties to access on-premise eDiscovery software. Initial cloud computing application deployment is proven to be much faster and on-going maintenance costs are proven to be much less expensive than on-premise software deployments.[3,4] Additionally, cloud-based eDiscovery software can provide highly predictable costs that eliminate the expense spikes typically associated with on-premise software, hardware, and human capital.

There has been a lot of misinformation equating "bringing eDiscovery in-house" with the purchase, installation and on-going management of on-premise software for various eDiscovery tasks. The true nature of bringing eDiscovery in-house is that corporate legal teams and their executives are trending toward retaining control of eDiscovery decision-making, creating and owning the overall eDiscovery process and acting as collaborative partners throughout the life cycle of a particular matter. The delivery model for eDiscovery software and services, cloud-based or on-premise, is not directly related to the notion of "bringing eDiscovery in-house."

According to Forrester Research, Inc.[3] the benefits of cloud-based applications include:

Dimension	Software-as-a-service helps by...
Reduced cost of adoption	Reducing the licensing, training, and support costs of adding additional users.
Quicker adoption	Decreasing the time to ramp up new users, maximizing their productivity from using the application.
Improved adoption	Enabling more users to use the application.
On-premise cost avoidance	■ Eliminating maintenance costs. ■ Reducing full-time help desk and server support, and transferring staff to higher value, proactive roles.
Improved flexibility	Reducing spend on excess capacity.

Public Clouds and Private Clouds: Why public clouds are wrong for eDiscovery

The difference between public and private clouds is very important for those performing eDiscovery. A public cloud uses shared hardware, software and applications that are available to the public. Examples include Amazon EC2, AWS and Google Apps. This approach is very effective when used for consumer-based applications or business applications that do not have the same security and access control requirements or the level of legal and regulatory scrutiny that eDiscovery data has. A private cloud, whether deployed by a company behind the firewall (aka "internal cloud") or deployed by a provider, uses hardware, software and applications only for subscribing users.

Private clouds have specific advantages over public clouds when it comes to eDiscovery: With a public cloud you don't know where (including what country, state or server) the files are stored, and don't know if you can really control document retention and destruction. And you may not be receiving the level of disaster recovery and business continuity that you require. Clients need to know that they are completely in control of their data, and a private, trusted cloud is the only way to do that.

(continued)

(continued)

As recently cited in the *Electronic Commerce & Law Report*, a non-private cloud pools resources to serve multiple clients, which "implies both an increased risk of inadvertent access to data by others in the cloud and an inability to pinpoint with any specificity where data resides at a given moment."

With private clouds, subscribers understand where their data resides, so their information aligns with proper jurisdiction, security and applicable document retention.[5]

[3]"The ROI of Software-as-a-Service," by Forrester Research, Inc., Liz Herbert and Jon Erickson, July 13, 2009

[4]"Talking To Your CFO About Cloud Computing," by Forrester Research, October 29, 2008

[5]Sotto, Lisa J., Bridget C. Treacy, and Melinda L. McLellan. "Privacy and Data Security Risks in Cloud Computing," *Electronic Commerce & Law Report*, February 3, 2010

Reproduced in part from Blueprint for Cloud-Based eDiscovery–On Demand Technology

The full article may be viewed at: www.CaseCentral.com/cloudblueprint.php

a single command. Documents associated with a case are stored on the computer in electronic folders. These folders may be set up to include transcripts, pleadings, text files (from OCR or otherwise), casts of characters, and core databases. Some versions of these programs are designed to work on standalone systems such as a laptop carried into court. Others permit concurrent use by many users over a network and some permit remote access over the Internet.

Concordance

Concordance (a LexisNexis company) is a litigation support system program that provides litigation document management. According to LexisNexis, "Concordance is a highly focused text database management program that features sophisticated text search and retrieval functions. Text database management differs substantially from traditional database management in that its focus is searching for, retrieving, and categorizing specific words, phrases, or combinations of words. The ability to perform detailed text searches is particularly important for individuals whose work is heavily text-concentrated, for example attorneys, scientific researchers, marketing researchers, librarians, and personnel managers for resume retrieval."

CaseCentral

Founded in 1994, CaseCentral provides secure, **private cloud**–based e-discovery software for corporations and law firms. CaseCentral's software was the industry's first web-based discovery management system that supported clients throughout the various stages of litigation and e-discovery.

private cloud
An Internet-based service that allows restricted access to information stored on servers of a third party host company.

The company's e-discovery platform integrates early case assessment, processing, search, analysis, review, and production capabilities with a private cloud delivery model.

CaseCentral allows authorized users from anywhere to log in through the Internet, and create and load new cases almost immediately, with CaseCentral providing the necessary technology infrastructure, thus eliminating the need for corporations and law firms to provide in-house infrastructure.

Users can perform early case assessment, review, and production using one online environment to conduct advanced searches that cull and filter to identify just the groups of documents necessary for further review. Using the same system, documents may then be reviewed before preparing them for opposing counsel.

The steps in the e-discovery process are shown in Exhibit 6.6.

Litigation support and attorneys can also search, analyze, code, and prepare documents for production, as shown in Exhibits 6.7 to 6.10.

Exhibit 6.6 Steps in the e-discovery process

Step 1. Early Case Assessment

Search and analyze large sets of data to quickly determine what ultimatelly needs active review

Step 2. Integrated Review

Evaluate and tag document and groups of documents in preparation for production

- Responsiveness and Privilege review
- Redaction and issue coding
- Witness preparation and trial strategy

Step 3. Post Review Utilization

Utilize the work product to guide your litigation hold or preservation strategy for further ECA or case management

Source: Copyright © casecentral.com.

CaseCentral's unique multi-matter support allows hundreds or even thousands of cases to be managed within the same repository, sharing workflow, security roles, production processes, and even work product between cases. (For example, prior to production, an administrator can verify if any documents have ever been withheld from any case.) Exhibit 6.10 shows how all cases, reviewers, time lines, and counsel may be monitored from a single Administrator Dashboard.

Exhibit 6.7 Documents view and related review criteria tagging window

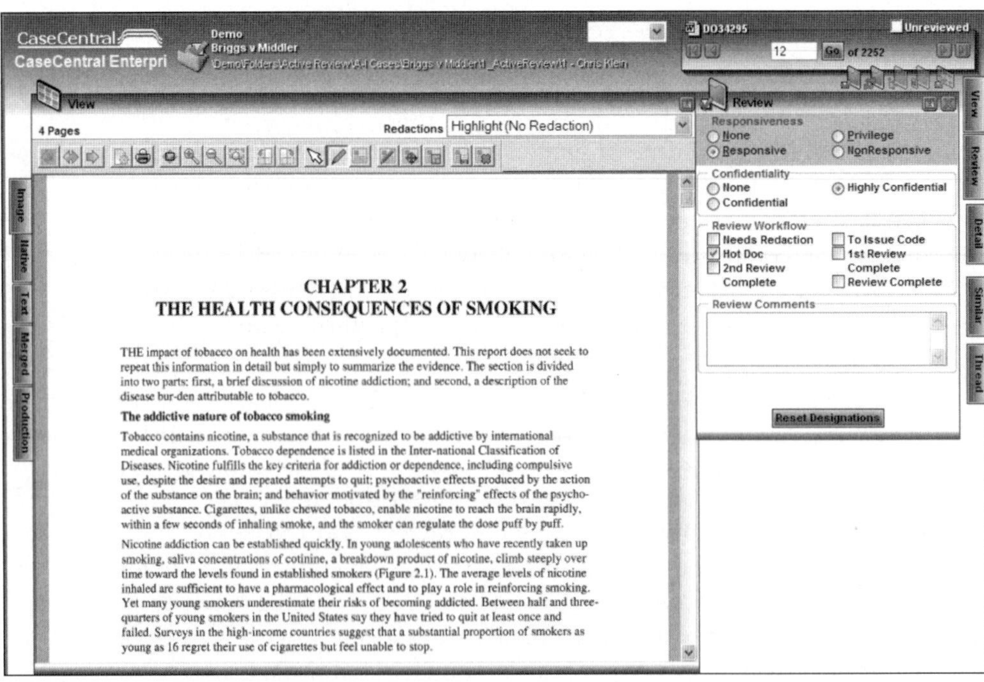

Source: Copyright © casecentral.com.

Exhibit 6.8
CaseCentral's report on near-duplicate documents

Similar

Document	Similarity
DO33584	100%
DO33805	100%
DO34295	99%
DO34330	99%
DO43900	96%
DO44068	94%
DO47559	87%
DO50990	85%
DO32941	85%
DO37803	85%
DO39144	84%
DO40411	84%
DO43904	84%
DO45560	77%
DO50976	77%

Include Documents Not In Folder

Compare Designate

Source: Copyright © casecentral.com.

Exhibit 6.9
Related email threads of near-duplicate documents

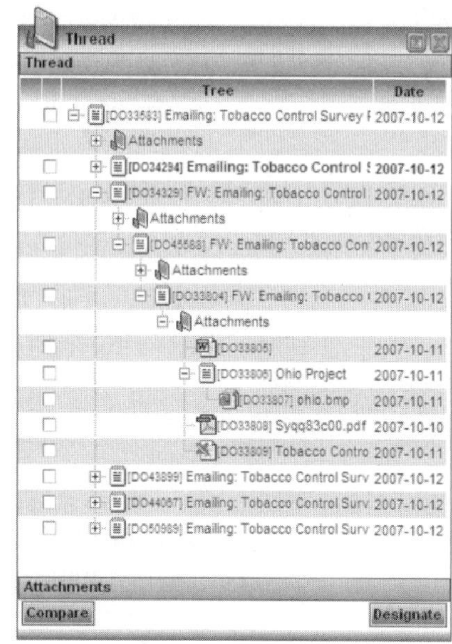

Source: Copyright © casecentral.com.

Exhibit 6.10 CaseCentral's Administrator Dashboard monitor of all cases and counsel

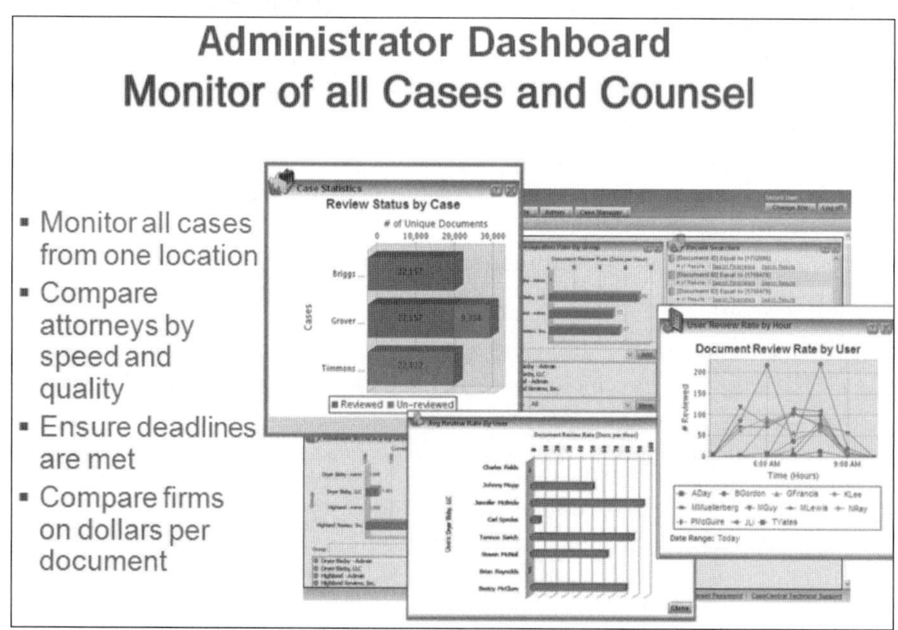

Source: Copyright © casecentral.com.

CONCEPT REVIEW AND REINFORCEMENT

KEY TERMS

Electronic Discovery Reference Model 136
Safe Haven 139
Information Management Reference Model (IMRM) 139
interrogatories 143
deposition 144
search query 148
Boolean 148
sampling 151
chain of custody 153
private cloud 157

CHAPTER SUMMARY

Introduction to Evidence and Discovery	For the plaintiff's attorney discovery is a matter of finding relevant evidence to present the case. For the plaintiff, it may also be a question of the timing of the action and where to institute suit. The defendant frequently is in the position of not knowing if or when a suit will be brought for which he or she will need a defense, and therefore not necessarily knowing what records need to be preserved or for how long.
Electronic Discovery—The Process	Electronic discovery, or e-discovery, should be thought of as a process and not a single event. It consists of a number of steps or individual processes as shown in the Electronic Discovery Reference Model in Exhibit 6.1: information management; identification; preservation and collection; processing, review and analysis; production; and presentation.
Information Management	The first step for the litigation team is learning the details and procedures of each party's retention policy and that of any potential third parties, such as a supplier of the parties that may have relevant supporting information.
Cost of Saving ESI	Technology has both advantages and disadvantages. One of the biggest advantages are computer systems for the efficient, economical creation and sharing of information in electronic form. One of the disadvantages that the explosion of ESI has created is the business and legal issue of how much information to save and for how long. Saving and archiving ESI in secure, multi-location storage facilities as required by court action, company policy, and government regulation incurs a cost that increases as the volume increases.
Identification	The initial step in the discovery process, both traditional and electronic, is to determine what documents are needed, who has those documents, what format the documents are in, the value of those documents in the case, and the potential costs of retrieving those documents.
Locating Evidence	Finding the desired document requires an appreciation of the types of records kept, by whom they are kept, where they are kept, and the language used by the creators of the records and those indexing them. Every occupation has its own lexicon of terms and type of document used to record its activity. Without the knowledge of the terms and phrases used, a search may not produce the desired documents.

Interrogatories and Depositions	Interrogatories are written questions that are required to be answered by the opposing party. These questions rarely result in any surprises, such as might be obtained in a face-to-face question session. They are submitted to opposing counsel, who reviews both the questions and the answers of the client carefully to ensure that only required information is supplied. With the information from the interrogatories, the next step in obtaining the needed information that may lead to existing or destroyed ESI is the Rule 30 deposition of a person knowledgeable in the opposing party's system.
Collection	Collection is the part of the e-discovery process that includes finding and obtaining electronically stored information for review and analysis. The collection process may require retaining outside professionals who are experienced in the techniques of searching databases. Depending on the computer systems used or the programs for creating, storing, or archiving the ESI, the specialist may be required to retrieve the data in a usable form.
Search Queries	A search query is a set of parameters that are used to search through electronic data to find relevant material. Lawyers and paralegals are trained to use keywords in conducting searches of legal literature. The most familiar search query is the keyword search method using the Boolean model. Boolean search queries are acknowledged to not have the degree of accuracy desired. A number of other search methods have been developed and are used by different search engines and electronic discovery software in an attempt to improve search accuracy.
Sampling	Sampling is the testing of a search query by running it against a limited set of documents to measure the accuracy of the response to a search query.
Computer Forensics	The goal of computer forensics is to perform a structured investigation while maintaining a documented chain of evidence to find out exactly what happened on a computer and who was responsible for it. There are times when one has the belief that documents have been modified or deleted. In this case, the dates of the original creation and those of any modifications or changes may be very relevant and material. The metadata for documents will typically show these relevant dates of creation and changes.
Chain of Custody	Steps are taken to ensure that evidence is properly collected and preserved, and that the possession of the evidence is properly documented and accounted for at all steps of the processing, pretrial, and trial phases.
Resources That Support E-Discovery	Law firms often retain a service bureau or consulting company to help in the electronic discovery process. There are many reasons for using an outside consultant—possibly a lack of in-house expertise or a workload that will not permit another case to be handled in-house. Some full-service companies offer a range of services from the basic, like scanning paper documents into electronic form, to the complex, like forensic recovery and investigation of lost, destroyed, or missing files.

REVIEW QUESTIONS AND EXERCISES

1. List the elements of the electronic discovery process.
2. What is the goal of the electronic discovery process?
3. What is information management?
4. Is the destruction of electronic documents permitted? Explain.
5. Has the change from paper to electronically stored information reduced the number of documents being created and stored?
6. What role does email play in the communications process?
7. What is meant by a Safe Haven?
8. Under what circumstances do the Federal Rules of Civil Procedure permit the destruction of documents without sanctions?
9. What is the obligation of a party who is aware of litigation with regard to documentation?
10. What role do document retention costs play in the retention of documents by businesses?
11. What are some of the elements with regard to identification of electronically stored documents?
12. How do the courts define a record for discovery purposes?
13. What information is needed to locate potential evidence?
14. Why is knowledge of the vocabulary of different professions and industries necessary for the litigation team?
15. What is the purpose of interrogatories?
16. What information can be obtained through the use of interrogatories that will help in locating electronically stored information?
17. How can interrogatories be used in preparing for depositions?
18. What are the requirements for giving notice of the taking of a Rule 30 deposition?
19. What kind of information can be learned in a Rule 30 deposition that will aid in electronic discovery?
20. What is the obligation to make voluntary disclosures of information in civil litigation under the federal rules?
21. When might the litigation team need the help of outside consultants in collecting electronically stored information?
22. What is the purpose of a search query in electronic discovery?
23. In electronic discovery, how effective is the Boolean model of searching?
24. What are some examples of other types of search methods that might be used in electronic discovery?
25. What is the significance of the Legal Track of the Information Technology Laboratory's annual simulation?
26. Why is sampling an important element in reducing the cost of electronic discovery?
27. What is the role of computer forensics in electronic discovery?
28. What is meant by the chain of custody?
29. Why is a properly maintained chain of custody important in the electronic discovery situation?
30. What role do service companies play in supporting electronic discovery?

BUILDING YOUR PARALEGAL SKILLS

INTERNET AND TECHNOLOGY EXERCISES

1. Locate the websites of companies that support electronic discovery and list the services that they offer.
2. Review the current information on the Electronic Discovery Reference Model at www.EDRM.net.
3. Use the Internet to locate ethics opinions with regard to electronic discovery in your jurisdiction.
4. Use the Internet to find information on other search query methods used in the legal profession.

CIVIL LITIGATION VIDEO CASE STUDIES

Scheduling Conference with Judge: Discovery Issue Resolution

At a scheduling conference in the judge's chambers, the attorneys and the judge discuss discovery issues in the case and motions for sanctions. The plaintiffs' attorney has been denied access to the truck involved in the collision, including the brake parts that may have failed, in order to inspect them. There is concern that the evidence needed by the plaintiffs to prove their case has been disposed of and no longer exists.

After viewing the video in MyLegalStudiesKit, answer the following questions.

1. What are the option open to the court to insure cooperation?
2. Does this constitute spoliation of evidence for which sanctions are appropriate?
3. What sanctions would be appropriate?

CHAPTER OPENING SCENARIO CASE STUDY

1. Use the Opening Scenario for this chapter to answer the following questions.
   a. Prepare an electronic discovery plan for use in the school bus case with the expanded details that include the potential for a product defect or negligent truck maintenance.
   b. Prepare a discovery plan for use in a complex litigation case like the airplane crash in Appendix III.
2. For the assigned case study:
   a. Prepare a set of interrogatories for use in this case.
   b. Prepare a Rule 30 deposition notice for use in this case.

COMPREHENSIVE CASE STUDY

SCHOOL BUS–TRUCK ACCIDENT CASE

1. Prepare a list of potential items that might have been destroyed.
2. Prepare a list of interrogatories to identify potentially destroyed evidence.

BUILDING YOUR PROFESSIONAL PORTFOLIO

CIVIL LITIGATION TEAM AT WORK

1. Prepare a standard set of interrogatories for use in a case involving electronic discovery.
2. Prepare a deposition notice for a corporation involving any federal Rule 30 deposition.

Contacts and Resources

1. Prepare a list, including website information and local contact information, of companies providing forensic services to the legal profession.
2. Prepare a list of local companies that provide e-discovery support services to the legal profession.
3. Prepare a list of companies, including their contact information, that provide cloud computing electronic discovery support.

"The power of the lawyer is in the uncertainty of the law."

–Jeremy Bentham,
Philosopher and Activist, 1748–1832

Analysis and Review

CHAPTER 7

OPENING SCENARIO

The litigation teams working on the school bus accident case and the airplane crash case were meeting with an information technology support specialist to discuss discovery issues. The IT specialist had been asked to sit in on the meeting to advise the team members in case there were any issues that they were not aware of in the discovery process. The school bus group indicated that they did not see any issues in how the documents were produced and delivered to them. The defendant company was so small that the team did not see how there could be any issues in electronic discovery and planned to just make a request in interrogatories for all documents related to the truck and its maintenance and repair. The IT specialist advised them not to assume that there would not be problems even with a small company since in her experience, some of the smaller companies use legacy computer systems or old computer systems with older forms of proprietary software that are not easy to replicate or read in the native form of the document. Her biggest concern was in the air crash litigation case because of the overwhelming amounts of information that the team would have to deal with—both the information being created as a part of the investigation by the state and federal agencies and the findings of records that the national air carrier was required to keep as part of government regulations and oversight. Owen Mason, as the senior partner, expressed great concern that they might not have the resources in-house to handle large-scale electronic document discovery and asked his litigation support paralegal to look into the options that might be available.

LEARNING OBJECTIVES

After studying this chapter, you should be able to:

1. Describe the issues in reviewing material as part of discovery.
2. Describe the purpose of privilege review and how items may be protected from disclosure.
3. Describe the reason and the process for authentication of documents.

VIDEO INTRODUCTION

An introduction to the paperless office.

After watching the video in MyLegalStudiesKit, answer the following question.

- What is a paperless office?

INTRODUCTION TO ANALYSIS AND REVIEW OF E-DISCOVERY

Once the potentially discoverable information needed has been identified and made available to the client's attorney, it must be reviewed by the litigation team for relevancy to the discovery request and for attorney-client privileged or confidential information and any attorney work product that must be logged and removed. It is generally agreed that the attorney review function is the most costly part of electronic discovery because it potentially requires the manual review of every document obtained in the identification and collection phases of e-discovery. With the cost factors involved, efforts are made to reduce the total number of documents that must be reviewed. Where possible, efforts are made to use computers to identify items that may be removed because they are out of the time range of the requested documents or are duplicates. In some cases, outside contract attorneys, law students, and paralegals are hired to make the physical review. But with all the effort to review the documents, some items that should not be released are mistakenly released to the other side. Depending on the circumstances and the particular court, this may result in a waiver of the privilege or confidential nature of the information.

REVIEWING ELECTRONIC DOCUMENTS

LEARNING OBJECTIVE 1
Describe the issues in reviewing material as part of discovery.

review
Checking documents for confidential, privileged or work product content.

One of the biggest costs in electronic discovery is incurred in document **review.** Initially this involves reviewing the material obtained from clients to find information relevant to the discovery request and to identify privileged, confidential, or protected documents, such as those containing trade secrets. In small cases with a limited amount of information, the easiest method may be to make copies of the electronically created files using the original programs used to create the files, like the process for making a backup copy. The client delivers the files after copying them from his or her computer system onto a portable storage device like a CD, DVD, flash drive, or memory card. File review is then performed by using the program used to create the original file, such as Microsoft Word, Excel, or Access, and viewing the material on a computer screen or from a printed hard copy.

After obtaining the documents, decisions must be made about how to process the client supplied material. Nearly all business documents will be in a computer-generated and -stored electronic format such as emails, spreadsheets, word processing documents, database documents, graphic images, or a number

VIDEO ADVICE FROM THE FIELD

Janet Laquintano–Vice President Document Review, Sanction Solutions

A discussion of the document review process, the qualifications and skills required to perform document review.

After watching the video in MyLegalStudiesKit, answer the following questions.

1. What is document review?
2. What are review platforms?
3. Who is qualified to perform document review?

of electronic file format variations within each category. The good news is that electronic files, as opposed to paper documents, lend themselves to electronic or computer processing, search, and review.

When documents are delivered in a number of different electronic file formats, such as word processor, database, or spreadsheet file formats, review usually requires multiple programs that can open and view the original files. When the number of documents is in the thousands, tens of thousands, or in complex cases, in the millions, this process can be very time-consuming. One solution is to convert all of the different types of documents into one common program format that can be searched and indexed with a common computer program.

Forms of Delivery of ESI

The delivery of information in response to a discovery request may be in electronic form, paper form, or a combination of both. Documents from clients provided for review before sending them to the other side may be in various forms and different formats. Thus one of the first issues to be considered by the litigation team as the producing party is the format for document delivery to the opposing side after review.

The federal procedural rules (rule 34) allow the requesting party to specify a desired format for the delivery of responsive information. If there is no specially requested form for production of documents rule 34 provides that unless an objection is raised and sustained by the court, they may be delivered in the form they are kept in the usual course of business or in another reasonably usable form.

Rule 34. Producing Documents, Electronically Stored Information, and Tangible Things, or Entering onto Land, for Inspection and Other Purposes

(b) Procedure.

(1) Contents of the Request.

The request:

(A) must describe with reasonable particularity each item or category of items to be inspected;

(B) must specify a reasonable time, place, and manner for the inspection and for performing the related acts; and

(C) may specify the form or forms in which electronically stored information is to be produced.

Format of Delivery

Federal Rules of Civil Procedure Rule 34. Producing Documents, Electronically Stored Information, and Tangible Things, or Entering onto Land, for Inspection and Other Purposes

(b)(2) Responses and Objections.

(E) *Producing the Documents or Electronically Stored Information.* Unless otherwise stipulated or ordered by the court, these procedures apply to producing documents or electronically stored information:

(i) A party must produce document s as they are kept in the usual course of business or must organize and label them to correspond to the categories in the request;

(ii) If a request does not specify a form for producing electronically stored information, a party must produce it in a form or forms in which it is ordinarily maintained or in a reasonably usable form or forms; and

(iii) A party need not produce the same electronically stored information in more than one form.

The rule provides for delivery, if not otherwise requested, in the "form in which it is ordinarily maintained or in a reasonably usable form." But as noted by U.S. Magistrate Judge Facciola in a March 2010 case involving a continuing series of cases of *Covad v. Revonet*, it may not be absolutely necessary that it include metadata.

> . . . I noted that the strips of spreadsheet were clearly not produced in the form that they were ordinarily maintained, nor were they produced in a reasonably usable form. Id. Revonet's suggestion that the documents be pasted together was pure impertinence and simply not acceptable to the Court; I found that it is improper to "take an electronically searchable document and either destroy or degrade the document's ability to be searched." Id. (citing *Dahl v. Bain Capital Partners, Inc.*, 655 F. Supp. 2d 146, 150 (D. Mass. 2009)) (requiring production of spreadsheets in native format); In re *Classicstar Mare Lease Litig.*, No. 07-CV-353, 2009 WL 260954, at *3 (E.D. Ky. Feb. 2, 2009) (production may not degrade searchability); *Goodbys Creek, LLC v. Arch Ins. Co.*, No. 07-CV-947, 2008 WL 4279693, at *3 (M.D. Fla. Sept. 15, 2008) (same; conversion of e-mails from native to PDF not acceptable); *White v. Graceland Coll. Ctr. for Prof'l Dev. & Lifelong Learning*, 586 F. Supp. 2d 1250, 1264 (D. Kan. 2008). . . . Earlier in this case, I found the production of 35,000 e-mails in hard copy to be unacceptable, because no reasonable person could believe that Revonet, in its day to day operations, prints out all of its electronic communications on paper and then preserves them. *Covad II*, 254 F.R.D. at 150-51. The conversion to paper was therefore a bit of gamesmanship that I was not obliged to tolerate.
>
> Covad, however, would like me to take the current case law a step further and determine that electronically stored data produced in hard copy is inherently unusable and unacceptable under the Rules, because it lacks the metadata available in the native format. Mot. Hr'g Tr. 121:18-23. Thus, Covad asks the Court to hold that only native production, with metadata, of electronically stored information, is reasonably usable under Rule 34(b)(2)(E)(ii). But, the rule itself permits production *either* in the format in which e-mail is ordinarily maintained, *i.e.* "native format," *or* another usable format. Thus, by its exact terms, the Rule provides an alternative to the native format, contradicting Covad's claim that native, electronic format is absolutely obligatory. . . .

Source: Covad v. Revonet civ action no 06-1892 at page 7-9

■ FORMS OF PRODUCTION—METADATA

Obtaining the metadata for all of the documents produced or delivered may or may not be an issue. Having the metadata delivered with the document is also not an issue when there is no question as to the authenticity and accuracy of the document. If the copies produced are the same as the requesting party already has in her or his possession, there may not be any need for the metadata.

Metadata

Every electronic document has **metadata,** which is simply information about the document. This information may include the location of the file, referred to as **resource (system) metadata,** and the content and author of the file, **content (application) metadata.** For example, Exhibit 7.1 shows the metadata for this chapter as displayed in Microsoft Word 2010.

The method used to create the electronic file can impact the metadata delivered. If the document is delivered in its **native format,** the metadata is part of the document. However, if the document is delivered in a copied format, such as **TIFF,** which is a document *image*, the hidden data or metadata is not part of the document delivered. This may be an advantage or disadvantage, depending on whether one are the sender who wants to conceal the metadata information or the recipient who might learn more about the creation of the original document.

metadata
Information about a particular data set that may describe, for example, how, when, and by whom it was received, created, accessed, and/or modified and how it is formatted.

resource (system) metadata
The data such as file names, size, and location.

content (application) metadata
Information about the contents of a document.

native file format
An associated file structure defined by the original creating application of electronic documents.

TIFF
Tagged Image File Format, one of the most widely used formats for storing images. TIFF graphics can be black and white, gray-scaled, or color.

Exhibit 7.1 Microsoft Word 2010 metadata display

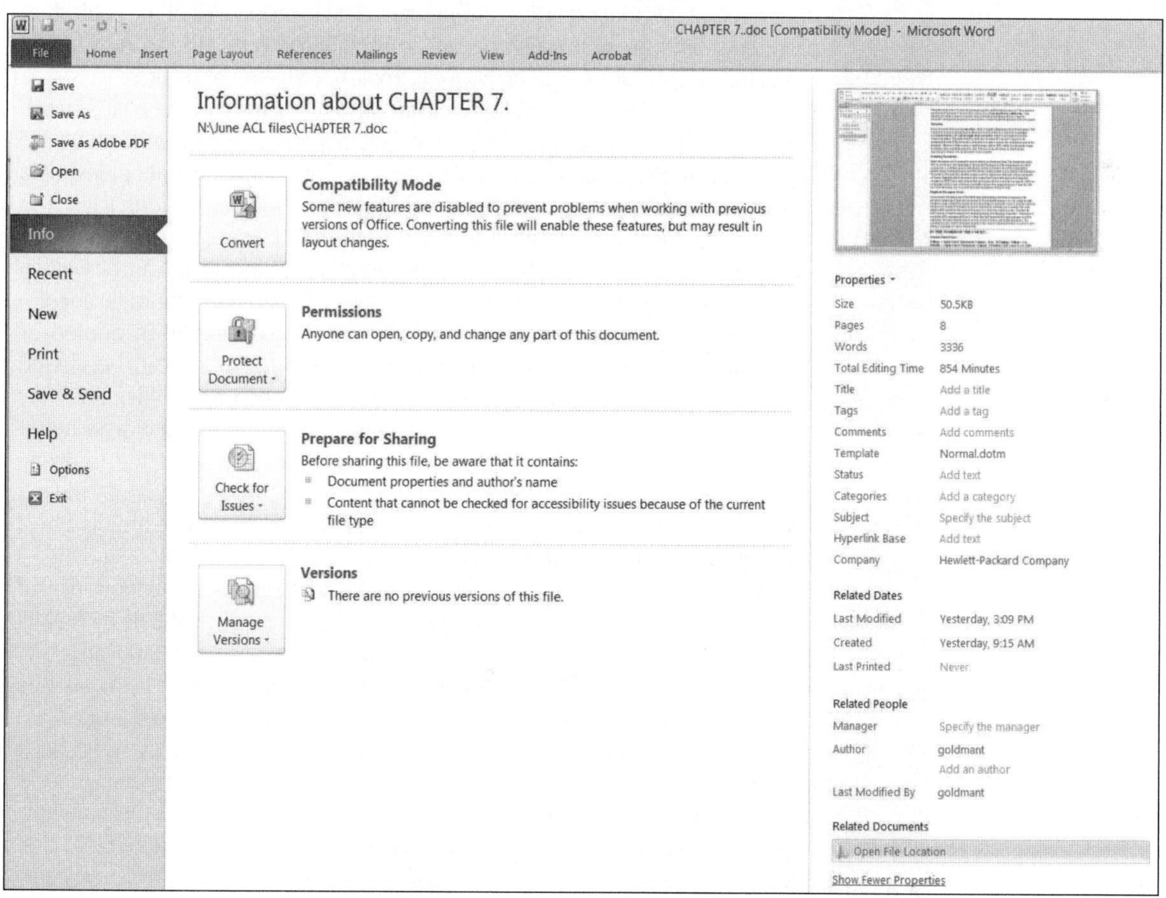

Source: Microsoft product screen shot(s) reprinted with permission from Microsoft Corporation; Metadata® is a registered trademark of Metadata, LLC.

IN THE WORDS OF THE COURT...

METADATA ETHICAL ISSUES

Williams v. Sprint/United Management Company,
(Kan. 2005) ***Shirley Williams et al.,***
Plaintiffs, v. Sprint/United Management Company, Defendant.
Civil Action No. 03-2200-JWL-DJW.
United States District Court, D. Kansas.
September 29, 2005.

1. Emerging standards of electronic discovery with regard to metadata.

a. What is metadata?

Before addressing whether Defendant was justified in removing the metadata from the Excel spreadsheets prior to producing them to Plaintiffs, a general discussion of metadata and its implications for electronic document production in discovery is instructive.

Metadata, commonly described as "data about data," is defined as "information describing the history, tracking, or management of an electronic document."

Appendix F to *The Sedona Guidelines: Best Practice Guidelines & Commentary for Managing Information & Records in the Electronic Age* defines metadata as "information about a particular data set which describes how, when and by whom it was collected, created, accessed, or modified and how it is formatted (including data demographics such as size, location, storage requirements and media information.)" Technical Appendix E to the *Sedona Guidelines* provides an extended description of metadata. It further defines metadata to include "all of the contextual, processing, and use information needed to identify and certify the scope, authenticity, and integrity of active or archival electronic information or records."

Some examples of metadata for electronic documents include: a file's name, a file's location (e.g., directory structure or pathname), file format or file type, file size, file dates (e.g., creation date, date of last data modification, date of last data access, and date of last metadata modification), and file permissions (e.g., who can read the data, who can write to it, who can run it). Some metadata, such as file dates and sizes, can easily be seen by users; other metadata can be hidden or embedded and unavailable to computer users who are not technically adept.

Most metadata is generally not visible when a document is printed or when the document is converted to an image file. Metadata can be altered intentionally or inadvertently and can be extracted when native files are converted to image files. Sometimes the metadata can be inaccurate, as when a form document reflects the author as the person who created the template but who did not draft the document. In addition, metadata can come from a variety of sources; it can be created automatically by a computer, supplied by a user, or inferred through a relationship to another document.

Appendix E to *The Sedona Guidelines* further explains the importance of metadata: Certain metadata is critical in information management and for ensuring effective retrieval and accountability in record-keeping. Metadata can assist in proving the authenticity of the content of electronic documents, as well as establish the context of the content. Metadata can also identify and exploit the structural relationships that exist between and within electronic documents, such as versions and drafts. Metadata allows organizations to track the many layers of rights and reproduction information that exist for records and their multiple versions. Metadata may also document other legal or security requirements that have been imposed on records; for example, privacy concerns, privileged communications or work product, or proprietary interests.

(*continued*)

The Microsoft Office Online website lists several examples of metadata that may be stored in Microsoft Excel spreadsheets, as well as other Microsoft applications such as Word or PowerPoint: author name or initials, company or organization name, identification of computer or network server or hard disk where document is saved, names of previous document authors, document revisions and versions, hidden text or cells, template information, other file properties and summary information, non-visible portions or embedded objects, personalized views, and comments.

It is important to note that metadata varies with different applications. As a general rule of thumb, the more interactive the application, the more important the metadata is to understanding the application's output. At one end of the spectrum is a word processing application where the metadata is usually not critical to understanding the substance of the document. The information can be conveyed without the need for the metadata. At the other end of the spectrum is a database application where the database is a completely undifferentiated mass of tables of data. The metadata is the key to showing the relationships between the data; without such metadata, the tables of data would have little meaning. A spreadsheet application lies somewhere in the middle. While metadata is not as crucial to understanding a spreadsheet as it is to a database application, a spreadsheet's metadata may be necessary to understand the spreadsheet because the cells containing formulas, which arguably are metadata themselves, often display a value rather than the formula itself. To understand the spreadsheet, the user must be able to ascertain the formula within the cell.

Due to the hidden, or not readily visible, nature of metadata, commentators note that metadata created by any software application has the potential for inadvertent disclosure of confidential or privileged information in both litigation and non-litigation setting[s], which could give rise to an ethical violation. One method commonly recommended to avoid this inadvertent disclosure is to utilize software that removes metadata from electronic documents. The process of removing metadata is commonly called "scrubbing" the electronic documents. In a litigation setting, the issue arises of whether this can be done without either the agreement of the parties or the producing party providing notice through an objection or motion for protective order.

IN THE WORDS OF THE COURT...

EMAIL METADATA

Wiginton v. CB Richard Ellis, Inc.*, (N.D. Ill. 2004) *Amy Wiginton, Kristine Moran, Norma Plank Fethler, Andrea Corey and Olivia Knapp, individually and on behalf of all persons similarly situated, Plaintiffs, v. CB Richard Ellis, Inc., Defendant.

Case No. 02 C 6832. United States District Court, N.D. Illinois, Eastern Division. August 9, 2004.

...Plaintiffs filed this class action complaint against CBRE alleging a nationwide pattern and practice of sexual harassment at the CBRE offices. As evidence of the hostile work environment prevalent at the offices of CBRE, Plaintiffs seek discovery of pornographic material that they claim was distributed electronically (i.e., via e-mail) and displayed on computers throughout the offices.

(*continued*)

> CBRE initially produced 94 monthly e-mail backup tapes from 11 offices. The backup tapes consist of the e-mails that existed on a given server at the time the backup is made. They are not a complete depiction of every e-mail that existed on the CBRE system during a month.
>
> ...At this point, we note that discussing documents in terms of numbers is somewhat inexact. For example, an e-mail containing a search term that hexists in a user's outbox, and also exists in another user's inbox, counts as two hits, even though it is really one document. A document containing a search term that is sent from one user to another, and returned under the "reply with history" option available on CBRE's e-mail system[,] counts as two hits. But, because of de-duplication, an e-mail that is present multiple times in one user's mailbox is not counted multiple times. So although talking about documents in terms of numbers is not entirely accurate, the search system was designed to get an idea of how frequently the documents containing search terms were being passed around by CBRE users within or between the offices. Because spam was eliminated, it means the picture does not present an entirely accurate view of any other pornographic e-mails that maybe have been available on the CBRE e-mail system, or how often users are opening such documents in view of other people. The numbers also do not reflect e-mails that were not captured on backup tapes.

Sometimes the most important information about a document is found not in the metadata but right on the face of the original document. Estate probate officials and Recorders of Wills frequently look at original documents to see if there is an excess number of staple holes, indicating that the document may have been taken apart after originally prepared and therefore raising the question of a removed or substituted page.

The color ink used in creating the document may offer important information as well—for example, in a paper-based medical record where each nursing shift used different-colored ink to make notes in the patient record (chart), or where the person signed using a red pen that appears black on a photocopy.

For example, in the case of *Robinson-Reeder v American Council on Education* 262 F.R.D. 41, the court ruled:

> ...Although ACE is correct that, in general, black and white copied documents satisfy a party's discovery obligations, here ACE has put a color or a mark on the original enrollment form at issue. Therefore, ACE must either arrange for Ms. Robinson Reeder to inspect the original enrollment form at counsel's office, or provide her with a color copy of the original form.

Obtaining Documents via Paper Discovery

Not all documents are in electronic form. Many public agencies, like police and fire departments, may still file paper-based reports. Litigation that involves a time frame prior to the age of electronic document preparation also has paper-based documents. These cases often involve a large volume of material that must be processed by the legal team. Converting the paper documents to electronic forms may be a solution.

The typical response to a paper document request is the delivery of a photocopy of the requested item. As with electronic discovery, the number of documents can be in the thousands or even millions (for example, a class action suit involving tobacco companies). Before the computer era, these documents had to be reviewed manually, which provided work for many contract lawyers, law students, and paralegals. Computer technology allows these paper documents to be converted into electronic files that can be processed like other electronic files. Typically the documents are copied or scanned and saved in some electronic file format.

Scanning Documents

Paper documents can be scanned to convert them to an electronic form. The format into which they are saved may vary depending on the use and the purpose of the scanning process. Most scanners have a software program that allows a choice of formats for viewing and saving the files. One of the most popular graphic image–scanning formats is the PDF format, which permits easy portability and sharing of the resulting electronic file and as the required format for filing documents in many courts. Modern scanners used in conjunction with such software programs such as Nuance PaperPort allow documents to be scanned and converted using **optical character recognition (OCR)** into a native format that can be processed like a word processing file. OCR is a technology used to create a full-text, searchable version of an image document. Using the full-text OCR document, you can search for words and phrases within its body.

optical character recognition (OCR)
A technology that takes data from a paper document and turns it into editable text data. The document is first scanned, then OCR software searches the document for letters, numbers, and other characters.

Some versions of Adobe Acrobat can be used to search documents and computer systems, as shown in the search of a computer and a search of the current document in Adobe Acrobat X Pro in Exhibit 7.2.

File Formats for Electronic Documents

In the e-discovery phase of litigation, the terms you will hear most often are *native file format*—meaning the document is saved in the same format in which it was created—and *TIFF* and **PDF,** which are the formats most frequently used in converting documents.

PDF
Portable Document Format.

Exhibit 7.2 Search of computer and document using Adobe Acrobat

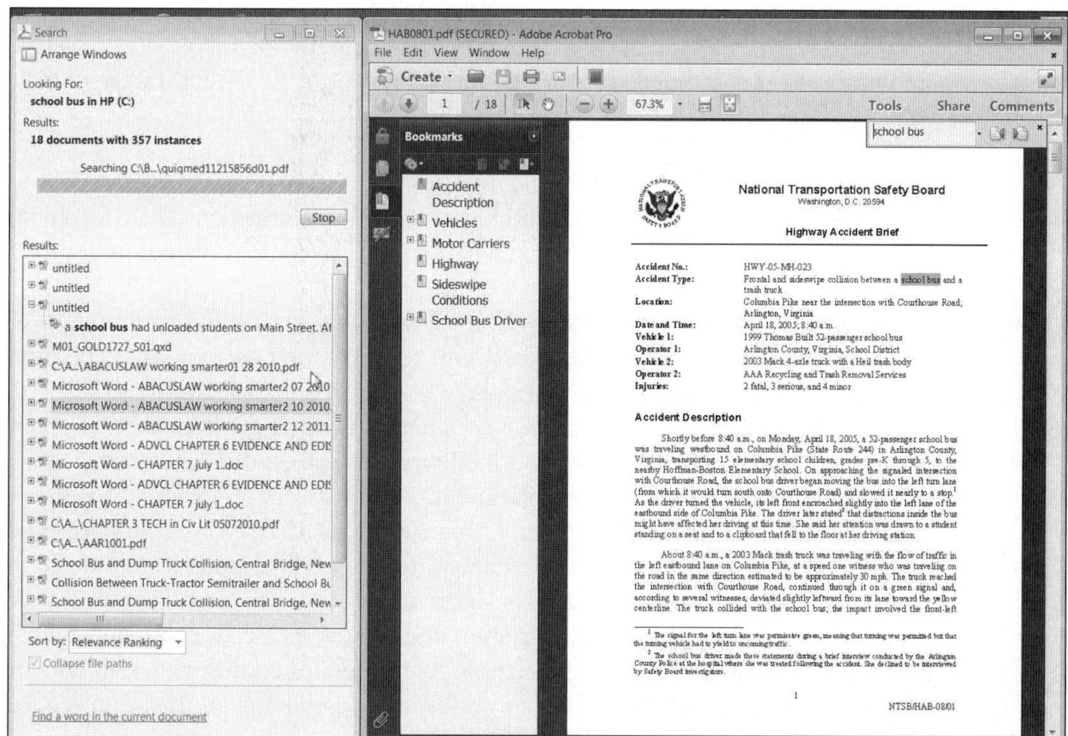

Source: Adobe product screenshot(s) reprinted with permission from Adobe Systems Incorporated.

Native file format is the format used by a program to save the data produced by the program, for example, Microsoft Word or WordPerfect, Excel or Access. "Deliver documents in native format" refers to delivering the files in the same format in which the documents were created and saved originally.

TIFF is short for "tagged image file format." It is one of the most widely used formats for storing images. TIFF graphics can be black and white, gray-scaled, or color. Files in TIFF format often end with a .tif extension.

PDF is short for "portable document format" created by Adobe.

Reducing ESI to Manageable Levels

The number of electronic documents supplied in response to the discovery request may be in the hundreds, thousands, or millions. Some or most of the documents produced (supplied) may not be relevant or have value as potential evidence in the litigation. From the EDRM, it is clear that there are typically more documents available than are relevant. Thus the documents need to be reduced to a reasonable number of relevant documents.

filtering
The process used to scan or search documents for relevant terms in an attempt to narrow the focus, such as filtering to eliminate documents created before or after a certain date.

de-duplication/de-duping
The process of comparing electronic records based on their characteristics and removing duplicate records from the data set.

Filtering is the process used to scan or search the documents for relevant terms in an attempt to narrow the search focus, such as filtering to eliminate documents created before or after a certain date.

Another process used to narrow the number of items to review involves eliminating duplicate copies of the same document by the de-duplication process. **De-duplication,** or **de-duping,** is the process of electronically eliminating the duplicates of the same document. For example, if all of the emails say the same thing, is it necessary to have all of the copies in the discovery material? Normally the answer is no, one is enough. But what might still be needed are the names of the parties to whom the email was sent. In a defamation or harassment case, it is necessary to prove, for example, that a branch manager was sending harassing or defamatory comments. In these types of cases, it would be important to know the names of recipients of the messages and those to whom they had forwarded the same message. The same situation may be true for invoices, letters, and similar documents. The metadata on each email or document might in some cases be important if there is a need to show changes, recipients, or similar information.

Document Processing

To be effectively sorted, retrieved, and identified for further review, each document must be identified by distinguishing characteristics, like date created and author. This process is known as coding.

coding
The process of capturing case-relevant information (i.e., author, date authored, date sent, recipient, date opened, etc.) from a document.

objective coding
Also referred to as a bibliographic indexing. This includes the author, type of document, recipient, and date.

subjective coding
Identifies keywords within the document or other criteria not related to bibliographic information.

auto coding
The electronic scanning and coding of documents by selected key terms and dates.

Coding is the process of capturing case-relevant information from a document—for example, author, date authored, date sent, recipient, and date opened. The most basic type of coding is **objective coding,** also referred to as bibliographic indexing. This includes the author, type of document, recipient, and date. Additional coding may include **subjective coding,** which identifies keywords within the document or other criteria not related to bibliographic information.

Obviously the manual coding of this information is time-consuming and costly. To reduce coding costs, some companies offer outsourcing to service companies in foreign locations where the labor rates are lower than in the United States. With modern scanning techniques and high-speed scanners, some companies provide **auto coding**—the electronic scanning and coding of documents by selected key terms and dates. In some cases, the documents are first auto-coded and then selected documents are manually coded.

ADVICE FROM THE FIELD

AUTOMATIC DOCUMENT CODING

By Lisa Rosen

Document coding has historically been the most expensive and time-intensive step of the entire process required for creating document production databases. On average, a coding professional can manually code approximately 20 documents (based on a five-page document) and 10 bibliographic fields per hour. In order to reduce the time and cost associated with manual coding, a movement began to send documents offshore to areas of cheap labor. However, many law firms and government agencies cannot or will not send their documents offshore for security reasons. The cost and time associated with manual document coding is significantly reduced with the use of document coding software, such as ALCoder, which allows the case team to focus efforts on the case at hand.

The new federal rules pertaining to ESI (Electronically Stored Information) [have] created an increased awareness of the need for coding and the need for auto-coding. ESI or native files/emails are often processed and imported into existing databases such as CT Summation and LexisNexis Concordance. During the extraction process, metadata (or data about the data) is identified and populated into those databases for searching and sorting purposes. Many believe that the metadata is accurate or complete, when that is often not the case. The metadata reflects the "profile" of a document, not the bibliographic information contained within the document. ALCoder goes into the native files, emails and attachments and extracts the bibliographic information from the document, supplementing the metadata with accurate bibliographic information. The improvement in Optical Character Recognition (OCR) technology in quality and price (through the availability of off-the-shelf software) has resulted in OCR frequently replacing slower and often prohibitively expensive manual document coding. The problem with searching databases limited to OCR is that critical information such as document dates and authors are not able to be searched and sorted. For example, if the documents need to be assembled in chronological order, they must be coded. Automatic coding software, like ALCoder, solve[s] the problem.

Source: Copyright © Lisa Rosen. Reprinted by permission of Rosen Technology Resources, Inc.

Exhibit 7.3 Bates stamper

Although page numbers are added to paper documents with a mechanical numbering device such as the Bates stamper, computer document management programs sometimes have a feature that electronically adds the sequential page numbers to the documents.

The same documents may be required in multidistrict litigation—for example, pages of an employer's policy manual that will be referenced in employment discrimination suits filed in different courts across the country. Using one set of identifying production numbers (Bates numbers) simplifies identification for the litigation team. With the same document numbers used in all cases filed, the chances of confusion when documents are referred to or introduced into evidence by production number will be eliminated. These numbers also allow for inventorying the documents. If a number is missing, it is clear that someone has removed or not delivered all the documents. Counsel in each case should be asked to agree to the same numbering system.

PRACTICE TIP

The pages in paper documents supplied in response to a request for production are frequently numbered sequentially to aid in the review and for identification purposes in pleadings and at trial. Plaintiffs use the letter *P* before the document number, and the defense uses a *D*. The sequential numbering of documents was and still is referred to as **Bates production numbering**, after the Bates numbering stamp shown in Exhibit 7.3.

Bates production numbering

A Bates production number is a tracking number assigned to each page of each document in the production set.

PRIVILEGE REVIEW

LEARNING OBJECTIVE 2
Describe the purpose of privilege review and how items may be protected from disclosure.

privilege review
A review of documents for privileged or confidential content or attorney work product.

Privilege review is the process of reviewing client's documents to identify those that contain privileged communication, confidential information, or attorney work product. Protection against disclosure is provided in the federal rules, such as the Rule 26 protection for privileged matter and work product.

Rule 26. Duty to Disclose; General Provisions Governing Discovery.

(b) Discovery Scope and Limits.

(1) Scope in General.

Unless otherwise limited by court order, the scope of discovery is as follows: Parties may obtain discovery regarding any nonprivileged matter that is relevant to any party's claim or defense—including the existence, description, nature, custody, condition, and location of any documents or other tangible things and the identity and location of persons who know of any discoverable matter. For good cause, the court may order discovery of any matter relevant to the subject matter involved in the action. Relevant information need not be admissible at the trial if the discovery appears reasonably calculated to lead to the discovery of admissible evidence. All discovery is subject to the limitations imposed by Rule 26(b)(2)(C).

. . .

(3) Trial Preparation: Materials.

(A) *Documents and Tangible Things*. Ordinarily, a party may not discover documents and tangible things that are prepared in anticipation of litigation or for trial by or for another party or its representative (including the other party's attorney, consultant, surety, indemnitor, insurer, or agent). But, subject to Rule 26(b)(4), those materials may be discovered if:

(i) they are otherwise discoverable under Rule 26(b)(1); and

(ii) the party shows that it has substantial need for the materials to prepare its case and cannot, without undue hardship, obtain their substantial equivalent by other means.

(B) *Protection Against Disclosure*. If the court orders discovery of those materials, it must protect against disclosure of the mental impressions, conclusions, opinions, or legal theories of a party's attorney or other representative concerning the litigation.

Documents identified as privileged can be removed from the documents produced to the opposing side. The excluded documents must be identified on a privilege log that states the basis for the claim of privilege. The privilege protection may be lost if steps are not taken to protect the information against inadvertent disclosure. Voluntary disclosure traditionally acts as a waiver of the various privileges. Even with careful privilege review, documents that are considered privileged may still be accidentally produced to the opposing side; this is referred to as **inadvertent disclosure.** The question raised by inadvertent disclosure is whether the privilege is waived. When very large numbers of documents are involved, inadvertent disclosure may happen, even after careful review to eliminate the contents of these documents. It is generally agreed that privilege review is the most costly phase of the discovery process. When the funds necessary for individual manual review by multiple layers of reviewers are not infinite, some items will slip through.

inadvertent disclosure
An unintended disclosure of privileged, confidential or work product information to the opposing side.

With larger and larger numbers of ESI being demanded as part of discovery, the time and costs of privilege review and the incidents of inadvertent disclosure are also increasing. Initial efforts to address inadvertent disclosure were included in the 2006 federal rules changes, which provided for a claw-back provision under Rule 26 that required parties to discuss "claw-back" or non-waiver agreements, and empowered the courts under Rule 16(b)(6) to include these agreements in the courts' scheduling order:

> 26(f)(3)(D) . . . any issues about claims of privilege or of protection as trial-preparation materials, including—if the parties agree on a procedure to assert these claims after production—whether to ask the court to include their agreement in an order. . . .

Rule 502 of the Federal Rules of Evidence was passed in 2009 as a solution to the inconsistent application of the claw-back provisions in different jurisdictions. The court ruling on the effect of inadvertent disclosure varied based on the reasons for the disclosure and the steps taken by the disclosing party after the disclosures. The new evidence rule seeks to offer, at least in federal court, protection when the disclosure is inadvertent, when reasonable steps were taken to avoid inadvertent production, when action is taken promptly to correct the inadvertent production, and when there is the existence of a claw-back agreement. What constitute "reasonable steps" and "prompt action" still remain an issue for court determination.

Even with claw-back agreements and the potential benefit of FRE 502, there is a duty to use reasonable efforts to protect confidential, privileged, or work product documents against inadvertent disclosure. Once an inadvertent disclosure is made, the recipient still has the information even if he or she cannot in theory use it, or if no further use can be made by a claim of waiver. Almost certainly, when the information inadvertently disclosed is important enough to the potential for success of the other side, an argument can be expected that a waiver existed. Even the provisions of the Federal Rules of Evidence have the qualifying word "reasonable." The federal rule does not apply in state courts, each of which may have its own standard and case law, some of which hold that any disclosure is an automatic waiver.

It should be noted that any waiver or claw-back agreement between the parties governs only their conduct, not the conduct of third parties, unless the court issues an order that contains the agreement and applies it to third parties. It is therefore good practice to reduce all non-waiver or claw-back agreements to writing and request their inclusion in the court's scheduling order.

Conducting the Privilege Review

Those conducting the actual document review must be familiar with not only the attorney–client privilege and work product rules, but also any definitive statutory privileges, such as in attorney–client privilege under statute and federal laws or rules of evidence, and the conditional privileges such as those that apply to trade secrets or other confidential material that could be damaging to a client if publicly disclosed, such as the contents of pharmaceutical research or new cell phone technology for which patents have not yet been obtained.

Redaction

In documents that contain confidential information, privileged material may be redacted. **Redaction** is the removal of confidential information, or material prepared for trial under the work product doctrine. With paper documents, the process has usually been to use a black marker to block out the desired material

redaction
The removal of confidential information (or at least that which is claimed to be confidential) or material prepared for trial under the work product doctrine.

before making copies. Although the process is not as easy with electronic documents, material can be deleted using a program that electronically blacks out the information and then allows for a copy to be made either electronically or in hard copy.

Claims of improper redaction or non-delivery of documentation frequently result in motions to the court for orders to disclose. The federal rules specifically address the process for the protection of this type of information. The party seeking to exclude a document from production to the other side because of a claim of privilege must make an objection in a timely manner and identify the items and the reason for the objection in a privilege log.

RULE 37. Failure to Make Disclosures or to Cooperate in Discovery; Sanctions

(a) Motion for an Order Compelling Disclosure or Discovery.

(1) In General.

On notice to other parties and all affected persons, a party may move for an order compelling disclosure or discovery. The motion must include a certification that the movant has in good faith conferred or attempted to confer with the person or party failing to make disclosure or discovery in an effort to obtain it without court action. . . .

(3) Specific Motions.

(A) *To Compel Disclosure.* If a party fails to make a disclosure required by Rule 26(a), any other party may move to compel disclosure and for appropriate sanctions.

(B) *To Compel a Discovery Response.* A party seeking discovery may move for an order compelling an answer, designation, production, or inspection. This motion may be made if:

(i) a deponent fails to answer a question asked under Rules 30 or 31;

(ii) a corporation or other entity fails to make a designation under Rule 30(b)(6) or 31(a)(4);

(iii) a party fails to answer an interrogatory submitted under Rule 33, or

(iv) a party fails to respond that inspection will be permitted—or fails to permit inspection—as requested under Rule 34.

(4) Evasive or Incomplete Disclosure, Answer, or Response.

For purposes of this subdivision (a), an evasive or incomplete disclosure, answer, or response must be treated as a failure to disclose, answer, or respond.

Privilege Logs

privilege log
A list of documents claimed by the submitting party to contain material subject to privilege or work product exclusion.

A **privilege log** is a list of documents claimed by the submitting party to contain material subject to a privilege or work product exclusion. Exhibit 7.4 shows a sample privilege log.

Rule 26. Duty to Disclose; General Provisions Governing Discovery

(5) Claiming Privilege or Protecting Trial-Preparation Materials.

(A) *Information Withheld.* When a party withholds information otherwise discoverable by claiming that the information is privileged or subject to protection as trial-preparation material, the party must:

(i) expressly make the claim; and

(ii) describe the nature of the documents, communications, or tangible things not produced or disclosed—and do so in a manner that, without revealing information itself privileged or protected, will enable other parties to assess the claim.

Exhibit 7.4 Privilege log

Public Records Request — **Privilege Log** — **July 18, 2008**

Ivy Frye's and Frank Bailey's February 2008 E-mails

Date	Author	Recipient	Document Description	Privilege
02/01/08	C. Fredeen. PDC Eng.	F. Bailey, GOV	6:59 am *E-mail re Request for Reappointment for Craig Freeden to AELS Board	Deliberative Process / Executive
01/24/08	D. Ogg	F. Bailey, GOV	9:21 am *E-mail re Education	Deliberative Process / Executive
02/01/08	D. Ogg	F. Bailey, GOV	8:32 am *E-mail re Education	Deliberative Process / Executive
02/01/08	S. Leighow, GOV	F. Bailey, GOV	8:46 am *E-mail re Appointment of member to the state Board of Game	Deliberative Process / Executive
2/1/2008	S. Parnell, GOV	S. Palin, GOV	7:41 am *E-mail re Andrew Halcro	Deliberative Process / Executive
2/1/2008	S. Parnell, GOV	F. Bailey, GOV K. Perry, GOV T. Palin	8:22 am *E-mail re Andrew Halcro	Deliberative Process / Executive
2/1/2008	S. Palin, GOV	F. Bailey, GOV K. Perry, GOV T. Palin	8:28 am *E-mail re Andrew Halcro	Deliberative Process / Executive
2/1/2008	S. Palin, GOV	F. Bailey, GOV K. Perry, GOV T. Palin	8:30 am *E-mail re Andrew Halcro	Deliberative Process / Executive
2/1/2008	I. Frye, GOV	S. Palin, GOV F. Bailey, GOV K. Perry, GOV T. Palin	8:42 am *E-mail re Andrew Halcro	Deliberative Process / Executive
2/1/2008	S. Palin, GOV	I. Frye, GOV K. Perry, GOV F. Bailey, GOV T. Palin	10:10 am *E-mail re Andrew Halcro	Deliberative Process / Executive
2/1/2008	I. Frye, GOV	S. Palin, GOV F. Bailey, GOV K. Perry, GOV T. Palin	10:23 am *E-mail re Andrew Halcro	Deliberative Process / Executive

Page 1

IN THE WORDS OF THE COURT...

In Re ***Grand Jury Subpoena***, 274 F.3d 563 (1st Cir. 2001)

In re ***Grand Jury Subpoena (Custodian of Records, Newparent, Inc.), A. Nameless Lawyer (A Pseudonym) et al., Intervenors, Appellants.***

No. 01-1975.

United States Court of Appeals, First Circuit.

Heard September 14, 2001.

Decided November 8, 2001.

1. *Individual Attorney-Client Privilege Claims.* The attorney-client privilege protects communications made in confidence by a client to his attorney. *See, e.g., United States v. Mass. Inst. of Tech.*, 129 F.3d 681, 684 (1st Cir. 1997)

...

3. *The Work Product Privilege.* The claim of work product privilege raises a similar set of issues anent joint privilege. The work product rule protects work done by an attorney in anticipation of, or during, litigation from disclosure to the opposing party. *E.g., Sealed Case*, 29 F.3d at 718. The rule facilitates zealous advocacy in the context of an adversarial system of justice by ensuring that the sweat of an attorney's brow is not appropriated by the opposing party. *Hickman v. Taylor*, 329 U.S. 495, 511, 67 S.Ct. 385, 91 L.Ed. 451 (1947)

(*continued*)

B. *Fed.R.Civ.P. 45(d)(2).*

As an alternate ground for our decision, we note that the motion to quash was properly denied because the intervenors failed to present sufficient information with respect to the items to which their claim of privilege attaches. The Civil Rules specifically provide that:

> When information subject to a subpoena is withheld on a claim that it is privileged or subject to protection as trial preparation materials, the claim shall be made expressly and shall be supported by a description of the nature of the documents, communications or things not produced that is sufficient to enable the demanding party to contest the claim.

Fed.R.Civ.P. 45(d)(2). The operative language is mandatory and, although the rule does not spell out the sufficiency requirement in detail, courts consistently have held that the rule requires a party resisting disclosure to produce a document index or privilege log. *See, e.g., Bregman v. Dist. of Columbia,* 182 F.R.D. 352, 363 (D.D.C. 1998); *First American Corp. v. Al-Nahyan,* 2 F.Supp.2d 58, 63 n. 5 (D.D.C. 1998); *see also Avery Dennison Corp. v. Four Pillars,* 190 F.R.D. 1, 1 (D.D.C. 1999) (describing privilege logs as "the universally accepted means" of asserting privilege claims in the federal courts); *cf. Vaughn v. Rosen,* 484 F.2d 820 (D.C.Ct.App. 1973) (articulating the justifications for requiring privilege logs in the context of the FOIA). A party that fails to submit a privilege log is deemed to waive the underlying privilege claim. *See Dorf & Stanton Communications, Inc. v. Molson Breweries,* 100 F.3d 919, 923 (Fed. Cir. 1996) (holding that failing "to provide a complete privilege log demonstrating sufficient grounds for taking the privilege" waives the privilege). Although most of the reported cases arise in the context of a claim of attorney-client privilege, the "specify or waive" rule applies equally in the context of claims of work product privilege. *See, e.g., Smith v. Conway Org., Inc.,* 154 F.R.D. 73, 76 (S.D.N.Y. 1994).

In a somewhat indirect fashion, the intervenors suggest that they were hampered in their ability to present a list of privileged documents by the district court's refusal to hold an evidentiary hearing. This suggestion does not withstand scrutiny. After all, the intervenors were not without knowledge of the communications to which the subpoena pertained; Lawyer originally had possession of them and turned them over to Smith & Jones only when Newparent decided to change counsel. Despite this knowledge, the intervenors made no effort to prepare a privilege log. That omission is fatal.

Privilege logs do not need to be precise to the point of pedantry. Thus, a party who possesses some knowledge of the nature of the materials to which a claim of privilege is addressed cannot shirk his obligation to file a privilege log merely because he lacks infinitely detailed information. To the contrary, we read Rule 45(d)(2) as requiring a party who asserts a claim of privilege to do the best that he reasonably can to describe the materials to which his claim adheres.

(B) *Information Produced.* If information produced in discovery is subject to a claim of privilege or of protection as trial preparation material, the party making the claim may notify any party that received the information of the claim and the basis for it. After being notified, a party must promptly return, sequester, or destroy the specified information and any copies it has; must not use or disclose the information until the claim is resolved; must take reasonable steps to retrieve the information if the party disclosed it before being notified; and may promptly present the information to the court under seal for a determination of the claim. The producing party must preserve the information until the claim is resolved.

Exhibit 7.5 Admissibility of Electronic Evidence

ADMISSIBILITY OF ELECTRONIC EVIDENCE

Paul W. Grimm & Kevin F. Brady

Checklist of Potential Authentication Methods

E-MAIL

- Witness with personal knowledge (901(b)(1))
- Expert testimony or comparison with authenticated examples (901(b)(3))
- Distinctive characteristics including circumstantial evidence (901(b)(4))
- Trade inscriptions (902(7))
- Certified copies of business record (902(11))

INTERNET WEBSITE POSTINGS

- Witness with personal knowledge (901(b)(1))
- Expert testimony or comparison with authenticated examples (901(b)(3))
- Distinctive characteristics including circumstantial evidence (901(b)(4))
- Public records (901(b)(7))
- System or process capable of proving a reliable result (901(b)(9))
- Official publications (902(5))

TEXT MESSAGES, TWEETS, AND THE LIKE

- Witness with personal knowledge (901(b)(1))
- Circumstantial evidence of distinctive characteristics (901(b)(4))
- Expert testimony or comparison with authenticated examples (901(b)(3))

COMPUTED STORED RECORDS AND DATA

- Witness with personal knowledge (901(b)(1))
- Expert testimony or comparison with authenticated examples (901(b)(3))
- Distinctive characteristics including circumstantial evidence (901(b)(4)
- System or process capable of proving a reliable result (901(b)(9))

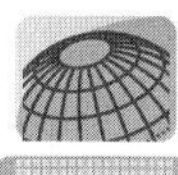

COMPUTER ANIMATIONS AND COMPUTER SIMULATIONS

- Witness with personal knowledge (901(b)(1))
- Expert testimony or comparison with authenticated examples (901(b)(3))
- System or process capable of proving a reliable result (901(b)(9)

DIGITAL PHOTOGRAPHS

- Witness with personal knowledge (901(b)(1))
- System or process capable of providing reliable result (901(b)(9)

CONNOLLY BOVE LODGE & HUTZ LLP
ATTORNEYS AT LAW

Exhibit 7.5 Continued

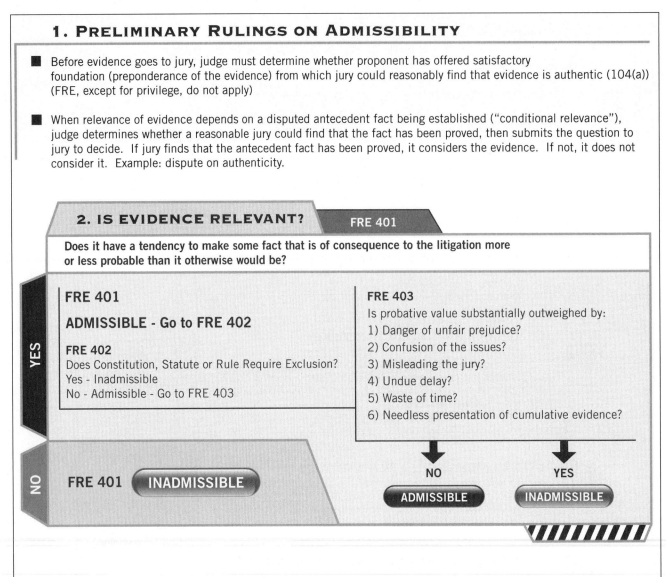

1. Preliminary Rulings on Admissibility

- Before evidence goes to jury, judge must determine whether proponent has offered satisfactory foundation (preponderance of the evidence) from which jury could reasonably find that evidence is authentic (104(a)) (FRE, except for privilege, do not apply)
- When relevance of evidence depends on a disputed antecedent fact being established ("conditional relevance"), judge determines whether a reasonable jury could find that the fact has been proved, then submits the question to jury to decide. If jury finds that the antecedent fact has been proved, it considers the evidence. If not, it does not consider it. Example: dispute on authenticity.

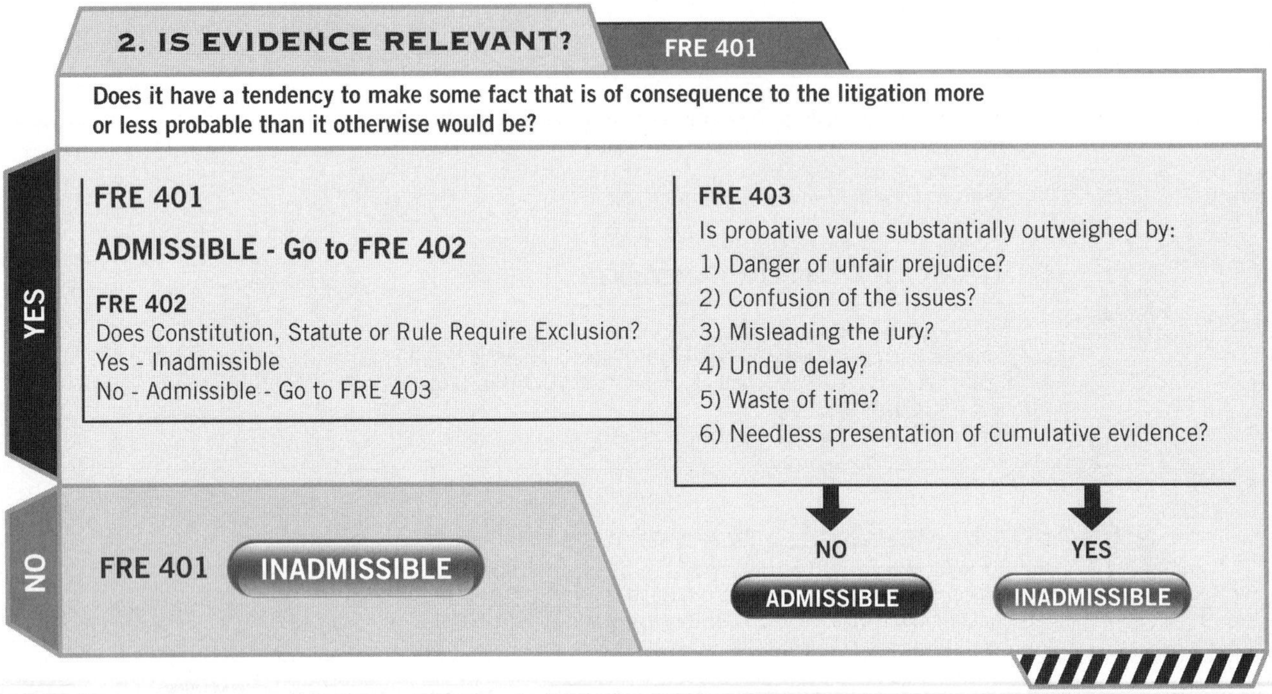

2. Is Evidence Relevant? FRE 401

Does it have a tendency to make some fact that is of consequence to the litigation more or less probable than it otherwise would be?

YES

FRE 401

ADMISSIBLE - Go to FRE 402

FRE 402
Does Constitution, Statute or Rule Require Exclusion?
Yes - Inadmissible
No - Admissible - Go to FRE 403

FRE 403
Is probative value substantially outweighed by:
1) Danger of unfair prejudice?
2) Confusion of the issues?
3) Misleading the jury?
4) Undue delay?
5) Waste of time?
6) Needless presentation of cumulative evidence?

NO → ADMISSIBLE

YES → INADMISSIBLE

NO

FRE 401 INADMISSIBLE

3. If Relevant, Is It Authentic? FRE 901– 902

- **FRE 901(a)** Is the evidence sufficient to support a finding that the matter in question is what proponent claims?

  Determining the degree of foundation required to authenticate electronic evidence depends on the quality and completeness of the data input, the complexity of the computer processing, the routines of the computer operation and the ability to test and verify the results.

- **FRE 901(b)**
  Non-exclusive list of examples includes:
  (1) Testimony of witness with knowledge;
  (3) Comparison by trier or expert witness;
  (4) Distinctive characteristics and the like (e-mail address, hash values, "reply" doctrine);
  (7) Public records or report; and
  (9) Process or system capable of producing a reliable result.

- **FRE 902**
  Methods by which information may be authenticated WITHOUT EXTRINSIC EVIDENCE:

  Ways to authenticate e-records:
  - 902(1)-(4) Public Records/Documents
  - 902(5) Official publications
  - 902(6) Newspapers, Magazines, Similar Publications
  - 902(7) Trade inscriptions
  - 902(11) Certified domestic records of regularly conducted activity (authenticate business records under FRE 803(6)).

Exhibit 7.5 Continued

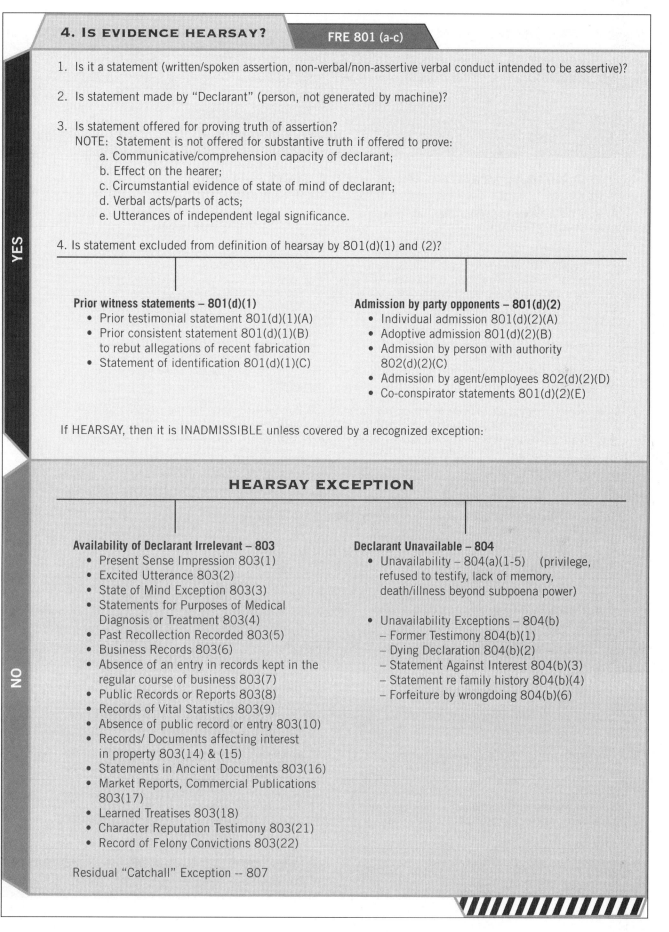

4. Is Evidence Hearsay?

FRE 801 (a-c)

YES

1. Is it a statement (written/spoken assertion, non-verbal/non-assertive verbal conduct intended to be assertive)?
2. Is statement made by "Declarant" (person, not generated by machine)?
3. Is statement offered for proving truth of assertion?
   NOTE: Statement is not offered for substantive truth if offered to prove:
   a. Communicative/comprehension capacity of declarant;
   b. Effect on the hearer;
   c. Circumstantial evidence of state of mind of declarant;
   d. Verbal acts/parts of acts;
   e. Utterances of independent legal significance.
4. Is statement excluded from definition of hearsay by 801(d)(1) and (2)?

Prior witness statements – 801(d)(1)
- Prior testimonial statement 801(d)(1)(A)
- Prior consistent statement 801(d)(1)(B) to rebut allegations of recent fabrication
- Statement of identification 801(d)(1)(C)

Admission by party opponents – 801(d)(2)
- Individual admission 801(d)(2)(A)
- Adoptive admission 801(d)(2)(B)
- Admission by person with authority 802(d)(2)(C)
- Admission by agent/employees 802(d)(2)(D)
- Co-conspirator statements 801(d)(2)(E)

If HEARSAY, then it is INADMISSIBLE unless covered by a recognized exception:

NO

HEARSAY EXCEPTION

Availability of Declarant Irrelevant – 803
- Present Sense Impression 803(1)
- Excited Utterance 803(2)
- State of Mind Exception 803(3)
- Statements for Purposes of Medical Diagnosis or Treatment 803(4)
- Past Recollection Recorded 803(5)
- Business Records 803(6)
- Absence of an entry in records kept in the regular course of business 803(7)
- Public Records or Reports 803(8)
- Records of Vital Statistics 803(9)
- Absence of public record or entry 803(10)
- Records/ Documents affecting interest in property 803(14) & (15)
- Statements in Ancient Documents 803(16)
- Market Reports, Commercial Publications 803(17)
- Learned Treatises 803(18)
- Character Reputation Testimony 803(21)
- Record of Felony Convictions 803(22)

Declarant Unavailable – 804
- Unavailability – 804(a)(1-5) (privilege, refused to testify, lack of memory, death/illness beyond subpoena power)
- Unavailability Exceptions – 804(b)
  - Former Testimony 804(b)(1)
  - Dying Declaration 804(b)(2)
  - Statement Against Interest 804(b)(3)
  - Statement re family history 804(b)(4)
  - Forfeiture by wrongdoing 804(b)(6)

Residual "Catchall" Exception -- 807

6 Original Writing Rule – FRE 1001 – 1008

- Is the evidence "original", "duplicate", "writing", "recording" (1001)
- Rule 1002 requires the original to prove the contents of a writing, recording or photograph unless "secondary evidence" (any evidence other than original or duplicative) is admissible. Rules 1004, 1005, 1006, 1007.
- Duplicates are co-extensively admissible as originals unless there is a genuine issue of authenticity of the original or circumstances indicate that it would be unfair to admit duplicate in lieu of original (1003)
- Permits proof of the contents of writing, recording or paragraph by use of "secondary evidence" – any proof of the contents of a writing, recording or photograph other than the original or duplicate (1004) if:
    - i. Non-bad faith loss/destruction of original/duplicate
    - ii. Inability to subpoena original/duplicate
    - iii. Original/duplicate in possession, custody, control of opposing party
    - iv. "Collateral record" (i.e., not closely related to controlling issue in case)
- Admission of summary of voluminous books, records or documents (1006)
- Testimony or deposition of party against whom offered or by that party's written admission (FRCP 30, 33, 36) (1007)
- If admissibility depends on the fulfillment of a condition or fact, question of whether condition has been fulfilled is for fact finder to determine under 104(b) (1008)
- But, the issue is for the trier of fact, if it is a question:
    - (a) whether they asserted writing ever existed;
    - (b) whether another writing, recording or photograph produced at trial is the original; or
    - (c) whether other evidence of contents correctly reflects the contents, the issue is for the trier of fact.

7 Practice Tips

1 Be prepared. Start with a defensible and comprehensive records management program.

2 Think strategically about the case and the evidence from the beginning of the case.

3 Memorialize each step of the collection and production process to bolster reliability.

4 Use every opportunity during discovery to authenticate potential evidence.

Examples:

a) For pretrial disclosures under F.R.C.P. 26(a)(3), you have 14 days to file objections or possible waiver;

b) Documents produced by opposing party are presumed to be authentic – burden shifts

c) F.R.C.P. 36 Requests for Admissions

d) Request stipulation of authenticity from opposing counsel

5 Be prepared to provide the court with enough information to understand the technology issues as they relate to the reliability of the evidence at hand.

6 Be creative and consider whether there are case management tools that might assist the court and the other parties in addressing evidentiary problems concerning some of the more complex issues (such as "dynamic" data in a database or what is a "true and accurate copy" of ESI).

7 Keep your audience in mind... will this be an issue for the judge or the jury? (e.g., Rule 104(a) or (b).

For more information contact:
Kevin F. Brady at: KBrady@cblh.com

DOCUMENT AUTHENTICATION

One of the recurring themes in all cases is the **authentication of documents.** Before a document may be admitted into evidence, it must be authenticated. For example, in the federal courts, Rule 901 of the Federal Rules of Evidence provides the groundwork for authentication:

LEARNING OBJECTIVE 3
Describe the reason and the process for authentication of documents.

authentication of documents
The process of determining that the proposed evidence is what it purports to be and is genuine.

> (a) General Provision. The requirement of authentication or identification as a condition precedent to admissibility is satisfied by evidence sufficient to support a finding that the matter in question is what its proponent claims. F.R.E. 901 (a)

Some records have inherent authenticity, such as public records, which are authenticated by proof of custody, even when they consist of data stored electronically. For example, section 1530 of the California Evidence Code provides:

> (a) A purported copy of a writing in the custody of a public entity, or of an entry in such a writing, is prima facie evidence of the existence and content of such writing or entry if:
>
> (1) The copy purports to be published by the authority of the nation or state, or public entity therein in which the writing is kept;...

Other documents are considered self-authenticating under Rule 902 of the Federal Rules of Evidence:

1. Domestic public documents under seal
2. Domestic public documents not under seal
3. Foreign public documents
4. Certified copies of public records
5. Official publications
6. Newspapers and periodicals
7. Trade inscriptions and the like
8. Acknowledged documents
9. Commercial paper and related documents
10. Certified domestic records of regularly conducted activity
11. Certified foreign records of regularly conducted activity

Original documents, while preferable, are not required if the originals cannot be obtained or if they have been lost or stolen "...unless the proponent lost or destroyed them in bad faith..." F.R.E. 1004.

For the most part, the great body of law on authentication developed during the time when paper documents dominated. However, the rules do not prevent the opposing party from challenging the authenticity of the documents. Handwriting experts and forensic experts in paper, ink characteristics, and material aging may still be called in if there is a question of authenticity, such as when the authenticity of a will, date of execution, or signature of the testator is questioned.

Electronically stored documents when reproduced in printed form do not have the same physical characteristics of original paper documents. Thus challenges to their authenticity are based not on the physical characteristics of the material on which they are created, but on the electronic characteristics of their creation and storage, the metadata.

IN THE WORDS OF THE COURT...

Lorraine v. Markel American Insurance Company (Md. 5-4-2007) *Jack R. Lorraine and, Beverly Mack Plaintiffs v. Markel American Insurance Company Defendants.*

CIVIL ACTION NO. PWG-06-1893.

United States District Court, D. Maryland.

May 4, 2007

Memorandum Opinion

PAUL GRIMM, Magistrate Judge

Whether ESI is admissible into evidence is determined by a collection of evidence rules that present themselves like a series of hurdles to be cleared by the proponent of the evidence. Failure to clear any of these evidentiary hurdles means that the evidence will not be admissible. Whenever ESI is offered as evidence, either at trial or in summary judgment, the following evidence rules must be considered: (1) is the ESI relevant as determined by Rule 401 (does it have any tendency to make some fact that is of consequence to the litigation more or less probable than it otherwise would be); (2) if relevant under 401, is it authentic as required by Rule 901(a) (can the proponent show that the ESI is what it purports to be); (3) if the ESI is offered for its substantive truth, is it hearsay as defined by Rule 801, and if so, is it covered by an applicable exception (Rules 803, 804 and 807); (4) is the form of the ESI that is being offered as evidence an original or duplicate under the original writing rule, o[r] if not, is there admissible secondary evidence to prove the content of the ESI (Rules 1001-1008); and (5) is the probative value of the ESI substantially outweighed by the danger of unfair prejudice or one of the other factors identified by Rule 403.

CONCEPT REVIEW AND REINFORCEMENT

KEY TERMS

review 166
metadata 169
resource (system) metadata 169
content (application) metadata 169
native file format 169
TIFF 169
optical character recognition (OCR) 173
PDF 173
filtering 174
de-duplication/de-duping 174
coding 174
objective coding 174
subjective coding 174
auto coding 174
Bates production numbering 175
privilege review 176
inadvertent disclosure 176
redaction 177
privilege log 178
authentication of documents 185

CHAPTER SUMMARY

Introduction to Analysis and Review of E-Discovery	Once the information needed has been identified and made available to a client's attorney, it must be reviewed for relevancy to the request and for privileged or confidential information and attorney work product that must be identified, logged, and removed.

Reviewing Electronic Documents	One of the biggest costs in electronic discovery is incurred in review. Initially it is reviewing the material obtained from clients to find relevant items and to identify privileged, confidential, or protected documents. After obtaining the documents, decisions must be made about how to process the material supplied.
Forms of Delivery of ESI	The response to a discovery request may be in electronic form or in paper form or a combination of both. Documents from clients provided for a review before sending them to the other side may be in various forms and different formats. One of the first issues to be considered is the format for document delivery to the opposing side after review.
Forms of Production—Metadata	Every electronic document has metadata, which is simply information about the document. This information may include the location of the file, referred to as resource (system) metadata, and content (application) metadata, which is the content and author.
Obtaining Documents via Paper Discovery	Not all documents are in electronic form. Many public agencies, like police and fire departments, may still file paper-based reports. Litigation that involves a time frame prior to the age of electronic document preparation also requires paper-based documents. These cases often involve a large volume of material that must be processed by the legal team. Converting the paper documents to electronic forms may shorten the processing time.
Scanning Documents	Paper documents can be scanned to convert them to an electronic form. The format into which they are saved may vary depending on the use and the purpose of the scanning process. Most scanners have a software program that allows a choice of format. One of the most popular graphic image–scanning formats is the PDF format.
File Formats for Electronic Documents	Native file format is the format used by a program to save the data produced by the program. TIFF is short for "tagged image file format." It is one of the most widely used formats for storing images. PDF is short for "portable document format."
Reducing ESI to Manageable Levels	It is clear that there are more documents available that are relevant. The documents need to be reduced to a reasonable number. Filtering is the process used to scan or search the documents for relevant terms in an attempt to narrow the focus, such as eliminating documents created before or after a certain date. De-duplication, or de-duping, is the term used to describe the process of electronically eliminating duplicates of the same document.
Document Processing	Each document must be identified by certain characteristics to allow it to be effectively sorted, retrieved, and identified for further review. This process is known as coding. The most basic type of coding is objective coding, also referred to as bibliographic indexing. This includes the author, type of document, recipient, and date. Additional coding may include subjective coding, which identifies keywords within the document or other criteria not related to bibliographic information.
Privilege Review	Privilege review is the process of reviewing documents to identify those that contain privileged communication, confidential information, or attorney work product.

	Documents identified as privileged can then be removed from the documents produced to the opposing side. But, the protection may be lost if steps are not taken to protect the information against disclosure. Voluntary disclosure traditionally acts as a waiver of the various privileges. Even with careful privilege review, sometimes documents that are considered privileged are still produced to the opposing side; this is referred to as inadvertent disclosure. Rule 502 of the Federal Rules of Evidence was passed in 2009 as a solution to the inconsistent application of the claw-back provisions based on the reasons and steps taken after the disclosures. It seeks to offer, at least in federal court, protection when the disclosure is inadvertent, when reasonable steps were taken to avoid inadvertent production, when steps are taken promptly to correct the inadvertent production, and when there is the existence of a claw-back agreement.
Conducting the Privilege Review	Those conducting the actual document review must be familiar with not only the attorney–client privilege and work product rules, but also any definitive statutory privileges, such as in the attorney–client privilege under statute and federal laws or rules of evidence, and the conditional privileges for such items as trade secrets or other confidential material, the public disclosure of which could be damaging to a client, such as pharmaceutical research or new cell phone technology for which patents have not yet been obtained.
Redaction	In documents that contain confidential information, privileged material may be redacted. Redaction is the removal of confidential information, or at least that which is claimed to be confidential, or material prepared for trial under the work product doctrine.
Document Authentication	Before a document may be admitted into evidence, it must be authenticated. Some records have inherent authenticity, such as public records, which are authenticated by proof of custody, even when they are comprised of data stored electronically. Other documents are considered self-authenticating under Rule 902 of the Federal Rules of Evidence. Original documents, while preferable, are not required if the originals cannot be obtained or they have been lost or stolen "... unless the proponent lost or destroyed them in bad faith..." F. R. E. 1004.

REVIEW QUESTIONS AND EXERCISES

1. What is the purpose of document review?
2. What is a solution to receiving documents in different formats and types?
3. Is there a required format for producing documents in discovery?
4. If the requesting party does not specify a format for production of the documents, what form may the producing party use?
5. Must all documents be produced with metadata?
6. What is metadata?
7. What is resources metadata?
8. What is content metadata?
9. Can metadata be removed from documents?
10. Is metadata the only way to determine the authenticity of a document?
11. How can paper documents be converted to electronic form?
12. What are the advantages to having documents in electronic form?
13. What is meant by native format?
14. What is the purpose of filtering in discovery? Give an example of a filtering term.
15. What is the purpose of de-duplication? Why is that an issue in e-discovery?

16. What is the purpose of coding documents?
17. What is the difference between objective and subjective coding?
18. What is auto coding? What are its advantages?
19. What is privilege review?
20. What documents can a party not provide to the other side?
21. What is inadvertent disclosure? What is the effect of inadvertent disclosure?
22. What is a claw-back clause?
23. What is the purpose of redaction?
24. Why must documents be authenticated?
25. Do any documents have automatic authenticity?
26. How is the claim of privilege made?
27. What is the purpose of a privilege log?

BUILDING YOUR PARALEGAL SKILLS

INTERNET AND TECHNOLOGY EXERCISES

1. Locate information about removing metadata from word processor documents.
2. Use the Internet to find redaction software.

CHAPTER OPENING SCENARIO CASE STUDY

Use the Opening Scenario for this chapter to answer the following questions.

1. In what form should each team request the documents be produced to them?
2. What are the potential problems with not specifying a format for production?
3. How can software programs or outside consultants be of advantage in either case?
4. What are the firm's options in discovery?

COMPREHENSIVE CASE STUDY

1. Review the issues that must be considered in each case as it relates to e-discovery and trial preparation. Prepare a list of the issues.
2. Use the list of issues to prepare instructions to client from initial inception of a case.
3. Use the Comprehensive case assigned or the demonstration school bus–truck accident case to:
   a. Prepare a litigation hold letter to your client. Explain the reasons and the penalties.
   b. Prepare a memo to members of the firm on the necessary steps and actions they must take regarding litigation hold procedures.
   c. Instruct your client on what documents you wish to review and the reasons for the review, including instructions and the reasons for the requested file format of the files.
   d. Prepare a template for use in preparing a privilege log.
   e. Prepare a list of witness you will require to authenticate documents to be admitted as evidence.

BUILDING YOUR PROFESSIONAL PORTFOLIO

CIVIL LITIGATION TEAM AT WORK

Procedures

1. Locate any rules of procedure or evidence in your jurisdiction on requirements for producing privileged material.
2. Prepare a checklist of the steps that must be taken in your jurisdiction to prevent inadvertent disclosure of confidential information from being treated as a waiver of the privilege.

"Mere access to the courthouse doors does not by itself assure a proper functioning of the adversary process."

—Thurgood Marshall

The Electronic Courthouse

CHAPTER 8

OPENING SCENARIO

It had been a very event-filled six months preparing the school bus accident case in which twenty-five clients were seeking damages. The facts were not in great dispute, but the challenge remained of how to show the jury the physical evidence, or at least a good representation of it, and how the product defects in the truck and the bus contributed to the severity of the injuries. The court's technical support person assured the litigation team that all they had to do was bring a laptop to court and hook it up. The lead attorney, Owen Mason, was nervous and not sure he could handle presenting the case to the jury while working the laptop computer, and presenting the graphics. There was a lot of documentation, including the electronically stored documents they had obtained during discovery that contained the "smoking gun" language that proved the liability part of the case. They all knew they were lucky to get the case into a court that had an electronic courtroom, unlike the local state courthouse, which did not even have TV monitors to present video depositions.

However, the question that had yet to be answered was whether they should present the case electronically or use photographic enlargements. The multimedia tools were all available, if a little costly, but what would make the best impression on the court and the jury? A major problem was that the engineering expert they were counting on would be out of the country the week the trial was scheduled. Getting the individual treating physicians to appear at the last minute was also a major problem. In planning for the trial, the firm had anticipated the problem of getting all the medical experts away from their practices to attend the trial. The firm had incurred considerable expenses in videotaping

LEARNING OBJECTIVES

After studying this chapter, you should be able to:

1. Describe how courts are implementing technology.
2. Describe the elements of an electronic courtroom.
3. Explain the use of trial presentation programs.
4. Describe the process of working with the court staff and issues of using electronic equipment in the courthouse.

VIDEO INTRODUCTION

A video introduction to the electronic courthouse.

After watching the video in MyLegalStudiesKit, answer the following question.

- Why has computer technology been adopted in the litigation process?

depositions of all the medical experts, treating doctors and the plaintiffs. The hope was that by using a high-technology electronic courtroom in federal court, the entire case could be presented with graphics and videotape.

INTRODUCTION TO THE ELECTRONIC COURTHOUSE

Computer technology is changing the way law offices and court systems perform traditional functions. The ease of creating electronic documents, including traditional letters and contracts and electronic communications in the form of emails, has resulted in a document explosion. At the same time, cases are coming to trial faster because of the demand for "quicker justice," which allows less time to prepare and present a case in court. The result has been growth in the use of electronic documentation, computerized case management, and the use of computers in litigation.

ELECTRONIC FILING

LEARNING OBJECTIVE 1
Describe how courts are implementing technology.

One of the most significant changes for a large segment of the legal community is the implementation of electronic filing by some courts. As of 2009, all of the federal district courts have implemented e-filing. The state courts have not embraced this technology as completely, with only a relative few making the use of e-filing either optionally available or mandating its use.

Some states such as Connecticut have mandated e-filing and set up websites such as that shown in Exhibit 8.1. In the Connecticut system, counsel are advised in the court requirements that:

> If an attorney or law firm without an exclusion form E-Services requirements submits, on paper, any document that is required to be filed electronically, the clerk will not file the document and will write "Not Accepted" across the file stamp on the document. The clerk will then return the document to the sender with a notice explaining why it was not filed.

VIDEO ADVICE FROM THE FIELD

Debra Weaver–Certified real time court reporter

A discussion explaining Real Time Reporting.

After watching the video in MyLegalStudiesKit, answer the following questions.

1. What is Real Time Reporting?
2. What are the advantages to a real time reporting transcript?

Exhibit 8.1 Connecticut e-filing website

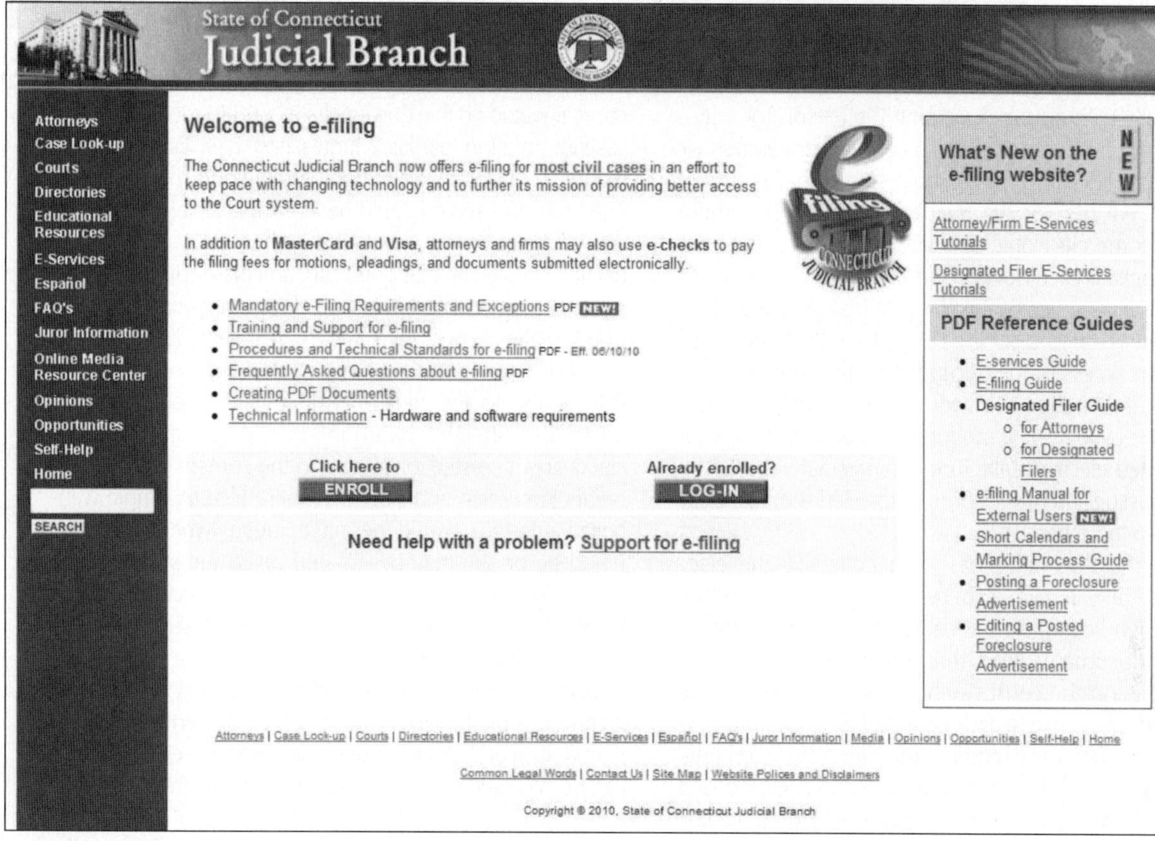

What can be expected is that more courts will adopt an e-filing system. Thus the legal team must be prepared to use the e-filing systems where required and stay current on the implementation status in the courts in which they practice.

ADVICE FROM THE FIELD

E-FILING IN STATE APPELLATE COURTS: AN APPRAISAL

by David Schanker, Clerk, Wisconsin Supreme Court and Court of Appeals, on behalf of the NCACC

...

E-Filing Systems

In fact, the e-filing systems offered by most e-filing vendors resemble each other far more than they differ. Nearly all are based on the federal model and provide interfaces designed with the differing perspectives of filers, the clerk's office, and the courts in mind.

In a typical (or ideal) e-filing system, filers prepare the document using conventional word processing software, then save it as a PDF file. The filer then (1) logs onto the court's e-filing interface with a court-issued username and password, (2) enters basic information relating to the case and the document, (3) uploads the document, (4) submits it to the system, and (5) pays any applicable filing fees online. The filer receives a notice verifying the submission of the document.

The appellate court clerk's office receives notification that the document has been submitted to the system, usually by the appearance of the newly submitted document in an e-filing review queue. A clerk's office employee reviews the document for compliance with the rules and deadlines and either accepts it or rejects it.

(continued)

(continued)

If the document is rejected, it is returned to the attorney electronically with a note describing the reason for rejection. If it is accepted, (1) the document is file-stamped or receive-stamped with an electronic stamp that is added to the PDF version of the document, (2) the document is added to the electronic case file, (3) the filing is noted on the appellate case docket, and (4) the other parties to the case receive notice of the filing. At that time, the other parties either receive a service copy of the PDF document or are given access to the document on the court's server. If the filing is a motion that requires immediate consideration by the court (e.g., a motion for extension of time), it is transmitted electronically to the appropriate court. The court then issues an order (through the clerk's office) electronically to the parties.

Once the document has been added to the electronic case file, it can also be made available to the public, depending upon the court's policy. In a number of states, documents filed through the e-filing system are available on the court's website, either as part of the appellate docket case search or as a briefs database. In states where the court requires the filing of documents in text-searchable PDF, the database can be configured to be searchable by terms and phrases, making it a valuable tool for attorneys and judges who want to read how other attorneys have handled a particular issue.

If, in addition, the system had an interface with the trial court, it would enable the appellate court to receive not only case information (parties, charges, case type, financial information, etc.) electronically but the trial court record as well. The trial court record could be as simple as a scanned version of the paper record, or it could be a set of links to electronic versions of trial court documents—including e-filed pleadings, scanned exhibits, and electronic transcripts. Most of this material could thereby be in text-searchable form.

The typical interface for judges would provide them with access to the electronic documents associated with a case in a straightforward manner; judges and their law clerks are interested, of course, in the content of the documents, not when and how they were filed. A simple web-based interface would permit a judge (wherever in the world he or she may be) to sign on to the system, enter a case number, and retrieve a list of the electronic documents in that case. Double-clicking on a document would open that document in Adobe Reader. Once open, the document can be saved, printed, downloaded, or e-mailed; it can be copied; pieces of text can be copied from within it; and, if hyperlinks have been included, cases or statutes can be accessed via the Internet from within the document.

Source: E-Filing in State Appellate Courts: An Appraisal by David Shankar, et al. Reprinted by permission of the National Conference of Appellate Court Clerks.

WEB RESOURCES

Read the entire article at: http://www.appellatecourtclerks.org/NCACC_E-Filing_White_Paper.pdf

WEB RESOURCES

Access PACER at www.pacer.gov

Pacer

The federal courts use a standardized system for access, Public Access to Court Electronic Records (PACER). As shown in Exhibit 8.2, the PACER website provides links to all of the individual websites of the federal courts. The PACER system is open to anyone who registers for an account at the PACER website, www.pacer.gov.

Training in the use of the PACER system is available from the website specific to the various courts, such as the Appellate, Bankruptcy, or District Courts, as shown in Exhibit 8.3.

THE ELECTRONIC COURTROOM

LEARNING OBJECTIVE 2
Describe the elements of the electronic courtroom.

Increasingly, judges are embracing the use of electronics and computer-based systems in the courtroom. The initial reluctance to allow the "newfangled" technology is giving way to acceptance of tools that enhance the speedy administration of justice. One of the earliest uses of technology in the courtroom was the playing of videotaped depositions of expert witnesses on TV monitors in court.

Getting experts to testify is difficult when the time and day for presenting their testimony is uncertain because of the uncertainty of trial schedules. Many experts, such as noted surgeons and medical forensics experts, have active, lucrative practices, and demand compensation that can run to the thousands of dollars per hour for the

Exhibit 8.2 PACER website links

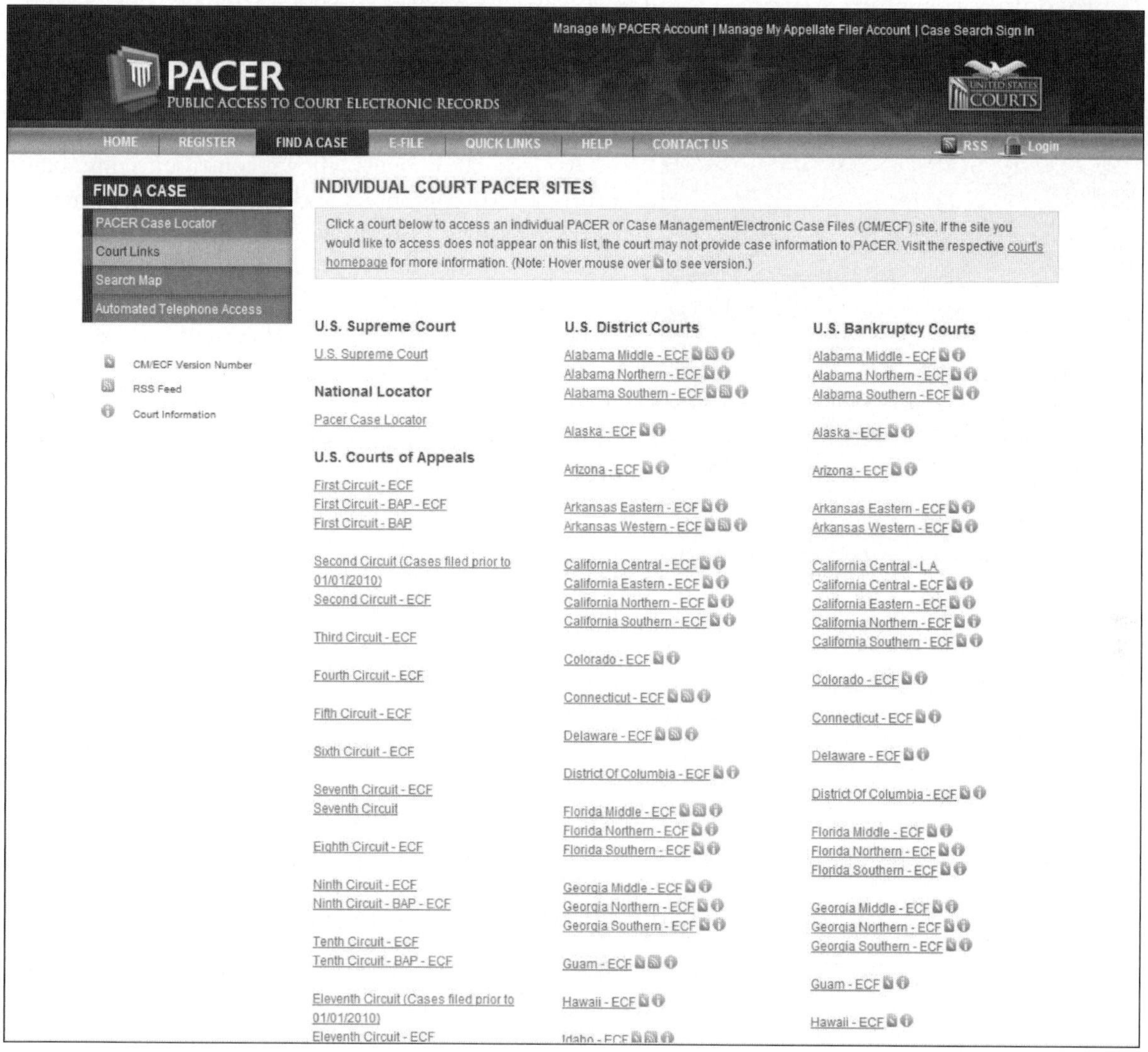

Manage My PACER Account | Manage My Appellate Filer Account | Case Search Sign In
PACER
PUBLIC ACCESS TO COURT ELECTRONIC RECORDS
UNITED STATES COURTS
HOME REGISTER FIND A CASE E-FILE QUICK LINKS HELP CONTACT US
RSS Login
FIND A CASE
PACER Case Locator
Court Links
Search Map
Automated Telephone Access
CM/ECF Version Number
RSS Feed
Court Information
INDIVIDUAL COURT PACER SITES
Click a court below to access an individual PACER or Case Management/Electronic Case Files (CM/ECF) site. If the site you would like to access does not appear on this list, the court may not provide case information to PACER. Visit the respective court's homepage for more information. (Note: Hover mouse over to see version.)
U.S. Supreme Court
U.S. Supreme Court
National Locator
Pacer Case Locator
U.S. Courts of Appeals
First Circuit - ECF
First Circuit - BAP - ECF
First Circuit - BAP
Second Circuit (Cases filed prior to 01/01/2010)
Second Circuit - ECF
Third Circuit - ECF
Fourth Circuit - ECF
Fifth Circuit - ECF
Sixth Circuit - ECF
Seventh Circuit - ECF
Seventh Circuit
Eighth Circuit - ECF
Ninth Circuit - ECF
Ninth Circuit - BAP - ECF
Tenth Circuit - ECF
Tenth Circuit - BAP - ECF
Eleventh Circuit (Cases filed prior to 01/01/2010)
Eleventh Circuit - ECF
U.S. District Courts
Alabama Middle - ECF
Alabama Northern - ECF
Alabama Southern - ECF
Alaska - ECF
Arizona - ECF
Arkansas Eastern - ECF
Arkansas Western - ECF
California Central - ECF
California Eastern - ECF
California Northern - ECF
California Southern - ECF
Colorado - ECF
Connecticut - ECF
Delaware - ECF
District Of Columbia - ECF
Florida Middle - ECF
Florida Northern - ECF
Florida Southern - ECF
Georgia Middle - ECF
Georgia Northern - ECF
Georgia Southern - ECF
Guam - ECF
Hawaii - ECF
Idaho - ECF
U.S. Bankruptcy Courts
Alabama Middle - ECF
Alabama Northern - ECF
Alabama Southern - ECF
Alaska - ECF
Arizona - ECF
Arkansas Eastern - ECF
Arkansas Western - ECF
California Central - L.A.
California Central - ECF
California Eastern - ECF
California Northern - ECF
California Southern - ECF
Colorado - ECF
Connecticut - ECF
Delaware - ECF
District Of Columbia - ECF
Florida Middle - ECF
Florida Northern - ECF
Florida Southern - ECF
Georgia Middle - ECF
Georgia Northern - ECF
Georgia Southern - ECF
Guam - ECF
Hawaii - ECF

Exhibit 8.3 PACER training website

Manage My PACER Account | Manage My Appellate Filer Account | Case Search Sign In
PACER
PUBLIC ACCESS TO COURT ELECTRONIC RECORDS
UNITED STATES COURTS
HOME REGISTER FIND A CASE E-FILE QUICK LINKS HELP CONTACT US
RSS Login
HELP
Frequently Asked Questions
Forgot Your Login/Password?
County/District Locators
Training
Resources
TRAINING
Click the links below to become familiar with the various CM/ECF products.
Appellate Courts
Computer-Based Training Modules
District Courts
Computer-Based Training Modules
Version 3.+ Electronic Learning Modules
Bankruptcy Courts
Computer-Based Training Modules
Version 3.+ Electronic Learning Modules
Streaming Video
"CM/ECF: The Attorney's Perspective" streaming video

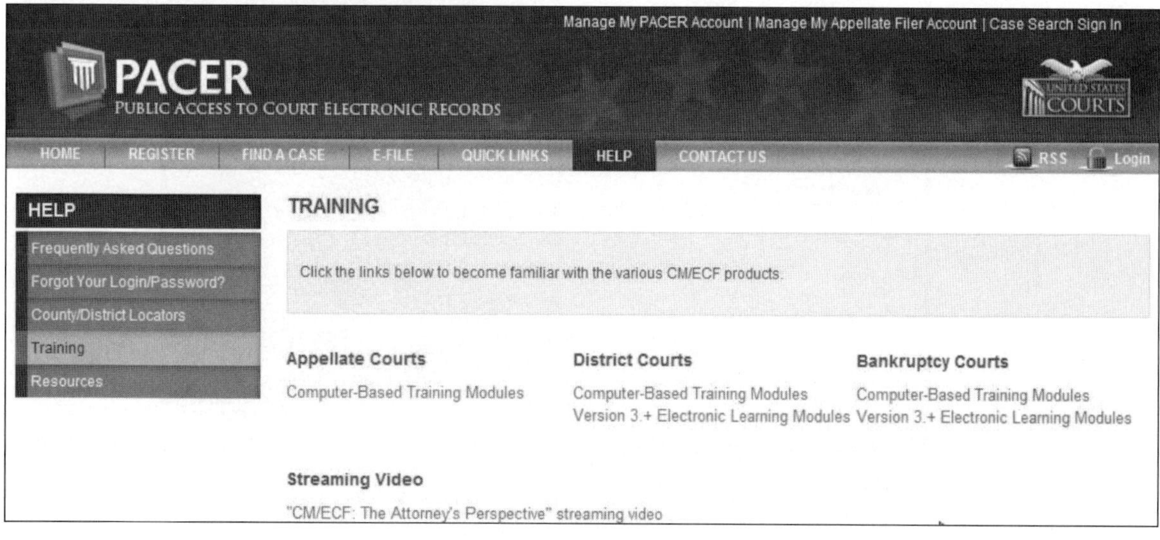

Exhibit 8.4 Electronic courtroom visual presentation system, Corpus Christi Federal Courthouse

time lost waiting to testify. The average litigant can rarely afford this litigation cost. However, a videotape or electronic recording of a deposition can be used in trial as a cost-effective method of presenting expert witnesses, or for witnesses who for reasons of health or distance would not otherwise be available to testify personally at a trial.

As judicial budgets allow, courtrooms are being outfitted with computers and audiovisual presentation systems. Exhibit 8.4 shows the new Corpus Christi Federal Courthouse technology courtrooms for the Honorable Hayden W. Head and the Honorable Janis Graham Jack, which have visual presentation systems.

Computerized courtrooms can be seen frequently on Court TV trials, in which computer terminals are present at each lawyer's table, at the judge's bench, and for each of the court support personnel, while the jury views a display monitor.

Litigation support software is used in trial to display documentary evidence, graphic presentations, and computer simulations of accident cases. Relevant portions of documents can be displayed as the witness testifies and identifies the document for everyone in the courtroom to see at the same time, without the need to pass paper copies to everyone. Lawyers can rapidly search depositions and documents, sometimes in the tens of thousands of pages, on their laptop computers to find pertinent material for examination or cross-examination of witnesses. Exhibit 8.5 shows another way in which litigation support software, in this case Sanction, is used to display part of a transcript and the video presentation at the same time.

Exhibit 8.5 Transcript and deposition display in Sanction

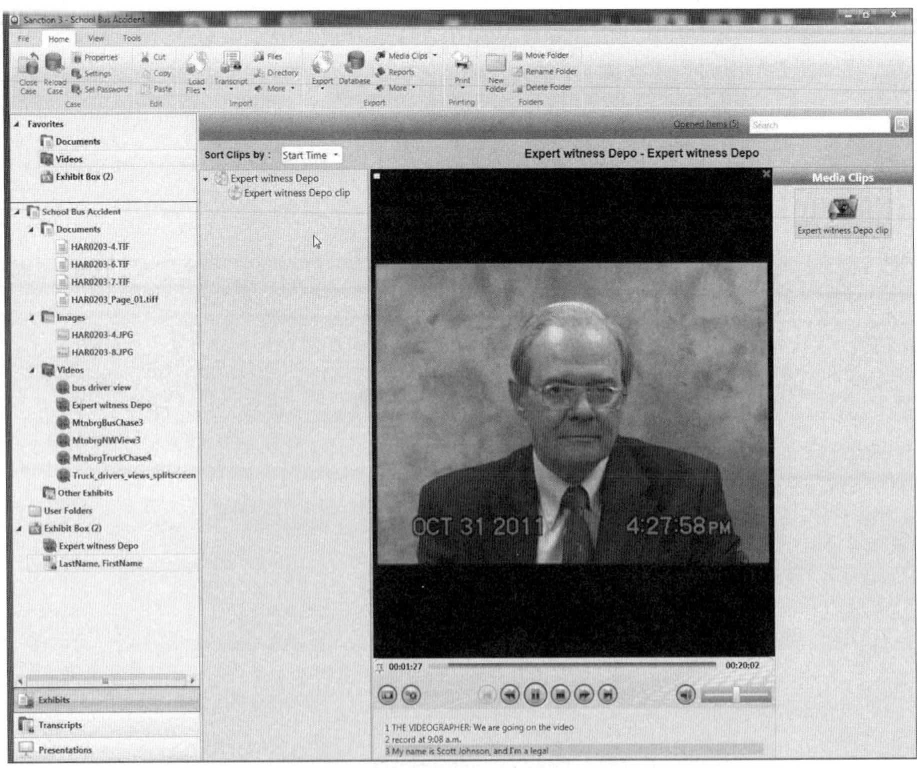

The Wired Courtroom

The extent to which courtrooms are set up for technology ranges from the basic, with only wall outlets for power, to the advanced, with installed wiring and equipment. Some courts have started the process toward the wired courtroom by eliminating the traditional court reporters, replacing them with an audio-wired courtroom with microphones at each needed location—witness box, counsel table, judge's bench—and a recording system located either in the courtroom or at a remote location. For example, the Delaware County courthouse in Pennsylvania has wired all of its courtrooms with microphones and playback equipment that is monitored from a separate location in the courthouse. Requests to repeat what was said are handled by the audio operator, who plays back an audio segment.

ELECTRONIC TRIAL PRESENTATION PROGRAMS

LEARNING OBJECTIVE 3
Explain the use of trial presentation programs.

More and more courtrooms are providing, or allowing litigants to provide for their trial, computer-based electronic display systems. Some see this as nothing more than a logical outgrowth of the multimedia presentations that started with the use of chalkboards, movie clips, and slide projectors.

Modern trial presentations frequently include videotaped depositions and images, photos, videos, computer simulations, and portions of documents. These may be on personal monitors at the lawyer's table, judge's bench, and in the jury box, or large-screen displays.

Managing the hundreds of individual components in the courtroom can be a trial nightmare unless they are organized and easily accessible for presentation. Sanction Solutions, TrialDirector, and similar **trial presentation programs** allow the legal team to organize and control the documents, depositions, photographs, and other data as exhibits for trial, and then display them as evidence when needed in depositions and trial. Exhibit 8.6 shows a sample screen from Sanction displaying the image files and a selected image from the NTSB case study in Appendix II.

trial presentation program
Computer program that organizes and controls documents, depositions, photographs, and other data as exhibits for trial and displays them as evidence when needed.

WEB RESOURCES
Try out a training module for Sanction at www.sanction.com/training/online9020module

Limitations on Presentation Graphics

The limitation on using presentation graphics is determined by the equipment in the courtroom. If the courtroom is not set up with appropriate power sources, screens, or monitors, computer presentations will not work, and print exhibits may still be needed. A key issue for the legal support staff is to determine well in advance the availability of technical resources in the courtroom in which the trial will take place. If the courtroom is not equipped for computer presentations, will the court allow the installation and use of equipment? And, if all of the equipment must be supplied, will the client be willing to pay for the costs associated with acquiring or renting and installing the needed hardware? In cases like the notorious O. J. Simpson case, if the courtroom had not been wired for computer use, the defendant certainly could have afforded the associated cost if advised of its benefits by counsel and allowed by the court.

WEB RESOURCES
For complete information and documentation on the Matthew J. Perry, Jr. Courthouse in Columbia, South Carolina, go to http://www.scd.uscourts.gov/

The following information and Exhibit 8.7 are from the online material available at the website of the U.S. District Court for the District of South Carolina, which opened its first fully **electronic courtrooms** at the Matthew J. Perry, Jr. Federal Courthouse in Columbia, South Carolina. They offer a glimpse into the features and equipment that may be found in other courtrooms and courthouses.

electronic courtroom
Courtroom equipped with electronic equipment for use in trial presentations.

Exhibit 8.6 Case file images available and selected image in Sanction

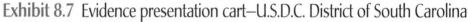

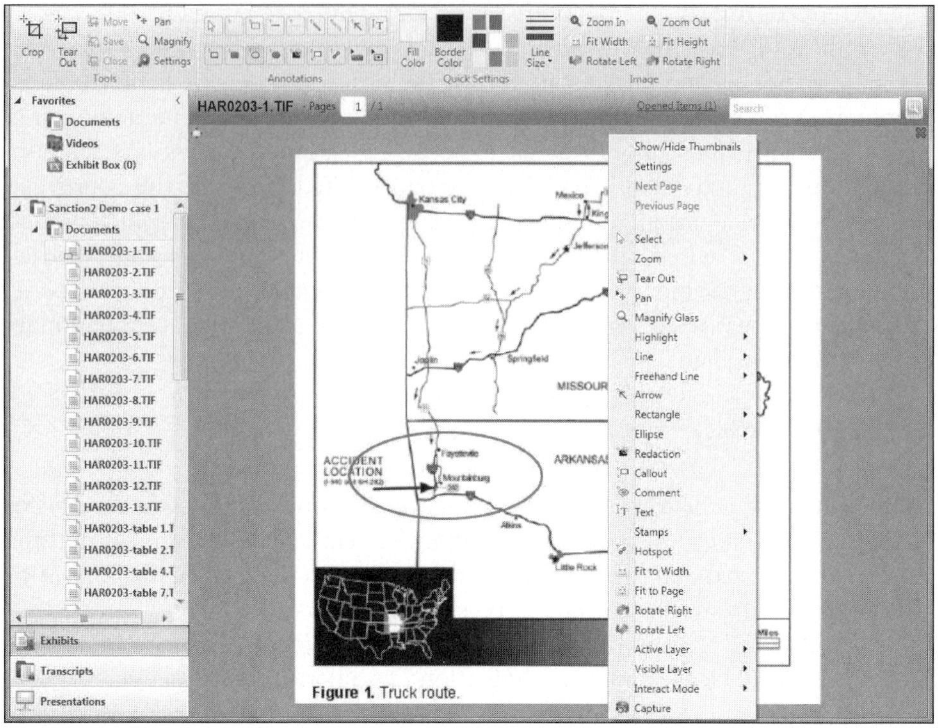

Source: Copyright © AG/Sanction LLC. Used with permission.

Exhibit 8.7 Evidence presentation cart–U.S.D.C. District of South Carolina

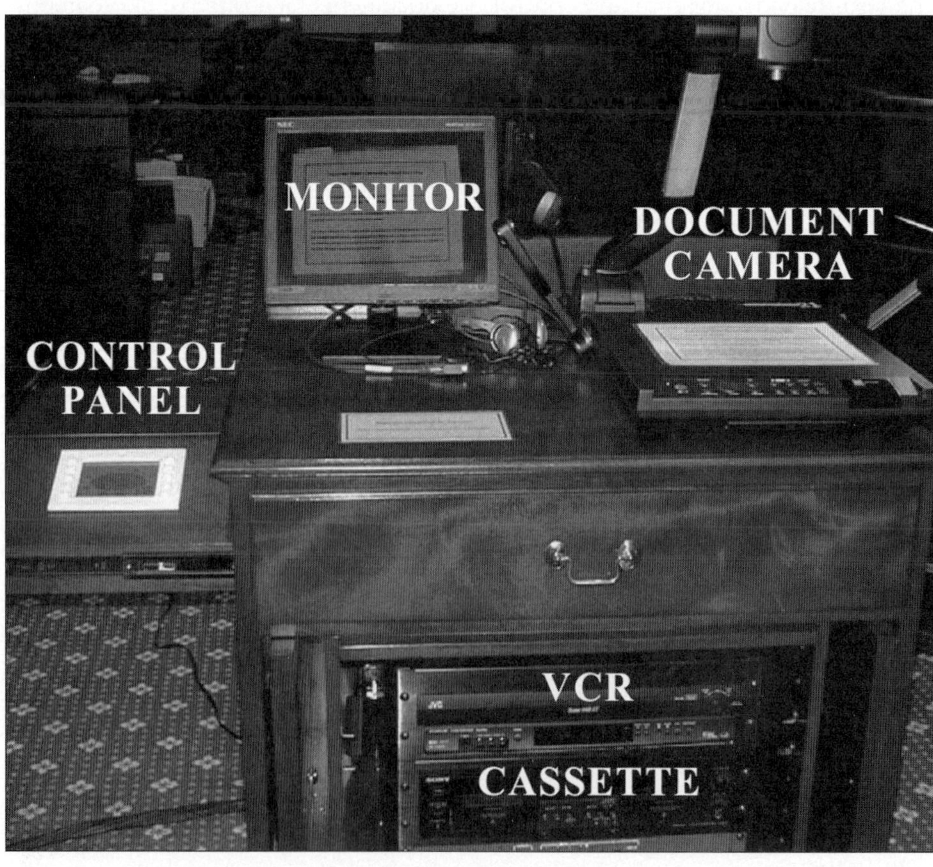

Video monitors are strategically placed around the courtroom. The judge's bench, the witness stand, the courtroom deputy, and each of the counsel tables and the jury box have video monitors to view the display of evidence. The jury box has one flat-panel monitor placed between every two juror chairs.

There are also **large-screen monitors** for display of evidence using a document camera or other electronic media just inside the well of the court, so those in the gallery may view evidence displayed through the system.

At the heart of the electronic courtroom is the **visual presentation cart,** or media center, which contains most of the presentation electronics. These items include:

Annotation monitor—Allows a witness to easily make on-screen annotations with the touch of a finger.
Document camera—A portable evidence presentation system equipped with a high-resolution camera.
Infrared headphones—Used as an assisted listening device for the hearing impaired.

large-screen monitor
A video monitor conveniently located in the courtroom and large enough for all to see the graphics displayed.

visual presentation cart
Media center located in the courtroom.

annotation monitor
Monitor that allows a witness to easily make on-screen annotations with the touch of a finger.

document camera
A portable evidence presentation system equipped with a high-resolution camera.

infrared headphones
An assisted listening device for the hearing impaired.

ADVICE FROM THE FIELD

TRIAL SUPPORT

Lone Stars: Enron trial support and the* SPECIALISTS *who made it happen
By Hillary Easom

Anyone who's stepped onto a dance floor knows that a waltz, a tango, and a two-step all require partners to move in sync. Working together, partners move smoothly and gracefully, creating a perfect rhythm. The relationship between attorneys and trial support specialists is another dance, demanding careful choreography, smooth movements, and excellent communication both before and during the trial.

In recent years, technology has helped make the trial dance less cumbersome. At the same time, glitches with technology can trip up one or both partners, creating awkward moments in the courtroom. The job of trial technology specialists is to develop a method of seamless presentation, supporting the attorneys without the need to count out each and every step.

A classic example of this vital "choreography" was the recent Enron criminal trial (*U.S. vs. Kenneth Lay and Jeffrey Skilling*). Over the course of several months, attorneys and support personnel had to practice their moves so as not to step on each other's toes during trial. One misstep in the litigation support process on either side could have been a serious factor in the trial's outcome.

Similar to a dance, the key to courtroom success can be summed up in one word: Preparation.

Expect the Unexpected

Scott Parreno knows the importance of careful pretrial groundwork. Parreno, from the Los Angeles office of O'Melveny & Myers, was the lead defense paralegal in the Enron case. He and four other paralegals acted as middlemen between the defense attorneys and other support personnel, ensuring that witness preparation binders and exhibits were complete and reproduced for relevant parties.

A 16-week trial with 56 witnesses inevitably presents surprises. "One thing that was constantly changing was the witnesses that were going to testify," says Parreno. This could be frustrating, as the team would put in a lot of time and effort in preparation to cross-examine a witness called by the prosecution, and suddenly the witness would be dropped and replaced by an alternate. "We'd be right back at square one preparing for a witness. The Judge maintained that each side had to know five witnesses ahead of time who the other side planned to call, but how important that witness was to either side really affected how much work we all would put into preparing."

In addition, preparations had to be made in advance for witnesses the defense believed might possibly be called further into the case. "For instance," says Parreno, "we thought that the government would be calling Richard

(continued)

(continued)

Causey at some point during the trial, so we not only had to compile prep materials for him in case he was called, but we also had to work on the other five witnesses that the government had already disclosed."

Sounds pretty high-stress. But Parreno maintains that the team got along famously. "Sort of like sailors in a submarine, we learned to depend on each other," he says. "We really did have a great crew, and we all thought of each other as family."

One of those "family" members was Pam Radford, a trial consultant with Houston-based Legal Media Inc. Radford and her colleague Trevor Brock ran all of the trial presentations for the defense.

A Stitch in Time

Skilling's attorneys required more help with preparation than Lay's due to the greater number of securities and wire fraud counts being tried–28 versus 6. On a typical day, Radford and Brock arrived at Skilling's office at 6:30 AM. By 7:45 or 8:00 they were in the courtroom preparing for the day's events. After a full day of presenting evidence, they adjourned to Skilling's office to prepare for the next day. Despite the long hours, the attorney-support relationship was positive. "They were some of the best attorneys in the country, by far," says Radford....

Similarly, the Legal Media Inc. team was structured so that they could take over for each other if necessary. This alleviated some of the stress that could otherwise come with such a long, drawn-out trial. Radford and Brock were able to take turns meeting late into the night with the attorneys, preparing for the next day's proceedings.

The pair created all demonstratives for the Skilling team and a small portion for the Lay team. Thanks to technology's growing presence in the courtroom, Radford and Brock needed only two laptop computers. Radford used Trial Director to organize document[s], and Brock used Sanction to present video and audio evidence in court.

Exhibits included between 800,000 and 1 million pages of documents, stored on two external hard drives. Almost a terabyte of video evidence was stored on additional hard drives. Every day during this trial, some 200 documents were added to the cache.

Courtroom Tech 101

Technology in the courtroom was limited. "Judge Lake was very strict about not bringing additional monitors in," says Radford. The courtroom had one large monitor, and at the Judge's insistence the federal courts brought their own additional monitors. *Legal Media Inc. needed only to provide additional audio mixers and filters, equipment to help regulate sound in the courtroom.*

"We did have some glitches with their system because of the way it was wired," says Radford. For example, sometimes the audio would get out of sync after a recess. However, learning how the system functioned made these problems easy to fix.

The Enron Broadband case, which tried five former Enron Broadband Services executives, presented a different set of technological hurdles. Unlike the one used in the criminal trial, this courtroom was not equipped for technology, and cables had to be installed for video distribution during the trial. This was no easy task, as there were almost 20 video outputs used in the trial.

Arizona-based Verdict Systems (Sanction) handled technology support for this case under the direction of Dan Bowen, acting COO of the company. "The source set of data was somewhere in excess of 100 million pages," Bowen recalls. "At the trial site, we had access to 25 million pages of paper. We ultimately went into trial every day with over 4700 exhibits that made up almost 75,000 pages of paper, and over 500 video clips. And that was a subset."

Whereas in the past these documents would have to be lugged back and forth each day to court, modern technology helps prevent countless backaches: a single laptop with additional external hard drives is all that's needed. This was unheard of as recently as 5 or 6 years ago....

"In a case of this complexity, there was literally so much volume that things got pushed right up until almost the day of trial," Bowen says. "We were doing a lot of data management trying to not just identify from the client what their exhibit lists were going to be, but then convert those lists down into usable electronic data so that it could be used in Sanction for the electronic presentation." This required months of pre-trial preparation. "We literally worked around the clock writing custom applications to strip out the pertinent data and create it into a usable format."

The efforts proved worthwhile, however, once the trial started, allowing the attorneys to think about the law and not have to worry about the technology. "Because of the way that the [Enron Broadband trial] database was structured, with very simple naming conventions," says Bowen, "the attorneys were able to say something as simple as, 'Let me show you Exhibit 4000," and the technology support specialist was able to quickly pull up the document. A labeling system that used the defendant's initials followed by a 4-digit number simplified the process; Exhibit 4000 was labeled "JH4000" and could be retrieved by typing 6 keys and hitting "Enter." This, in addition to prepping with the attorneys and trial team, helped greatly facilitate communication in court.

Room for Error

Still, no matter how well a team prepares, there is always room for a glitch. "We had hard drives fail," says Bowen,

(continued)

stressing that backups are essential in any trial situation. Radford agrees and adds, "Always have it somewhere else inside the courtroom with you."

Experienced support personnel know to have extra hard drives on hand with backups of all documents and video or audio evidence, in case the primary computer should fizzle. But what good does this equipment do if it's not there when an emergency strikes?

During the Lay/Skilling Enron trial, Radford tried to power up her computer with the opening statements, and the machine refused to boot. Fortunately, she was prepared with another machine containing the same information, and when she pulled out the mirrored backup everything went smoothly.

In another instance during the trial, an attorney accidentally kicked a plug out under a table. "When we went to test the audio, it wasn't playing," says Radford. "It had been playing 30 minutes before." This emphasizes the importance of testing equipment ahead of time; Radford and Brock were able to troubleshoot before the trial resumed. They also had backup speakers and computers on hand in case of emergency; fortunately, none of these had to be used.

For Radford and Brock, working the Enron case required stopping work on all other cases 2-1/2 months before the trial began....

Most pre-trial work was done via e-mail between the support specialists and the attorneys. Pre-trial work for Brock included digitizing and synchronizing video and audio evidence–a daunting task–and organizing all media exhibits. Radford's time was spent meeting with attorneys to work on demonstrative ideas, exhibit structure, and graphic design.

And in this Corner...

Technology in the courtroom, for the prosecutors, was a new bag. This required some special choreographing by CACI, Inc.–Commercial, the firm providing litigation support for the government, to facilitate communications between the person in the hot seat and the attorneys.

Brian Katz was CACI, Inc.–Technical Support Services Manager at the time of the trial. "Some of these attorneys had never used technology or used it very little," he says. "This was a technology-driven case. Some attorneys would turn to the person in the hot seat and say, 'Could you zoom in to paragraph 2?'" Others simply mention an exhibit, and the technology support specialist must take the cue.

It is critical, notes Katz, to understand how each attorney operates. "They're going to blame you at the end of the day if a document didn't come up quick enough."

Chris Sasso, Michael Denault, and Matthew Mehler made up Katz's team, working with attorneys and running presentations during the trial. Katz's job was to ensure that the other three were able to get into a rhythm.

Sasso and Denault were in the hot seat running trial presentations, while Mehler worked behind the scenes, preparing and scanning documents and exhibits to be passed on for review. He essentially built the case in the "war room" and passed it on to his teammates to present in the courtroom....

The team prepared for over a year before the trial began, processing e-mails and documents for exhibits. This came to a head about 2-1/2 weeks before the trial, as they honed in on detailed preparations. Though another company prepared and presented opening statements, CACI, Inc.–Commercial, continued to work with the prosecution for the extent of the trial....

About the Author: Hillary Easom is a freelance writer and photographer whose work has appeared internationally in various print and online publications including *Better Investing, Marie Claire, Cruise Magazine,* and *American Fitness*. Ms. Easom lives in Bethesda, Maryland, with her husband, son, and lop-eared rabbit. Her interests include travel, yoga, and pop culture.

Source: "Lone Stars: Enron trial support and the specialists who made it happen," *Litigation Support Today*, August 2006. Copyright © 2006 Conexion. Used with permission.

Laptop port—A connection into which a laptop may be plugged.
Interpreter box—Routes language translations from an interpreter to the witness/defendant's headphones or the courtroom's public address system.
VCR and **dual-cassette player**—For video and audio playback.

In addition to the electronic courtroom capabilities, videoconferencing technology is available in any courtroom at the Matthew J. Perry, Jr. Courthouse.

laptop port
A connection into which a laptop may be plugged.

interpreter box
Routes language translations from an interpreter to the witness/defendant's headphones or the courtroom's public address system.

VCR
Equipment that plays back video and audio.

dual-cassette player
Equipment that plays back audio.

ELECTRONIC EQUIPMENT IN THE COURTROOM

Document Camera

The document camera (Exhibit 8.8) is an easy-to-operate, portable evidence-presentation system. This unit is equipped with a high-resolution camera and features a 12:1 magnification zoom lens with a high-accuracy auto-focusing system. The

Exhibit 8.8 Document camera

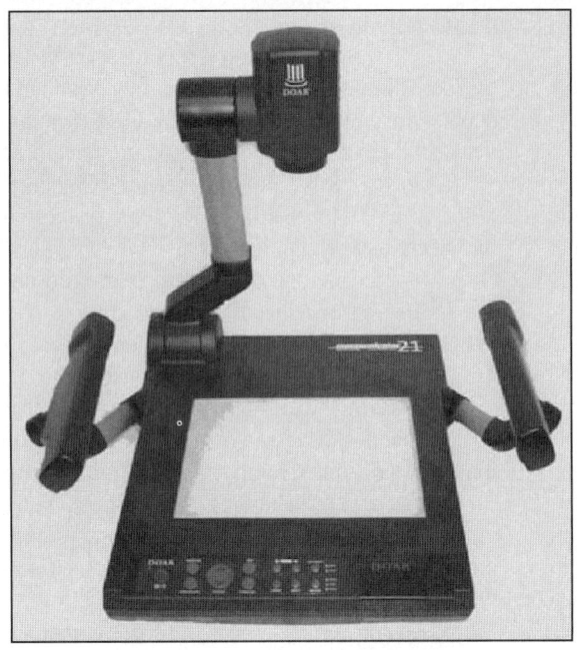

Exhibit 8.9 Annotation monitors

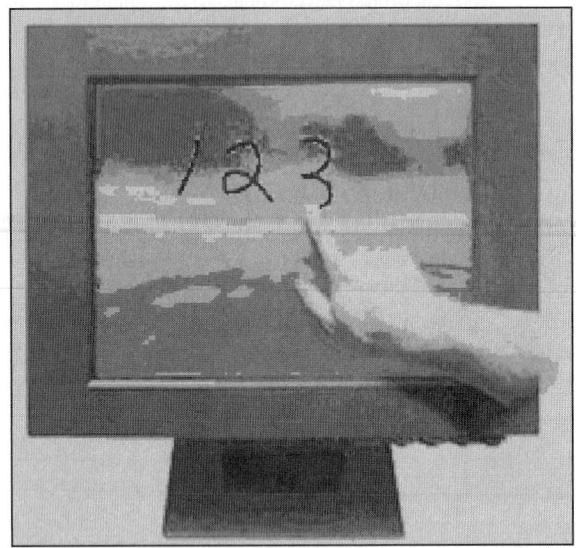

Exhibit 8.10 The interpreter box

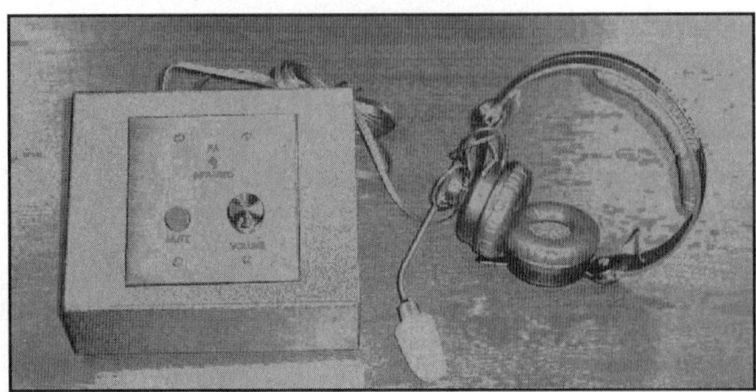

document camera can present evidence (e.g., 3-D objects, paper documents, transparencies, X-rays, etc.) for display on monitors throughout the courtroom.

Annotation Monitor

Annotation monitors (Exhibit 8.9) allow a witness to easily make on-screen annotations with the touch of a finger. Annotations can be made by pressing lightly and dragging your finger as you would a pen.

Interpreter Box

The interpreter box (Exhibit 8.10) routes language translations from an interpreter to the witness/defendant's headphones or the courtroom's public address system.

Infrared Headphones

Infrared headphones (Exhibit 8.11) are used as an assisted listening device for the hearing impaired. The Americans with Disabilities Act requires that this type of device be available for any individual needing it. It can also be used in conjunction with the interpreter box, for language interpretations.

Typical of the information available online about electronic courtrooms is that on the website for the U.S. District Court for Middle District of Pennsylvania (Exhibit 8.12), which can be viewed at http://www.pamd.uscourts.gov/docs/elec-cr.pdf.

Exhibit 8.11 Infrared headphones

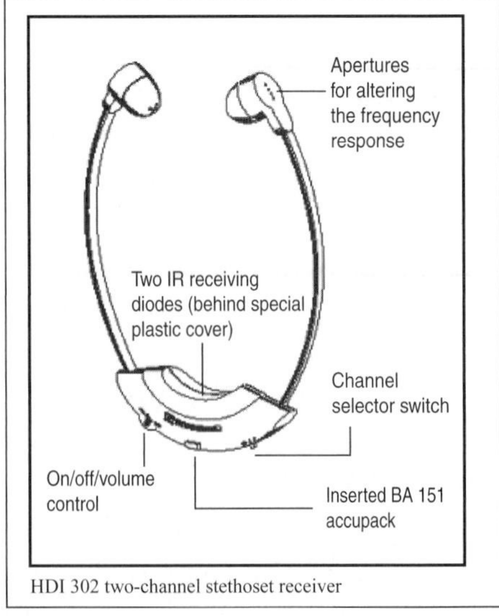

HDI 302 two-channel stethoset receiver

VIDEO ADVICE FROM THE FIELD

Richard Manfredi–Videographer

A videographer discusses the role of the videographer in video depositions.

After watching the video in MyLegalStudiesKit, answer the following question.

- What is the role of the videographer in the deposition?

WORKING WITH COURTHOUSE TECHNOLOGY STAFF

LEARNING OBJECTIVE 4
Describe the process of working with the court staff and issues of using electronic information in the courthouse.

Within each courthouse and each courtroom are numerous people more than willing to help the legal team if properly approached and consulted. These people have specialty knowledge developed from working in their area on a daily basis that occasional users of the services like members of a litigation trial team cannot expect to have unless they also spend considerable time learning the ropes. And even then, because courthouse technology staff are familiar with the idiosyncrasies peculiar to their own installation, they can make the process flow smoothly and help solve the problems that inevitably occur at some point.

Exhibit 8.13 shows an example of how the U.S. District Court for the Northern District of Illinois invites users to become familiar with electronic support in the courtroom. The IT or technical support office should be the first place to go or contact if any technology will be needed or used in the courthouse, whether in a deposition or a trial. Find out what the procedures are first. Members of the support staff are usually the ones who also know how the different judges feel about the use of technology. Some may not approve of any large-screen displays, while others may think a single large-projection screen is appropriate. Some may have individual monitors all over the courtroom and yet not want them used for things like presenting a video deposition, preferring instead a single monitor placed for the judge and the jury to view.

The technical support person may also be the one to help clear the hardware through security, saving time and stress on the day of trial by getting everything into the building in time to set it up and try it out beforehand. Remember, the courtrooms IT staff are usually the ones with the master keys to unlock the courtroom. It is also an advantage for the legal team to have someone who speaks the same technical jargon and can interface at the same knowledge level. A little goodwill can go a long way.

Exhibit 8.12 The Electronic Courtroom Brochure for the U.S.D.C. Middle District of Pennsylvania

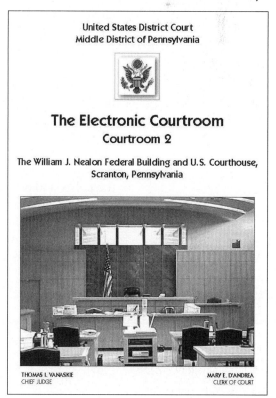

United States District Court
Middle District of Pennsylvania

The Electronic Courtroom
Courtroom 2

The William J. Nealon Federal Building and U.S. Courthouse, Scranton, Pennsylvania

THOMAS I. VANASKIE
CHIEF JUDGE

MARY E. D'ANDREA
CLERK OF COURT

Clearing the Right to Bring in the Equipment Beforehand

Anyone who has been in a courthouse in the past few years knows of the increased security measures in place: metal scanners, X-ray machines, and briefcase searches.

Exhibit 8.13 Electronic courtroom technology website

Source: http://www.ilnd.uscourts.gov/home/CourtRoomTechnology.aspx

Anything out of the ordinary, particularly electronic equipment, can result in special scrutiny. In the ideal setting, the only thing the legal team needs to bring is the CD, videotape, or other electronic storage media—because all the equipment is provided by the courthouse.

Rarely does everything work so smoothly as the ideal. Most attorneys carry the electronic files on their laptops. The trial presentation plan may be to use the software and files on a laptop by connecting it to the courtroom equipment with a cable. Where the court system is not compatible or the equipment is not provided, the legal team must bring the needed equipment into the courthouse. It is highly recommended that the security office be contacted ahead of time to learn the policy and procedures for bringing everything into the courthouse and setting it up. In a number of courthouses, this will mean using the loading dock of the courthouse or other alternate entrance and waiting for clearance. Pre-clearing equipment can save valuable time on the day of trial, not to mention stress and concern that everything will work as planned.

Checklist ✓ A PRESENTATION APPROACH

Getting Technology to Work in the Courtroom–

- Try it out ahead of time.
- Have backup equipment.
- Have a separate operator.
- Have the passwords.

WHAT HAPPENS WHEN THE LIGHTS GO OUT

Even the best plans can be sidetracked when the equipment fails or when the power needed is not available. In many parts of the country, the reaction to excess power demand is to reduce the voltage, sometimes called a brownout. Some equipment will work at a lower-than-optimum voltage while other items must have a constant power supply. For example, many homeowners have found their refrigerators not working after a brownout because the motors could not operate at the lower voltage supplied by the power company, and the motors burned out. While there are options like battery-powered backup systems, these may not be practical. In anticipation of "when all else fails," it is always good to have backup hard copies of graphs and charts.

Many legal teams bring a backup of important files and software on extra laptop computers, just in case. Particularly well-prepared or overly concerned legal teams check the equipment in advance and bring extra projection bulbs for the computer projector, and even bring backup projectors, monitors, and in some cases printers. To paraphrase an old adage, if anything can go wrong, it will, at the worst possible moment—and in the middle of trial.

CONCEPT REVIEW AND REINFORCEMENT

KEY TERMS

trial presentation program 197
electronic courtroom 197
large-screen monitors 199
visual presentation cart 199
annotation monitor 199
document camera 199
infrared headphones 199
laptop port 201
interpreter box 201
VCR 201
dual-cassette player 201

CHAPTER SUMMARY

Introduction to the Electronic Courthouse	Technology is changing the way that courts perform their traditional function of recognizing the demand for swift justice.
Electronic Filing	As of 2009, all of the federal district courts have implemented e-filing. The state courts have not embraced this technology as completely, with only a relative few making the use of e-filing either optionally available or mandatory.
The Electronic Courtroom	Electronic court-based systems are increasingly being used in the courts. As budgets allow, courtrooms are being outfitted with computers and audiovisual presentation systems.
The Wired Courtroom	Courtrooms are being wired with technology ranging from the very basic to high-technology monitors and computers at every workstation for lawyers, the judge, and the jury.
Electronic Trial Presentation Programs	Courtrooms are providing, or allowing litigants to provide for their trial, computer-based electronic display systems. Trial presentations frequently include videotaped depositions and the presentation of images, photos, videos, and portions of documents.

	Trial presentation programs allow the legal team to organize and control the documents, depositions, photographs, and other data as exhibits for trial, and then display them as evidence when needed. ■ Sanction This is an electronic trial presentation software application. ■ Supported formats Not all native formats can be used in all trial presentation programs. It is wise to check the formats supported by the trial presentation program selected for trial early in the preparation process to ensure compatibility.
Working with Courthouse Technology Staff	Courtrooms generally have support personnel who are available to assist the members of the litigation team in the use of the technology available in the courtroom or the courthouse. They are also the key contact for obtaining a right to bring equipment into the courthouse on the day of trial. Good working relations with the technical support staff can be invaluable when everything goes wrong and backup equipment is needed on an emergency basis.

REVIEW QUESTIONS AND EXERCISES

1. List and explain some of the advantages to the use of technology in litigation.
2. What are the functions for which the litigation team uses the litigation presentation programs?
3. How may the legal team use presentation graphics programs? Give examples of both litigation and nonlitigation legal teams.
4. Explain the use of trial presentation programs.
5. What can you do when the power fails?
6. List and explain considerations in the creation of presentation graphics.
7. List and explain limitations on presentation graphics used at trial.
8. Why is the courthouse technology team important to the legal team?

BUILDING YOUR PARALEGAL SKILLS

INTERNET AND TECHNOLOGY EXERCISES

1. Use the Internet to locate resources for e-filing in your federal and state jurisdictions.
2. Use the Internet to find information on the electronic courthouse and courtroom in your federal and state jurisdictions.

CIVIL LITIGATION VIDEO CASE STUDIES

Signing Documents: Zealous Representation Issue

A paralegal takes a document to be filed before the statute of limitation expires, but is told it must be signed by the attorney and a fee paid.

After viewing the video in MyLegalStudiesKit, answer the following questions.

1. May a paralegal sign the attorney's name to a document filed with the court?
2. How could this time problem have been avoided?
3. Could the papers have been filed electronically in your local federal court? Your local state court?

CHAPTER OPENING SCENARIO CASE STUDY

Use the Opening Scenario for this chapter to answer the following questions.

1. What equipment will the trial team need to display the photographs electronically?
2. What are the advantages and disadvantages of electronic display?
3. What are the advantages and disadvantages of using photographic enlargements?
4. How should the team plan to present the evidence of the medical experts and treating doctors? What equipment or arrangements will need to be made?

COMPREHENSIVE CASE STUDY

1. Prepare a list of the electronic equipment available in the federal and state courts in your jurisdiction where you may be assigned to try a case.
2. Prepare a memo to the trial team explaining the local rules for bringing in and using multimedia equipment in trial.
3. Prepare a list of the potential multimedia exhibits you would use in the school bus–truck accident case in Appendix II or for the assigned comprehensive case.

BUILDING YOUR PROFESSIONAL PORTFOLIO

CIVIL LITIGATION TEAM AT WORK

Procedures

1. Prepare a memo on the requirements for using the federal court electronic filing system.
2. Prepare a checklist of the steps for electronically filing documents in the federal court and your state court, or if e-filing is not available in your state, the requirements for filing including the physical locations (street address and room number) and required items and fees.

"A picture shows me at a glance what it takes dozens of pages of a book to expound."

Ivan Turgenev (1818–1883)

Presentation and Trial Graphics

CHAPTER 9

OPENING SCENARIO

The legal team had worked hard for the past six months preparing the case for trial. It was a big case for a small firm. A lot of the young firm's resources in time and money had been invested in the case, and success was essential. The firm had been notified by the court that the trial was scheduled to begin in three weeks. Everyone agreed that it was a great case; they just needed to get the jury's attention with all the facts and evidence that the legal team had prepared. They had been assigned to the new electronic courtroom that was equipped with individual monitors and large projection screens. All members of the legal team agreed that the photos they had would make everyone take notice of where and how it all happened. Good-quality graphics would also be essential to showing the jury what had happened and gaining their sympathy and a good verdict. Owen Mason, the lead attorney, and his partner were adamant that they not make the mistakes they had seen other lawyers make, using poor graphics that did not help the case or that the trial judge excluded for lack of veracity. With limited additional resources, they knew they had to prepare the graphics in-house.

LEARNING OBJECTIVES

After studying this chapter, you should be able to:

1. Explain how ordinary office suite and presentation graphics programs may be used in litigation.
2. Create a basic PowerPoint presentation.
3. Create an accident scene exhibit using a graphic software program.

VIDEO INTRODUCTION

A. A video introduction to graphics creation software.

After watching the video in MyLegalStudiesKit, answer the following questions.

1. What is the advantage to graphics creation software to the legal team?
2. What are the uses of graphics in the litigation process?

B. A video introduction to Smartdraw.

After watching the video in MyLegalStudiesKit, answer the following question.

- How can graphic creation programs be used in the litigation process?

INTRODUCTION TO PRESENTATION AND TRIAL GRAPHICS

It has been said that one picture is worth ten thousand words. Properly prepared graphics are an excellent way of telling a story and making a point whether to a jury, a client, or to a group of concerned residents in a public meeting. On the other hand, poorly prepared graphics can be boring and can distract from the main message. Everyone has seen a PowerPoint presentation. Some hit home and everyone in the audience wishes they had copies. Others convey a confusing message at best or offer a few minutes of sleep to the audience at worst. More and more people now use graphics in presentations, as the software to create them has become easier to use and more affordable.

Among the most accessible presentation graphics software programs are those included as part of the office suites of programs from Microsoft, including PowerPoint, and WordPerfect's Presentation and Quattro Pro. Because these program suites are already part of the software in many offices, they are often used to create high-quality slide shows and drawings that include text, data charts, and graphic objects.

GRAPHICS AND PRESENTATIONS IN LITIGATION

Electronic Graphics Creation

LEARNING OBJECTIVE 1
Explain how ordinary office suite and presentation graphics programs may be used in litigation.

It used to be that when you walked into a courthouse, you could identify who was trying the case by the armload of poster board graphics and easels being carried by the legal support staff. The use of photographs has always been a common form of exhibit, and is a good lesson in what is appropriate for a presentation graphic. While some lawyers carry snapshot-size photos (4 × 5 in.) and others carry larger photos (8 × 10 in.), it is good to remember the words of a wise old judge to an novice trial attorney: If it's important enough to use a photo, make sure that the last person in the jury box and the judge can see it at the same time. Many wiser trial attorneys, with the introduction of overhead projectors and slide and computer projectors, have given up using costly photo enlargements (30 × 40 in.) in favor of computer-projected versions (where size is limited only by the size of the screen or wall). The same is true of the size of drawings and diagrams. But always remember the advice about poorly prepared graphics—do not use them.

Graphics and Presentations in Litigation

Most think of litigation graphics as being useful only in courtroom presentations. However, graphics and presentations play an increasingly important role not just in the actual trial but also in the stages leading up to trial. Using photographs, videos, computer simulations, and other graphic representations of the incident like time lines, the litigation team frequently obtains a better understanding of the issues that have to be proven and the facts available to do so. With a legal theory in place, it is common practice to try to settle the case and avoid actual trial. Thus, settlement brochures are increasingly sent to the opposing side to graphically lay out the case, the damages, and the potential evidence that will be used if the case goes to trial, and demonstrate why the case is so strong that it is better to settle the case. Where the case does not settle before trial, the graphics used in the settlement brochure or created in the pretrial process may be used as trial exhibits. In cases where the potential verdict justifies the expense, the settlement brochure may be a video of a day in the life of the victim, showing the impact the accident has had on the person—in extreme cases, what daily life is like for a formerly able-bodied person so seriously injured that she or he must spend the rest of her or his life in a wheelchair.

Using the Office Suite Applications

Information about the case, the activities of the litigation team working on the case, and items that need to be completed must be organized from the beginning of the case. Even if case management or office management software is not being used to capture and organize information, the same types of information still need to be captured in the form of time records, to-do lists, contact lists, and lists of investigative and discovery items. Sample forms for each of these types of items are available in the Microsoft office suite and the WordPerfect office suite. While technically not part of litigation graphics, they nevertheless illustrate the types of graphics tools that are available without needing to purchase additional pieces of software. Each of these types of graphics presentations can be used to create charts and tables for inclusion within written communications, as part of a presentation, or ultimately as an exhibit in trial.

Spreadsheets. The following examples are from the free samples that may be downloaded from the Microsoft Office Excel spreadsheet program. You can use an **electronic spreadsheet** or download a preset spreadsheet such as the one shown in Exhibit 9.1, which was downloaded from Microsoft. The screen that appears when opening a new document in Excel is shown in Exhibit 9.2.

electronic spreadsheet
A computer software program with rows and columns in which primarily numeric data may be manipulated using formulas. Also sometimes called electronic accounting worksheets.

The sample time sheet shown in Exhibit 9.1 has a formula built in that automatically totals the time column as each entry is added. The same type of spreadsheet can also be set up with columns that identify and track expenses, individual client medical expenses, or any other set of financial information where keeping track of the items and amounts is important.

The information tracked, or any portion of the information in the spreadsheet, may be imported to a Word document using the table menu in Word as shown in Exhibit 9.3. This can be a time-saver when demand letters are sent to the opposing side and information is to be included within the letters.

Exhibit 9.1 Excel time sheet

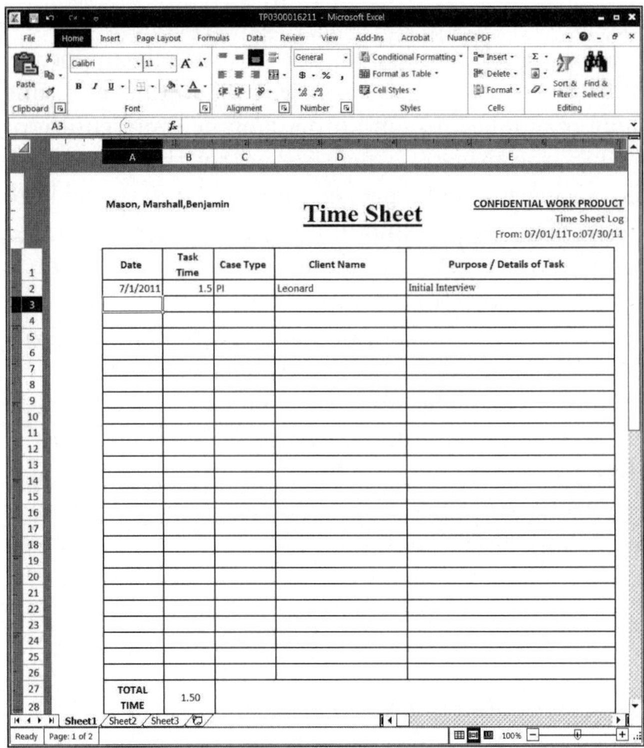

Source: Microsoft product screen shot(s) reprinted with permission from Microsoft Corporation.

electronic database
An electronic repository of information of all types that can be sorted by a computer program and presented in a meaningful manner.

Databases. Task lists, or as they are frequently referred to, "to-do lists," can be created using the **electronic database** in the office suite—for example, the Microsoft Access Task List shown in Exhibit 9.4—by choosing the sample Task List from the Access start menu, which is similar to the Excel spreadsheet start menu shown in Exhibit 9.2. With the database, the information for each task is captured as a record, "Task Details." In the particular database shown, the

Exhibit 9.2 Sample Excel spreadsheet downloads

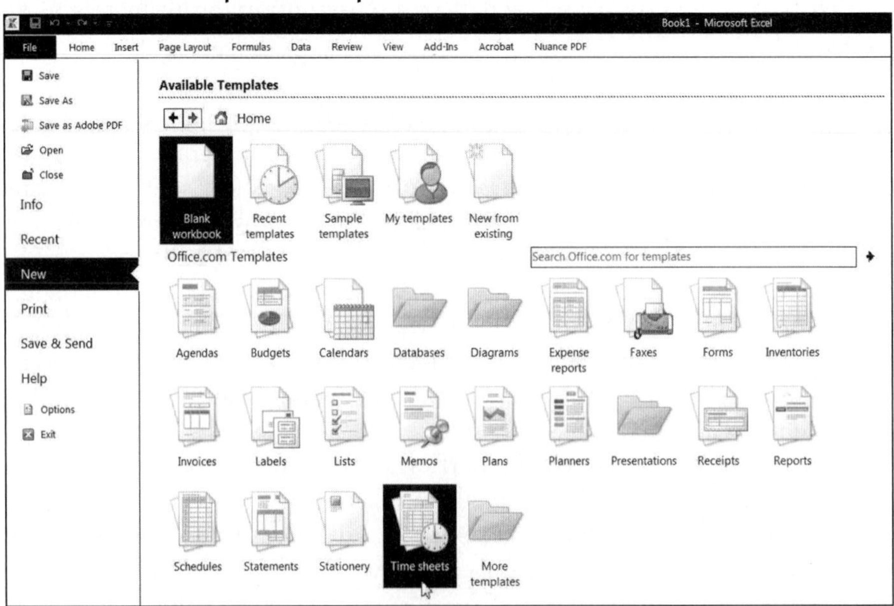

Source: Microsoft product screen shot(s) reprinted with permission from Microsoft Corporation.

Exhibit 9.3 Excel information imported to Word

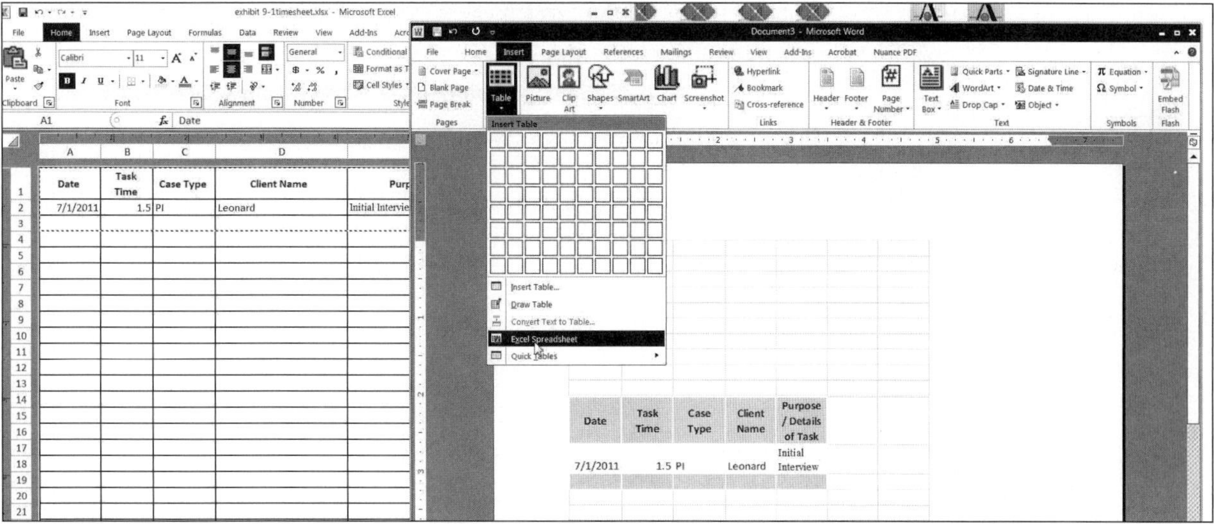

Source: Microsoft product screen shot(s) reprinted with permission from Microsoft Corporation.

program also allows the capture of contact information as part of the input of the information, as shown in Exhibit 9.5.

Word processor. The **word processor** in the modern office suite can be used for more than just writing letters. Among its features are the ability to vary type

word processor
A computer software program for creating, editing, and producing word documents in various formats.

Exhibit 9.4 Access task list database

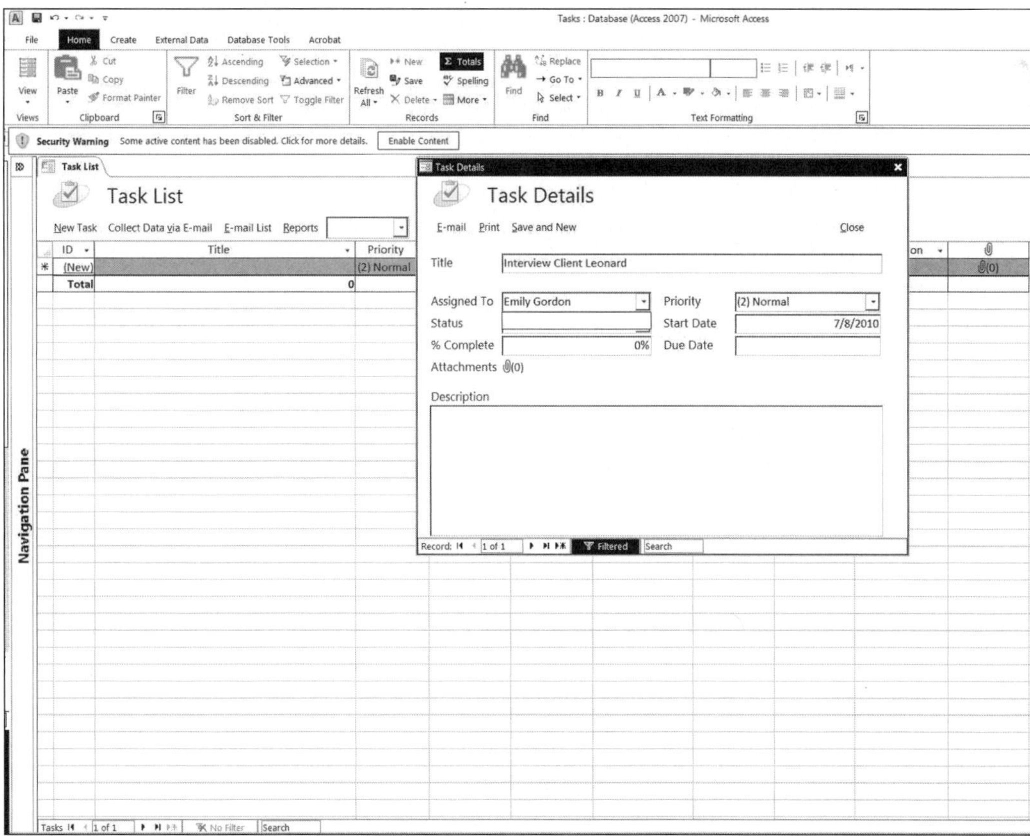

Source: Microsoft product screen shot(s) reprinted with permission from Microsoft Corporation.

Exhibit 9.5 Access task list contact entry

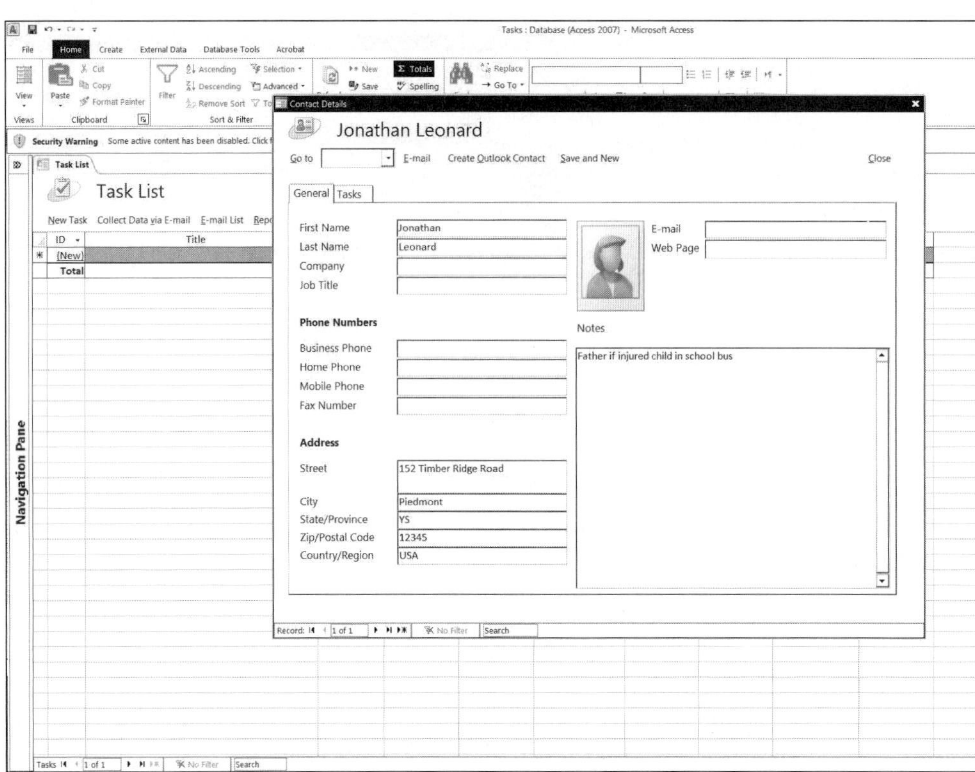

Source: Microsoft product screen shot(s) reprinted with permission from Microsoft Corporation.

fonts, sizes, and colors, making it possible to create letterheads with different fonts and sizes, as shown in Exhibit 9.6. The content of the actual letter can then be set using a traditional type font and size. In addition to the ability to insert spreadsheet information as shown above, images and pictures can be inserted when needed.

Using the various office suite tools, settlement brochures can be created in-house, saving the cost of media services, and when available, can be printed in color with low-cost color printers and high-quality paper or can be sent electronically to a printing service for printing, such as Staples and Kinkos. The sample shown in Exhibit 9.7 was created using a word processor and inserting pictures and a pictorial index via the Microsoft Word table feature.

Poster-size prints can be made of any of the images. In addition, each page of the settlement brochure can be used in face-to face settlement conferences or, if authenticated and permitted by the court, can be used in trial as part of the opening statement, during the trial as individual exhibits, or in the closing summary argument.

CREATING LITIGATION PRESENTATIONS USING *MICROSOFT POWERPOINT*

LEARNING OBJECTIVE 2
Create a basic PowerPoint presentation.

Microsoft PowerPoint can be used to present graphics and documents created by PowerPoint or other programs. Graphics and document files may be imported from such programs as LexisNexis TimeMap, SmartDraw, Adobe Acrobat, and Nuance PDF Converter.

Exhibit 9.6 Word processor–created letterhead and letter with image inserted

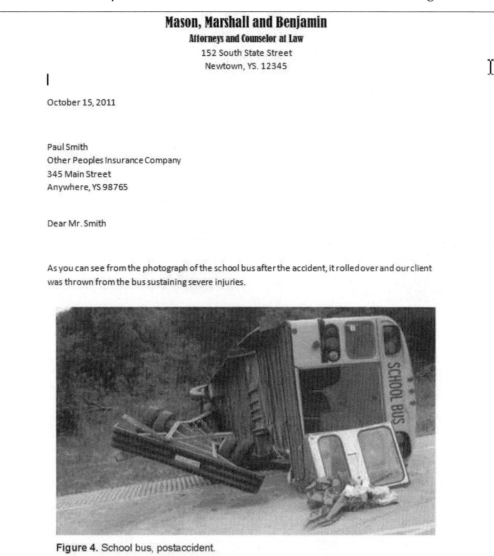

Mason, Marshall and Benjamin
Attorneys and Counselor at Law
152 South State Street
Newtown, YS. 12345

October 15, 2011

Paul Smith
Other Peoples Insurance Company
345 Main Street
Anywhere, YS 98765

Dear Mr. Smith

As you can see from the photograph of the school bus after the accident, it rolled over and our client was thrown from the bus sustaining severe injuries.

Figure 4. School bus, postaccident.

Program Integration

Many of these programs provide a link or menu option to import or export files. Some of these links are added automatically to other programs when the software is installed on a computer on which the other program is already installed. For example, the PDF Converter Pro link used in Exhibit 9.8 was added to PowerPoint (a previously installed program on the computer) when PDF Converter Pro was installed. Exhibit 9.8 shows the result of using the Import/Export link. Each page of the original document, saved as a single PDF file with many pages, has first been converted into a usable format by PDF Converter, and then imported into PowerPoint as an individual page, each a separate screen or slide.

Program integration is a time-saver when using different presentation and case management tools. Integration allows a single mouse click or keystroke

Exhibit 9.7 Sample settlement brochure created using a word processor

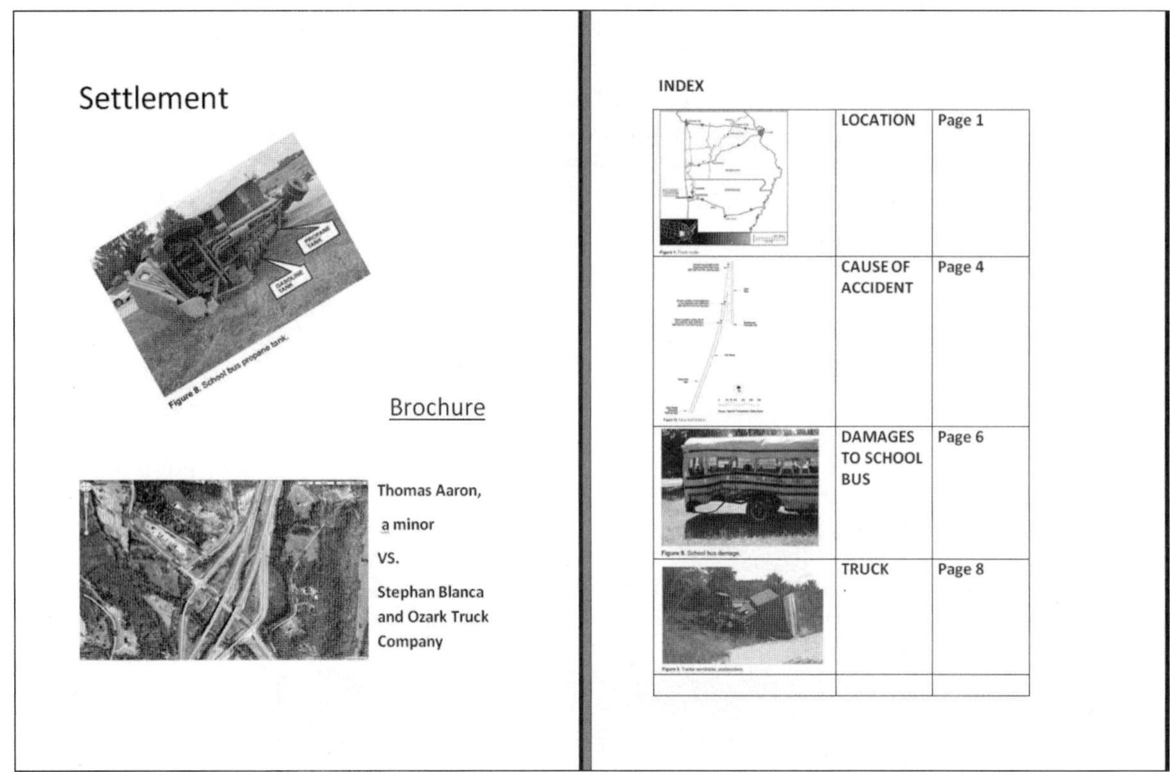

Exhibit 9.8 PDF images created from a single PDF file using PDF Converter 5

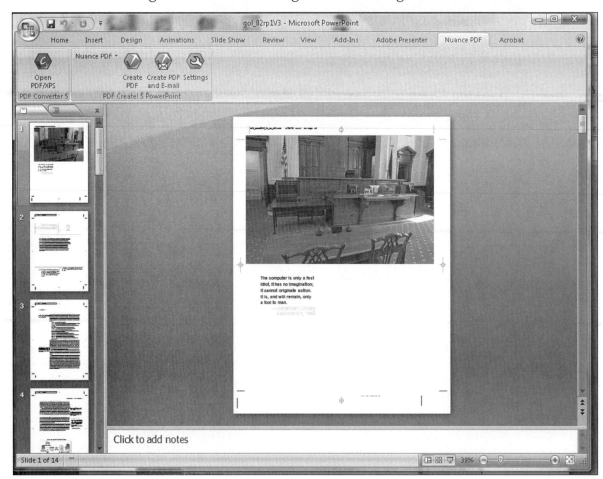

Exhibit 9.9 SmartDraw export options

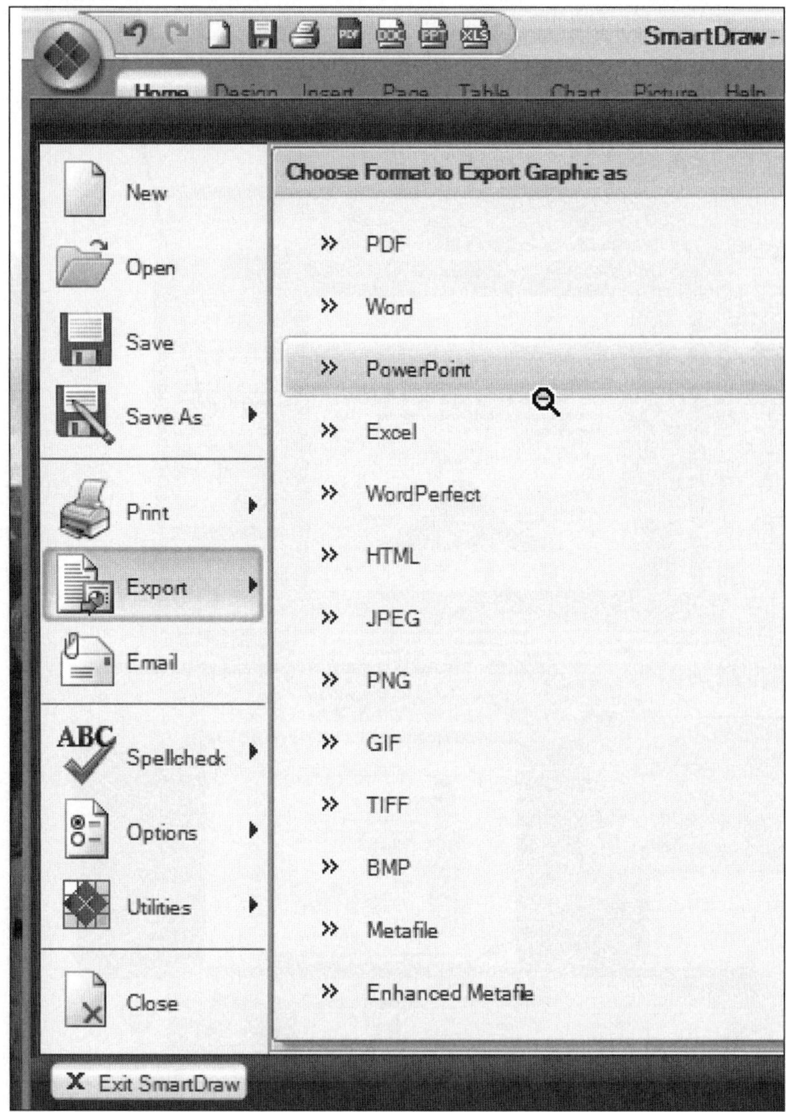

to start a process that would otherwise require starting up multiple programs and using multiple functions in each program to achieve a common end, the transfer in a usable format of information from one program to another. This is similar to the integration features available in suites of office programs, like Microsoft Office Suite or Corel WordPerfect Suite. Exhibit 9.9 shows another example, a link to automatically export a SmartDraw graphic directly into PowerPoint with a single mouse click. The user has the choice of showing a separate slide per entry, or a combined single-entry slide showing multiple time points, all with one keystroke.

Creating the Presentation

Creating a PowerPoint presentation starts with the New command in the PowerPoint menu. This command creates a new working window and a single slide. Text, graphics, sound, video, and animation can be added to the slide. The Insert menu displays a number of options for inserting graphics. A popular method

Exhibit 9.10 Microsoft PowerPoint

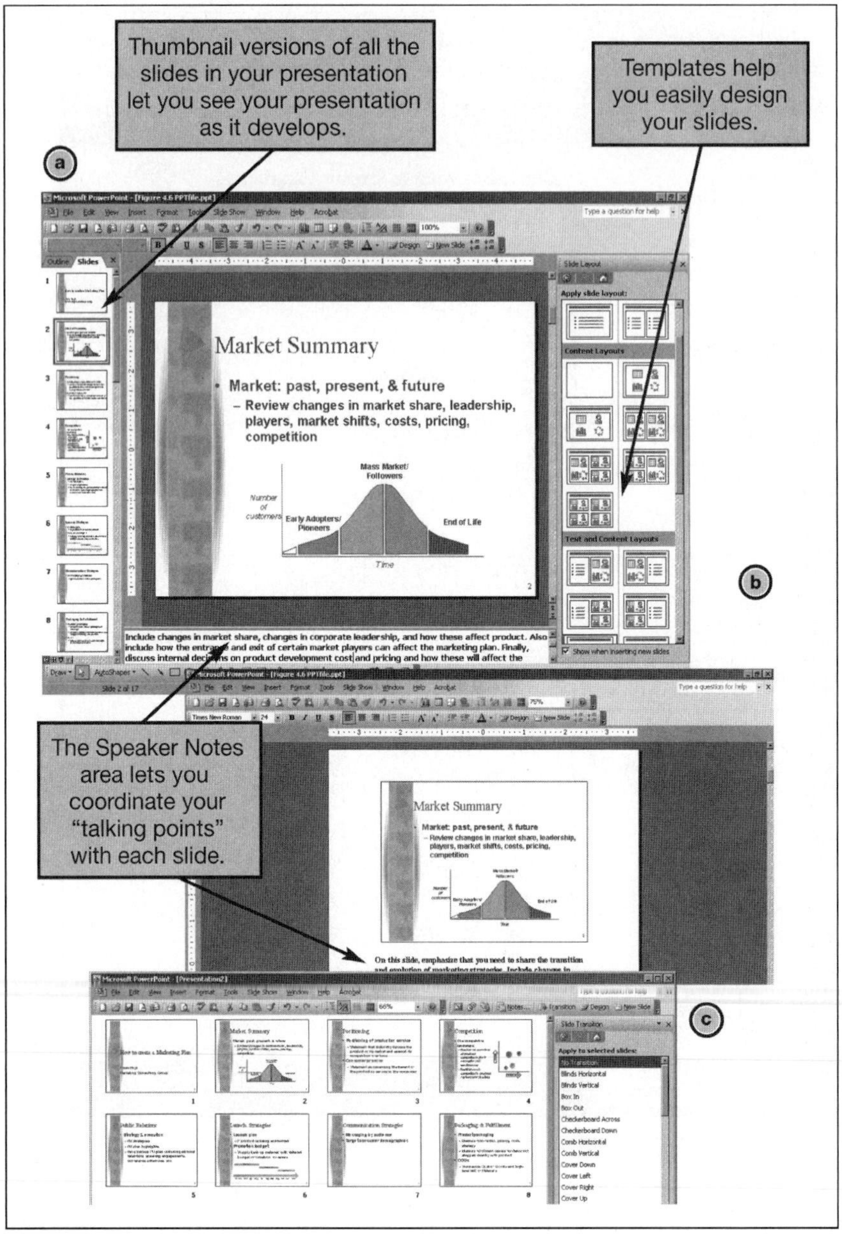

Thumbnail versions of all the slides in your presentation let you see your presentation as it develops.

Templates help you easily design your slides.

The Speaker Notes area lets you coordinate your "talking points" with each slide.

Source: Microsoft product screen shot(s) reprinted with permission from Microsoft Corporation.

is to insert graphics from clip art. The Clip Art search menu opens as a panel with a search feature for finding available clip art and sounds that can be accessed using the drag-and-drop method. Exhibits 9.10 to 9.12 show a PowerPoint presentation being created using clip art. The search results of available clip art using the term "accident" provide a number of choices.

Presentations may be enhanced, when appropriate, by the introduction of sound. Sound clips may also be found in the Clip Art panel. The sounds may be added by clicking on the Insert selection that is part of the Items options menu or by the drag-and-drop method. Sounds may be programmed to play automatically when the slide opens or upon the user clicking the mouse or keyboard, as shown in Exhibit 9.11. The presence of the sound clip is represented by the speaker icon, as shown in Exhibit 9.12, which indicates that two separate sounds were added.

Exhibit 9.11 Adding sound to the presentation

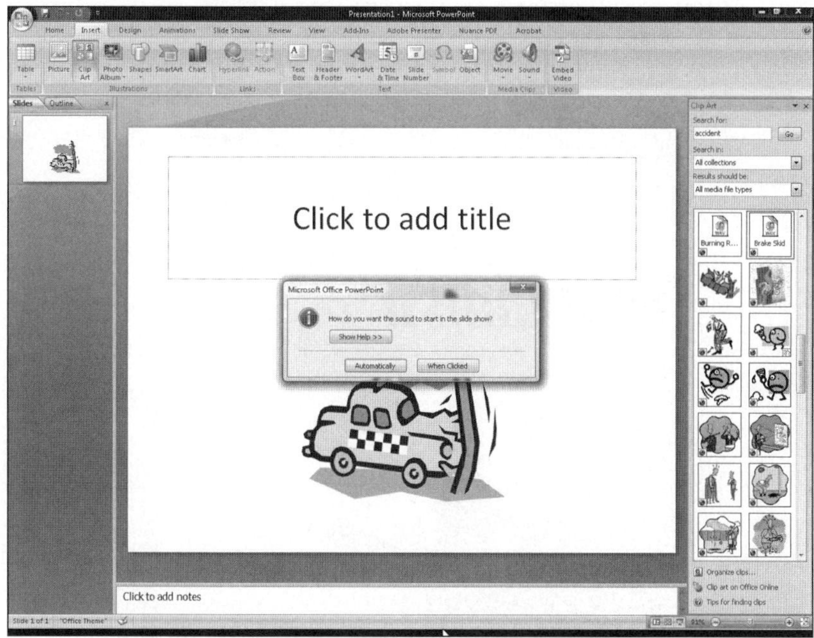

Source: Microsoft product screen shot(s) reprinted with permission from Microsoft Corporation.

Presentation Graphic Elements. Multiple graphic elements may be used in a single slide such as the taxi accident graphic and the arrow shape added from the Home tab Drawing options as shown in Exhibit 9.13. Any graphic element can be moved in front of or in back of another graphic in the slide to allow

Exhibit 9.12 Presentation slide showing that two sound clips are part of the presentation

Source: Microsoft product screen shot(s) reprinted with permission from Microsoft Corporation.

Exhibit 9.13 Menu for presentation options and addition of graphic feature

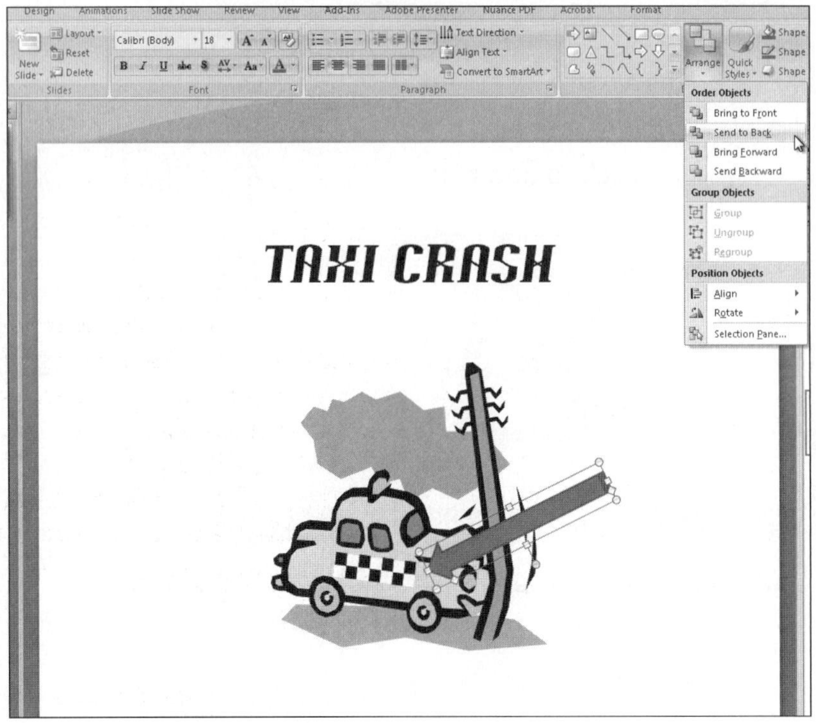

Source: Microsoft product screen shot(s) reprinted with permission from Microsoft Corporation.

one graphic to appear to overlay another, as shown in Exhibit 9.14, where the Send to Back option from the Home tab Design menu has been selected after the arrow graphic was selected as the object to which it would apply.

When an object has been selected, a dotted line appears around the object, as shown in Exhibit 9.13. Notice the corner and midline markers that

Exhibit 9.14 Graphic feature, the arrow sent to back

Source: Microsoft product screen shot(s) reprinted with permission from Microsoft Corporation.

also appear. These may be used to expand or contract the size of the selected object by a left mouse click on the desired point and moving the mouse in or out while holding the left mouse button. The marker in the middle of the line below the arrow in Exhibit 9.14 may be used in the same way to rotate the object.

There are many options available that may be used for a particular presentation depending on the situation and the audience. Microsoft makes available online tutorials and demos for learning about the program and the features desired. Tutorial and demos of PowerPoint features and options are available from the Help menu in the program and online at the Microsoft website.

Microsoft Visio

Microsoft Visio is a popular graphic drawing program. It provides many of the traditional engineering and architectural design elements frequently used in courtroom presentations for drawings of buildings and roadway diagrams. It also provides many of the elements necessary for the creation of business graphics and time lines. A sample of the work screen is shown in Exhibit 9.15.

Exhibit 9.15 Microsoft Visio sample work screen

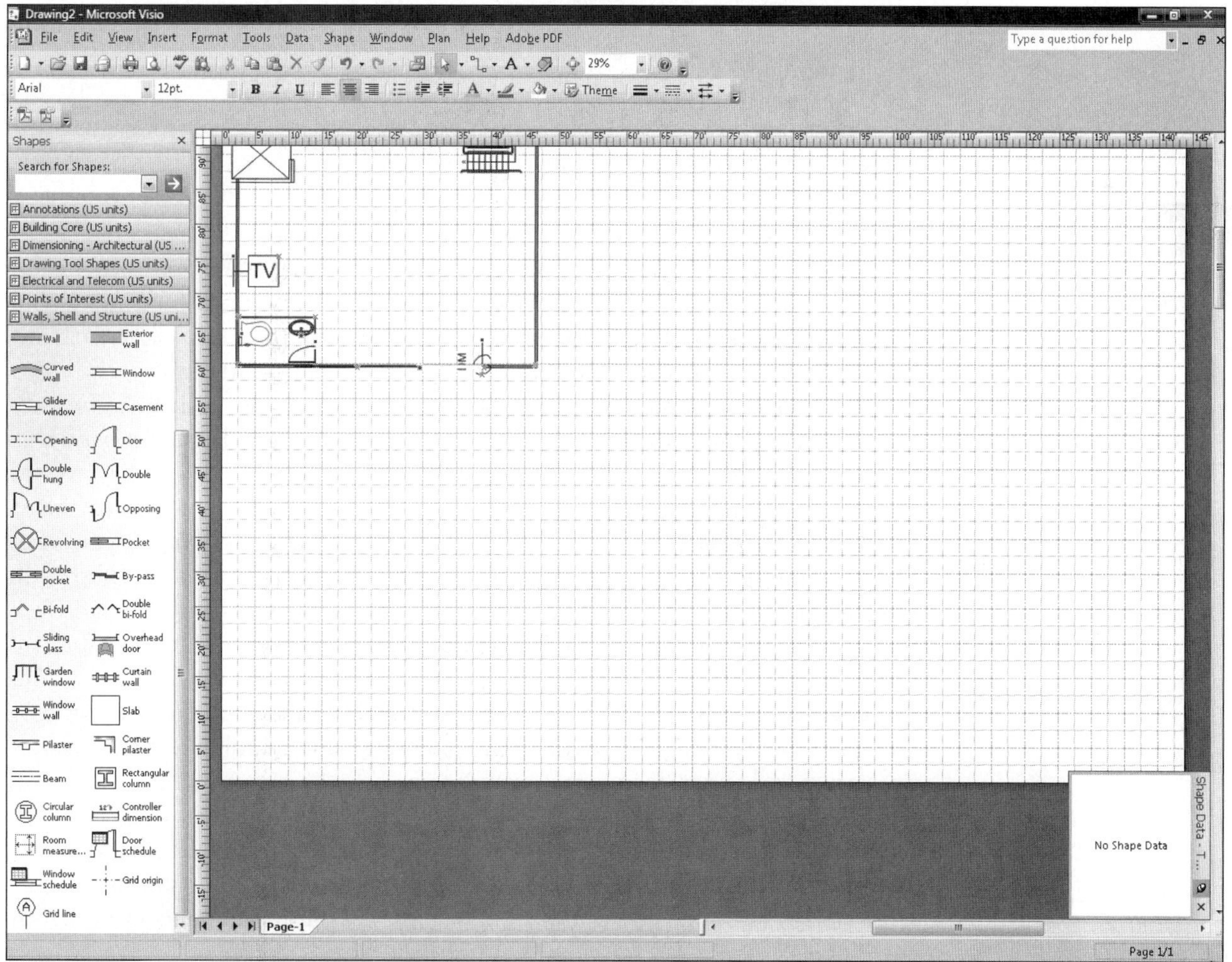

Source: Microsoft product screen shot(s) reprinted with permission from Microsoft Corporation.

Exhibit 9.16 Sample SmartDraw accident reconstruction graphic

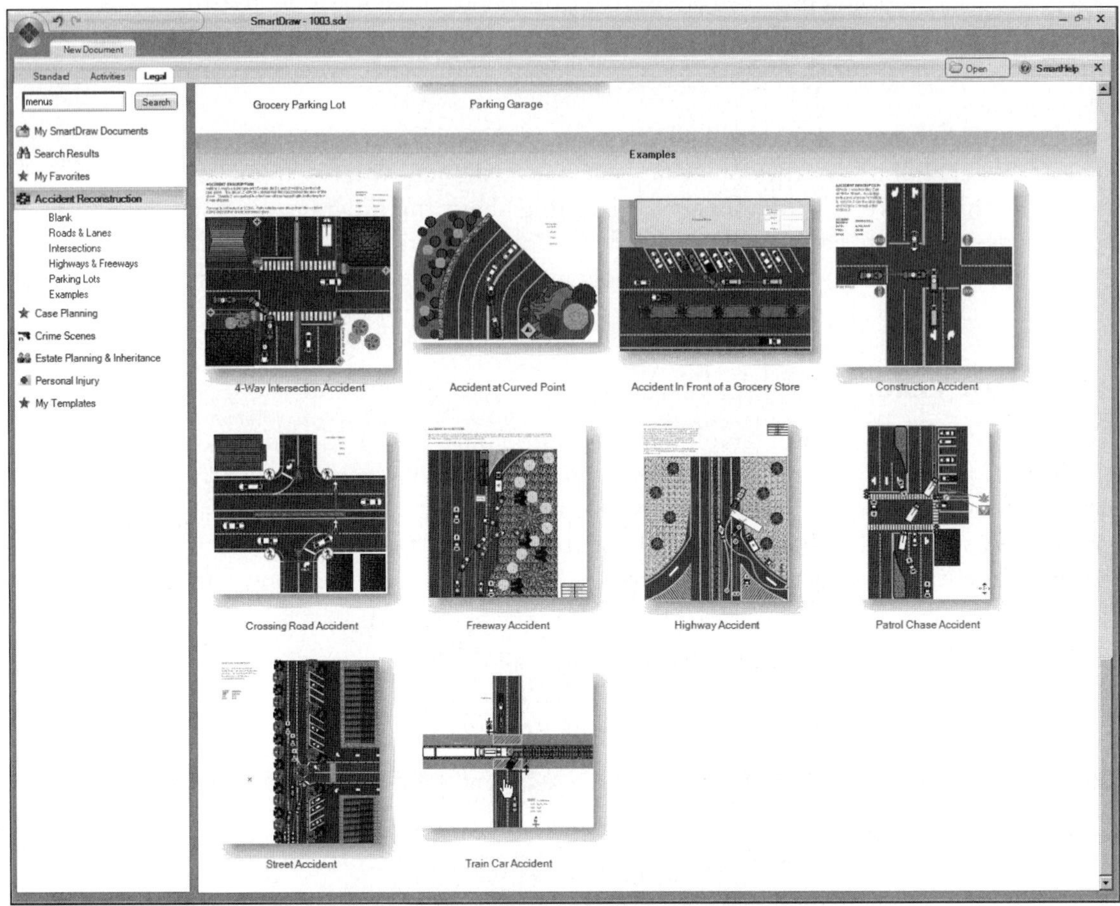

Graphic creation programs are used to create either standalone graphics or graphics that are part of a presentation such as a PowerPoint presentation. One of the newer classes of graphic software programs that offer templates is SmartDraw. Exhibit 9.16 shows examples of graphics prepared using SmartDraw.

The obvious advantage to this class of software is the ability it gives the legal team to create their own graphics and not need graphic artists and outside consultants. For example, it is possible for the legal team to create trial graphics in court on a laptop computer to meet an unexpected factual twist, and then to display the image using the laptop and projection unit. Even when the graphics are printed out, the software provides an electronic backup if the large display boards are delayed in transit, damaged, or destroyed by an overzealous cleaning staff. Exhibit 9.17 shows a sample graphic created for trial using SmartDraw.

PowerPoint has become the standard for making electronic presentations of all types to all types of audiences, from grade-schoolers (Exhibit 9.18) to business executives and to jury members in courtrooms.

Creating slide presentations in PowerPoint is made easier with the wide variety of templates and content slides available for download from the Microsoft website, for creating a new presentation using the provided templates in the program, and from online downloads available using the Internet connection within the program.

Exhibit 9.17 Intersection of accident scene created with SmartDraw

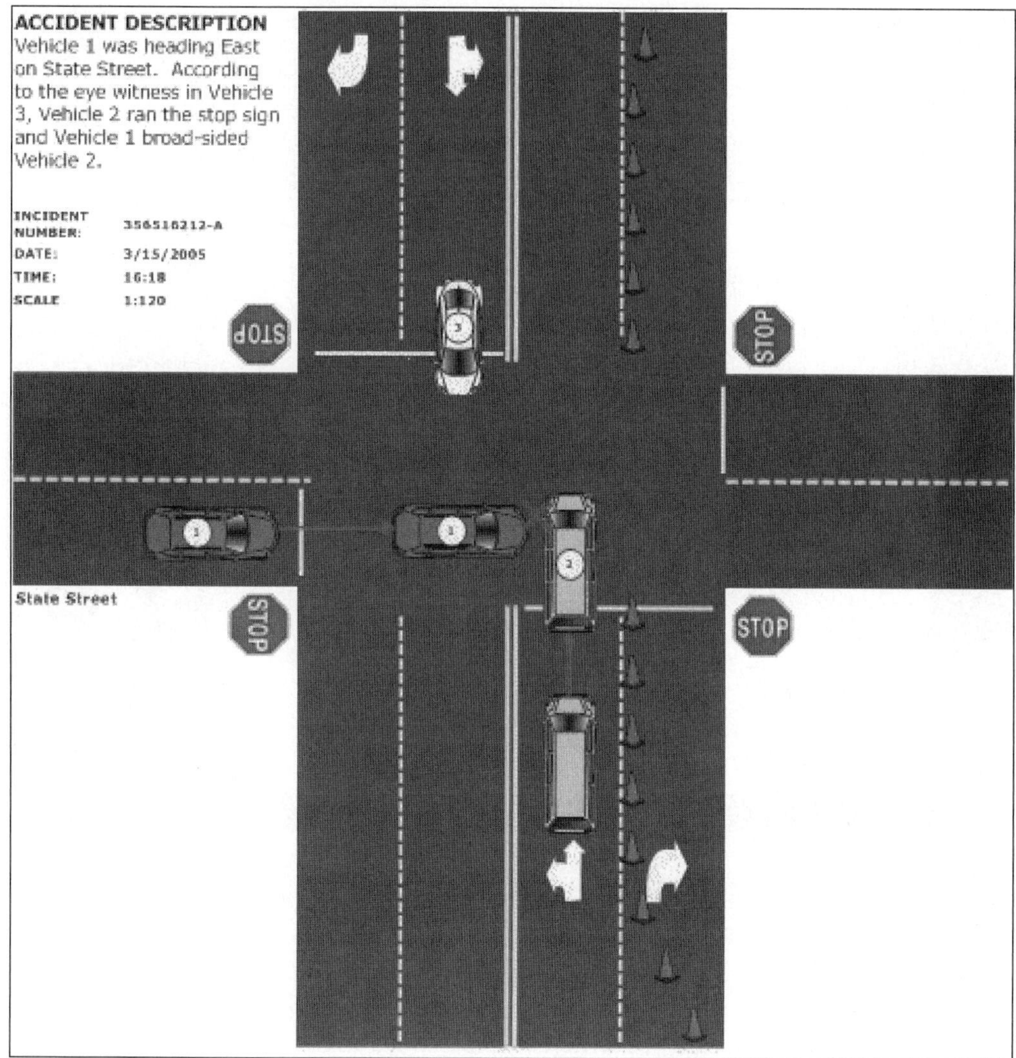

Exhibit 9.18 PowerPoint sample slide

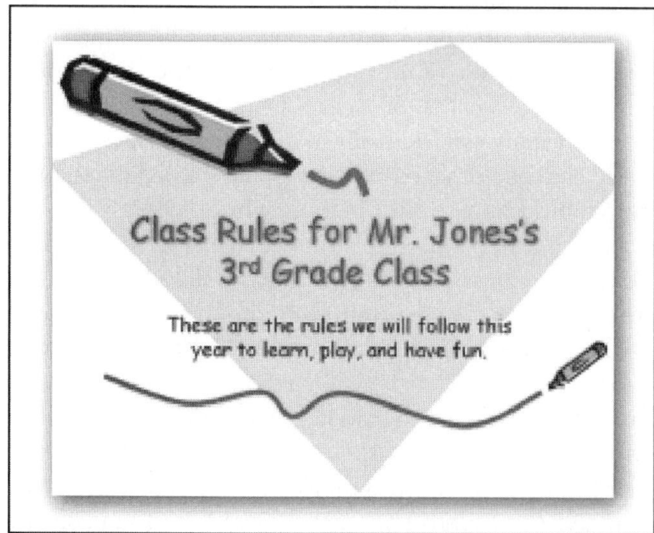

Source: Microsoft product screen shot(s) reprinted with permission from Microsoft Corporation.

PRACTICE TIP

As with all the programs in the Microsoft office suite, online tutorials and help are available to learn how to use PowerPoint and the features it contains.

Exhibit 9.19 PowerPoint first slide using the Clip Art search feature

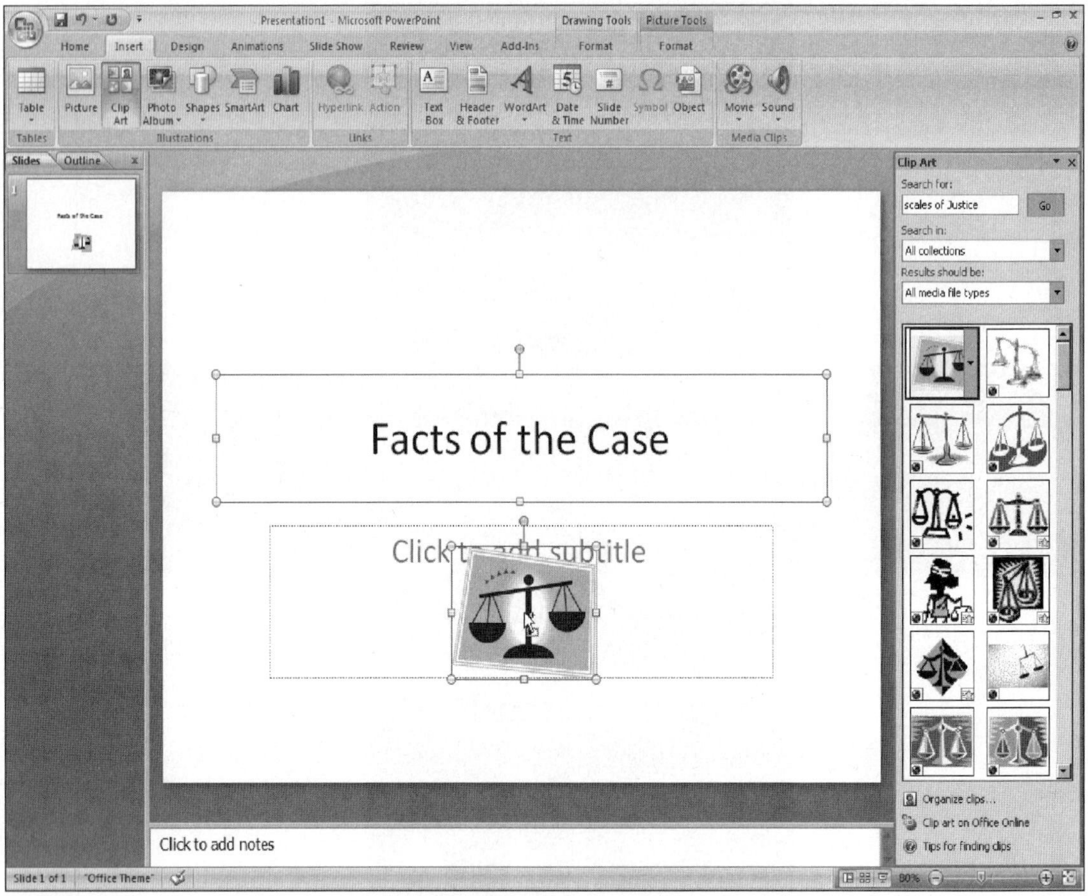

Source: Microsoft product screen shot(s) reprinted with permission from Microsoft Corporation.

Creating a new presentation starts with choosing a blank slide from the slide formats available, to which may be added text or graphics. Exhibit 9.19 shows a possible first slide for a trial presentation. The text of the first slide tells the jury and judge what the presenter is going to tell them, Facts of the Case. Depending on the audiences and the approach to the case, a graphic might be added, in this case the scales of justice. Graphic images can be found using the Clip Art command under the Insert tab, which is part of the Illustrations groups, as shown in Exhibit 9.19. A search of "scales of justice" in all collections produces many options in many styles, from modern art to classic black and white. The selected art can be "dragged and dropped" by a left click of the mouse pointer on the graphic and sliding it over while holding the left button and releasing the button when the graphic is correctly positioned on the PowerPoint slide. Additional adjustments to size are possible by using the mouse pointer on one of the circles or boxes surrounding the image or any place on the slide and dragging the mouse while holding the left button, a standard technique in many programs.

PowerPoint allows many enhancements to a slide presentation, such as slide transitions—like fading in and fading out and the addition of sounds during a slide transition. The standard transitions are selectable from the Animations tab on the PowerPoint Ribbon, and the sounds that may be used are found in the Transition to This Slide group, as shown in Exhibit 9.20.

A good PowerPoint presentation can reinforce and highlight the speaker's ideas and concepts, whereas a poor presentation can undermine all the hard

Exhibit 9.20 PowerPoint sound selections for enhancing a slide transition

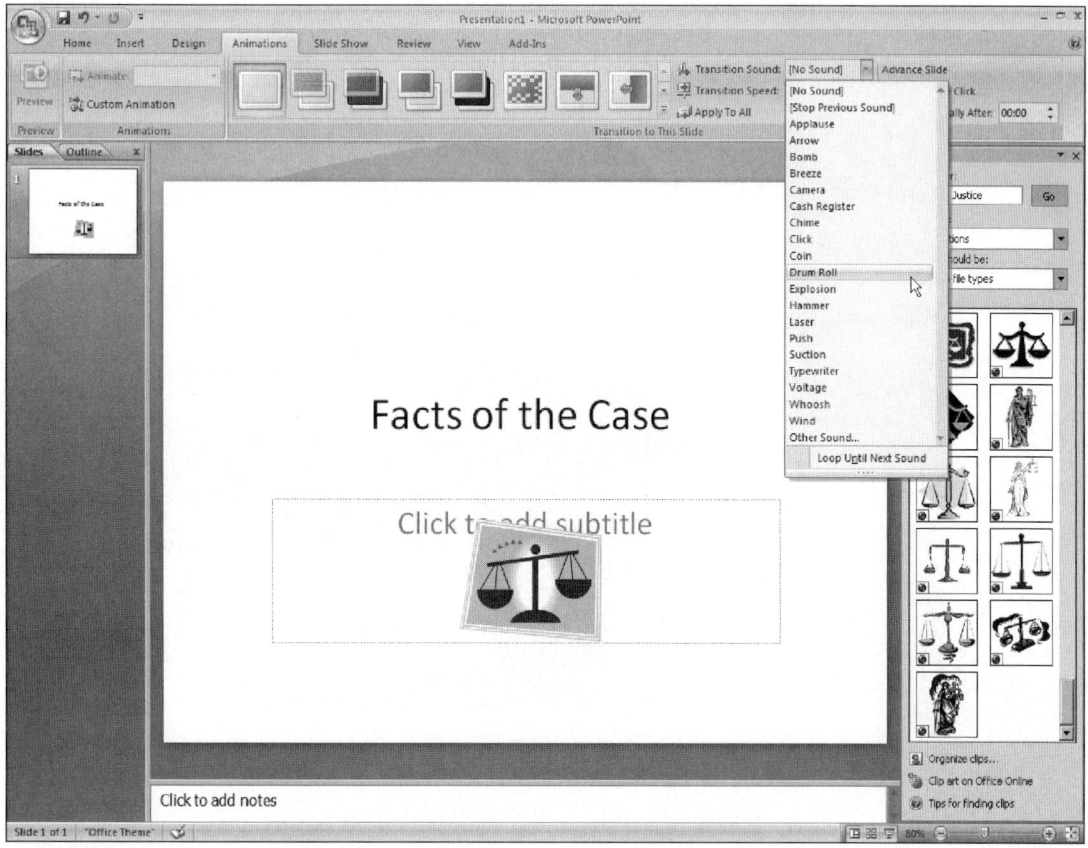

Source: Microsoft product screen shot(s) reprinted with permission from Microsoft Corporation.

work that went into it. While some presentations are designed for unattended viewing, presentations in the legal community are typically used to reinforce the ideas, concepts, and thoughts that the presenter wants to emphasize to the audience.

PRACTICE TIP

A few pointers on presentations using PowerPoint:

- ***Viewability***–Use background and text color combinations that can be seen by everyone in the room. Be aware of the issue of colorblindness and the effect of some colors, like soothing pastel colors and vivid, wake-up colors like red.
- ***Density***–Slides should support ideas in as few words as possible; no one wants to read a full page of text.
- ***Sounds***–Sounds can be very effective, when used appropriately. Overdo it and the impact is lost. Inappropriate sound effects used in a courtroom, like gunshots, may not be acceptable or permitted.
- ***Stand aside***–Even the best presentation is ineffective if the presenter is standing in front, blocking the viewers' ability to see the slides.
- ***Imagery***–As quoted elsewhere, one good picture is worth ten thousand words, but choose the picture wisely. What is the lasting impression you want to leave in the mind of, say, the jury, when it goes into deliberations? Among the most effective pictures in a personal injury case are those of the victim sitting in a wheelchair or lying in a hospital bed; in these cases, no words are necessary.

Exhibit 9.21 Export tab in SmartDraw

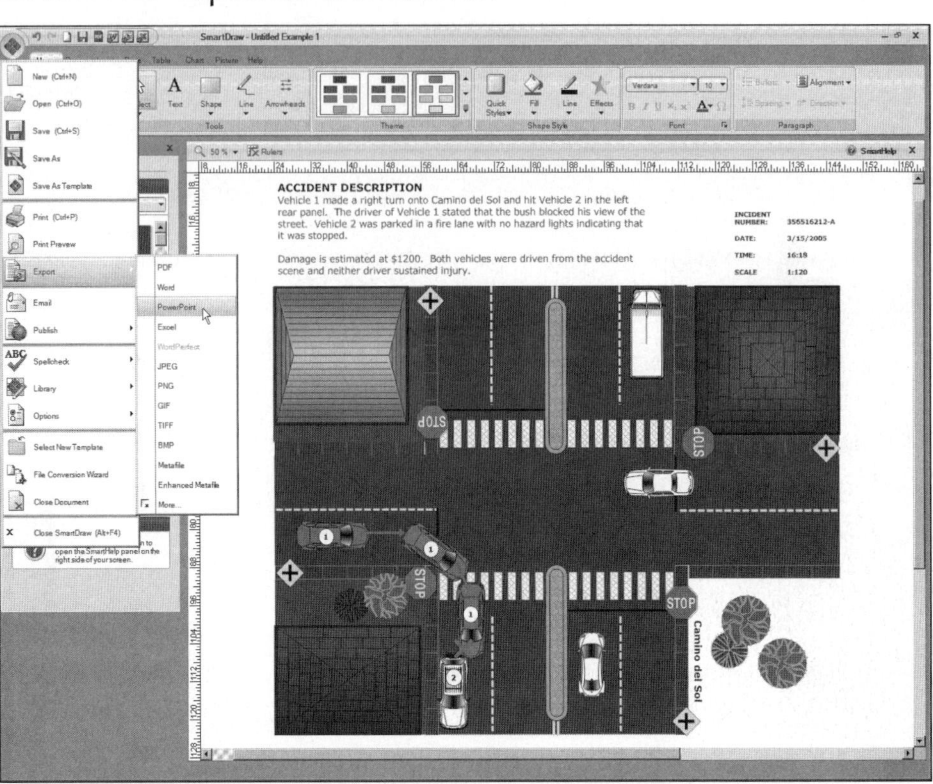

SmartDraw

SmartDraw is a graphics creation program that provides thousands of predesigned objects and elements, including specialty features for different professions and businesses. It can be used to create standalone graphic images, both in print form and for computer slide presentations. In addition to its intuitive user interface, one of SmartDraw's biggest advantages for the legal team is the thousands of templates and icons available for creating graphics quickly. Many of the predesigned graphics anticipate the needs of the legal community and require only minor modification (see Exhibit 9.16).

Each of the examples can be modified using the drag-and-drop technique with a left mouse click as described previously. Additional symbols can also be added easily from the stock symbols in the left panel of the SmartDraw user screen.

Finished graphics can be exported from SmartDraw using the Export tab and selecting the program to which the image is to be sent, in this case PowerPoint (see Exhibit 9.21).

The new graphic and any additional graphics can be added to the PowerPoint presentation as a slide, as shown in Exhibit 9.22.

CREATE A SMARTDRAW GRAPHIC

LEARNING OBJECTIVE 3
Create an accident scene exhibit using a graphics software program.

SmartDraw provides a number of templates of graphs and diagrams that are useful in litigation, some of which are shown in Exhibit 9.23.

The starting point is selecting the template or sample that most closely resembles the desired graphic—for example, an automobile accident at a four-way intersection being represented by the accident reconstruction SmartTemplate in Exhibit 9.24.

Exhibit 9.22 SmartDraw graphic exported to a PowerPoint presentation

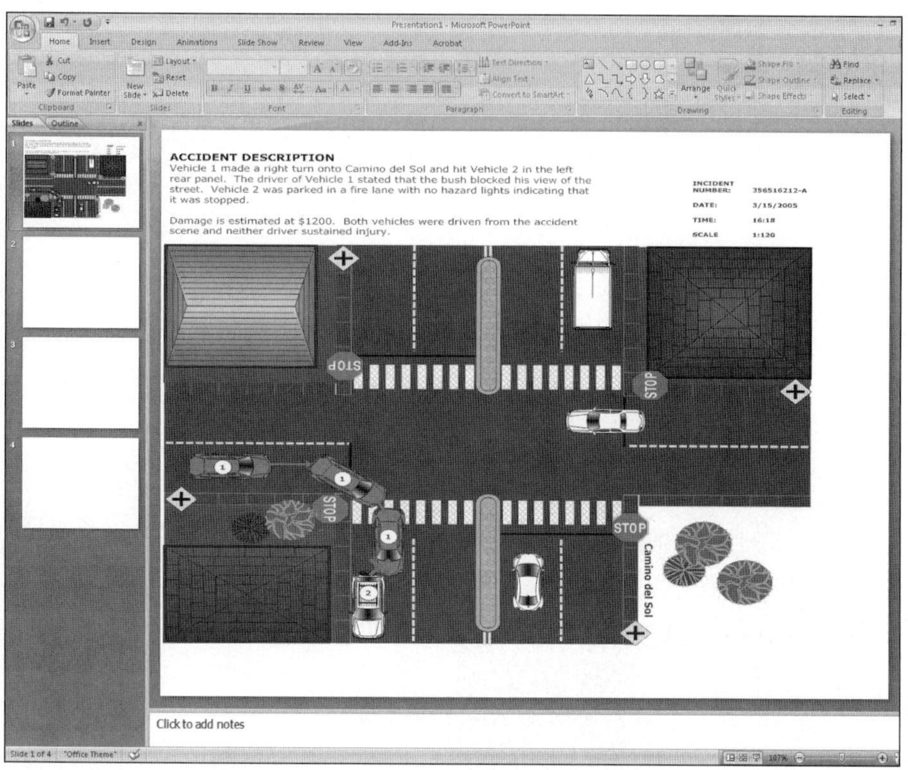

Exhibit 9.23 SmartDraw templates and sample graphics

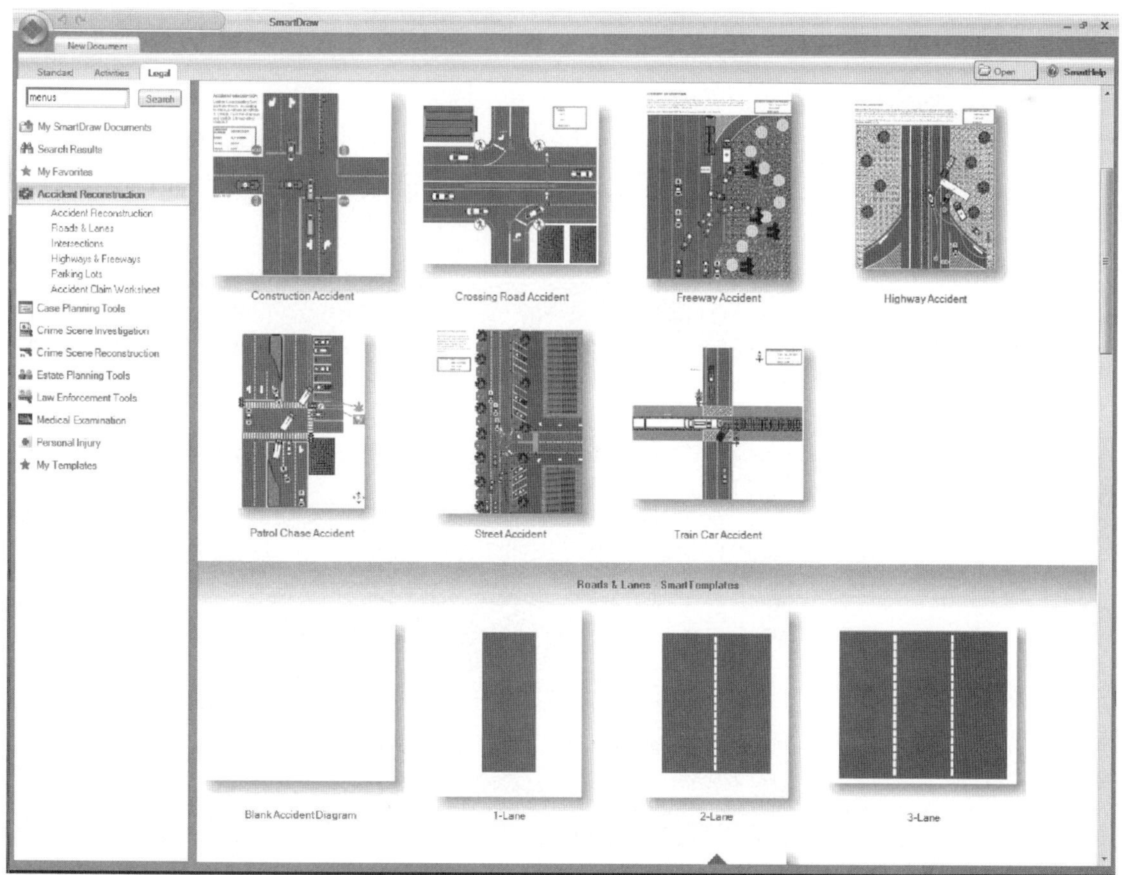

Exhibit 9.24 Accident reconstruction graphic created using SmartDraw

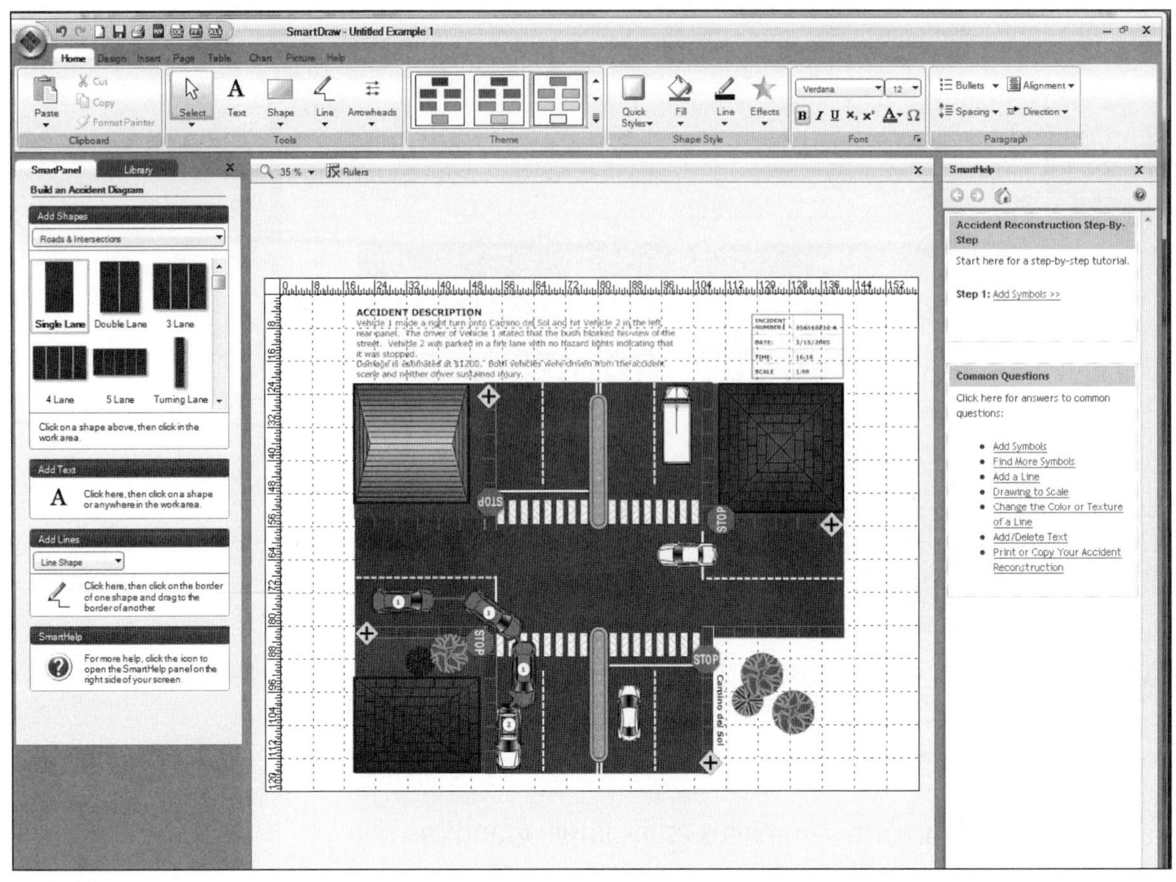

Exhibit 9.25 SmartDraw graphic with car on top of fire engine

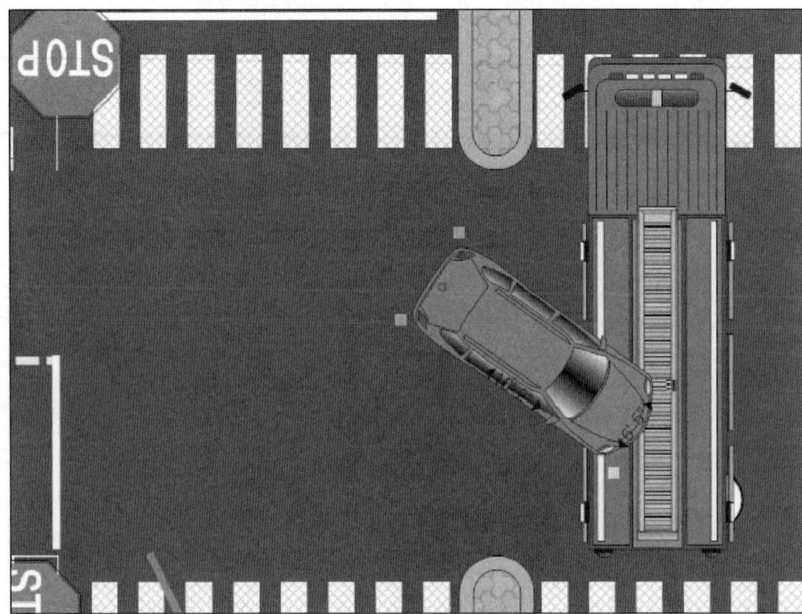

Each of the items shown in the main or center panel of the graphic can be moved, removed, or edited.

The right panel contains SmartHelp for using the specific functions and also contains the library of graphics that may be used in creating or modifying the graphic—for example, adding a fire engine from the SmartPanel to the graphic by the drop-and-drag method (Exhibit 9.25).

In Exhibit 9.25 Vehicle number 1 has been dragged on top of the fire truck graphic. Selecting the fire truck by a left mouse click highlights the selected graphic element. (The selected element is the one that has the corner boxes.) Selecting the option Bring to Front changes the view just as described in the PowerPoint discussion above, and the car appears to be under the truck, as shown in Exhibit 9.26.

Graphic elements may be further modified by adding text and color fill using the Ribbon Tabs and Menu items just as in the Microsoft Office software using the Ribbon menu.

Completed graphics may be saved in a variety of formats including PDF, and exported directly to PowerPoint and other software programs.

Exhibit 9.26 SmartDraw graphic with fire truck selected and brought to front

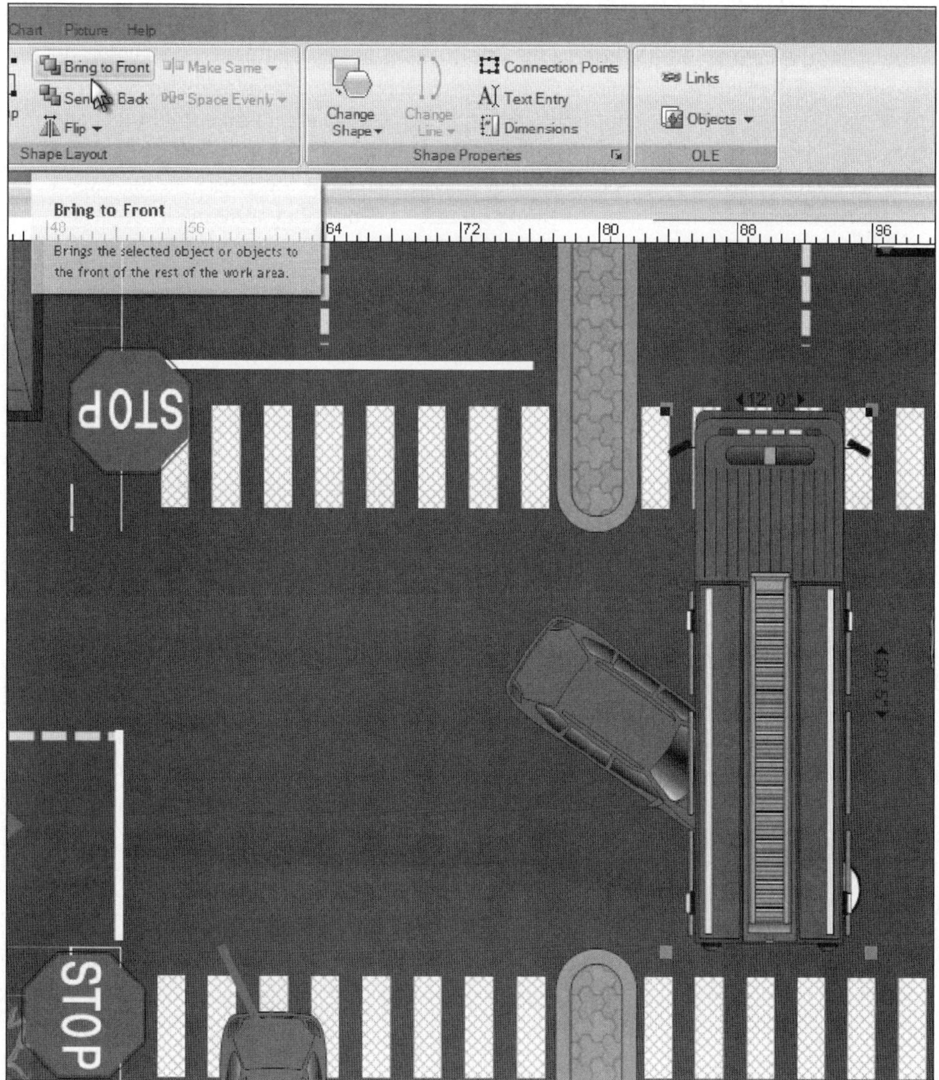

ADVICE FROM THE FIELD

THE "BUM" RULE—HOW TO CREATE EFFECTIVE DEMONSTRATIVE EVIDENCE

by John Cleaves

Remember Justice Potter Stewart's famous observation: "I shall not today attempt further to define the kinds of material I understand to be embraced... [b]ut I know it when I see it..."? This statement applies to effective demonstrative evidence just as well as it does to the original subject Justice Stewart had in mind.

What is effective demonstrative evidence? Nearly anything. Physical items, such as weapons, car bumpers, and computer chips; video shot at the scene of an accident, or showing the process by which an item is manufactured are typical examples. Other demonstratives include graphics illustrating events along a timeline, animation of a patent drawing, or diagrams of a medical procedure.

Attorneys occasionally fall into the trap of using bullet points to list their facts and arguments. But bullet points rarely help explain the facts and seldom convince jurors of the merits of the case. They do, however, bore everyone to tears as the attorney reads one after another. Bullet points are not effective demonstrative evidence.

As a Litigation Support professional you may be called upon to assist or manage the creation of demonstratives within your firm or corporate legal department. As trial time approaches the attorney team may be focusing on finalizing their exhibits and preparing witnesses. The creation of demonstratives may fall through the cracks or be a last minute detail left to you or your staff. Follow these tips to ensure you or you're (sic) staff create demonstratives that capture the attention of the jury and/or judge.

Believe, Understand and Remember

When considering that demonstrative evidence can be nearly anything (bounded by the rules of evidence, of course)—and often is an "I know it when I see it" type of thing—how do you as a litigation support professional come up with a demonstrative that is truly effective? One way is by using the "BUM" criteria: is the demonstrative believable, understandable and memorable? A demonstrative is believable if it appeals to the jurors' common sense, is straight-forward, and is honest. For example, in a case where a company was accused of fraud for selling "vaporware," the defense attorney used the product in opening. Not an image or photograph, but the actual item, putting it to the use it was intended. It is difficult to argue an item does not exist when it is sitting in court on counsel's table doing what it was supposed to do.

A demonstrative is understandable if it makes sense to the jurors without a long explanation. Attorneys often use clichés, logic and fundamentals (such as $2 + 2 = 4$) to create understandable demonstratives. For example, in a breach of contract case a graphic showing a man with his fingers crossed behind his back was used to demonstrate that one of the parties had ulterior motives. By referencing the simple childhood cliché of crossing one's fingers when making a promise the jury immediately understood the point made in the demonstrative.

An exhibit is memorable when it sticks with the jurors throughout the trial and deliberations. Unfortunately it is difficult to know what jurors will find memorable; jury research often shows jurors remembering items the attorneys find insignificant and missing points the attorneys stress repeatedly. One method to overcome this problem is to force the jurors to use several senses to process the information. Jurors typically rely on sight and sound, but adding touch to the mix helps fix the information in their minds. For example, in a patent infringement case involving the manufacture of computer chips, counsel distributed silicon wafers to the jurors as the expert explained the process by which they were made....

Overcoming the Problems and Pitfalls of Demonstratives

Two kinds of problems tend to come up when using demonstratives. The first is procedural: are they legally relevant, was a proper foundation laid, or are they argumentative? These are important questions [for Litigation Support professionals] to keep in mind as they consider and use the demonstratives.

The second type of problem is substantive. Demonstratives work best when they are straight-forward, clear of piles of money saved by the defendants by not enacting safety measures are often used to sway jurors['] feelings.

Another good source of demonstratives is to give jurors visual displays of the sheer volume of evidence, on the theory that a lot of evidence on one side probably means that is the party that should prevail, even if the small amount of evidence on the other side is very effective.

Seeing from the Jurors' Point of View

When selecting physical items as demonstrative evidence, consider if the item is relevant, if it adds to the story, or if it

(continued)

(continued)

is something a layperson would be curious to see. In civil cases it may be difficult to come up with an item, often and concise. When full of information, perhaps lots of text or images, they can become confusing and even intimidating to jurors. If jurors are overwhelmed with a tidal wave of data they may simply tune out. At the same time, it can be difficult for attorneys to avoid this pitfall because they are so intimately informed about every aspect of the case and have only a short time to teach and convince the jurors about a case they have been working on for months or years.

There are several ways to avoid these risks. One is to be very conscientious about limiting the number of words in a graphic. Most billboards['] ads are effective because they have very few words. The same is true of demonstratives–the fewer words the better.

Next, remove all extraneous information. This can be as simple as removing the decimal points if every number in a chart ends in .00, or cropping a photo to center it on the primary subject, or showcasing only the portion of a machine that's at issue rather than an entire piece of equipment. When jurors are first exposed to a new demonstrative they do not necessarily know what is most important. If it is cluttered with extra information, they may be distracted or confused and miss your crucial point.

Finally, build slowly. Introduce the components of the demonstrative one at a time so they can be explained individually. If the jurors are presented with information in small bites it is more likely they will understand and follow along. Even though it may be tempting to put the multi-variable formula or the hyper-detailed flowchart up all at once, if it causes even one juror to stop paying attention it has not helped the case.

There are rewards for the attorney who effectively uses demonstrative evidence. In addition to showing common sense is on their side–which is one of the keys to consistent success in trial–effective demonstratives help entertain, and therefore engage the jurors in the proceedings. Think back to those warm spring days in high school science class when the professor would show a video instead of dryly lecturing. Weren't those classes more interesting and memorable? Demonstrative evidence can also speed up the trial by teaching the jury the facts in a more concise and therefore quicker way. One example is a timeline which ties together various facts into a chain of events. Another could be a theme signpost which can help add structure to the disjointed way in which facts are presented in a case and can help jurors fit the facts together in a way that is logical and makes sense.

Finally, demonstrative evidence can be a very effective way of showing the other sides' motive. This is a key piece of information for jurors. Whether it is a physical item, as in a criminal case, or a smoking gun document in a civil case, showing the item or document repeatedly and reminding the jurors of the motive again and again will help cement it in their memories. Andy Warhol once said, "I'm afraid that if you look at a thing long enough, it loses all its meaning." The same can be true of the evidence in a case. Documents, testimony and other exhibits can be spun one way or the other. They can be forgotten or ignored by a jury. Or, worst of all, they can be misinterpreted in favor of the opposition. But by using demonstratives the jurors will believe, understand and remember to add meaning to the evidence, the chances of success are dramatically improved.

About the Author: John Cleaves is the Director of Forensic and Litigation Consulting at FTI Consulting.

Source: John Cleaves, "The "Bum" Rule–how to create effective demonstrative evidence," *Litigation Support Today,* May/July 2007.

CONCEPT REVIEW AND REINFORCEMENT

KEY TERMS

electronic spreadsheet 211 | electronic database 212 | word processor 213

CHAPTER SUMMARY

Introduction to Presentation and Trial Graphics	Properly prepared graphics are an excellent way of telling a story and making a point. The most accessible presentation software program is Microsoft PowerPoint.

Electronic Graphic Creation	Graphic creation programs are used to create either standalone graphics for presentations or graphics that are part of a presentation. An advantage of this class of software is the ability of the legal team to create their own graphics without the need of graphic artists and outside consultants.
PowerPoint	Microsoft PowerPoint is standard for making electronic presentations. Templates and content slides are available for download from the Microsoft website when creating a new PowerPoint presentation. PowerPoint allows many enhancements to a slide presentation, including transitions, animation, and sounds. A good PowerPoint presentation can reinforce and highlight the speaker's ideas and concepts. PowerPoint presentation pointers: Use color combinations that can be seen by everyone in the room. Use as few words per slide as possible. Use sounds only when appropriate. Don't block the slides during the presentation. Choose pictures wisely.
SmartDraw	SmartDraw is a graphic creation program that provides thousands of templates and icons for creating graphics quickly. Template examples can be modified using the drop-and-drag technique.

REVIEW QUESTIONS AND EXERCISES

1. How may the legal team use presentation graphics programs? Give examples of both litigation and nonlitigation legal teams.
2. Create an accident scene graphic exhibit using SmartDraw.
3. Create a graphic of a room using Microsoft Visio.
4. Explain the use of trial presentation programs.
5. Create a basic PowerPoint presentation on the use of PowerPoint in litigation.
6. Present a PowerPoint presentation to a group. You may want to use the PowerPoint in exercise 5. Describe the positive and negative reactions to the presentation. What changes would you make to the presentation if you were to give it again?
7. Create a basic PowerPoint presentation on the use of PowerPoint by the legal team, including an explanation of how to make a slide.
8. Create a PowerPoint presentation using clip art and at least one sound element.
9. Use TimeMap to create a time line of at least ten time elements; these may be personal items like birthdays and anniversaries or course-related deadlines. Export the time line to PowerPoint, with each item on a separate slide. Create another PowerPoint presentation with all the time line elements on one slide.

BUILDING YOUR PARALEGAL SKILLS

INTERNET AND TECHNOLOGY EXERCISES

1. Use the Internet to locate resources for learning how to use Microsoft PowerPoint. List the topics available and the web address for accessing this information.
2. What Internet resources are available for obtaining maps and aerial views of locations that might be used for trial preparation?
3. Locate resources for learning SmartDraw online.

CIVIL LITIGATION VIDEO CASE STUDIES

Final Pretrial Evidentiary issues

Trial counsel are meeting with the judge prior to the trial. Counsels have opposing views of the use of graphic pictures. The court agrees to take the use under consideration.

After viewing the video in MyLegalStudiesKit, answer the following questions.

1. How important is the use of photographs and graphics in a trial?
2. Are there any issues that should be reviewed about the use of videotaped depositions?
3. Is the final pretrial conference an appropriate time to determine the judge's willingness to allow multimedia presentations?

CHAPTER OPENING SCENARIO CASE STUDY

Use the Opening Scenario for this chapter to answer the following questions.

1. Prepare a memo for the attorneys of the firm on the issues involved in using outside sources for the preparation of trial graphics.
2. How can all the needed equipment be used in court without requiring a truck to carry all the documents and exhibits?
3. How can graphics be used in the trial?
4. What are the advantages and disadvantages of the different trial graphics options, in software cost and in time for preparation? Explain using specific software costs.
5. What cautions should the trial attorney consider in using graphics at trial?
6. What pretrial measures should be taken if trial graphics are going to be used?

COMPREHENSIVE CASE STUDY

SCHOOL BUS–TRUCK ACCIDENT CASE

For the assigned case study from Appendix III:

1. From the Technology Resources Website, www.pearsonhighered.com/goldman, download and install on your computer the demo version of SmartDraw.
2. If you do not have PowerPoint or Visio on your computer, download a demo version from the Microsoft Office link at www.pearsonhighered.com/goldman or directly from the Microsoft website.
3. Prepare a diagram of the case study accident scene using SmartDraw and showing the vehicles:
   a. Before the impact.
   b. After the collisions and all of the vehicles had come to rest.
4. Prepare a settlement brochure using SmartDraw.
5. Prepare a PowerPoint presentation for use in trial using the exhibits in the comprehensive accident case study in Appendix II and the graphics prepared using SmartDraw and TimeMap.

BUILDING YOUR PROFESSIONAL PORTFOLIO

CIVIL LITIGATION TEAM AT WORK

Form

1. Create an electronic time sheet using a computerized spreadsheet like Microsoft Excel to create an electronic time sheet that automatically totals the time column. Print a copy for your portfolio.
2. Create a personal letterhead using a word processor program and save the file as a template.
3. Print out and include in your portfolio the Settlement brochure in the comprehensive case study assignment above.
4. Print the lecture notes version of the PowerPoint presentation prepared in the comprehensive case study assignment above.

"Simplicity means the achievement of maximum effect with minimum means."

—Dr. Koichi Kawana, Architect

Electronic Trial Presentation

CHAPTER 10

OPENING SCENARIO

The trial teams handling the school bus case and the airplane crash case were having their regular meeting to discuss common issues in preparing the cases for trial. Efforts to settle the cases had not, as of yet, met with any success, and it was time to get the trial materials finalized. With some relief and some concern, Owen Mason informed everyone that the school bus case had been assigned to the new, very high-tech courtroom. The technology consultant who had been sitting in on the case meeting indicated that this was a blessing and a curse. Shocked, Ethan Benjamin looked at her and asked, "How can it not be the best thing?" She calmly told him that while it is nice having all the toys, the jury would expect the toys to be used to entertain them, like people see on television. Owen jumped in to add that he had been meeting with the technologist to determine the cost of using all the multimedia. With a small trial budget and potentially a lot of evidence, it might be more than they could afford, especially with two major cases coming to trial at the same time. Ariel Marshall, the third partner, spoke up and commented, "At least I don't have that problem with my case because they have put us in the large courtroom that is not equipped with any electronics except wall outlets."

LEARNING OBJECTIVES

After studying this chapter, you should be able to:

1. Describe the types of multimedia equipment found in typical electronic courtrooms.
2. Explain how presentation software is used in litigation.
3. Create a case presentation.

VIDEO INTRODUCTION

A video introduction to Using Trial Presentation Programs.

After watching the video in MyLegalStudiesKit, answer the following question.

- What is the advantage to using a trial presentation program?

INTRODUCTION TO ELECTRONIC TRIAL PRESENTATION

More and more courts are providing, or allowing litigants to bring into the courtroom, computer-based electronic display systems for use in trial. Some see this as nothing more than a logical outgrowth of the multimedia presentations that started with the use of overhead projectors, movie clips, and slide projectors.

Modern trial presentations frequently include videotaped depositions and the electronic presentation of document images, photos, videos, and computer simulations. These may be shown on projection screens, personal monitors, or large-panel displays.

Managing the hundreds of individual multimedia elements in the courtroom can be a nightmare unless they are organized and easily accessible for presentation. Sanction by Sanction Solutions, inData's TrialDirector, and similar trial presentation programs allow the legal team to organize and control the documents, depositions, photographs, and other data as exhibits for trial, and then display them as evidence when needed in depositions and trial.

MULTIMEDIA IN THE COURTROOM

LEARNING OBJECTIVE 1
Describe the types of multimedia equipment found in typical electronic courtrooms.

The types of electronic and computerized equipment available for litigating a case vary, even within the same courthouse from courtroom to courtroom. This may be because of budgetary issues and/or the personal preferences of the jurist using that particular courtroom. Just as some trial attorneys are not comfortable using computerized multimedia presentation tools, some judges may feel that multimedia takes away from the ultimate task of determining the facts with which to

VIDEO ADVICE FROM THE FIELD

Mike Hahn–Managing Director, Sanction Solutions

A discussion on the use of trial presentation software.

After watching the video in MyLegalStudiesKit, answer the following questions.

1. What is trial presentation software?
2. Should every case presentation use multimedia presentations?
3. Can trial presentation software be used by the litigator without any support in court?

make a judgment. The trial team has to be prepared to make the best presentation of their client's case whether in a traditional courtroom or a contemporary multimedia courtroom.

In most traditional courtrooms, litigants have access to court-provided easels, or they may bring in easels with large display boards, blackboards, or erasable whiteboards. These may be used to display previously created exhibits, to list items, or to provide an area on which witnesses may draw diagrams.

In more contemporary courtrooms, the use of basic, traditional tools has given way to the use of more modern tools like the overhead projector, the VCR, and the computer projector. More complex arrangements include computer monitors at counsel's table, Exhibit 10.1; on the judge's bench, Exhibit 10.2; in some cases in the jury box, Exhibit 10.3, or witness stand; and possibly a large-screen monitor to replace the computer projector and projection screen, Exhibit 10.4.

As technology has advanced, some courts have installed multimedia podiums for lawyers to use that include special projection devices like the popular Elmo document projector, VCR, or DVD player, as seen in Exhibit 10.5.

Exhibit 10.1 Counsel tables

Exhibit 10.2 The judge's bench

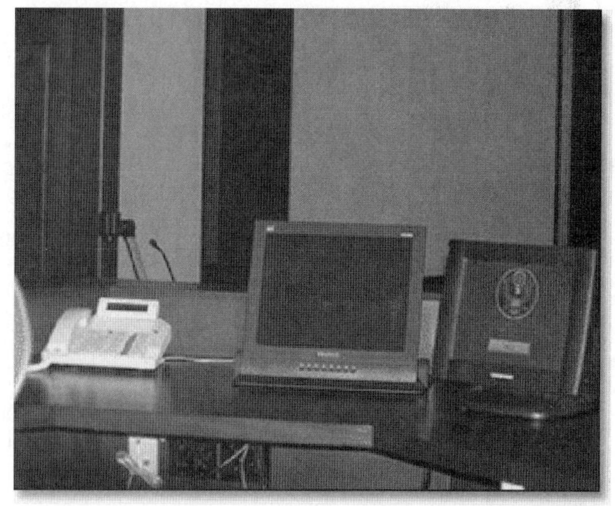

Exhibit 10.3 The jury box

Exhibit 10.4 Large screen and projector

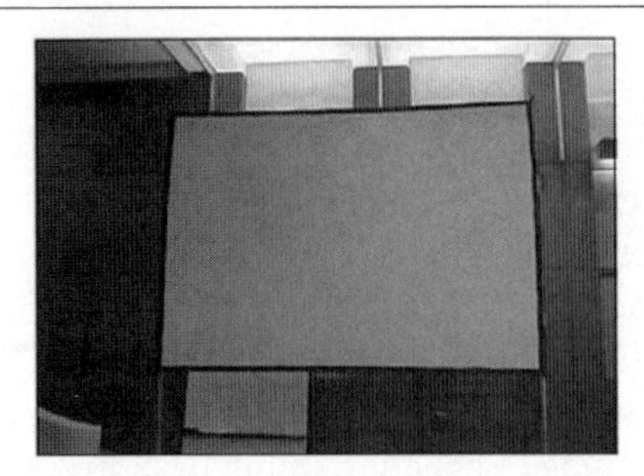

In some cases, judges who do not have a multimedia-equipped courtroom will permit the attorneys to bring in equipment. Typically, such permission is granted when each side can afford the shared cost or when the better-financed litigant, to avoid any unfair advantage, agrees to make full access to the equipment available to the other side.

Learning how to use the different types of equipment is not difficult, but may take a little practice. Everyone on the trial team should be comfortable with the operation and use of the equipment before the start of trial.

PRACTICE TIP

All of the equipment used in the electronic courtroom is similar in type and purpose to that used in classrooms. Most teachers colleges offer courses in the operation and use of multimedia equipment; in some cases, these courses are required for teaching certification. Litigation team members may learn the use and techniques of electronic equipment by taking these and refresher courses.

Electronic Setup in the Courtroom

The most basic courtroom setup includes a projector with a projection screen, positioned for viewing by the court and the jury, to which each litigation team may hook up a computer or other multimedia tool, such as a VCR or CD player.

Exhibit 10.5 Attorney lectern with document camera

Exhibit 10.6 Basic Courtroom Setup A

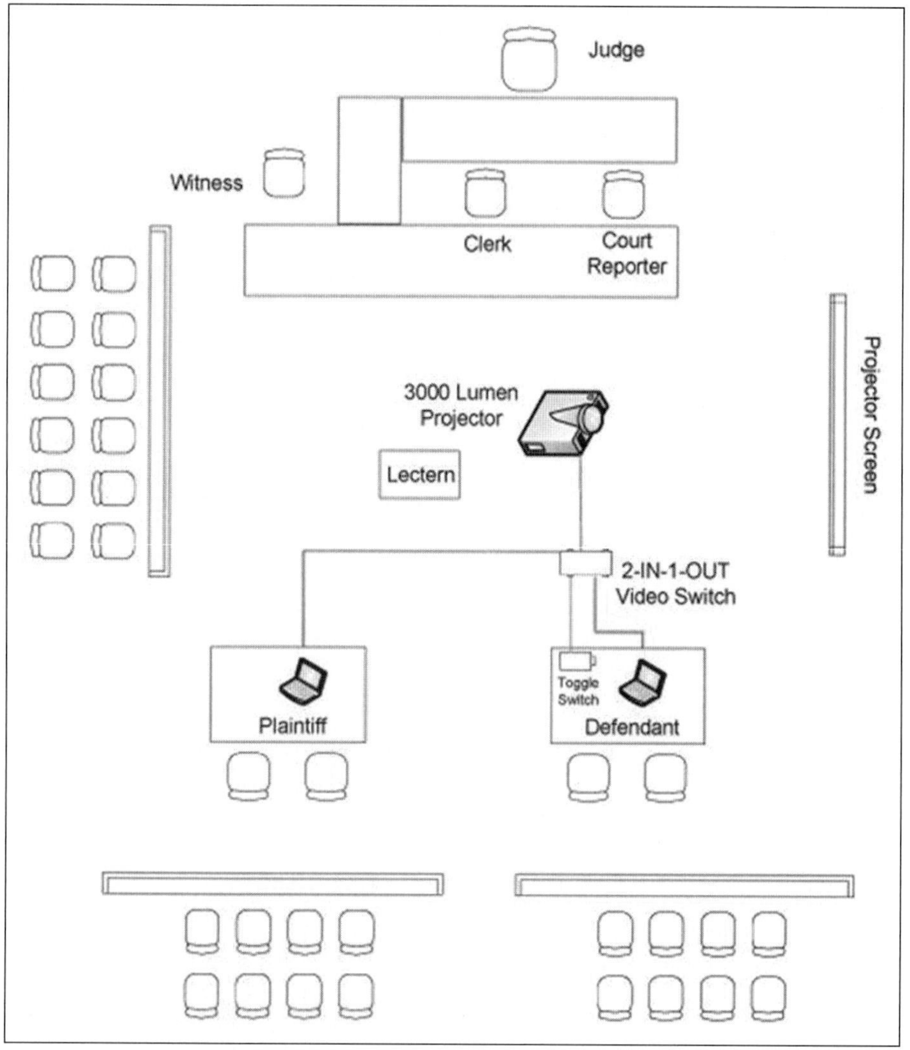

Source: Copyright © AG/Sanction LLC. Used with permission.

This setup allows both counsel teams to simultaneously share the projector using a 2-input, 1-output video connector switch, as shown in Exhibit 10.6. With each side's laptop plugged into an input, the video switch controls which laptop image is projected onto the screen. Audio on a video or sound track can be played back using the courtroom's sound system or played from speakers plugged into the laptop computer.

Judge Control of Multimedia During Trial

The trial judge may initially determine in a meeting with trial counsel what, if any, multimedia may be used during trial. This determination may take place during a meeting to discuss motions or objections raised by one or the other counsel to the use of specific evidence. Such a meeting may also take place because photographs are claimed to be prejudicial, objections were raised in traditional depositions, or videotaped depositions need to be resolved before allowing their presentation in trial. In some cases, trial judges may be concerned that additional objections will be raised during trial and may thus want the ability to prevent any presentation until the court rules on the objection. If so, a "kill switch" that

Exhibit 10.7 Courtroom Setup B with judge-controlled kill switch

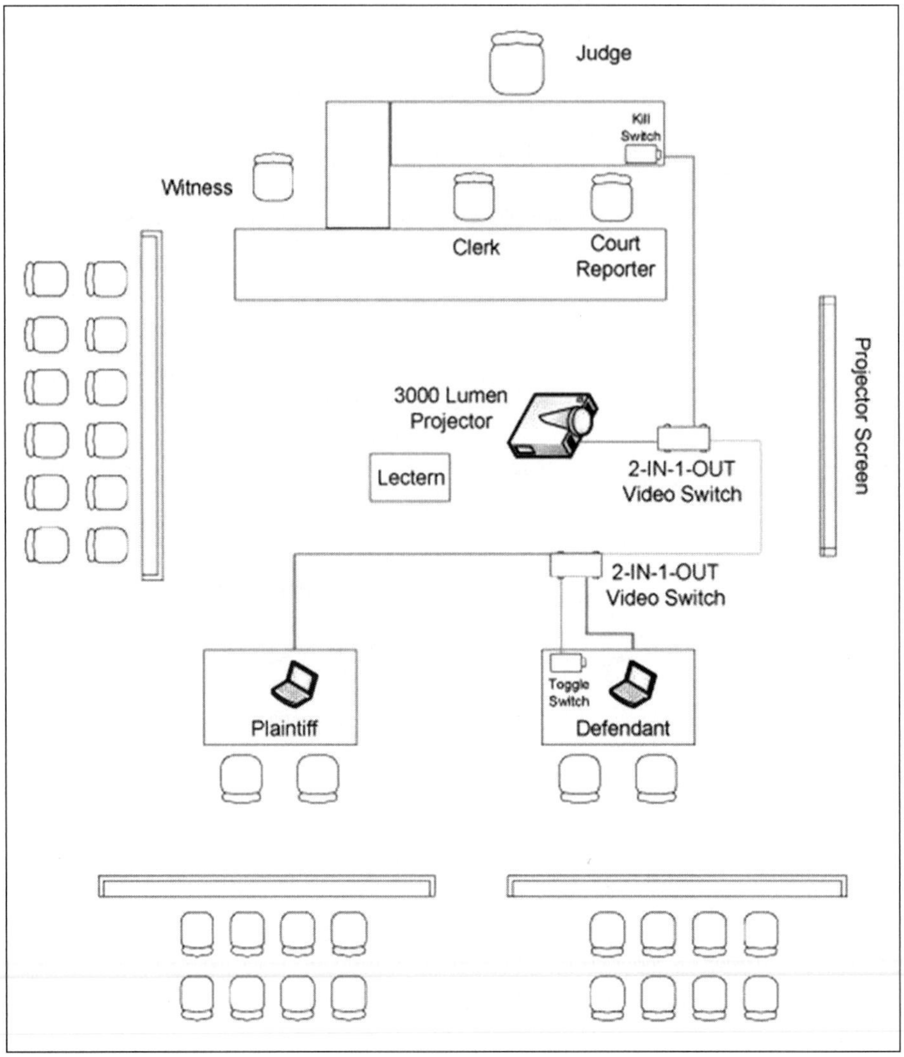

Source: Copyright © AG/Sanction LLC. Used with permission.

gives the court the ability to "kill" the video display (by temporarily blacking it out) may be required. This is accomplished by introducing a second video switch between the first video switch and the projector, as seen in Exhibit 10.7. This is the same basic configuration as in Exhibit 10.6 except that the judge has ultimate control over whether or not an image gets sent to the projector.

More and more courtrooms have monitors at counsel's table, on the judge's bench, at witness stands, and in jury boxes, as shown schematically in Exhibit 10.8. This setup builds on the basic components shown in Exhibits 10.6 and 10.7. Setup C adds an additional connector that allows multiple outputs—in this drawing, one input and six outputs.

Exhibit 10.9 adds the use of jury flat-panel screens in conjunction with a projector. This setup takes into consideration the additional monitors added in Courtroom Setup C because it has additional connections for the jury monitors. Notice that the feed to the jury monitors comes after the judge's kill switch, thus giving the judge the power to control what the jury sees.

Since every court is different and each judge controls his or her own courtroom, it is essential for the legal team to consult the appropriate court personnel or check the court's website for local rules and procedures.

Exhibit 10.8 Courtroom Setup C

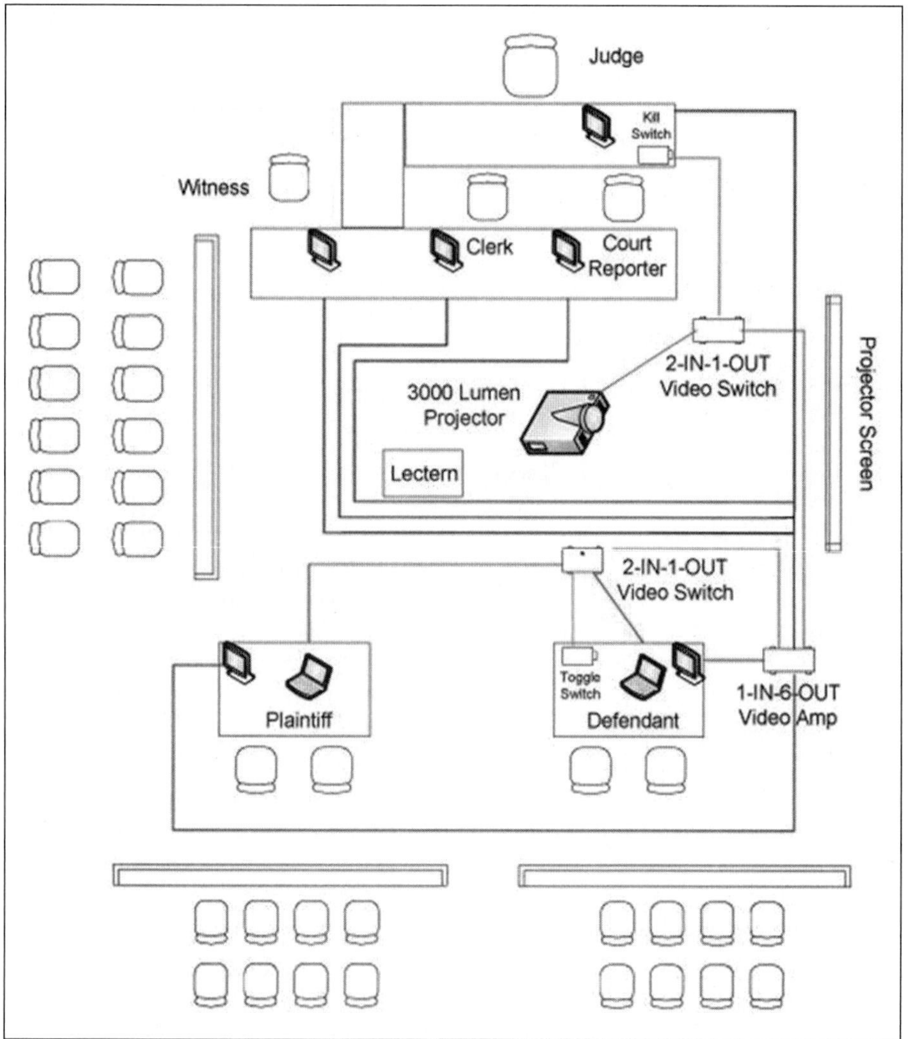

Source: Copyright © AG/Sanction LLC. Used with permission.

PRACTICE TIP

TRIAL

Local and national trial consulting and support firms are available to provide the necessary equipment and technical support during trial. Depending on the type of case and the types of audiovisual tools needed, the litigation team may need to bring in a specialist if the case budget allows.

USING TECHNOLOGY TO PRESENT THE CASE

LEARNING OBJECTIVE 2
Explain how presentation software is used in litigation.

The primary goal of every trial attorney is to make the best possible presentation of the case and obtain a favorable verdict. The most effective method of presenting a case may be a simple handwritten chart that trial counsel creates during the case to show the individual elements of the case as the evidence is presented, which at the end of the presentation then serves as a summary of the evidence presented. More frequently, however, effective presentation requires the use of photographs, videos, computer simulations, and other multimedia elements that will appeal to a jury of citizens who have been raised in an era of multimedia presentations and television and expect to see in the courtroom what they have seen on television in real and fictitious cases.

Exhibit 10.9 Courtroom Setup D

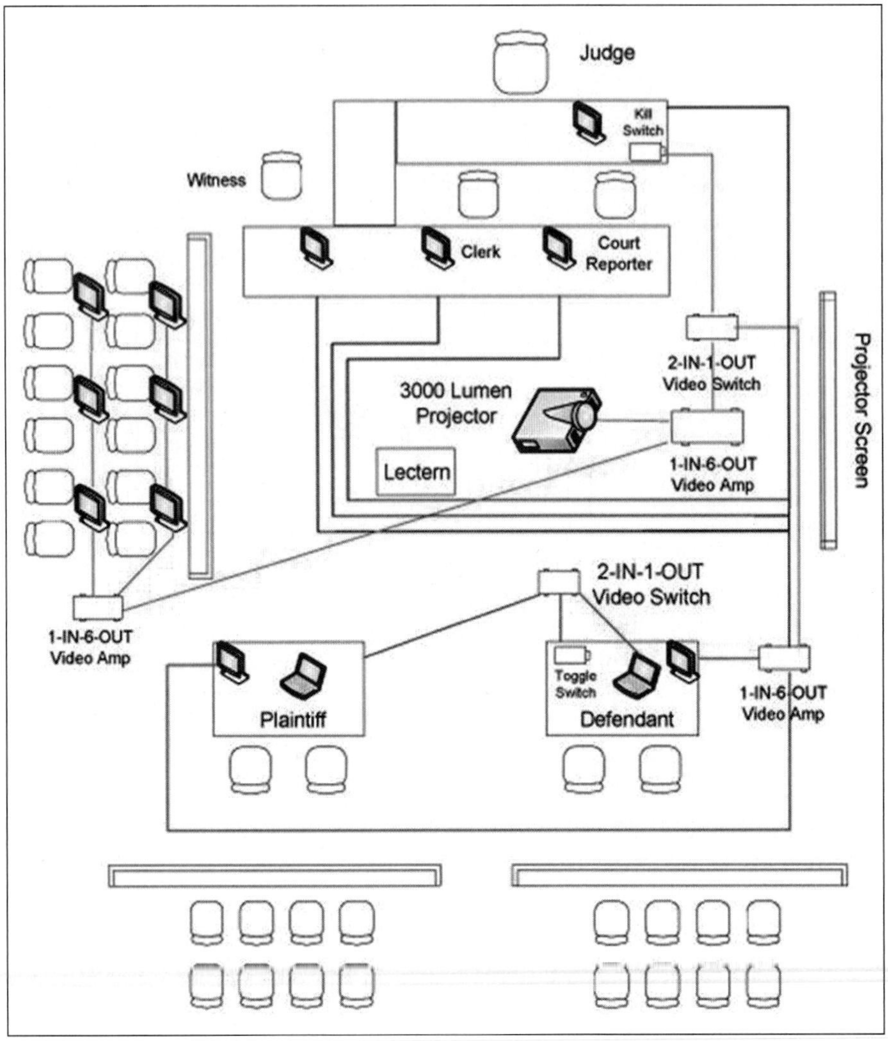

Source: Copyright © AG/Sanction LLC. Used with permission.

Presentation Programs

Trial presentation programs are software programs that allow different types of media—including still photographs, text documents, video and sound clips, and computer simulation—to be organized and displayed using a single common presentation program. Consider the different types of potential documentary evidence and the number of programs that would have to be installed and running on a computer to show all of these media types. For example, Word documents would need the original word processor program, like MS Word or WordPerfect; videos would require a multimedia player like Apple's Quicktime or Microsoft Windows Media

> **PRACTICE TIP**
> **SUPPORTED FORMATS**
> Not all native file formats can be used with all trial presentation programs, just as not all music files can be played on every brand of portable music player. It is thus wise, early in the preparation process, to check the formats supported by the trial presentation program selected for trial in order to ensure compatibility and avoid a rush near trial to convert or find suitable replacements.

Exhibit 10.10 Sanction with case file images

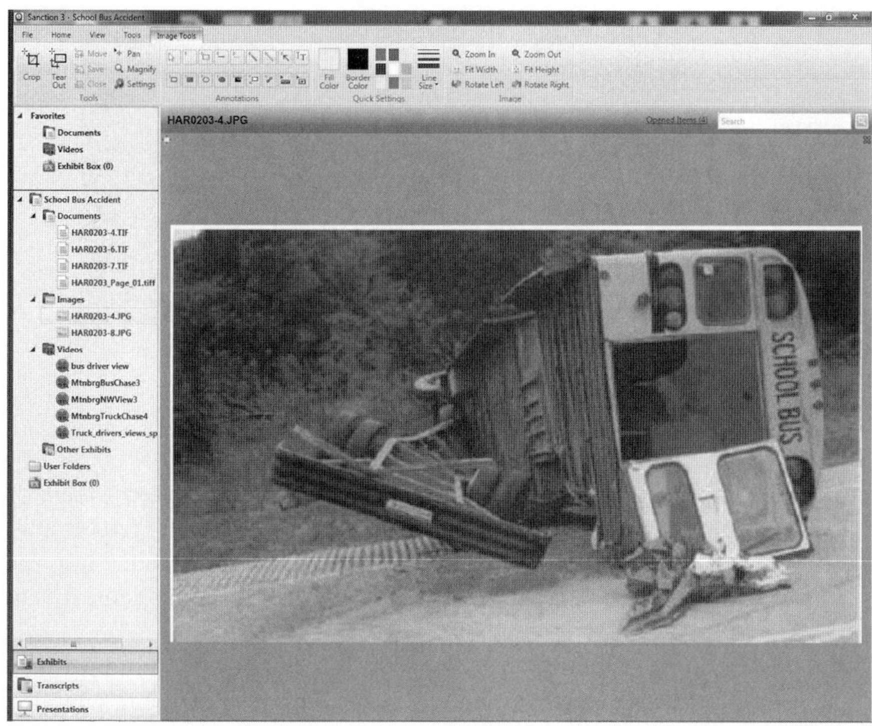

Player; and PDF files would need Adobe Reader. Trial presentation programs provide all the necessary viewers and all the files in one package in a linked database.

Litigation presentation programs, like Sanction by Sanction Solutions and TrialDirector by inData, are multifaceted. As exhibit management tools, they provide a single source of access to exhibits of different types, like Microsoft Explorer, which allows access to different items on a computer or network, as shown in the Tree View of available files in Exhibit 10.10.

Selected files can then be previewed on counsels' personal computer monitors before projecting the items onto the court's presentation system. Documents can then be annotated using highlighting tools, graphics like arrows, or underlining. Another common feature is the ability to integrate a videotaped deposition of a witness with the related written transcript and display both on a split screen, as shown in Exhibit 10.11.

These programs allow existing documents and files to be presented with no more effort than copying them into the program data file and making a selection for presentation.

The advantage of these higher-level presentation programs is their ability to work with a variety of file types including video, which is an increasingly popular tool in the courtroom. Video presentations provide a convenient method of showing prerecorded depositions of witnesses, particularly experts who might not be available on short notice to appear in a trial when called from the trial list. They are also used for elderly and very young witnesses who cannot travel or for whom the trial itself might be too emotionally upsetting. As shown in Exhibit 10.12, the video may be annotated with highlighting to show only the desired questions and answers. The video and sound may also be presented with the written transcript on the screen, or the transcript may be presented alone—for example, it might be used to point out what the witness on the witness stand had stated in a pretrial deposition.

Exhibit 10.11 Preview and presentation screens with annotated document

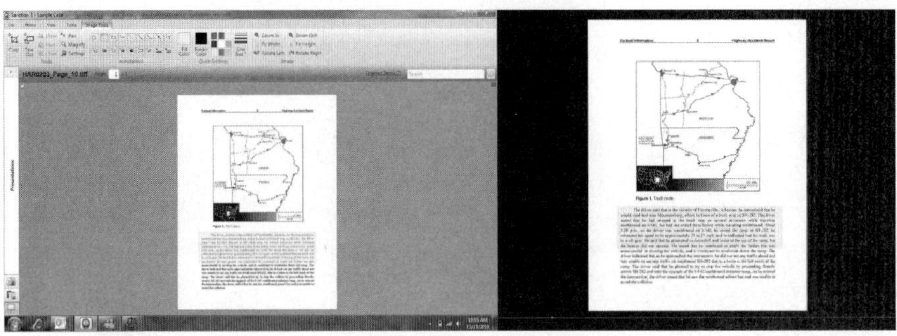

Source: Copyright © AG/Sanction LLC. Used with permission.

Bringing It All Together

Presentation programs like Sanction and TrialDirector allow the legal team to assemble all of the electronically storable evidence in one program. Photographs, video, document images, transcripts, and sound files can all be preloaded into the program for use in trial. In courtrooms equipped with display equipment, it is as simple as hooking up the laptop to the system.

With everything stored electronically, it is not difficult to find and show almost anything on a moment's notice when testimony or strategy changes. With coordination between the trial attorney and the litigation support team running the equipment, the presentation to the court and the jury may appear flawless.

Using presentation software, as with using any software, requires some training and practice. When the use is a for public forum like the courtroom, it is best to be up to speed and take advantage of available training and refresher courses or, in appropriate cases, to bring in a trial support consultant to manage the system and free up the litigation support staff for other trial functions.

Exhibit 10.12 Sanction video transcript screen

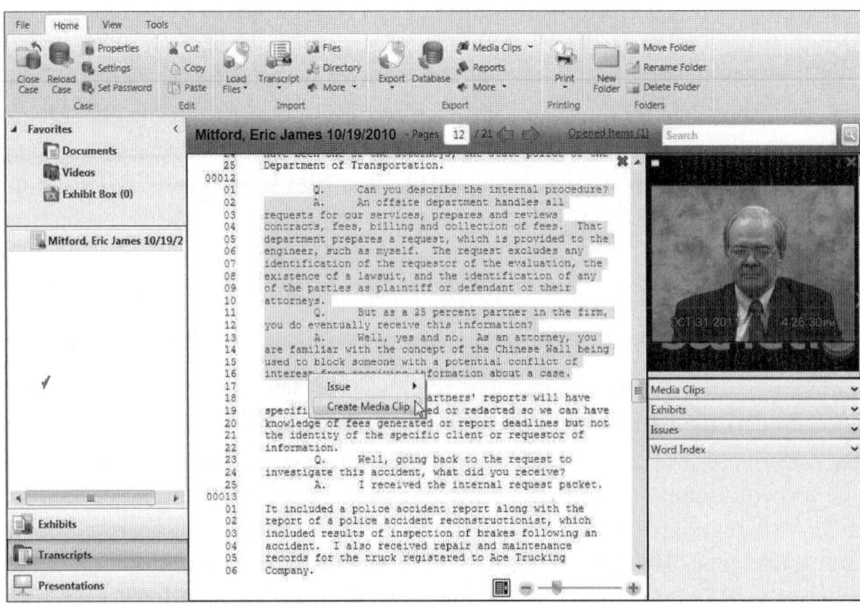

Source: Copyright © AG/Sanction LLC. Used with permission.

Another advantage of these programs is their flexibility. They can be used to prepare and present the graphic presentation electronically using a computer, with or without a projector, and to print out paper copies for distribution.

PRACTICE TIP

Before creating a case, make sure all of the items you wish to use are in formats that are supported by the selected presentation program. Make copies or move all the items into a separate folder or groups of folders for easy access and use.

CREATE A CASE PRESENTATION

LEARNING OBJECTIVE 3
Create a case presentation.

Setting up a basic presentation requires an understanding of a few basic Windows tools, including the use of Windows Explorer, creating new folders, copying and pasting files and "dragging" folders, and "dragging and dropping" files from one folder or program to another. In Windows, using the copy and paste functions leaves the files in the original location and pastes a copy of the file in the new location; the original is not moved or deleted. On the other hand, the drag-and-drop method moves the file from one location to another, deleting the file from the original location.

When using Windows, it is always recommended that the copy-and-paste method be used, just as it is always recommended that the Save As function be used instead of the Save function to avoid overwriting or erasing the original files. In Sanction, either method (copy and paste or drag and drop) *leaves* the original file in its original location. Desired documents, images, videos, and transcripts can thus be safely added to the Sanction case by dragging and dropping them from a folder on the computer or memory media, because the drag-and-drop feature in Sanction sets up a link to the original location rather than actually removes the file. This is similar to the way document management programs set up links to the document, like a web address in a web search engine tells the program where to look, but does not change the file or physically move it.

The first step is to create a new case, as shown in Exhibit 10.13.

Items for each category may be dragged from their original folder on the computer, in this case, from the Sanction Demo Folder on a removable thumb drive to the location in the program (as shown in Exhibit 10.14), where documents are dragged from a folder on the computer to the Documents category in Sanction or imported using the import function in Sanction.

Exhibit 10.13 Creating a new case

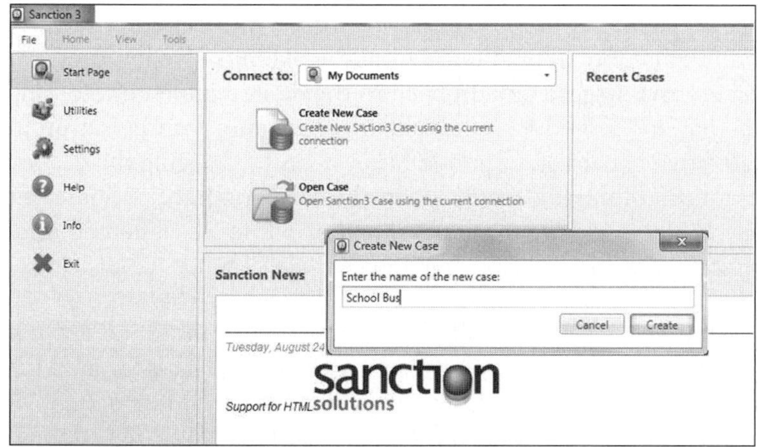

Source: Copyright © AG/Sanction LLC. Used with permission.

PRACTICE TIP

Making backups is critical for safety and security. Remember this author's adage: "If anything can go wrong it will, at the worst possible moment—in the middle of a trial." Many others besides myself have been known to bring a complete backup system to trial, including extra copies of electronic files and extra computers. In smaller cases, files may be backed up using removable media cards and thumb drives, and in larger cases, they may be backed up on relatively inexpensive portable hard drives.

Exhibit 10.14 Adding multiple documents from Windows folder on computer to new case in Sanction

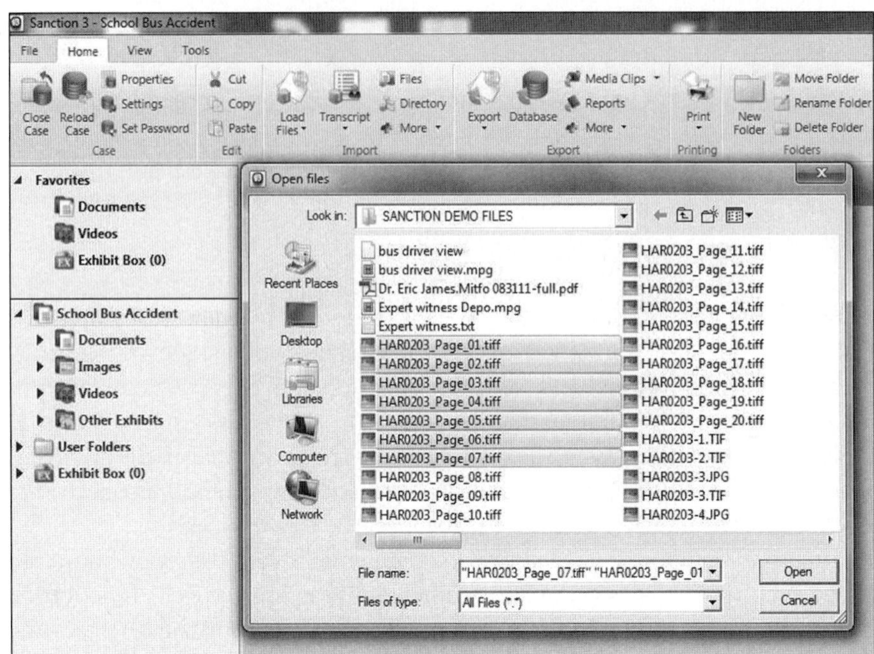

Source: Copyright © AG/Sanction LLC. Used with permission.

PRACTICE TIP

Multiple files can be selected in Windows Explorer by holding down the Crtl (control) key and pointing and clicking on each desired file with the left mouse button.

Again, dragging the individual files to a Sanction case does not actually move them; it only creates a link to the location for the program to use when you want to view those items. In this sample case, all the desired items that will be used have been moved to one folder on a removable memory media. When the Sanction program is run, the memory media must be in the computer for the program to access the link to the files.

PRACTICE TIP

The optimal process is to have the data files on an internal hard drive on the computer, *not* on the flash drive. This prevents data being left behind.

When items have been entered into the program, they can be previewed by highlighting the item in the Sanction Tree Views, as in Exhibit 10.15, which shows the cover page of the NTSB report of the school bus–truck accident in the preview screen and a thumbnail view.

Preparing a Presentation

A presentation may contain any of the various files loaded into Sanction. To create a presentation in Sanction, desired items from the exhibits listed in the Tree View may be selected and dragged and dropped to the desired presentation using the mouse. Items that are desired for a particular presentation can be set up in advance as an individual collection of presentation items by dragging the desired items to the presentation folder. Depending on the case, a number of different presentations may be created—for example, different witnesses, different legal theories, opening statement, and closing argument.

Special Features and Tools. As with all sophisticated programs, Sanction has numerous tools and features. For example, Sanction has a set of tools for marking up and annotating items presented, as shown in Exhibit 10.16. This image shows a number of potential annotations and the menu (selected with a right mouse click) used to select and change the annotation desired.

Exhibit 10.15 Sanction Tree View with document and thumbnail view

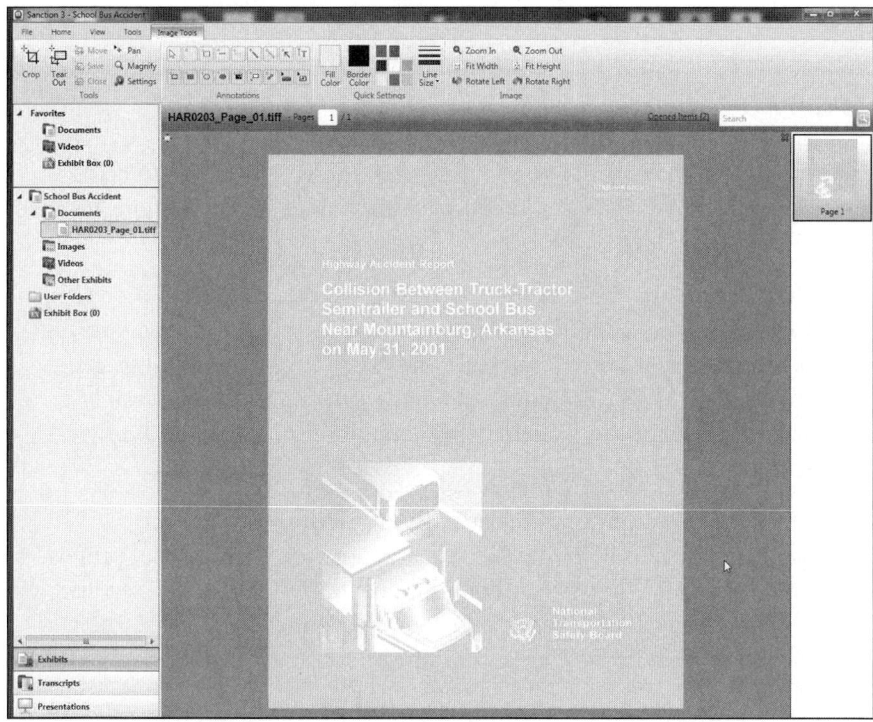

Source: Copyright © AG/Sanction LLC. Used with permission.

Exhibit 10.16 Annotation tools and menus

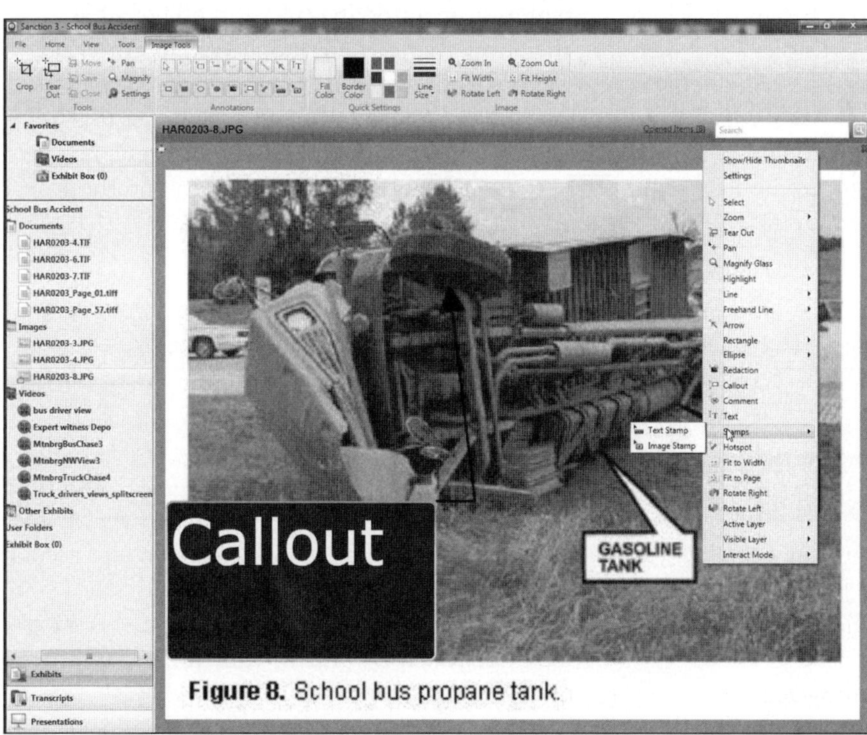

Source: Copyright © AG/Sanction LLC. Used with permission.

CONCEPT REVIEW AND REINFORCEMENT

CHAPTER SUMMARY

ELECTRONIC TRIAL PRESENTATION

Introduction to Electronic Trial Presentation	More and more courts are providing, or allowing litigants to bring into the courtroom, computer-based electronic display systems for use in trial.
The Electronic Courtroom	The basic electronic courtroom uses a computer projector, a projection screen, and a laptop computer. More complex arrangements include computer monitors at counsel's table, on the judge's bench, and in some cases in the jury box and witness stand, and possibly a large-screen monitor to replace the computer projector and projection screen.
Using Technology to Present the Case	Litigation presentation programs, like Sanction by Sanction Solutions and TrialDirector by inData, are multifaceted trial presentation programs that offer a comprehensive approach to presenting all types of exhibits in the courtroom, including documents, photographs, graphic images, video presentations, and recorded depositions.
Bringing it All Together	Presentation programs like Sanction and TrialDirector allow the legal team to assemble all of the electronically storable evidence in one program. Photographs, video, document images, transcripts, and sound files can all be preloaded into the program for use in trial. In courtrooms equipped with display equipment, it is as simple as hooking the laptop up to the system.
Create a Case Presentation	Setting up a basic presentation requires an understanding of a few basic Windows tools, including the use of Windows Explorer to find files, create new folders, copy and paste, and "drag and drop" to move files from one folder to another. Dragging the individual files to a Sanction case does not actually move them, but only creates a link to the location for the program to use when you want to find those items.
Preparing a Presentation	A presentation may contain any of the case items (data) in the program. Items that are desired for a particular presentation can be set up in advance as an individual collection of presentation items.

REVIEW QUESTIONS AND EXERCISES

1. What types of equipment are found in the electronic courtroom?
2. What are the features of a basic electronic courtroom?
3. What is the purpose of a judge's kill switch?
4. What are some of the items that might be found on the attorney's lectern?
5. Who determines what may be used in a particular courtroom?
6. What are factors to be considered in bringing a technology expert into a trial to help with the presentation?
7. What is required in order to use existing images and documents with a trial presentation program?

8. What is the advantage of using video as part of a trial presentation?
9. How are objections to the materials handled in a trial presentation program?
10. What is the advantage of having a trial consultant handle the trial presentation program?
11. Why is copy and paste preferred over drag and drop in Windows Explorer?
12. What happens to files that are dragged and dropped into the Sanction program?
13. What is the importance of backups of trial materials?
14. Why do some trial lawyers carry backup equipment to trial?
15. How are individual presentation sets created in Sanction?
16. How can annotation tools be used in Sanction?

BUILDING YOUR PARALEGAL SKILLS

INTERNET AND TECHNOLOGY EXERCISES

1. Search the Internet for your local court's website on trial technology.
2. Locate any website for local judges' rules on technology in their courtrooms.
3. Conduct a search of the Internet for multimedia trial consultants.

CIVIL LITIGATION VIDEO CASE STUDIES

Arbitration Before 3-Member Panel

A civil case is presented before a three member arbitration panel including showing a video tape of the incident that is the basis for the lawsuit.

After viewing the video in MyLegalStudiesKit, answer the following questions.

1. Is the use of trial presentation software useful in an arbitration?
2. Should multimedia and trial presentation software be used in a small setting like arbitration or only in a large setting like a courtroom?
3. What are the advantages and disadvantages to using trial presentation software in an arbitration?

CHAPTER OPENING SCENARIO CASE STUDY

Use the Opening Scenario for this chapter to answer the following questions.

1. Prepare an outline of the potential multimedia elements that might be used in trial.
2. Prepare a memo explaining how a trial presentation program might be used to present the case.
3. What are the items that will be needed in order to use a presentation program?
4. Answer the question raised by one of the attorneys: "Can we present the case without a presentation program?"
5. How can using a program like Sanction help in preparing for trial and during trial?

COMPREHENSIVE CASE STUDY

SCHOOL BUS–TRUCK ACCIDENT CASE

1. For the assigned case study from Appendix II:
   a. From the Technology Resources Website, www.pearsonhighered.com/goldman, download and install on your computer the demo version of Sanction.
   b. Download the Sanction Demo Files to a removable memory device.
   c. Use Sanction to set up a new case.
   d. Prepare a presentation for the case study in Appendix II.

BUILDING YOUR PROFESSIONAL PORTFOLIO

CIVIL LITIGATION TEAM AT WORK

Prepare a policy on access to the information in the trial presentation program. Cite any local case law or ethics opinions on confidentiality, privilege, and work product.

Forms

1. Obtain any forms necessary to preauthorize or bring audiovisual equipment into the courthouse.
2. Prepare a template for a trial equipment checklist.

Procedures

Prepare a step-by-step procedure for bringing trial presentation equipment into your jurisdiction's federal and state courts.

Contacts and Resources

1. Prepare a contact list with email address, phone number, physical address, and mailing address of the technology contact in the federal and state courts in your jurisdiction.
2. Prepare a contact list with email address, phone number, physical address, and mailing address of each individual judge's contact person who can advise on the judge's rules and procedures for that court.
3. Prepare a contact list with email addresses, phone numbers, physical addresses, and mailing addresses of the local trial presentation consultants in your area.
4. Prepare a contact list with email addresses, phone numbers, physical addresses, and mailing addresses of the local companies that rent or repair audiovisual equipment or computers.

APPENDIX I

CHAPTER OPENING CASE STUDY

Each chapter has an Opening Scenario that focuses on the issues presented in the chapter. The scenarios follow the activities of the law firm of Mason, Marshall and Benjamin, Attorneys and Counselors at Law. The firm started in a small town near the local state courthouse. With the increased volume of litigation cases, it was determined that a satellite office in the city of Oldtown was essential to service the cases in federal court. A new location was established across the street from the federal district court with Ethan Benjamin, Esq., as the office's managing partner. Benjamin, a former litigation paralegal for the suburban office, graduated from law school, passed the state bar, and was admitted, on the motion of the senior partner, Owen Mason, Esq., to the federal district court. Owen Mason had been a law clerk to a federal judge in the same court.

Edith Hannah, an experienced paralegal from a prestigious downtown law firm, was the first employee hired by Mr. Mason to run the original office in the suburban town of Newtown across from the local state trial court building. Ariel Marshall, a former prosecution attorney, and her litigation support paralegal, Emily Gordon, joined the firm shortly after its formation, after they had worked a major multiparty tort action. Ms. Marshall became a partner of Mr. Mason. With the growth of both offices, Mrs. Hannah became the office manager for both offices, and soon hired Emily's twin sister, Caitlin, as an additional paralegal to work in the center city office with Mr. Benjamin. Cary Eden, Esq., was hired by Mr. Benjamin as an associate in the center city office to assist him in federal court litigation.

LAW OFFICE INFORMATION

Mason, Marshall and Benjamin
Attorneys and Counselors
at Law
Newtown Office
2 South State Street
Newtown, Your State
Office Phone 555-111-2222

Oldtown Office
1 Federal Street
Oldtown, Your State
Office Phone 555-222-1111

Owen Mason, Esquire
138 South Main Street
Newtown, Your State
Social Security Number 123-45-6789
Office Phone 555-111-2222
Home Phone 555-345-3333
Date of Birth 08-19-1961

Ariel Marshall, Esquire
621 Merion Road
Old Station, Your State
Social Security Number 123-45-6792
Office Phone 555-222-2224
Home Phone 555-432-5673
Date of Birth 08-06-1968

Ethan Benjamin, Esquire
138 City Court
Oldtown, Your State
Social Security Number 555-22-7890
Office Phone 555-222-1111
Home Phone 555-987-6543
Date of Birth 06-23-1968

Cary Eden, Esquire
12 Schan Drive
Richboro, Your State
Office Phone 555-222-1111
Home Phone 555-518-9166
Date of Birth 08-12-1964

Mrs. Hannah
43 Washington Avenue
Newtown, Your State
Social Security Number 123-45-6790
Home Phone 555-453-3134
Date of Birth 01-12-1960

Emily Gordon
2916 Boulevard Avenue
Forest Park, Your State and Zip
Social Security Number 123-45-6793
Home Phone 555-468-3335
Date of Birth 01-28-1984

Caitlin Gordon
76 Medford Road
Lawnview, Your State
Social Security Number 999-11-0000
Home Phone 555-444-8888
Date of Birth 01-28-1984

Billing Rates

Owen Marshall, senior partner, attorney—$350 hour
Ariel Marshall, partner, attorney—$300 hour
Ethan Benjamin, managing partner, attorney—$250 hour
Cary Eden, associate attorney—$200 hour
Mrs. Hannah, paralegal—$90
Emily Gordon, litigation paralegal—$90 hour
Caitlin Gordon, paralegal—$90 hour

YOUR HOURLY BILLING RATE $40 Hour

APPENDIX II

COMPREHENSIVE CASE STUDY: SCHOOL BUS–TRUCK ACCIDENT CASE STUDY

The Comprehensive Case Study: School Bus–Truck Accident Case is used as the basis for the pleading and forms throughout the text to allow users to follow a single case from beginning to end. Many of the elements of the case are illustrated with videos presented in chapters where appropriate in the video case study material.

The comprehensive case study is based on actual facts as reported in a National Transportation Safety Board (NTSB) report. Content has been edited and reproduced in the words of the report to provide as much authenticity as possible. Figures are reproduced from the same report. Some liberty has been taken with the identity of the parties, and no names used represent or are actual parties involved in the tragic accident reported. We use an actual incident to allow you to perform basic legal and factual research that will present actual information that would be found in a real case on which you might work in the future.

Multi-Vehicle Collision between Truck and School Bus
Near Mountainburg, Arkansas
May 31, 2001

Abstract

On May 31, 2001, near Mountainburg, Arkansas, a Gayle Stuart Trucking, Inc., truck-tractor semitrailer collided with a 65-passenger school bus operated by the Mountainburg, Arkansas, Public Schools. Three school bus passengers were fatally injured; two other passengers received serious injuries. Four passengers, the school bus driver, and the truck driver sustained minor injuries.

Passengers

Refer to seat numbers on National Transportation Safety Board (NTSB) seating chart:

1A Alice Bates

2A Amy Francs
2C Clarisa Howard
2E Doris Isaacs

9A Harry Allen
9C Charles Barley

10A Dan Thomas
10E David Thompson

11A Thomas Aaron

Other Drivers and Parties

School Bus Driver:	Robert Howard
Tractor-Trailer Driver:	Stephen Blanca
Trucking Company:	Gayle Stuart Trucking, Inc

Highway Accident Report

EXECUTIVE SUMMARY

On May 31, 2001, about 3:28 p.m. central daylight time, a southbound Gayle Stuart Trucking, Inc., truck-tractor semitrailer exited Interstate 540 at State Highway 282 near Mountainburg, Arkansas. The driver was unable to stop at the stop sign at the bottom of the ramp. The 79,040-pound combination unit was traveling approximately 48 mph when it entered the intersection and collided with the right side of a westbound, 65-passenger, 1990 Blue Bird Corporation school bus operated by the Mountainburg, Arkansas, Public Schools. The school bus rotated approximately 300 degrees clockwise and overturned; the body, which partially separated from the chassis, came to rest on its right side on the eastbound shoulder of State Highway 282. The tractor semitrailer continued across the roadway, rotated about 60 degrees clockwise, overturned, and came to rest on its left side.

Three school bus passengers seated across from the impact area were fatally injured; one was partially ejected. Two other passengers, one of whom was seated in the impact area, received serious injuries, and four passengers had minor injuries. The school bus driver and the truck driver both sustained minor injuries.

The Safety Board determines that the probable cause of the accident was the truck driver's inability to stop the tractor semitrailer at the stop sign at the bottom of the ramp due to the reduced braking efficiency of the truck's brakes, which had been poorly maintained and inadequately inspected. Contributing to the school bus passengers' injuries during the side impact were incomplete compartmentalization and the lack of energy-absorbing material on interior surfaces.

NOTE: The complete National Transportation Safety Board report is available and may be downloaded from the Technology Resources Website, www.pearsonhighered.com/goldman, together with selected exhibits and accident simulations.

APPENDIX III

SUPPLEMENTAL CASE STUDIES

Additional case studies are provided for use in completing independent case analysis, using the Comprehensive Case Study: School Bus–Truck Accident Case as an example.

Two of the additional case studies, New York School Bus Accident and Virginia School Bus Accident, are similar in nature to the Comprehensive Case Study: School Bus–Truck Accident Case. Additional cases are provided for a property damage case, a simple personal injury case, a tort action based on a civil assault, a commercial breach of contract, and an airplane crash.

List of Additional Cases:

- **Case 1: Simple motor vehicle accident with property damage claim**
- **Case 2: Student injured on school bus with a delay in treatment**
- **Case 3: Civil assault on a school bus and failure to protect**
- **Case 4: Breach of commercial contract**
- **Case 5: New York school bus accident**
- **Case 6: Virginia school bus accident**
- **Case 7: Aircraft fatality**

Several of the scenarios and parties in the non-NTSB cases are semi-fictional and loosely based on facts and situations from a number of sources woven together to provide a variety of case types. Some liberty has been taken with the identity of the parties, and no names used represent or are actual parties involved in the tragic accidents reported in the NTSB-based case studies.

CASE 1: SIMPLE MOTOR VEHICLE ACCIDENT WITH PROPERTY DAMAGE CLAIM

Joel Wilkenson is a regular client of the law firm. He recently had a fender bender for which there is no insurance coverage. He was stopped at the traffic light at Fourteenth and Market Streets waiting to make a left-hand turn when an SUV driven by a woman talking on her cell phone ran the red light from the other direction. He is seeking to sue the woman who hit him to recover the costs of the repair to his automobile.

Parties

Joel Wilkenson

Mary Smith
Mike Pope of Acme Garage—to testify for damage and repair to car
Tom Horton—a fact witness who observed the accident

CASE 2: STUDENT INJURED ON A SCHOOL BUS WITH A DELAY IN TREATMENT

Mandy Stein was returning from a class trip. She was seated in the rear of the school bus. Located directly behind her at the back of the bus were some boxes containing supplies and beverages. The bus stopped suddenly and a box fell on Mandy's head, injuring her. Mandy was taken to the emergency room, where treatment was provided until her mother arrived at the hospital. Mrs. Stein's religious beliefs do not allow submission to traditional medical treatment, but rather rely on higher powers for healing and recovery. She insisted that any treatment be stopped and took Mandy home. Mandy's father does not hold the same religious beliefs, and he sought court permission to have Mandy's injuries treated. Mandy suffered a head/scalp laceration, which was stitched in the emergency room, but there was no follow-up treatment or care until her father received court permission to have her treated by Dr. Lee. Because of the delay in treatment, the stitches became infected and surgery was required to remove the dead and infected skin, facial muscle, and nerves. She has permanent scarring and some loss of the use of her facial muscles.

Parties

Mandy Stein, a minor

Larry Stein, her father
Samantha Stein, her mother
Dr. Lee, plastic surgeon
Ron Clemmons, bus driver
Yourtown School District

CASE 3: CIVIL ASSAULT ON A SCHOOL BUS AND FAILURE TO PROTECT

Davis Hilary was riding home from school when Bobby Jones confronted him and prevented him from exiting the bus at his regular stop. Bobby held Davis down and threatened to harm him. A girl shouted that Bobby had a knife and the bus driver stopped the bus to investigate the matter. Bobby was restrained and taken back to school, where an investigation began.

Parties

Bobby Jones, a minor

Robert Jones, Sr., Bobby's father
Davis Hilary, a minor
Katy Hilary, Davis's mother
Lower Council School District
Ron Clemmons, bus driver

CASE 4: BREACH OF COMMERCIAL CONTRACT

The comprehensive case study is based on actual facts as reported in public documents. Content has been edited and reproduced in the words of the original documents to provide as much authenticity as possible. The use of an actual case is to allow you to perform basic legal and factual research that will present actual information that would be found in a real case on which you may in the future work.

Breach of Commercial Contract
Abstract

Melford Olson Honey, Inc. (Mel-O), a Minnesota honey wholesaler, sued Richard Adee (Richard) doing business as Adee Honey Farms (Adee Honey), a South Dakota honey farmer, in a Minnesota state court for breach of contract and specific performance, alleging Adee Honey failed to provide the requisite quantity of honey set forth in a June 2002 contract. Adee Honey removed the case to federal court on diversity jurisdiction and counterclaimed for money owed under the same contract. The district court denied both parties' motions for partial summary judgment, and the case proceeded to a jury trial.

Parties

Richard Adee, doing business as Adee Honey Farms

Bruce, SD
with regional offices in Bakersfield, CA, Cedar Rapids, NE, Roscoe, SD, and Woodville, MS, USA

Melford Olson Honey, Inc

Cannon Falls, MN

EXECUTIVE SUMMARY

Adee Honey, formed by Richard in 1957, operates honey farms in California, Nebraska, Mississippi, and South Dakota. Adee Honey's principal place of business is in South Dakota. Mel-O is owned by William Sill, and Curt and Darcy Riess. They bought the company in 1997 and were referred to Richard by Mel-O's prior owners.

In March 2002, Adee Honey and Mel-O entered into an oral agreement for the sale of honey. At the time, Adee Honey possessed a sufficient inventory of honey and agreed to sell approximately thirty loads, or 1.5 million pounds, to Mel-O for 82¢ per pound. Shortly thereafter, Mel-O sent a purchase order to Adee Honey memorializing the sale of 1.5 million pounds of honey for 82¢ per pound. The purchase order noted it was a contract with a "Good Thru" date of April 11, 2002. It was sent to Adee Honey's South Dakota office although Mel-O allegedly knew Richard was working at the Mississippi facility until mid-June.

At approximately the same time, Adee Honey called Mel-O to discuss the possibility of selling up to twelve loads of its inventoried honey to a competitor.

According to Adee Honey, Mel-O agreed, thereby altering the quantity term of the March 2002 contract. According to Mel-O, it permitted Adee Honey to sell twelve loads of inventoried honey to another distributor, provided the terms of the March 2002 contract were fulfilled with other honey. Between the months of May and September 2002, Adee Honey sent Mel-O eighteen loads of honey at 82¢ per pound.

In May 2002, honey prices began to rise due to a contamination in major Chinese honey supplies. In June 2002, Mel-O contacted Adee Honey about purchasing an additional 3.2 million pounds, and the parties agreed on a $1.00 per pound purchase price for the additional quantity. Mel-O sent a contract to Adee

Honey detailing the new arrangement, and Richard added a handwritten *force majeure* clause, specifically excusing performance in the event of "an act of God such as a drought or flood."

Later in the summer of 2002, South Dakota was experiencing drought-like conditions, and Adee Honey unilaterally stopped performing its obligations under the June contract. According to Mel-O, Richard contacted it to discuss the possibility of increasing the price of honey by 10¢ per pound to cover losses Adee Honey would suffer due to the production shortage. By the time Mel-O grudgingly decided to accept the terms, Adee Honey instead stated that the new price would be $1.55 per pound instead of $1.00 to $1.10 per pound.

In the early fall of 2002, Adee Honey began delivering honey to Mel-O at an invoice price of $1.55 per pound. Mel-O, however, refused to pay for this honey. By November 2002, its account was roughly $1.7 million in arrears. In November and December, Mel-O paid Adee Honey 82¢ per pound for approximately 575,000 pounds received, claiming this honey fulfilled the terms of the March 2002 contract. Mel-O did not pay anything for an additional 602,206 pounds received. Mel-O admits owing $1.00 per pound on this quantity, subject to some adjustments.

Adee Honey admits it contracted with Mel-O for eighteen loads of honey.

Miscellaneous Information

The Minnesota statute of frauds provides that oral contracts for the sale of goods for $500.00 or more are unenforceable "unless there is some writing sufficient to indicate that a contract for sale has been made between the parties and signed by the party against whom enforcement is sought." Minn. Stat. § 336.2-201(1).

The statute is applicable because the March 2002 contract for the sale of honey, goods priced over $500.00, was not reduced to writing and signed by Adee Honey, the party against whom enforcement was sought.

> *Under the merchant exception, Minnesota law provides:*
>
> (2) Between merchants if within a reasonable time a writing in confirmation of the contract and sufficient against the sender is received and the party receiving it has reason to know its contents, it satisfies the requirements of subsection (1) [regarding the general applicability of the statute of frauds] against such party unless written notice of objection to its contents is given within ten days after it is received.

The June 2002 contract contains a handwritten *force majeure* clause. Next to the 3.2 million-pound quantity, Richard added: "provided production of said pounds is NOT impeded by an Act of God such as by drought or flood."

> *Minnesota law provides:*
>
> Except so far as a seller may have assumed a greater obligation and subject to the preceding section on substituted performance:
>
> (a) Delay in delivery or nondelivery in whole or in part by a seller who complies with paragraphs (b) and (c) is not a breach of duty under a contract for sale if performance as agreed has been made impracticable by the occurrence of a contingency the nonoccurrence of which was a basic assumption on which the contract was made or by compliance in good faith with any applicable foreign or domestic governmental regulation or order whether or not it later proves to be invalid.

(b) Where the causes mentioned in paragraph (a) affect only a part of the seller's capacity to perform, the seller must allocate production and deliveries among the seller's customers but may include regular customers not then under contract as well as the seller's own requirements for further manufacture. The seller may so allocate in any manner which is fair and reasonable.

(c) The seller must notify the buyer seasonably that there will be delay or non-delivery and, when allocation is required under paragraph (b), of the estimated quota thus made available for the buyer.

CASE 5: NEW YORK SCHOOL BUS ACCIDENT

The comprehensive case study is based on actual facts as reported in a National Transportation Safety Board (NTSB) report. Content has been edited and reproduced in the words of the report to provide as much authenticity as possible. Figures are reproduced from the same report. Some liberty has been taken with the identity of the parties, and no names used represent or are actual parties involved in the tragic accident reported. We use an actual incident to allow you to perform basic legal and factual research that will present actual information that would be found in a real case on which you might in the future work.

School Bus and Dump Truck Collision
Central Bridge, New York
October 21, 1999

Abstract

On October 21, 1999, about 10:30 a.m. near Central Bridge, New York, a school bus was transporting 44 students and 8 adults on a field trip. The bus was traveling north on State Route 30A as it approached the intersection with State Route 7. Concurrently, a dump truck, towing a utility trailer, was traveling west on State Route 7. As the bus approached the intersection, it failed to stop as required and was struck by the dump truck. Seven bus passengers sustained serious injuries; 28 bus passengers and the truck driver received minor injuries. Thirteen bus passengers, the bus driver, and the truck passenger were uninjured.

Passengers

Refer to seat numbers on the National Transportation Safety Board (NTSB) seating chart (NTSB report Figure 4) on page 260.

Other Drivers and Parties

School Bus Driver:	Sam Carole
School Bus Company:	*Kinnicutt Bus Company*
Tractor-Trailer Driver:	Dave Smith
Trucking Company	*MVF Construction Company*

EXECUTIVE SUMMARY

About 10:30 a.m. on October 21, 1999, in Schoharie County, New York, a Kinnicutt Bus Company school bus was transporting 44 students, 5 to 9 years old, and 8 adults on an Albany City School No. 18 field trip. The bus was traveling north on State Route 30A as it approached the intersection with State Route 7, which is about 1.5 miles east of Central Bridge, New York. Concurrently, an MVF Construction Company dump truck, towing a utility trailer, was traveling west on

Figure 4 School bus seating and injury diagram.

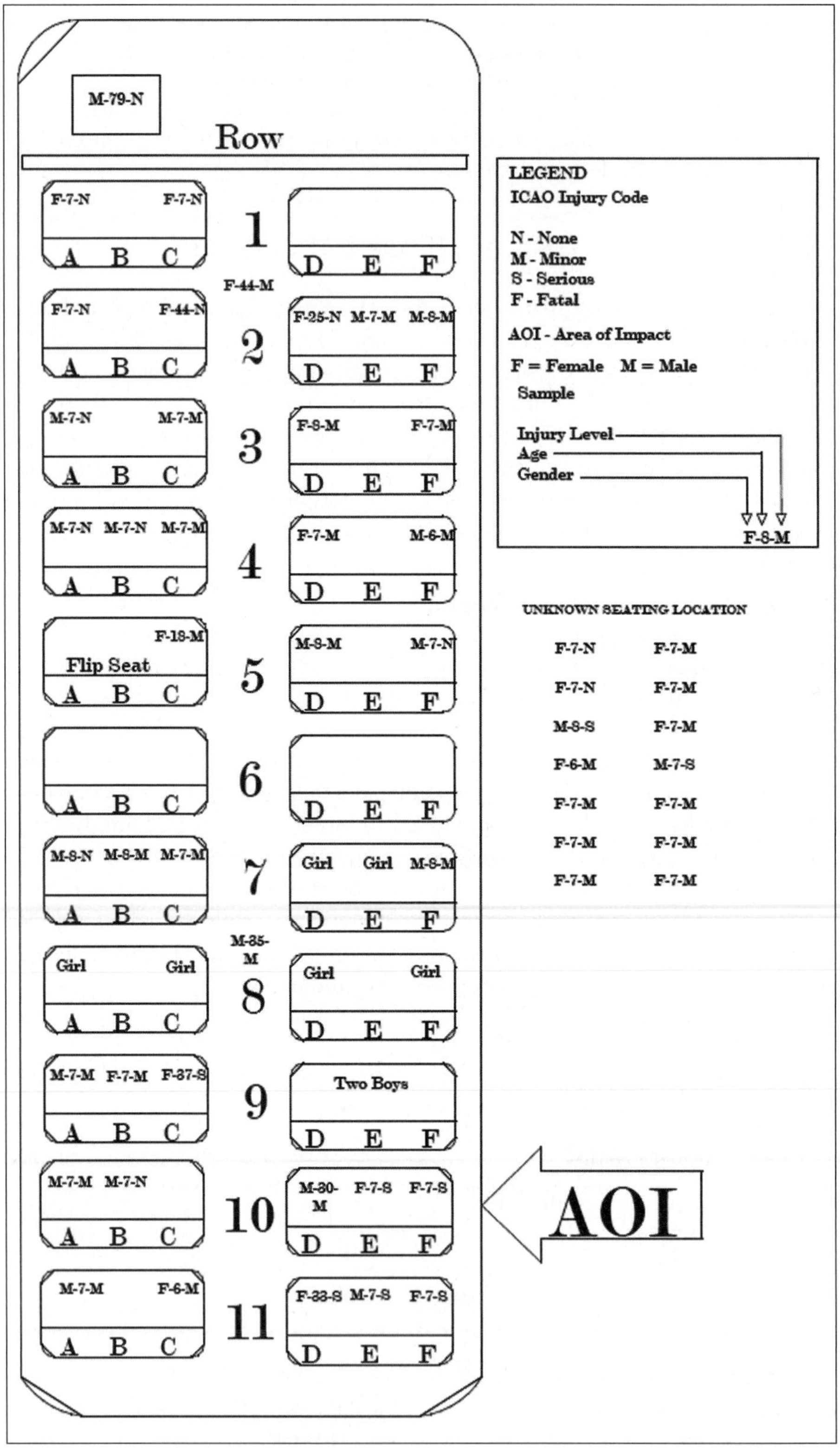

State Route 7. The dump truck was occupied by the driver and a passenger. As the bus approached the intersection, it failed to stop as required and was struck by the dump truck. Seven bus passengers sustained serious injuries; 28 bus passengers and the truck driver received minor injuries. Thirteen bus passengers, the bus driver, and the truck passenger were uninjured.

The National Transportation Safety Board determines that the probable cause of this accident was the school bus driver's failure to stop for the stop sign due to his degraded performance or lapse of attention as a result of factors associated with aging or his medical condition or both.

The following major safety issues were identified in this accident:

- the potential for passenger injuries as a result of the school bus emergency exit door design,
- the potential for passenger injuries as a result of school bus seat cushion bottoms that are removable or hinged, and
- the adequacy of commercial vehicle airbrake inspections.

The medical fitness of commercial drivers and the medical examination for the commercial driver's license were also identified as safety issues; however, these issues will be analyzed in a forthcoming Safety Board special investigation report.

Factual Information

Accident Narrative

About 7:20 a.m. on October 21, 1999, in Albany, New York, a 79-year-old school bus driver began transporting students to school on his regular morning route. He drove a 1997 American Transportation Corporation (AmTran) full-size school bus, owned and operated by the Kinnicutt Bus Company (Kinnicutt). About 8:50 a.m., after finishing his regular route, he drove to Albany City School No. 18 and loaded 44 children, 5 to 9 years old, and 8 adults (chaperons) for a scheduled field trip to the Pumpkin Patch in Central Bridge, New York, about 40 miles from the school.

The bus driver stated that he had never been to the Pumpkin Patch. No directions to the site had been provided by Kinnicutt for him to use. According to one chaperon, the bus driver said that he knew the general area to which he was going vaguely but not specifically. The chaperon said that the bus driver asked him for directions. The chaperon then went into the school and was able to obtain a map and directions from a teacher for the bus driver to use.

Each school bus passenger seat was equipped with three color-coded lap belts. These belts were attached to the seat frame at the juncture between the seatback and seat cushion bottom. According to the adult passengers, all of the children were restrained by a lap belt before the trip began. The chaperons said that, to better supervise the children, the adults, except the one seated next to the emergency exit door, were unrestrained.

The bus departed the school about 9:20 a.m. The bus driver took the New York State Thruway west to exit 25A onto Interstate-88 (I-88) and then traveled west on I-88 toward exit 23, the intended exit. The chaperons stated that the bus driver seemed confused about the directions to the Pumpkin Patch and that he turned off at exit 24, the wrong exit.

He ultimately stopped the bus on the exit 24 ramp. One chaperon reported that the driver appeared confused when he stopped on the ramp. She stated that she was concerned about where he positioned the bus on the ramp when he stopped; she feared that it would be struck by another vehicle. After the bus driver received directions from a chaperon, the driver returned to I-88 and continued traveling to exit 23, the correct exit.

The bus driver stated that at the top of the exit 23 ramp, he turned right onto State Route 30A (SR-30A) and started looking for State Route 7 (SR-7). About 10:30 a.m., the bus was traveling north on SR-30A between 15 and 25 mph as it approached the intersection with SR-7. The intersection was about 1.5 miles east of Central Bridge. The north- and southbound traffic on SR-30A were controlled by an advance warning sign that indicated a stop ahead, a stop sign, flashing red intersection control beacons, and pavement markings that included the word "stop" and a stop bar.

At the same time, an MVF Construction Company (MVF) dump truck, towing a utility trailer, was traveling about 45 mph west on SR-7. East- and westbound traffic on SR-7 at the intersection were controlled by flashing yellow intersection control beacons. The dump truck was occupied by its 52-year-old driver and a passenger. As the school bus approached the intersection, according to the chaperons, several children on board saw the sign for the Pumpkin Patch that was beyond the intersection and yelled. These children may also have released their belt buckles. One child reportedly stood up in the seating compartment. The bus driver, who was looking for SR-7, told investigating police that he saw the posted stop sign, slowed, but did not stop the bus, which then entered the intersection where the dump truck struck it on the right side behind the rear axle. (See Figure 1.)

Figure 1 Exterior crush damage of school bus

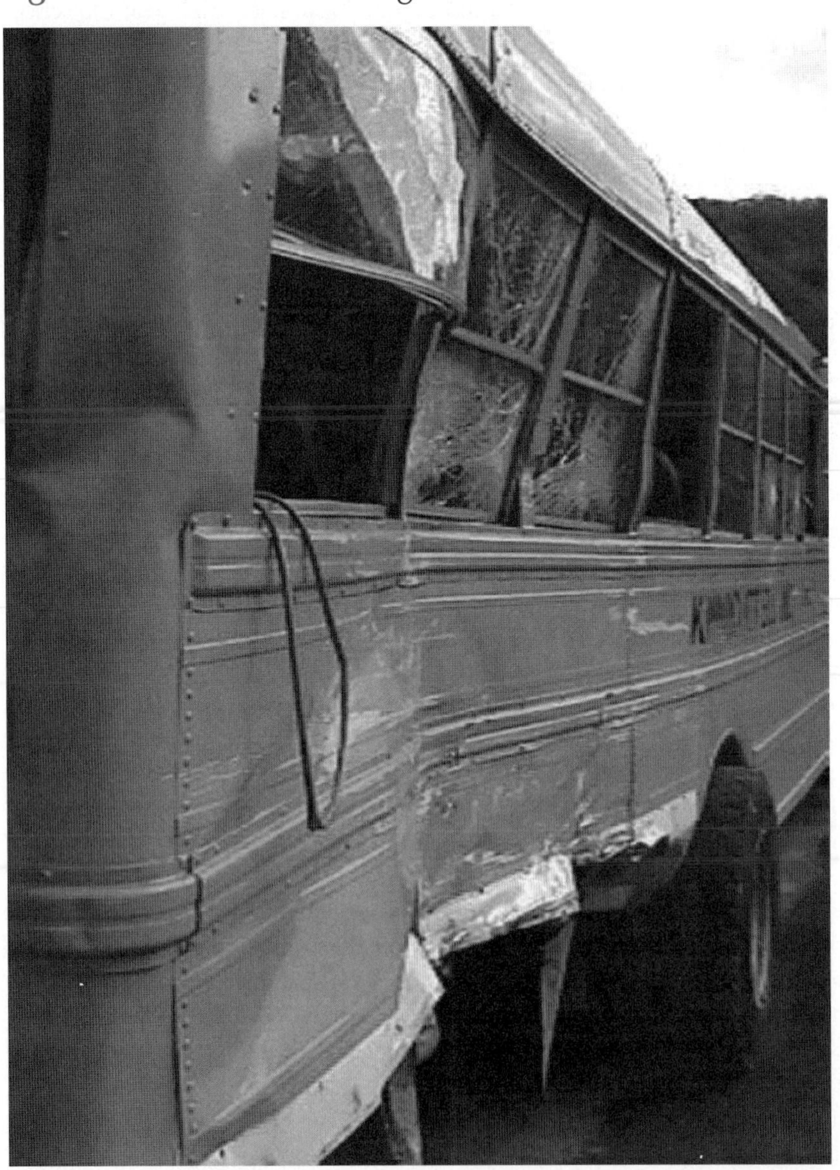

Figure 3 Final rest position

The school bus, after rotating about 145 degrees clockwise, slid approximately 100 feet and came to rest facing south. The dump truck, after rotating about 150 degrees clockwise, struck three highway guide signs and a utility pole; it then came to rest facing northeast. (See Figure 3.)

The complete National Transportation Safety Board report is available and may be downloaded from the Technology Resources Website, www.pearsonhighered.com/goldman, together with selected exhibits.

SOURCE: http://www.ntsb.gov/publictn/2000/HAR0002.pdf

CASE 6: VIRGINIA SCHOOL BUS ACCIDENT

The comprehensive case study is based on actual facts as reported in a National Transportation Safety Board (NTSB) report. Content has been edited and reproduced in the words of the report to provide as much authenticity as possible. Figures are reproduced from the same report. Some liberty has been taken with the identity of the parties, and no names used represent or are actual parties involved in the tragic accident reported. We use an actual incident to allow you to perform basic legal and factual research that will present actual information that would be found in a real case on which you might in the future work.

Multi-Vehicle Collision between Trash Truck and School Bus
Arlington, Virginia
April 18, 2005

Abstract

A 52-passenger school bus was traveling westbound on Columbia Pike (State Route 244) in Arlington County, Virginia, transporting 15 elementary school children, grades pre-K through 5, to the nearby Hoffman-Boston Elementary School. On approaching the signaled intersection with Courthouse Road, the school bus driver began moving the bus into the left turn lane and slowed it

Passengers

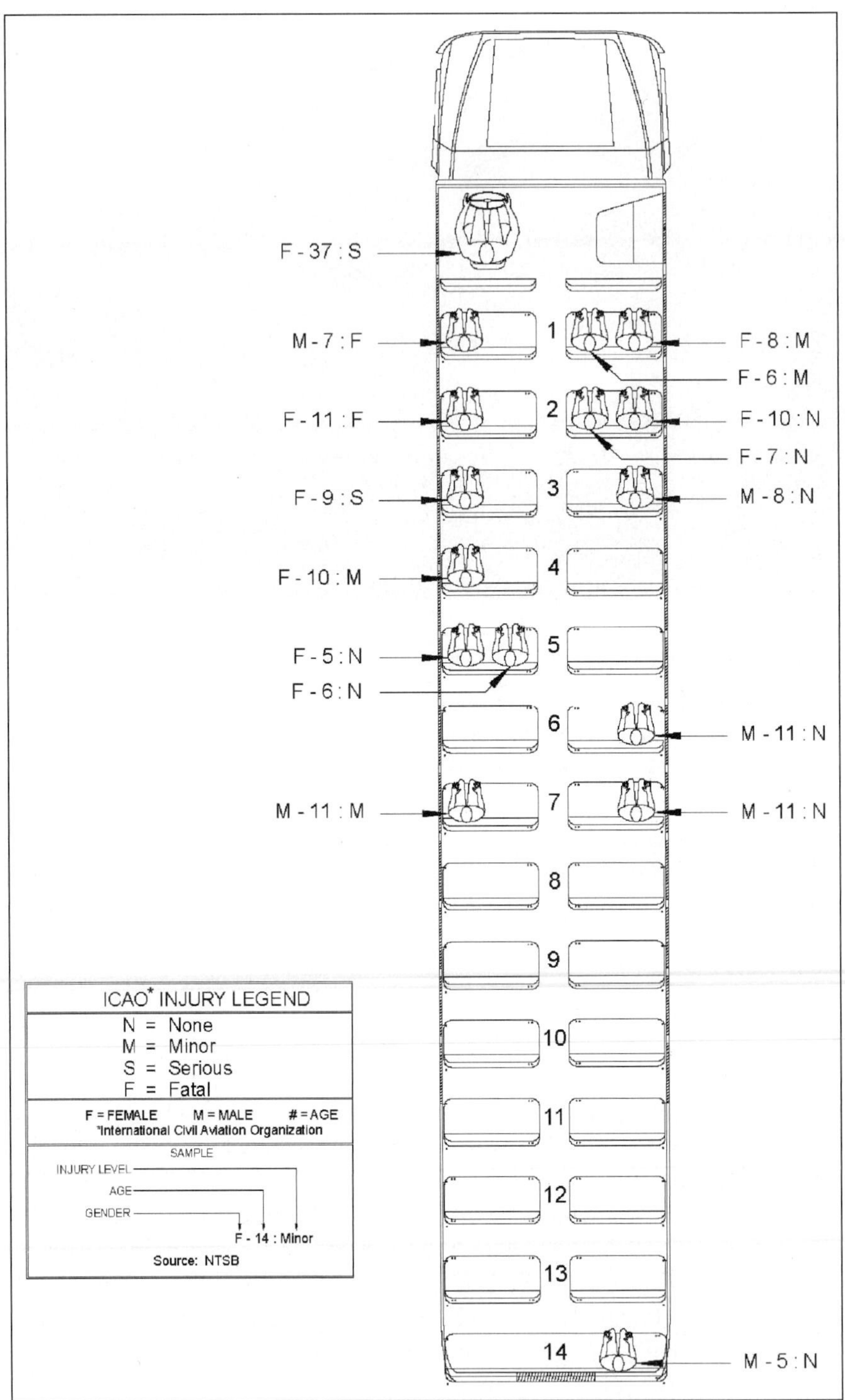

nearly to a stop. As the driver turned the vehicle, its left front encroached slightly into the left lane of the eastbound side of Columbia Pike. A 2003 Mack trash truck was traveling with the flow of traffic in the left eastbound lane on Columbia Pike. The truck reached the intersection with Courthouse Road, continued through it on a green signal, and deviated slightly leftward from its lane toward the yellow centerline. The truck collided with the school bus; the impact involved the front-left corners of both vehicles and a sideswipe.

Drivers and Parties

School Bus Driver:	Kathryn Salvatore
School Bus Operator:	Arlington County School District
Truck Driver:	John Gonzales
Trucking Company:	AAA Recycling and Trash Removal Services

EXECUTIVE SUMMARY

Accident Description

Shortly before 8:40 a.m., on Monday, April 18, 2005, a 52-passenger school bus was traveling westbound on Columbia Pike (State Route 244) in Arlington County, Virginia, transporting 15 elementary school children, grades pre-K through 5, to the nearby Hoffman-Boston Elementary School. On approaching the signaled intersection with Courthouse Road, the school bus driver began moving the bus into the left turn lane (from which it would turn south onto Courthouse Road) and slowed it nearly to a stop. As the driver turned the vehicle, its left front encroached slightly into the left lane of the eastbound side of Columbia Pike. The driver later stated that distractions inside the bus might have affected her driving at this time. She said her attention was drawn to a student standing on a seat and to a clipboard that fell to the floor at her driving station.

About 8:40 a.m., a 2003 Mack trash truck was traveling with the flow of traffic in the left eastbound lane on Columbia Pike, at a speed one witness who was traveling on the road in the same direction estimated to be approximately 30 mph. The truck reached the intersection with Courthouse Road, continued through it on a green signal and, according to several witnesses, deviated slightly leftward from its lane toward the yellow centerline. The truck collided with the school bus; the impact involved the front-left corners of both vehicles and a sideswipe. (See Figures 1 and 2 for a map of the accident location area and a diagram representing the vehicles at the point of impact.)

During the collision, the school bus was pushed backward, but it remained in the left turn lane following the accident. The trash truck continued eastbound about 200 feet, crossed the right eastbound lane, jumped the right curb of Columbia Pike, and came to rest.

One student died at the scene and one student died 3 days later in the hospital. The truck driver, school bus driver, and one student on the bus sustained serious injuries; four students sustained minor injuries; and the remaining eight students were uninjured. The bus driver, who had been wearing her seat belt, was ejected through the broken windshield when the shoulder portion of the belt was sheared in half. Emergency responders needed approximately 1 hour to extricate the trash truck driver from the truck cab because of his legs being trapped in the wreckage. The students who suffered the most severe injuries were seated behind the driver on the left side, near the front, of the bus.

Weather conditions at the time of the accident were clear and dry. The school bus sustained impact damage to its front and left side. (See Figure 5.) The damage continued along the left side of the bus to near the sixth passenger row behind the driver's seat, approximately 20 feet rearward from the front bumper. Intrusion into the occupant compartment extended inboard to a depth of about 6 1/2 inches.

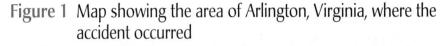

Figure 1 Map showing the area of Arlington, Virginia, where the accident occurred

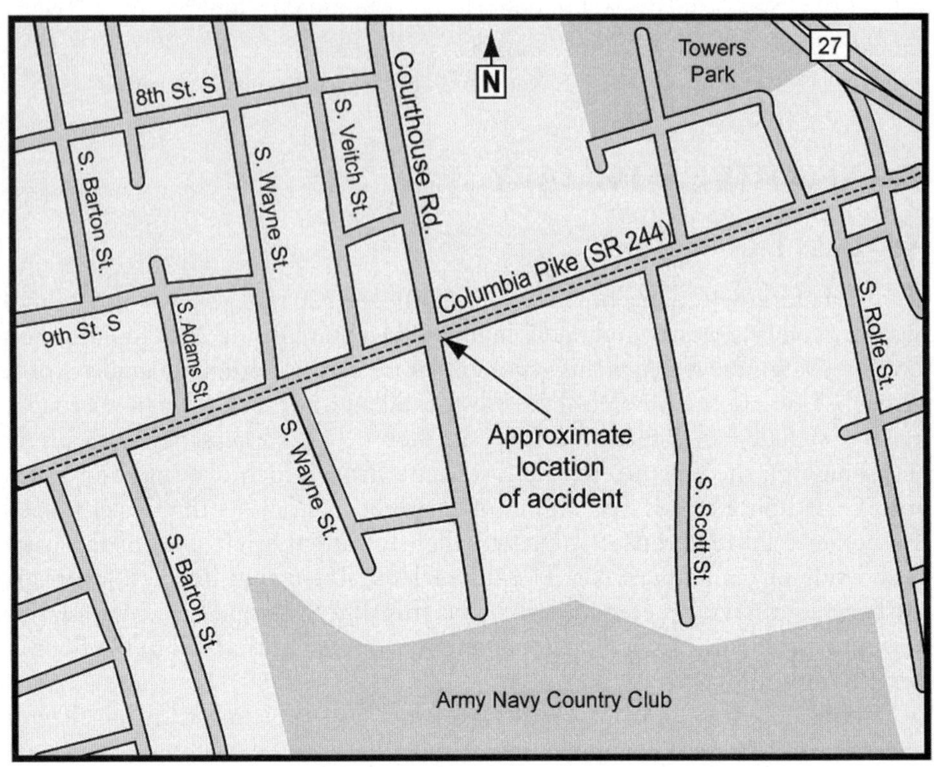

Figure 2 Diagram showing the estimated positions of the school bus and the trash truck at the point of impact

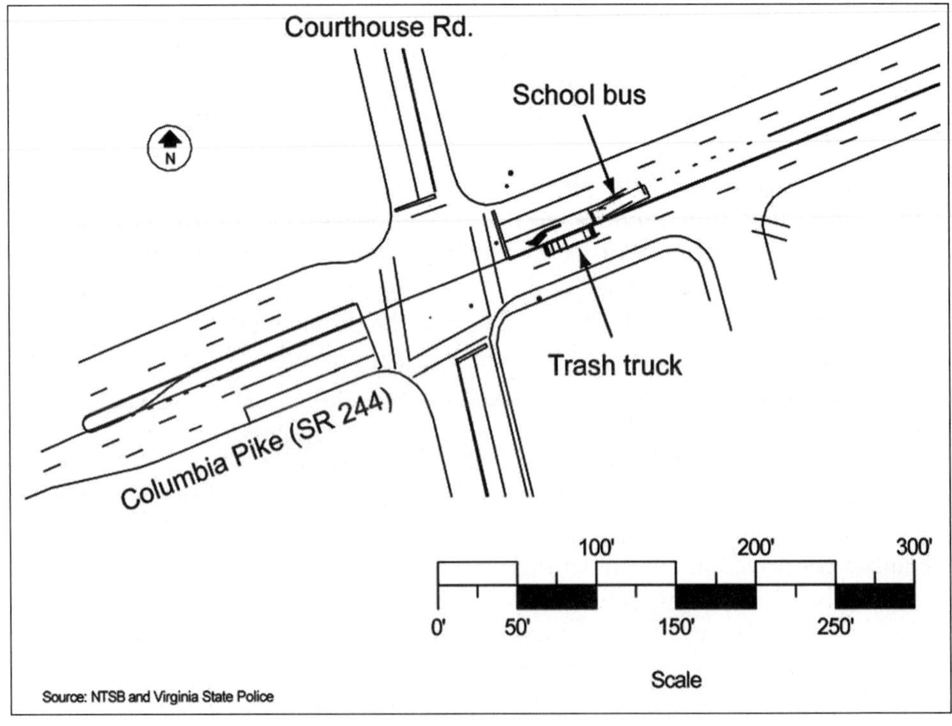

Figure 5 Damage to the school bus

Probable Cause

The National Transportation Safety Board determines that the probable cause of this accident was the school bus driver's encroachment into the trash truck's lane and the trash truck driver's failure to maintain proper lane position, for undetermined reasons, causing the front-left sides of the two vehicles to collide and the vehicles to sideswipe each other.

The complete National Transportation Safety Board report is available and may be downloaded from the Technology Resources Website, www.pearsonhighered.com/goldman, together with selected exhibits.

SOURCE: http://www.ntsb.gov/publictn/2008/HAB0801.pdf

CASE 7: NEW YORK AIRPLANE CRASH

The comprehensive case study is based on actual facts as reported in a National Transportation Safety Board (NTSB) report. Content has been edited and reproduced in the words of the report to provide as much authenticity as possible. Figures are reproduced from the same report. Some liberty has been taken with the identity of the parties, and no names used represent or are actual parties involved in the tragic accident reported. We use an actual incident to allow you to perform basic legal and factual research that will present actual information that would be found in a real case on which you might in the future work.

Aircraft Accident
Clarence Center, New York
February 12, 2009

Abstract

On February 12, 2009, about 2217 (10:17 p.m.) eastern standard time, a Colgan Air, Inc., Bombardier DHC-8-400, N200WQ, operating as Continental Connection flight 3407, was on an instrument approach to Buffalo-Niagara International Airport, Buffalo, New York, when it crashed into a residence in Clarence Center, New York, about 5 nautical miles northeast of the airport. The 2 pilots, 2 flight attendants, and 45 passengers aboard the airplane were killed, one person on the ground was killed, and the airplane was destroyed by impact forces and a post crash fire.

EXECUTIVE SUMMARY

On February 12, 2009, about 2217 eastern standard time, a Colgan Air, Inc., Bombardier DHC-8-400, N200WQ, operating as Continental Connection flight 3407, was on an instrument approach to Buffalo-Niagara International Airport, Buffalo, New York, when it crashed into a residence in Clarence Center, New York, about 5 nautical miles northeast of the airport. The 2 pilots, 2 flight attendants, and 45 passengers aboard the airplane were killed, one person on the ground was killed, and the airplane was destroyed by impact forces and a post-crash fire. The flight was operating under the provisions of 14 *Code of Federal Regulations* Part 121. Night visual meteorological conditions prevailed at the time of the accident.

The home base of operations for both the captain and the first officer was Liberty International Airport (EWR), Newark, New Jersey. On February 11, 2009, the captain had completed a 2-day trip sequence, with the final flight of the trip arriving at EWR at 1544. Also that day, the first officer began her commute from her home near Seattle, Washington, to EWR at 1951 Pacific standard time (PST), arriving at EWR (via Memphis International Airport [MEM], Memphis, Tennessee) on the day of the accident at 0623. The captain and the first officer were both observed in Colgan's crew room on February 12 before their scheduled report time of 1330. The flight crew's first two scheduled flights of the day, from EWR to Greater Rochester International Airport (ROC), Rochester, New York, and back, had been canceled because of high winds at EWR and the resulting ground delays at the airport.

The company dispatch release for flight 3407 was issued at 1800 and showed an estimated departure time of 1910 and an estimated en route time of 53 minutes. The airplane to be used for flight 3407, N200WQ, arrived at EWR at 1854. A first officer whose flight arrived at EWR at 1853 saw, as he exited his airplane, the flight 3407 captain and first officer walking toward the accident airplane. The airplane's aircraft communications addressing and reporting system (ACARS) showed a departure clearance request at 1930 and pushback from the gate at 1945. According to the cockpit voice recorder (CVR) recording, the EWR ground controller provided taxi instructions for the flight at 2030:28, which the first officer acknowledged.

About 2041:35, the first officer stated, "I'm ready to be in the hotel room," to which the captain replied, "I feel bad for you." She continued, "this is one of those times that if I felt like this when I was at home there's no way I would have come all the way out here." She then stated, "if I call in sick now I've got to put myself in a hotel until I feel better... we'll see how... it feels flying. If the pressure's just too much... I could always call in tomorrow at least I'm in a hotel on the company's buck but we'll see. I'm pretty tough." The captain responded by stating that the first officer could try an over-the-counter herbal supplement, drink orange juice, or take vitamin C.

The CVR recorded the tower controller clearing the airplane for takeoff about 2118:23. The first officer acknowledged the clearance, and the captain stated, "alright cleared for takeoff it's mine." According to the dispatch release, the intended cruise altitude for the flight was 16,000 feet mean sea level (msl) The flight data recorder (FDR) showed that, during the climb to altitude, the propeller deice and airframe deice equipment were turned on (the pitot static deicing equipment had been turned on before takeoff) and the autopilot was engaged.

The airplane reached its cruising altitude of 16,000 feet about 2134:44. The cruise portion of flight was routine and uneventful. The CVR recorded the captain and the first officer engaged in an almost continuous conversation throughout that portion of the flight, but these conversations did not conflict with the sterile cockpit rule, which prohibits nonessential conversations within the cockpit during critical phases of flight. About 2149:18, the CVR recorded the captain making a sound similar to a yawn. About 1 minute later, the captain interrupted his own conversation to point out, to the first officer, traffic that was crossing left to right. About 2150:42, the first officer reported the winds to be from 250° at 15 knots gusting to 23 knots; afterward, the captain stated that runway 23 would be used for the landing.

About 2153:40, the first officer briefed the airspeeds for landing with the flaps at 15° (flaps 15) as 118 knots (reference landing speed [Vref]) and 114 knots (go-around speed [Vga]), and the captain acknowledged this information. About 2156:26, the first officer stated, "might be easier on my ears if we start going down sooner." About 2156:36, the captain instructed the first officer to "get discretion to twelve [thousand feet]." Less than 1 minute later, a controller from Cleveland Center cleared the flight to descend to 11,000 feet, and the first officer acknowledged the clearance.

About 2203:38, the Cleveland Center controller instructed the flight crew to contact BUF approach control, and the first officer acknowledged this instruction. The first officer made initial contact with BUF approach control about 2203:53, stating that the flight was descending from 12,000 to 11,000 feet with automatic terminal information service (ATIS) information "romeo," and the approach controller provided the airport altimeter setting and told the crew to plan an instrument landing system (ILS) approach to runway 23.

About 2204:16, the captain began the approach briefing. About 2205:01, the approach controller cleared the flight crew to descend and maintain 6,000 feet, and the first officer acknowledged the clearance. About 30 seconds later, the captain continued the approach briefing, during which he repeated the airspeeds for a flaps 15 landing. FDR data showed that the airplane descended through 10,000 feet about 2206:37. From that point on, the flight crew was required to observe the sterile cockpit rule.

About 2207:14, the CVR recorded the first officer making a sound similar to a yawn. About 2208:41 and 2209:12, the approach controller cleared the flight crew to descend and maintain 5,000 and 4,000 feet, respectively, and the first officer acknowledged the clearances. Afterward, the captain asked the first officer about her ears, and she indicated that they were stuffy and popping.

About 2210:23, the first officer asked whether ice had been accumulating on the windshield, and the captain replied that ice was present on his side of the windshield and asked whether ice was present on her windshield side. The first officer responded, "lots of ice." The captain then stated, "that's the most I've seen—most ice I've seen on the leading edges in a long time. In a while anyway I should say." About 10 seconds later, the captain and the first officer began a conversation that was unrelated to their flying duties. During that conversation, the first officer indicated that she had accumulated more actual flight time in icing conditions on her first day of initial operating experience (IOE) with

Colgan than she had before her employment with the company. She also stated that, when other company first officers were "complaining" about not yet having upgraded to captain, she was thinking that she "wouldn't mind going through a winter in the northeast before [upgrading] to captain." The first officer explained that, before IOE, she had "never seen icing conditions . . . never deiced . . . never experienced any of that."

> About 2212:18, the approach controller cleared the flight crew to descend and maintain 2,300 feet, and the first officer acknowledged the clearance. Afterward, the captain and the first officer performed flight-related duties but also continued the conversation that was unrelated to their flying duties. About 2212:44, the approach controller cleared the flight crew to turn left onto a heading of 330°. About 2213:25 and 2213:36, the captain called for the descent and approach checklists, respectively, which the first officer performed. About 2214:09, the approach controller cleared the flight crew to turn left onto a heading of 310°, and the autopilot's altitude hold mode became active about 1 second later as the airplane was approaching the preselected altitude of 2,300 feet. The airplane reached this altitude about 2214:30; the airspeed was about 180 knots at the time.

About 2215:06, the captain called for the flaps to be moved to the 5° position, and the CVR recorded a sound similar to flap handle movement. Afterward, the approach controller cleared the flight crew to turn left onto a heading of 260° and maintain 2,300 feet until established on the localizer for the ILS approach to runway 23. The first officer acknowledged the clearance.

The captain began to slow the airplane less than 3 miles from the outer marker to establish the appropriate airspeed before landing. According to FDR data, the engine power levers were reduced to about 42° (flight idle was 35°) about 2216:00, and both engines' torque values were at minimum thrust about 2216:02. The approach controller then instructed the flight crew to contact the BUF air traffic control tower (ATCT) controller. The first officer acknowledged this instruction, which was the last communication between the flight crew and air traffic control (ATC). Afterward, the CVR recorded sounds similar to landing gear handle deployment and landing gear movement, and the FDR showed that the propeller condition levers had been moved forward to their maximum RPM position and that pitch trim in the airplane- nose-up direction had been applied by the autopilot.

About 2216:21, the first officer told the captain that the gear was down; at that time, the airspeed was about 145 knots. Afterward, FDR data showed that additional pitch trim in the airplane-nose-up direction had been applied by the autopilot and that an "ice detected" message appeared on the engine display in the cockpit. About the same time, the captain called for the flaps to be set to 15° and for the before landing checklist. The CVR then recorded a sound similar to flap handle movement, and FDR data showed that the flaps had been selected to 10°. FDR data also showed that the airspeed at the time was about 135 knots.

At 2216:27.4, the CVR recorded a sound similar to the stick shaker. (The stick shaker warns a pilot of an impending wing aerodynamic stall through vibrations on the control column, providing tactile and aural cues.) The CVR also recorded a sound similar to the autopilot disconnect horn, which repeated until the end of the recording. FDR data showed that, when the autopilot disengaged, the airplane was at an airspeed of 131 knots. FDR data showed that the control columns moved aft at 2216:27.8 and that the engine power levers were advanced to about 70° (rating detent was 80°) 1 second later. The CVR then recorded a sound similar to increased engine power, and FDR data showed that engine power had increased to about 75 percent torque.

FDR data also showed that, while engine power was increasing, the airplane pitched up; rolled to the left, reaching a roll angle of 45° left wing down; and then rolled to the right. As the airplane rolled to the right through wings level, the stick pusher activated (about 2216:34), and flaps 0 was selected. (The Q400 stick pusher applies an airplane-nose-down control column input to decrease the wing angle-of-attack [AOA] after an aerodynamic stall.) About 2216:37, the first officer told the captain that she had put the flaps up. FDR data confirmed that the flaps had begun to retract by 2216:38; at that time, the airplane's airspeed was about 100 knots. FDR data also showed that the roll angle reached 105° right wing down before the airplane began to roll back to the left and the stick pusher activated a second time (about 2216:40). At the time, the airplane's pitch angle was −1°.

About 2216:42, the CVR recorded the captain making a grunting sound. FDR data showed that the roll angle had reached about 35° left wing down before the airplane began to roll again to the right. Afterward, the first officer asked whether she should put the landing gear up, and the captain stated, "gear up" and an expletive. The airplane's pitch and roll angles had reached about 25° airplane nose down and 100° right wing down, respectively, when the airplane entered a steep descent. The stick pusher activated a third time (about 2216:50). FDR data showed that the flaps were fully retracted about 2216:52. About the same time, the CVR recorded the captain stating, "we're down," and a sound of a thump. The airplane impacted a single-family home (where the ground fatality occurred), and a postcrash fire ensued. The CVR recording ended about 2216:54.

ABBREVIATIONS

AC	advisory circular
ACARS	aircraft communications addressing and reporting system
AFM	airplane flight manual
agl	above ground level
AOA	angle-of-attack
ATC	air traffic control
ATCT	air traffic control tower
ATIS	automatic terminal information service
ATOS	air transportation oversight system
BTV	Burlington International Airport
BUF	Buffalo-Niagara International Airport
CVR	cockpit voice recorder
CWA	Center Weather Advisory
eice	en route ice accumulation
FDR	flight data recorder
IFR	instrument flight rules
ILS	instrument landing system
msl	mean sea level
nm	nautical mile
PIC	pilot-in-command
SIC	second-in-command

The complete National Transportation Safety Board report is available and may be downloaded from the Technology Resources Website, www.pearsonhighered .com/goldman, together with selected exhibits and simulation, or in PDF format.

SOURCE: http://www.ntsb.gov/publictn/2010/AAR1001.pdf

APPENDIX IV

ABACUSLAW TUTORIAL

HOW DO I DOWNLOAD ABACUSLAW FROM THE ABACUSLAW WEBSITE?

Some Internet browsers may give you a choice to **Save** or to **Run.**

You may download and **save** the **installer program** or immediately **run** it on your computer. Depending on the speed of your Internet connection, it may take from 1 to 10 minutes. It is recommended that you save the program and then run the program after closing your web browser and antivirus program. When you save the program, make a note where the program was saved so you can locate it and install it at a later time.

For example, the location where the program is saved includes

Drive designation**\Folder** name**\File**name

or

C:\Downloads\AbacusLaw2010ALL.exe

The location C:\Downloads\AbacusLaw2010ALL.exe is called the **path.**

When you download the program, record the path for your computer below.

*Enter your Drive:*______:\

*Enter your download folder:*______\

File name: AbacusLaw2010ALL.exe

DOWNLOADING AND INSTALLING ABACUSLAW FROM WEBSITE

GOAL	ACTION	RESULT
DOWNLOAD AND SAVE ABACUSLAW INSTALLER PROGRAM FROM ABACUSLAW WEBSITE	**START** Your Internet web browser **ENTER** http://media.pearsoncmg.com/ph/chet/chet_goldman_techresources_1/ for 120-day demo or www.abacuslaw.com for 30-day demo **CLICK** *Save*	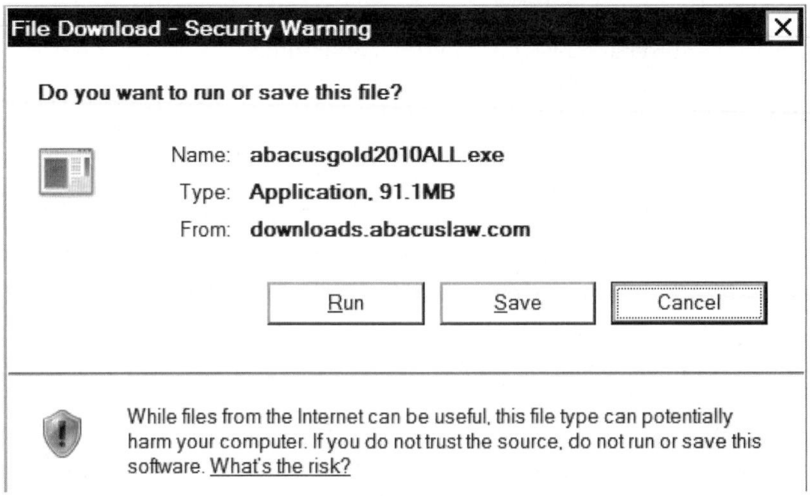 File Download - Security Warning **Do you want to run or save this file?** Name: **abacusgold2010ALL.exe** Type: **Application, 91.1MB** From: **downloads.abacuslaw.com** Run Save Cancel While files from the Internet can be useful, this file type can potentially harm your computer. If you do not trust the source, do not run or save this software. What's the risk?

Reproduced from: *AbacusLaw: A Hands-On Tutorial and Guide*, by Thomas F. Goldman, Pearson/Prentice Hall, copyright 2011.

When you run the installer program, it installs the actual program files, sets up the necessary AbacusLaw folder, and adds necessary entries on your computer hard drive to allow it to run and function.

HOW DO I VERIFY MY FIRM INFORMATION?

Firm information is needed to use the Practice Manager. The basic firm information is entered as part of the AbacusLaw installation registration and verification process. The firm information is provided to AbacusLaw when the program is purchased, a demo version requested, or the academic version is preregistered. It is a good idea to check the accuracy of the information and make any necessary changes or update the information. Additional information about the firm may need to be entered during the Abacus Accounting installation and setup.

Verifying My Firm Information

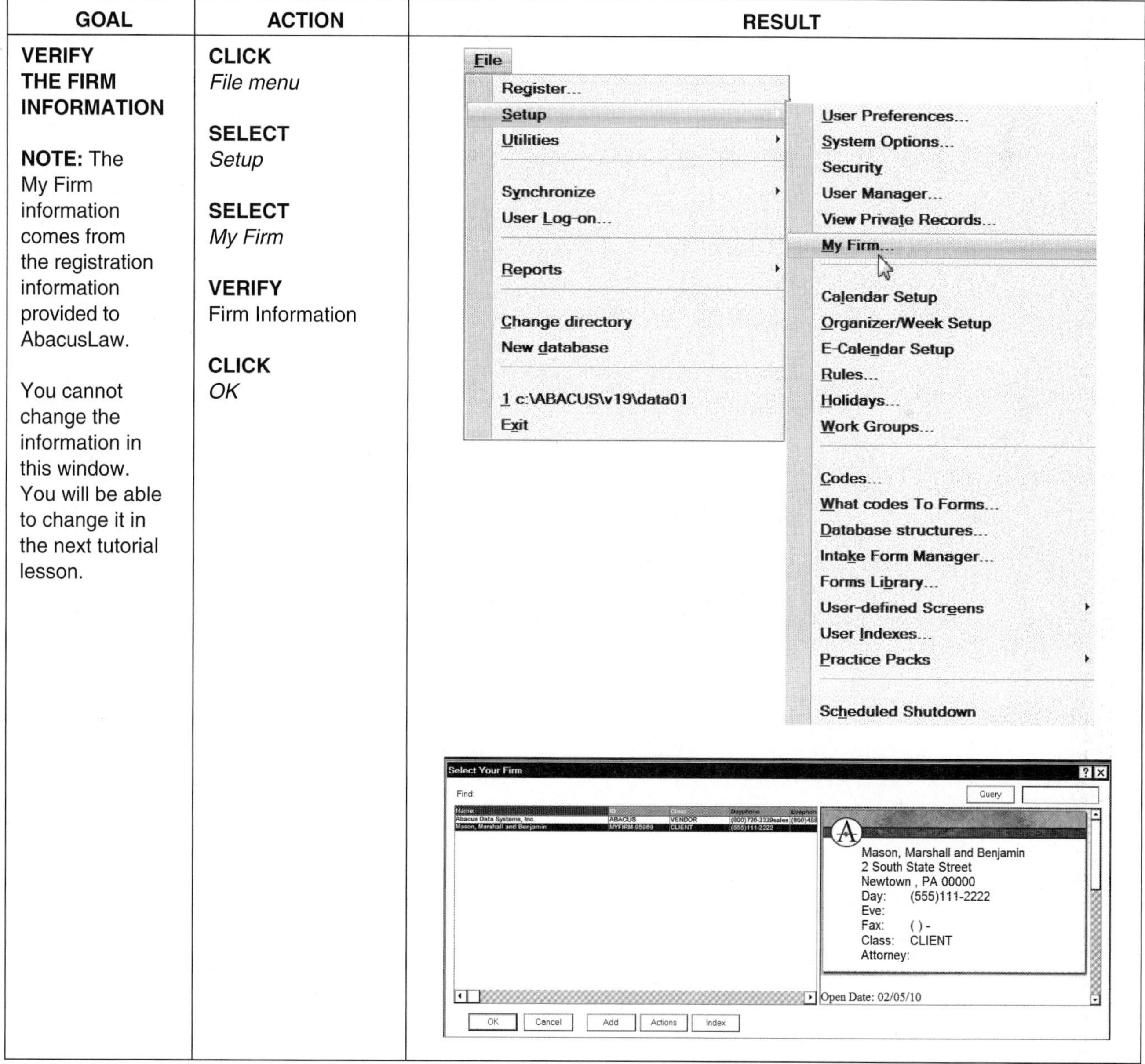

GOAL	ACTION	RESULT
VERIFY THE FIRM INFORMATION **NOTE:** The My Firm information comes from the registration information provided to AbacusLaw. You cannot change the information in this window. You will be able to change it in the next tutorial lesson.	**CLICK** *File menu* **SELECT** *Setup* **SELECT** *My Firm* **VERIFY** Firm Information **CLICK** *OK*	

Continue with the following tutorial before exiting the program.

HOW DO I CHANGE THE FIRM INFORMATION?

Firm information is shown in a Names window like all contacts and names, including clients, vendors, opposing counsel, and parties. Names window can be accessed using the Names menu, Browse command, or the Names Browse window.

Substitute your personal information. Fill in the information before starting.

	TUTORIAL INFORMATION	YOUR INFORMATION
Firm Name	Mason, Marshall and Benjamin	
Attorney	Owen Mason	
ID	OM	
Email	mason@masonmarshallandbenjamin.com	
Attorney	Ariel Marshall	
ID	AM	
Address	138 North Street	
City	Newtown	
State	PA	
Zip	18940	
Day Phone	555 111 2222	
Fax	555 111 3333	
Printer Reports	HP LASERJET 4250	
Printer Labels	SMARTLABEL PRINTER	
Printer Envelopes	HP LASERJET 4050	
Word Processor		
Word Processor Executable	C:\programfiles\microsoft office\winword	

CHANGE FIRM INFORMATION ON THE NAMES WINDOW

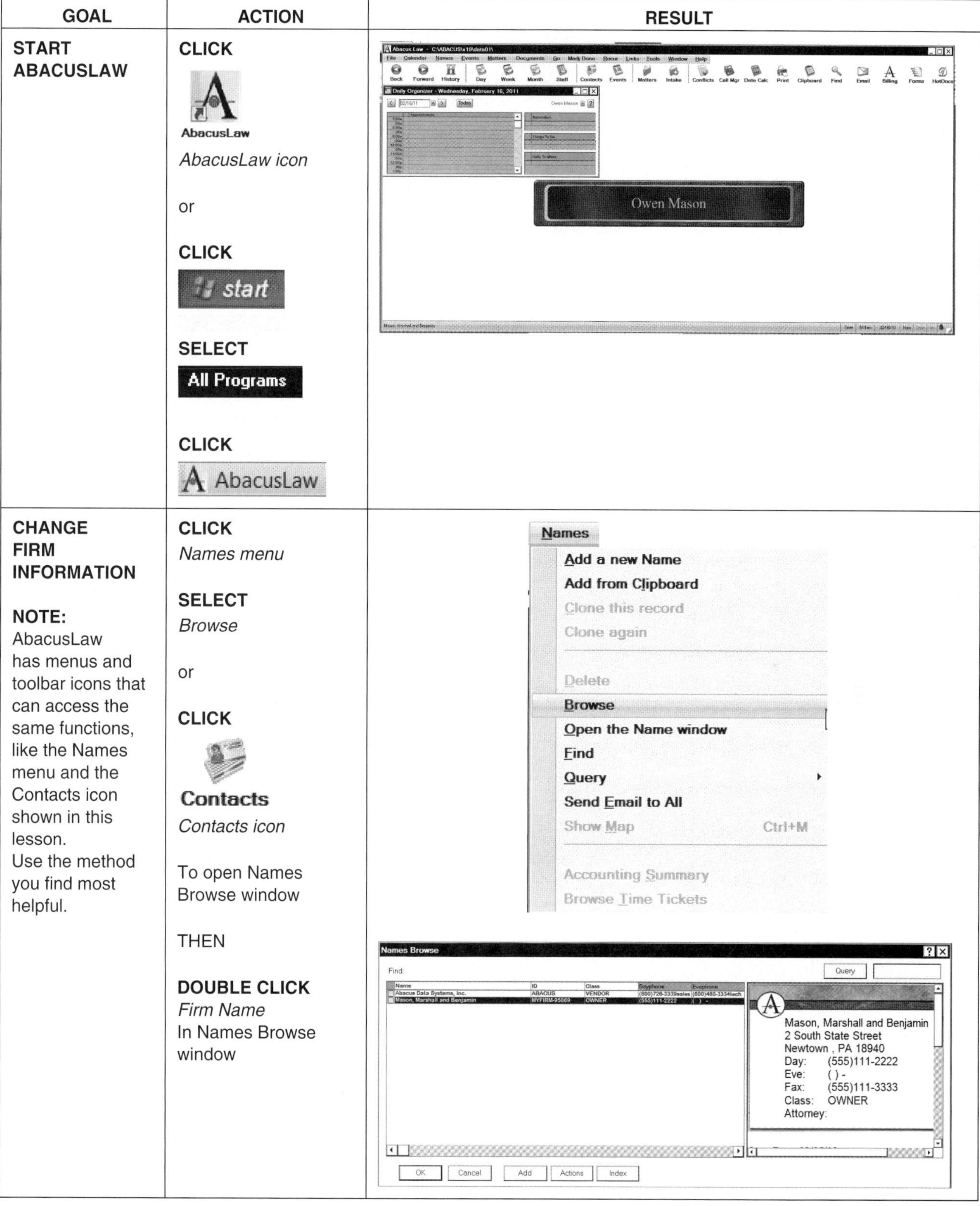

GOAL	ACTION	RESULT
START ABACUSLAW	**CLICK** AbacusLaw *AbacusLaw icon* or **CLICK** start **SELECT** All Programs **CLICK** AbacusLaw	
CHANGE FIRM INFORMATION **NOTE:** AbacusLaw has menus and toolbar icons that can access the same functions, like the Names menu and the Contacts icon shown in this lesson. Use the method you find most helpful.	**CLICK** *Names menu* **SELECT** *Browse* or **CLICK** Contacts *Contacts icon* To open Names Browse window THEN **DOUBLE CLICK** *Firm Name* In Names Browse window	

(continued)

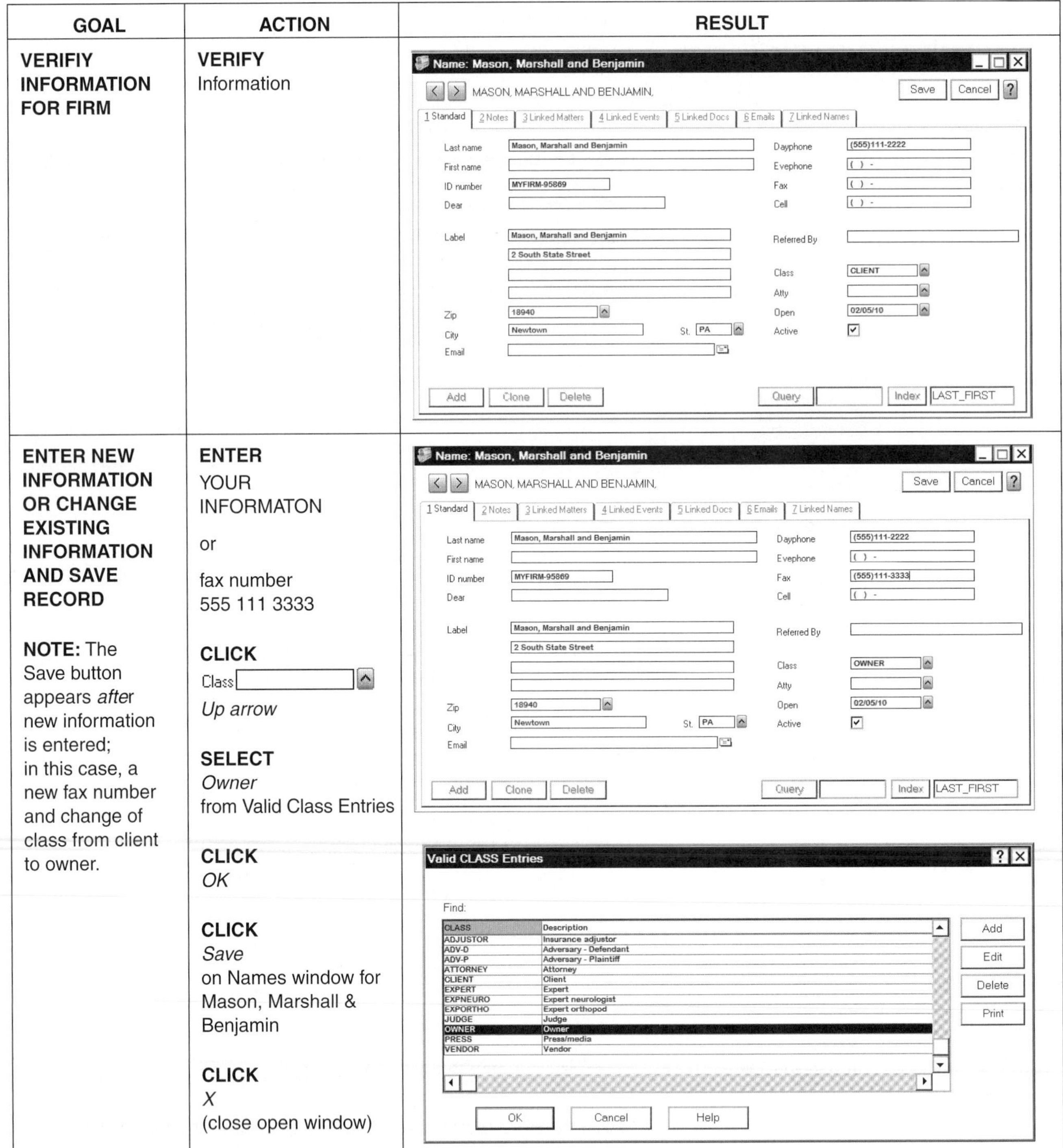

GOAL	ACTION	RESULT
VERIFIY INFORMATION FOR FIRM	**VERIFY** Information	
ENTER NEW INFORMATION OR CHANGE EXISTING INFORMATION AND SAVE RECORD **NOTE:** The Save button appears *after* new information is entered; in this case, a new fax number and change of class from client to owner.	**ENTER** YOUR INFORMATON or fax number 555 111 3333 **CLICK** Class *Up arrow* **SELECT** *Owner* from Valid Class Entries **CLICK** *OK* **CLICK** *Save* on Names window for Mason, Marshall & Benjamin **CLICK** *X* (close open window)	

Continue with the following lesson before exiting the program.

HOW DO I SET UP MY PERSONAL USER INFORMATION?

Each AbacusLaw user may enter his or her personal information, including ID initials used to log on to AbacusLaw, personal email address, and how the program will appear on the desktop when AbacusLaw is started (such as with or without a nameplate). Each user may have a different printer or word processor; these may also be customized for individual users' workstations. In some cases there may be different printers used for documents, labels, and envelopes.

The User Preference window has four tabbed screens for entering preferences: User Info, Appearance, Printing/Email Program, and Queries & Miscellaneous.

User Preferences

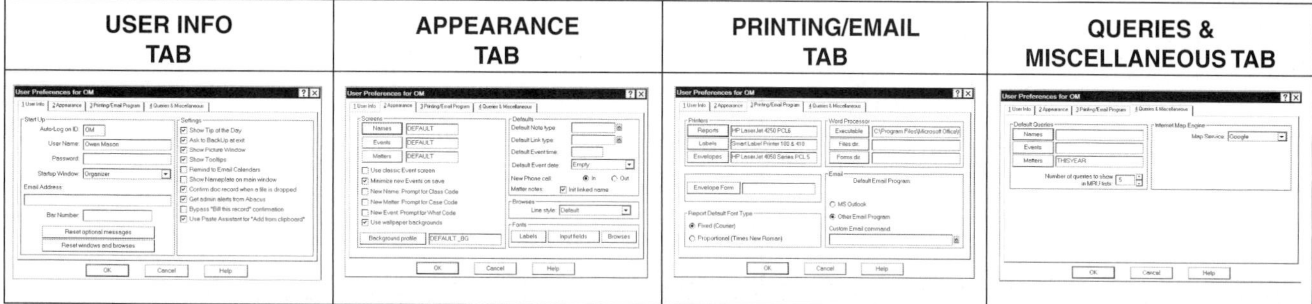

Setting Up Personal Preferences

GOAL	ACTION	RESULT
SET UP YOUR PERSONAL USER PREFERENCES	**CLICK** *File menu* **SELECT** *Setup* **SELECT** *User Preferences*	File Register... Setup Utilities Synchronize User Log-on... Reports Change directory New database 1 C:\ABACUS\v19\data01 2 \\Tomhp-pc\c$\ABACUS\v19\data01 Exit User Preferences... System Options... Security User Manager... View Private Records... My Firm... Calendar Setup Organizer/Week Setup E-Calendar Setup Rules... Holidays... Work Groups... Codes... What codes To Forms... Database structures... Intake Form Manager... Forms Library... User-defined Screens User Indexes... Practice Packs Scheduled Shutdown
ENTER YOUR PERSONAL INFORMATION **NOTE:** You can change the settings at any time by checking or unchecking the settings boxes.	**ENTER YOUR PERSONAL INFORMATION** or *OM* In Auto-Log on ID **ENTER** *Owen Mason* in User Name	User Preferences for OM 1 User Info | 2 Appearance | 3 Printing/Email Program | 4 Queries & Miscellaneous Start Up Auto-Log on ID: OM User Name: Owen Mason Password: Startup Window: Main Menu Main Menu Monthly Calendar Weekly Calendar Organizer Names Matters Events Today's Docs Staff Calendar Email Address: Bar Number: Reset Reset windows and browses Settings Show Tip of the Day Ask to BackUp at exit Show Picture Window Show Tooltips Remind to Email Calendars Show Nameplate on main window Confirm doc record when a file is dropped Get admin alerts from Abacus Bypass "Bill this record" confirmation Use Paste Assistant for "Add from clipboard" OK Cancel Help

(continued)

GOAL	ACTION	RESULT
NOTE: You may personalize the look of the desktop by selecting one of the calendar options, such as organizer selected in this lesson.	**CLICK** Down arrow by Startup Window field **SELECT** *Organizer* **CHECK** *Show Nameplate* on *main window* **CHECK** *Ask to backup at exit*	
SELECT OR ENTER THE NAME OF THE PRINTER YOU USE TO PRINT DOCUMENTS AND REPORTS **NOTE:** Your **default printer** will appear as the Name on the **Print Setup** Window (HP LaserJet 4250PCL6 is shown only as an example). You must enter *your* printer to be able to print AbacusLaw report. Change this by selecting your printer in the Printing Setup window; click on the down arrow at the end of the Name. If you use a different printer for labels or envelopes, repeat the process of selecting the printer.	**CLICK** *Printing/Email Program* tab **CLICK** *Reports* tab In Printers **SELECT** *Your printer for reports* from the Print Setup window **CLICK** *OK* In Print Setup window	User Preferences for OM 1 User Info · 2 Appearance · 3 Printing/Email Program · 4 Queries & Miscellaneous Printers: Reports · Labels · Envelopes Word Processor: Executable Envelope Form Report Default F… · Fixed (Couri… · Proportional **Print Setup** Printer — Name: HP LaserJet 4250 PCL6 · Properties... Status: Toner low; 0 documents waiting Type: HP LaserJet 4250 PCL6 Where: 192.168.2.101 Comment: Paper — Size: Letter · Source: Automatically Select Orientation — Portrait · Landscape Network... · OK · Cancel
SELECT YOUR WORD PROCESSOR FROM YOUR COMPUTER PROGRAM FILES **TIP:** Find your word processor on your computer using Windows Explorer.	**CLICK** *Executable* tab in word processor option on Printing/Email tab **FIND** Path to your word processor using Windows Explorer window	User Preferences for OM 1 User Info · 2 Appearance · 3 Printing/Email Program · 4 Queries & Miscellaneous Printers — Reports: HP LaserJet 4250 PCL6 · Labels: Smart Label Printer 100 & 410 · Envelopes: HP LaserJet 4050 Series PCL 5 Word Processor — Executable: C:\Program Files\Microsoft Office\ · Files dir. · Forms dir. Envelope Form Email — Default Email Program: MS Outlook · Other Email Program · Custom Email command: Report Default Font Type — Fixed (Courier) · Proportional (Times New Roman) OK · Cancel · Help

(continued)

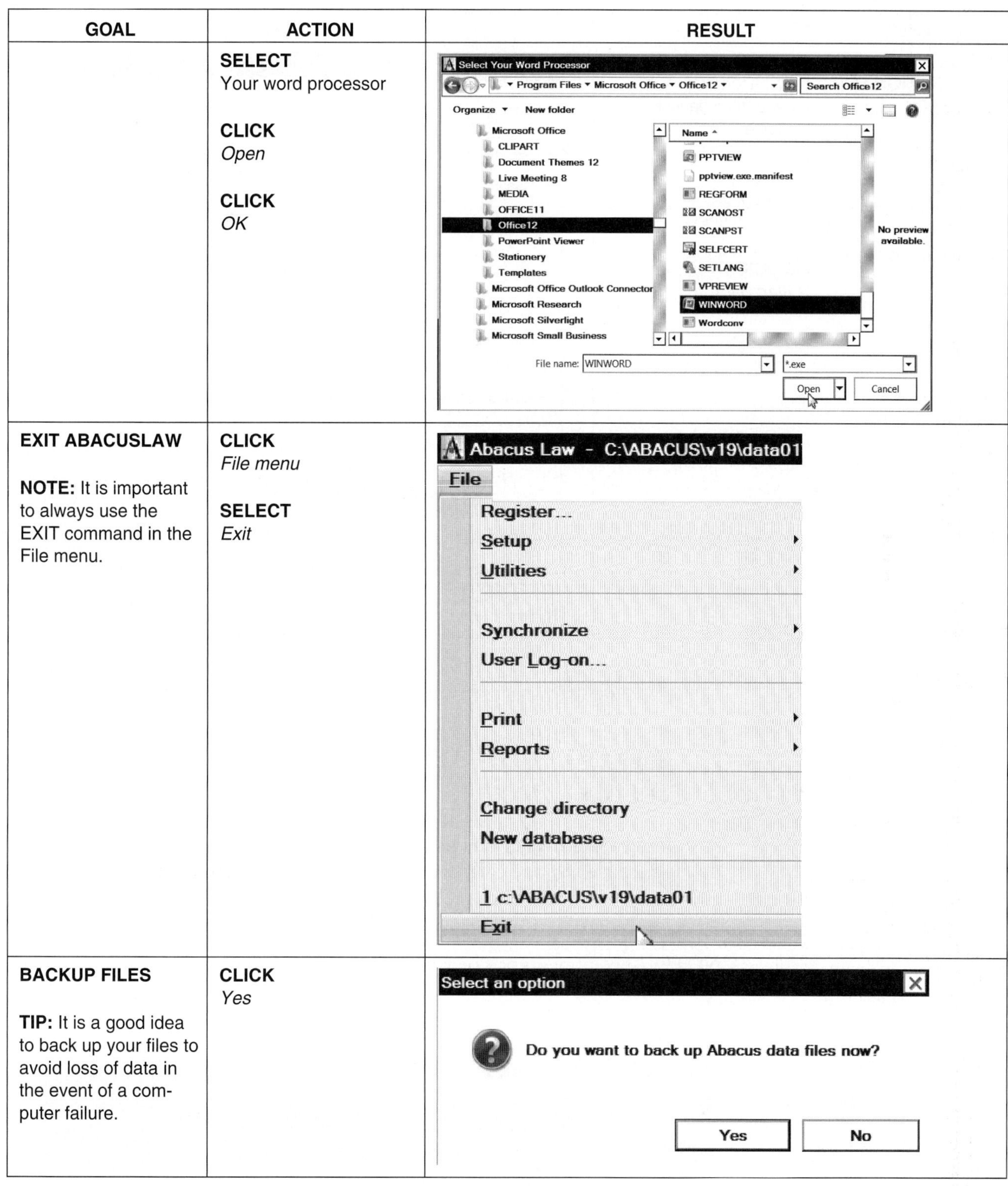

GOAL	ACTION	RESULT
	SELECT Your word processor **CLICK** *Open* **CLICK** *OK*	
EXIT ABACUSLAW **NOTE:** It is important to always use the EXIT command in the File menu.	**CLICK** *File menu* **SELECT** *Exit*	
BACKUP FILES **TIP:** It is a good idea to back up your files to avoid loss of data in the event of a computer failure.	**CLICK** *Yes*	

(continued)

GOAL	ACTION	RESULT
SELECT THE DESTINATION FOR THE BACKUP **TIP:** You should back up to a removable storage device by indicating that device as the DESTINATION in the backup options window. To locate other storage devices connected to your computer, click the DESTINATION button.	**ENTER** Path to your removable backup device or *C:\Abacus* As destination **CLICK** *Start Backup*	**Backup Abacus Files** Directories Destination: C:\ Source: C:\ABACUS\v19\data01\ Number of backup files to retain: 7 Include along with main data ☐ Abacus MessageSlips ☐ Forms .AF files (only recommended if you design forms) ☐ Accounting data ☐ Saved PDF bills (may be huge!) Current file: File Compression Overall Progress Cancel · Start Backup · ☐ Send in email

When you restart AbacusLaw, the changes in user preferences, including the nameplate and daily organizer calendar, will appear on your personal desktop.

HOW DO I ADD APPPOINTMENTS (EVENTS) TO CALENDAR?

Appointments or events may be added for each person or item listed on a calendar. Items added to one calendar view, such as daily calendar, will also be added and shown on the other calendar views. Events may be entered for any person, place, or thing with a WHO code.

NOTE: Appointments or scheduled activity in the calendar are referred to as *events*.

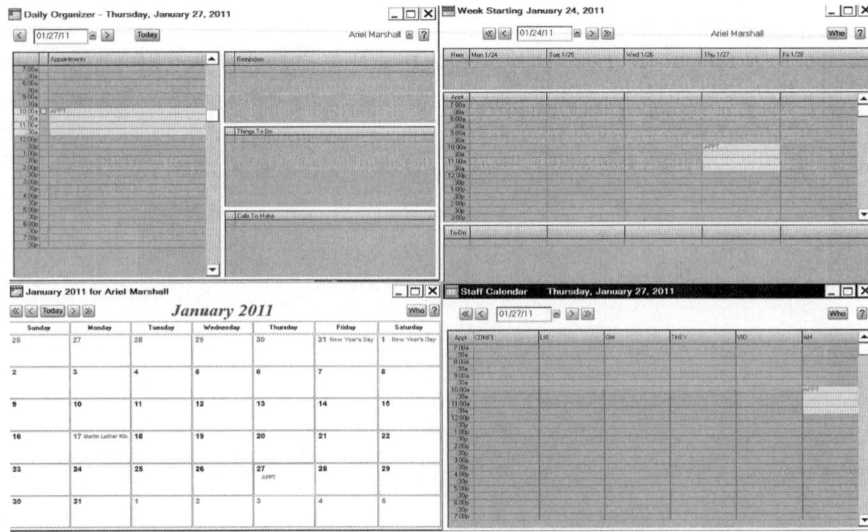

Add an Event to Calendar for Specific Person

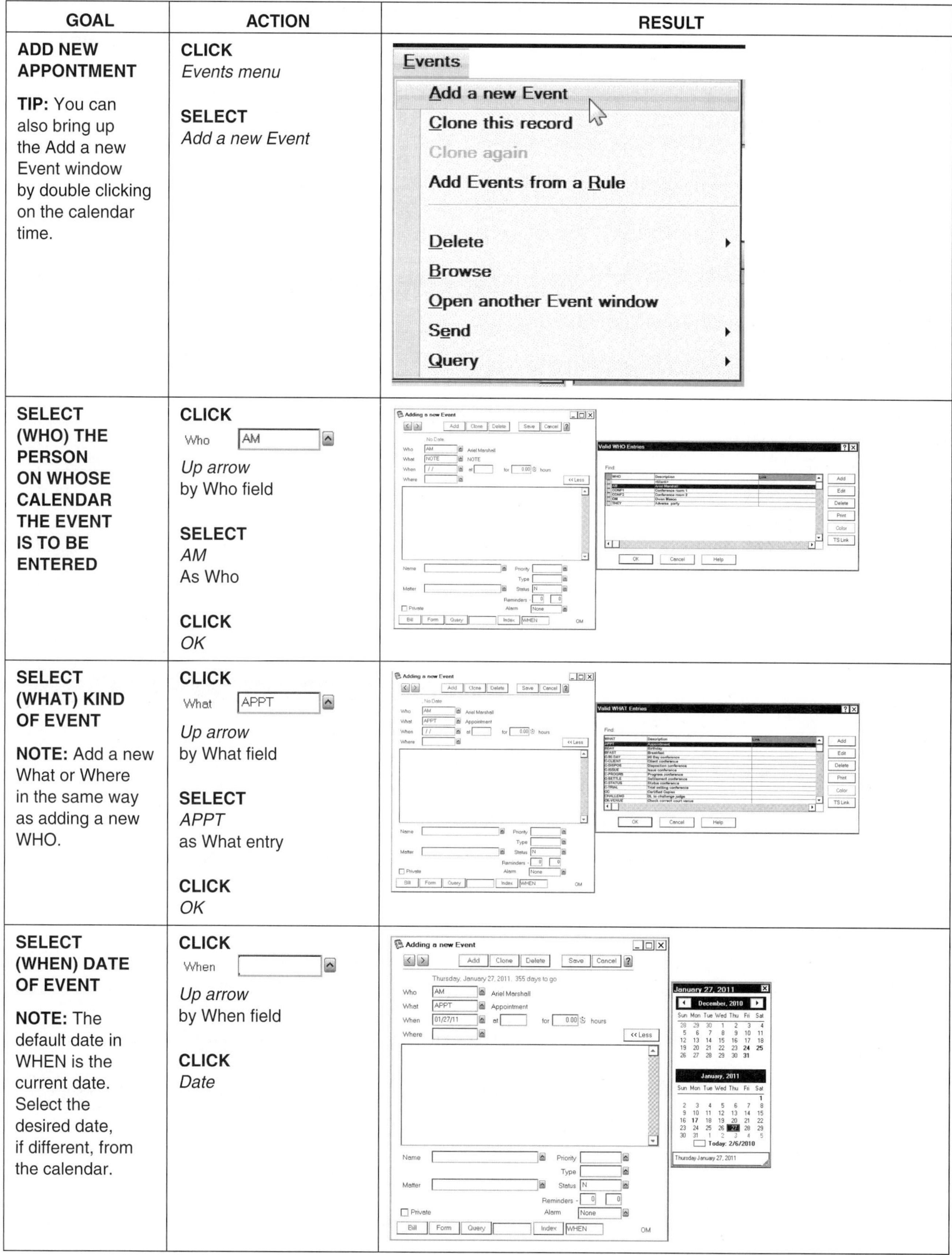

GOAL	ACTION	RESULT
ADD NEW APPONTMENT **TIP:** You can also bring up the Add a new Event window by double clicking on the calendar time.	**CLICK** *Events menu* **SELECT** *Add a new Event*	
SELECT (WHO) THE PERSON ON WHOSE CALENDAR THE EVENT IS TO BE ENTERED	**CLICK** Who AM *Up arrow* by Who field **SELECT** *AM* As Who **CLICK** *OK*	
SELECT (WHAT) KIND OF EVENT **NOTE:** Add a new What or Where in the same way as adding a new WHO.	**CLICK** What APPT *Up arrow* by What field **SELECT** *APPT* as What entry **CLICK** *OK*	
SELECT (WHEN) DATE OF EVENT **NOTE:** The default date in WHEN is the current date. Select the desired date, if different, from the calendar.	**CLICK** When *Up arrow* by When field **CLICK** *Date*	

(continued)

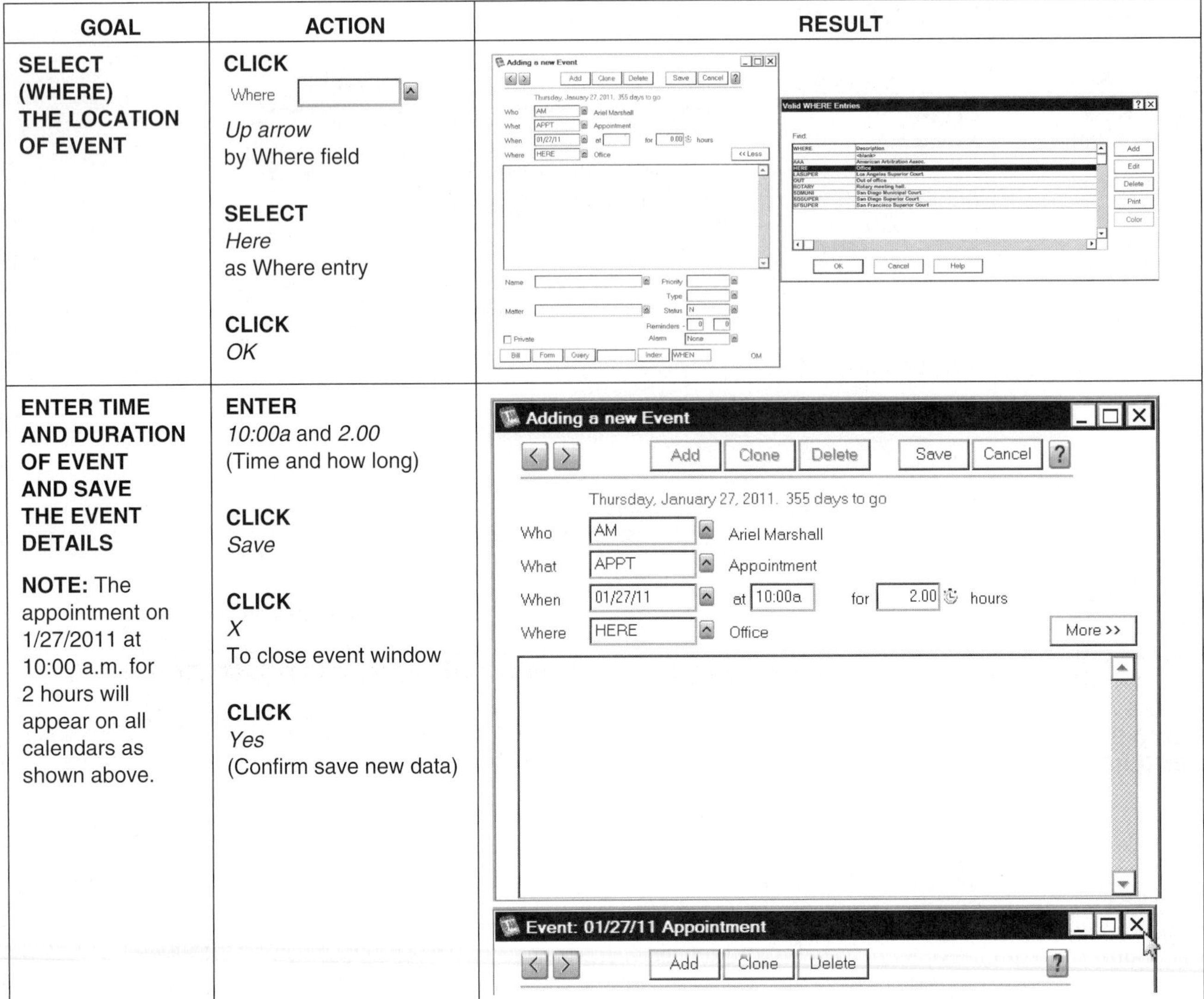

GOAL	ACTION	RESULT
SELECT (WHERE) THE LOCATION OF EVENT	**CLICK** Where *Up arrow* by Where field **SELECT** *Here* as Where entry **CLICK** *OK*	
ENTER TIME AND DURATION OF EVENT AND SAVE THE EVENT DETAILS **NOTE:** The appointment on 1/27/2011 at 10:00 a.m. for 2 hours will appear on all calendars as shown above.	**ENTER** *10:00a* and *2.00* (Time and how long) **CLICK** *Save* **CLICK** *X* To close event window **CLICK** *Yes* (Confirm save new data)	

You may exit the program or continue the next tutorial.

HOW DO I ADD CONTACTS (NAMES)?

A contact (person, firm, client, or counsel) is any name in your address book, email list, or whose information you want to record for future use. It may be information that has been kept in the firm's or personal address book on individual index cards or in a paper conflicts file or note cards. It may be current clients, prospective clients, other attorneys and paralegals, or other professionals or friends. All of the contacts' names and information when entered into the AbacusLaw program is saved and stored in the Names database. You can add new names and contacts at any time or during the new matter setup.

Adding Contacts (Names)

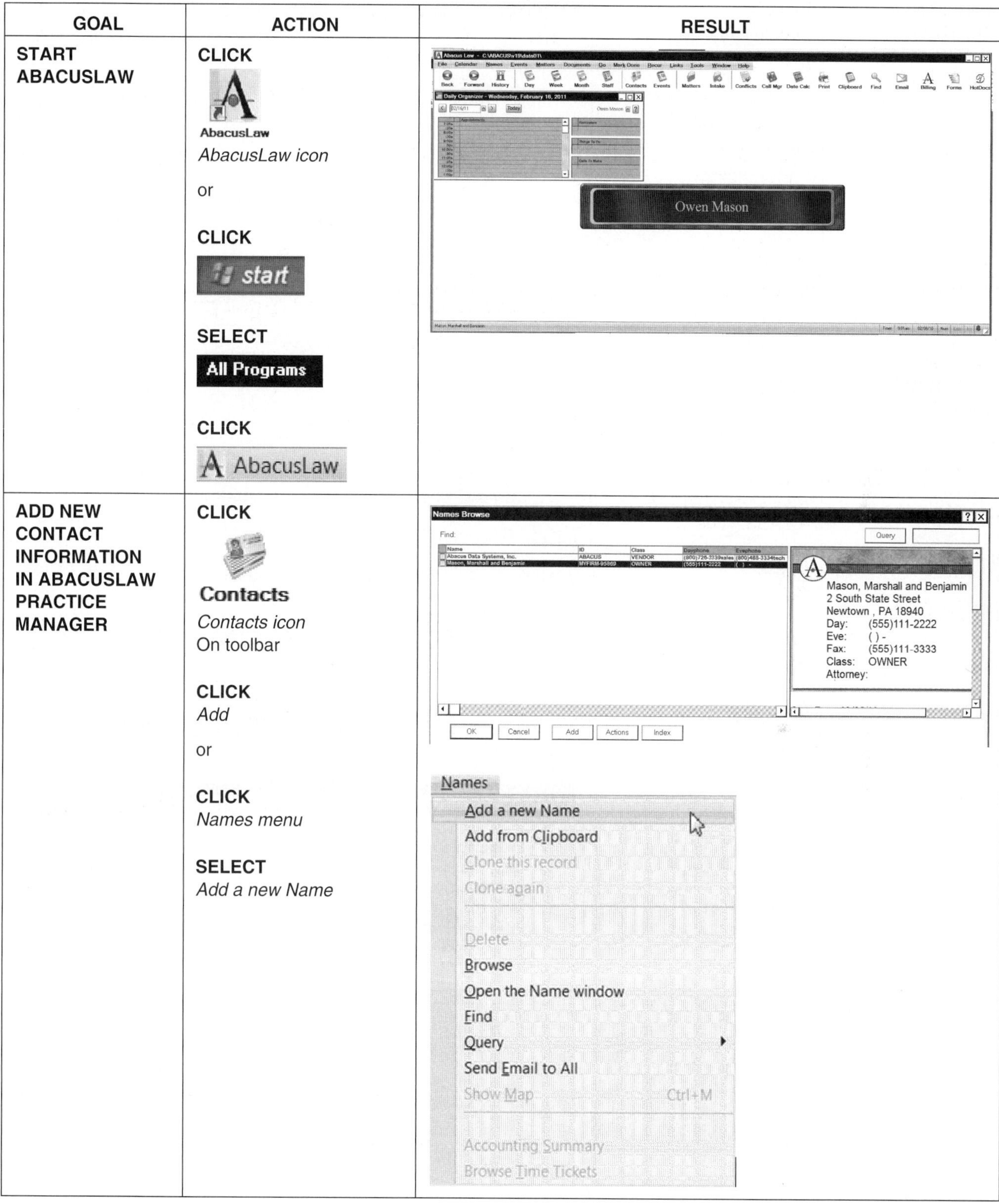

GOAL	ACTION	RESULT
START ABACUSLAW	CLICK AbacusLaw *AbacusLaw icon* or CLICK start SELECT All Programs CLICK AbacusLaw	Owen Mason
ADD NEW CONTACT INFORMATION IN ABACUSLAW PRACTICE MANAGER	CLICK Contacts *Contacts icon* On toolbar CLICK *Add* or CLICK *Names menu* SELECT *Add a new Name*	Names Browse Names Add a new Name Add from Clipboard Clone this record Clone again Delete Browse Open the Name window Find Query Send Email to All Show Map Ctrl+M Accounting Summary Browse Time Tickets

(*continued*)

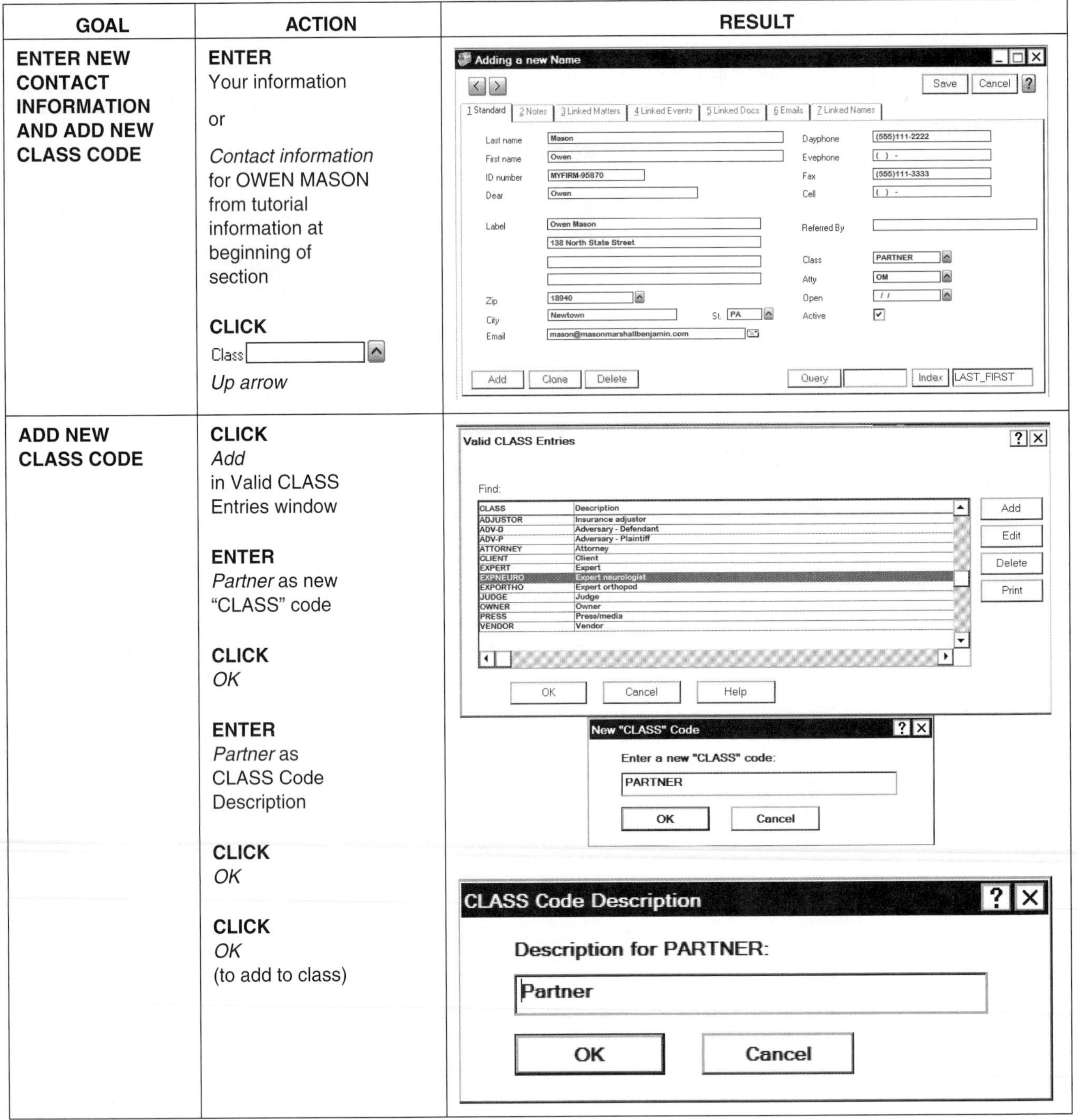

GOAL	ACTION	RESULT
ENTER NEW CONTACT INFORMATION AND ADD NEW CLASS CODE	**ENTER** Your information or *Contact information* for OWEN MASON from tutorial information at beginning of section **CLICK** Class [ ] ^ *Up arrow*	
ADD NEW CLASS CODE	**CLICK** *Add* in Valid CLASS Entries window **ENTER** *Partner* as new "CLASS" code **CLICK** *OK* **ENTER** *Partner* as CLASS Code Description **CLICK** *OK* **CLICK** *OK* (to add to class)	

(*continued*)

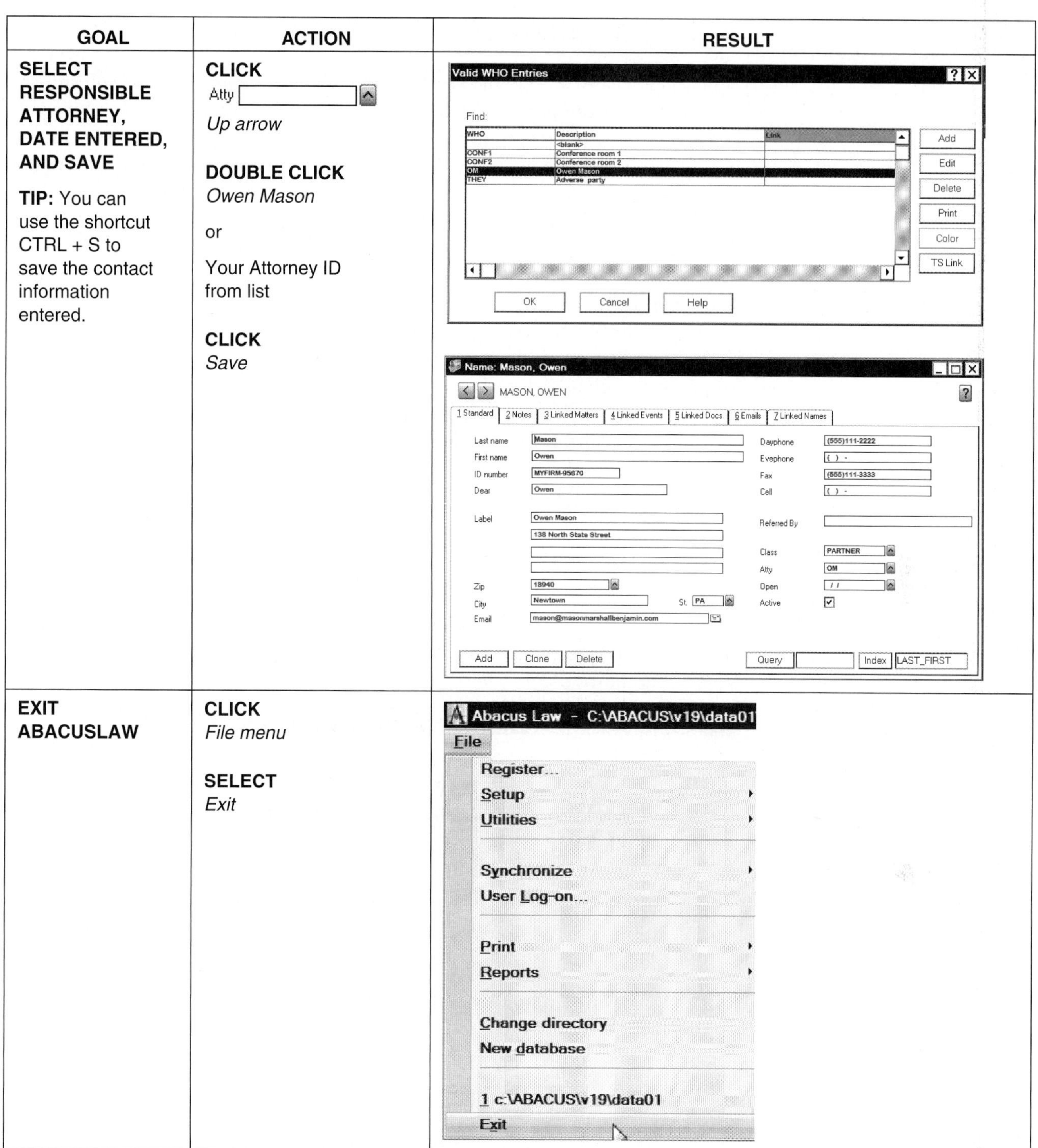

GOAL	ACTION	RESULT
SELECT RESPONSIBLE ATTORNEY, DATE ENTERED, AND SAVE **TIP:** You can use the shortcut CTRL + S to save the contact information entered.	**CLICK** Atty *Up arrow* **DOUBLE CLICK** *Owen Mason* or Your Attorney ID from list **CLICK** *Save*	
EXIT ABACUSLAW	**CLICK** *File menu* **SELECT** *Exit*	

SETTING UP A NEW MATTER

A matter is a case for a client. There may be a single client for whom you are handling a number of matters; for example, preparing a will, defending a breach of contract action, and representing the client seeking damages for a personal injury from a motor vehicle accident. You only need to input the client information once and then use the same information in each matter as it is set up.

All of the information about the case may be entered using the Matters window, including items related to the matter, like notes, people, documents, and events. These are referred to in AbacusLaw as *linked: linked notes*, *linked names*, *linked events*, and *linked documents*.

Depending on the type of matter (kind of case or area of law), you may use the generic Matter window to enter the information or use an AbacusLaw add-on product, such as the personal injury practice pack intake forms and specialty matters windows. The basic information is the same, but the specialty practice screens have additional linked information.

In this tutorial you will need to enter the information about the court in which the case will be filed.

The Jurisdiction ID

To be able to enter a code in the Jurisdiction ID, the court must be listed in the Valid Court entries. If the specific court is not listed, you will need to add the court and jurisdiction information, and then add the desired court from the list of Valid Court entries.

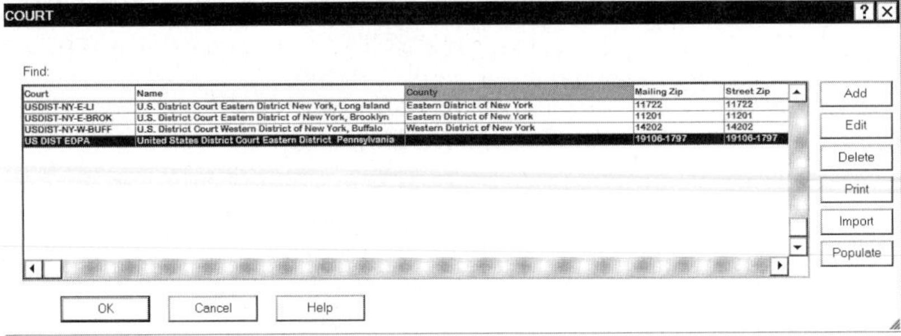

TIP: If you will be using the timekeeping functions, it is a good practice to set up the client or other party, such as the insurance company or corporation who is paying the legal fees, as the "bill to" party when setting up the individual case matter.

HOW DO I ADD CLIENTS USING AN INTAKE FORM?

Client information can be entered as contact information using the Names window or as part of a new case setup, as shown above. Information may be entered using a new contact or new matter intake form, which contains the basic contact information and details of the new contact or matter.

Adding Clients Using PI Case Intake Form

GOAL	ACTION	RESULT
ADD NEW MATTER AND CLIENT INFORMATION USING PI CASE INTAKE FORM **NOTE:** Many forms can be accessed in different ways including the menu bar or toolbar icon, as well as from within other forms.	**CLICK**  Intake *Intake icon* **CLICK** *PI Case Intake Form* or **CLICK** *Matters menu* **SELECT** *Intake Forms* **SELECT** *PI Case Intake Form*	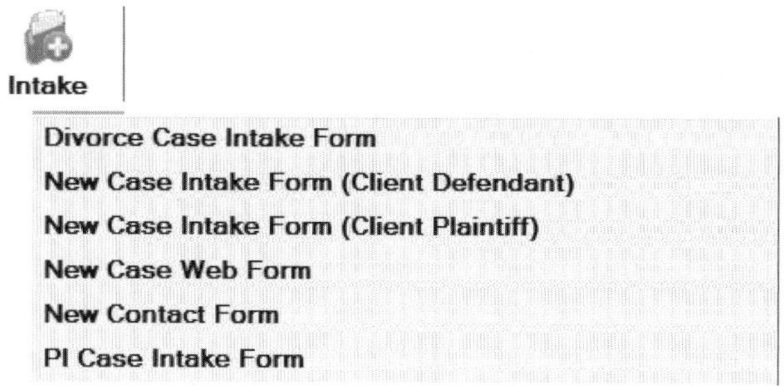 Intake Divorce Case Intake Form New Case Intake Form (Client Defendant) New Case Intake Form (Client Plaintiff) New Case Web Form New Contact Form PI Case Intake Form or Matters Add a new Matter Clone this record Clone again Intake Forms Delete Browse Open the Matter window Find Query Accounting Summary Browse Time Tickets Download and import web data... Import web data Intake Form Manager... Divorce Case Intake Form New Case Intake Form (Client Defendant) New Case Intake Form (Client Plaintiff) New Case Web Form New Contact Form PI Case Intake Form 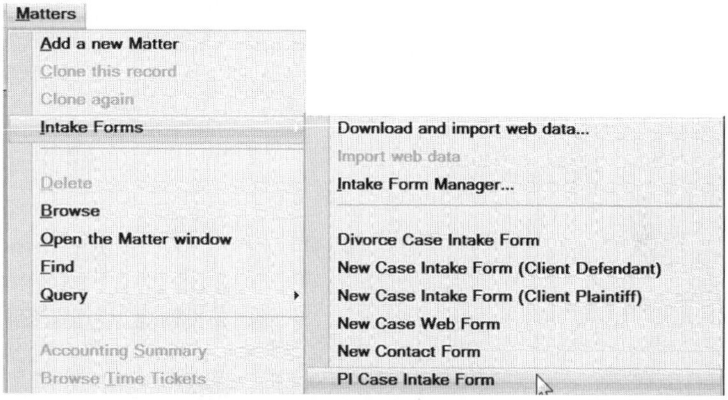
ENTER NEW CLIENT AND MATTER INFORMATION **ENTER OPPOSING PARTY INFORMATION** **NOTE:** The top half of the intake form is the same information entered in the New Matter screen and the New Names input screen. **NOTE:** After you save the intake form, a Billing Information screen will open, as shown below.	**ENTER** Information as shown **CLICK** *Save*	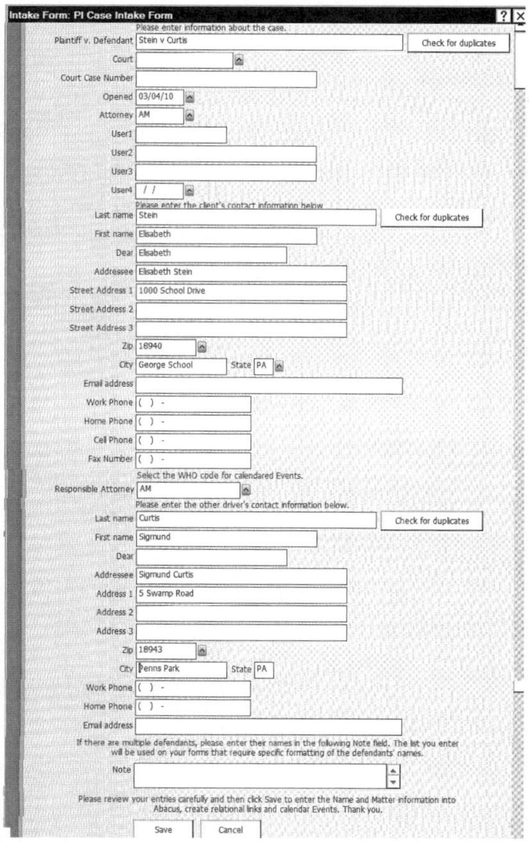 Intake Form: PI Case Intake Form Please enter information about the case. Plaintiff v. Defendant: Stein v Curtis — Check for duplicates Court: Court Case Number: Opened: 03/04/10 Attorney: AM User1: User2: User3: User4: / / Please enter the client's contact information below Last name: Stein — Check for duplicates First name: Elisabeth Dear: Elisabeth Addressee: Elisabeth Stein Street Address 1: 1000 School Drive Street Address 2: Street Address 3: Zip: 18940 City: George School State: PA Email address: Work Phone: ( ) - Home Phone: ( ) - Cell Phone: ( ) - Fax Number: ( ) - Select the WHO code for calendared Events. Responsible Attorney: AM Please enter the other driver's contact information below. Last name: Curtis — Check for duplicates First name: Sigmund Dear: Addressee: Sigmund Curtis Address 1: 5 Swamp Road Address 2: Address 3: Zip: 18943 City: Penns Park State: PA Work Phone: ( ) - Home Phone: ( ) - Email address: If there are multiple defendants, please enter their names in the following Note field. The list you enter will be used on your forms that require specific formatting of the defendants' names. Note: Please review your entries carefully and then click Save to enter the Name and Matter information into Abacus, create relational links and calendar Events. Thank you. Save Cancel

(*continued*)

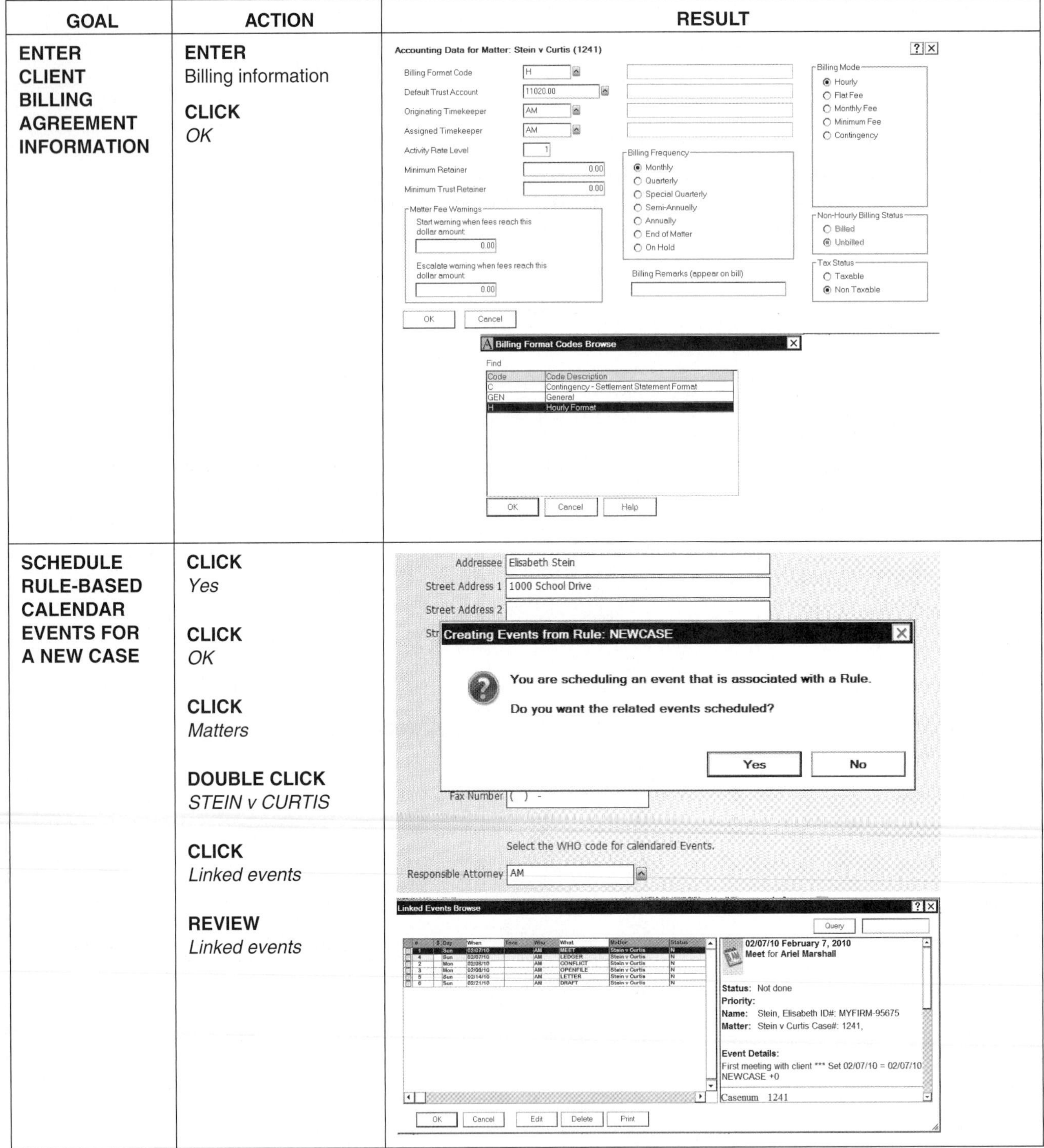

GOAL	ACTION	RESULT
ENTER CLIENT BILLING AGREEMENT INFORMATION	**ENTER** Billing information **CLICK** *OK*	
SCHEDULE RULE-BASED CALENDAR EVENTS FOR A NEW CASE	**CLICK** *Yes* **CLICK** *OK* **CLICK** *Matters* **DOUBLE CLICK** *STEIN v CURTIS* **CLICK** *Linked events* **REVIEW** *Linked events*	

HOW DO I CREATE TIME TICKETS IN ABACUS ACCOUNTING?

Time is billed to clients and to matters (cases) for events (things that happen). The linked events in matters are usually billable activities and can be set to be billed to that matter. A separate time ticket may also be created for each activity on each matter. This may be a result of entering paper time records or a record of time spent on a matter while out of the office and away from a computer.

NOTE: To enter a time ticket, you must identify the matter.

NOTE: *Task-based billing codes* were established by the American Bar Association (ABA) and are used to organize time entries by category to meet the ABA billing standards. Abacus Accounting is preloaded with the ABA task-based billing codes. You do not need to modify or delete these codes unless the ABA changes its code set.

Creating a Time Ticket in a Contingency Fee Case

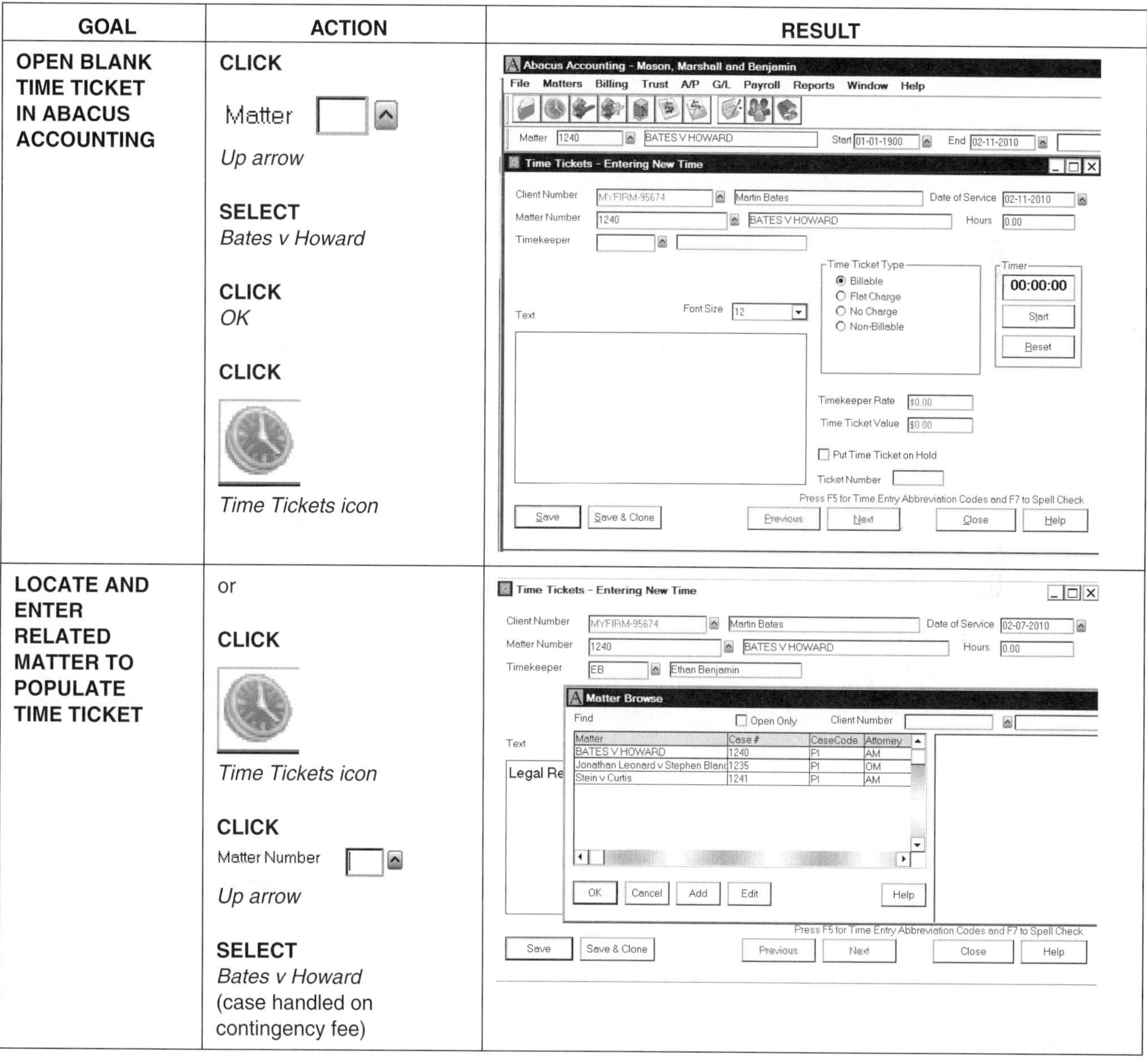

GOAL	ACTION	RESULT
OPEN BLANK TIME TICKET IN ABACUS ACCOUNTING	**CLICK** Matter *Up arrow* **SELECT** *Bates v Howard* **CLICK** *OK* **CLICK** *Time Tickets icon*	
LOCATE AND ENTER RELATED MATTER TO POPULATE TIME TICKET	or **CLICK** *Time Tickets icon* **CLICK** Matter Number *Up arrow* **SELECT** *Bates v Howard* (case handled on contingency fee)	

(continued)

GOAL	ACTION	RESULT
IDENTIFY NATURE OF CHARGE USING TIME TICKET CODES **NOTE:** Activity code will only appear if you have Task-Based Billing selected as the billing format for the selected matter or client, or if you have the firm preferences set to Force Activity Code on Time Tickets.	**CLICK**  Timekeeper *Up arrow* **SELECT** *EB* *as Timekeeper* **CLICK** *OK* in Timekeeper Browse window **ENTER** *12-07-2010* (Date of Service field) *1.00* (Hours field) **CHECK** *No Charge* **CLICK CURSOR** In Text box **CLICK** *F5 key* **SELECT** *Legal Research* **CLICK** *OK* **CLICK** *Save*	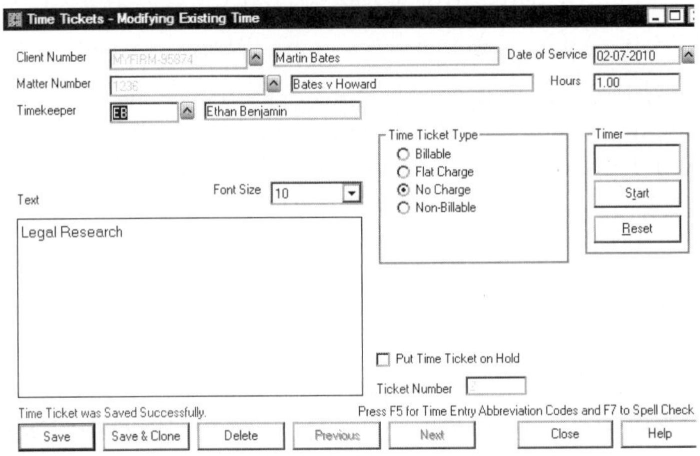 Time Tickets - Modifying Existing Time Client Number MYFIRM-95874 Martin Bates Date of Service 02-07-2010 Matter Number 1236 Bates v Howard Hours 1.00 Timekeeper EB Ethan Benjamin Time Ticket Type: Billable, Flat Charge, No Charge, Non-Billable Timer: Start, Reset Text Font Size 10 Legal Research Put Time Ticket on Hold Ticket Number Time Ticket was Saved Successfully. Press F5 for Time Entry Abbreviation Codes and F7 to Spell Check Save, Save & Clone, Delete, Previous, Next, Close, Help
VERIFY INFORMTION FOR ACCURACY	**CLICK** *Close*	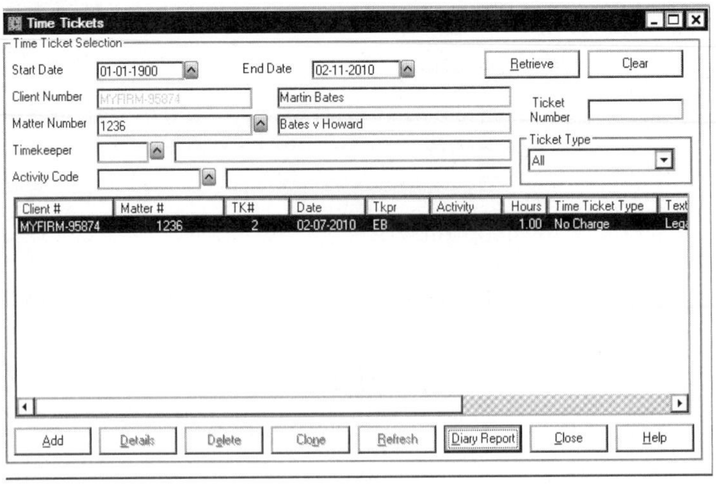 Time Tickets Time Ticket Selection Start Date 01-01-1900 End Date 02-11-2010 Retrieve Clear Client Number MYFIRM-95874 Martin Bates Ticket Number Matter Number 1236 Bates v Howard Timekeeper Ticket Type All Activity Code Client # | Matter # | TK# | Date | Tkpr | Activity | Hours | Time Ticket Type | Text MYFIRM-95874 | 1236 | 2 | 02-07-2010 | EB | | 1.00 | No Charge | Leg Add, Details, Delete, Clone, Refresh, Diary Report, Close, Help

Close Abacus Accounting.

HOW DO I ENTER TIME CHARGES FOR EVENTS FROM THE ABACUSLAW PRACTICE MANAGER?

Events within a matter may be set up as time tickets within the Practice Manager. Events include time spent working with a client or on a client case, including conferences, drafting, research, and other billable time. These events may be charged as time tickets using the same method as entering an event into a calendar.

Enter Chargeable Event in Practice Manager

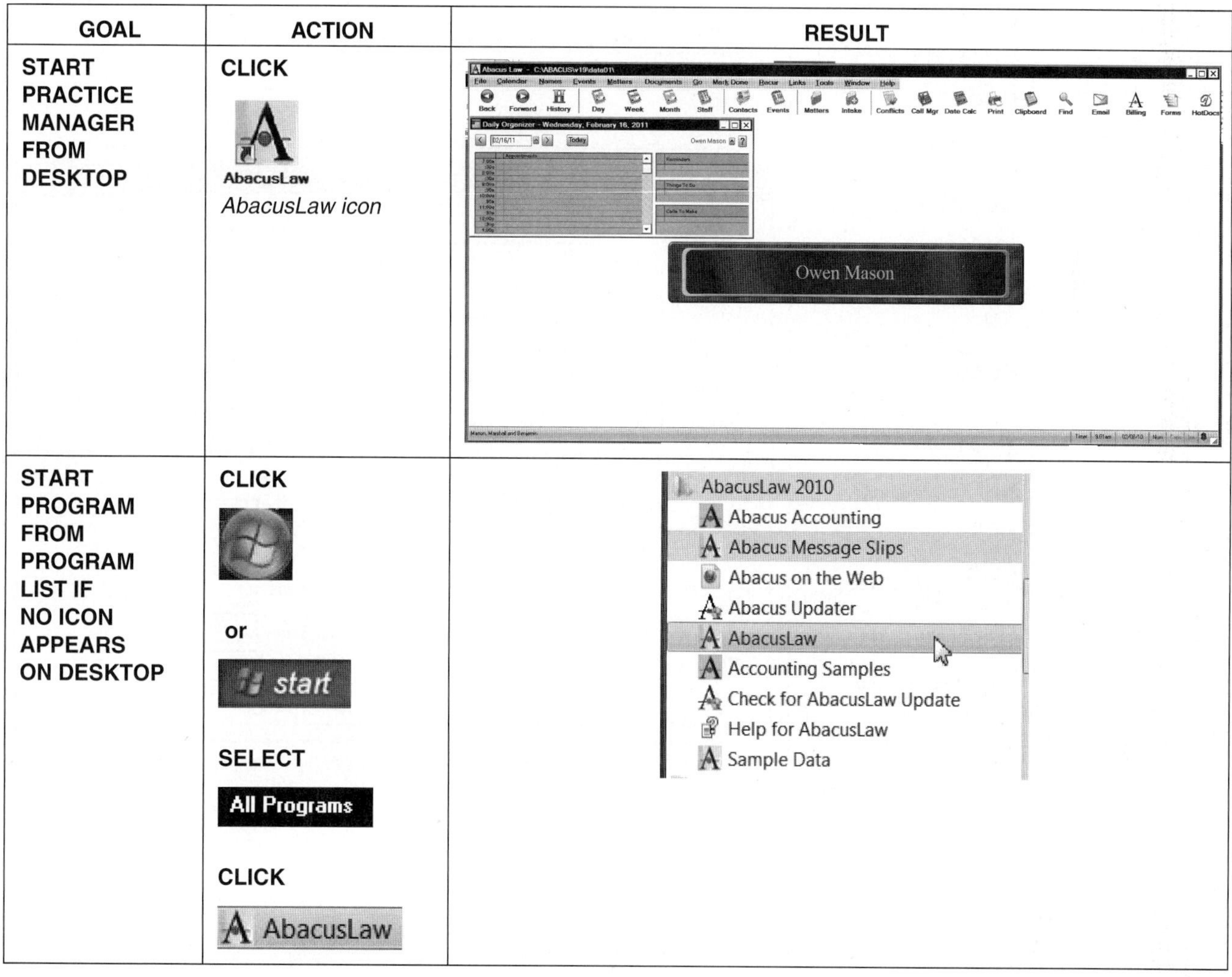

GOAL	ACTION	RESULT
START PRACTICE MANAGER FROM DESKTOP	CLICK AbacusLaw *AbacusLaw icon*	Owen Mason
START PROGRAM FROM PROGRAM LIST IF NO ICON APPEARS ON DESKTOP	CLICK or start SELECT All Programs CLICK AbacusLaw	AbacusLaw 2010 Abacus Accounting Abacus Message Slips Abacus on the Web Abacus Updater AbacusLaw Accounting Samples Check for AbacusLaw Update Help for AbacusLaw Sample Data

(*continued*)

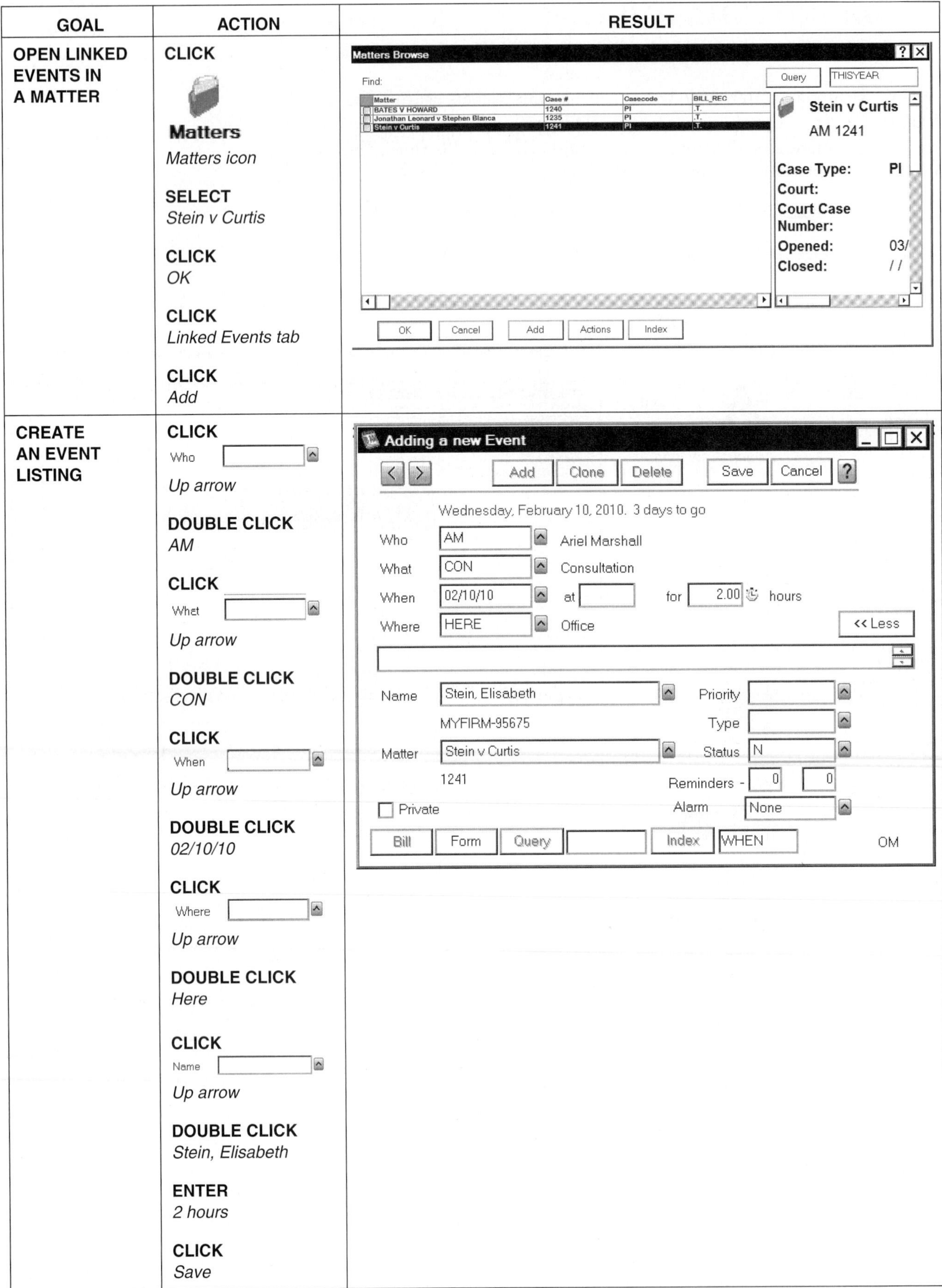

GOAL	ACTION	RESULT
OPEN LINKED EVENTS IN A MATTER	CLICK Matters *Matters icon* SELECT *Stein v Curtis* CLICK *OK* CLICK *Linked Events tab* CLICK *Add*	
CREATE AN EVENT LISTING	CLICK Who *Up arrow* DOUBLE CLICK *AM* CLICK What *Up arrow* DOUBLE CLICK *CON* CLICK When *Up arrow* DOUBLE CLICK *02/10/10* CLICK Where *Up arrow* DOUBLE CLICK *Here* CLICK Name *Up arrow* DOUBLE CLICK *Stein, Elisabeth* ENTER *2 hours* CLICK *Save*	

(continued)

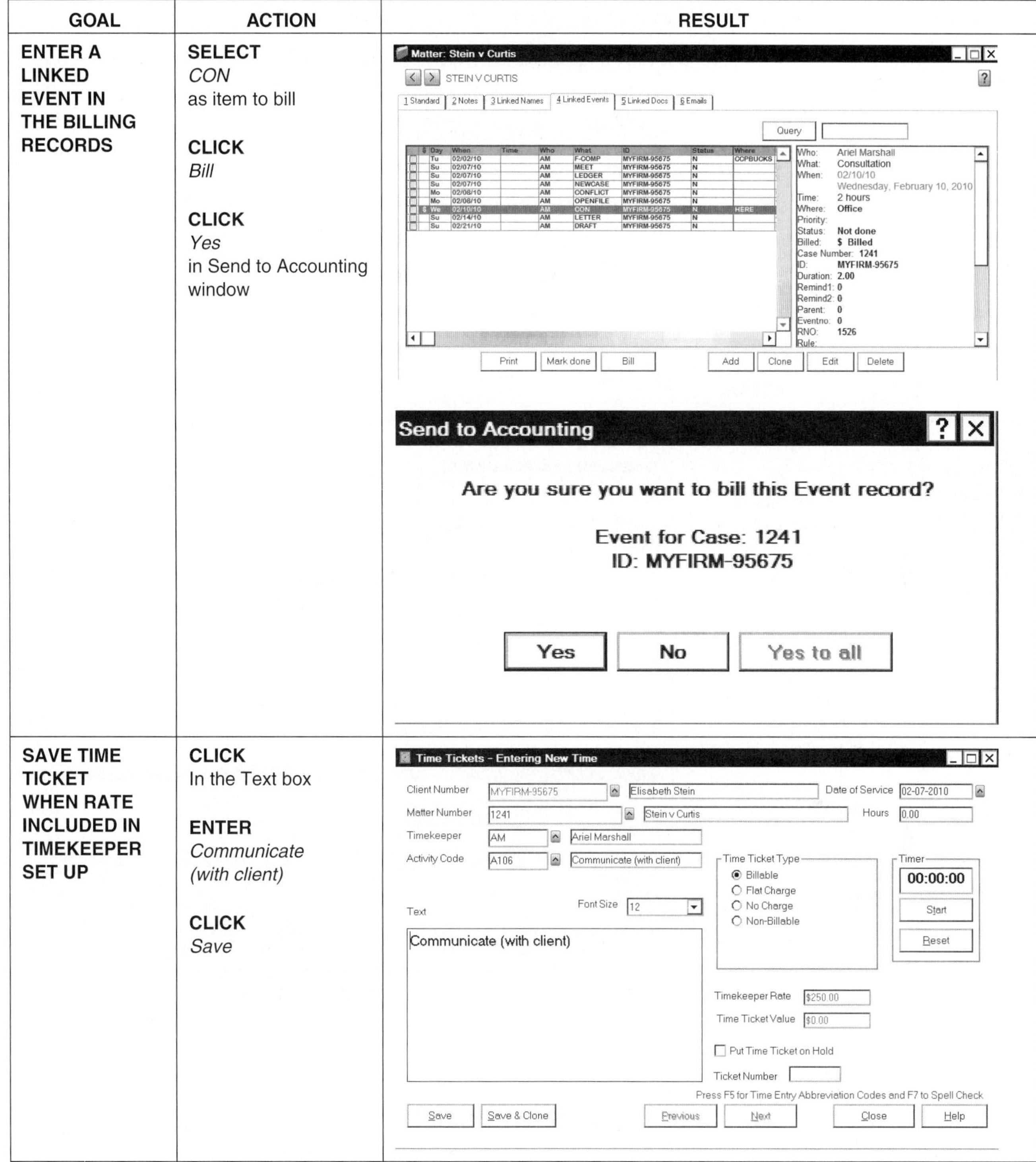

GOAL	ACTION	RESULT
ENTER A LINKED EVENT IN THE BILLING RECORDS	**SELECT** *CON* as item to bill **CLICK** *Bill* **CLICK** *Yes* in Send to Accounting window	
SAVE TIME TICKET WHEN RATE INCLUDED IN TIMEKEEPER SET UP	**CLICK** In the Text box **ENTER** *Communicate (with client)* **CLICK** *Save*	

Continue without closing and go on to next tutorial.

HOW DO I PREPARE A TIME REPORT?

Time reports are a useful way of tracking activity on files and matters. In weekly or monthly legal team meetings, they may be used to determine what has been done by members of the legal team and what remains to be done. Partners will frequently want to see the productivity or efforts being made by associates or others in the firm.

They are also an important source of information when a court asks what has been done on a case, to justify a billing request to the court for court-assigned cases, or to request reimbursement for paralegal time spent on a case.

Prepare a Time Report—Time Ticket Diary

GOAL	ACTION	RESULT
OPEN ABACUS ACCOUNTING USING LINK FROM ABACULAW PRACTICE MANAGER DESKTOP	**CLICK** **Billing** *Billing icon* on AbacusLaw desktop	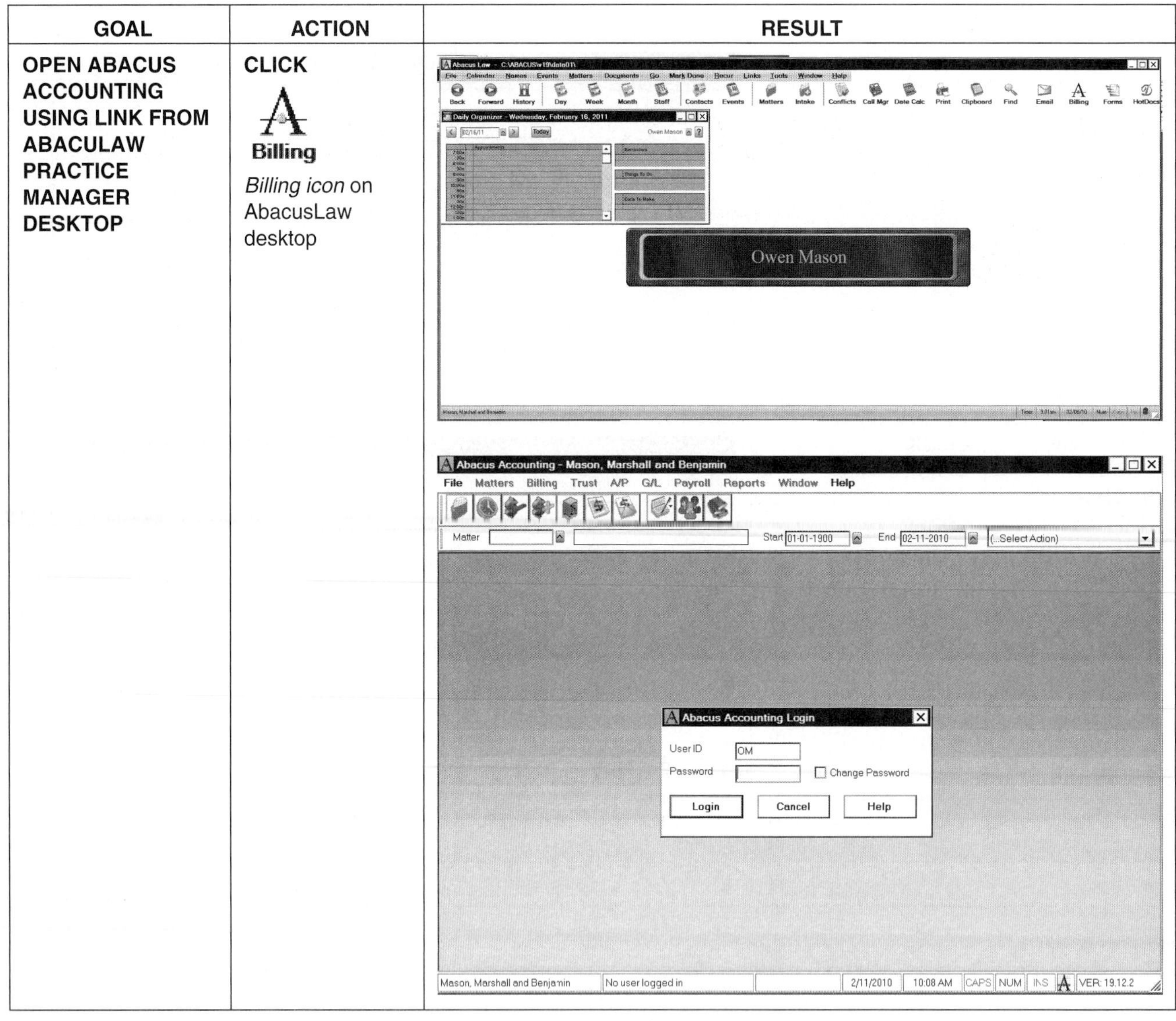

(continued)

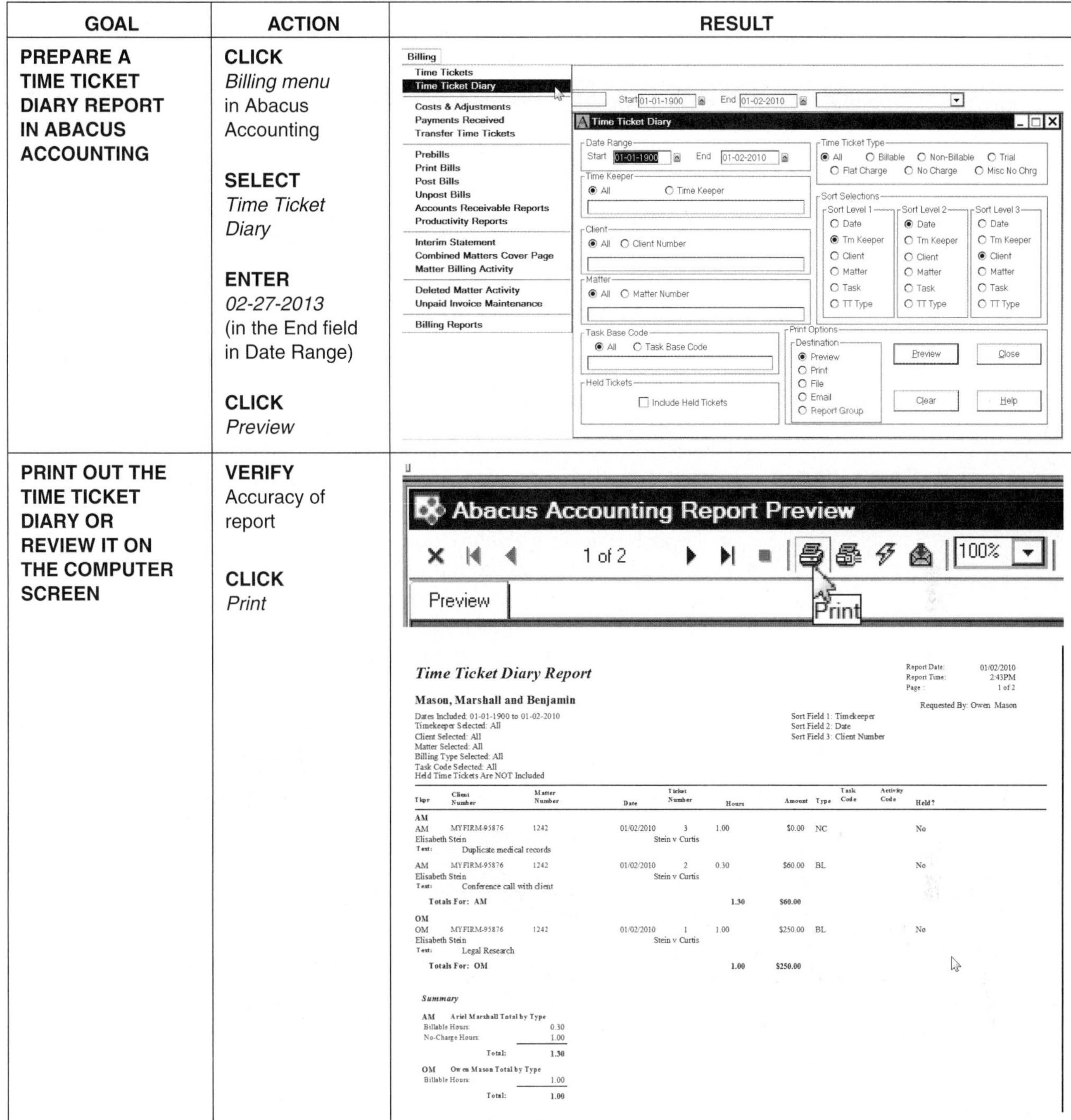

GOAL	ACTION	RESULT
PREPARE A TIME TICKET DIARY REPORT IN ABACUS ACCOUNTING	**CLICK** *Billing menu* in Abacus Accounting **SELECT** *Time Ticket Diary* **ENTER** *02-27-2013* (in the End field in Date Range) **CLICK** *Preview*	
PRINT OUT THE TIME TICKET DIARY OR REVIEW IT ON THE COMPUTER SCREEN	**VERIFY** Accuracy of report **CLICK** *Print*	

Additional tutorial information is available at
http://media.pearsoncmg.com/ph/chet/chet_goldman_techresources_1/

or on the Technology Resources Website:
www.pearsonhighered.com/goldman

APPENDIX V

SMARTDRAW TUTORIAL

- How Can I Create Map Exhibits?
  - *Tutorial—Creating Map Exhibits Using Live Maps*
- How Can I Create an Exhibit Showing How the Accident Happened?
  - *Tutorial—Creating Map and Photo Exhibits*
- How Can I Create a Timeline of a Case?
  - *Tutorial—Creating a Case Timeline*
- How Can I Annotate a Timeline to Make It More Dramatic?
  - *Tutorial—Adding Pictures and Maps to a Timeline*
- How Can I Change the Line Directions of Labels?
  - *Tutorial—Changing Arrow Directions and Shapes*
- How Can I Animate an Exhibit to Show What Happened?
  - *Tutorial—Animating an Accident Presentation*
- How Can I Use SmartDraw to Create a Settlement Brochure?
  - *Tutorial—Creating a Settlement Brochure*

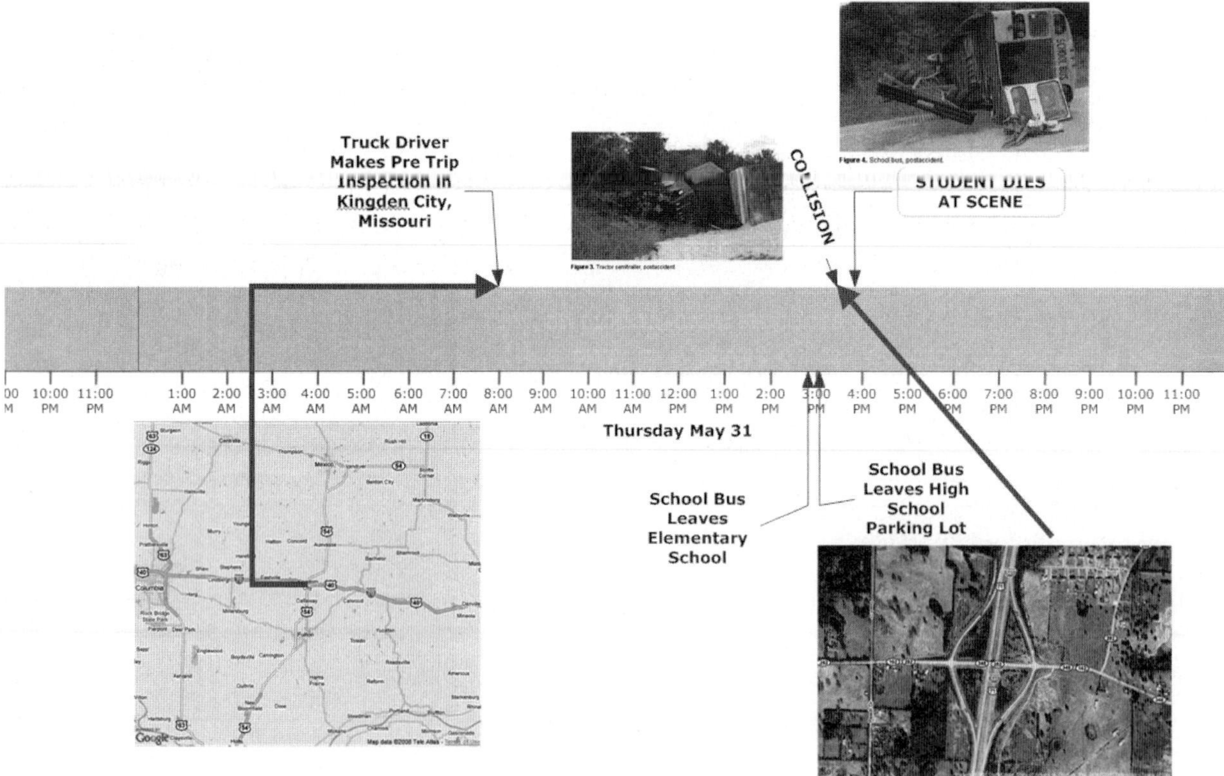

Source: Timeline created with SmartDraw.

HOW CAN I CREATE MAP EXHIBITS?

SmartDraw provides a full set of traditional international, national, and local maps. SmartDraw also provides direct access to Google maps through an Internet connection. The Maps category in the Document Browser has a category of Live Maps; these show a specific area, such as a state and the surrounding area. A mouse click on a highlighted area connects to the Google map for that area over the Internet. Other maps can be created using the Blank Map template and the Map tool in the Insert tab.

An actual accident case reported by the National Transportation Safety Board is used for purposes of this tutorial. The same fact pattern, dates, and location will be used in the following group of legal application tutorials.

CREATING MAP EXHIBITS USING LIVE MAPS

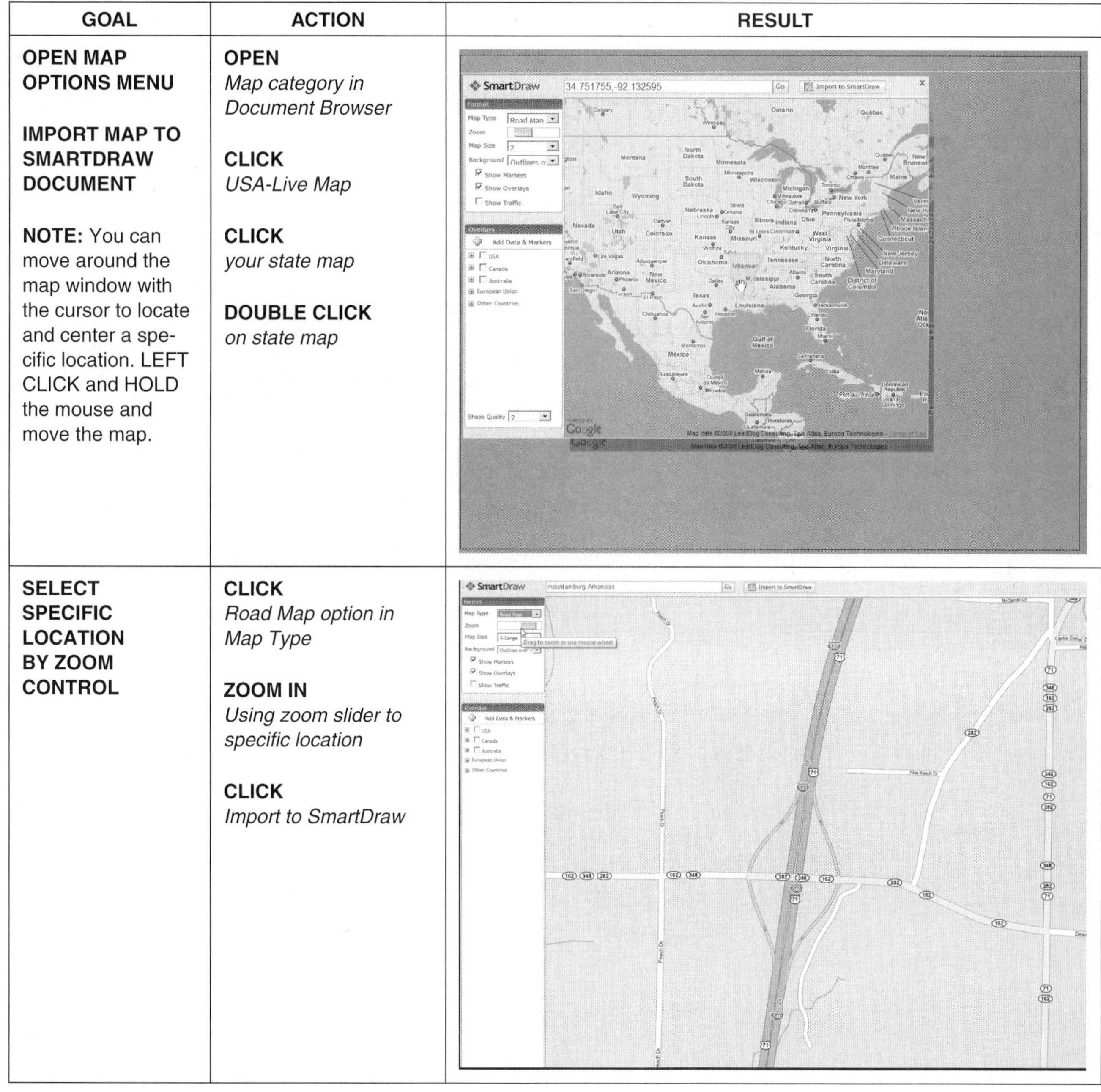

GOAL	ACTION	RESULT
OPEN MAP OPTIONS MENU **IMPORT MAP TO SMARTDRAW DOCUMENT** **NOTE:** You can move around the map window with the cursor to locate and center a specific location. LEFT CLICK and HOLD the mouse and move the map.	**OPEN** *Map category in Document Browser* **CLICK** *USA-Live Map* **CLICK** *your state map* **DOUBLE CLICK** *on state map*	
SELECT SPECIFIC LOCATION BY ZOOM CONTROL	**CLICK** *Road Map option in Map Type* **ZOOM IN** *Using zoom slider to specific location* **CLICK** *Import to SmartDraw*	

(continued)

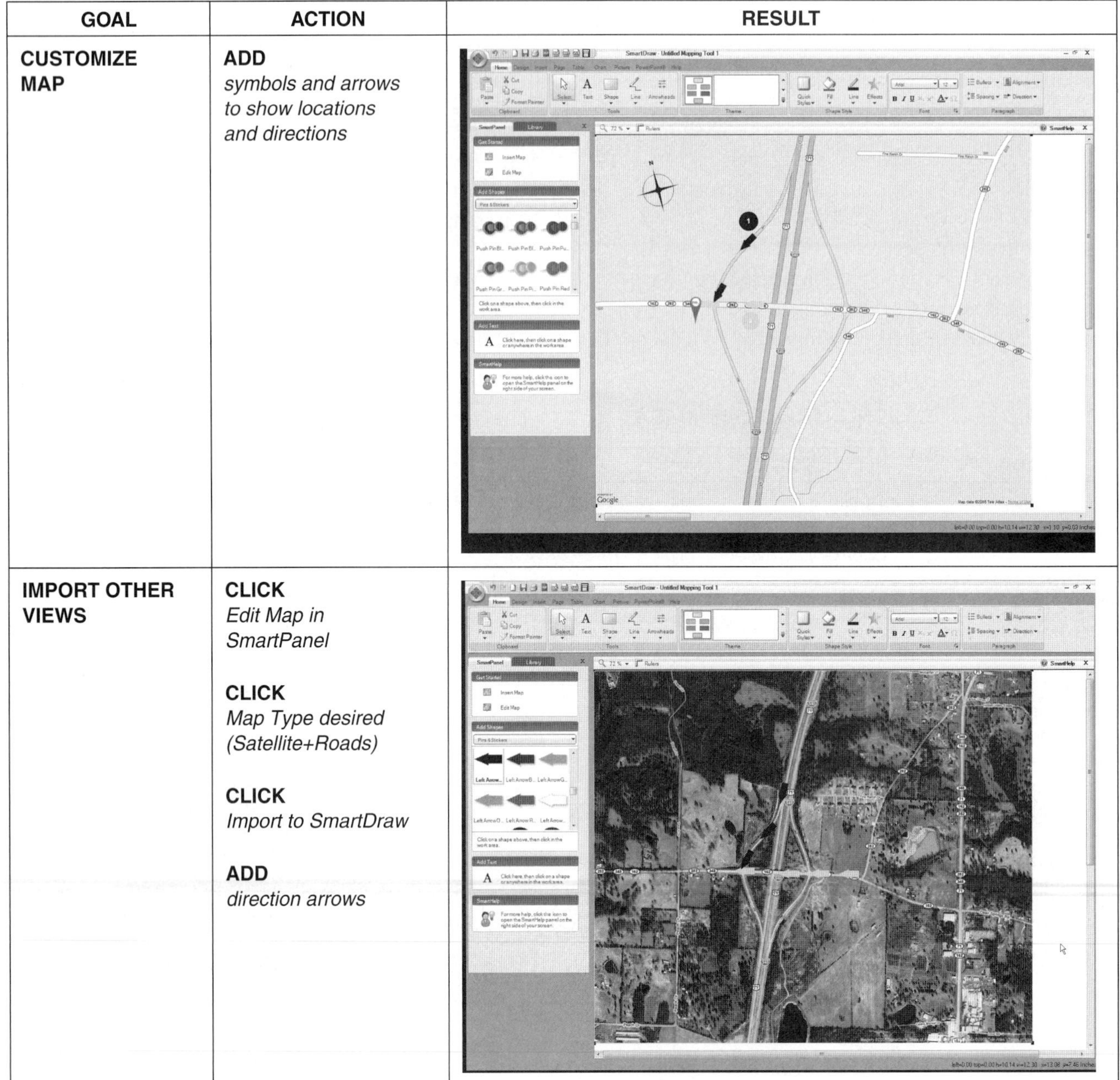

GOAL	ACTION	RESULT
CUSTOMIZE MAP	**ADD** *symbols and arrows to show locations and directions*	
IMPORT OTHER VIEWS	**CLICK** *Edit Map in SmartPanel* **CLICK** *Map Type desired (Satellite+Roads)* **CLICK** *Import to SmartDraw* **ADD** *direction arrows*	

HOW CAN I CREATE AN EXHIBIT SHOWING HOW THE ACCIDENT HAPPENED?

Annotated maps and photos are frequently used as exhibits in pretrial activities and in trial. Visual representations of how an accident occurred can be easily prepared using the SmartDraw Accident Reconstruction SmartTemplates. In many cases you will be able to find an example of a scene close enough to the one you need in the Accident Reconstruction SmartTemplates.

Creating Map and Photo Exhibits

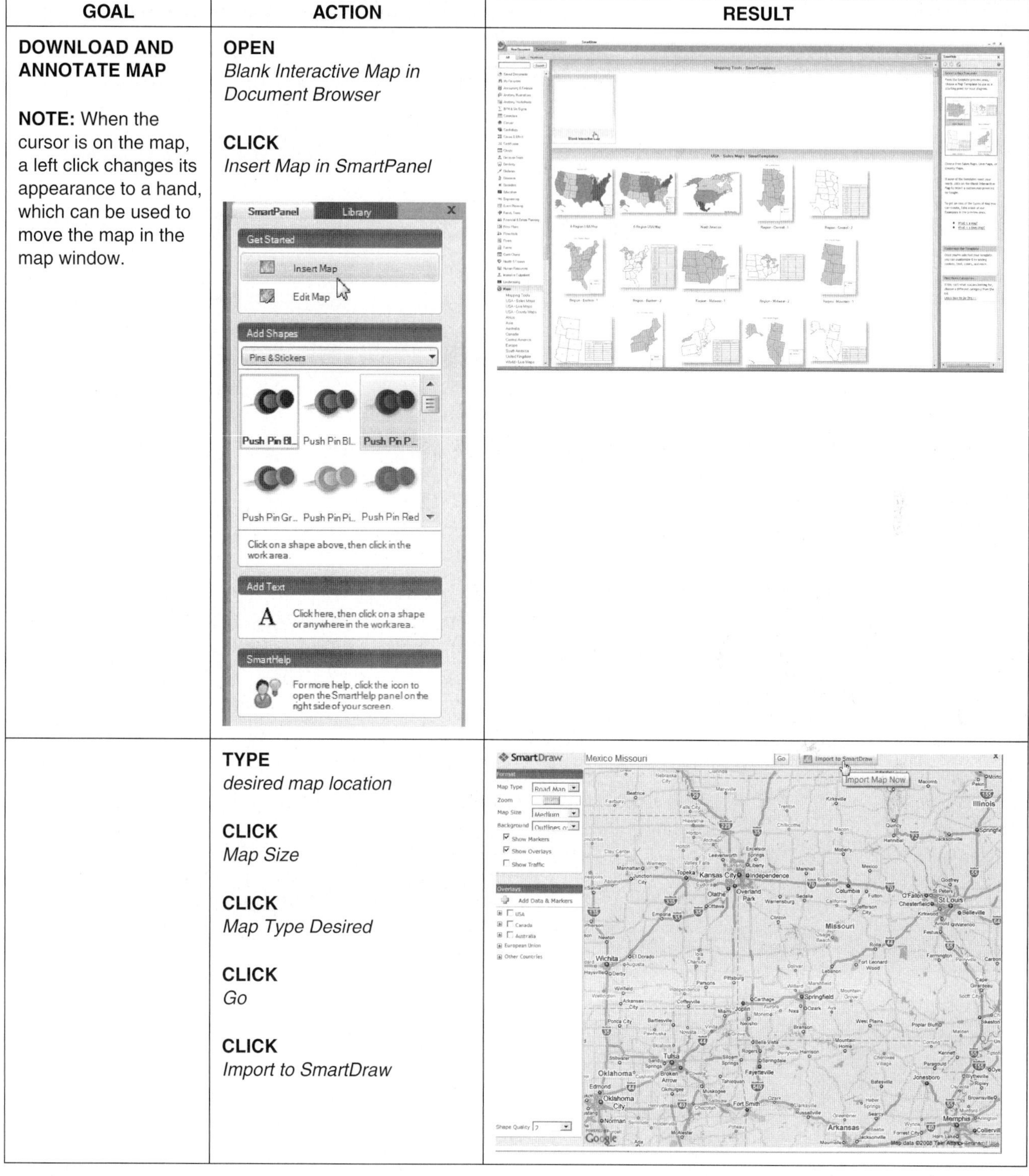

GOAL	ACTION	RESULT
DOWNLOAD AND ANNOTATE MAP **NOTE:** When the cursor is on the map, a left click changes its appearance to a hand, which can be used to move the map in the map window.	**OPEN** *Blank Interactive Map in Document Browser* **CLICK** *Insert Map in SmartPanel*	
	TYPE *desired map location* **CLICK** *Map Size* **CLICK** *Map Type Desired* **CLICK** *Go* **CLICK** *Import to SmartDraw*	

(continued)

GOAL	ACTION	RESULT
EDIT MAP **TIPS:** The Pan and Zoom tools can be used to "lasso," and then zoom in on a desired area of a map. Save your work as a SmartDraw file for future use and to print as an exhibit poster or a settlement brochure.	**SELECT** *Map* **CLICK** *Picture tab* **CLICK** *Pan and Zoom* 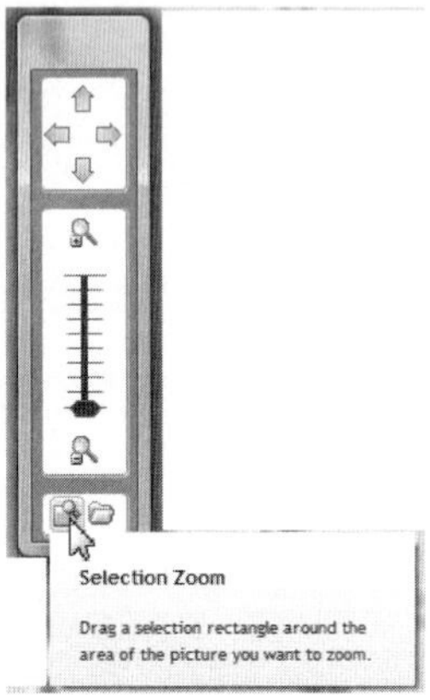 Selection Zoom Drag a selection rectangle around the area of the picture you want to zoom. **LASSO and ZOOM** 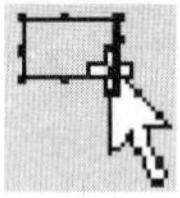 *desired map area* **CLICK** *Trim to Shape* **CLICK** *Continue*	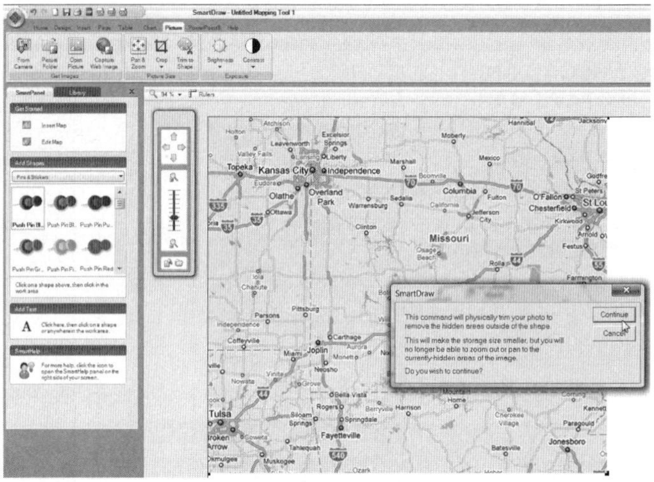
ANNOTATE MAP	**SELECT and MOVE** *symbols from SmartPanel to annotate* **CLICK** *Add Text In SmartPanel* **TYPE** *descriptive text*	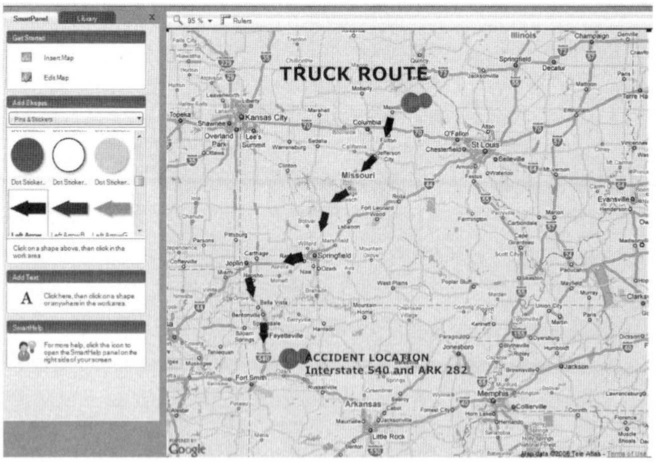 TRUCK ROUTE ACCIDENT LOCATION Interstate 540 and ARK 282

(continued)

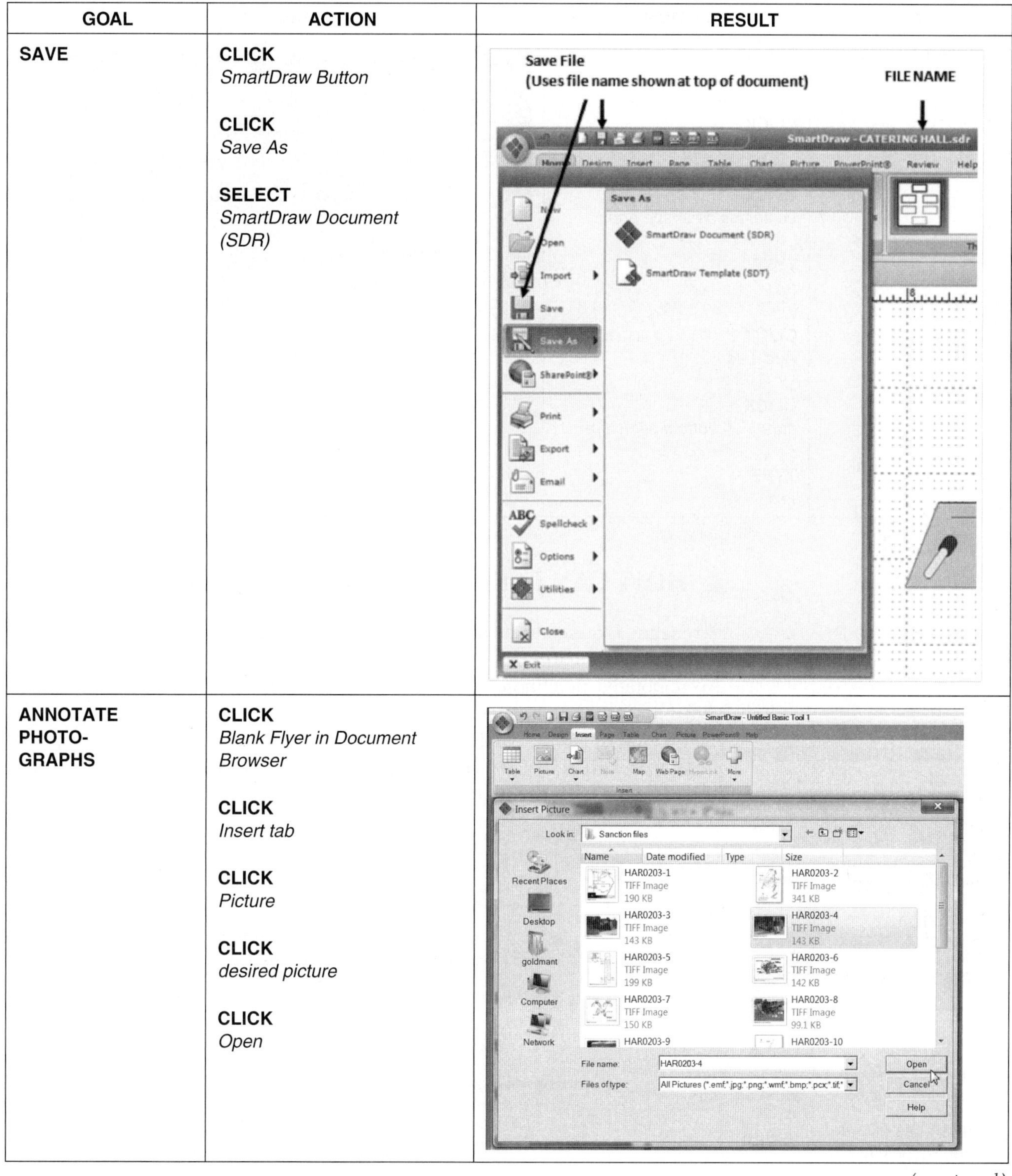

GOAL	ACTION	RESULT
SAVE	**CLICK** *SmartDraw Button* **CLICK** *Save As* **SELECT** *SmartDraw Document (SDR)*	
ANNOTATE PHOTO-GRAPHS	**CLICK** *Blank Flyer in Document Browser* **CLICK** *Insert tab* **CLICK** *Picture* **CLICK** *desired picture* **CLICK** *Open*	

(continued)

GOAL	ACTION	RESULT
ENTER TEXT	**SELECT and MOVE** *shape* **CLICK** *Add Text in SmartPanel* **CLICK** *cursor inside shape and* **TYPE** *text* **CLICK** *Add Text* **CLICK** *cursor on bottom of picture* **TYPE** *text*	 POINT of IMPACT SCHOOL BUS SCHOOL BUS AFTER ACCIDENT

HOW CAN I CREATE A TIMELINE OF A CASE?

A timeline is a useful way to quickly present a full sequence of events. It can also be used to summarize a series of events leading to a claim for injury or death. An annotated timeline can be used to show what happened and when it happened in making an argument to a claims adjuster, arbitration panel, or jury. The SmartDraw timeline templates may be annotated with pictures and maps. As mentioned earlier, the case used to illustrate this tutorial is an actual case reported by the National Transportation Study Board.

CREATING A CASE TIMELINE

GOAL	ACTION	RESULT
CREATE TIMELINE STARTING EVENT **NOTES:** You can use different Connector Styles in the same timeline. You can use different Event Shapes in the same timeline.	**CLICK** *Timeline in Document Browser* **CLICK** *Start Date for timeline in SmartPanel* **ENTER** *date*	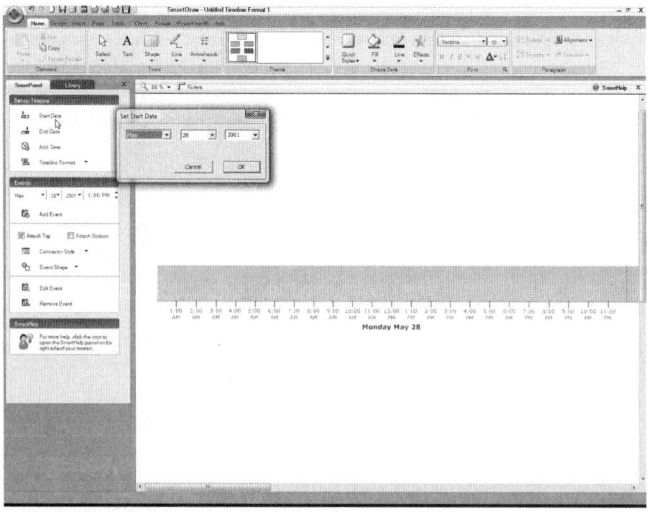 Set Start Date Cancel OK Monday May 28

(continued)

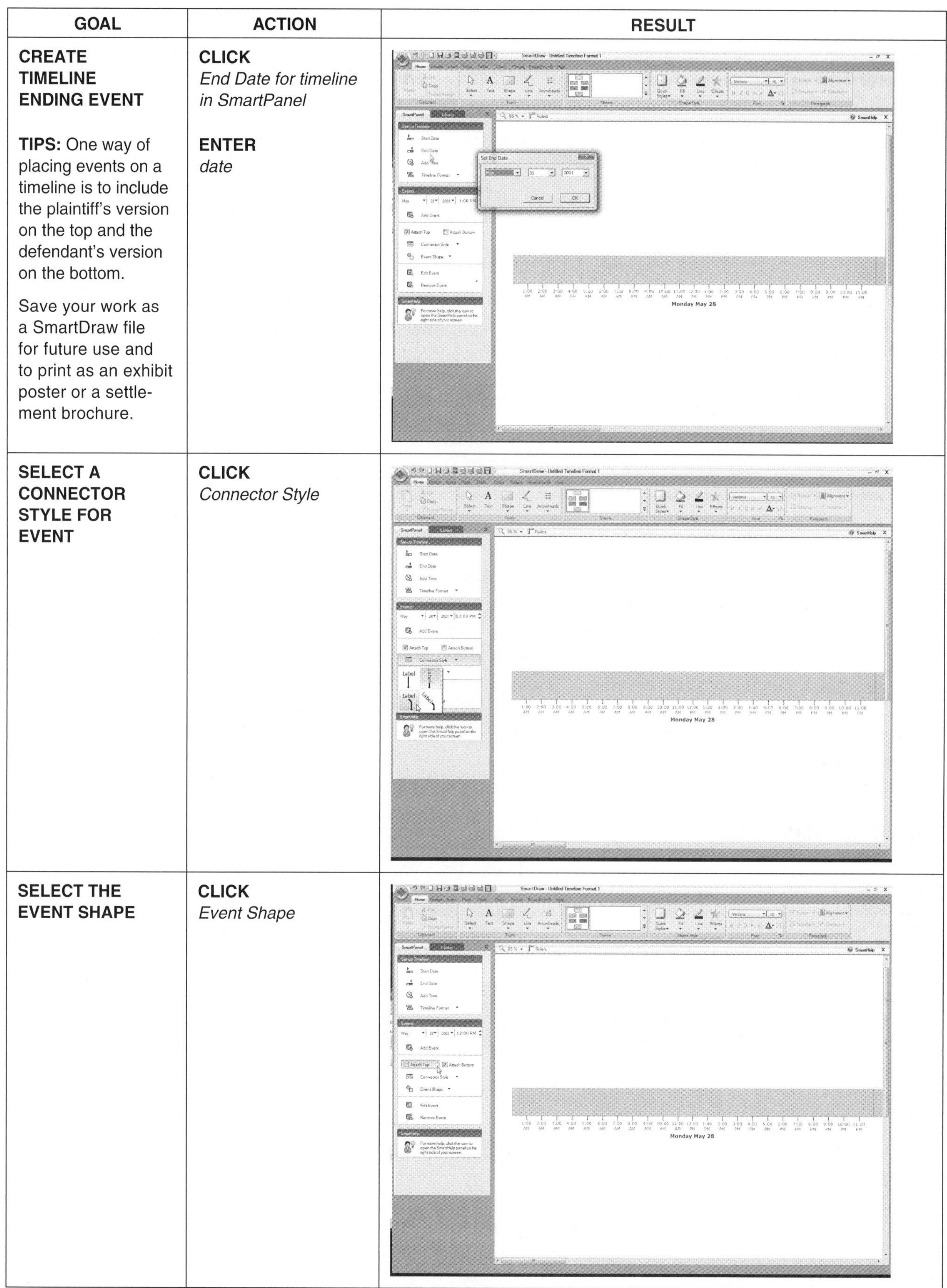

GOAL	ACTION	RESULT
CREATE TIMELINE ENDING EVENT **TIPS:** One way of placing events on a timeline is to include the plaintiff's version on the top and the defendant's version on the bottom. Save your work as a SmartDraw file for future use and to print as an exhibit poster or a settle-ment brochure.	**CLICK** *End Date for timeline in SmartPanel* **ENTER** *date*	
SELECT A CONNECTOR STYLE FOR EVENT	**CLICK** *Connector Style*	
SELECT THE EVENT SHAPE	**CLICK** *Event Shape*	

(continued)

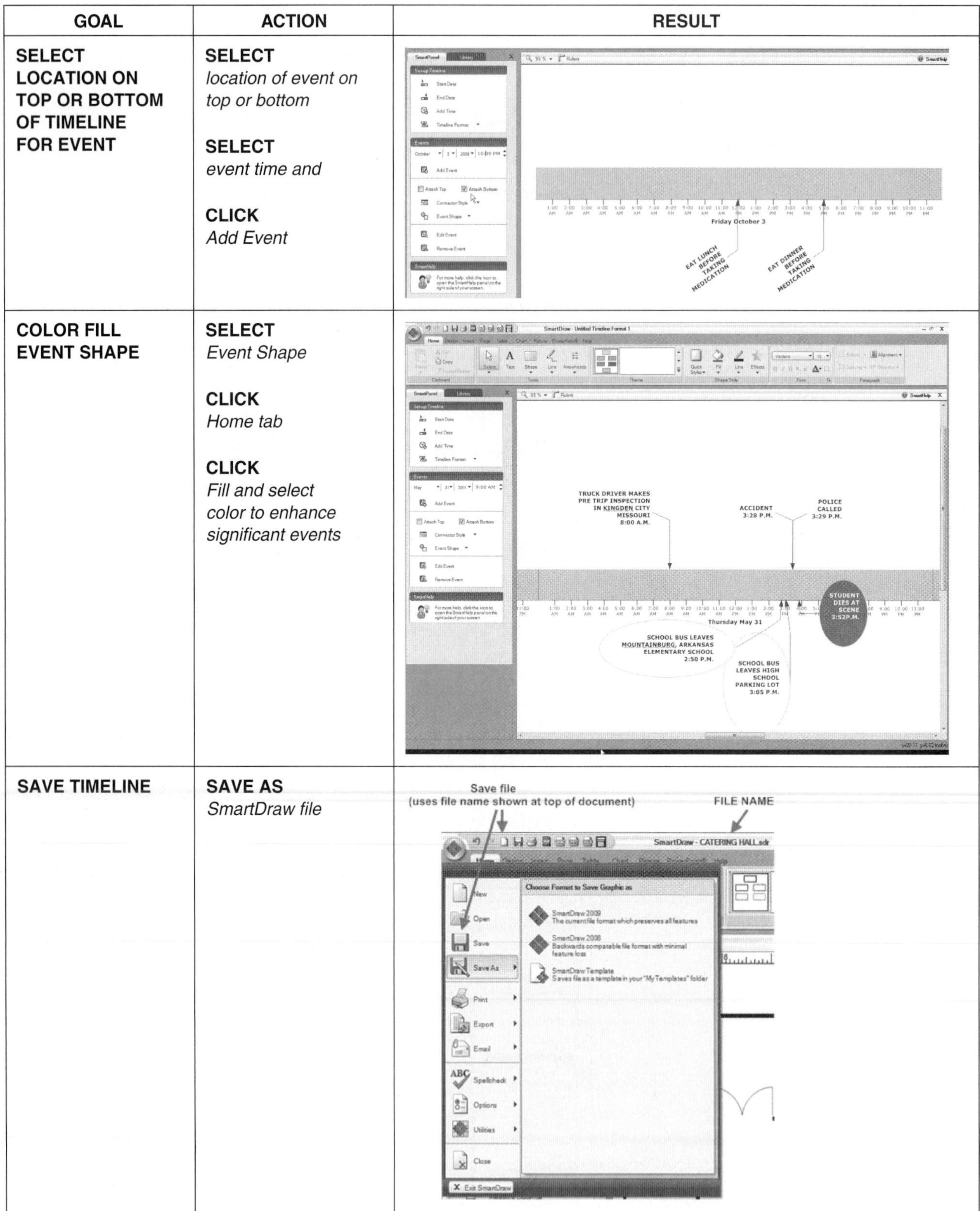

GOAL	ACTION	RESULT
SELECT LOCATION ON TOP OR BOTTOM OF TIMELINE FOR EVENT	**SELECT** *location of event on top or bottom* **SELECT** *event time and* **CLICK** *Add Event*	
COLOR FILL EVENT SHAPE	**SELECT** *Event Shape* **CLICK** *Home tab* **CLICK** *Fill and select color to enhance significant events*	
SAVE TIMELINE	**SAVE AS** *SmartDraw file*	

You may use this timeline in the next tutorial or start a new one.

HOW CAN I ANNOTATE A TIMELINE TO MAKE IT MORE DRAMATIC?

A basic timeline can be very useful in showing facts. But a timeline annotated with pictures and maps, when permitted in court or in pretrial settlement activities, can communicate the story even more effectively. The timeline used in the previous tutorial is used in the following tutorial with the addition of maps and pictures. This tutorial provides the steps to add pictures. Before you start, locate a few sample pictures on your computer that you can use to practice inserting pictures in a timeline.

Adding Pictures and Maps to a Timeline

GOAL	ACTION	RESULT
INSERT PICTURE IN TIMELINE	**CLICK** *Insert tab* **CLICK** *Picture* **CLICK** *Add a New Picture*	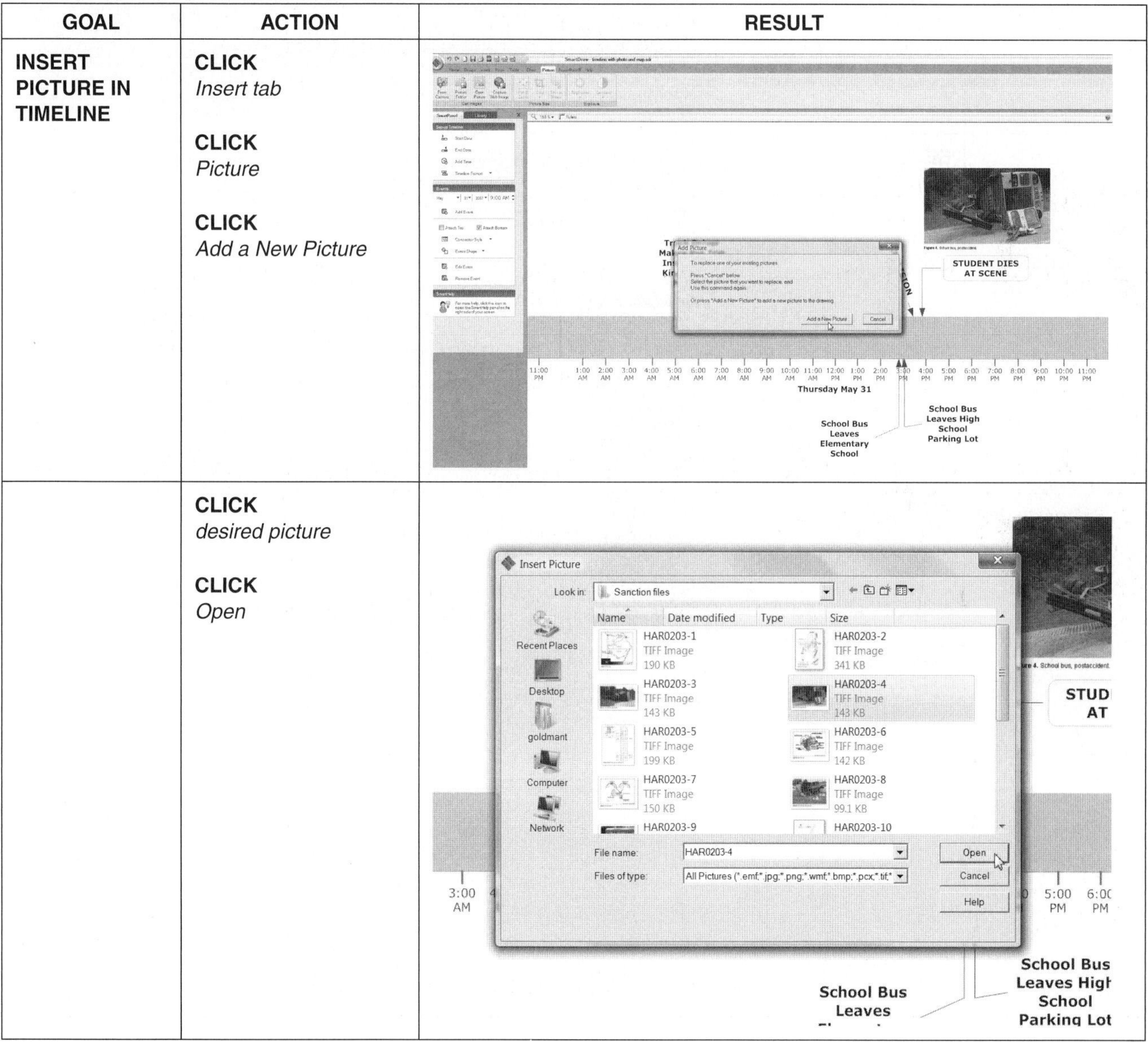
	CLICK *desired picture* **CLICK** *Open*	

(*continued*)

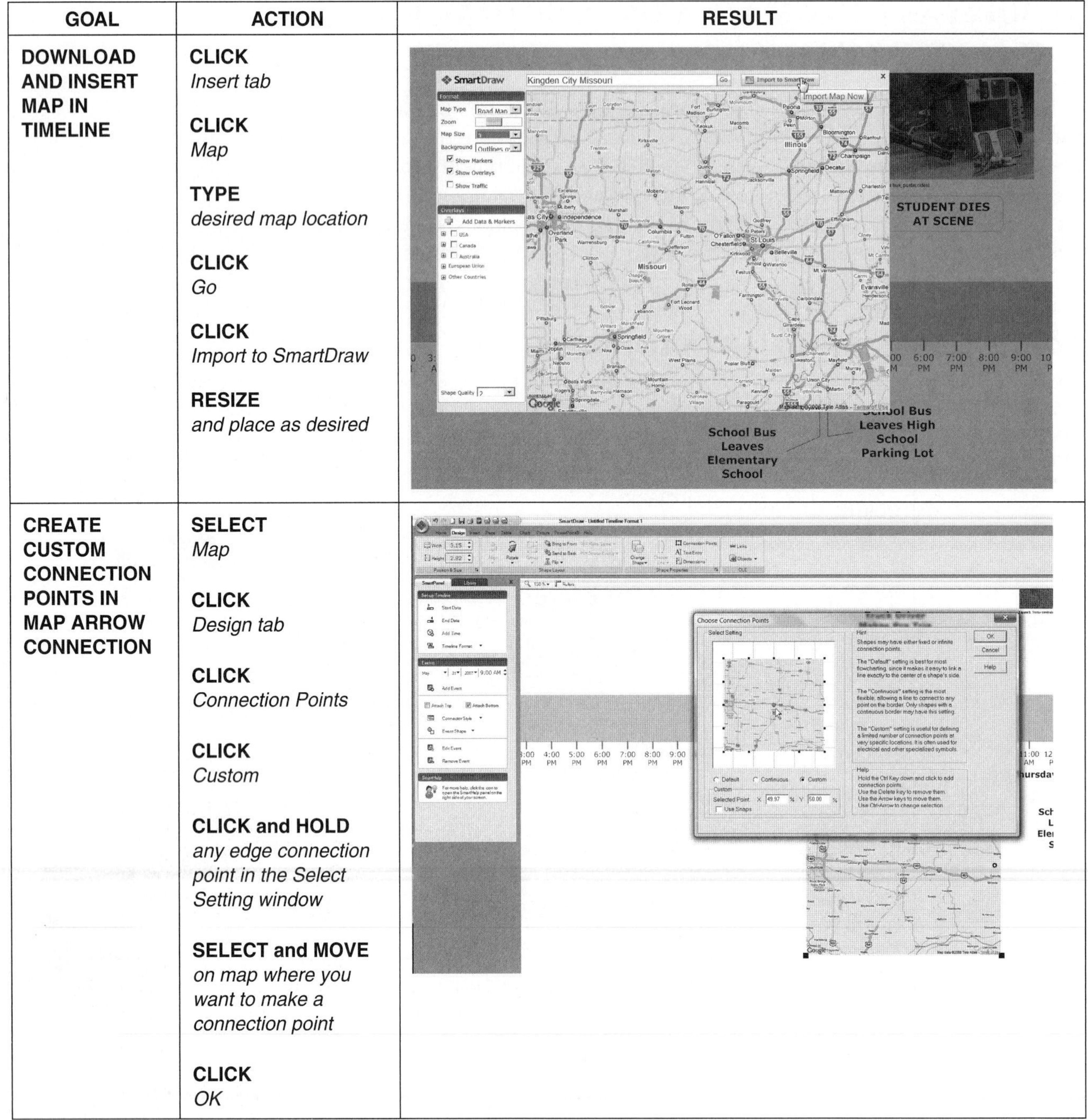

GOAL	ACTION	RESULT
DOWNLOAD AND INSERT MAP IN TIMELINE	**CLICK** *Insert tab* **CLICK** *Map* **TYPE** *desired map location* **CLICK** *Go* **CLICK** *Import to SmartDraw* **RESIZE** *and place as desired*	
CREATE CUSTOM CONNECTION POINTS IN MAP ARROW CONNECTION	**SELECT** *Map* **CLICK** *Design tab* **CLICK** *Connection Points* **CLICK** *Custom* **CLICK and HOLD** *any edge connection point in the Select Setting window* **SELECT and MOVE** *on map where you want to make a connection point* **CLICK** *OK*	

(continued)

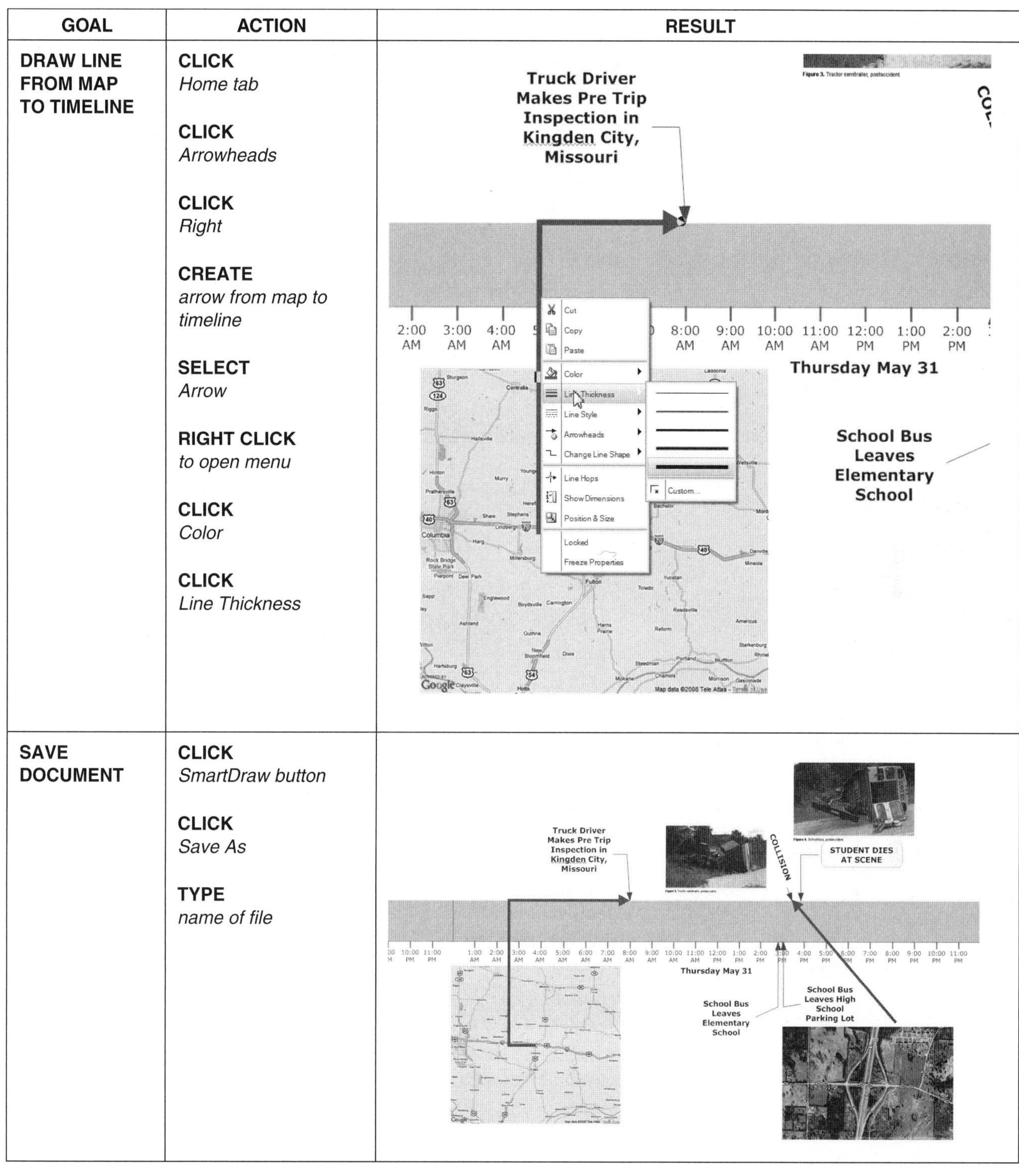

GOAL	ACTION	RESULT
DRAW LINE FROM MAP TO TIMELINE	**CLICK** *Home tab* **CLICK** *Arrowheads* **CLICK** *Right* **CREATE** *arrow from map to timeline* **SELECT** *Arrow* **RIGHT CLICK** *to open menu* **CLICK** *Color* **CLICK** *Line Thickness*	
SAVE DOCUMENT	**CLICK** *SmartDraw button* **CLICK** *Save As* **TYPE** *name of file*	

HOW CAN I CHANGE THE LINE DIRECTIONS OF LABELS?

Arrows in timelines have selection handles. Depending on the type of label selected these may be fixed as a straight arrow, or have intermediate handles that can be moved to change direction or shape.

CHANGING ARROW DIRECTIONS AND SHAPES

GOAL	ACTION	RESULT
EDIT LINES IN TIMELINE **NOTE:** The label lines in a timeline may be edited by using the end or middle handles to move, rotate, or bend the line.	**SELECT** *Arrow* **CLICK** *handles* **MOVE** *to new location*	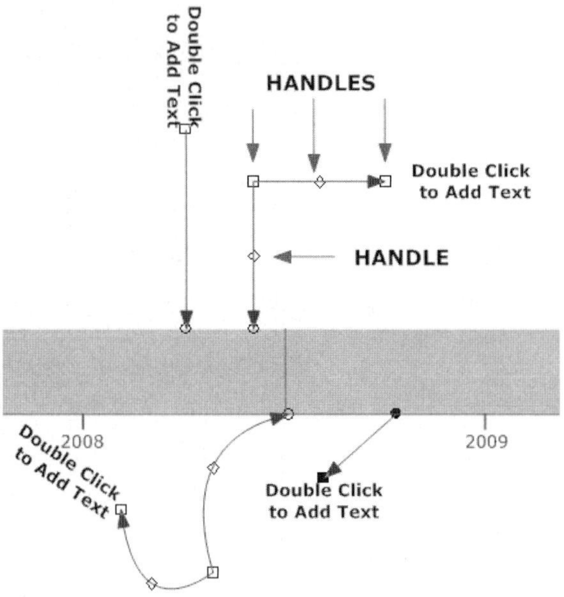 Double Click to Add Text HANDLES Double Click to Add Text HANDLE 2008 2009 Double Click to Add Text Double Click to Add Text

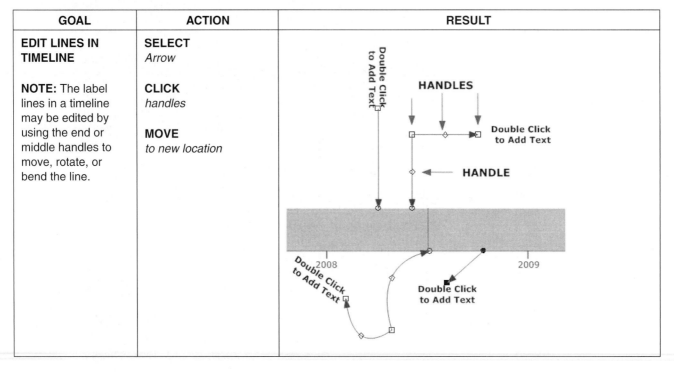

HOW CAN I ANIMATE AN EXHIBIT TO SHOW WHAT HAPPENED?

Your client says the other car struck her car while it was parked. Creating an animated recreation would be nice, but the case does not justify the cost of a full-scale animation. SmartDraw enables you to create a step-by-step presentation of the position of the vehicles based on testimony or depositions.

Animating an Accident Presentation

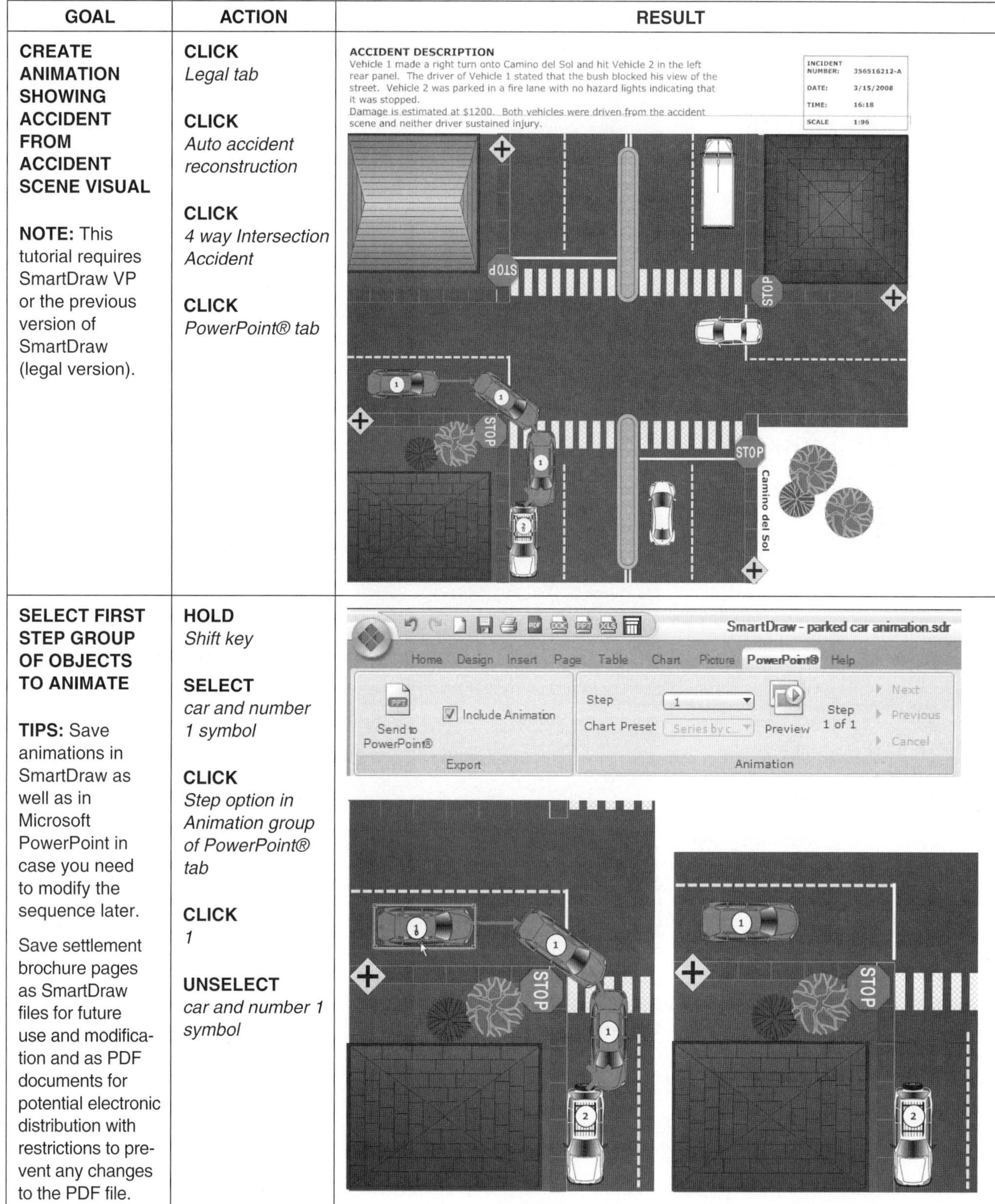
ACCIDENT DESCRIPTION
Vehicle 1 made a right turn onto Camino del Sol and hit Vehicle 2 in the left rear panel. The driver of Vehicle 1 stated that the bush blocked his view of the street. Vehicle 2 was parked in a fire lane with no hazard lights indicating that it was stopped.
Damage is estimated at $1200. Both vehicles were driven from the accident scene and neither driver sustained injury.
INCIDENT NUMBER: 356516212-A
DATE: 3/15/2008
TIME: 16:18
SCALE 1:96
STOP
Camino del Sol
SmartDraw - parked car animation.sdr
Home Design Insert Page Table Chart Picture PowerPoint® Help
Send to PowerPoint®
Include Animation
Export
Step
Chart Preset
Preview
Step 1 of 1
Next
Previous
Cancel
Animation

GOAL	ACTION	RESULT
CREATE ANIMATION SHOWING ACCIDENT FROM ACCIDENT SCENE VISUAL **NOTE:** This tutorial requires SmartDraw VP or the previous version of SmartDraw (legal version).	**CLICK** *Legal tab* **CLICK** *Auto accident reconstruction* **CLICK** *4 way Intersection Accident* **CLICK** *PowerPoint® tab*	
SELECT FIRST STEP GROUP OF OBJECTS TO ANIMATE **TIPS:** Save animations in SmartDraw as well as in Microsoft PowerPoint in case you need to modify the sequence later. Save settlement brochure pages as SmartDraw files for future use and modification and as PDF documents for potential electronic distribution with restrictions to prevent any changes to the PDF file.	**HOLD** *Shift key* **SELECT** *car and number 1 symbol* **CLICK** *Step option in Animation group of PowerPoint® tab* **CLICK** *1* **UNSELECT** *car and number 1 symbol*	

(continued)

GOAL	ACTION	RESULT
SELECT SECOND STEP OBJECT TO ANIMATE	**SELECT** *arrow symbol* **CLICK** *Step option in Animation group of PowerPoint® tab* **CLICK** *2* **UNSELECT** *Arrow symbol*	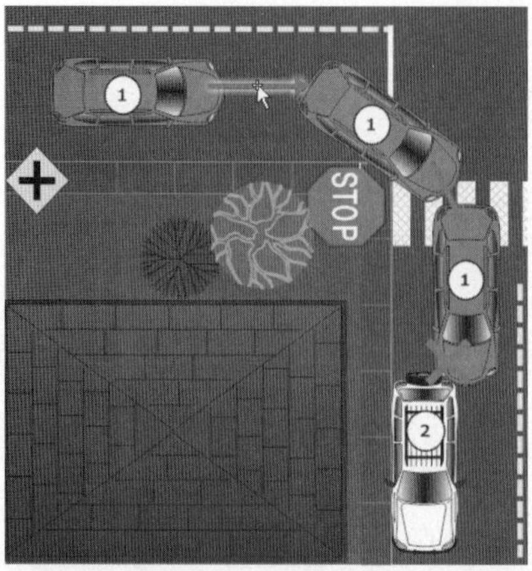 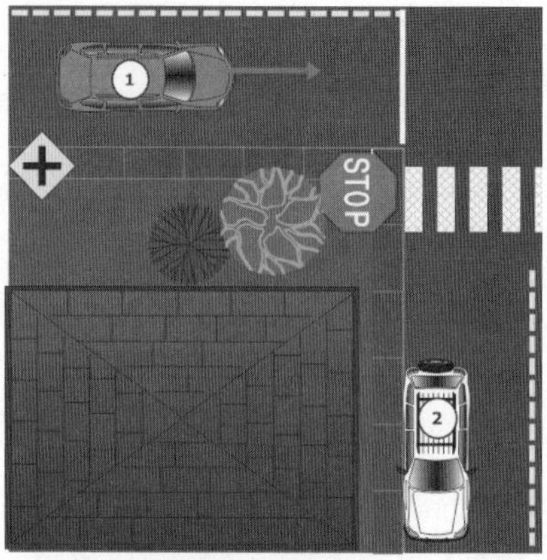 STOP STOP
SELECT THIRD STEP GROUP OF OBJECTS TO ANIMATE	**SELECT** *car and number symbol* **CLICK** *Step option in Animation group of PowerPoint® tab* **CLICK** *3* **UNSELECT** *car and number symbol*	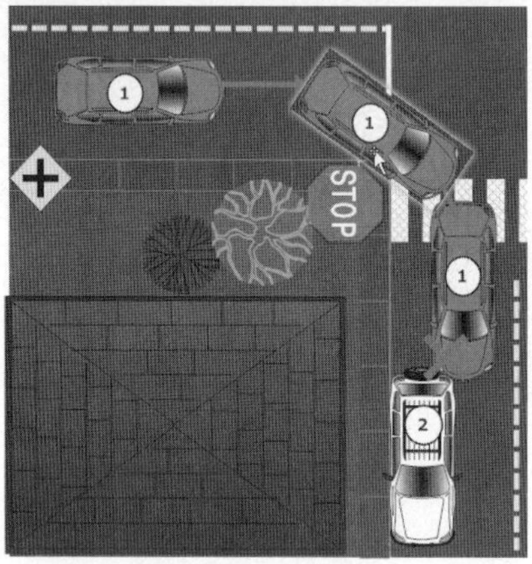 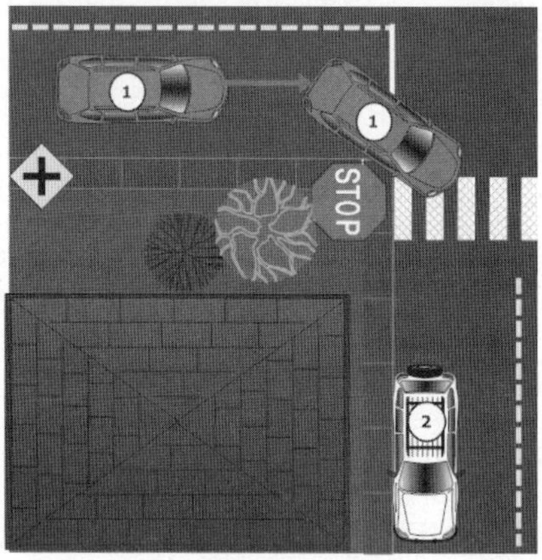 STOP STOP
SELECT FOURTH STEP OBJECT TO ANIMATE	**SELECT** *arrow symbol* **CLICK** *Step option in Animation group of PowerPoint® tab* **CLICK** *4* **UNSELECT** *arrow symbol*	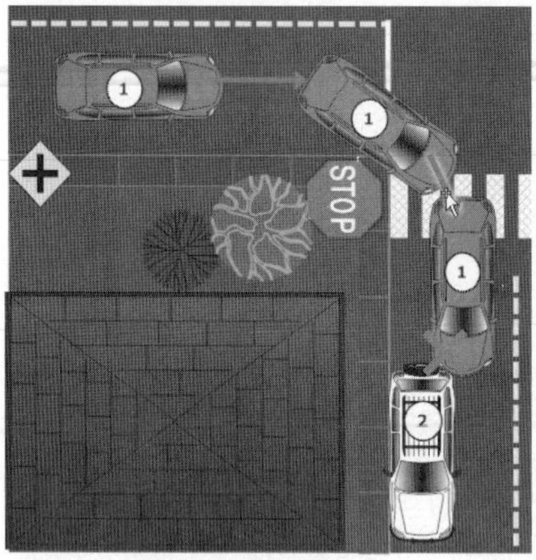 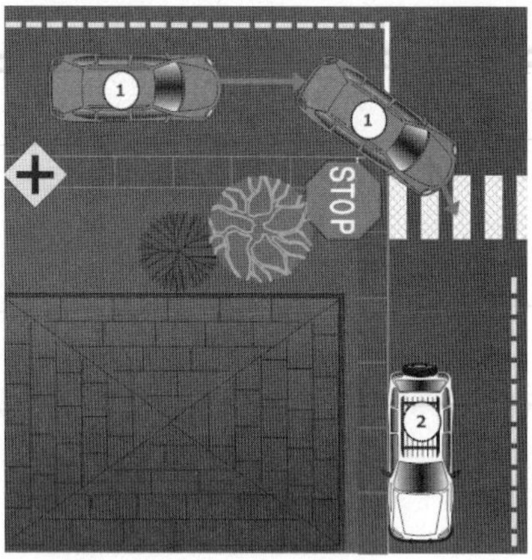 STOP STOP

(*continued*)

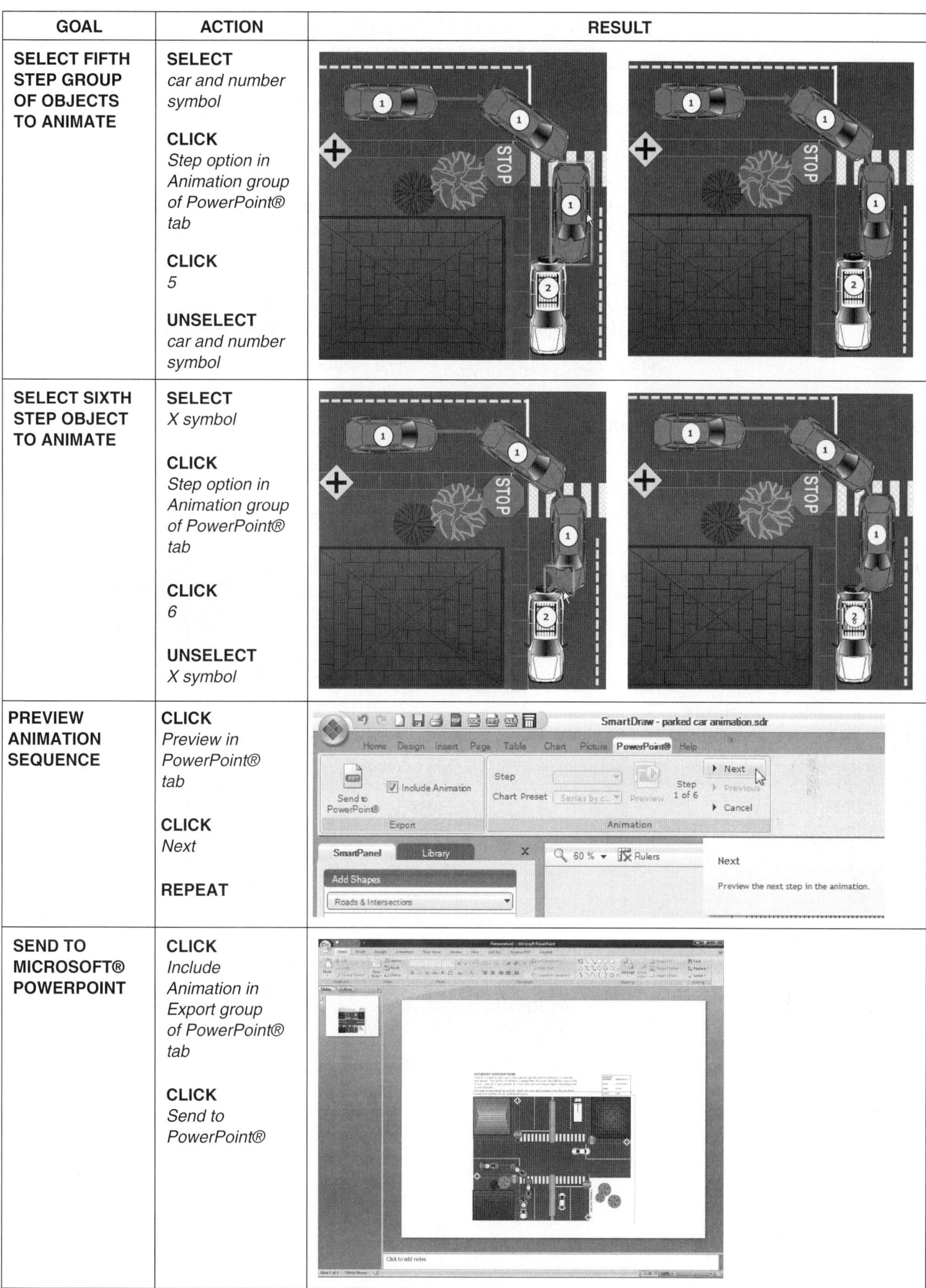

GOAL	ACTION	RESULT
SELECT FIFTH STEP GROUP OF OBJECTS TO ANIMATE	**SELECT** *car and number symbol* **CLICK** *Step option in Animation group of PowerPoint® tab* **CLICK** *5* **UNSELECT** *car and number symbol*	
SELECT SIXTH STEP OBJECT TO ANIMATE	**SELECT** *X symbol* **CLICK** *Step option in Animation group of PowerPoint® tab* **CLICK** *6* **UNSELECT** *X symbol*	
PREVIEW ANIMATION SEQUENCE	**CLICK** *Preview in PowerPoint® tab* **CLICK** *Next* **REPEAT**	
SEND TO MICROSOFT® POWERPOINT	**CLICK** *Include Animation in Export group of PowerPoint® tab* **CLICK** *Send to PowerPoint®*	

HOW CAN I USE SMARTDRAW TO CREATE A SETTLEMENT BROCHURE?

A properly prepared settlement brochure can be an effective way to obtain the best possible settlement before trial. The exhibits in the brochure can also be enlarged and used as trial exhibits if the case does not settle. Photographs of injuries can show the visible signs of an injury, but not the underlying cause of the pain and suffering. An anatomically correct exhibit can show the specific body part affected by the injury, such as a spinal injury. SmartDraw Healthcare includes a wide assortment of medically accurate drawings that can be submitted in a brochure to the insurance company or opposing counsel, or enlarged for use as exhibits in trial. One of the obvious advantages of creating brochures is avoiding the cost of buying large exhibits or storing a collection.

NOTE: See page 314 for a medical exhibit from the Healthcare version.

CREATING A SETTLEMENT BROCHURE

GOAL	ACTION	RESULT
CREATE COVER **TIP:** Exhibits in a brochure can also be printed poster size or used in electronic format in trial as exhibits. Exhibits in brochures can also be printed poster size or used in electronic format as exhibits in trial. Local printer companies can provide the desired file format for large-scale printing.	**SELECT** *Blank Flyer template* **OR** **OPEN** *SmartDraw document* **IMPORT** *photographs and images*	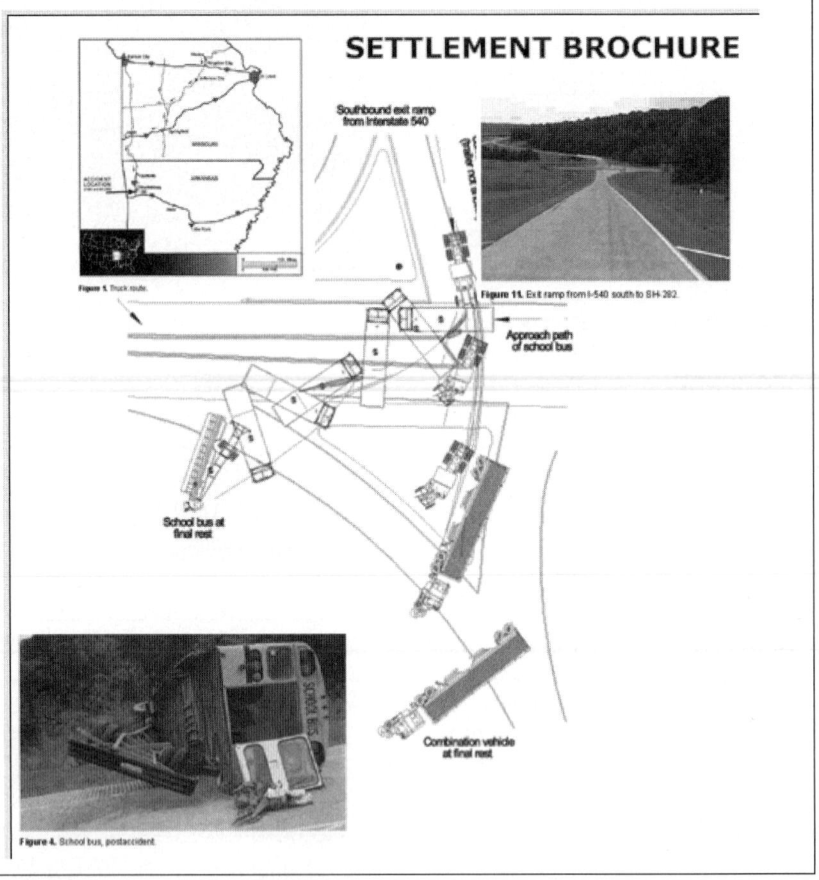 SETTLEMENT BROCHURE

(*continued*)

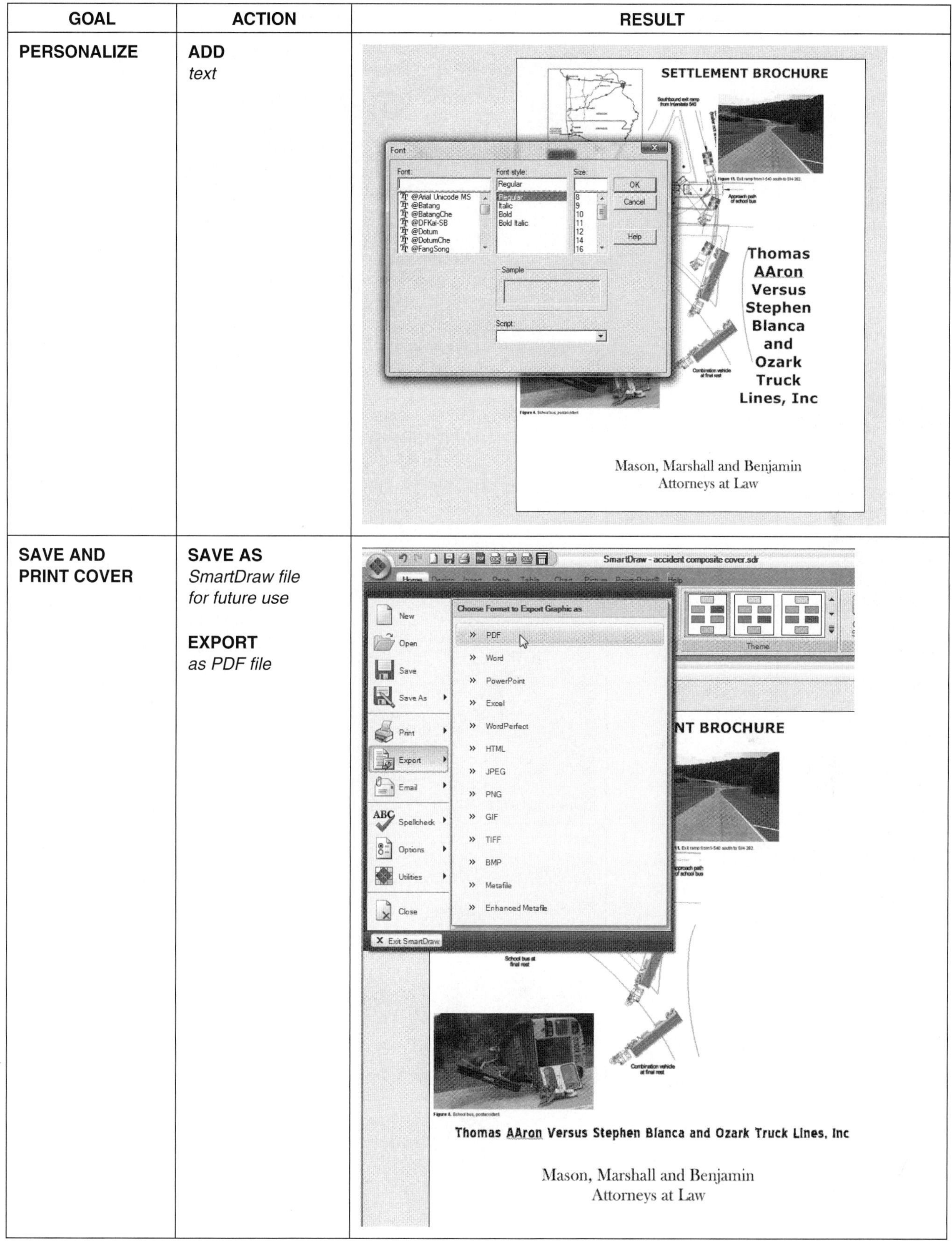

GOAL	ACTION	RESULT
PERSONALIZE	**ADD** *text*	
SAVE AND PRINT COVER	**SAVE AS** *SmartDraw file for future use* **EXPORT** *as PDF file*	

(*continued*)

GOAL	ACTION	RESULT
ADD PICTURES **EXPORT SMARTDRAW DOCUMENTS TO ADD TO SETTLEMENT BROCHURE**	**EXPORT** *as PDF file*	 SCHOOL BUS AFTER ACCIDENT
ADD ANNOTATED MAPS **EXPORT SMARTDRAW DOCUMENTS TO ADD TO SETTLEMENT BROCHURE**	**EXPORT** *as PDF file*	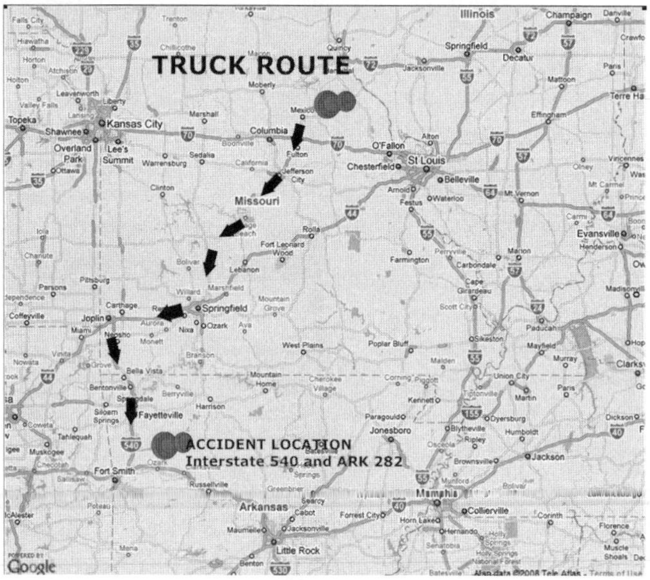
CREATE EXHIBITS **EXPORT SMARTDRAW DOCUMENTS TO ADD TO SETTLEMENT BROCHURE**	**CLICK** *Personal Injury in Document Browser* **CLICK** *Spine* **ANNOTATE** *by adding arrow symbols and text showing area of injury*	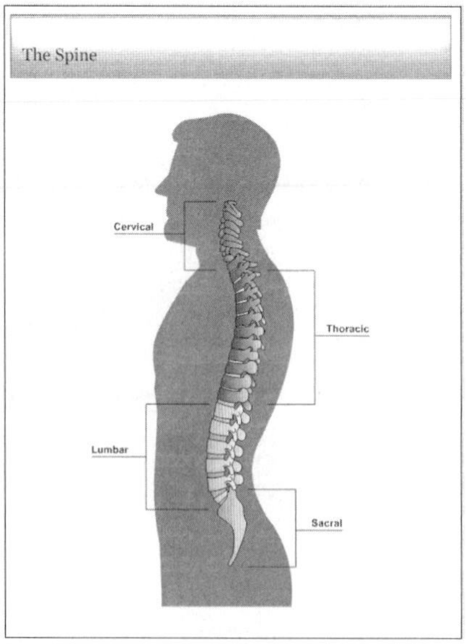

(*continued*)

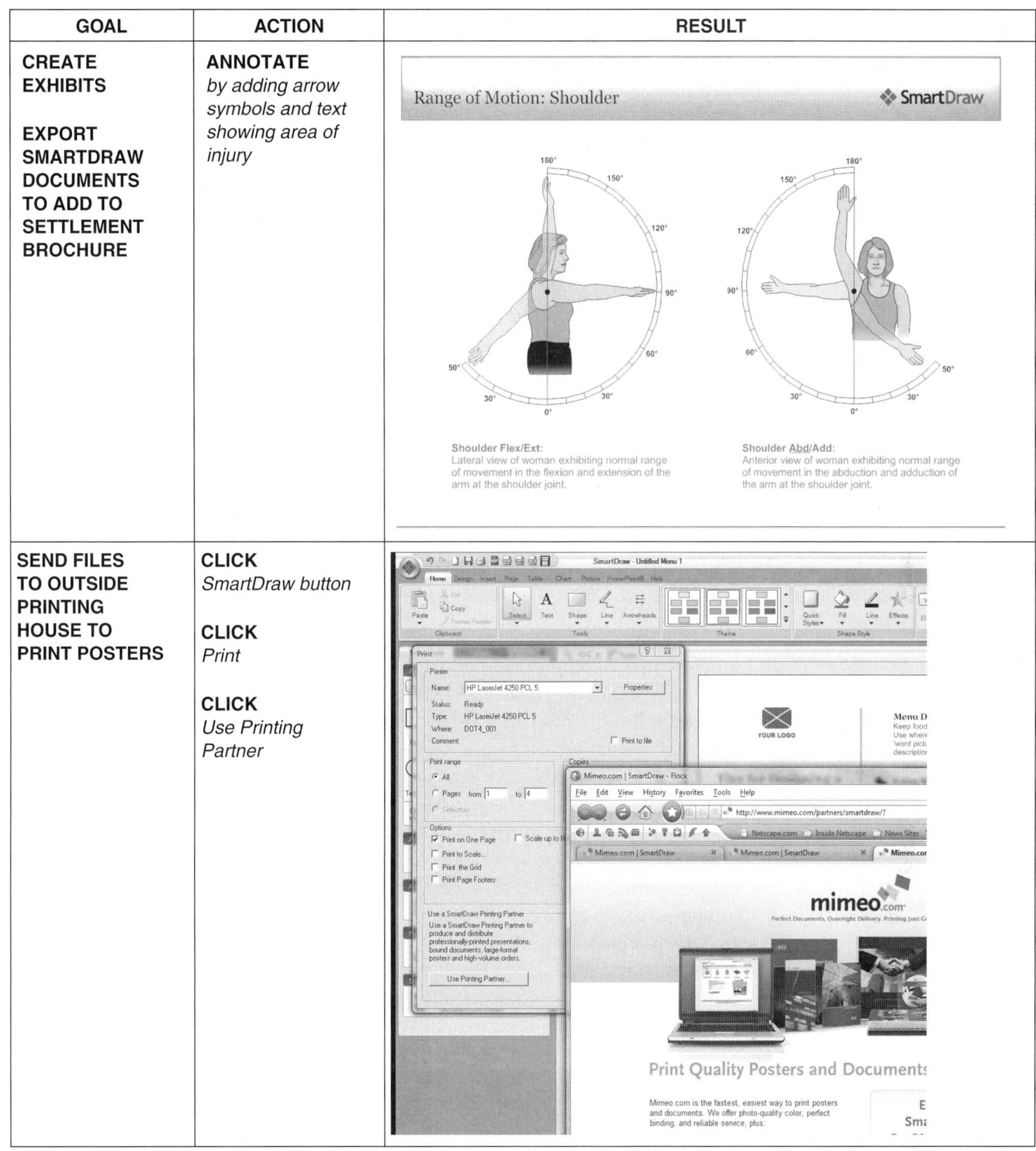
Range of Motion: Shoulder
SmartDraw
Shoulder Flex/Ext:
Lateral view of woman exhibiting normal range of movement in the flexion and extension of the arm at the shoulder joint.
Shoulder Abd/Add:
Anterior view of woman exhibiting normal range of movement in the abduction and adduction of the arm at the shoulder joint.
SmartDraw - Untitled Menu 1
Print
Use a SmartDraw Printing Partner
Use Printing Partner...
Mimeo.com | SmartDraw - Flock
mimeo.com
Print Quality Posters and Documents

GOAL	ACTION	RESULT
CREATE EXHIBITS **EXPORT SMARTDRAW DOCUMENTS TO ADD TO SETTLEMENT BROCHURE**	**ANNOTATE** *by adding arrow symbols and text showing area of injury*	
SEND FILES TO OUTSIDE PRINTING HOUSE TO PRINT POSTERS	**CLICK** *SmartDraw button* **CLICK** *Print* **CLICK** *Use Printing Partner*	

APPENDIX VI

SANCTION TUTORIAL

sanction™

CREATING A TRIAL PRESENTATION

Trial presentation programs may be used to display different types of evidence and trial exhibits including photographs or written documents, videotaped depositions of witnesses not present in the courtroom, computer simulations, or videos showing how an accident happened, on large screens or multimedia monitors for identification by a witness or to the court.

Sanction is used to assemble all of the potential items to be presented: paper-based exhibits, text transcripts of depositions, video depositions, and simulation videos. It may also be used to annotate on the screen passages in documents, or show enlarged sections of documents for emphasis.

The school bus–truck accident case presented in the text and detailed in Appendix II is used in this short tutorial. The sample files of the related exhibits, computer simulations, videotaped deposition and transcript, may be download from MyLegalStudiesKit, www.mylegalstudieskit.com.

TUTORIAL DEMONSTRATION FILES

Before starting the tutorial: create a folder such as C:\Sanction Files on your computer, or on a removable storage media, for the sample files; then download all of these materials to that folder from MyLegalStudiesKit.

Files may be downloaded individually or using the compressed file that contains all the files. To open the compressed file requires an unzip program be installed on your computer, such as WinZip.

Tutorial Requirements

Minimum Hardware Requirements

PC Users.

	Minimum Configuration	Optimal Configuration
Processor	2GHz or faster Single Core	2GHz or faster Core2 Duo
Processor Memory	1GB RAM	4GB RAM
Operating System	Windows XP (Service Pack 3)	Windows XP or Windows 7
Data Storage	80GB Internal Hard Drive	160GB Internal Hard Drive
Video	128MB Video Display Card	256MB Video Display Card

MAC Users. To use this program on a MAC requires a Mac computer that can run PC software.

DOWNLOADING DEMONSTRATION FILES FROM MYLEGALSTUDIESKIT WEBSITE

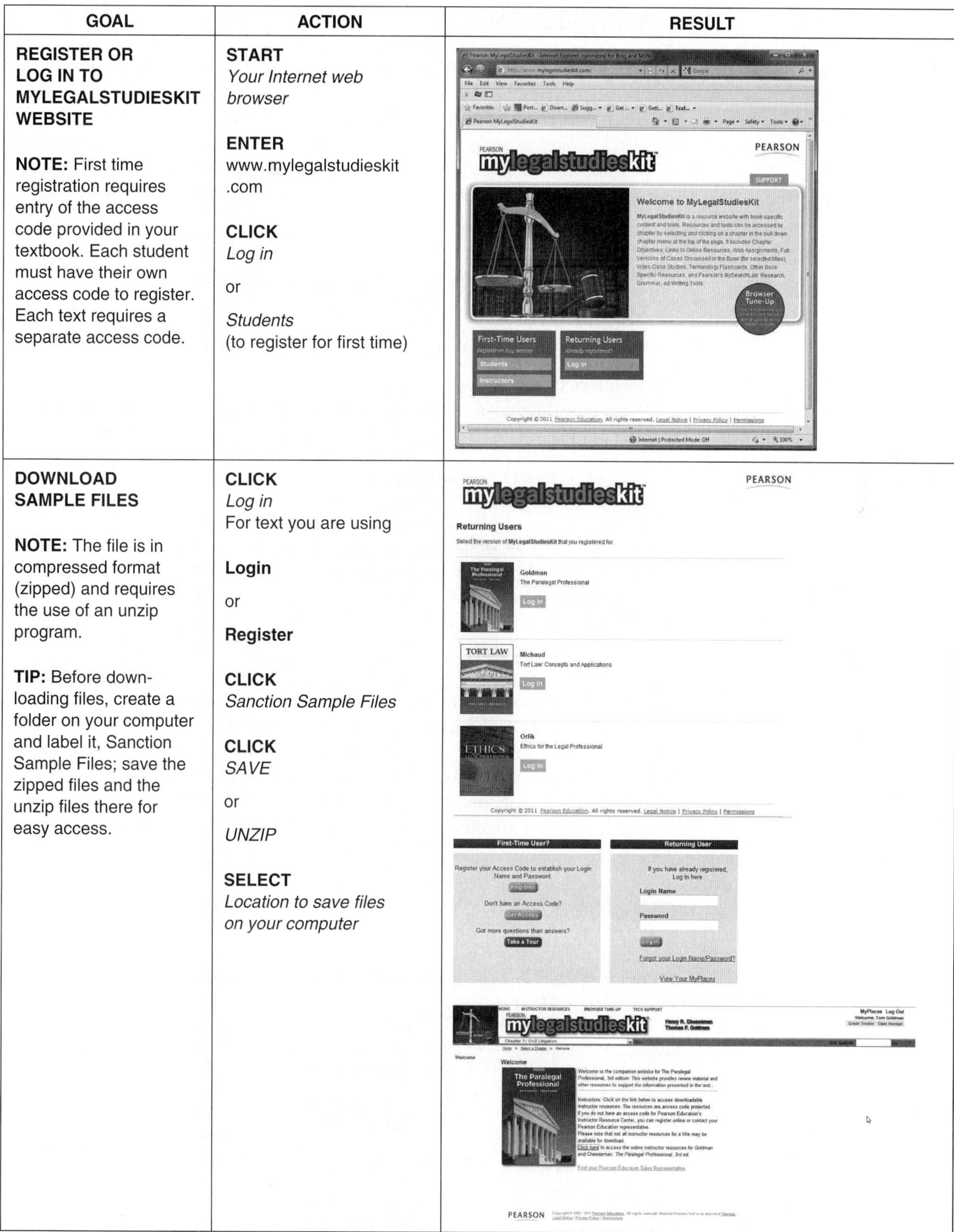

GOAL	ACTION	RESULT
REGISTER OR LOG IN TO MYLEGALSTUDIESKIT WEBSITE **NOTE:** First time registration requires entry of the access code provided in your textbook. Each student must have their own access code to register. Each text requires a separate access code.	**START** *Your Internet web browser* **ENTER** www.mylegalstudieskit .com **CLICK** *Log in* or *Students* (to register for first time)	
DOWNLOAD SAMPLE FILES **NOTE:** The file is in compressed format (zipped) and requires the use of an unzip program. **TIP:** Before down-loading files, create a folder on your computer and label it, Sanction Sample Files; save the zipped files and the unzip files there for easy access.	**CLICK** *Log in* For text you are using **Login** or **Register** **CLICK** *Sanction Sample Files* **CLICK** *SAVE* or *UNZIP* **SELECT** *Location to save files on your computer*	

HOW DO I DOWNLOAD SANCTION FROM THE SANCTION SOLUTIONS WEBSITE?

When downloading the demo program your Internet browser may ask if you want to **save** the **program** first and later run it, or immediately **run** it on your computer. Depending on the speed of your Internet connection, the download may take from 1 to 10 minutes. It is recommended that you save the program and then run the program after closing your web browser and antivirus program. When you save the program, remember where you saved the program so you can locate it and install it at a later time.

For example, the location where the program is saved includes

Drive designation**\Folder** name**\Filename**

or

C: \Downloads\Sanction 3.exe

The location: C:\Downloads\Sanction 3.exe is called the **path.**

When you download the program, record the path for your computer below.

*Enter Drive:*________:\

Enter download folder: _____________\

File name: Sanction 3.exe

When you run the program it installs the actual program files, sets up a Sanction Solution folder in the Program folder of the computer, and adds necessary entries on your computer hard drive to allow it to run.

The program will run more efficiently if the sample files are also saved in a folder on the computer on which the Sanction program is installed.

However, if you are going to use Sanction with the sample case files on a removable storage media, it must be plugged into the computer each time you use the program. When you set up a case in Sanction, such as the School Bus–Truck case study, the program creates a path to the source of the sample files. For example, if you are using a Toshiba portable hard drive, Sanction will setup the path to the sample files on that device. Every time you use Sanction to review this School Bus–Truck case, the Toshiba portable hard drive would need to be accessible.

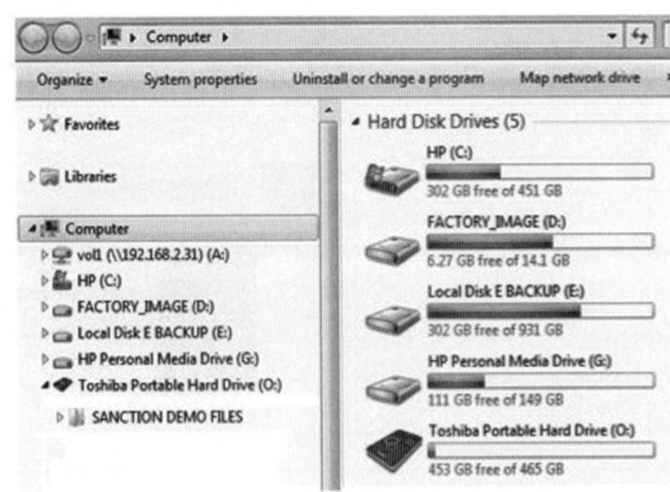

DOWNLOADING AND INSTALLING SANCTION FROM WEBSITE

GOAL	ACTION	RESULT
DOWNLOAD SANCTION DEMO PROGRAM FROM THE SANCTION SOLUTIONS WEBSITE	**START** *Your Internet web browser* **ENTER** http://media.pearsoncmg .com/ph/chet/chet_goldman _techresources_1/ **CLICK** *Sanction icon tab* Follow instructions on website	

■ STARTING SANCTION

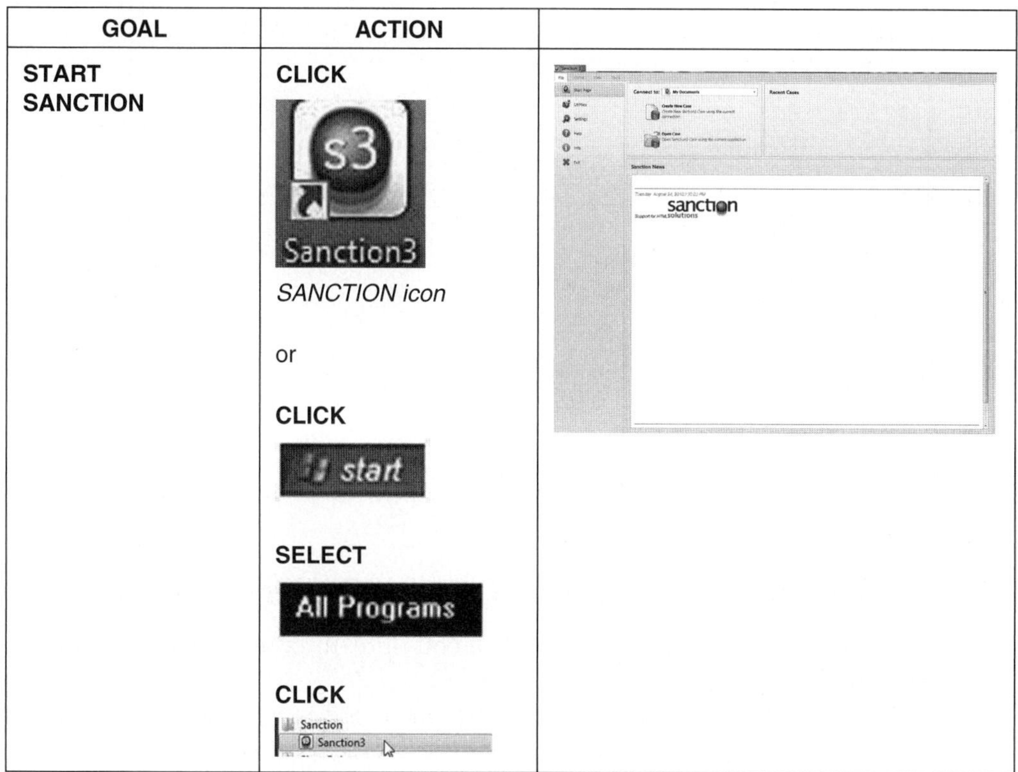

GOAL	ACTION	
START SANCTION	**CLICK** *SANCTION icon* or **CLICK** **SELECT** **CLICK**	

CREATING A NEW CASE

GOAL	ACTION	RESULT
CREATE A NEW CASE FILE IN SANCTION	**CLICK** *Open Case*	Connect to: My Documents Create New Case Create New Sanction3 Case using the current connection Open Case Open Sanction3 Case using the current connection Create New Case Enter the name of the new case: Cancel Create
ENTER NAME OF NEW CASE FILE	**TYPE** *School Bus* **CLICK** *Create*	Connect to: My Documents Create New Case Create New Sanction3 Case using the current connection Open Case Open Sanction3 Case using the current connection Create New Case Enter the name of the new case: School Bus Cancel Create

Exhibit 1 New case created in Sanction

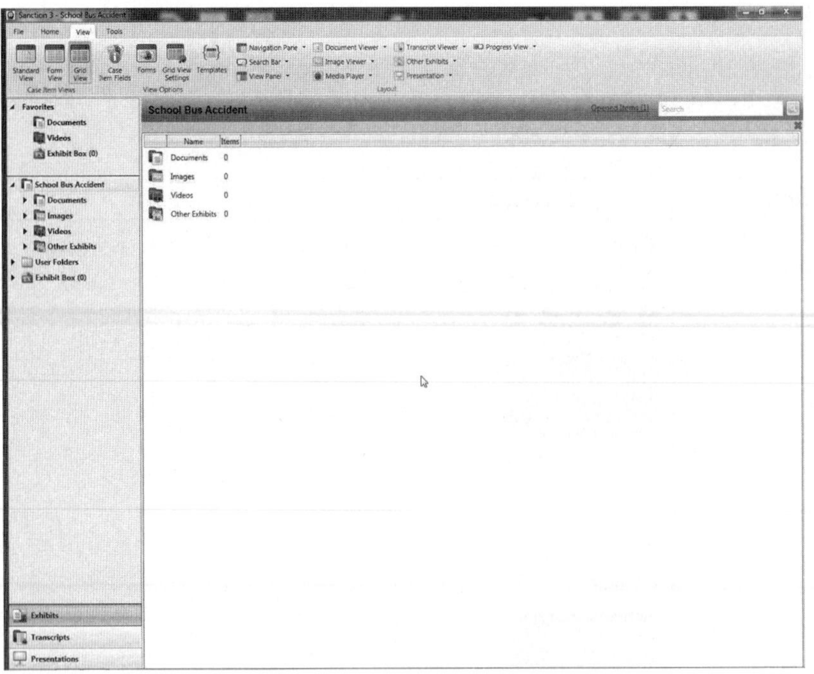

Adding Items to a Sanction Case for Presentation

Sanction divides the presentation elements into three main category folders: Exhibits, Transcripts, and Presentations.

Exhibits include documents, images, video, and other exhibits. Transcripts of deposition and trial are imported into the Transcripts folder. After adding exhibits and transcripts to a Sanction Case File they may be added to the specific Presentation folder for later use. Presentations folders are just convenient folders for sorting the different items that may be used in specific presentations such as that for a specific witness, an opening statement, or closing argument.

There are a number of different ways to add items to a Sanction case including the use of tab menu options and traditional Microsoft file selection, drag and drop.

You can add documents, images, videos, transcripts, and other exhibits that are in a computer format recognized by Sanction. Like other computer programs, Sanction must be able recognize the file format to access it within the program. Sanction supports the following file formats:

Document types supported: TIF, PDF
Image types supported: JPG, GIF, BMP, PNG
Media types supported: MPG, WAV, MP3

TIP

The Open Files window may be set to show the same files in detail or in icons. It may be easier to set your option to icons to locate files.

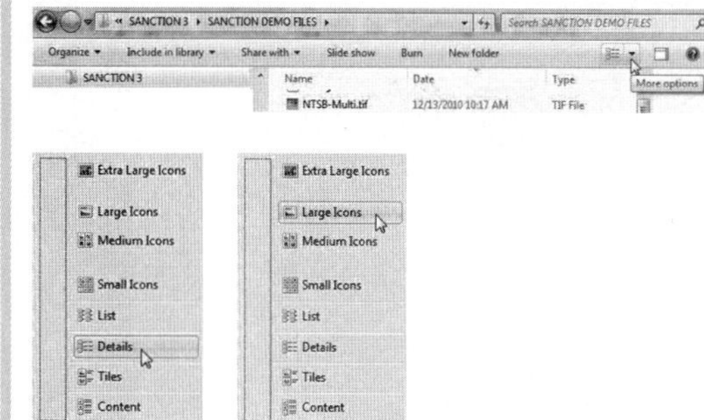

ADDING DOCUMENTS TO A SANCTION CASE

GOAL	ACTION	RESULT
ADD DOCUMENT TO SANCTION SCHOOL BUS CASE	**CLICK** *Files* in the import options on the Home Tab **BROWSE** *Open files* window to folder containing Sanction sample files **CLICK** *Desired document* **CLICK** *Open*	

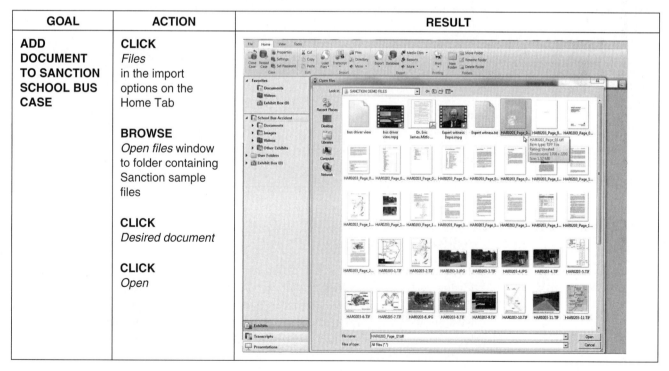

ADDING IMAGES TO A SANCTION CASE

GOAL	ACTION	RESULT
SELECT AND ADD IMAGES TO SANCTION SCHOOL BUS CASE	**CLICK** *Files* in the import options in the Home Tab **BROWSE** *Open files* window to folder containing image files **CLICK** *Desired image* **CLICK** *Open*	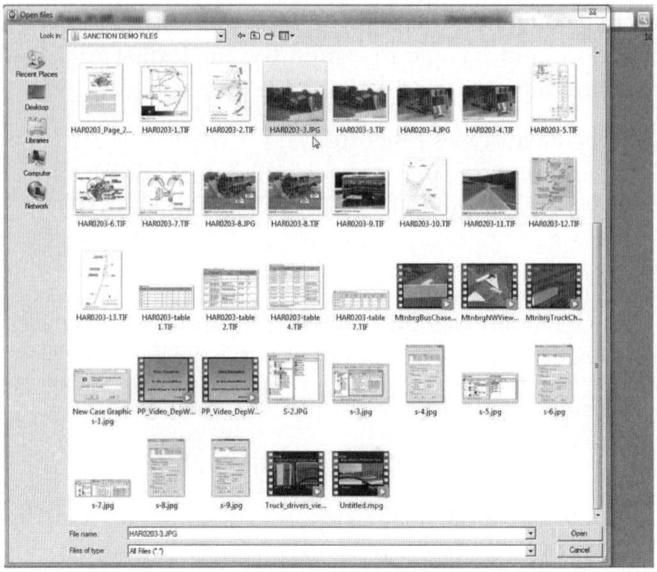

ADDING VIDEO SIMULATIONS TO A SANCTION CASE

GOAL	ACTION	RESULT
ADD A VIDEO FILE TO SANCTION SCHOOL BUS CASE	**CLICK** *Files* in the import options in the Home Tab **BROWSE** *Open files* window to folder containing video files **CLICK** *Desired video* **CLICK** *Open*	 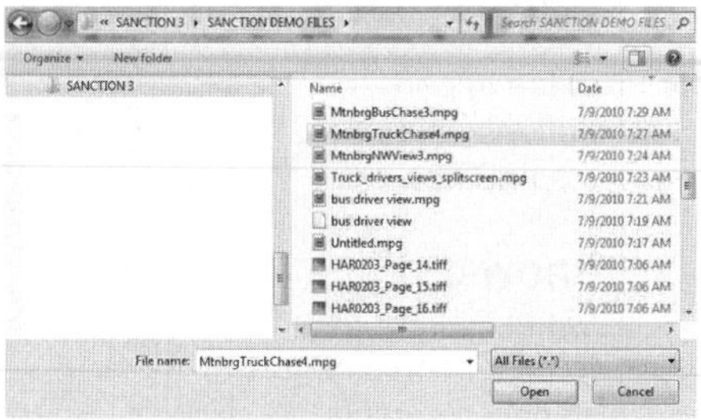

Adding Transcripts

Transcript may be provided in different formats. Typical is the ASCII or text file format. When a deposition is videotaped, the deposition may be provided with a linked text file and the video file. In Sanction this may be in a proprietary format that allows video and text to scroll together. For demonstration purposes you have been provided with the coordinated file (Esquireview Deposition) and the traditional text file.

Exhibit 2 Sanction video transcript screen

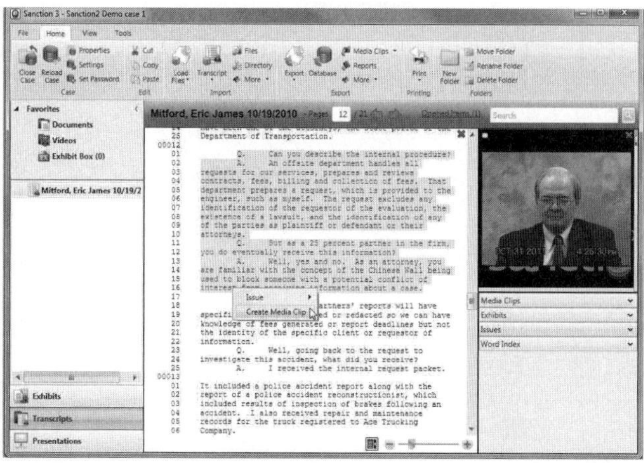

ADDING AN ASCII TRANSCRIPT TO A SANCTION CASE

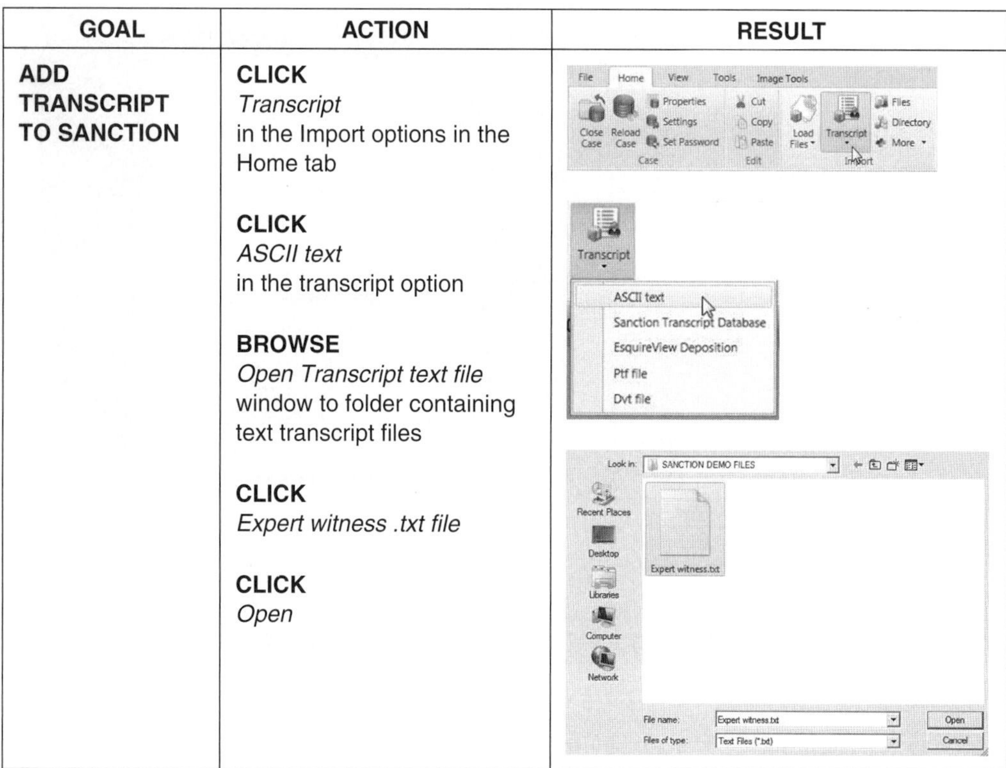

GOAL	ACTION	RESULT
ADD TRANSCRIPT TO SANCTION	**CLICK** *Transcript* in the Import options in the Home tab **CLICK** *ASCII text* in the transcript option **BROWSE** *Open Transcript text file* window to folder containing text transcript files **CLICK** *Expert witness .txt file* **CLICK** *Open*	

Items are managed in a folder of similar type items—Exhibits, Transcripts and Presentations—shown on the bottom of the left panel-Tree. Selecting the folder shows the items in that category, which may then be displayed in the viewing area.

VIEWING ITEMS IN THE PREVIEW SCREEN

GOAL	ACTION	RESULT
OPEN CATEGORY AND EXPAND LIST OF ITEMS	**CLICK** *Exhibits* **RIGHT CLICK** with cursor on *Documents* **CLICK** *Expand*	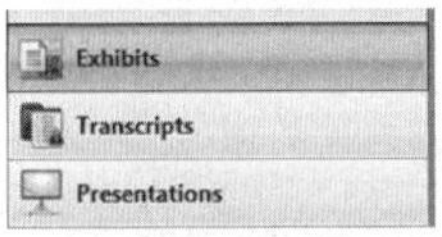 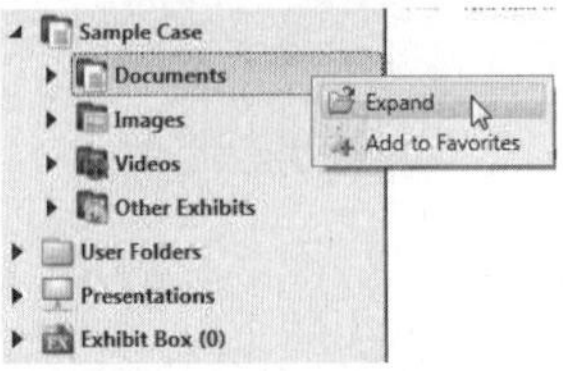 Exhibits Transcripts Presentations Sample Case Documents Images Videos Other Exhibits User Folders Presentations Exhibit Box (0) Expand Add to Favorites
SELECT FILE TO OPEN INTO THE VIEWING AREA	**RIGHT CLICK** *Documents* **CLICK** *Open*	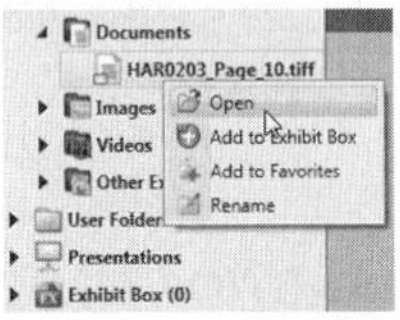 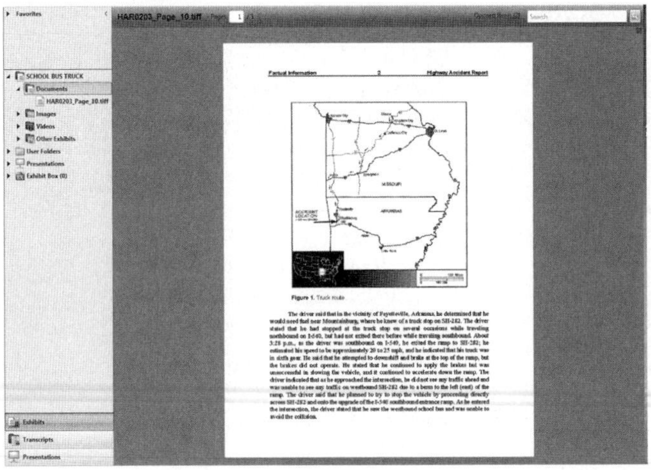 Documents HAR0203_Page_10.tiff Images Videos Other Exhibits User Folders Presentations Exhibit Box (0) Open Add to Exhibit Box Add to Favorites Rename

■ PRESENTATION ON THE COURT MONITOR

Presentations in Sanction are collections of documents, images, videos, and other exhibits that may be organized in individual presentation folders. The Presentation Mode allows the items in the individual presentation folders to be displayed on the court monitor. All of the items may be previewed in the viewing area of the legal team monitor before presentation.

Exhibit 3 Working screen with viewing area and Presentation Mode Screen

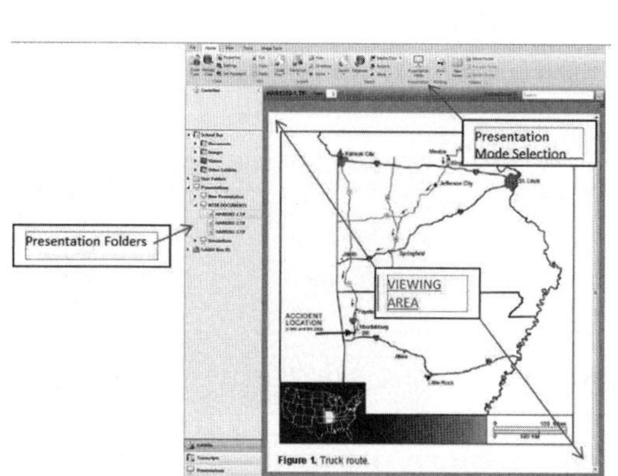

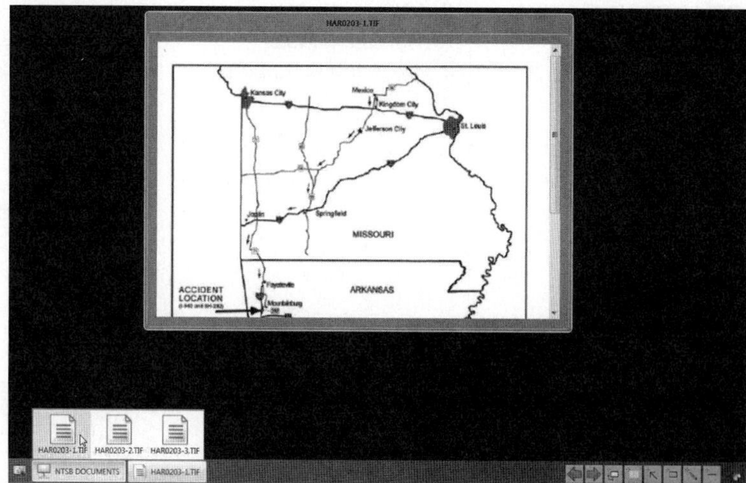

PRESENTING ITEMS ON THE COURT MONITOR

GOAL	ACTION	RESULT
CREATE PRESENTATION FOLDERS WITH EXHIBITS FOR USE IN PRESENTATION MODE **NOTE:** This requires a two monitor display system.	**RIGHT CLICK** with cursor on *Presentations* **CLICK** *Create New Presentation* rename the folder **RIGHT CLICK** with cursor on *Documents* **CLICK** *Expand* **CLICK and Hold Mouse button** on document drag it to new presentation folder **RELEASE CURSOR**	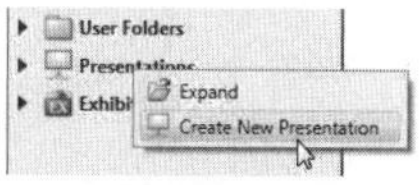 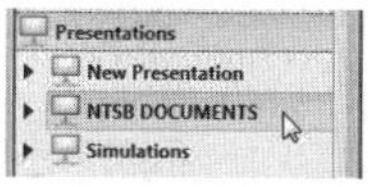  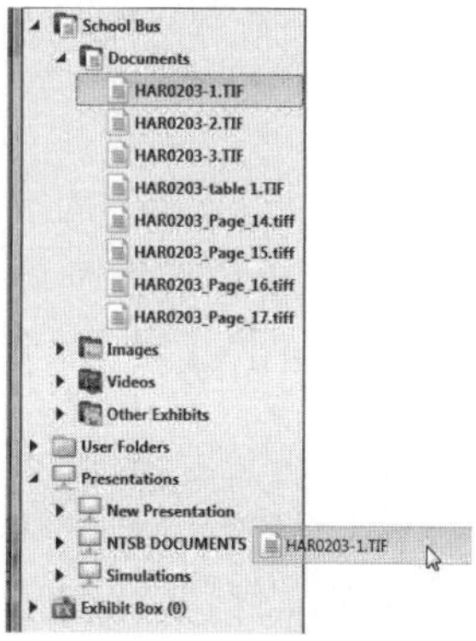

(*continued*)

GOAL	ACTION	RESULT
OPEN PRESENTATION MODE SCREEEN	**CLICK** *Presentation Mode* in Home tab on ribbon	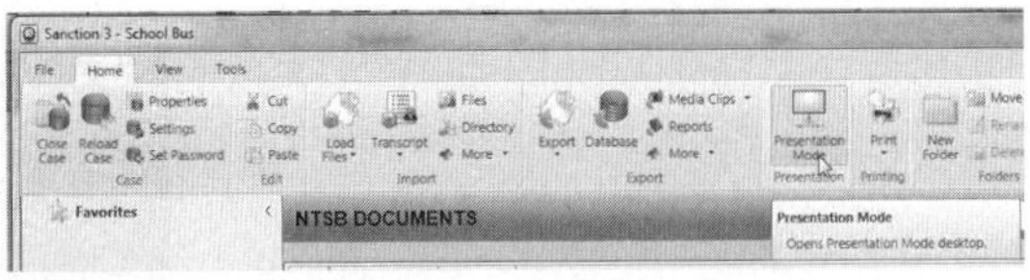 
SHOW SELECTED ITEM IN VIEWING AREA ON PERSONAL DISPLAY AND ON COURT DISPLAY	**RIGHT CLICK** *Icon* to open Presentation option **CLICK** *NTSB Document* **CLICK** *Item to display*	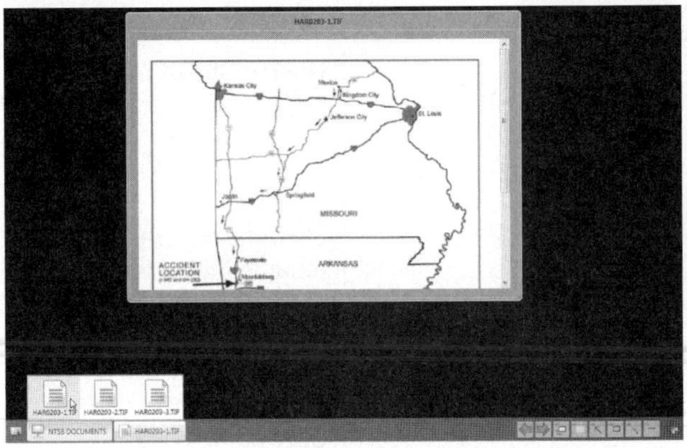

ANNOTATIONS

A complete set of annotations tools can be used to mark up documents. The annotation tools are located in the Image Tools tab on the ribbon as shown below. An annotation menu is also accessible by a right click of the mouse when a document is opened in the preview area.

Adding Annotations

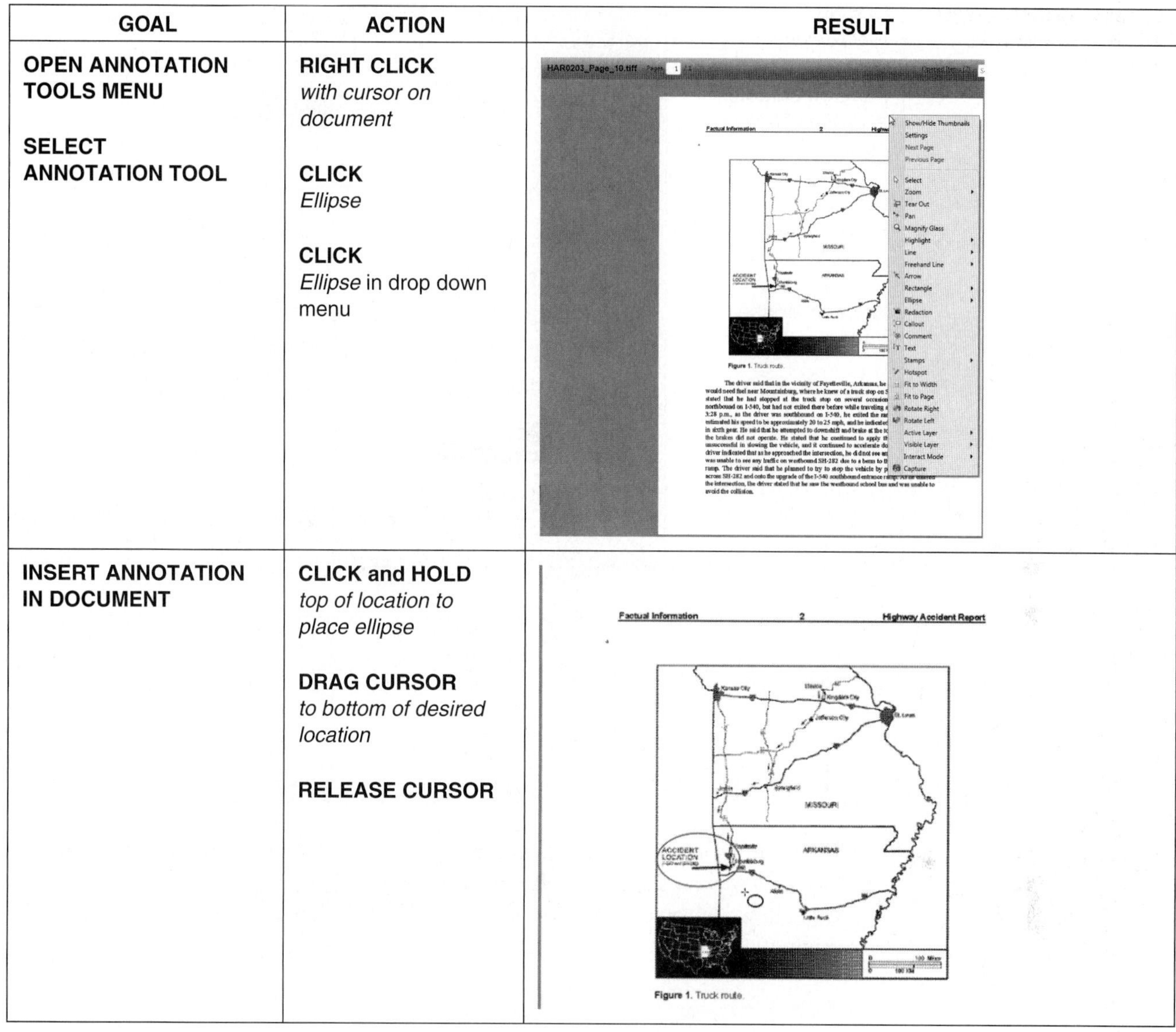

GOAL	ACTION	RESULT
OPEN ANNOTATION TOOLS MENU **SELECT ANNOTATION TOOL**	**RIGHT CLICK** *with cursor on document* **CLICK** *Ellipse* **CLICK** *Ellipse* in drop down menu	
INSERT ANNOTATION IN DOCUMENT	**CLICK and HOLD** *top of location to place ellipse* **DRAG CURSOR** *to bottom of desired location* **RELEASE CURSOR**	

(continued)

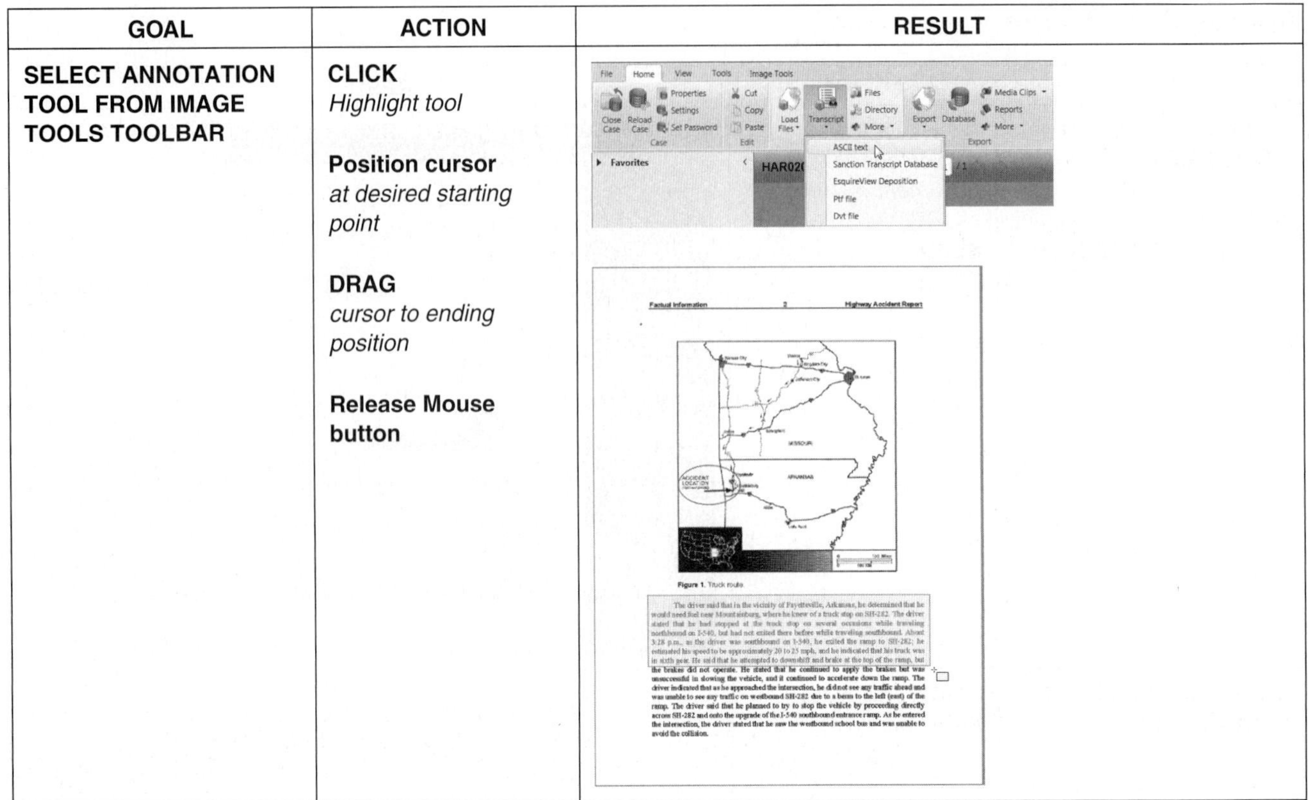

GOAL	ACTION	RESULT
SELECT ANNOTATION TOOL FROM IMAGE TOOLS TOOLBAR	**CLICK** *Highlight tool* **Position cursor** *at desired starting point* **DRAG** *cursor to ending position* **Release Mouse button**	

TEAR OUT A SECTION OF A DOCUMENT

There are portions of documents that may need to be shown clearly and in a larger view than the rest of the document of which it is a part. The tear out feature allows selected text to be shown in a larger separate window on top of the original document.

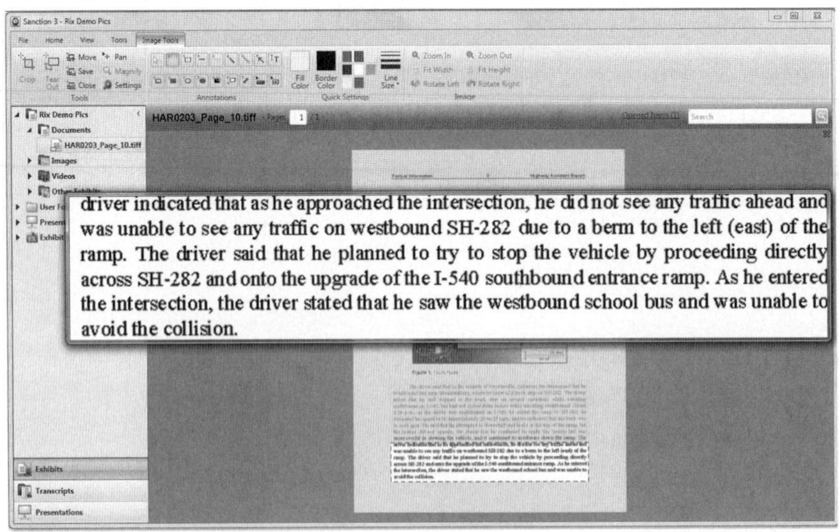

TEAR OUT A SECTION OF A DOCUMENT

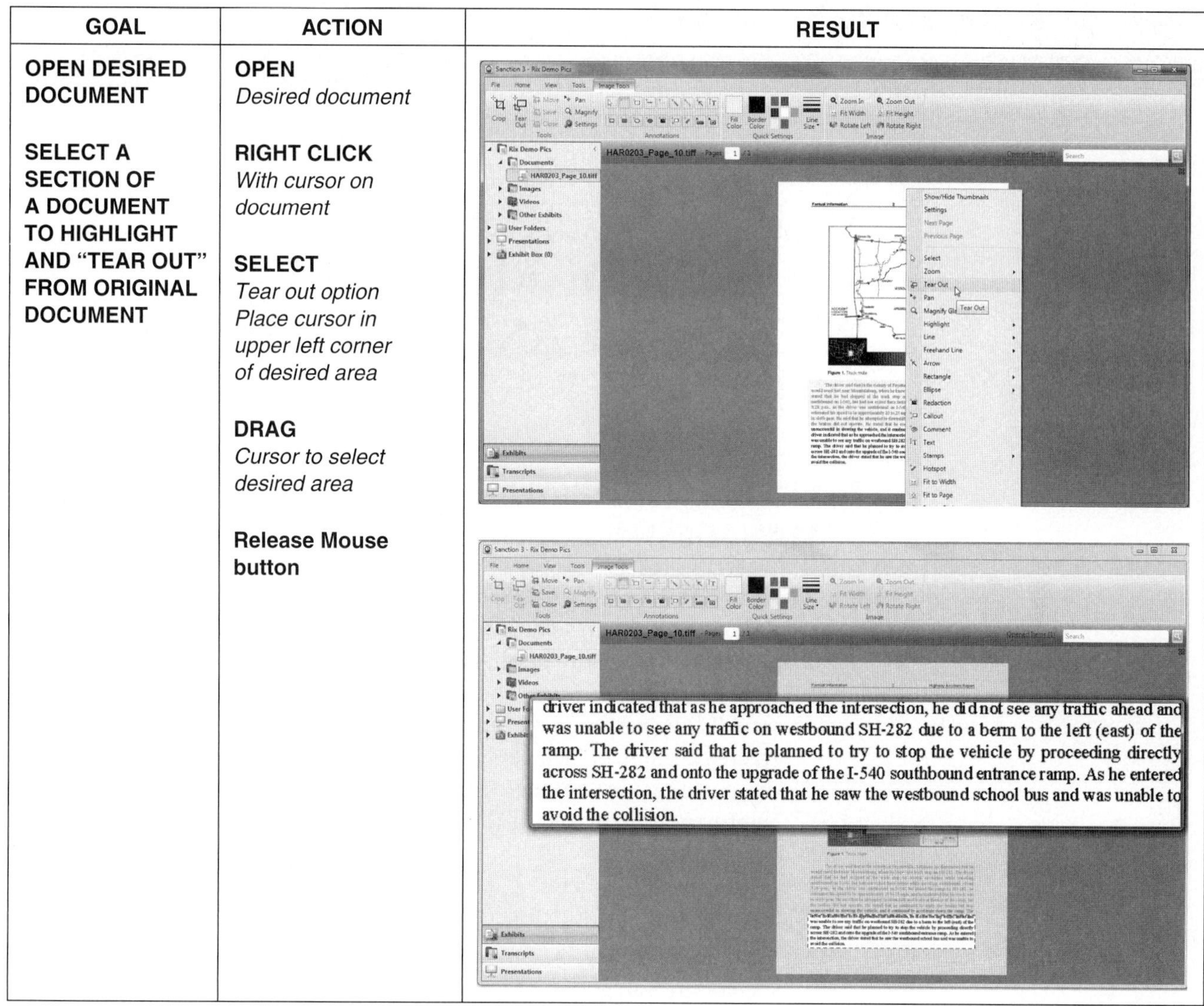

GOAL	ACTION	RESULT
OPEN DESIRED DOCUMENT **SELECT A SECTION OF A DOCUMENT TO HIGHLIGHT AND "TEAR OUT" FROM ORIGINAL DOCUMENT**	**OPEN** *Desired document* **RIGHT CLICK** *With cursor on document* **SELECT** *Tear out option* *Place cursor in upper left corner of desired area* **DRAG** *Cursor to select desired area* **Release Mouse button**	

Additional tutorial information is available at
http://media.pearsoncmg.com/ph/chet/chet_goldman_techresources_1/

or on the Technology Resources Website:
www.pearsonhighered.com/goldman

APPENDIX VII

SELECTED PORTIONS OF THE FEDERAL RULES OF CIVIL PROCEDURE AND FEDERAL RULES OF EVIDENCE

RULE 16. PRETRIAL CONFERENCES; SCHEDULING; MANAGEMENT

(a) Purposes of a Pretrial Conference.
In any action, the court may order the attorneys and any unrepresented parties to appear for one or more pretrial conferences for such purposes as:
(1) expediting disposition of the action;
(2) establishing early and continuing control so that the case will not be protracted because of lack of management;
(3) discouraging wasteful pretrial activities;
(4) improving the quality of the trial through more thorough preparation, and;
(5) facilitating settlement.

(b) Scheduling.
(1) Scheduling Order.
Except in categories of actions exempted by local rule, the district judge—or a magistrate judge when authorized by local rule—must issue a scheduling order:
(A) after receiving the parties' report under Rule 26(f); or
(B) after consulting with the parties' attorneys and any unrepresented parties at a scheduling conference or by telephone, mail, or other means.

(2) Time to Issue.
The judge must issue the scheduling order as soon as practicable, but in any event within the earlier of 120 days after any defendant has been served with the complaint or 90 days after any defendant has appeared.

(3) Contents of the Order.
(A) *Required Contents*. The scheduling order must limit the time to join other parties, amend the pleadings, complete discovery, and file motions.
(B) *Permitted Contents*. The scheduling order may:
(i) modify the timing of disclosures under Rules 26(a) and 26(e)(1);
(ii) modify the extent of discovery;

(iii) provide for disclosure or discovery of electronically stored information;
(iv) include any agreements the parties reach for asserting claims of privilege or of protection as trial-preparation material after information is produced;
(v) set dates for pretrial conferences and for trial; and
(vi) include other appropriate matters.

(4) Modifying a Schedule.
A schedule may be modified only for good cause and with the judge's consent.

(c) Attendance and Matters for Consideration at a Pretrial Conference.

(1) Attendance.
A represented party must authorize at least one of its attorneys to make stipulations and admissions about all matters that can reasonably be anticipated for discussion at a pretrial conference. If appropriate, the court may require that a party or its representative be present or reasonably available by other means to consider possible settlement.

(2) Matters for Consideration.
At any pretrial conference, the court may consider and take appropriate action on the following matters:

(A) formulating and simplifying the issues, and eliminating frivolous claims or defenses;
(B) amending the pleadings if necessary or desirable;
(C) obtaining admissions and stipulations about facts and documents to avoid unnecessary proof, and ruling in advance on the admissibility of evidence;
(D) avoiding unnecessary proof and cumulative evidence, and limiting the use of testimony under Federal Rule of Evidence 702;
(E) determining the appropriateness and timing of summary adjudication under Rule 56;
(F) controlling and scheduling discovery, including orders affecting disclosures and discovery under Rule 26 and Rules 29 through 37;
(G) identifying witnesses and documents, scheduling the filing and exchange of any pretrial briefs, and setting dates for further conferences and for trial;
(H) referring matters to a magistrate judge or a master;
(I) settling the case and using special procedures to assist in resolving the dispute when authorized by statute or local rule;
(J) determining the form and content of the pretrial order;
(K) disposing of pending motions;
(L) adopting special procedures for managing potentially difficult or protracted actions that may involve complex issues, multiple parties, difficult legal questions, or unusual proof problems;
(M) ordering a separate trial under Rule 42(b) of a claim, counterclaim, crossclaim, thirdparty claim, or particular issue;
(N) ordering the presentation of evidence early in the trial on a manageable issue that might, on the evidence, be the basis for a judgment as a matter of law under Rule 50(a) or a judgment on partial findings under Rule 52(c);

(O) establishing a reasonable limit on the time allowed to present evidence; and

(P) facilitating in other ways the just, speedy, and inexpensive disposition of the action.

(d) Pretrial Orders.
After any conference under this rule, the court should issue an order reciting the action taken. This order controls the course of the action unless the court modifies it.

(e) Final Pretrial Conference and Orders.
The court may hold a final pretrial conference to formulate a trial plan, including a plan to facilitate the admission of evidence. The conference must be held as close to the start of trial as is reasonable, and must be attended by at least one attorney who will conduct the trial for each party and by any unrepresented party. The court may modify the order issued after a final pretrial conference only to prevent manifest injustice.

(f) Sanctions.

(1) In General.
On motion or on its own, the court may issue any just orders, including those authorized by Rule 37(b)(2)(A)(ii)-(vii), if a party or its attorney:

(A) fails to appear at a scheduling or other pretrial conference;

(B) is substantially unprepared to participate—or does not participate in good faith—in the conference; or

(C) fails to obey a scheduling or other pretrial order.

(2) Imposing Fees and Costs.
Instead of or in addition to any other sanction, the court must order the party, its attorney, or both to pay the reasonable expenses—including attorney's fees—incurred because of any noncompliance with this rule, unless the noncompliance was substantially justified or other circumstances make an award of expenses unjust.

RULE 26. DUTY TO DISCLOSE; GENERAL PROVISIONS GOVERNING DISCOVERY

(a) Required Disclosures.

(1) Initial Disclosures.

(A) In General. Except as exempted by Rule 26(a)(1)(B) or as otherwise stipulated or ordered by the court, a party must, without awaiting a discovery request, provide to the other parties:

(i) the name and, if known, the address and telephone number of each individual likely to have discoverable information—along with the subjects of that information—that the disclosing party may use to support its claims or defenses, unless the use would be solely for impeachment;

(ii) a copy—or a description by category and location—of all documents, electronically stored information, and tangible things that the disclosing party has in its possession, custody, or control and may use to support its claims or defenses, unless the use would be solely for impeachment;

(iii) a computation of each category of damages claimed by the disclosing party—who must also make available for inspection and copying as under Rule 34 the documents or other evidentiary material, unless privileged or protected from disclosure, on which each computation is based, including materials bearing on the nature and extent of injuries suffered; and

(iv) for inspection and copying as under Rule 34, any insurance agreement under which an insurance business may be liable to satisfy all or part of a possible judgment in the action or to indemnify or reimburse for payments made to satisfy the judgment.

(B) Proceedings Exempt from Initial Disclosure. The following proceedings are exempt from initial disclosure:

(i) an action for review on an administrative record;

(ii) a forfeiture action in rem arising from a federal statute;

(iii) a petition for habeas corpus or any other proceeding to challenge a criminal conviction or sentence;

(iv) an action brought without an attorney by a person in the custody of the United States, a state, or a state subdivision;

(v) an action to enforce or quash an administrative summons or subpoena;

(vi) an action by the United States to recover benefit payments;

(vii) an action by the United States to collect on a student loan guaranteed by the United States;

(viii) a proceeding ancillary to a proceeding in another court; and

(ix) an action to enforce an arbitration award.

(C) Time for Initial Disclosures—In General. A party must make the initial disclosures at or within 14 days after the parties' Rule 26(f) conference unless a different time is set by stipulation or court order, or unless a party objects during the conference that initial disclosures are not appropriate in this action and states the objection in the proposed discovery plan. In ruling on the objection, the court must determine what disclosures, if any, are to be made and must set the time for disclosure.

(D) Time for Initial Disclosures—For Parties Served or Joined Later. A party that is first served or otherwise joined after the Rule 26(f) conference must make the initial disclosures within 30 days after being served or joined, unless a different time is set by stipulation or court order.

(E) Basis for Initial Disclosure; Unacceptable Excuses. A party must make its initial disclosures based on the information then reasonably available to it. A party is not excused from making its disclosures because it has not fully investigated the case or because it challenges the sufficiency of another party's disclosures or because another party has not made its disclosures.

(2) Disclosure of Expert Testimony.

(A) In General. In addition to the disclosures required by Rule 26(a)(1), a party must disclose to the other parties the identity of any witness it may use at trial to present evidence under Federal Rule of Evidence 702, 703, or 705.

(B) Written Report. Unless otherwise stipulated or ordered by the court, this disclosure must be accompanied by a written report—prepared and signed by the witness—if the witness is one retained or specially employed to provide expert testimony in the case or one whose duties as the party's employee regularly involve giving expert testimony. The report must contain:

(i) a complete statement of all opinions the witness will express and the basis and reasons for them;

(ii) the data or other information considered by the witness in forming them;

(iii) any exhibits that will be used to summarize or support them;

(iv) the witness's qualifications, including a list of all publications authored in the previous 10 years;

(v) a list of all other cases in which, during the previous 4 years, the witness testified as an expert at trial or by deposition; and

(vi) a statement of the compensation to be paid for the study and testimony in the case.

(C) Time to Disclose Expert Testimony. A party must make these disclosures at the times and in the sequence that the court orders. Absent a stipulation or a court order, the disclosures must be made:

(i) at least 90 days before the date set for trial or for the case to be ready for trial; or

(ii) if the evidence is intended solely to contradict or rebut evidence on the same subject matter identified by another party under Rule 26(a)(2)(B), within 30 days after the other party's disclosure.

(D) Supplementing the Disclosure. The parties must supplement these disclosures when required under Rule 26(e).

(3) **Pretrial Disclosures.**

(A) In General. In addition to the disclosures required by Rule 26(a)(1) and (2), a party must provide to the other parties and promptly file the following information about the evidence that it may present at trial other than solely for impeachment:

(i) the name and, if not previously provided, the address and telephone number of each witness—separately identifying those the party expects to present and those it may call if the need arises;

(ii) the designation of those witnesses whose testimony the party expects to present by deposition and, if not taken stenographically, a transcript of the pertinent parts of the deposition; and

(iii) an identification of each document or other exhibit, including summaries of other evidence—separately identifying those items the party expects to offer and those it may offer if the need arises.

(B) Time for Pretrial Disclosures; Objections. Unless the court orders otherwise, these disclosures must be made at least 30 days before trial. Within 14 days after they are made, unless the court sets a different time, a party may serve and promptly file a list of the following objections: any objections to the use under Rule 32(a) of a deposition designated by another party under Rule 26(a)(3)(A)(ii);

and any objection, together with the grounds for it, that may be made to the admissibility of materials identified under Rule 26(a)(3)(A)(iii). An objection not so made—except for one under Federal Rule of Evidence 402 or 403—is waived unless excused by the court for good cause.

(4) Form of Disclosures.

Unless the court orders otherwise, all disclosures under Rule 26(a) must be in writing, signed, and served.

(b) Discovery Scope and Limits.

(1) Scope in General.

Unless otherwise limited by court order, the scope of discovery is as follows: Parties may obtain discovery regarding any nonprivileged matter that is relevant to any party's claim or defense—including the existence, description, nature, custody, condition, and location of any documents or other tangible things and the identity and location of persons who know of any discoverable matter. For good cause, the court may order discovery of any matter relevant to the subject matter involved in the action. Relevant information need not be admissible at the trial if the discovery appears reasonably calculated to lead to the discovery of admissible evidence. All discovery is subject to the limitations imposed by Rule 26(b)(2)(C).

(2) Limitations on Frequency and Extent.

(A) When Permitted. By order, the court may alter the limits in these rules on the number of depositions and interrogatories or on the length of depositions under Rule 30. By order or local rule, the court may also limit the number of requests under Rule 36.

(B) Specific Limitations on Electronically Stored Information. A party need not provide discovery of electronically stored information from sources that the party identifies as not reasonably accessible because of undue burden or cost. On motion to compel discovery or for a protective order, the party from whom discovery is sought must show that the information is not reasonably accessible because of undue burden or cost. If that showing is made, the court may nonetheless order discovery from such sources if the requesting party shows good cause, considering the limitations of Rule 26(b)(2)(C). The court may specify conditions for the discovery.

(C) When Required. On motion or on its own, the court must limit the frequency or extent of discovery otherwise allowed by these rules or by local rule if it determines that:

(i) the discovery sought is unreasonably cumulative or duplicative, or can be obtained from some other source that is more convenient, less burdensome, or less expensive;

(ii) the party seeking discovery has had ample opportunity to obtain the information by discovery in the action; or

(iii) the burden or expense of the proposed discovery outweighs its likely benefit, considering the needs of the case, the amount in controversy, the parties' resources, the importance of the issues at stake in the action, and the importance of the discovery in resolving the issues.

(3) Trial Preparation: Materials.

(A) Documents and Tangible Things. Ordinarily, a party may not discover documents and tangible things that are prepared in anticipation of litigation or for trial by or for another party or its representative (including the other party's attorney, consultant, surety, indemnitor, insurer, or agent). But, subject to Rule 26(b)(4), those materials may be discovered if:

(i) they are otherwise discoverable under Rule 26(b)(1); and

(ii) the party shows that it has substantial need for the materials to prepare its case and cannot, without undue hardship, obtain their substantial equivalent by other means.

(B) Protection Against Disclosure. If the court orders discovery of those materials, it must protect against disclosure of the mental impressions, conclusions, opinions, or legal theories of a party's attorney or other representative concerning the litigation.

(C) Previous Statement. Any party or other person may, on request and without the required showing, obtain the person's own previous statement about the action or its subject matter. If the request is refused, the person may move for a court order, and Rule 37(a)(5) applies to the award of expenses. A previous statement is either:

(i) a written statement that the person has signed or otherwise adopted or approved; or

(ii) a contemporaneous stenographic, mechanical, electrical, or other recording—or a transcription of it—that recites substantially verbatim the person's oral statement.

(4) Trial Preparation: Experts.

(A) **Expert Who May Testify.** A party may depose any person who has been identified as an expert whose opinions may be presented at trial. If Rule 26(a)(2)(B) requires a report from the expert, the deposition may be conducted only after the report is provided.

(B) **Expert Employed Only for Trial Preparation.** Ordinarily, a party may not, by interrogatories or deposition, discover facts known or opinions held by an expert who has been retained or specially employed by another party in anticipation of litigation or to prepare for trial and who is not expected to be called as a witness at trial. But a party may do so only:

(i) as provided in Rule 35(b); or

(ii) on showing exceptional circumstances under which it is impracticable for the party to obtain facts or opinions on the same subject by other means.

(C) **Payment.** Unless manifest injustice would result, the court must require that the party seeking discovery:

(i) pay the expert a reasonable fee for time spent in responding to discovery under Rule 26(b)(4)(A) or (B); and

(ii) for discovery under (B), also pay the other party a fair portion of the fees and expenses it reasonably incurred in obtaining the expert's facts and opinions.

(5) Claiming Privilege or Protecting Trial- Preparation Materials.

(A) Information Withheld. When a party withholds information otherwise discoverable by claiming that the information is privileged or subject to protection as trial-preparation material, the party must:

(i) expressly make the claim; and

(ii) describe the nature of the documents, communications, or tangible things not produced or disclosed—and do so in a manner that, without revealing information itself privileged or protected, will enable other parties to assess the claim.

(B) Information Produced. If information produced in discovery is subject to a claim of privilege or of protection as trial preparation material, the party making the claim may notify any party that received the information of the claim and the basis for it. After being notified, a party must promptly return, sequester, or destroy the specified information and any copies it has; must not use or disclose the information until the claim is resolved; must take reasonable steps to retrieve the information if the party disclosed it before being notified; and may promptly present the information to the court under seal for a determination of the claim. The producing party must preserve the information until the claim is resolved.

(c) Protective Orders.

(1) In General.

A party or any person from whom discovery is sought may move for a protective order in the court where the action is pending—or as an alternative on matters relating to a deposition, in the court for the district where the deposition will be taken. The motion must include a certification that the movant has in good faith conferred or attempted to confer with other affected parties in an effort to resolve the dispute without court action. The court may, for good cause, issue an order to protect a party or person from annoyance, embarrassment, oppression, or undue burden or expense, including one or more of the following:

(A) forbidding the disclosure or discovery;

(B) specifying terms, including time and place, for the disclosure or discovery;

(C) prescribing a discovery method other than the one selected by the party seeking discovery;

(D) forbidding inquiry into certain matters, or limiting the scope of disclosure or discovery to certain matters;

(E) designating the persons who may be present while the discovery is conducted;

(F) requiring that a deposition be sealed and opened only on court order;

(G) requiring that a trade secret or other confidential research, development, or commercial information not be revealed or be revealed only in a specified way; and

(H) requiring that the parties simultaneously file specified documents or information in sealed envelopes, to be opened as the court directs.

(2) Ordering Discovery.

If a motion for a protective order is wholly or partly denied, the court may, on just terms, order that any party or person provide or permit discovery.

(3) Awarding Expenses.

Rule 37(a)(5) applies to the award of expenses.

(d) Timing and Sequence of Discovery.

(1) Timing.

A party may not seek discovery from any source before the parties have conferred as required by Rule 26(f), except in a proceeding exempted from initial disclosure under Rule 26(a)(1)(B), or when authorized by these rules, by stipulation, or by court order.

(2) **Sequence.**
Unless, on motion, the court orders otherwise for the parties' and witnesses' convenience and in the interests of justice:
(A) methods of discovery may be used in any sequence; and
(B) discovery by one party does not require any other party to delay its discovery.

(e) **Supplementation of Disclosures and Responses.**

(1) **In General.**
A party who has made a disclosure under Rule 26(a)—or who has responded to an interrogatory, request for production, or request for admission—must supplement or correct its disclosure or response:
(A) in a timely manner if the party learns that in some material respect the disclosure or response is incomplete or incorrect, and if the additional or corrective information has not otherwise been made known to the other parties during the discovery process or in writing; or
(B) as ordered by the court.

(2) **Expert Witness.**
For an expert whose report must be disclosed under Rule 26(a)(2)(B), the party's duty to supplement extends both to information included in the report and to information given during the expert's deposition. Any additions or changes to this information must be disclosed by the time the party's pretrial disclosures under Rule 26(a)(3) are due.

(f) **Conference of the Parties; Planning for Discovery**

(1) **Conference Timing.**
Except in a proceeding exempted from initial disclosure under Rule 26(a)(1)(B) or when the court orders otherwise, the parties must confer as soon as practicable—and in any event at least 21 days before a scheduling conference is to be held or a scheduling order is due under Rule 16(b).

(2) **Conference Content; Parties' Responsibilities.**
In conferring, the parties must consider the nature and basis of their claims and defenses and the possibilities for promptly settling or resolving the case; make or arrange for the disclosures required by Rule 26(a)(1); discuss any issues about preserving discoverable information; and develop a proposed discovery plan. The attorneys of record and all unrepresented parties that have appeared in the case are jointly responsible for arranging the conference, for attempting in good faith to agree on the proposed discovery plan, and for submitting to the court within 14 days after the conference a written report outlining the plan. The court may order the parties or attorneys to attend the conference in person.

(3) **Discovery Plan.**
A discovery plan must state the parties' views and proposals on:
(A) what changes should be made in the timing, form, or requirement for disclosures under Rule 26(a), including a statement of when initial disclosures were made or will be made;
(B) the subjects on which discovery may be needed, when discovery should be completed, and whether discovery should be conducted in phases or be limited to or focused on particular issues;
(C) any issues about disclosure or discovery of electronically stored information, including the form or forms in which it should be produced;

(D) any issues about claims of privilege or of protection as trial-preparation materials, including—if the parties agree on a procedure to assert these claims after production—whether to ask the court to include their agreement in an order;

(E) what changes should be made in the limitations on discovery imposed under these rules or by local rule, and what other limitations should be imposed; and

(F) any other orders that the court should issue under Rule 26(c) or under Rule 16(b) and (c).

(4) Expedited Schedule.

If necessary to comply with its expedited schedule for Rule 16(b) conferences, a court may by local rule:

(A) require the parties' conference to occur less than 21 days before the scheduling conference is held or a scheduling order is due under Rule 16(b); and

(B) require the written report outlining the discovery plan to be filed less than 14 days after the parties' conference, or excuse the parties from submitting a written report and permit them to report orally on their discovery plan at the Rule 16(b) conference.

(g) Signing Disclosures and Discovery Requests, Responses, and Objections.

(1) Signature Required; Effect of Signature.

Every disclosure under Rule 26(a)(1) or (a)(3) and every discovery request, response, or objection must be signed by at least one attorney of record in the attorney's own name—or by the party personally, if unrepresented—and must state the signer's address, e-mail address, and telephone number. By signing, an attorney or party certifies that to the best of the person's knowledge, information, and belief formed after a reasonable inquiry:

(A) with respect to a disclosure, it is complete and correct as of the time it is made; and

(B) with respect to a discovery request, response, or objection, it is:

(i) consistent with these rules and warranted by existing law or by a nonfrivolous argument for extending, modifying, or reversing existing law, or for establishing new law;

(ii) not interposed for any improper purpose, such as to harass, cause unnecessary delay, or needlessly increase the cost of litigation; and

(iii) neither unreasonable nor unduly burdensome or expensive, considering the needs of the case, prior discovery in the case, the amount in controversy, and the importance of the issues at stake in the action.

(2) Failure to Sign.

Other parties have no duty to act on an unsigned disclosure, request, response, or objection until it is signed, and the court must strike it unless a signature is promptly supplied after the omission is called to the attorney's or party's attention.

(3) Sanction for Improper Certification.

If a certification violates this rule without substantial justification, the court, on motion or on its own, must impose an appropriate sanction on the signer, the party on whose behalf the signer was acting, or both. The sanction may include an order to pay the reasonable expenses, including attorney's fees, caused by the violation.

RULE 33. INTERROGATORIES TO PARTIES

(a) In General.

(1) Number.

Unless otherwise stipulated or ordered by the court, a party may serve on any other party no more than 25 written interrogatories, including all discrete subparts. Leave to serve additional interrogatories may be granted to the extent consistent with Rule 26(b)(2).

(2) Scope.

An interrogatory may relate to any matter that may be inquired into under Rule 26(b). An interrogatory is not objectionable merely because it asks for an opinion or contention that relates to fact or the application of law to fact, but the court may order that the interrogatory need not be answered until designated discovery is complete, or until a pretrial conference or some other time.

(b) Answers and Objections.

(1) Responding Party.

The interrogatories must be answered:

(A) by the party to whom they are directed; or

(B) if that party is a public or private corporation, a partnership, an association, or a governmental agency, by any officer or agent, who must furnish the information available to the party.

(2) Time to Respond.

The responding party must serve its answers and any objections within 30 days after being served with the interrogatories. A shorter or longer time may be stipulated to under Rule 29 or be ordered by the court.

(3) Answering Each Interrogatory.

Each interrogatory must, to the extent it is not objected to, be answered separately and fully in writing under oath.

(4) Objections.

The grounds for objecting to an interrogatory must be stated with specificity. Any ground not stated in a timely objection is waived unless the court, for good cause, excuses the failure.

(5) Signature.

The person who makes the answers must sign them, and the attorney who objects must sign any objections.

(c) Use.

An answer to an interrogatory may be used to the extent allowed by the Federal Rules of Evidence.

(d) Option to Produce Business Records.

If the answer to an interrogatory may be determined by examining, auditing, compiling, abstracting, or summarizing a party's business records (including electronically stored information), and if the burden of deriving or ascertaining the answer will be substantially the same for either party, the responding party may answer by:

(1) specifying the records that must be reviewed, in sufficient detail to enable the interrogating party to locate and identify them as readily as the responding party could; and

(2) giving the interrogating party a reasonable opportunity to examine and audit the records and to make copies, compilations, abstracts, or summaries.

RULE 34. PRODUCING DOCUMENTS, ELECTRONICALLY STORED INFORMATION, AND TANGIBLE THINGS, OR ENTERING ONTO LAND, FOR INSPECTION AND OTHER PURPOSES

(a) In General.

A party may serve on any other party a request within the scope of Rule 26(b):

(1) to produce and permit the requesting party or its representative to inspect, copy, test, or sample the following items in the responding party's possession, custody, or control:

(A) any designated documents or electronically stored information—including writings, drawings, graphs, charts, photographs, sound recordings, images, and other data or data compilations—stored in any medium from which information can be obtained either directly or, if necessary, after translation by the responding party into a reasonably usable form; or

(B) any designated tangible things; or

(2) to permit entry onto designated land or other property possessed or controlled by the responding party, so that the requesting party may inspect, measure, survey, photograph, test, or sample the property or any designated object or operation on it.

(b) Procedure.

(1) Contents of the Request.

The request:

(A) must describe with reasonable particularity each item or category of items to be inspected;

(B) must specify a reasonable time, place, and manner for the inspection and for performing the related acts; and

(C) may specify the form or forms in which electronically stored information is to be produced.

(2) Responses and Objections.

(A) *Time to Respond.* The party to whom the request is directed must respond in writing within 30 days after being served. A shorter or longer time may be stipulated to under Rule 29 or be ordered by the court.

(B) *Responding to Each Item.* For each item or category, the response must either state that inspection and related activities will be permitted as requested or state an objection to the request, including the reasons.

(C) *Objections.* An objection to part of a request must specify the part and permit inspection of the rest.

(D) *Responding to a Request for Production of Electronically Stored Information.* The response may state an objection to a requested form for producing electronically stored information. If the responding party objects to a requested form—or if no form was specified in the request—the party must state the form or forms it intends to use.

(E) *Producing the Documents or Electronically Stored Information.* Unless otherwise stipulated or ordered by the court, these procedures apply to producing documents or electronically stored information:

(i) A party must produce documents as they are kept in the usual course of business or must organize and label them to correspond to the categories in the request;

(ii) If a request does not specify a form for producing electronically stored information, a party must produce it in a form or forms in which it is ordinarily maintained or in a reasonably usable form or forms; and

(iii) A party need not produce the same electronically stored information in more than one form.

(c) Nonparties.
As provided in Rule 45, a nonparty may be compelled to produce documents and tangible things or to permit an inspection.

RULE 37. FAILURE TO MAKE DISCLOSURES OR TO COOPERATE IN DISCOVERY; SANCTIONS

(a) Motion for an Order Compelling Disclosure or Discovery.

(1) In General.
On notice to other parties and all affected persons, a party may move for an order compelling disclosure or discovery. The motion must include a certification that the movant has in good faith conferred or attempted to confer with the person or party failing to make disclosure or discovery in an effort to obtain it without court action.

(2) Appropriate Court.
A motion for an order to a party must be made in the court where the action is pending. A motion for an order to a nonparty must be made in the court where the discovery is or will be taken.

(3) Specific Motions.

(A) To Compel Disclosure. If a party fails to make a disclosure required by Rule 26(a), any other party may move to compel disclosure and for appropriate sanctions.

(B) To Compel a Discovery Response. A party seeking discovery may move for an order compelling an answer, designation, production, or inspection. This motion may be made if:

(i) a deponent fails to answer a question asked under Rules 30 or 31;

(ii) a corporation or other entity fails to make a designation under Rule 30(b)(6) or 31(a)(4);

(iii) a party fails to answer an interrogatory submitted under Rule 33, or

(iv) a party fails to respond that inspection will be permitted—or fails to permit inspection—as requested under Rule 34.

(C) Related to a Deposition. When taking an oral deposition, the party asking a question may complete or adjourn the examination before moving for an order.

(4) Evasive or Incomplete Disclosure, Answer, or Response.
For purposes of this subdivision (a), an evasive or incomplete disclosure, answer, or response must be treated as a failure to disclose, answer, or respond.

(5) Payment of Expenses; Protective Orders.

(A) If the Motion Is Granted (or Disclosure or Discovery Is Provided After Filing). If the motion is granted—or if the disclosure or requested discovery is provided after the motion was filed—the court must, after giving an opportunity to be heard, require the party or deponent whose conduct necessitated the motion, the party or attorney advising that conduct, or both to pay the movant's reasonable expenses incurred in making the motion, including attorney's fees. But the court must not order this payment if:

(i) the movant filed the motion before attempting in good faith to obtain the disclosure or discovery without court action;

(ii) the opposing party's nondisclosure, response, or objection was substantially justified; or

(iii) other circumstances make an award of expenses unjust.

(B) If the Motion Is Denied. If the motion is denied, the court may issue any protective order authorized under Rule 26(c) and must, after giving an opportunity to be heard, require the movant, the attorney filing the motion, or both to pay the party or deponent who opposed the motion its reasonable expenses incurred in opposing the motion, including attorney's fees. But the court must not order this payment if the motion was substantially justified or other circumstances make an award of expenses unjust.

(C) If the Motion Is Granted in Part and Denied in Part. If the motion is granted in part and denied in part, the court may issue any protective order authorized under Rule 26(c) and may, after giving an opportunity to be heard, apportion the reasonable expenses for the motion.

(b) Failure to Comply with a Court Order.

(1) Sanctions in the District Where the Deposition Is Taken.
If the court where the discovery is taken orders a deponent to be sworn or to answer a question and the deponent fails to obey, the failure may be treated as contempt of court.

(2) Sanctions in the District Where the Action Is Pending.

(A) For Not Obeying a Discovery Order. If a party or a party's officer, director, or managing agent—or a witness designated under Rule 30(b)(6) or 31(a)(4)—fails to obey an order to provide or permit discovery, including an order under Rule 26(f), 35, or 37(a), the court where the action is pending may issue further just orders. They may include the following:

(i) directing that the matters embraced in the order or other designated facts be taken as established for purposes of the action, as the prevailing party claims;

(ii) prohibiting the disobedient party from supporting or opposing designated claims or defenses, or from introducing designated matters in evidence;

(iii) striking pleadings in whole or in part;

(iv) staying further proceedings until the order is obeyed;

(v) dismissing the action or proceeding in whole or in part;

(vi) rendering a default judgment against the disobedient party; or

(vii) treating as contempt of court the failure to obey any order except an order to submit to a physical or mental examination.

(B) For Not Producing a Person for Examination. If a party fails to comply with an order under Rule 35(a) requiring it to produce another person for examination, the court may issue any of the orders listed in Rule 37(b)(2)(A)(i)-(vi), unless the disobedient party shows that it cannot produce the other person.

(C) Payment of Expenses. Instead of or in addition to the orders above, the court must order the disobedient party, the attorney advising that party, or both to pay the reasonable expenses, including attorney's fees, caused by the failure, unless the failure was substantially justified or other circumstances make an award of expenses unjust.

(c) Failure to Disclose; to Supplement an Earlier Response, or to Admit.

(1) Failure to Disclose or Supplement.

If a party fails to provide information or identify a witness as required by Rule 26(a) or 26(e), the party is not allowed to use that information or witness to supply evidence on a motion, at a hearing, or at a trial, unless the failure was substantially justified or is harmless. In addition to or instead of this sanction, the court, on motion and after giving an opportunity to be heard:

(A) may order payment of the reasonable expenses, including attorney's fees, caused by the failure;

(B) may inform the jury of the party's failure; and

(C) may impose other appropriate sanctions, including any of the orders listed in Rule 37(b)(2)(A)(i)-(vi).

(2) Failure to Admit.

If a party fails to admit what is requested under Rule 36 and if the requesting party later proves a document to be genuine or the matter true, the requesting party may move that the party who failed to admit pay the reasonable expenses, including attorney's fees, incurred in making that proof. The court must so order unless:

(A) the request was held objectionable under Rule 36(a);

(B) the admission sought was of no substantial importance;

(C) the party failing to admit had a reasonable ground to believe that it might prevail on the matter; or

(D) there was other good reason for the failure to admit.

(d) Party's Failure to Attend Its Own Deposition, Serve Answers to Interrogatories, or Respond to a Request for Inspection.

(1) In General.

(A) Motion; Grounds for Sanctions. The court where the action is pending may, on motion, order sanctions if:

(i) a party or a party's officer, director, or managing agent—or a person designated under Rule 30(b)(6) or 31(a)(4)—fails, after being served with proper notice, to appear for that person's deposition; or

(ii) a party, after being properly served with interrogatories under Rule 33 or a request for inspection under Rule 34, fails to serve its answers, objections, or written response.

(B) Certification. A motion for sanctions for failing to answer or respond must include a certification that the movant has in good faith conferred or attempted to confer with the party failing to act in an effort to obtain the answer or response without court action.

(2) Unacceptable Excuse for Failing to Act.

A failure described in Rule 37(d)(1)(A) is not excused on the ground that the discovery sought was objectionable, unless the party failing to act has a pending motion for a protective order under Rule 26(c).

(3) Types of Sanctions.

Sanctions may include any of the orders listed in Rule 37(b)(2)(A)(i)-(vi). Instead of or in addition to these sanctions, the court must require the party failing to act, the attorney advising that party, or both to pay the reasonable expenses, including attorney's fees, caused by the failure, unless the failure was substantially justified or other circumstances make an award of expenses unjust.

(e) Failure to Provide Electronically Stored Information.
Absent exceptional circumstances, a court may not impose sanctions under these rules on a party for failing to provide electronically stored information lost as a result of the routine, good-faith operation of an electronic information system.

(f) Failure to Participate in Framing a Discovery Plan.
If a party or its attorney fails to participate in good faith in developing and submitting a proposed discovery plan as required by Rule 26(f), the court may, after giving an opportunity to be heard, require that party or attorney to pay to any other party the reasonable expenses, including attorney's fees, caused by the failure.

RULE 45. SUBPOENA

(a) In General.

(1) Form and Contents.

(A) *Requirements—In General.* Every subpoena must:

(i) state the court from which it issued;

(ii) state the title of the action, the court in which it is pending, and its civil-action number;

(iii) command each person to whom it is directed to do the following at a specified time and place: attend and testify; produce designated documents, electronically stored information, or tangible things in that person's possession, custody, or control; or permit the inspection of premises; and

(iv) set out the text of Rule 45(c) and (d).

(B) *Command to Attend a Deposition—Notice of the Recording Method.* A subpoena commanding attendance at a deposition must state the method for recording the testimony.

(C) *Combining or Separating a Command to Produce or to Permit Inspection; Specifying the Form for Electronically Stored Information.* A command to produce documents, electronically stored information, or tangible things or to permit the inspection of premises may be included in a subpoena commanding attendance at a deposition, hearing, or trial, or may be set out in a separate subpoena. A subpoena may specify the form or forms in which electronically stored information is to be produced.

(D) *Command to Produce; Included Obligations.* A command in a subpoena to produce documents, electronically stored information, or tangible things requires the responding party to permit inspection, copying, testing, or sampling of the materials.

(2) Issued from Which Court.
A subpoena must issue as follows:

(A) for attendance at a hearing or trial, from the court for the district where the hearing or trial is to be held;

(B) for attendance at a deposition, from the court for the district where the deposition is to be taken; and

(C) for production or inspection, if separate from a subpoena commanding a person's attendance, from the court for the district where the production or inspection is to be made.

(3) Issued by Whom.
The clerk must issue a subpoena, signed but otherwise in blank, to a party who requests it. That party must complete it before service. An attorney also may issue and sign a subpoena as an officer of:
(A) a court in which the attorney is authorized to practice; or
(B) a court for a district where a deposition is to be taken or production is to be made, if the attorney is authorized to practice in the court where the action is pending.

(b) Service.

(1) By Whom; Tendering Fees; Serving a Copy of Certain Subpoenas.
Any person who is at least 18 years old and not a party may serve a subpoena. Serving a subpoena requires delivering a copy to the named person and, if the subpoena requires that person's attendance, tendering the fees for 1 day's attendance and the mileage allowed by law. Fees and mileage need not be tendered when the subpoena issues on behalf of the United States or any of its officers or agencies. If the subpoena commands the production of documents, electronically stored information, or tangible things or the inspection of premises before trial, then before it is served, a notice must be served on each party.

(2) Service in the United States.
Subject to Rule 45(c)(3)(A)(ii), a subpoena may be served at any place:
(A) within the district of the issuing court;
(B) outside that district but within 100 miles of the place specified for the deposition, hearing, trial, production, or inspection;
(C) within the state of the issuing court if a state statute or court rule allows service at that place of a subpoena issued by a state court of general jurisdiction sitting in the place specified for the deposition, hearing, trial, production, or inspection; or
(D) that the court authorizes on motion and for good cause, if a federal statute so provides.

(3) Service in a Foreign Country.
28 U.S.C. § 1783 governs issuing and serving a subpoena directed to a United States national or resident who is in a foreign country.

(4) Proof of Service.
Proving service, when necessary, requires filing with the issuing court a statement showing the date and manner of service and the names of the persons served. The statement must be certified by the server.

(c) Protecting a Person Subject to a Subpoena.

(1) Avoiding Undue Burden or Expense; Sanctions.
A party or attorney responsible for issuing and serving a subpoena must take reasonable steps to avoid imposing undue burden or expense on a person subject to the subpoena. The issuing court must enforce this duty and impose an appropriate sanction—which may include lost earnings and reasonable attorney's fees—on a party or attorney who fails to comply.

(2) Command to Produce Materials or Permit Inspection.
(A) *Appearance Not Required.* A person commanded to produce documents, electronically stored information, or tangible things, or to permit the

inspection of premises, need not appear in person at the place of production or inspection unless also commanded to appear for a deposition, hearing, or trial.

(B) *Objections*. A person commanded to produce documents or tangible things or to permit inspection may serve on the party or attorney designated in the subpoena a written objection to inspecting, copying, testing or sampling any or all of the materials or to inspecting the premises—or to producing electronically stored information in the form or forms requested. The objection must be served before the earlier of the time specified for compliance or 14 days after the subpoena is served. If an objection is made, the following rules apply:

(i) At any time, on notice to the commanded person, the serving party may move the issuing court for an order compelling production or inspection.

(ii) These acts may be required only as directed in the order, and the order must protect a person who is neither a party nor a party's officer from significant expense resulting from compliance.

(3) Quashing or Modifying a Subpoena.

(A) When Required. On timely motion, the issuing court must quash or modify a subpoena that:

(i) fails to allow a reasonable time to comply;

(ii) requires a person who is neither a party nor a party's officer to travel more than 100 miles from where that person resides, is employed, or regularly transacts business in person—except that, subject to Rule 45(c)(3)(B)(iii), the person may be commanded to attend a trial by traveling from any such place within the state where the trial is held;

(iii) requires disclosure of privileged or other protected matter, if no exception or waiver applies; or

(iv) subjects a person to undue burden.

(B) When Permitted. To protect a person subject to or affected by a subpoena, the issuing court may, on motion, quash or modify the subpoena if it requires:

(i) disclosing a trade secret or other confidential research, development, or commercial information;

(ii) disclosing an unretained expert's opinion or information that does not describe specific occurrences in dispute and results from the expert's study that was not requested by a party; or

(iii) a person who is neither a party nor a party's officer to incur substantial expense to travel more than 100 miles to attend trial.

(C) Specifying Conditions as an Alternative. In the circumstances described in Rule 45(c)(3)(B), the court may, instead of quashing or modifying a subpoena, order appearance or production under specified conditions if the serving party:

(i) shows a substantial need for the testimony or material that cannot be otherwise met without undue hardship; and

(ii) ensures that the subpoenaed person will be reasonably compensated.

(d) Duties in Responding to Subpoena.

(1) Producing Documents or Electronically Stored Information. These procedures apply to producing documents or electronically stored information:

(A) *Documents.* A person responding to a subpoena to produce documents must produce them as they are kept in the ordinary course of business or must organize and label them to correspond to the categories in the demand.

(B) *Form for Producing Electronically Stored Information Not Specified.* If a subpoena does not specify a form for producing electronically stored information, the person responding must produce it in a form or forms in which it is ordinarily maintained or in a reasonably usable form or forms.

(C) *Electronically Stored Information Produced in Only One Form.* The person responding need not produce the same electronically stored information in more than one form.

(D) *Inaccessible Electronically Stored Information.* The person responding need not provide discovery of electronically stored information from sources that the person identifies as not reasonably accessible because of undue burden or cost. On motion to compel discovery or for a protective order, the person responding must show that the information is not reasonably accessible because of undue burden or cost. If that showing is made, the court may nonetheless order discovery from such sources if the requesting party shows good cause, considering the limitations of Rule 26(b)(2)(C). The court may specify conditions for the discovery.

(2) Claiming Privilege or Protection.

(A) *Information Withheld.* A person withholding subpoenaed information under a claim that it is privileged or subject to protection as trial-preparation material must:

(i) expressly make the claim; and

(ii) describe the nature of the withheld documents, communications, or tangible things in a manner that, without revealing information itself privileged or protected, will enable the parties to assess the claim.

(B) *Information Produced.* If information produced in response to a subpoena is subject to a claim of privilege or of protection as trial-preparation material, the person making the claim may notify any party that received the information of the claim and the basis for it. After being notified, a party must promptly return, sequester, or destroy the specified information and any copies it has; must not use or disclose the information until the claim is resolved; must take reasonable steps to retrieve the information if the party disclosed it before being notified; and may promptly present the information to the court under seal for a determination of the claim. The person who produced the information must preserve the information until the claim is resolved.

(e) Contempt.

The issuing court may hold in contempt a person who, having been served, fails without adequate excuse to obey the subpoena. A nonparty's failure to obey must be excused if the subpoena purports to require the nonparty to attend or produce at a place outside the limits of Rule 45(c)(3)(A)(ii).

UNITED STATES DISTRICT COURT
for the
<________________> DISTRICT OF <________________>

<Name(s) of plaintiff(s)>,	)	
Plaintiff(s)	)	Civil Action No. <Number>
v.	)	
<Name(s) of defendant(s)>,	)	
Defendant(s)	)	

REPORT OF THE PARTIES' PLANNING MEETING

1. The following persons participated in a Rule 26(f) conference on <Date> by <State the method of conferring>:
   <Name>, representing the <plaintiff>
   <Name>, representing the <defendant>
2. Initial Disclosures. The parties [have completed] [will complete by <Date>] the initial disclosures required by Rule 26(a)(1).
3. Discovery Plan. The parties propose this discovery plan:
   <Use separate paragraphs or subparagraphs if the parties disagree.>
   (a) Discovery will be needed on these subjects: <Describe>.
   (b) <Dates for commencing and completing discovery, including discovery to be commenced or completed before other discovery.>
   (c) <Maximum number of interrogatories by each party to another party, along with the dates the answers are due.>
   (d) <Maximum number of requests for admission, along with the dates responses are due.>
   (e) <Maximum number of depositions by each party.>
   (f) <Limits on the length of depositions, in hours.>
   (g) <Dates for exchanging reports of expert witnesses.>
   (h) <Dates for supplementations under Rule 26(e).>
4. Other Items:
   (a) <A date if the parties ask to meet with the court before a scheduling order.>
   (b) <Requested dates for pretrial conferences.>
   (c) <Final dates for the plaintiff to amend pleadings or to join parties.>
   (d) <Final dates for the defendant to amend pleadings or to join parties.>
   (e) <Final dates to file dispositive motions.>
   (f) <State the prospects for settlement.>
   (g) <Identify any alternative dispute resolution procedure that may enhance settlement prospects.>
   (h) <Final dates for submitting Rule 26(a)(3) witness lists, designations of witnesses whose testimony will be presented by deposition, and exhibit lists.>
   (i) <Final dates to file objections under Rule 26(a)(3).>
   (j) <Suggested trial date and estimate of trial length.>
   (k) <Other matters.>

Date: <Date>

<Signature of the attorney or unrepresented party>

____

<Printed name>
<Address>
<E-mail address>
<Telephone number>

Date: <Date>

<Signature of the attorney or unrepresented party>

____

<Printed name>
<Address>
<E-mail address>
<Telephone number>

Source: http://www.uscourts.gov/uscourts/RulesAndPolicies/Rules/Usable_Rules_Forms_Civil/ CIV52-Report_of_the_Parties-_Planning_Meeting.wpd

ARTICLE V. PRIVILEGES

Rule 501. General Rule

Except as otherwise required by the Constitution of the United States or provided by Act of Congress or in rules prescribed by the Supreme Court pursuant to statutory authority, the privilege of a witness, person, government, State, or political subdivision thereof shall be governed by the principles of the common law as they may be interpreted by the courts of the United States in the light of reason and experience. However, in civil actions and proceedings, with respect to an element of a claim or defense as to which State law supplies the rule of decision, the privilege of a witness, person, government, State, or political subdivision thereof shall be determined in accordance with State law.

Notes

Rule 502. Attorney-Client Privilege and Work Product; Limitations on Waiver

(a) **Scope of waiver.**
In federal proceedings, the waiver by disclosure of an attorney-client privilege or work product protection extends to an undisclosed communication or information concerning the same subject matter only if that undisclosed communication or information ought in fairness to be considered with the disclosed communication or information.

(b) **Inadvertent disclosure.**
A disclosure of a communication or information covered by the attorney-client privilege or work product protection does not operate as a waiver in a state or federal proceeding if the disclosure is inadvertent and is made in connection with federal litigation or federal administrative proceedings—and if the holder of the privilege or work product protection took reasonable precautions to prevent disclosure and took reasonably prompt measures, once the holder knew or should have known of the disclosure, to rectify the error, including (if applicable) following the procedures in Fed. R. Civ. P. 26(b)(5)(B).

(c) **Selective waiver.**
In a federal or state proceeding, a disclosure of a communication or information covered by the attorney-client privilege or work product protection—when made to a federal public office or agency in the exercise of its regulatory, investigative, or enforcement authority—does not operate as a waiver of the privilege or protection in favor of non-governmental persons or entities. The effect of disclosure to a state or local government agency, with respect to non-governmental persons or entities, is governed by applicable state law. Nothing in this rule limits or expands the authority of a government agency to disclose communications or information to other government agencies or as otherwise authorized or required by law.

(d) Controlling effect of court orders.
A federal court order that the attorney-client privilege or work product protection is not waived as a result of disclosure in connection with the litigation pending before the court governs all persons or entities in all state or federal proceedings, whether or not they were parties to the matter before the court, if the order incorporates the agreement of the parties before the court.

(e) Controlling effect of party agreements.
An agreement on the effect of disclosure of a communication or information covered by the attorney-client privilege or work product protection is binding on the parties to the agreement, but not on other parties unless the agreement is incorporated into a court order.

(f) Included privilege and protection.
As used in this rule:
(1) "attorney-client privilege" means the protection provided for confidential attorney-client communications, under applicable law; and
(2) "work product protection" means the protection for materials prepared in anticipation of litigation or for trial, under applicable law.

ARTICLE IX. AUTHENTICATION AND IDENTIFICATION

Rule 901. Requirement of Authentication or Identification

(a) General provision.
The requirement of authentication or identification as a condition precedent to admissibility is satisfied by evidence sufficient to support a finding that the matter in question is what its proponent claims.

(b) Illustrations.
By way of illustration only, and not by way of limitation, the following are examples of authentication or identification conforming with the requirements of this rule:
(1) *Testimony of witness with knowledge*. Testimony that a matter is what it is claimed to be.
(2) *Nonexpert opinion on handwriting*. Nonexpert opinion as to the genuineness of handwriting, based upon familiarity not acquired for purposes of the litigation.
(3) *Comparison by trier or expert witness*. Comparison by the trier of fact or by expert witnesses with specimens which have been authenticated.
(4) *Distinctive characteristics and the like*. Appearance, contents, substance, internal patterns, or other distinctive characteristics, taken in conjunction with circumstances.
(5) *Voice identification*. Identification of a voice, whether heard firsthand or through mechanical or electronic transmission or recording, by opinion based upon hearing the voice at any time under circumstances connecting it with the alleged speaker.
(6) *Telephone conversations*. Telephone conversations, by evidence that a call was made to the number assigned at the time by the telephone company to a particular person or business, if (A) in the case of a person, circumstances, including self-identification, show the person answering

to be the one called, or (B) in the case of a business, the call was made to a place of business and the conversation related to business reasonably transacted over the telephone.

(7) *Public records or reports.* Evidence that a writing authorized by law to be recorded or filed and in fact recorded or filed in a public office, or a purported public record, report, statement, or data compilation, in any form, is from the public office where items of this nature are kept.

(8) *Ancient documents or data compilation.* Evidence that a document or data compilation, in any form, (A) is in such condition as to create no suspicion concerning its authenticity, (B) was in a place where it, if authentic, would likely be, and (C) has been in existence 20 years or more at the time it is offered.

(9) *Process or system.* Evidence describing a process or system used to produce a result and showing that the process or system produces an accurate result.

(10) *Methods provided by statute or rule.* Any method of authentication or identification provided by Act of Congress or by other rules prescribed by the Supreme Court pursuant to statutory authority.

Notes

Rule 902. Self-authentication

Extrinsic evidence of authenticity as a condition precedent to admissibility is not required with respect to the following:

(1) Domestic public documents under seal. A document bearing a seal purporting to be that of the United States, or of any State, district, Commonwealth, territory, or insular possession thereof, or the Panama Canal Zone, or the Trust Territory of the Pacific Islands, or of a political subdivision, department, officer, or agency thereof, and a signature purporting to be an attestation or execution.

(2) Domestic public documents not under seal. A document purporting to bear the signature in the official capacity of an officer or employee of any entity included in paragraph (1) hereof, having no seal, if a public officer having a seal and having official duties in the district or political subdivision of the officer or employee certifies under seal that the signer has the official capacity and that the signature is genuine.

(3) Foreign public documents. A document purporting to be executed or attested in an official capacity by a person authorized by the laws of a foreign country to make the execution or attestation, and accompanied by a final certification as to the genuineness of the signature and official position (A) of the executing or attesting person, or (B) of any foreign official whose certificate of genuineness of signature and official position relates to the execution or attestation or is in a chain of certificates of genuineness of signature and official position relating to the execution or attestation. A final certification may be made by a secretary of an embassy or legation, consul general, consul, vice consul, or consular agent of the United States, or a diplomatic or consular official of the foreign country assigned or accredited to the United States. If reasonable opportunity has been given to all parties to investigate the authenticity and accuracy of official documents, the court may, for good cause shown, order that they be treated as presumptively authentic without final certification or permit them to be evidenced by an attested summary with or without final certification.

(4) **Certified copies of public records.** A copy of an official record or report or entry therein, or of a document authorized by law to be recorded or filed and actually recorded or filed in a public office, including data compilations in any form, certified as correct by the custodian or other person authorized to make the certification, by certificate complying with paragraph (1), (2), or (3) of this rule or complying with any Act of Congress or rule prescribed by the Supreme Court pursuant to statutory authority.

(5) **Official publications.** Books, pamphlets, or other publications purporting to be issued by public authority.

(6) **Newspapers and periodicals.** Printed materials purporting to be newspapers or periodicals.

(7) **Trade inscriptions and the like.** Inscriptions, signs, tags, or labels purporting to have been affixed in the course of business and indicating ownership, control, or origin.

(8) **Acknowledged documents.** Documents accompanied by a certificate of acknowledgment executed in the manner provided by law by a notary public or other officer authorized by law to take acknowledgments.

(9) **Commercial paper and related documents.** Commercial paper, signatures thereon, and documents relating thereto to the extent provided by general commercial law.

(10) **Presumptions under Acts of Congress.** Any signature, document, or other matter declared by Act of Congress to be presumptively or prima facie genuine or authentic.

(11) **Certified domestic records of regularly conducted activity.** The original or a duplicate of a domestic record of regularly conducted activity that would be admissible under Rule 803(6) if accompanied by a written declaration of its custodian or other qualified person, in a manner complying with any Act of Congress or rule prescribed by the Supreme Court pursuant to statutory authority, certifying that the record:

(A) was made at or near the time of the occurrence of the matters set forth by, or from information transmitted by, a person with knowledge of those matters;

(B) was kept in the course of the regularly conducted activity; and

(C) was made by the regularly conducted activity as a regular practice.

A party intending to offer a record into evidence under this paragraph must provide written notice of that intention to all adverse parties, and must make the record and declaration available for inspection sufficiently in advance of their offer into evidence to provide an adverse party with a fair opportunity to challenge them.

(12) **Certified foreign records of regularly conducted activity.** In a civil case, the original or a duplicate of a foreign record of regularly conducted activity that would be admissible under Rule 803(6) if accompanied by a written declaration by its custodian or other qualified person certifying that the record:

(A) was made at or near the time of the occurrence of the matters set forth by, or from information transmitted by, a person with knowledge of those matters;

(B) was kept in the course of the regularly conducted activity; and

(C) was made by the regularly conducted activity as a regular practice.

The declaration must be signed in a manner that, if falsely made, would subject the maker to criminal penalty under the laws of the country where the declaration is signed. A party intending to offer a record into evidence under this paragraph must provide written notice of that intention to all adverse parties, and must make the record and declaration available for inspection sufficiently in advance of their offer into evidence to provide an adverse party with a fair opportunity to challenge them.

Notes

Rule 903. Subscribing Witness' Testimony Unnecessary

The testimony of a subscribing witness is not necessary to authenticate a writing unless required by the laws of the jurisdiction whose laws govern the validity of the writing.

Notes

GLOSSARY

Annotation monitor Monitor that allows a witness to easily make on-screen annotations with the touch of a finger.

Attorney–client privilege Rule of evidence that protects the client from the attorney being required to reveal the confidential information.

Authentication of documents The process of determining that the proposed evidence is what it purports to be and is genuine.

Auto coding The electronic scanning and coding of documents by selected key terms and dates.

Bates production numbering A Bates production number is a tracking number assigned to each page of each document in the production set.

Boolean search A search model that uses keywords and connectors.

Candor Ethical obligation to not mislead the court or opposing counsel with false statements of law or of facts that the lawyer knows to be false.

Case management system Software for organizing the parts of a case in a central repository that can be shared by all members of the legal team.

Cell In a spreadsheet, the box at the intersection of a row and column for text or numerical data.

Chain of custody A written record showing the identity of everyone accessing evidence and showing that the evidence was not altered while in possession of the law firm.

Civil litigation Resolution of legal disputes between parties seeking a remedy for a civil wrong or to enforce a contract.

Claim of privilege The person claiming the privilege—usually the client—has the burden to establish its existence.

Claw-back provision A provision contained in the report of counsel's meet and confer and included in the court's scheduling order that describes what to do with privileged materials that are disclosed inadvertently through e-discovery. The provision should address return of the materials and waiver of the privilege.

Cloud computing The access over the Internet of a secure depository by authorized users.

Coding The process of capturing case-relevant information (i.e., author, date authored, date sent, recipient, date opened, etc.) from a document.

Competent Having the requisite knowledge and skill, thoroughness, and preparation necessary for representation.

Confidentiality Ethical obligation to keep client information confidential (not disclose) founded on the belief that clients should be able to tell their attorneys everything about their case so the attorney can give proper legal advice to the client.

Conflict of interest Situations where the interests or loyalties of the lawyer and client may be or may appear to be adverse or divided.

Conflict report generator A preconfigured report in a contacts database.

Content (application) metadata Information about the contents of a document.

Database A collection of similar records.

De-duplication/De-duping The process of comparing electronic records based on their characteristics and removing duplicate records from the data set.

Deposition A form of discovery available to ask questions and obtain oral answers under oath from a witness or party to a lawsuit. Questions and answers are recorded stenographically.

Document camera A portable evidence presentation system equipped with a high-resolution camera.

Documentary evidence Writings, recordings, and photographs, which include X-ray films, electronic recordings, or any other data compilation.

Dual-cassette player Equipment that plays back audio.

E-Discovery Discovery of documents created, disseminated, and stored via electronic means.

Electronic courtroom Courtroom equipped with electronic equipment for use in trial presentations.

Electronic database An electronic repository of information of all types that can be sorted by a computer program and presented in a meaningful manner.

Electronic Discovery Reference Model A suggested model of the procedures in electronic discovery.

Electronic spreadsheet A computer software program with rows and columns in which primarily numeric data may be manipulated using formulas. Also sometimes called electronic accounting worksheets.

Electronically stored information (ESI) Any type of information that can be stored electronically.

Encryption Technology that allows computer users to put a "lock" around information to prevent discovery by others.

Entry of appearance An attorney for one of the litigants files papers officially identifying himself or herself as representing the client before the court.

E-Repository(online document repository) An electronic data storage facility accessed using the Internet.

Ethics Minimally acceptable standards of conduct in a profession.

Evidence Testimony, documents, and tangible things that tend to prove or disprove a fact.

Expert witness A person qualified by education, training, or experience to render an opinion based on a set of facts that are outside the scope of knowledge of the fact finder.

Fields Information located in vertical columns.

Filtering The process used to scan or search documents for relevant terms in an attempt to narrow the focus, such as filtering to eliminate documents created before or after a certain date.

Graphic image format A computer image that is stored and displayed as a set of colored points in a rectangular grid.

Inadvertent disclosure An unintended disclosure of privileged, confidential or work product information to the opposing side.

Information Management Reference Model (IMRM) A proposed model for e-discovery that balances business and litigation needs.

Information technologist A member of the legal team who has legal and technological skills and primarily support electronic discovery activities.

Infrared headphones An assisted listening device for the hearing impaired.

Intake form A template used to enter information into a computer program such as a case management program.

Interpreter box Routes language translations from an interpreter to the witness/defendant's headphones or the courtroom's public address system.

Interrogatories A form of discovery in which written questions are addressed to a party to a lawsuit requiring written answers made under oath.

Laptop port A connection into which a laptop may be plugged.

Large-screen monitor A video monitor conveniently located in the courtroom and large enough for all to see the graphics displayed.

Legal hold An affirmative duty to preserve potential evidence.

Litigation hold A process whereby a company or individual determines that an unresolved dispute may result in litigation and as a result, documents should not be destroyed or altered.

Metadata Information about a particular data set that may describe, for example, how, when, and by whom it was received, created, accessed, and/or modified and how it is formatted.

Model Rules of Professional Conduct The American Bar Association set of proposed ethical standards for the legal profession.

Native form Electronic documents have an associated file structure defined by the original creating application. This file structure is referred to as the "native format" of the document. Because viewing or searching documents in the native format may require the original application (e.g., viewing a Microsoft Word document may require the Microsoft Word application), documents are often converted to a standard file format (e.g., TIFF) as part of electronic document processing.

Native format (native file format) An associated file structure defined by the original creating application of electronic documents.

Non-waiver agreement An agreement between counsel that any privileged or confidential information inadvertently submitted does not lose its status as privileged or confidential. Also called a claw back clause. Agreement may be included in courts discover order.

Objective coding Also referred to as a bibliographic indexing. This includes the author, type of document, recipient, and date.

Optical character recognition (OCR) A technology that takes data from a paper document and turns it into editable text data. The document is first scanned, then OCR software searches the document for letters, numbers, and other characters.

Portable document format (PDF) An open standard format for document exchange that enables a document to be processed and printed on any computer.

Private cloud An Internet-based service that allows restricted access to information stored on servers of a third party host company.

Privilege log A list of documents claimed by the submitting party to contain material subject to privilege or work product exclusion.

Privilege review A review of documents for privileged or confidential content or attorney work product.

Proportionality Weighing the cost against the benefits of preserving and obtaining evidence against the amount in controversy.

Record In a database, the information in a horizontal row.

Record retention Keeping documents and electronically stored information for a period of time.

Redaction The removal of confidential information (or at least that which is claimed to be confidential) or material prepared for trial under the work product doctrine.

Relevant That which tends to prove the existence of facts important to the resolution of a case or may lead to such evidence which is admissible.

Reports Information from a search of a database or databases.

Resource (system) metadata The data such as file names, size, and location.

Retention policy A formal process for retaining and destroying files and electronically stored information.

Review Checking documents for confidential, privileged or work product content.

Rules-based calendaring A calendar or date calculator based on rules of court that set time limits and deadlines for cases and procedures in court.

Safe Haven Procedures and circumstances under which a party will not be penalized.

Sampling The testing of a search query by running it against a limited set of documents to measure the accuracy of the response to a search query.

Scanning Copying a document by converting the image into an electronic format

Search queries Specific words used in a computerized search.

Spoliation of evidence Destruction of records that may be relevant to ongoing or anticipated litigation, government investigation, or audit. Courts differ in their interpretation of the level of intent required before sanctions may be warranted.

Statute of limitations The time frame within which an action must be commenced or the party will lose their right to use the courts to seek redress.

Subjective coding Identifies keywords within the document or other criteria not related to bibliographic information.

Supervising attorney Member of the legal team to whom all others on the team report and who has the ultimate responsibility for the actions of the legal team.

System metadata Data such as file name, size, and location.

Table Data that is organized in a format of horizontal rows and vertical columns.

TIFF Tagged Image File Format, one of the most widely used formats for storing images. TIFF graphics can be black and white, gray-scaled, or color.

Timeline A graphic representation of the facts or procedural steps in a case.

Trial notebook A summary of the case, usually contained in a tabbed, three-ring binder with sections such as pleadings, motions, law, pretrial memos, and witnesses.

Trial presentation program Computer program that organizes and controls documents, depositions, photographs, and other data as exhibits for trial and displays them as evidence when needed.

VCR Equipment that plays back video and audio.

Visual presentation cart Media center located in the courtroom.

Word processor A computer software program for creating, editing, and producing word documents in various formats.

Work product doctrine A limited protection for material prepared by the attorney, or those working for the attorney, in anticipation of litigation or for trial.

CASE INDEX

SUBJECT INDEX